LIST OF PERSONS
WHOSE
NAMES HAVE BEEN CHANGED
IN
MASSACHUSETTS

1780 - 1892

Collated and Published by
the Secretary of the Commonwealth,
under Authority of Chapter 191 of
the Acts of the Year 1893

CLEARFIELD

First published
1885

Second Edition
Boston, 1893

Reprinted by
Genealogical Publishing Company
Baltimore, Maryland, 1972

Library of Congress Cataloging in Publication Data
Massachusetts. Secretary of the Commonwealth.
  List of persons whose names have been changed in Massachusetts, 1780-1892.
  Reprint of the 1893 ed.
  1. Names, Personal - Massachusetts. I. Title.
F63.A5 1972   929.4'09744   75-39364
ISBN 978-0-8063-0498-4

LIST OF PERSONS

WHOSE

NAMES HAVE BEEN CHANGED IN THIS COMMONWEALTH.

1780–1892.

AN ACT for altering the Name of Thomas Jackson Greenwood, of Newton, in the County of Middlesex, and permitting him to take the Name of Alexander Shephard.

Whereas the said Thomas Jackson Greenwood, by the death of his natural father was in infancy left an orphan, whose education has been attended to by Mr. Alexander Shephard, who having no son, the said Thomas Jackson Greenwood desires to take the name of his benefactor :

Be it therefore enacted by the Senate and House of Representatives, in General Court assembled, and by the authority of the same,

That Thomas Jackson Greenwood be, and he hereby is allowed to take the name of Alexander Shephard, and on all and every occasion hereafter to make the name of Alexander Shephard his proper Christian and surname ; and by that name he shall be considered in all processes and records whatever. ' [*May 8, 1781.*

AN ACT for changing the name of Thomas Greaves Russell, to Thomas Russell Greaves.

Whereas Thomas Greaves Russell, of Boston, in the county of Suffolk, gentleman, being the lineal descendant of the Honorable Thomas Greaves, late of Charlestown, Esq., deceased, and being desirous from respect to his memory to be called by his surname :

Be it enacted, etc., as follows :

That from and after the passing this act, the said Thomas Greaves Russell shall be allowed to take the name of Thomas Russell Greaves, and by that name, instead of his present Christian and surname, to be called and known, and that to all legal purposes, the said name of Thomas Russell Greaves shall be considered as his own, proper and only name, and avail accordingly.   [*July 6, 1787.*

An Act to enable Dudley Atkins, Esq., to take the Surname of Tyng.

Whereas Dudley Atkins, of Newbury, in the county of Essex, Esquire, has petitioned this court, setting forth that he is descended from the family of Tyng ; that Mrs. Sarah Winslow, of Tyngsborough, in the county of Middlesex, being a descendant from the same family, and having no children, has devised to him a considerable part of her estate, and has requested him to take the surname of Tyng, and therefore praying the interposition of this court for that purpose :

Be it therefore enacted, etc., as follows :

That the said Dudley Atkins be, and he hereby is enabled to take upon himself the surname of Tyng, in addition to his present name, and that he be hereafter known and called by the name of Dudley Atkins Tyng. [*January 16, 1790.*

An Act for changing the Name of Samuel Turner, to Samuel James Longman.

Whereas some advantages are expected to accrue to Samuel Turner, son of William Turner, Esq., of Boston, in the county of Suffolk, by said Samuel's having the name of Samuel James Longman ; and upon the petition of the said William therefor :

Be it enacted, etc., as follows :

That from and after the passing of this act, the said Samuel Turner shall be allowed to take the name of Samuel James Longman, and by that name, instead of his present Christian and surname, to be called and known, and that to all legal purposes, the said name of Samuel James Longman shall be considered as his own proper and only name, and avail accordingly. [*February 25, 1792.*

An Act authorizing Lewis Ansart de Maresquelle, to omit the addition of De Maresquelle, and to be called and known by the Names of Lewis Ansart.

Whereas Lewis Ansart de Maresquelle, of Dracut, in the county of Middlesex, Esq., has petitioned this court, praying that he may be authorized to omit the addition of de Maresquelle, and that he may be called and known by the names Lewis Ansart, which are his Christian and family names :

Be it therefore enacted, etc., as follows :

That the said Lewis Ansart de Maresquelle be, and he hereby is allowed and authorized to omit the said addition of de Maresquelle, and that he be hereafter known and called by the name of Lewis Ansart.   [*June 6, 1793.*

An Act to change the Name of John Murdock, of Roxbury, in the County of Norfolk, to the Name of Robert Pierpont.

Whereas Hannah Pierpont, of Roxbury aforesaid, hath petitioned this court, for certain reasons set forth in her petition, that the name of John

Murdock, of said Roxbury, may be changed and altered to the name of
Robert Pierpont, and the said John Murdock hath assented to and joined in
said prayer : Therefore,
Be it enacted, etc., as follows :
   That from and after the passing of this act, the said John Murdock shall
be, and he hereby is authorized and impowered to take, use and bear the
name of Robert Pierpont, instead of the said name of John Murdock, and
to be called and known by that name, instead of his present Christian and
surname. [*February 28, 1795.*

An Act to change the Name of William Shelden, of Hadley, in the County
         of Hampshire, to the Name of Giles Crouch Kellogg.
   Whereas Enos Smith, of Hadley, in the county of Hampshire, guardian
to William Shelden, of said Hadley, a minor, hath petitioned this court,
that the name of the said William Shelden may be changed and altered to
the name of Giles Crouch Kellogg, and the said William Shelden hath
desired the same : Therefore,
Be it enacted, etc., as follows :
   That from and after the passing of this act, the said William Shelden
shall be, and hereby is authorized and impowered to take, use and bear the
name of Giles Crouch Kellogg instead of the name of William Shelden, and
to be called and known by that name forever hereafter. [*June 4, 1795.*

An Act giving the Surname of Darling to Leonard Warfield, of Mendon.
Be it enacted, etc., as follows :
   That from and after the passing of this act, the said Leonard Warfield,
of Mendon, shall be, and hereby is authorized and impowered to take, bear
and use the surname of Darling ; and shall be called and known by the
name of Leonard Warfield Darling. [*June 23, 1795.*

An Act to alter the Name of John Williams, to the Name of John Davis
                              Williams.
Be it enacted, etc., as follows :
   That John Williams, of Boston, in the county of Suffolk, son to John
Davis Williams, of Roxbury, in the county of Norfolk, be, and he hereby
is allowed to take the Christian name of John Davis, and on every occasion
hereafter to make the name of John Davis Williams his proper Christian
and surname, and by that name he shall be known and called in all
processes and records whatever. [*January 20, 1796.*

An Act altering the Christian name of Samuel Gardner.
Be it enacted, etc., as follows :
   That from and after the passing of this act, Samuel Gardner, formerly of
Salem, now of Boston, in the county of Suffolk, merchant, shall be, and
he hereby is authorized and empowered to take, bear and use the name of
Samuel Pickering Gardner, and shall be called and known by that name at
all times hereafter. [*February 15, 1796.*

AN ACT to change the name of Moses Porter Phelps, to the Name of
Charles Porter Phelps.

Be it enacted, etc., as follows:

That from and after the passing this act, Moses Porter Phelps, resident
in Boston, in the county of Suffolk, son of Charles Phelps, of Hadley, in
the county of Hampshire, be and he hereby is authorized and allowed to
take, use and bear the name of Charles Porter Phelps, instead of the name
of Moses Porter Phelps, and by that name, to be forever hereafter known
and called in all processes and records whatsoever. [*February 15, 1796.*

AN ACT to change the Name of Ephraim Farrar, to the Name of John
Farrar.

Be it enacted, etc., as follows:

That from and after the passing of this act, Ephraim Farrar, of Worcester, in the county of Worcester, son of John Farrar, late of Shrewsbury,
in the county of Worcester, deceased, be, and he hereby is authorized and
allowed to take, use, and bear the name of John Farrar, and by that name
to be forever hereafter known and called, in all precepts and records whatsoever. [*June 13, 1796.*

AN ACT altering the name of Thomas Amory, to the Name of Thomas C.
Amory.

Be it enacted, etc., as follows:

That from and after the passing of this act, Thomas Amory of Boston,
in the county of Suffolk, merchant, son of the late Thomas Amory,
deceased, shall be, and hereby is authorized and empowered to take, bear
and use the name of Thomas C. Amory, and shall be called and known by
that name at all times hereafter. [*June 14, 1796.*

AN ACT to alter the Name of Samuel Hewes.

Be it enacted, etc., as follows:

That from the passing of this act, Samuel Hewes, of Boston, in the
county of Suffolk, merchant, son of Samuel Hewes, late of said Boston,
deceased, be, and he hereby is authorized to take and use the name of
Samuel Hill Hewes, and that he be called and known by that name at all
times hereafter. [*November 24, 1796.*

AN ACT altering the Name of William White, to the Name of William
Charles White.

Be it enacted, etc., as follows:

That from and after the passing of this act, William White, of Boston,
in the county of Suffolk, son of William White, of said Boston, merchant,
shall be, and he hereby is authorized and empowered to take, bear and use
the name of William Charles White, and shall be called and known by that
name forever hereafter. [*November 25, 1796.*

AN ACT altering the Name of Isaac Davis to Isaac P. Davis.
Be it enacted, etc., as follows:
That from and after the passing this act, Isaac Davis, of Boston, in the county of Suffolk, rope-maker, son of Thomas Davis, late of Plymouth, in the county of Plymouth, merchant, deceased, shall be and hereby is authorized and empowered to take, bear and use the name of Isaac P. Davis, and shall be called and known by that name at all times hereafter. [*March 1, 1797.*

AN ACT to change the name of James Cody to the Name of James Cody Apthorp.
Be it enacted, etc., as follows:
That from and after the passing this act, James Cody, of Partridgefield, in the county of Berkshire, be, and he hereby is authorized and allowed to take, use and bear the name of James Cody Apthorp, and by that name to be forever hereafter known and called in all processes and records whatsoever. [*June 9, 1797.*

AN ACT altering the name of William Gray, the Fifth, to the Name of William Shepard Gray.
Be it enacted, etc., as follows:
That from and after the passing of this act, William Gray, the fifth, of Salem, in the county of Essex, son of William Gray, the third, of said Salem, shall be, and hereby is authorized and empowered to take, bear and use the name of William Shepard Gray, and shall be called and known by that name at all times hereafter. [*February 5, 1798.*

AN ACT altering the Name of Peter Greene to Peter W. Greene.
Be it enacted, etc., as follows:
That from and after the passing of this act, Peter Greene, of Boston, merchant, (son of Richard Greene, late of Warwick, in the state of Rhode Island, deceased) shall be, and he hereby is authorized and empowered to take, bear and use the name of Peter W. Greene, and shall be called and known by that name at all times hereafter. [*February 19, 1798.*

AN ACT for changing the Name of Isaac Vose to that of Isaac D. Vose.
Be it enacted, etc., as follows:
That from and after the passing of this act the said Isaac Vose, son of Joseph Vose, of Milton, Esq. shall be allowed to take the name of Isaac D. Vose, and by that name, instead of his present Christian and surnames, shall be known and called, and that the same shall, to all legal intents and purposes, be hereafter considered as the only and proper name of the said Vose, and shall avail him accordingly. [*February 12, 1799.*

AN ACT to change the Name of Gideon Thayer to Gideon Latimer Thayer.
Be it enacted, etc., as follows:
That from and after the passing of this act, Gideon Thayer, of Braintree, in the county of Norfolk, son of the Honorable Ebenezer Thayer, of said

town, be, and he hereby is authorized and allowed to take, use and bear the name of Gideon Latimer Thayer, and by that name to be hereafter known and called in all processes and records whatever. [*February 16, 1799.*

AN ACT to alter the Name of Jeremiah Williams to the Name of Jeremiah Wadsworth Williams.

Be it enacted, etc., as follows:
That from and after the passing this act, Jeremiah Williams, of Dalton, in the county of Berkshire, shall be, and he hereby is authorized and empowered to take, bear, and use the name of Jeremiah Wadsworth Williams, and shall be called and known by that name forever hereafter. [*February 21, 1799.*

AN ACT altering the Name of William Roberts to William Leate Roberts.

Be it enacted, etc., as follows:
That from and after the passing of this act, William Roberts, of Boston, in the county of Suffolk, son of John White Roberts, late of said Boston, deceased, be, and hereby is authorized and empowered to take, use and bear the name of William Leate Roberts, and by that name to be hereafter known and called in all processes and records whatsoever. [*February 26, 1799.*

AN ACT for changing the Name of William Boardman to that of William Henderson Boardman.

Be it enacted, etc., as follows:
That from and after the passing of this act, the said William Boardman, son of William Boardman, of Chelsea, shall be allowed to take the name of William Henderson Boardman, and by that name, instead of his present Christian and surnames, shall be known and called; and that the same shall to all legal intents and purposes be hereafter considered as the only and proper name of the said Boardman, and shall avail him accordingly. [*March 1, 1799.*

AN ACT altering the Name of Oliver Pond, 3d, to Oliver N. Pond.

Be it enacted, etc., as follows:
That from and after the passing of this act, Oliver Pond, the third of that name of Franklin, in the county of Norfolk, be, and he hereby is authorized and allowed to take, use and bear the name of Oliver N. Pond, and by that name be hereafter known and called in all processes and records whatever. [*June 14, 1799.*

AN ACT for changing the Name of Samuel Flagg the third, to that of Samuel H. Flagg.

Be it enacted, etc., as follows:
That from and after the passing of this act, the said Samuel Flagg, the third of that name, of Worcester, and son of Francis Flagg, of Worcester, in the county of Worcester, shall be allowed to take the name of Samuel H. Flagg, instead of his present Christian and surname, and shall be known and called thereby; and that the same shall, to all legal intents and pur-

poses, be hereafter considered as the only proper name of the said Flagg, and shall avail him accordingly. [*June 21, 1799.*

An Act to change the Name of Charles Cabot to that of Charles George Cabot.

Be it enacted, etc., as follows :
   That Charles Cabot, of Brookline, in the county of Norfolk, merchant, son of George Cabot, of the same place, Esquire, be, and he hereby is authorized to take and bear the name of Charles George Cabot ; and by that name shall henceforth be known and called. [*June 13, 1800.*

An Act to change the names of Billy Hager, Silvanus Coleman the third, Alexander McLeod Clark, John Tyler, Rodolphus Stratton, James Allen, and John Parkman.

Be it enacted, etc., as follows :
   That from and after the passing of this act, Billy Hager, of Marlborough, in the county of Middlesex, son of William Hager, of said Marlborough, shall be allowed to take the name of William Hager ; that Silvanus Coleman, the third of that name, of Nantucket, in the county of Nantucket, son of Jonathan Coleman, of said Nantucket, shall be allowed to take the name of Davis Coleman ; that Alexander McLeod Clark, of Medfield, in the county of Norfolk, son of Elias Clark, of said Medfield, shall be allowed to take the name of Alexander Clark ; that John Tyler, of Boston, in the county of Suffolk, son of John Tyler, late of Mendon, in the county of Worcester, deceased, shall be allowed to take the name of John Eugene Tyler ; that Rodolphus Stratton, of Northfield, in the county of Hampshire, shall be allowed to take the name of Adolphus Smith ; that James Allen, of Boston, in the county of Suffolk, son of Thomas Allen, of Pasquetank county, in the state of North Carolina, shall be allowed to take the name of James Armour Allen ; and that John Parkman, of said Boston, son of William Parkman, of Concord, in the county of Middlesex, shall be allowed to take the name of John Augustus Parkman ; and said persons shall in future be respectively known and called by the names which they are respectively allowed to take as aforesaid, and the same shall be considered as their only proper names, to all intents and purposes. [*March 7, 1801.*

An Act to change the Names of Joseph Sprague Stearns, John Parker, and Jedediah Baker the third.

Be it enacted, etc., as follows :
   That from and after the passing of this act, Joseph Sprague Stearns, of Salem, in the county of Essex, son of William Stearns, shall be allowed to take the name of Joseph Sprague ; that John Parker, of Boston, in the county of Suffolk, son of Isaac Parker, shall be allowed to take the name of John Williams Parker ; that Jedediah Baker the third, of Yarmouth, in the county of Barnstable, shall be allowed to take the name of Washington Baker ; and said persons shall, in future, be respectively known and called

by the names which they are respectively allowed to take as aforesaid, and
the same shall be considered as their only proper names to all intents and
purposes. [*June 19, 1801.*

———

AN ACT to alter the Names of certain Persons therein mentioned.
Be it enacted, etc., as follows:
That from and after the passing of this act, Humphry Stanwood, of Newburyport, in the county of Essex and Commonwealth aforesaid, cooper,
shall be allowed to take the name of Humphry Woodbury ; and that Judith
Stanwood and Agnes Stanwood, the said Humphry's daughters, shall also
be allowed to take the surname of Woodbury ; that Robert Hallowell the
younger, of Boston, in the county of Suffolk, gentleman, shall be allowed
to take the name of Robert Hallowell Gardiner ; that Thomas Denny the
second, of Leicester, in the county of Worcester, son of Samuel Denny, of
said Leicester, shall be allowed to take the name of Nathaniel P. Denny ;
that Levi H. Hardy, of Worcester, in the county of Worcester, shall be
allowed to take the name of Samuel Hardy ; that John Benson, of Boston,
in the county of Suffolk, merchant, son of Joseph Benson, of Scituate, in
the county of Plymouth, shall be allowed to take the name of John Henry
Benson ; that Josiah Vose, of Boston, son of Joseph Vose, of Milton, in
the county of Norfolk, Esq., shall be allowed to take the name of Josiah
Howe Vose ; that Nathaniel Thayer, of Boston, in the county of Suffolk,
and son of Ebenezer Thayer, Esq. of Braintree, in the county of Norfolk,
shall be allowed to take the name of Nathaniel Frederick Thayer ; and that
Samuel Curwen Ward, Jun. a minor, son of Samuel Curwen Ward, of
Salem, in the county of Essex, gentleman, shall be allowed to take the
name of Samuel Curwen ; and said persons shall in future be respectively
known and called by the names which they are respectively allowed to take
as aforesaid ; and the same shall be considered as their only proper names
to all intents and purposes. [*March 11, 1802.*

———

AN ACT to alter the Names of certain Persons therein mentioned.
Be it enacted, etc., as follows:
That from and after the passing of this act, Breck Brigham, of Worcester,
in the county of Worcester, shall be allowed to take the name of Robert
Breck Brigham ; and that John Ambourlain, of Roxbury, in the county of
Norfolk, a minor and ward of Martin Brimmer, shall be allowed to take
the name of John A. Brimmer ; and that William Orne, a minor, a son of
William Orne, of Salem, in the county of Essex, be allowed to take the
name of William Putnam Orne ; and that William Gray, a minor, son of
William Gray, Jun., of Salem, be allowed to take the name of William
Rufus Gray : and said persons shall in future be respectively known and
called by the names which they are respectively allowed to take as aforesaid, and the same shall be considered as their only proper names to all
intents and purposes. [*June 23, 1802.*

An Act to change the Names of Thomas Paine, Joseph Pope, David Child, Abijah Bond, Joseph Johnson, Abijah Savage, Jun., Jonathan Barney, Shubael Sowle, and James Jewett, Jun.

Be it enacted, etc., as follows:

That Thomas Paine, attorney at law, shall be allowed to take the name of Robert Treat Paine; that Joseph Pope, merchant, shall be allowed to take the name of Joseph Henry Pope; that David Child, merchant, shall be allowed to take the name of David Weld Child; that Abijah Bond, a minor, shall be allowed to take the name of William A. Bond; that Joseph Johnson, merchant, shall be allowed to take the name of Joseph Joy Johnson; that Abijah Savage, Jun., a minor, shall be allowed to take the name of Henry Savage; all of Boston, in the county of Suffolk: That Jonathan Barney, of the town and county of Nantucket, mariner, shall be allowed to take the name of Jonathan Jenkins Barney; that Shubael Sowle, of Brookfield, in the county of Worcester, shall be allowed to take the name of Shubael Lyman; and that James Jewett, Jun. of Portland, in the county of Cumberland, gentleman, shall be allowed to take the name of James Charles Jewett; and each of the persons before named shall, in future, be respectively known and called by the names which they are severally allowed to take as aforesaid; and the same shall be considered as their only proper names to all intents and purposes.   [*March 8, 1803.*

An Act to change the Names of Enoch Rust Ridgway, George Parbury, Catharine Powell Archbald, Bradstreet Story, Samuel Bradley, Jun. and Samuel Goddard.

Be it enacted, etc., as follows:

That Enoch Rust Ridgway, of Boston, shall be allowed to take the name of Enoch Henry Rust; that George Parbury, son of George Parbury, late of Baltimore, now resident in Boston, shall be allowed to take the name of George Parbury Pollen: that Catharine Powell Archbald, of Boston, daughter of Francis Archbald, of Penobscot, shall be allowed to take the name of Catharine Goldthwait Powell: that Bradstreet Story, of Boston, son of the Rev. Isaac Story, late of Marblehead, shall be allowed to take the name of Dudley Story Bradstreet: that Samuel Bradley, Jun. now resident in Boston, son of John Bradley, of Concord, in the state of New Hampshire, shall be allowed to take the name of Samuel Ayer Bradley; and that Samuel Goddard, of Boston, son of Samuel Goddard, of Roxbury, shall be allowed to take the name of Samuel Brewer Goddard : — and each of the persons before named shall, in future, be respectively known and called by the names which they are severally allowed to take as aforesaid ; and the same shall be considered as their only proper names to all intents and purposes.   [*June 22, 1803.*

An Act to change the Names of George Parker, Nathaniel Appleton, Charles Appleton, Henry Atwater, Nathaniel Sherman, John Andrews, and John Appleton.

Be it enacted, etc., as follows:

That George Parker, of Dunstable, in the county of Middlesex, a minor, son of Levi Parker, of Peterborough, in the state of New Hampshire, be, and hereby is allowed to take the name of George Wright: that Nathaniel

Appleton, son of Nathaniel Walker Appleton, late of Boston, physician, deceased, be allowed to take the name of Nathaniel Walker Appleton : that Charles Appleton, son of the said Nathaniel Walker Appleton, be allowed to take the name of Charles Henderson Appleton : that Henry Atwater, son of Russell Atwater, of Blandford, in the county of Hampshire, be allowed to take the name of Jedediah Smith Atwater : that Nathaniel Sherman, son of Isaac Sherman, of New Bedford, be allowed to take the name of Nathaniel Church Sherman : that John Andrews, of Boston, son of Benjamin Andrews, late of Boston, deceased, be allowed to take the name of John Hichborn Andrews : that John Appleton, Jun. son of John Appleton, of Salem, be allowed to take the name of John Sparhawk Appleton : and each of the persons before named shall in future be respectively known and called by the names which they are severally allowed to take as aforesaid, and the same shall be considered as their only proper names to all intents and purposes. [*March 8, 1804.*

An Act to change the Names of Ebenezer Morse, William Paine, Jun. William Stevens, Joseph B. Tinker, and James Crawford Bullock.

Be it enacted, etc., as follows :

That Ebenezer Morse, son of Seth Morse, of Westborough, in the county of Worcester, gentleman, be and he hereby is allowed to take the name of Ebenezer Belknap Morse ; that William Paine, Jun. son of William Paine, of Worcester, in the county of Worcester, physician, be and he hereby is allowed to take the name of William Fitz Paine ; that William Stevens, of Portland, in the county of ' Cumberland, son of Samuel Stevens, late of Gloucester, deceased, be and he hereby is allowed to take the name of William Samuel Stevens ; that Joseph B. Tinker, late of Windham, in the state of Connecticut, now resident in Boston, in the county of Suffolk, stationer, be and he hereby is allowed to take the name of Joseph Tinker Buckingham ; that James Crawford Bullock, of Boston, in the county of Suffolk, son of Nathaniel Bullock, late of Salem, in the county of Essex, be and he hereby is allowed to take the name of James Crawford Bullard : and each of the persons above named shall, in future, be respectively known and called by the names which they are severally allowed to take as aforesaid ; and the same shall be considered as their only proper names, to all intents and purposes. [*June 23, 1804.*

An Act to change the Name of Bela Nichols.

Be it enacted, etc., as follows :

That Bela Nichols, of Springfield, in the county of Hampshire, printer, be and he hereby is allowed to take the name of Francis D. Nichols ; and that he shall in future be known and called by the name of Francis D. Nichols, and the same shall be considered as his proper name to all intents and purposes. [*November 21, 1804.*

An Act to change the Name of Bela Snow.

Be it enacted, etc., as follows :

That Bela Snow, son of the late Sylvanus Snow, of Brewster, in the county of Barnstable, deceased, be and he hereby is allowed to take the name of Sylvanus Snow; and that he shall be in future known and called by the name which he is so allowed to take as aforesaid, and the same shall be considered as his only proper name to all intents and purposes. [*November 22, 1804.*

An ACT to alter the Names of certain Persons therein mentioned.
Be it enacted, etc., as follows:
That from and after the passing of this act, Oliver Ware, Jun. of Wrentham, in the county of Norfolk, shall be allowed to take the name of Arom Allchorous; that Samuel Hunt, Jun. of Boston, in the county of Suffolk, shall be allowed to take the name of John Dixwell; that David Curtiss, Jun. of Granville, in the county of Hampshire, shall be allowed to take the name of David Bishop Curtiss; that Charles Thayer, son of Ziphion Thayer, upholsterer, of Boston, in the county of Suffolk, shall be allowed to take the name of Charles Lambert Thayer; that Joseph How, of said Boston, shall be allowed to take the name of Joseph Neals How; that William Goodridge, of said Boston, shall be allowed to take the name of William Marcellus Goodrich; that Ebenezer Beckford, son of Ebenezer Beckford, of Salem, in the county of Essex, shall be allowed to take the name of Ebenezer Hunt Beckford; that Samuel Derby of said Salem, merchant, shall be allowed to take the name of Samuel Gardner Derby; that Jeremiah Fogg, of Boston aforesaid, son of Daniel Fogg, of Braintree, in the county of Norfolk, shall be allowed to take the name of Jeremiah Parsons Fogg; that Jonathan Weston, of Eastport, in the county of Washington, and son of Jonathan Weston, of Reading, in the county of Middlesex, shall be allowed to take the name of Jonathan De Lesdernier Weston; that William Brooks, of Medford, in the county of Middlesex, shall be allowed to take the name of William Smith Brooks; and said persons shall in future be respectively known and called by the names, which they are respectively allowed to take as aforesaid, and the same shall be considered as their only proper names to all intents and purposes. [*March 16, 1805.*

An ACT to alter the Names of certain Persons therein mentioned.
Be it enacted, etc., as follows:
That from and after the passing this act, James Bowdoin Temple, of Boston, in the county of Suffolk, gentleman, shall be allowed to take the name of James Temple Bowdoin; that Samuel Bass Wales, of Randolph, in the county of Norfolk, a minor, shall be allowed to take the name of Ephraim Wales; that John Allen the 4th, of Salem, in the county of Essex, shall be allowed to take the name of John Woodberry Allen; that George Smith, of Salem, in the county of Essex, housewright, and son of Isaac Smith, of Rowley, in said county, shall be allowed to take the name of George Hibbert Smith; that William Hobby, Jun. of Portland, in the county of Cumberland, shall be allowed to take the name of William Gardner Hobby; that John Rogers, of Charlestown, in the county of Middlesex, mariner, shall be allowed to take the name of John Weston Rogers: and said persons in future shall be respectively known and called by the names, which they are respectively allowed to take as aforesaid, and

the same shall hereafter be considered as their only proper names to all intents and purposes. [*June 15, 1805.*

An Act to alter the Names of certain Persons therein mentioned.
Be it enacted, etc., as follows:

That from and after the passing of this act, John O'Neil, Jun. of Madison, in the county of Kennebeck, shall be allowed to take the name of John Neil; James O'Neil, of said Madison, shall be allowed to take the name of James Neil; Samuel O'Neil, of Norridgewalk, in said county, shall be allowed to take the name of Samuel Neil; Benjamin Pickman, son of the Hon. Benjamin Pickman, Jun. of Salem, in the county of Essex, shall be allowed to take the name of Benjamin Toppan Pickman; Stephen Webb, son of Stephen Webb, of said Salem, shall be allowed to take the name of Stephen Palfrey Webb; William Richardson, of said Salem, shall be allowed to take the name of William Putnam Richardson; James Griffin, of said Salem, shall be allowed to take the name of Jonathan Griffin; John Edmands, the third, of Charlestown, in the county of Middlesex, shall be allowed to take the name of John Davis Edmands; Samuel Coolidge, of Boston, in the county of Suffolk, shall be allowed to take the name of Samuel Frederick Coolidge; Andrew Campbell Moses, of said Boston, shall be allowed to take the name of Andrew Campbell Jones; Benjamin Homer, of said Boston, shall be allowed to take the name of Benjamin Parrot Homer; William Hunt, of said Boston, shall be allowed to take the name of William Chamberlain Hunt; Job Prince, of said Boston, shall be allowed to take the name of Thomas J. Prince; Judith Parsons, daughter of Theophilus Parsons, of said Boston, Esq. shall be allowed to take the name of Mary Judith Parsons; John Winslow, Jun. of said Boston, shall be allowed to take the name of John D. Winslow; Joseph Neals How, of said Boston, shall be allowed to take the name of Joseph Neals Howe; Thomas Wales, of said Boston, shall be allowed to take the name of Thomas B. Wales; Francis Thayer, of Braintree, in the county of Norfolk, shall be allowed to take the name of Ebenezer Francis Thayer; Obed Broadbrooks, of Harwich, in the county of Barnstable, shall be allowed to take the name of Obed Brooks; Ebenezer Broadbrooks, of said Harwich, shall be allowed to take the name of Ebenezer Brooks; and the minor children of said Ebenezer Broadbrooks, to wit, Asenath, Jameson, Lucy, Ebenezer, Seth, and Sabra, shall respectively take the surname of Brooks, instead of Broadbrooks; and John Green, of Eastport, in the county of Washington, shall be allowed to take the name of John Le Baron Green; and each of the persons before named shall, in future, be respectively known and called by the names they are severally allowed to take as aforesaid, and the same shall be considered as their only proper names, to all intents and purposes. [*March 14, 1806.*

An Act to alter the Names of certain Persons therein mentioned.
Be it enacted, etc., as follows:

That from and after the passing of this act, William Hunt, of Boston, otherwise called William Chamberlain Hunt, be allowed to take the name of William Hunt Chamberlain; anything in the act passed the 14th day of

March last, and entitled, " An Act to alter the names of certain persons therein mentioned," to the contrary, notwithstanding ; that Samuel Williams, of Boston, in the county of Suffolk, merchant, son of Gideon Williams, of Taunton, in the county of Bristol, be allowed to take the name of Samuel Gideon Williams ; that Thomas Legate, the third, of Leominster, in the county of Worcester, be allowed to take the name of Thomas Charles Legate ; that Robert Cunningham, a minor, and grandson of David Murray, of the town of New Castle, in the county of Lincoln, be allowed to take the name of Robert Murray ; that Edmund Jewett, of Shirley, in the county of Middlesex, be allowed to take the name of Edmund Morrill Jewett. And each of the persons before named, shall in future, be respectively known and called by the names which they are severally allowed to take as aforesaid ; and the same shall be considered as their only proper names to all intents and purposes. [*June 24, 1806.*

An Act to alter the Names of certain Persons therein mentioned.
Be it enacted, etc., as follows :

That from and after the passing of this act, Mary Ann Avery, daughter of John Avery, late of Boston, in the county of Suffolk, Esquire, deceased, shall be allowed to take the name of Mary Ann Smith Avery ; that Tabitha Glover, daughter of Benjamin Stacey Glover, late of Marblehead, in the county of Essex, gentleman, deceased, shall be allowed to take the name of Malvina Tabitha Glover ; that Asa Hammond, of Boston, in the county of Suffolk, son of Samuel Hammond, late of Newton, in the Commonwealth of Massachusetts, deceased, shall be allowed to take the name of Samuel Hammond ; that Samuel Putnam, lately of Lynnfield, in the county of Essex, now of Salem, in said county, trader, shall be allowed to take the name of Samuel Kimbal Putnam ; that Henry Hills, of Boston, in the county of Suffolk, shall be allowed to take the name of Henry Woodbridge Hills ; that Mark Farley, of Leominster, in the county of Worcester, student at law, and son of Benjamin Farley, of the state of New Hampshire, shall be allowed to take the name of Benjamin Mark Farley ; that Jeremiah Smith Boies Hubbard, of Milton, in the county of Norfolk, a minor, and son of William Hubbard, Esquire of New Brunswick, shall be allowed to take the name of Jeremiah Smith Hubbard Boies ; that John Foster, of Salem, in the county of Essex, a minor, and son of John Foster, of said Salem, shall be allowed to take the name of John Burchmore Foster ; that Elizabeth Winslow, of Boston, in the county of Suffolk, single woman, shall be allowed to take the name of Elizabeth Jane Winslow ; that Stephen Blyth, of Salem, in the county of Essex, shall be allowed to take the name of Stephen Cleveland Blydon ; that Sarah Blyth, of Salem, aforesaid, the wife of said Stephen Blyth, be allowed to take the name of Sarah Blydon ; that Lucy Cleveland Blyth, of Salem, aforesaid, and daughter of said Stephen Blyth, shall be allowed to take the name of Sarah Cleveland Blydon ; that William Cleveland Blyth, of Salem, aforesaid, and son of said Stephen Blyth, shall be allowed to take the name of William Cleveland Blydon ; that Joseph Pike, of Newburyport, in the county of Essex, and son of Nicholas Pike, of said Newburyport, shall be allowed to take the name of Joseph Smith Pike ; that Joseph Pike, of Newburyport, aforesaid, and son of John Pike, of Somersworth, in the county of Strafford, and state of New Hampshire, shall be allowed to take the name of Joseph Trevet Pike ; that Hezekiah Stone, of Rutland, in the county of Worcester, gentleman, shall be allowed to take the name of Hezekiah Fletcher Stone ; that Alpheus Stone, of Greenfield, in the county of Hampshire, physician, shall be allowed to take the name of Alpheus Fletcher Stone ; that Samuel Foster, of Newburyport, in the county of Essex, merchant, shall be allowed to take the name of Samuel H. Foster ; that John Buffington Snupe, of Beverly, in the county of Essex, merchant, shall be allowed to take the name of John Buffington ; that Samuel Lee, a minor, and son of Jonas Lee, of Concord, in the county of Middlesex, shall be allowed to take the name of Samuel Cordis Lee ; that Samuel Willard, of Boston, in the county of Suffolk, and son of the late President Willard, of Cambridge, in the county of Middlesex, shall be allowed to take the name of Samuel Sheaf Willard ; that Francis Jones, of Sandwich, in the county of Barnstable, merchant, be allowed to take the name of Francis Freeman Jones ; that Catharine Low, of Chelmsford, in the county of Middlesex, single woman, be allowed to take the name of Catharine Mary Gibson ; and Samuel Loud, of Weymouth, be allowed to take the name of Samuel Prince Loud ; and said persons shall in future be respectively known and called by the names which they are respectively allowed to take as aforesaid ; and the same shall be considered as their only proper names, to all intents and purposes. [*Feb. 27, 1807.*

An Act to alter the Names of certain Persons therein named.
Be it enacted, etc., as follows :
   That from and after the passing of this act, John Hayward, of Boston, in the county of Suffolk, student at law, shall be allowed to take the name of John White Hayward ; that Jonathan Sprague, of Boston, aforesaid, physician, shall be allowed to take the name of John Sprague ; that John Wheelwright, of Boston, aforesaid, merchant, be allowed to take the name of John Hall Wheelwright ; that M'Gregory Bumside, of Andover, in the county of Essex, shall be allowed to take the name of Samuel M. Bumside ; that Habijah Weld Fuller, of Augusta, in the county of Kennebeck, attorney at law, be allowed to take the name of Henry Weld Fuller ; that Charles Vose, of Gardiner, in said county of Kennebeck, merchant, be allowed to take the name of Robert Charles Vose ; that Benjamin Tucker of Dartmouth, in the county of Bristol, merchant, be allowed to take the name of Benjamin Ricketson Tucker. And said persons shall in future be respectively known and called by the names which they are respectively allowed to take as aforesaid, and the same shall hereafter be considered as their only proper names, to all intents and purposes. [*June 20, 1807.*

An Act to alter the Names of certain Persons therein mentioned.
Be it enacted, etc., as follows :
   That from and after the passing of this act, Thomas Harris the third, of Charlestown, in the county of Middlesex, son of Richard Harris, late of Marblehead, deceased, be allowed to take the name of Richard Thomas Harris ; that Elisa Loyns Potter, a minor, and son of Job Potter, of Great Barrington, be allowed to take the name of Robert Loyns Potter ; that

Henry Orne, of Salem, in the county of Essex, and son of William Orne, of said Salem, merchant, be allowed to take the name of Charles Henry Orne ; that Richard Derby, of Boston, in the county of Suffolk, son of Elias Hasket Derby, late of Salem, in the county of Essex, deceased, be allowed to take the name of Richard C. Derby ; that Prince Tobey, of Augusta, in the county of Kennebeck, son of Stephen Tobey, of the same Augusta, gentleman, be allowed to take the name of Charles Edward Tobey ; that Thomas Smith, of Rowley, in the county of Essex, son of Isaac Smith, of the same Rowley, be allowed to take the name of Thomas Hibbert Smith ; that Samuel Page, of Salem, in the county of Essex, and son of Samuel Page, of the same Salem, deceased, be allowed to take the name of Samuel Lee Page ; that John Gilman, of Winslow, in the county of Kennebeck, be allowed to take the name of John Hancock Gilman ; that Andrew Mock, of Boston, in the county of Suffolk, minor, and son of William Mock, late of said Boston, deceased, be allowed to take the name of Andrew Jeremiah Allen ; that James King the third, of Salem, in the county of Essex, and son of James King, of said Salem, be allowed to take the name of James Charles King ; that James Purinton, late of Topsham, in the county of Lincoln, but now of the plantation of Little River, tanner, be allowed to take the name of James Woodbury Purinton ; that Daniel Hamant, Jun., of Medfield, in the county of Norfolk, minor, and son of Daniel Hamant, of said Medfield, be allowed to take the name of Caleb Strong Hamant ; that Zachariah Shed, of Boston, in the county of Suffolk, merchant, son of Ebenezer Shed, of Chelmsford, in the county of Middlesex, be allowed to take the name of George Shed ; that George Bruce, of Boston, in the county of Suffolk, minor, and son of the late Stephen Bruce, of said Boston, deceased, be allowed to take the name of George Appleton Bruce ; that Charles Bruce, of said Boston, minor, and son of said Stephen Bruce, be allowed to take the name of Charles Henry Bruce ; that Billey Richardson, of Billerica, in the county of Middlesex, blacksmith, son of Jacob Richardson, late of said Billerica, be allowed to take the name of William Richardson ; that Rosel Underwood, of Greenfield, in the county of Hampshire, be allowed to take the name of Rosel U. Deming.   And said persons shall, in future, be respectively known and called by the names which they are respectively allowed to take as aforesaid ; and the same shall be considered as their only proper names to all intents and purposes.   [*March 11, 1808.*

An Act to alter the Names of certain Persons therein named.
Be it enacted, etc., as follows :
That from and after the passing of this act, Samuel Knapp, of Haverhill, in the county of Essex, gentleman, be allowed to take the name of Samuel Lorenzo Knapp ; and that Samuel Fales, of Boston, in the county of Suffolk, trader, son of Nehemiah Fales, late of Dedham, in the county of Norfolk, yeoman, deceased, be allowed to take the name of Samuel Whiting Fales ; John Blake, of Boston, in the county of Suffolk, merchant, be allowed to take the name John H. Blake ; that Samuel Burling, of Boston, aforesaid, merchant, be allowed to take the name of Samuel Curson : and said persons shall, in future, be respectively known and called by the names which they are respectively allowed to take as aforesaid, and the

same shall be considered as their only proper names to all intents and purposes. [*June 10, 1808.*

An Act to change the Name of Samuel M. Bumside, of Charlestown, County of Middlesex, and to render valid the doings of said Samuel, under the Name of Samuel M. Burnside.
Be it enacted, etc., as follows:
That Samuel M. Bumside, of Charlestown, in the county of Middlesex, shall be allowed to take the name of Samuel M. Burnside, and that in future he be known by the same, as his only legal and proper name, and that all the acts which heretofore he may have done, and performed, by the name of Samuel M. Burnside be and hereby are ratified and confirmed as far as respects the use of said name. [*Nov. 17, 1808.*

An Act to change the Name of Harris Tuckerman.
Be it enacted, etc., as follows:
That from and after the passing of this act, Harris Tuckerman, of Boston, in the county of Suffolk, merchant, be allowed to take the name of Henry H. Tuckerman ; and said Tuckerman shall in future be known and called by the name he is hereby allowed to take as aforesaid, and the same shall be considered as his proper name to all intents and purposes. [*Nov. 17, 1808.*

An Act to alter the Names of certain Persons therein mentioned.
Be it enacted, etc., as follows:
That from and after the passing of this act, Joseph Clark, of Boston, in the county of Suffolk, shall be allowed to take the name of Joseph Dyar Clark, that Joseph Newell of Boston aforesaid, shall be allowed to take the name of Joseph Reynolds Newell ; that Daniel Parker of Boston aforesaid, shall be allowed to take the name of Daniel Pinckney Parker ; that William Hayes of Charlestown, in the county of Middlesex, shall be allowed to take the name of William Allen Hayes ; that William Hales (otherwise Littlehale) of Gloucester in the county of Essex, shall be allowed to take the name of William Hales ; that Micajah Marston of Salem, in the county of Essex, shall be allowed to take the name of Morrill Marston ; that Charles Curtis of Roxbury in the county of Norfolk, shall be allowed to take the name of Charles Dormer Curtis ; that Richard Williamson of Dedham in the county of Norfolk shall be allowed to take the name of Richard Leland ; that Bille Metcalf of Franklin in the county of Norfolk shall be allowed to take the name of William Haven Metcalf ; that Asa Bly, and Elizabeth Bly (otherwise both called Tripp) both of Westport, in the county of Bristol, shall be allowed to take the names of Asa Bly, and Elizabeth Bly ; that Josiah Linkhornew, Joshua Linkhornew, Dawson Linkhornew, Doane Linkhornew, Andrew Linkhornew, and Joseph Linkhornew, all of Eastham in the county of Barnstable, shall be severally allowed to take the names of Josiah Lincoln, Joshua Lincoln, Dawson Lincoln, Doane Lincoln, Andrew Lincoln, and Joseph Lincoln ; that Joseph Peiroe the second, of Dorchester in the county of Norfolk, (son of Joseph Peirce of Boston in the county of Suffolk, Esq.) shall be allowed to take the name of Joseph H. Peirce ; that McGregore Burnside of Charlestown in the

county of Middlesex, shall be allowed to take the name of Samuel M. Burnside; that Susanna Alexander, of Charlestown in the county of Middlesex, single woman, shall be allowed to take the name of Susanna Fowle; that George Smith the fifth, of Salem, in the county of Essex, shall be allowed to take the name of George Campbell Smith; and that Joseph Wingate of Bath, in the county of Lincoln, shall be allowed to take the name of Joseph Ferdinand Wingate. And each of the persons before named shall be severally allowed to assume the said names respectively, and they shall in future be called and known by the said names, and the same names shall hereafter be considered as their only proper names to all intents and purposes. [*March 4, 1809.*]

An Act to change the Names of certain Persons therein mentioned.
Be it enacted, etc., as follows:
That from and after the passing of this act, John O'Brien, the third, of Newbury, in the county of Essex, shall be allowed to take the name of John Maurice O'Brien; that John Hooper, of Marblehead, in the county aforesaid, shall be allowed to take the name of John Grist Hooper; that Josiah Clark, of Sharon, in the county of Norfolk, who has been known and called by the name of Joseph Huin, shall be allowed to take the name of Joseph Huin; that Samuel Bayley, Jun. of Weymouth, in the county of Norfolk, shall be allowed to take the name of Samuel Publius Bayley; that William Stickney, the third, of Newbury, in the county of Essex, shall be allowed to take the name of Albert Alonzo Stickney; that Joseph Sprague, Jun. of Salem, in the county of Essex, shall be allowed to take the name of Joseph E. Sprague; that Samuel Lee, of Boston, in the county of Suffolk, shall be allowed to take the name of William Raymond Lee; that Elijah White, of Boston, aforesaid, shall be allowed to take the name of Ferdinand Elliot White; that Israel Putnam the fourth, son of Eleazer Putnam of Danvers, in the county of Essex, Esq. shall be allowed to take the name of Israel Warburton Putnam. And the said persons shall, from and after the passing of this act, be known and called by the names which they are respectively allowed to take, as aforesaid, and the same shall be considered as their only proper names. [*June 19, 1809.*]

An Act to change the Names of certain Persons therein mentioned.
Be it enacted, etc., as follows:
That from and after the passing of this act, James Ayer (son of James Ayer, Jun.) of Haverhill, in the county of Essex, shall be allowed to take the names of James Hazen Bricket Ayer; that Prince Beal, of Kingston, in the county of Plymouth, shall be allowed to take the name of Thomas Prince Beal; that Grace Besom, of Marblehead, in the county of Essex, shall be allowed to take the name of Martha Besom; that John Hall, of Lee, in the county of Berkshire, shall be allowed to take the name of John Grafton Hall; that Joseph Huin, of Sharon, in the county of Norfolk, shall be allowed to take the name of Joseph Hewins; that John Phillips, of Bradford, in the county of Essex, shall be allowed to take the name of Alonzo Phillips; that Joseph Sprague (son of Ebenezer Sprague) of Dan-

vers, in the county of Essex, shall be allowed to take the name of Joseph George Sprague; that Sylvester Twiss, of Danvers, in the county of Essex, shall be allowed to take the name of Sylvester Proctor; that Elizabeth Thompson Tyler, of Boston, in the county of Suffolk, shall be allowed to take the names of Elizabeth Jones Thompson Tyler; that Asa Ward, Jun. of Boston, in the county of Suffolk, shall be allowed to take the name of Lauriston Ward; that Rhoda White, of Salem, in the county of Essex, shall be allowed to take the name of Elizabeth Cutter White; that James Hinkley, (also called James Evans) of Winthrop, in the county of Kennebeck, shall be allowed to take the name of James Wheeler; that George Fiske, of Boston, in the county of Suffolk, shall be allowed to take the name of George Boyle Fiske; that Samuel Ford, of Boston, in the county of Suffolk, shall be allowed to take the name of Samuel Bass Ford; that William Hall, of Boston, in the county of Suffolk, shall be allowed to take the name of William Chauncy Hall; that Abraham Howe, of Boston, in the county of Suffolk, shall be allowed to take the name of Abraham Fay Howe; that Rufus Lincoln, of Boston, in the county of Suffolk, shall be allowed to take the name of Rufus Warren Lincoln; that Thomas Hibbert Smith, of Salem, son of Isaac Smith of Rowley, in the county of Essex, shall be allowed to take the name of Lorain W. Smith; that Mussey Southwick, of Uxbridge, in the county of Worcester, shall be allowed to take the name of Thomas Mussey Southwick; that John Stephens, of Boston, in the county of Suffolk, shall be allowed to take the name of John Hathaway Stephens; that William Barry Turell, of Salem, in the county of Essex, shall be allowed to take the name of Charles Turell; that Sarah Morton, of Dorchester, in the county of Norfolk, shall be allowed to take the name of Sarah Wentworth Morton; and the said persons shall, from and after the passing of this act, be known and called by the names which they are respectively allowed to take as aforesaid, and the same shall be considered as their only proper names. [*March 6, 1810.*]

———

An ACT to alter the Names of the several Persons therein mentioned.
Be it enacted, etc., as follows:

That from and after the passing this act, Nathaniel Child, of Gardiner, in the county of Worcester, shall be allowed to take the name of Nathaniel Parks Child; that Samuel Stevens, Jun. of Newburyport, in the county of Essex, shall be allowed to take the name of Samuel Bingham Stevens, that Federal Brownell, of Westport, in the county of Bristol, shall be allowed to take the name of Frederick Brownell; that Benjamin Crowninshield, of Salem, in the county of Essex, shall be allowed to take the name of Benjamin Williams Crowninshield; that Abraham Priest, of Boston, in the county of Suffolk, shall be allowed to take the name of Abraham Priest Gibson; that Pepper Mixer, of Dedham, in the county of Norfolk, shall be allowed to take the name of Charles Mixer; and each of the persons before named shall be severally allowed to assume the said names respectively, and they shall in future be called and known by the said names, and the same names shall hereafter be considered as their only proper names to all intents and purposes. [*June 13, 1810.*]

AN ACT to alter the Names of certain Persons therein named.
Be it enacted, etc., as follows:
    That from and after the passing of this act, Roger King, of Brewster, in
the county of Barnstable, shall be allowed to take the name of Elkanah
King; that Quintus Carolus Turner, of Scituate, in the county of Plymouth,
be allowed to take the name of Charles Henry Turner; that George
Hodges, of Salem, in the county of Essex, be allowed to take the name of
George Atkinson Hodges; that John Stinson, of Woolwich, in the county
of Lincoln, be allowed to take the name of John Robinson Stinson; that
Isaac Rea, and Ebenezer Rea, both of Beverly, in the county of Essex, be
allowed to take the surname of Ray; that William Caldwell, the fourth, of
Newburyport, in the county of Essex, be allowed to take the name of
William Warner Caldwell; that Molly Clark, of Brewster, in the county of
Barnstable, take the name of Mary Paddock Clark; that William Bancroft,
Jun. of Charlestown, in the county of Middlesex, be allowed to take the
name of William Austin Bancroft; that Abel Coffin, son of Jonathan
Coffin, of Nantucket, in the county of Nantucket, take the name of Abel
C. Coffin; that Dyer Peters, of Ellsworth, in the county of Hancock, take
the name of Edward Dyer Peters; that John Saunders, of Danvers, in the
county of Essex, be allowed to take the name of John Wallis Saunders;
that Jonathan Crosby, of Stow, in the county of Middlesex, be allowed to
take the name of Salvo Crosby; that William Coolidge, of Boston, in the
county of Suffolk, take the name of William Clark Coolidge; that Alexander Wheelock, of Boston, in the county of Suffolk, be allowed to take
the name of Abel Wheelock; that Isaac Foster, of Brunswick, in the
county of Cumberland, be allowed to take the name of Ferris De Ayr
Foster; that Thomas Davis, of Sidney, in the county of Kennebeck, be
allowed to take the name of Charles Stewart Davis; that Samuel Derby,
of Salem, in the county of Essex, be allowed to take the name of Samuel
Barton Derby; that Samuel Ayer, the third, of Haverhill, in the county of
Essex, be allowed to take the name of Samuel W. Ayer; that John
Carter, of Boston, in the county of Suffolk, be allowed to take the name of
John S. Carter; that John Foster, Jun. of Boston, in the county of Suffolk,
son of the Reverend John Foster, of Brighton, be allowed to take the name
of John Standish Foster; that John Bacon, of Boston, in the county of
Suffolk, be allowed to take the name of John Arno Bacon; that Alderman
Hyde, of New Marlborough, in the county of Berkshire, be allowed to take
the name of James Alderman Hyde; that Asa Wildes, of Newburyport, in
the county of Essex, be allowed to take the name of Asa Waldo Wildes;
that Abijah Peirce Hoar, of Charlestown, son of Samuel Hoar, of Lincoln,
in the county of Middlesex, be allowed to take the name of Abijah Hoar
Peirce; that Peter Brigham, of Boston, in the county of Suffolk, be allowed
to take the name of Peter Welles Brigham; that Peter Thacher, of Boston,
in the county of Suffolk, Esq. be allowed to take the name of Peter Oxen-
bridge Thacher; — and each of the persons before named shall be severally allowed to assume the said names respectively, and they shall in future
be called and known by said names, and the same names shall hereafter be
considered as their only proper names, to all intents and purposes. [*Feb.
26, 1811.*

An Act to alter the Names of certain Persons therein mentioned.
Be it enacted, etc., as follows:

That from and after the passing of this act, Thomas Searle of Rowley, in the county of Essex, son of Joseph Searle, shall be allowed to take the name of Thomas Colman Searle; that Joseph Jones, of Boston, in the county of Suffolk, shall be allowed to take the name of Charles Henry Jones; that Abraham Quincy, of Boston aforesaid, shall be allowed to take the name of Abraham Howard Quincy; that Elizabeth Mock, of Boston aforesaid, single woman, shall be allowed to take the name of Elizabeth Allen; that William Rogers, of Boston aforesaid, shall take the name of William Charles Rogers; that John King, Jun. of Salem, in the county of Essex, shall be allowed to take the name of John Glen King; that John Harris, Jun. of Marblehead, in said county of Essex, shall be allowed to take the name of John Lord Harris; that Moses Atkinson, of Newbury, in said county of Essex, shall be allowed to take the name of Moses Little Atkinson; that Moses Moody Swan, of Haverhill, in said county of Essex, shall be allowed to take the name of Moses Swan Moody; that Levi Whitmore, of Framingham, in the county of Middlesex, shall be allowed to take the name of Levi Foster Whitmore; that Samuel B. Harris, of Charlestown, in said county, shall be allowed to take the name of Samuel Harris Bradstreet; that Batchellor Hussey, of Portland, in the county of Cumberland, shall be allowed to take the name of Henry Hussey; that Simeon Alden, Jun. of Randolph, in the county of Norfolk, shall be allowed to take the name of Horatio Bingley Alden; that Marilla Gurney, of the town of Abington, in the county of Plymouth, shall be allowed to take the name of Marilla Livingston Gurney; that Samuel Barnard, of Boston aforesaid, shall be allowed to take the name of George Edward Augustus Carpenter Barnard.

And each of the persons before named shall be allowed to assume the said names respectively, and they shall in future be called and known by the said names, and the said names shall hereafter be considered as their only proper names, to all intents and purposes. [*June 21, 1811.*]

––––––

An Act to change the Names of certain Persons herein mentioned.
Be it enacted, etc., as follows:

That from and after the date of passing this act, that William Andrews, the third son of John Andrews, of Boston, shall be allowed to take the name of William Barrell Andrews; that John Brown, of Boston, son of John Brown, of Sterling, in the county of Worcester, shall be allowed to take the name of John George Brown; that Elijah Clark, son of Humphry Clark, shall be allowed to take the name of Elijah Pope Clark; that William Jarvis shall be allowed to take the name of William Charles Jarvis; that Obadiah Johnson shall be allowed to take the name of William Henry Johnson; that Susan Ann Lovell, daughter of James Lovell, shall be allowed to take the name of Ann Bethune Lovell; that William Machett shall be allowed to take the name of William P. Matchett; that John Marston shall be allowed to take the name of John Melcher Marston; that Henry Parkman, son of Samuel Parkman, shall be allowed to take the name of Samuel Parkman, — all of Boston in the county of Suffolk; that John Buckminster, of Hamilton, shall be allowed to take the name of John

Butler; that Elisha Hogg, of Danvers, shall be allowed to take the name of Elisha Dana; that Asa Fletcher, of Danvers, shall be allowed to take the name of William Asa Fletcher; that Polly Smith, of Salem, shall be allowed to take the name of Mary Larkin Smith, — all of the county of Essex; that Samuel Tubbs, of Pembroke, shall be allowed to take the name of Samuel Tubbs Angier; that Calvin Dammon, of Scituate, shall be allowed to take the name of Calvin Damon Wilder, — all of the county of Plymouth; that Abner Gifford, of Westport, shall be allowed to take the name of Abner Browner Gifford; that Raiman Castino (alias Salisbury), and Abigail Castino (alias Salisbury), of Westport, shall be allowed to take the names of Raiman Castino, and Abigail Castino, only, — all of the county of Bristol; that Baxter Olds, of Brookfield, shall be allowed to take the name of Baxter Olds Minot; that Polycarp Putnam, of Sutton, shall be allowed to take the name of John Milton Putnam, — all of the county of Worcester; that Richard Lyman, of Northampton, shall be allowed to take the name of William Cornelius Lyman; that Chase Page Wedgewood Griffin, of Alfred, in the county of York, shall be allowed to take the name of Charles Griffin; that John Kimbal, of Augusta, in the county of Kennebeck, shall be allowed to take the name of John Sawyer Kimbal; that Ebenezer McIntosh, of Portland in the county of Cumberland, shall be allowed to take the name of Henry P. McIntosh; that Moses Chase, Jun. of Newburyport, shall be allowed to take the name of Moses James Chase; that Moses Chase the third, of Newburyport, shall be allowed to take the name of Moses Bailey Chase; that Benjamin Gould, Jun. of Newburyport, shall be allowed to take the name of Benjamin Apthorp Gould, — all of the county of Essex.   And the said several persons, from and after the passing of this act, be called and known by the names which by this act they are respectively allowed to take as aforesaid, and the same shall be considered as their only proper and legal names. [*Feb. 29, 1812.*]

An Act to change the Names of certain Persons therein named.
Be it enacted, etc., as follows:
That Joseph Freeland, Jun. of Boston shall be allowed to take the name of Joseph Freeland Bordman; James Perkins son of the late Colonel William Perkins of said Boston, shall be allowed to take the name of Charles James Perkins, all of the county of Suffolk; John Mudge, Jun. of Lynn, shall be allowed to take the name of Parker Mudge; Charles Kimball of Boxford shall be allowed to take the name of Charles Harrison Kimball; George Smith. the seventh of that name of Salem, shall be allowed to take the name of George King Smith; Jonathan Sargent the fourth of Amesbury, shall be allowed to take the name of Jonathan Adams Sargent; Jonathan Morrill, Jun. of said Amesbury, shall be allowed to take the name of Jonathan Currier Morrill, all in the county of Essex; Wiiliam Breck, of Northampton in the county of Hampshire, shall be allowed to take the name of Joseph Hunt Breck; Chauncy Taylor, of Blandford, in the county of Hampden, shall be allowed to take the name of Chauncy Taylor Knox; Rebecca Cutler of Sudbury, in the county of Middlesex, shall be allowed to take the name of Rebecca Maynard; James Child, Jun. of Augusta, in the county of Kennebeck, shall be allowed to take the name of James Loring Child; Barden Sylvester, merchant, of Bath in the county of Lin-

coln, shall be allowed to take the name of Thomas Barden Sylvester ; and the said several persons, from the time of passing this act, shall be called and known by the names which by this act they are severally allowed to take as aforesaid, and the same shall be considered as their only proper and legal names. [*June 22, 1812.*

AN ACT to change the Names of certain Persons therein mentioned.
Be it enacted, etc., as follows :
    That Ebenezer Stoddard of Salem, in the county of Essex, trader, shall be allowed to take the name of William Couillard Stoddard ; and that Moses Smith Fox of Williamsburgh, in the county of Hampshire, yeoman, shall be allowed to take the name of Augustine Washington Fox ; and the said persons, from the time of the passing this act, shall be called and known by the names which by this act are severally allowed to take as aforesaid, and the same shall be considered as their only proper and legal names. [*Oct. 24, 1812.*

AN ACT to alter the Name of Joshua Gee Whittemore, Jun.
Be it enacted, etc., as follows :
    That from and after the passing of this act, Joshua Gee Whittemore, Jun. of Gloucester, in the county of Essex, mariner, shall be allowed to take the name of Harvey C. Mackay, and he shall in future be called and known by the said name ; and the said name shall forever hereafter be considered as his only proper and legal name, to all intents and purposes. [*Feb. 13, 1813.*

AN ACT to alter and change the Names of certain Persons therein mentioned, and for other purposes.
Be it enacted, etc., as follows :
    That from and after the passing of this act, Samuel White, of Boston, in the county of Suffolk, shall be allowed to take the name of Samuel Kellogg White ; that Mary Leo Griffith, daughter of the widow Mary Griffith, of the same Boston, shall be allowed to take the name of Mary Elizabeth Newall Griffith ; that Johnston Brown, of Boston aforesaid, jeweller, son of Robert Brown, late of Plymouth, in the county of Plymouth, deceased, shall be allowed to take the name of Robert Johnston Brown ; that Abiah Williams, of said Boston, shall be allowed to take the name of Maria Williams ; that Charles Parsons, of Boston aforesaid, merchant, shall be allowed to take the name of Charles Chauncy Parsons ; and all acts heretofore lawfully done by the said Parsons, in the name of Charles Chauncy Parsons, are hereby ratified and confirmed ; that Lucy Ann Innes Whitwell, an infant daughter of Benjamin Whitwell, Esq. of the same Boston, shall be allowed to take the name of Lucy Cushing Whitwell ; that James Dickinson, of said Boston, comedian, shall be allowed to take the name of James Amos Dickson ; that Ebenezer Baker, of Boston aforesaid, son of Ebenezer Baker, late of Dorchester, in the county of Norfolk, deceased, shall be allowed to take the name of Ebenezer Richard Baker ; that William Wyer, of the same Boston, mariner, shall be allowed to take the name of William Fitspatrick Wyer ; that George Hall, of said Boston, son of Dr. George H. Hall, late of Brattleborough, Vermont, deceased, shall

be allowed to take the name of George Ward Hall; that John Browne, of Salem, in the county of Essex, cordwainer, shall be allowed to take the name of John D. Browne; that John Smith, Jun. of Newburyport, in said county of Essex, merchant, son of Leonard Smith, of the same Newburyport, shall be allowed to take the name of John Augustus Smith; that Salvador Sabate, of Cohasset, in the county of Norfolk, shall be allowed to take the name of Samuel Snow; that William Leonard, Jun. of Plymouth, in the county of Plymouth, son of Nathaniel Leonard, Esq. of Taunton, in the county of Bristol, shall be allowed to take the name of William B. Leonard; that Harry Sargent, of Leicester, in the county of Worcester, gentleman, shall be allowed to take the name of Henry Sargent; that Albert Lamberton, commonly called Albert Lewis, a minor and godson of Darius Lewis, of Egremont, in the county of Berkshire, shall be allowed to take the name of Albert Lewis; that Jesse Hunter, of Becket, in the said county of Berkshire, yeoman, shall be allowed to take the name of John Larkin Hunter; that Pardon Shippey, otherwise called Pardon Trask, of Cheshire, in the county of Berkshire aforesaid, yeoman, shall be allowed to take the name of Pardon Lincoln; that Harvy Needham, of South Brimfield, in the county of Hampden, gentleman, shall be allowed to take the name of James Harvey Needham; that John Tompson, the fourth, of Berwick, in the county of York, shall be allowed to take the name of John S. Tompson; that Abel Prescott, 2d of Concord, in the county of Middlesex, son of the late Willoughby Prescott, of the same Concord, deceased, shall be allowed to take the name of Abel Heywood Prescott; and the several persons before named, from the time of the passing of this act, shall be called and known by the names, which by this act they are respectively allowed to take and assume as aforesaid; and the said names shall forever hereafter be considered as their only proper and legal names, to all intents and purposes. [*Feb. 27, 1813.*

An Act to alter and change the Names of certain persons therein mentioned.

Be it enacted, etc., as follows:

    That from and after the passing of this act, Samuel Torrey of Boston, in the county of Suffolk, son of William Torrey of Mendon, in the county of Worcester, shall be allowed to take the name of Samuel Davenport Torrey; that Joseph Smith of Salem, in the county of Essex, son of Joseph Smith of Rowley, in said county, shall be allowed to take the name of Joseph Baker Smith; that Chauncey Whittlesey Coats of Middlefield, in the county of Hampshire, shall be allowed to take the name of Chauncey Coats; that Zebedee Macomber, 2d, of Westport, in the county of Bristol, shall be allowed to take the name of Zebedee Augustus Macomber; that William Woodbury of Hallowell, in the county of Kennebeck, printer, shall be allowed to take the name of William Augustus Woodbury; that James Bowdoin Winthrop, son of Thomas L. Winthrop, Esq. of Boston, in the county of Suffolk, a minor, shall be allowed to take the name of James Bowdoin. And the several persons before named, from the time of the passing of this act, shall be called and known by the names, which by this act they are respectively allowed to take and assume, as aforesaid; and the said names shall forever hereafter be considered as their only proper and legal names, to all intents and purposes. [*June 16, 1813.*

———

An Act to alter and change the Names of certain persons therein mentioned.

Be it enacted, etc., as follows:

That from and after the date of the passing of this act, Thomas Kendall, of Boston, in the county of Suffolk, sail-maker, shall be allowed to take the name of Thomas Boyd Kendall; that Silas Cheney, of the same Boston, shall be allowed to take the name of Samuel S. Cheney; that John Torrey, son of Samuel Torrey, of Boston aforesaid, shall be allowed to take the name of John Gore Torrey; that Asa Dennet, a citizen of the United States of America, and resident at said Boston, shall be allowed to take the name of Charles A. Dennet; that John Reed, of Boston aforesaid, son of Benjamin Reed, of Milton, in the county of Norfolk, shall be allowed to take the name of John Walter Reed; that Ebenezer Upton, Jun. of Danvers, in the county of Essex, shall be allowed to take the name of Eben Sprague Upton; that Mercy Smith, an infant daughter of James Smith, of Marblehead, in said county of Essex, merchant, shall be allowed to take the name of Mercy Abigail King Smith; that Moses Moody the 3d, of Newburyport, in the county of Essex aforesaid, merchant, shall be allowed to take the name of Moses Frederic Moody; that Lorenty Spitzenfield Colby, an infant son of John Colby, of Salisbury, in said county of Essex, shall be allowed to take the name of Edwin John Colby; that George Bartlett 2d, of Charlestown, in the county of Middlesex, son of the Hon. Josiah Bartlett, of the same place, shall be allowed to take the name of George Frederick Bartlett; that William Porter, of Charlestown aforesaid, shall be allowed to take the name of Frederick William Porter; that Timothy Burbank, of Sherburne, in said county of Middlesex, shall be allowed to take the name of Timothy Kendall; that Lysander Bascom Loveland, an orphan boy, and son of the late Epaphroditus Loveland, of Greenfield, in the county of Franklin, deceased, shall bo allowed to take the name of Lysander Loveland Bascom; that Mary Gifford, of Westport, in the county of Bristol, shall be allowed to take the name of Mary Ann Wilbour Gifford; that Adam Briggs, a minor, and son of the late Susanna Harrington, of Orange, in the county of Franklin, shall be allowed to take the name of Adams Harrington; that John Rice, of Boston, in the county of Suffolk, son of the late Major John Rice, of the same Boston, shall be allowed to take the name of John H. Rice.

And the several persons before named from the time of the passing of this act, shall be called and known by the names which, by this act, they are respectively allowed to take and assume as aforesaid; and the said names shall forever hereafter be considered as their only proper and legal names, to all intents and purposes. [*Feb. 26, 1814.*

AN ACT to alter and change the Names of certain Persons therein mentioned.

Be it enacted, etc., as follows:

That from and after the passing of this act, Charles Adams of Boston in the county of Suffolk, son of Elijah Adams, of Medfield, in the county of Norfolk, shall be allowed to take the name of Charles Jeremiah Adams; that Welcome Eager of Boston aforesaid, merchant, shall be allowed to take the name of William Eager; that John Bradford of said Boston, son of William B. Bradford of the same place, shall be allowed to take the name of John Rufus Bradford; that George Doane of the same Boston, shall be allowed to take the name of George Bartlett Doane; that William Couillard Stodderd, of Salem, in the county of Essex, trader, son of Ebed Stodderd, of the same Salem, shall be allowed to take the name of Ebenezer Couillard Stoddard; that John Babbidge, jun., of Salem aforesaid, mariner, shall be allowed to take the name of John Laurens Babbidge; that John Osgood, jun. of the same Salem, mariner, shall be allowed to take the name of John Babbidge Osgood; that William Low, of Salem aforesaid, a minor, and son of David Low, late of Haverhill, in said county, deceased, shall be allowed to take the name of William Henry Low; that John Browne, the sixth, of said Salem, son of Edward Browne of the same place, shall be allowed to take the name of Edward John Browne; that John Clarke, of Watertown, in the county of Middlesex, son of Thomas Clarke, Esq. of the same town, shall be allowed to take the name of John Henry Clarke; that Joseph Tufts, the third of Charlestown, in said county of Middlesex, son of Deacon Amos Tufts of the same place, shall be allowed to take the name of Joseph Frothingham Tufts; that Jesse Harlow Torrey, of Plymouth, in the county of Plymouth, merchant, shall be allowed to take the name of Harlow J. Torrey; that Thomas Damon of Truro, in the county of Barnstable, shall be allowed to take the name of William Frederick Josiah Damon; that Walter Johnson, 2d, of Leominster, in the county of Worcester, shall be allowed to take the name of Walter Rogers Johnson; that Obadiah Burnham, a minor, and son of Josiah Burnham, of Durham, in the county of Cumberland, shall be allowed to take the name of George Burnham; that Scott Wilkinson, of Thomastown, in the county of Lincoln, attorney at law, shall be allowed to take the name of Samuel Scott Wilkinson; and the several persons before named, from the time of the passing of this act, shall be called and known by the names, which by this act they are respectively allowed to take and assume as aforesaid; and the said names shall forever hereafter be considered, as their only proper and legal names, to all intent and purposes. [*June 14, 1814.*]

———

AN ACT to alter and change the Names of certain Persons therein mentioned.

Be it enacted, etc., as follows:

That from and after the passing of this act, Joseph Adams, of the late firm of Johnson & Adams, of Boston, in the county of Suffolk, shall be allowed to take the name of Joseph Henry Adams; that Thode Coats, of Middlefield, in the county of Hampshire, shall be allowed to take the name of Theodore Coats; and the several persons before named, from the time of the passing of this act, shall be called and known by the names, which by this act, they are respectively allowed to take and assume as aforesaid ; and the said names shall forever hereafter be considered as their only proper and legal names, to all intents and purposes. [*Oct. 19, 1814.*

AN ACT to alter and change the Names of certain Persons therein mentioned.

Be it enacted, etc., as follows :

That from and after the passing of this act, William Andrews, son of Ebenezer T. Andrews, Esq. of Boston, in the county of Suffolk, shall be allowed to take the name of William Turell Andrews ; that Theodore Baker of the same Boston, shall be allowed to take the name of George T. Baker ; that James Drew, of Boston, aforesaid, mariner, shall be allowed to take the name of James Clement Drew ; that Shirley Erving, eldest son of Dr. Shirley Erving, late of said Boston, deceased, shall be allowed to take the name of William Shirley Erving ; that James Moncrieff, of Boston aforesaid, late an indented apprentice to William H. H. Chealy of the same Boston, trader, shall be allowed to take the name of James Chealy Moncrieff ; that Jonathan Low, of Gloucester, in the county of Essex, shall be allowed to take the name of James Willis Low ; that Stephen Marston of Newburyport, in the county of Essex aforesaid, shall be allowed to take the name of Stephen Webster Marston ; that John Ropes, jun. a minor, and son of John Ropes Esq. of Salem, in the same county of Essex, shall be allowed to take the name of John Haradan Ropes ; that John Adams, of Roxbury, in the county of Norfolk, son of Nathan Adams, of Medford, in the county of Middlesex, shall be allowed to take the name of Edward Holyoke Adams ; that Howard Davis, of Westport, in the county of Bristol, shall be allowed to take the name of John Howard Davis ; that Lot Bumpus, jun. of Wareham in the county of Plymouth, shall be allowed to take the name of Lot Bumpus Sullivan ; that Major Goodale Ware, of Northampton, in the county of Hampshire, shall be allowed to take the name of Goodale Sylvester Ware ; that Elizabeth Hyde, of Sandisfield, in the county of Berkshire, daughter of Dr. Jabez Holden, of the same Sandisfield, and formerly the wife of Agur Hyde, of the same town, shall be allowed to take the name of Elizabeth Smith ; that Edwards Morse, of Charlestown, in the county of Middlesex, gentleman, son of the Rev. Jedediah Morse, D. D. of the same Charlestown, shall be allowed to take the name of Sydney Edwards Morse ; that Mary Emerson Baker, of Newburyport, in the county of Essex, aforesaid, single-woman, shall be allowed to take the name of Mary Jane Brown.

And the several persons before named, from the time of passing this act, shall be called and known by the names, which by this act they are respectively allowed to take and assume as aforesaid ; and the said names shall forever hereafter be considered as their only proper and legal names to all intents and purposes. [*March 2, 1815.*

AN ACT to alter and change the Names of certain Persons therein mentioned.

Be it enacted, etc., as follows :

That from and after the passing of this act, George Lewis Cushing, a minor, and son of the late George Augustus Cushing, of Boston, in the

county of Suffolk, shall be allowed to take the name of George Augustus
Cushing; that Elisha Goddard, of the same Boston, merchant, shall be
allowed to take the name of Francis Edward Goddard; that Pliny Colburn,
of South Reading, in the county of Middlesex, shall be allowed to take
the name of Augustus George Pliny Colburn'; that Henry Thacher, of
Biddeford, in the county of York, son of the Hon. George Thacher, of
the same Biddeford, shall be allowed to take the name of Henry Savage
Thacher; that Asa Peabody, of Boston aforesaid, Esq., shall be allowed
to take the name of Augustus Peabody; and the several persons before
named, from the time of the passing of this act, shall be called and known by
the names, which, by this act, they are respectively allowed to take and
assume as aforesaid; and the said names shall forever hereafter be considered as their only proper and legal names to all intents and purposes.
[*June 15, 1815.*

An Act to alter and change the Names of certain Persons therein mentioned.

Be it enacted, etc., as follows:
   That from and after the passing of this act, Isaiah Atkins of Boston, in
the county of Suffolk, gentleman, shall be allowed to take the name Isaiah
Strong Atkins; that John S. Carter of the same Boston, merchant, shall be
allowed to take the name of John Sigourney Carter; that Samuel Davis of
Boston aforesaid, son of Rufus Davis of Quincy, in the county of Norfolk,
shall be allowed to take the name of Samuel S. Davis; that George Foster,
son of Samuel Foster of said Boston, merchant, shall be allowed to take
the name of George Reginald Foster; that Henry Gray, a minor, and son
of Sylvanus Gray of the same Boston, merchant, shall be allowed to take
the name of Henry Gallison Gray; that John Loring of Boston aforesaid,
son of the late Dr. John Loring of the same place, shall be allowed to take
the name of John James Loring; that John Long of said Boston, trader,
son of John Long formerly of Oakham, in the county of Worcester, yeoman,
shall be allowed to take the name of John W. Long; that Daniel Farrar
Melony, of the same Boston, mariner, shall be allowed to take the name of
Daniel Farrar; that Ebenezer Wells Ramsay of Boston aforesaid, shall be
allowed to take the name of Ebenezer Wells; that Thomas Rice of the same
Boston, merchant, son of the Rev. Asaph Rice of Westminster, in the
county of Worcester, shall be allowed to take the name of Thomas Kinsey
Rice; that Thomas Smith, a minor, and son of William Smith, Esq. of
Boston aforesaid, shall be allowed to take the name of Thomas Carter Smith;
that Sally Shannon Goodhue, daughter of Samuel Goodhue of Newburyport, in the county of Essex, shall be allowed to take the name of Susan
Adams Goodhue; that Henry Small of the same Newburyport, gentleman,
shall be allowed to take the name of Henry Small Ellenwood; that Jacob
Jewett, Jun. of Rowley, in said county of Essex, shall be allowed to take
the name of Jacob Clark Jewett; that Harvey Richmond of Worthington,
in the county of Hampshire, shall be allowed to take the name of Harvey
Metcalf; that Job Kittridge of Hinsdale, in the county of Berkshire, shall
be allowed to take the name of William Kittridge; that Isaiah Atkins of
Roxbury, in the county of Norfolk, gentleman, son of Samuel Atkins of
Truro, in the county of Barnstable, shall be allowed to take the name of
Isaiah Malcomb Atkins; that John Batista, of Cohasset in said county of

Norfolk, mariner, shall be allowed to take the name of John Barker; that Robert Dunlap, 2d, of Brunswick, in the county of Cumberland, shall be allowed to take the name of Robert Pinckney Dunlap; that Jesse Barrows of Fryburg, in the county of Oxford, son of Deacon William Barrows, of Hebron, in the same county, shall be allowed to take the name of John Stuart Barrows; that David Fales, 3d, of Thomaston, in the county of Lincoln, Esq. son of David Fales, Esq. of the same Thomaston, shall be allowed to take the name of David Samuel Fales; and the several persons before named, from the time of the passing of this act, shall be called and known by the names which, by this act, they are respectively allowed to take and assume as aforesaid; and the said names shall forever hereafter be considered as their only proper and legal names, to all intents and purposes. [*Feb. 15, 1816.*

AN ACT to alter and change the Names of certain Persons therein mentioned.

Be it enacted, etc., as follows:

That from and after the passing of this act, Stephen Minot Thayer Fogg, of Braintree, in the county of Norfolk, student at law, shall be allowed to take the name of Ebenezer Thayer Fogg: Mehitable Miller Soper, of Braintree aforesaid, shall be allowed to take the name of Eliza Mary Thomas Soper: John Child, of Boston, in the county of Suffolk, merchant, son of Daniel Child of Newton, shall be allowed to take the name of John Richards Child: Daniel B. Strafford, of said Boston, shall be allowed to take the name of Kent B. Strafford: Lucy Foster, of Billerica, in the county of Middlesex, widow, shall be allowed to take the name of Lucy Hill Foster: John Child, of Boston aforesaid, merchant, son of Stephen Child, of Roxbury, shall be allowed to take the name of John Weld Child: Henry Coffin, of Boston, son of John Gorham Coffin, shall be allowed to take the name of Henry Rice Coffin: Loammi Hamilton, of Northampton, in the county of Hampshire, shall be allowed to take the name of Alexander Hamilton: Billy Hancock Grant, son of David Grant, of Wrentham, in the county of Norfolk, shall be allowed to take the name of William Hancock Grant: Israel Lakeman, of Boston aforesaid, merchant, son of Pelatiah Lakeman, shall be allowed to take the name of David Hinkley Lakeman: Gorham Benson, of Scituate, in the county of Plymouth, shall be allowed to take the name of William Gorham Benson: George Thacher, 2d, of Boston aforesaid, shall be allowed to take the name of George Churchill Thacher: Peace Lee, of Portland, in the county of Cumberland, shall be allowed to take the name of Caroline Peace Lee: David Brownell, of Westport, in the county of Bristol, son of George Brownell, late of said Westport, shall be allowed to take the name of David Milk Brownell; Rebecca Davis, daughter of Samuel Davis, of Newbury, in the county of Essex, shall be allowed to take the name of Rebeccah Kendall Davis: Jannah Ranny, of Northampton aforesaid, shall be allowed to take the name of George Jannah Ranny; William Bradford, of Boston aforesaid, merchant, shall be allowed to take the name of William Washer Bradford: Aaron Davis, son of Aaron Davis, of Newburyport, in the county of Essex, shall be allowed to take the name of Aaron Charles Davis; James Allen, of Boston aforesaid, merchant, son of Oliver Allen, of Bridgewater, in the county of Plymouth, shall be allowed to take the name of James Seymour Allen:

William Spooner, of Boston aforesaid, son of William Spooner, of said
Boston, physician, shall be allowed to take the name of William Jones
Spooner; and the several persons before mentioned, from and after the
passing of this act, shall be known and called by the names which by this
act they are respectively allowed to take and assume as aforesaid; and
said names shall forever hereafter be considered as their only proper and
legal names to all intents and purposes. [*June 20, 1816.*

An Act to change the Names of certain Persons therein mentioned.
Be it enacted, etc., as follows:
That from and after the passing of this act, John Platts of Rowley, in
the county of Essex, shall be allowed to take the name of Luther Platts
Palmer; that Zerubbabel Kemp of Marblehead, in the same county shall
be allowed to take the name of Henry Kemp; that Tirzah Newcomb of
Greenfield in the county of Franklin shall be allowed to take the name of
Tirzah Smead; that Amelia Greenough of Boston, in the county of Suffolk,
shall be allowed to take the name of Laura Ann Greenough; that Gideon
Snow, Jun. of said Boston, shall be allowed to take the name of Gideon
Theodore Snow; that Lemuel Billings of said Boston, shall be allowed to
take the name of Henry Lemuel Billings; that Ira Blanchard of Weymouth
in the county of Norfolk, shall be allowed to take the name of Ira Henry
Thomas Blanchard; that Joseph Cabot of said Boston shall be allowed to
take the name of Joseph Sebastian Cabot; that John Rice of Salem, shall
be allowed to take the name of John Parker Rice; that Asahel Plympton
of said Boston, shall be allowed to take the name of Alexander Plympton;
that Nathaniel Emmons, son of Samuel Emmons of said Boston, shall be
allowed to take the name of Nathaniel Henry Emmons; that James Moulton of Westborough, in the county of Worcester, shall be allowed to take
the name of Elijah Russell; and that George Lyman, son of Theodore Lyman of said Boston, shall be allowed to take the name of George Williams
Lyman; and said persons shall in future be respectively known and
called by the names which they are respectively allowed to take as aforesaid; and the same shall be considered as their only proper names to all
intents and purposes. [*Dec. 14, 1816.*

An Act to alter and change the Names of certain Persons therein mentioned.
Be it enacted, etc., as follows:
That from and after the passing of this act, Dudley Atkins Tyng, jun.,
of Cambridge in the county of Middlesex, shall be allowed to take the
name of Dudley Atkins; James Chever, the third of Salem, in the county
of Essex, shall be allowed to take the name of James W. Chever; Thomas
Smith shall be allowed to take the name of Thomas Tarlton Smith; Edward
Loring Davis, of Barnstable in the county of Barnstable, shall be allowed
to take the name of Lothrop Davis; George Kuhn, son of Jacob Kuhn,
of Boston, in the county of Suffolk, shall be allowed to take the name of
George Horatio Kuhn; Leonard Cummings Smith, of Leominster, in the
county of Worcester, shall be allowed to take the name of Crowninshield
Van Jerome Smith; John Platts Palmer, of Rowley, in the county of

Essex, shall be allowed to take the name of John Platts ; Luther Platts of said Rowley, shall be allowed to take the name of Luther Platts Palmer ; William Greenough, of Boston, aforesaid, shall be allowed to take the name of William Hardy Greenough ; Catharine Hay Weld, of the same Boston, shall be allowed to take the name of Catharine Weld Hay ; John Frost, of said Cambridge, shall be allowed to take the name of John Henry Augustus Frost ; Oliver Blackman Everett, of Dedham, in the county of Norfolk, shall be allowed to take the name of Oliver B. Everett ; Eliza Rider, of said Salem, shall be allowed to take the name of Eliza Rider Atkinson : Mary Fuller, of said Boston, shall be allowed to take the name of Ann Mary Fuller Weld ; Thomas Weld, of said Boston, shall be allowed to take the name of Thomas Greenleaf Weld ; Samuel Heywood, of said Boston, shall be allowed to take the name of Samuel P. Heywood ; William Ward, of said Boston, merchant, shall be allowed to take the name of William Haven Ward ; Charles Treadwell, jun., of said Salem, shall be allowed to take the name of Francis Charles Treadwell ; Nathan Webber, of Gloucester, shall be allowed to take the name of Edward Webber ; Francis Fay, Jun. of Southborough, shall be allowed to take the name of Francis Ball Fay ; Barnabas Blankinship, of Rochester, shall be allowed to take the name of Barnabas D. Nye ; Laurens Bascom, of Southampton, shall be allowed to take the name of Henry Laurens Bascom ; John Gifford, of Westport, in the county of Bristol, shall be allowed to take the name of John Winslow Gifford ; Harriot Bowers, of Billerica, shall be allowed to take the name of Silence Bowers ; Samuel Tenney, jun., of Newburyport, shall be allowed to take the name of Samuel Newell Tenney ; Harriet Swett, of Dracut, shall be allowed to take the name of Harriet Swett Varnum ; and the several persons before mentioned, from and after the passing of this act, shall be known and called by the names, which by this act, they are respectively allowed to take and assume, as aforesaid, and said names shall, forever hereafter, be considered as their only proper and legal names, to all intents and purposes. [*June 17, 1817.*]

———

An Act to alter and change the Names of certain Persons therein mentioned.

Be it enacted, etc., as follows:

   That from and after the passing of this act, Calvin Bailey, son of Calvin Bailey, of Hanover, in the county of Plymouth, shall be allowed to take the name of Bernard Calvin Bailey ; Edward Jenkins, of Scituate, in the same county, shall be allowed to take the name of Edward Henry Jenkins ; Lory Jones, of Greenwich, in the county of Hampshire, shall be allowed to take the name of Lorenzo Baldwin Jones ; John Deblois, son of Stephen Deblois, of Boston, in the county of Suffolk, shall be allowed to take the name of John A. Deblois ; Thomas Smalley Delano, of the same Boston, shall be allowed to take the name of Nathaniel Lewis Nickerson ; Thomas Carter, of Newburyport, in the county of Essex, shall be allowed to take the name of Thomas Duncan Carter ; George Carter, of the same place, shall be allowed to take the name of George Duncan Carter ; Ithamar Beard, jun., of Littleton, in the county of Middlesex, shall be allowed to take the name of Ithamar Ames Beard ; Pliny Cutler, 2d, of said Boston, shall be allowed to take the name of Henry Pliny Cutler ; John

Ward, of said Boston, merchant, shall be allowed to take the name of John George Ward ; Henry Gray, of said Boston, shall be allowed to take the name of Henry D. Gray ; Emery Brigham, of Southborough, in the county of Worcester, shall be allowed to take the name of Emery Cushing Brigham ; Thomas Williams, of Boston, aforesaid shall be allowed to take the name of Thomas Kendall Williams ; Henry Hale Gay, son of Mary Gay, of Dedham, in the county of Norfolk, shall be allowed to take the name of George Henry Gay ; Larkin Newton, of said Southborough, shall be allowed to take the name of Henry Martial Pinkney ; Samuel Putnam, jun., of Salem, in the county of Essex, shall be allowed to take the name of Samuel R. Putnam ; Washington Thayer, of said Boston, shall be allowed to take the name of George Washington Thayer ; John Parker Mc-Quillin, of Beverly, in the county of Essex, shall be allowed to take the name of John Hills Parker ; Thomas R. Amory, of Boston, aforesaid, shall be allowed to take the name of Thomas C. Amory ; Job Williams, son of Gideon Williams, of Taunton, in the county of Bristol, shall be allowed to take the name of Francis Job Williams.; Adolphus Frederick Packard, of Springfield, in the county of Hampden, shall be allowed to take the name of Frederick Adolphus Packard ; Jacob Thompson Wild, of Boston, aforesaid, shall be allowed to take the name of James Thompson Wild ; John Low, jun., of said Boston, shall be allowed to take the name of John Vaughan Low ; Charles Adams of said Boston, shall be allowed to take the name of Charles Frederick Adams ; Josiah Trott, of Woolwich, shall be allowed to take the name of Josiah Winship Trott ; Nathan Foster, of Boston aforesaid, silk dyer, shall be allowed to take the name of Nathan Orris Foster ; Daniel Rogers, jun., of Gloucester, in the county of Essex, shall be allowed to take the name of Daniel W. Rogers ; Harriet Walker, of Boston, aforesaid, shall be allowed to take the name of Harriet Walker Boardman ; Francis Shaw Blake, son of Sarah Blake, of Boston, shall be allowed to take the name of Edward Blake ; Lucy Ann Bradlee, daughter of Josiah Bradlee, of said Boston, shall be allowed to take the name of Lucy Hall Bradlee ; Edward Augustus Holyoke Turner, shall be allowed to take the name of Edward Augustus Holyoke ; and the said several persons shall hereafter be called and known by the names, which, by this act, they are severally and respectively allowed to take as aforesaid ; and the same shall be considered as their only proper and legal names. [*Feb. 24, 1818.*

An Act to change the Names of the several Persons therein mentioned.
Be it enacted, etc., as follows :
That from and after the passing of this act, George Mayo Edgar, of Boston shall be allowed to take the name of Mayo Graves Edgar ; that John Harris, son of the late Samuel Harris, of Boston, shall be allowed to take the name of John Welsh Harris ; that Daniel Johnson, of Boston, shall be allowed to take the name of Daniel Bridges Johnson ; that John Wilkins, of Boston, trader, shall be allowed to take the name of John Fox Wilkins ; that Robert Breck Williams, son of Thomas Williams, of Boston, shall be allowed to take the name of Robert Breck Garven Williams ; that Daniel Chase Hazeltine resident in Boston, (late of New-Hampshire,) shall be allowed to take the name of Daniel Hazeltine Chase, all of the county of Suffolk ; that Benjamin Browne, the third, of Salem, apothecary, shall

be allowed to take the name of Benjamin F. Browne; that Josiah Newhall, of Lynn, shall be allowed to take the name of Josiah Selkirk Newhall; that Jonathan Phillips, of said Lynn, shall be allowed to take the name of Benjamin Jonathan Phillips, all of the county of Essex; that the name of Clementina Harrington, of Southbridge be, and hereby is confirmed to her the said Clementina; that Henry Martial Pinkney, of Southborough, shall be allowed to take the name of Larkin Newton; that Lucius Paige, son of Timothy Paige, Esq., of Hardwick, shall be allowed to take the name of Lewis Robinson Paige, all of the county of Worcester; that Elijah Hoar, of Montague, shall be allowed to take the name of Elijah Hanson, and that his several minor children shall be allowed to take the same name, viz.: Lucretia Hanson, Erastus Gunn Hanson, Morilla Hanson, Asahel Gunn Hanson, and Elijah Shaw Hanson; that William Hoar, of Deerfield, shall be allowed to take the name of William Hanson, and that his several minor children shall be allowed to take the same name, viz.: Lucy Hanson, Ariel Hanson, Submit Hanson, Flavilla Hanson, John Milton Hanson, Caroline Hanson, Melinda Hanson, Persis Hanson, and Edwin Hanson; that John Hoar, of Greenfield, shall be allowed to take the name of John Hoar Wheeler; that John Cheney, of Orange, shall be allowed to take the name of John Cheney Hill, all of the county of Franklin; that Eliza Stebbins Snow, of Northampton, in the county of Hampshire, shall be allowed to take the name of Eliza Snow Stebbins; that Briggs Sampson, of Duxbury, in the county of Plymouth, shall be allowed to take the name of Henry Briggs Sampson; that Benjamin Sisson, of Westport, in the county of Bristol, shall be allowed to take the name of Benjamin Baylies Sisson; that Marsena Graton, of Sandwich, in the county of Barnstable, shall be allowed to take the name of Alwin M. Graton; that Randolph Codman, of Limerick, in the county of York, shall be allowed to take the name of Randolph Augustus Lawrence Codman; and the said several persons, shall hereafter be called and known by the names, which, by this act they are severally and respectively allowed to take as aforesaid, and the same shall be considered as their only proper and legal names. [*June 12, 1818.*]

An ACT to change the Names of certain Persons therein mentioned.
Be it enacted, etc., as follows:
That Joseph Bartlett, 3d, of Plymouth, shall be allowed to take the name of Joseph Henry Bartlett; that Nathaniel Bishop, jun., of Winthrop, shall be allowed to take the name of Nathaniel Cony Bishop; that John Brewer, of Framingham, shall be allowed to take the name of John Maitland Brewer; that Abigail Brooks, wife of John Brooks, of Boston, shall be allowed to take the name of Mary Abigail Brooks; that Mary Hart Bull, daughter of James Bull, of Northampton, shall be allowed to take the name of Elizabeth Miller Hart Bull; that Charles Forbes, of Northampton, shall be allowed to take the name of Charles E. Forbes; that George Cary, of Chelsea, shall be allowed to take the name of George Blankern Cary; that Charles Dexter, of Boston, son of Aaron Dexter, shall be allowed to take the name of Charles Parker Dexter; that Susanna Lewis Nickolson Delano, daughter of Mercy Delano, of Boston, shall be allowed to take the name of Mary Elizabeth Nickolson; that Edward Gannet, of Salem, shall be allowed to take the name of Edward Farley; that Samuel Gooch, of

Boston, shall be allowed to take the name of Samuel Davenport Gooch; that Susan Elizabeth Green, daughter of Andrew Green, of Boston, shall be allowed to take the name of Elizabeth Heath Green; that Charles Hayward, son of Caleb Hayward, of Boston, shall be allowed to take the name of Charles Rice Hayward; that Stephen Little, jun., of Newbury, shall be allowed to take the name of Stephen William Little; that Lewis Robinson Paige, son of Timothy Paige, of Hardwick, shall be allowed to take the name of Lucius Robinson Paige; that William Paige, of Boston, shall be allowed to take the name of James William Paige; that Samuel Parker, son of Samuel Lillie Parker, of Boston, shall be allowed to take the name of Lucius Champlin Parker; that Joseph Peabody, 3d, of Salem, shall be allowed to take the name of Joseph William Peabody; that John Proctor, of Danvers, shall be allowed to take the name of John W. Proctor; that Peter Smith, of Boston, shall be allowed to take the name of Francis Peter Smith; that Joel Thayer, of Boston shall be allowed to take the name of Joel Frederick Thayer; that Sarah Atherton Thayer, daughter of Stephen Thayer, of Boston shall be allowed to take the name of Sarah Jackson Thayer; that Joseph Henry Jackson Thayer, son of the said Stephen Thayer, shall be allowed to take the name of Joseph Henry Jackson; that John Glover Teague, of Boston, shall be allowed to take the name of John Glover; that Charles Torrey, of Scituate, shall be allowed to take the name of Charles Turner Torrey; that Stephen Twist, of Danvers, shall be allowed to take the name of George T. Cook; that Jesse Walcutt, a native of Bolton, now resident in Cambridge, shall be allowed to take the name of Samuel Baker Walcutt; that Samuel Watson, 2d, of Leicester, shall be allowed to take the name of Samuel Dexter Watson; that Caleb Winship, of Boston, son of Abiel Winship, shall be allowed to take the name of Charles Shepard Winship; that Isaac Van Deuson, 3d, of Great Barrington, shall be allowed to take the name of Isaac Laird Van Deuson; and the said several persons, shall hereafter be called and known by the names which, by this act, they are severally and respectively allowed to take as aforesaid; and the same shall be considered as their only proper and legal names. [*Feb. 18, 1819.*

AN ACT to change the Names of certain Persons therein mentioned.
Be it enacted, etc., as follows:
That George Joy, son of Benjamin Joy, of Boston, in the county of Suffolk, shall be allowed to take the name of John Joy; Sally Sumner Homer, daughter of George Homer, of said Boston, shall be allowed to take the name of Sarah Sumner Homer; Joseph Emery, of said Boston, housewright, shall be allowed to take the name of Joseph D. Emery; Major Arms Dickerman, of said Boston, trader, shall be allowed to take the name of William Arms Dickerman; Benjamin Hichborn Fosdick, of Charlestown, in the county of Middlesex, shall be allowed to take the name of Benjamin Hichborn; John Russell Estabrooks, of Cambridge, in said county of Middlesex, son of John Estabrooks, late of said Cambridge, deceased, shall be allowed to take the name of John Brooks Russell; Benjamin Walton, son of John Walton, of Pepperell, in said county of Middlesex, Esquire, shall be allowed to take the name of Benjamin Allen Walton; Sumner Walton, son of said John Walton, shall be allowed to

take the name of James Sumner Walton ; Joseph Jewett, 3d, of Rowley, in the county of Essex, shall be allowed to take the name of Joseph
M. Jewett ; Nathan Brown, junior, of Newburyport, in said county of Essex,
shall be allowed to take the name of Nathan William Brown ; Henry Kendall, of Leominster, in the county of Worcester, shall be allowed to take
the name of Jonas Henry Kendall ; Isaac Van Deusen, of Great Barrington, in the county of Berkshire, son of Isaac Van Deusen, deceased, shall
be allowed to take the name of Isaac I. Van Deusen ; Isaac White, of
Buxton, in the county of York, shall be allowed to take the name of Isaac
Lamb White ; Enoch Bearce, of Hebron, in the county of Oxford, shall be
allowed to take the name of Enoch Fogg Bearce ; William Smith, of Portland, in the county of Cumberland, shall be allowed to take the name of
William Rufus Smith ; Luke Barton, of Augusta, in the county of Kenne-
beck, gentleman, shall be allowed to take the name of Luke Nickols Barton ;
Lydia Sears Hall, infant daughter of Hezekiah Hall, of New Sharon, in
said county of Kennebeck, shall be allowed to take the name of Maria Louisa
Hall ; Joseph Cox, jun., son of Joseph Cox, resident in the town of Concord, in the county of Middlesex, shall be allowed to take the name of
Joseph Wyman ; Samuel Turner, jun., of Scituate, in the county of
Plymouth, gentleman, shall be allowed to take the name of Samuel Adams
Turner.   And the said persons, from the time of the passing of this act,
shall be called and known by the names, which, by this act, they are
severally allowed to take, as aforesaid, and the same shall be considered
as their only proper and legal names, to all intents and purposes.   [*June
19, 1819.*

An Act to alter and change the Names of certain Persons therein mentioned.

Be it enacted, etc., as follows :
    That Charles Blake, of Boston, in the county of Suffolk, librarian, son
of James Blake, shall be allowed to take the name of Charles Lloyd Blake ;
Betsey G. Bray, of said Boston, single-woman, daughter of John Bray,
shall be allowed to take the name of Elizabeth Goodwin Bray ; Charles
Bullard, of said Boston, son of Eli Bullard, of Framingham, shall be
allowed to take the name of Charles Buckminster Bullard ; James Russell
Dutton, son of Warren Dutton, of said Boston, Esq., shall be allowed to
take the name of James Dutton Russell ; William French, son of Thomas
French, of said Boston, shall be allowed to take the name of William
Page French ; John Howe, of said Boston, victualler, shall be allowed to
take the name of John Jay Howe ; Henry Jones, son of Ephraim Jones,
of said Boston, shall be allowed to take the name of Henry Hartwell
Jones ; John Vinton, of said Boston, shall be allowed to take the name of
John Calder Vinton ; Miriam Hayden, of said Boston, shall be allowed to
take the name of Miriam Sumner Hayden ; Asa Penniman, of Dedham, in
the county of Norfolk, shall be allowed to take the name of Henry Asa
Penniman ; Ezra Prior, of Quincy, in said county of Norfolk, mariner, son
of Ezra Prior, late of Duxbury, in the county of Plymouth, deceased, shall
be allowed to take the name of Ezra William Prior ; Edward Fisher Keith,
of Wrentham, in said county of Norfolk, shall be allowed to take the name
of Edward Comstock Fisher ; Freeman Josselyn, of Pembroke, in the
county of Plymouth, shall be allowed to take the name of Freeman Mar-

shall Josselyn ; Aurora Oldham, of said Pembroke, shall be allowed to take the name of Aurora Williams Oldham ; Nehemiah Stockbridge Tubbs, of said Pembroke, shall be allowed to take the name of Nehemiah Bisbee Stockbridge ; Zadoc Leonard, of New Bedford, in the county of Bristol, cabinet maker, shall be allowed to take the name of William Henry Leonard ; Eber Baker, of Westport, in said county of Bristol, shall be allowed to take the name of Eber Davis Baker ; Perry Maccomber, jun., of Dartmouth in said county, shall be allowed to take the name of Perry Russell Maccomber ; Joseph Long, of Cambridge, in the county of Middlesex, shall be allowed to take the name of Joseph Augustus Edwin Long ; Joseph Allen, son of Shobal C. Allen, Esq., late of Townsend, in said county of Middlesex, deceased, shall be allowed to take the name Joseph Shobal Allen ; and William Allen, son of said Shobal C. Allen, shall be allowed to take the name of William Child Allen ; Warwick Palfray, 3d, of Salem, in the county of Essex, shall be allowed to take the name of William W. Palfray ; Nancy Mackey, of Andover, in said county of Essex, single-woman, shall be allowed to take the name of Nancy Lois Gardner Mackey ; Jonathan Hoar, of New Salem, in the county of Franklin, shall be allowed to take the name of Jonathan Hanson ; and Joseph S. Hopy, and Azuby, children of the said Jonathan, shall be allowed to take the surname of Hanson, instead of Hoar ; Anthony Logo, of Ashfield, in the said county of Franklin, trader, shall be allowed to take the name of John Clark ; Nathan Keep, of Longmeadow, in the county of Hampden, shall be allowed to take the name of Nathan Cooley Keep ; Winthrop Farrin, of Bath, in the county of Lincoln, shipwright, shall be allowed to take the name of Winthrop G. Farrin ; Jonathan Freeman Dana, of Cambridge aforesaid, physician, shall be allowed to take the name of James Freeman Dana ; Henry Andrews, of said Boston, shall be allowed to take the name of Henry Perkins Andrews ; Job Pierce Porter, of Middleborough, in said county of Plymouth, shall be allowed to take the name of Job Pierce ; and Babbit Blanchard, of Harvard, in the county of Worcester, shall be allowed to take the name of Grove B. Blanchard ; and the said persons, from the time of the passing of this act, shall be called and known by the names, which, by this act, they are severally allowed to take as aforesaid, and the same shall be considered as their only proper and legal names, to all intents and purposes. [*Feb. 21, 1820.*

An Act to alter and change the Names of the Persons therein mentioned. *Be it enacted, etc., as follows :*
That Asa Lawrence, 4th, of Groton, shall be allowed to take the name of Asa Farnsworth Lawrence ; Rachel Thayer Soper, of Cambridge, shall be allowed to take the name of Mary Francis Soper, both of the county of Middlesex ; Elisha Dogget Beckford, of Salem, a minor, son of Joshua Beckford, shall be allowed to take the name of John Beckford ; Ephraim Bailey Horne, of Haverhill, combmaker, shall be allowed to take the name of Ephraim Bailey Orne ; William Newhall, of Lynn, ward of Doctor John Lummers, shall be allowed to take the name of Hewson Parrish ; John Morse, jun., of Amesbury, shall be allowed to take the name of John S. Morse ; Polly Osgood, of Salem, widow, shall be allowed to take the name of Mary Osgood ; Stephen Phillips, jun., of Salem, merchant, shall be

allowed to take the name of Stephen Claredon Phillips, all of the county
of Essex; that John Moulton, of Boston, shall be allowed to take the name
of John Roberts; Charles Wells, of Boston, bookbinder, shall be allowed
to take the name of Charles Allen Wells; Charles Lowell Clapp, son of
William W. Clapp, shall be allowed to take the name of Charles William
Clapp; Masa Willis, of Boston, shall be allowed to take the name of
Horatio M. Willis; John Henry Parker, a minor, of Boston, son of the
Hon. Isaac Parker, shall be allowed to take the name John Brooks
Parker; Joseph Queen, of Boston, trader, shall be allowed to take the name
of Joseph French Edwards; John Wheelwright, of Boston, merchant, shall
be allowed to take the name of John Tower Wheelwright; Henry Felt, of
Boston, shall be allowed to take the name of Henry Felt Baker; Samuel
Whitwell, of Boston, son of Benjamin Whitwell, shall be allowed to take
the name of Samuel Sprague Whitwell, all in the county of Suffolk; Jonathan Ferry, jun., of Brimfield in the county of Hampden, shall be allowed
to take the name of Jonathan Saunders Ferry; John Shaw shall be allowed
to take the name of John Forsyth Shaw; Prince Shaw shall be allowed to
take the name of Edward Shaw, both of New Marlborough, in the county
of Berkshire; Joseph Adams, jun., student in Harvard University, son of
Joseph Adams, of Roxbury, shall be allowed to take the name of Joseph
Thornton Adams; Rebecca Miller Thayer of Braintree, daughter of the late
Atherton Thayer, Esq., shall be allowed to take the name of Rebecca
Atherton Thayer, both of the county of Norfolk; Theodore Mayhew,
student at law, of Chilmark, in the county of Dukes' county, shall be
allowed to take the name of Theodore Gardner Mayhew; Giles Hosier,
of Nantucket, in the county of Nantucket, trader, shall be allowed to take
the name of William Giles Hosier; Samuel Fosket shall be allowed to take
the name of Samuel Bradley; Robert M. Fosket shall be allowed to take
the name of Robert M. Bradley; John Fosket shall be allowed to take
the name of John Bradley; Hugh Fosket shall be allowed to take the
name of Hugh Bradley; that the minor children of Samuel Fosket aforesaid, viz.: Bethuel Fosket shall be allowed to take the name of Bethuel
Bradley; Josiah Fosket shall be allowed to take the name of Josiah Bradley; David Fosket shall be allowed to take the name of David Bradley;
Samuel Fosket, jun., shall be allowed to take the name of Samuel Bradley;
Abigail Fosket shall be allowed to take the name of Abigail Bradley;
James Fosket shall be allowed to take the name of James Bradley; Jane
Fosket shall be allowed to take the name of Jane Bradley; Alonzo Fosket
shall be allowed to take the name of Alonzo Bradley; and William
Fosket shall be allowed to take the name of William Bradley, all of Colraine,
in the county of Franklin; and the several persons before mentioned, from
and after the passing of this act shall be known and called by the names,
which, by this act, they are respectively allowed to take and assume as
aforesaid, and said names shall forever hereafter, be considered as their
only proper and legal names, to all intents and purposes. [*June 17, 1820.*

An Act to change the Names of the Persons therein mentioned.

Sect. 1. *Be it enacted, etc., as follows:*

That John Hayden, jun., son of John Hayden, of Cambridge, trader,
shall be allowed to take the name of John Cole Hayden; that Abel Wrif-

ford, of Boston, writing master, may take the name of Allison Wrifford;
that Sarah Davis Dorr, daughter of William Dorr, of Dorchester, may take
the name of Sarah Whitney Davis Dorr; that Thomas Green, of Boston,
printer, may take the name of Thomas Allen Green; that Jacob Read,
junior, of Salem, trader, may take the name of John Read; that Nathaniel
Fisher, of Boston, merchant, may take the name of George N. Fisher;
that William Luscomb, 3d, of Salem, son of William Luscomb, junior,
late of Salem, painter, deceased, may take the name of William George
Luscomb; that Thomas Woodbridge Hooper, of Boston, may take the
name of Thomas Woodbridge; that Flavel Fay of Northborough, trader,
may take the name of John Flavel Fay; that Charles Parsons, of Boston, merchant, son of Thomas Parsons, of said Boston, merchant, may
take the name of Charles Thomas Parsons; that Consider Howland Hammatt, of Boston, merchant, may take the name of Charles Howland Hammatt; that Elizabeth Stickney, daughter of Thomas Stickney, late of
Worcester, deceased, may take the name of Elizabeth Stickney Ward; that
Tilley Rice, of Worcester, may take the name of George Tilley Rice; that
John Tappan, junior, son of John Tappan, of Boston, merchant, may take
the name of John Gallison Tappan; that Darius Holbrook, jun., of Boston, merchant, may take the name of Darius Blake Holbrook; that Phineas
James Whitney, of Shirley, son of Thomas Whitney, Esquire, may take the
name of James Phineas Whitney; that John Jones, of Boston, jeweller,
may take the name of John Belknap Jones; that De Lucena Palmer, of
Amherst, may take the name of Frederick Augustus Palmer; that Agnes
Bradlee, daughter of John W. Bradlee, of Boston, may take the name of
Agnes Love Bradlee; that Thomas H. Oliver, of Salem, gentleman, may
take the name of Henry Kemble Oliver; that Lillie Phelps, of Charlestown,
may take the name of Elisha Lillie Phelps; that Argalus Thomas, of Western, innholder, may take the name of Samuel B. Thomas; that Abraham
Hammatt, son of William Hammatt, late of Boston, deceased, may take
the name of Abraham Barker Hammatt; that Joseph Stanley, of Danvers,
shoemaker, may take the name of Joseph Ober Prescott; that Daniel
Sigourney, of Boston, son of Daniel Sigourney, late of Chelsea, may take
the name of Daniel Andrew Sigourney; that Nathan Tufts, 3d, of
Charlestown, son of Amos Tufts, blacksmith, may take the name of Nathan
Adams Tufts; that Abigail Stone, of Lincoln, single-woman, and daughter
of Gregory Stone, may take the name of Abigail Hartwell Stone; that
Silas Prouty, of Scituate, mariner, may take the name of Silas Penniman;
that Benjamin Downes, of Newburyport, may take the name of Benjamin
Robert Downes; that John Harris, of Boston, of the firm of Gores and
Harris, may take the name of John Sharrad Harris; that Henry Weed, of
Dana, may take the name of Henry Stintson Weed; that Pelham Bonney,
of Pembroke, may take the name of Pelham Winslow Bonney; that Wil-
liam Josselyn, of the said Pembroke, may take the name of William
Warren Josselyn.

SECT. 2. *Be it further enacted,*
That from and after the passing of this act, the several persons herein-
before named, shall be known and called by the names, which by this act,
they are respectively allowed to take and assume as aforesaid; and that
said names shall forever hereafter be considered as their only proper and
legal names, to all intents and purposes. [*Feb. 14, 1821.*

AN ACT to change the Names of the Persons therein mentioned, and to change the Name of the Second Social Library, in Charlestown.

SECT. 1. *Be it enacted, etc., as follows:*

That from and after the passing of this act, the several persons herein named, shall be known and called by the names, which by this act, they are respectively allowed to assume; and that the said names shall forever hereafter be considered as their only proper and legal names, to all intents and purposes; viz.: Ebenezer Dorr, jun., may take the name of Ebenezer Ritchie Dorr; that Peter Albertus Von Hagen, jun., may take the name of Davis Coolidge Ballard; that Ebenezer May Meriam, may take the name of George May Meriam; that James Otis, jun., merchant, may take the name of James Allen Gardner Otis; that John Cooper Russell, may take the name of John Brown Frazier Russell; that Rachel Coddington Thayer, may take the name of Caroline C. Thayer; that Ebenezer C. Thayer, may take the name of Nathaniel Thayer; that Thomas Goodwin, son of Thomas Goodwin, formerly of Portland, may take the name of Thomas Croswell Goodwin; that Ira Smith, printer, may take the name of Fernando Victor Smith, all of Boston, in the county of Suffolk; that William Balch, 3d, of Bradford, may take the name of William Savory Balch; that Daniel Stickney, jun., of Bradford, may take the name of Daniel Balch Stickney; that Samuel Stickney, jun., of Rowley, may take the name of Samuel Warren Stickney; that Joseph Moody Stickney, of Rowley, may take the name of Joseph Pike Stickney; that Samuel Lunt, jun., of Newbury, son of Nicholas Lunt, may take the name of Samuel Laban Scott Lunt, all of the county of Essex; that Eleazer Bradshaw Edes, son of the late Peter Edes, of Charlestown, may take the name of Eleazer Edes Bradshaw; that Calvin Sanger, jun., son of Calvin Sanger, Esq., of Sherburne, may take the name of Calvin Phipps Sanger; that Asa Jarvis, of Concord, son of Francis Jarvis, of Concord, may take the name of Edward Asa Jarvis; that Josiah Nottage, trader, of Cambridge, may take the name of Josiah Nottage Marshall; that Marshall Stone, of East Sudbury, may take the name of Marshall Damon Spring Stone, all of the county of Middlesex; that Asa Augustus Miles, of Ashburnham, son of Captain Isaac Miles, of Waltham, may take the name of Augustus Strong; that David Stone, of Grafton, son of Gregory Stone, may take the name of Gregory David Stone, all of the county of Worcester; that Solomon Sylvester Ware, of Chesterfield, in the county of Hampshire, may take the name of Jonathan Sylvester Ware; that John Van Deusen, of Great Barrington, in the county of Berkshire, may take the name of John C. Van Deusen; that Helen Bartlett, of Roxbury, daughter of Doctor John Bartlett, may take the name of Ann Matilda Bartlett; that Jonathan Battle, of Dover, may take the name of Jonathan Battell; and that each of his children, viz.: Jonathan, Ralph, Leonard, Clarissa, Adeline, and Mehitable, may take the name of Battell, all of the county of Norfolk; that Meshack Fifield, of Nantucket, trader, son of Mark Fifield, of New Hampshire, may take the name of Henry Fifield; that Atkins Dyer Pocock, of Wellfleet, in the county of Barnstable, may take the name of Atkins Dyer; that John Woodward Perry, of Seekonk, in the county of Bristol, may take the name of John Perry Woodward.

SECT. 2. *Be it further enacted,*

That from and after the passing of this act, the proprietors of the Second

Social Library in Charlestown shall be allowed to assume the name of the Charlestown Union Library, any thing contained in their act of incorporation to the contrary notwithstanding. [*June 15, 1821.*]

An Act to change the Names of the Persons therein mentioned.
Be it enacted, etc., as follows:

That from and after the passing of this act, the several persons herein named, shall be known and called by the names they are respectively allowed to assume, viz.: That William Hart Bowles, bookseller, may take the name of William Ralph Hart Bowles; that John Dana, merchant, may take the name of John Bridge Dana; that Deborah Eunson may take the name of Deborah Lincoln; that Peter Nathaniel Greene, printer, may take the name of Nathaniel Greene; that Pelham Holmes, jun., merchant, may take the name of James Lobdell Holmes; that Joseph Eckley Huntington, son of the late Rev. Joshua Huntington, may take the name of Joshua Huntington; that Jason Jay Jerome, broker, may take the name of John Jay Jerome; that Sophia Lapham, widow, may take the name of Sophia Dunbar; and that her son, Charles Howard Lapham, a minor, may take the name of Charles Howard Dunbar; that Charles Spring, merchant, may take the name of Charles Augustus Spring; that Edward Stevens, gentleman, may take the name of Edward Lowe Stevens; that John Thayer, a minor, son of the Rev. Nathaniel Thayer, of Lancaster, may take the name of John Eliot Thayer; that John Trull, distiller, son of John Trull, late of Tewksbury, husbandman, deceased, may take the name of John Wyman Trull; that Edward Erving, son of the late Doctor Shirley Erving, deceased, may take the name of Edward Shirley Erving; that Jonathan Stearns, grocer, son of David Stearns, late of Weston, may take the name of Jonathan Parkard Stearns, all of Boston, in the county of Suffolk; that Elizabeth Cleaveland, a minor, daughter of Parker Cleaveland, of Rowley, may take the name of Elizabeth Abigail Cleaveland; that Hannah Hardy, of Bradford, single-woman, daughter of Reuben Hardy, of said Bradford, deceased, may take the name of Hannah Coves Hardy; that Joseph Hoyt, jun., of Amesbury, chaise maker, may take the name of Job Hoyt; that Jacob Boardman Patten, of Amesbury, gentleman, may take the name of Charles Boardman Patten; that Herbert Peabody, a minor, son of Samuel Peabody, jun., of Salem, may take the name of Herbert Cheever Peabody; that Ebenezer Sargent, of Amesbury, chaise maker, may take the name of Noah Sargent; that Edmund Sargent, of Amesbury, potter, may take the name of Smith Sargent; that Mary Ann Cleaveland Spalding, of Byfield, may take the name of Mary Ann Cleaveland; that Sarah Toppan Boardman, a minor, daughter of Offin Boardman, of Newburyport, may take the name of Sarah Greenleaf Boardman; that Clement Trickey, of Salem, trader, may take the name of Clement Tracy, all of the county of Essex; that William Blanchard, a minor, son of Isaac Blanchard, of Charlestown, may take the name of Sampson Stoddard Blanchard; that Napoleon Bonaparte Hemenway, of Framingham, may take the name of Charles Hemenway; that Billey Onthank, of Holliston, may take the name of William Newton Onthank; that Amos Prescott, laborer, of Westford, now resident in Pepperell, may take the name of Amos Fletcher Prescott; that Frederick Manson, jun., of Cambridge,

printer, may take the name of Frederick Hurlburt Manson ; that Ira Sawyer, of Marlborough, laborer, may take the name of Alfred Ira Sawyer ;
that Nathan Weston, of Charlestown, schoolmaster, may take the name of
Alexander Nathan Weston ; that Amos Cox, of Weston, son of Joseph
Cox, of Waltham, may take the name of Daniel Wyman, all of the county
of Middlesex ; that Silas Allen, of Dorchester, may take the name of
William Winthrop Allen ; that George Minott, 3d, of Dorchester, may
take the name of George Nathaniel Minott ; that Willard Savage, of Needham, may take the name of Alonzo Temple ; that Alice Sumner, of Brookline, may take the name of Alice Elizabeth Sumner, all of the county of
Norfolk ; that William Mendell, 2d, of Rochester, in the county of
Plymouth may take the name of William P. Mendell ; that John Thurston,
3d, of Lancaster, trader, in the county of Worcester, may take the name
of John Gates Thurston ; that Peter Hunt, jun., of Seekonk, in the
county of Bristol, may take the name of Peter Brown Hunt ; that Darius
Morris, of Springfield, in the county of Hampden, student at law, may
take the name of Richard Darius Morris. And the said several persons
before named, shall hereafter, be called and known by the names which,
by this act, they are respectively allowed to assume as aforesaid ; and the
same shall be considered as their only proper and legal names. [*Feb. 18,
1822.*

An Act to change the Names of the Persons therein described.
Be it enacted, etc., as follows :

That from and after the passing of this act, the several persons herein
named, shall be known and called by the names they are respectively
allowed to assume, viz. : That Jesse Holbrook, of Boston, merchant,
may take the name of Henry I. Holbrook ; that George Howe, of Boston,
bookbinder, may take the name of George Gedney Howe, both of the
county of Suffolk ; that John Tarbox Balch, of Newburyport, merchant,
may take the name of John Theodoric Balch ; that Amos Buss, of Salem,
trader, may take the name of Amos Sawyer Thornton ; that Richard
Wheatland, 3d, of Salem, gentleman, may take the name of Richard
Goodhue Wheatland ; that Francis Huntress, of Salisbury, a minor, may take
the name of Joshua Follensbee ; all of the county of Essex ; that Timothy
Brown, of Reading, painter, may take the name of Timothy Noyes Brown ;
that Sarah Brown, of Billerica, may take the name of Sarah Putnam Brown ;
children of Timothy Brown of Tewksbury, all of the county of Middlesex ;
that Daniel Hunt of Weymouth, cordwainer, may take the name of Albert
Hunt, of the county of Norfolk ; that Jahleel Brenton, of Plymouth, in the
county of Plymouth, printer, may take the name of James Jahleel Brenton ;
that Joseph Carpenter, 2d, of Rehoboth, housewright, in the county of
Bristol, may take the name of Joseph Carpenter Brown ; that Sherebiah
Hunt, jun., of Ashburnham, may take the name of Charles S. Hunt ;
that Benjamin Savage, of Grafton, husbandman, may take the name of
Benjamin Dillingham Phelps ; that Zenas Studley, of Western, housewright, may take the name of Henry Zenas Studley ; that Squire Wood, of
Grafton, may take the name of Abijah Wood, all of the county of Worcester ; that George Williams, of Deerfield, in the county of Franklin, may
take the name of John George Williams ; and the said several persons
herein named, shall hereafter be called and known by the names, which, by

this act, they are respectively allowed to assume as aforesaid; and the same shall be considered as their only proper and legal names. [*June 15, 1822.*

An Act to change the Names of the Persons therein mentioned.
Be it enacted, etc., as follows:

That the several persons herein named, shall hereafter be known and called by the names they are hereby respectively allowed to assume, viz. : — That Grace Baker, single-woman, may take the name of Lucretia Baker; that Isaac Brown, druggist, may take the name of John Isaac Brown; that Ebenezer Dorr Child, son of David W. Child, may take the name of Edward Vernon Child; that Charles Fessenden may take the name of Charles Phillips Fessenden; that Charles Lee, merchant, may take the name of Charles Henry Lee; that Isaac Osgood, counsellor at law, may take the name of Isaac Peabody Osgood; that William Parker, son of Jonas Parker, of Pepperell, may take the name of William Gay Parker; that Lucy Parsons, daughter of the late Hon. Theophilus Parsons, may take the name of Lucy Greenleaf Parsons; that George Roulston, son of John Roulston, riding-master, may take the name of John Stephen Roulston; that George Shepherd, trader, may take the name of George Adams Shepherd; that Robert Gibbs Southack may take the name of Robert Southack Gibbs; that Edward Williams, merchant, may take the name of Edward Alexander Williams; that William Winchester, son of Edmund Winchester, may take the name of William Parsons Winchester; all of Boston, in the county of Suffolk; that Benjamin Deland Cox, of Lynn, cordwainer, may take the name of William Benjamin Dana; that Edward Stanley Dean, son of Thomas Dean, of Salem, mariner, may take the name of Edward Dean; that Jonathan Osborn, 3d, son of Richard Osborn, of Danvers, may take the name of Jonathan W. Osborn; that Paine Sargent, of Newbury, chaise maker, may take the name of Paine Wingate Sargent; that Cornelius L. Wyatt, laborer, of Wenham, may take the name of Cornelius Larcom Preston; that Samuel Wyatt, laborer, of said Wenham, may take the name of Samuel Preston; all of the county of Essex; that Elizabeth Hedley, of Rochester, in the county of Plymouth, may take the name of Elizabeth Wing Hedley; that Harriot Dinsmore, daughter of Amos Parker, of Reading, may take the name of Harriot Brigden Parker; that Elijah Bingham Wright, of Pepperell, house-wright, may take the name of William Otis; both of the county of Middlesex; that James Carter, of Lancaster, son of James Carter, of Leominster, may take the name of James Gordon Carter; that Henry Hills, of Leominster may take the name of George Henry Hills; both of the county of Worcester : that Nathan Fisher, of Dover, trader, may take the name of Nathan Mason Fisher; that James Thayer, of Weymouth, cordwainer, may take the name of James Eliphas Thayer; both of the county of Norfolk : that Rebecca Smith Rice, adopted daughter of Moses Smith, physician, of Hawley, in the county of Franklin, may take the name of Rebecca Ann Smith; that Henry Sheldon, son of Charles Sheldon, late of Springfield, deceased, may take the name of Henry W. Sheldon. And the said several persons herein named, shall hereafter be called and known by the names, which, by this act, they are respectively allowed to assume as aforesaid; and the same shall be considered as their only proper and legal names. [*Feb. 8, 1823.*

An Act to change the Names of Persons therein mentioned.
Be it enacted, etc., as follows:

That from and after the passing of this act, the several persons herein named, shall be known and called by the names they are respectively allowed to assume, viz. : that William Adams, of Boston, schoolmaster, may take the name of William Joseph Adams ; that Guy Middleton, of Lee, laborer, may take the name of John Middleton ; that John Andrews, of Boston, founder, may take the name of George Canning Franklin Andrews ; that Mary Poor, of Haverhill, single-woman, may take the name of Mary Sargeant Poor ; that Minerva Parker, of Hawley, may take the name of Catharine Minerva Lilley ; that John Bridge, jun., of Boston, may take the name of John Dana Bridge ; that Timothy Morrill, jun., of Salisbury, trader, may take the name of Timothy Pilsbury Morrill ; that Catharine Hannah Adams Willard, of Charlestown, may take the name of Catharine Hannah Adams ; that Peter Dow, of Haverhill, housewright, may take the name of Charles W. Dow ; that Ezra Gates, of Ashby, may take the name of Ezra Coolidge Gates ; that John Stevens, of West Newbury, may take the name of Luther Green Stevens ; that Reuben Stackpole, of Boston, may take the name of Reuben Markham Stackpole ; that Tabitha Henderson, of Charlestown, single-woman, may take the name of Tabitha Wilder ; that Elisha Williams, of Boston, may take the name of Elisha Scott Williams ; that Edmund Colburn, of Boston, may take the name of Edmund Wesley Colburn ; that William Trowbridge, of Worcester, mechanic, may take the name of William Frederick Trowbridge ; that Mariet Jones, of Boston, single-woman, may take the name of Maria Jones ; that Asa Green, of Northborough, may take the name of Asahel Wood Green ; that Oliver Webster, of Otis, a minor, may take the name of Oliver Post Webster ; that George Wells, a member of Harvard University, may take the name of George Wadsworth Wells. And the said several persons before named shall hereafter be called and known by the names, which by this act they are respectively allowed to assume as aforesaid ; and the same shall be considered as their only proper and legal names. [*June 14, 1823.*

An Act to change the Names of the Persons therein mentioned.
Be it enacted, etc., as follows:

That the several persons herein named, shall hereafter be known and called by the names they are hereby allowed to assume, viz. :

That William Cleverly, of Weymouth, may take the name of William Coolidge ; that Rachel Cleverly, wife of William Cleverly of Weymouth, may take the name of Rachel Coolidge ; that Phebe Thayer Cleverly, of Weymouth, minor, may take the name of Phebe Thayer Coolidge ; that William Beal Cleverly, of Weymouth, minor, may take the name of William Beal Cooledge ; that Charles Cleverly, of Weymouth, minor, may take the name of Charles Coolidge ; that Lucy Ann Cleverly, of Weymouth, minor, may take the name of Lucy Ann Coolidge ; that Thomas Haskins, may take the name of Thomas Waldo Haskins ; that Mary Holden Jackson, may take the name of Mary Howard Jackson ; that James Brewer, of Boston, a minor, son of Elizabeth Brewer, may take the name of James Hamilton Brewer ; that Elam Clark, jun., of Easthampton, may take the name of Elam Calhoun Clarke ; that George Callender, of Boston, son of the late Joseph Callender, grocer, may take the name of George Henry Callender; that Ashbell Brigham, of Boston, may take the name of William Ashbell Brigham ; that John Andrews, of Boston, may take the name of John Brooks Andrews ; that Jesse J. Sleeper, of Boston, may take the name of Romanzo Warwick Montgomery ; that Hervey Divol, of Winchendon, county of Worcester, may take the name of Abel Hervey Wilder ; that Lilbourne Boyd Drane, a member of Harvard University, may take the name of Robert Brent Drane ; that William Metcalf Cobb, of Holden, minor, may take the name of William Cobb Metcalf ; that Bela Burns, of Boston, may take the name of William Lovejoy Burns ; that Jeremiah Sprague, of Boston, may take the name of George James Sprague ; that John Haven Dexter, of Boston, merchant, son of Aaron Dexter, physician, may take the name of John Coffin Dexter ; that Elizabeth Knapp, of Newburyport, a minor, daughter of Mary Knapp, widow, may take the name of Jane Knapp ; that Mary Adams, of Newburyport, may take the name of Mary Hills Adams ; that Lyman Stetson, son of Bela Stetson, of Chesterfield, may take the name of William Lyman Stetson ; that Mary Emerson Knight, daughter of Joseph Knight, of Newbury, minor, may take the name of Mary Jane Knight ; that John Peirce Batchelder, of Danvers, may take the name of John Batchelder Peirce ; that James New, of Boston, may take the name of James Edwards New ; that Shepherd Gifford, of Westport, may take the name of Charles Shepherd Gifford ; that Barker Gifford, of Westport, may take the name of Stephen Barker Gifford ; that James Laha, of Gloucester, may take the name of James Green ; that Jonathan Hitchcock, of West Stockbridge, may take the name of Jonathan Wright Hitchcock ; that Josiah Foster, 5th, son of Josiah Foster, 3d, of Beverly, may take the name of Josiah Lovett Foster ; that Benjamin Knight Dunbering, of Salem, may take the name of Benjamin Knight; that Tryphosa Kendrick, of Newton, may take the name of Mary Eleanor Kendrick ; that Archelaus Fuller, of Middleton, may take the name of Archelaus Putnam Fuller ; that Samuel Hazen, of Westborough, cooper, may take the name of Henry Otis ; that Stephen Glover Spurr, of Quincy, may take the name of Stephen Elisha Glover ; that Russell Glover Spurr, of Quincy, may take the name of Russell Edward Glover ; that Ebenezer Tarbox, jun., of Charlestown, may take the name of Ebenezer Thorndike ; that Nathaniel Tarbox, son of Ebenezer Tarbox, jun., of Charlestown, may take the name of Nathaniel Thorndike ; that Ebenezer Tarbox, son of Ebenezer Tarbox, jun., of Charlestown, may take the name of Ebenezer Thorndike ; that Catherine Tarbox, daughter of Ebenezer Tarbox, jun., of Charlestown, may take the name of Catherine Thorndike. And the several persons herein named shall hereafter be called and known by the names which by this act they are respectively allowed to assume aforesaid ; and the same shall be considered as their only proper and legal names. [*Feb. 7, 1824.*

AN ACT to change the Names of the Persons therein mentioned.
Be it enacted, etc., as follows :

That from and after the passing of this act, the several persons herein named shall be called and known by the names which by this act they are respectively allowed to assume, viz. : William Andrews, of Boston, merchant, may take the name of William Stutson Andrews ; that Joseph Bradford, of Boston, merchant, may take the name of Joseph Nash Bradford ; that

Joseph Haydn Von Hagen, a minor, may take the name of Joseph Adams Ballard; that Joanette Catherine Elizabeth Von Hagen, a minor, may take the name of Joanette Catherine Elizabeth Ballard; that Robert Dyer, printer, may take the name of Robert Spencer Dyer; that John Haskell, machinist, may take the name of John Augustus Haskell; that Benjamin Holmes, the third, a minor, may take the name of Benjamin Salter Holmes; that Chloe Lincoln, mantua-maker, may take the name of Martha Ann C. Lincoln; that Nancy Lovejoy, mantua-maker, may take the name of Ann Frances Lovejoy; that William S. Newman, cordwainer, may take the name of William Homer Newman; that David Murphy Rupp, a minor, may take the name of David Collson Moseley Rupp; that Matilda Sleeper, may take the name of Matilda Ormond Montgomery; that John Smith, may take the name of John Henry Smith; that James Scott Thorndike, may take the name of James Franklin Thorndike; that Edward Tuckerman, 2d, may take the name of Francis Edward Tuckerman; that Woodis Lee Wheeler, trader, may take the name of Woodhouse Lee Wheeler; that Thomas Herrick Waterman, may take the name of Thomas Waterman Herrick; that Thomas Frederick Palmer, may take the name of Thomas Frederick Temple Palmer; that William James Palmer, may take the name of William Bowdoin Palmer; all of Boston in the county of Suffolk; that John Clarke Fillis, a minor, of Salem, may take the name of John L. Clarke; that Luther Britton, of Salem, cordwainer, may take the name of Luther Reed; that Aaron Field, of Lynn, may take the name of Aaron Chauncey Clark Field; that Equality Weston, of Lynn, may take the name of John Equality Weston; that Thomas Lambert, jun., of Rowley, may take the name of Thomas Merrill Lambert; that Elizabeth Ann Tyler, of Newburyport, may take the name of Sarah Elizabeth Tyler; all of the county of Essex; that Amos Baker, jun., of Lincoln, may take the name of Amos Prescott Baker; that Luther Fish, of Sudbury, may take the name of Luther Richardson; that Mary G. Tarbox, of Charlestown, may take the name of Mary G. Thorndike; that Alexander White McQuillin, of East Sudbury, may take the name of Alexander White; all of the county of Middlesex; that William Marble, 2d, of Charlton, may take the name of William Proctor Marble; that Otis McLane, of the town of Worcester, husbandman, may take the name of Otis David Lane; that Haliburton McLane, son of the said Otis McLane, may take the name of Haliburton Lane; that Joseph Jennings McLane, son of said Otis McLane, may take the name of Joseph Jennings Lane; that Caleb Henry Mellen Prentiss, of Leominster, may take the name of Caleb M. Prentiss; that Cornelius Rix, of Harvard, may take the name of Eleazer Rix; that Cephas Whitcomb, of Bolton, may take the name of James Bedingfield Whitcomb; all of the county of Worcester; that Warham Crooks, of Springfield, in the county of Hampden, may take the name of James Warham Crooks; that Luther Frink, of Greenwich, may take the name of William Field; that Samuel Partridge, 3d, of Hatfield, may take the name of Samuel Dwight Partridge; both of the county of Hampshire; that Joseph Atkins Montenari, of Plymouth, mariner, may take the name of Joseph Atkins; and the several persons herein named, shall hereafter be called and known by the names which by this act, they are respectively allowed to assume as aforesaid; and the same shall be considered as their only proper and legal names. [*June 12, 1824.*

An Act to change the Names of the several Persons therein mentioned.
Be it enacted, etc., as follows:
That the several persons herein named shall hereafter be known and
called by the names they are hereby respectively allowed to assume, viz. :
that Samuel Baker Palmer, mariner, may take the name of Samuel Baker ;
that Phineas Sargent Denny, may take the name of Thomas Denny ; that
Edward Edes Eayres, a minor, may take the name of Edward Edes Eayres
Gardner ; that William Holbrook, may take the name of William Read Hol-
brook ; that Noah Langley, trader, may take the name of Nathan Lang ;
that Jacob Noyes may take the name of Jacob Wyatt Noyes ; that Salome
Noyes may take the name of Salome Hooper Noyes ; that Charles Parker,
a minor, may take the name of Charles Hamilton Parker ; that Asa
Raymond, jun., may take the name of Edward Asa Raymond ; .that
Catharine Russell may take the name of Catharine Graves Russell ; that
Philander Shaw, jun., may take the name of Joseph Philander Shaw ;
that David Weld may take the name of Aaron Davis Weld ; that William
Frickey may take the name of William Tracy ; that John George Booth
may take the name of George Frederick Noble ; all of Boston, in the county
of Suffolk ; that James Brown, 3d, mariner, of Salem, may take the name
of William James Brown ; that Ruth Ward Bott, a minor, may take the
name of Ruth Susan Safford Bott ; that Betsey Frye, of Salem, a single-
woman, may take the name of Martha Elizabeth Grey ; that Bracket Fur-
bush, of Salem, may take the name of Bracket Lord ; that Mary Parrott,
of Gloucester, may take the name of Mary Georgianna Parrot ; that Calvin
Colman, a minor, of Rowley, may take the name of William Colman Searle ;
that Samuel Miller Searle, a minor, of Rowley, may take the name
of Thomas Samuel Searle ; that Joseph Vincent, 4th, of Salem, may
take the name of Joseph Clarkson Vincent ; that Hiram McGlathlen, of
Salem, may take the name of Hiram West, all of the county of Essex ;
that Nathaniel Brown, of Charlestown, may take the name of Nathaniel
Brown Winship ; that Charles Chase Gordon, of said Charlestown, may
take the name of Robert Gordon ; that Isiah King, jun., of Framingham,
may take the name of Isiah Francis King ; that Elizabeth Townsend, of
Waltham, may take the name of Mary Elizabeth Townsend ; that John
Prince Seaver, a minor, of Newton, may take the name of John Seaver ;
that James Warren, a minor, of Brighton, may take the name of James
Lloyd La Fayette Warren, all of the county of Middlesex ; that Samuel
Arnold, of Braintree, may take the name of John Boss Arnold ; that Ebenezer Perry Chase, of Bellingham, may take the name of Ebenezer Chase ;
that James Ward, of Roxbury, may take the name of James Otis Ward ;
that Noah Worcester, of Brookline, may take the name of Henry Aiken
Worcester, all of the county of Norfolk ; that David Ryder, of Dartmouth,
in the county of Bristol, may take the name of David Cummings Ryder ;
that Thomas Allen, of New Bedford, in said county, may take the name of
Thomas Munroe Allen ; that William Fessenden, 3d, of Sandwich, in the
county of Barnstable, may take the name of William H. Fessenden ; that
Comfort Haven, a minor, of Bolton, may take the name of Clymena
Matilda Haven ; that Mary Aikin Paige, of Hardwick, may take the name
of Mary Ann Aikin Paige ; that Harriet Phelps, of Hubbardston, may take
the name of Mary Harriet Phelps, all of the county of Worcester ; that
Augusta Demond, of Ware, may take the name of Mary Augusta Demond ;

that Reuben Field, of Williamsburg, may take the name of Luther Franklin Sanderson; that Henry Strong of Northampton, may take the name of William Augustus Strong, all of the county of Hampshire; that Payson Kendall, of Boston, in the county of Suffolk, may take the name of Henry Payson Kendall; that Mary Warren, of Lincoln, in the county of Middlesex, may take the name of Mary Fassit: that Caroline Emery, of Newburyport, in the county of Essex, may take the name of Caroline Smith Emery; and the several persons herein named, shall hereafter be called and known by the names which by this act they are respectively allowed to assume as aforesaid, and the same shall be considered as their only proper and legal names. [*Feb. 24, 1825.*

An Act to change the Names of the several Persons therein described.
Be it enacted, etc., as follows:
That John Dunn may take the name of John C. Dunn; that John Fessenden, may take the name of John Peirce Fessenden; that Asaph Churchill Leeds may take the name of Theodore Churchill Leeds; that Pierre Francois Henry Thomas Wilson Melvill, a minor, may take the name of Thomas Wilson Melvill; that Lucius Champlin Parker may take the name of Samuel Parker; that Thomas Jefferson Shed may take the name of Samuel Adams Shed, all of Boston, in the county of Suffolk; that Charles Holland may take the name of Lucius Deluce; that Charles Putnam may take the name of Charles Fisk Putnam, both of Salem, in the county of Essex; that John Park, jun., of Groton, in the county of Middlesex, may take the name of John Gray Park; that Eliza Gardner, may take the name of Elizabeth Greenleaf Gardner; that Esther Sewall Gardner may take the name of Ann Sewall Gardner, both of Leominster; that Henry Lane, of Lancaster, may take the name of Jonas Henry Lane; that Clarissa Lee, of Douglas, may take the name of Clarissa Johnson, all of the county of Worcester; that Richard Lard, of Enfield, in the county of Hampshire, may take the name of Richard Gardner; that Ebenezer Penniman, jun., of Braintree, in the county of Norfolk, may take the name of Daniel Penniman; that John Clapp, may take the name of Henry Porter Clark; that Abigail Clapp, his wife, may take the name of Abigail Jackson Clark, both of Easton; that Zebina Sumner, of Taunton, may take the name of Edward H. Sumner, all of the county of Bristol; that Asa Briggs, of West Bridgewater, may take the name of Henry Ellis Briggs; that Henry Wade, of Scituate, may take the name of Henry Stockbridge Wade, both of the county of Plymouth; that Aaron Ayres, of Boston, in the county of Suffolk, physician, may take the name of Aaron Andrews. And the said several persons herein named shall hereafter be called and known by the names which, by this act, they are respectively allowed to assume as aforesaid, and the same shall be considered as their only proper and legal names. [*June 18, 1825.*

An Act to change the Name of Christopher Gillpatrick.
Be it enacted, etc., as follows:
That Christopher Gillpatrick, of Boston, shall hereafter be known and called by the name of Christopher Gill, and the same shall be considered as his only proper and legal name. [*Jan. 26, 1826.*

An Act to change the Names of the several Persons therein mentioned.
Be it enacted, etc., as follows:
 That Mark Alcock, of Boston, trader, may take the name of Mark Allcut ;
that Jonathan Gardner Brewer, a minor, son of Thomas Brewer, merchant,
of Boston, may take the name of Gardner Brewer ; that William Brown, of
Boston, merchant, may take the name of William Austin Brown ; that
David Hale, of Boston, may take the name of David Ward Hale ; that
Jane Ann Hutchings, child of the late Fitz Edward Hutchings, of the state
of Illinois, and adopted child of William Hales, of Boston, may take the
name of Jane Ann Hutchings Hales ; that Edmund Wyatt Harring, of Boston, hat manufacturer, may take the name of Wyatt Harrington ; that
Charles Jones, of Boston, may take the name of Charles Faneuil Jones ;
that William Kelton, of Boston, may take the name of William Leeds Carlton ; that Mary Jane Kelton, wife of said William Kelton, may take the
name of Mary Jane Carlton ; and that their six children, all minors, and
under the age of twenty-one years, may take the name of Carlton, viz. :
Elizabeth Stuart Kelton, may take the name of Elizabeth Stuart Carlton ;
that William Tolman Kelton, may take the name of William Tolman Carlton ; that Margaret Dommet Kelton, may take the name of Margaret
Dommet Carlton ; that Harriet Maria Kelton, may take the name of Harriet Maria Carlton ; that Daniel Filmore Kelton, may take the name of
Daniel Filmore Carlton ; that Sarah Jane Kelton, may take the name of
Sarah Jane Carlton ; that William Lang, jun., of Boston, merchant, may
take the name of William Bailey Lang ; that Nancy Newman, of Boston,
widow, may take the name of Ann Jane Newman ; that Ludovicus Reed,
of Boston, merchant, may take the name of Henry Ludovicus Reed ; that
Edward Ross McLachlan, of Boston may take the name of Edward McLachlan Ross ; all of the county of Suffolk ; that Mary Bagley, a minor, child
of Joseph Bagley, of Newburyport, deceased, may take the name of Mary
Lucy Bagley ; that John Mason Bird, of Salem, may take the name of John
Mason ; that Methuseleh Boynton, of Bradford, a minor, may take the
name of Alfred Boynton ; that Martha Davis, of Newburyport, may take
the name of Martha Ann Davis ; that Polly Davis, of Newburyport, may
take the name of Mary Wheelwright Davis ; that Samuel Cloon Fortune, of
Marblehead, may take the name of Samuel Cloon ; that William Hewes
Hunkings, of Beverly, may take the name of William Hunkings Hewes ;
that Aaron Kimball, a minor, son of David Kimball, of Gloucester, may
take the name of John Stacy Kimball ; that Joseph Jackman, of Newbury,
may take the name of Joseph Noyes Jackman ; that John Knight, a minor,
son of Adams Knight, of Newbury, may take the name of John Little
Knight ; that Mark Newman, jun., a minor, son of Mark Newman, of
Andover, may take the name of Mark Haskell Newman ; that Hannah
Newman, a minor, child of the said Mark Newman, may take the name of
Hannah Haskell Newman ; that Lucy Grafton Pickman, a minor, child of
Dudley L. Pickman, Esq., of Salem, may take the name of Catherine Saunders Pickman ; that Peter Edmund Russell, of Marblehead, may take the
name of Edmund Peter Russell ; that Joseph Grafton Treadwell, a minor,
son of John W. Treadwell, of Salem, may take the name of Joseph Treadwell Grafton — all of the county of Essex ; that Roxalana Edmands, a
minor, a child of Benjamin Edmands, of Charlestown, may take the name
of Roxalana Graves Edmands ; that Francis Cook Foxcroft, now resident

at Harvard College, son of Francis Augustus Foxcroft, late of Boston,
merchant, may take the name of Francis Augustus Foxcroft; that Reuben
Jones, of Concord, may take the name of William Jones — all of the county
of Middlesex; that Catherine Sturgis Nye Peirce, a minor and orphan
child, adopted by her uncle, Baalis Bullard, of Uxbridge, may take the
name of Catherine Sturgis Nye Peirce Bullard; that Richard Carter, son
of Oliver Carter, of Lancaster, may take the name of Richard Bridge Carter;
that Henry Carter, the 2d, of Leominster, may take the name of Henry
Wadsworth Carter; that James Carter, the 2d, of Leominster, may take
the name of James H. Carter; that Charles Colburn, 2d, a minor, son of
Elisha Colburn, of Leominster, may take the name of Charles Henry Col-
burn; that Josiah Johnson, 2d, of Leominster, may take the name of Josiah
Clemmons Johnson; that Dana Rugg, of Templeton, may take the name
of Francis Dana; that Samuel W. Smith, of Barre, may take the name of
Warner Smith; all of the county of Worcester; that Nathaniel Weld
Davis Crane, of Dorchester, may take the name of Nathaniel Crane; that
Ezra Glover Spurr, of Quincy, mariner, may take the name of Ezra Elijah
Glover; both of the county of Norfolk; that Abraham Borden, 4th, of
Troy, may take the name of Abraham G. Borden, that Isaac Hathaway, of
Dartmouth, may take the name of Isaac Tobey Hathaway; that Humphrey
Howland, 2d, of Westport, may take the name of Humphrey Daniel How-
land; that Reuben Jenney, of New Bedford, bricklayer, may take the name
of Reuben Jennings; all of the county of Bristol; that Carlow Allen, only
son of Seth Allen, late of Falmouth, in the county of Barnstable, may take
the name of Seth Allen; that Shove Howland, of Amherst, may take the
name of Warren Shove Howland; that Wright Strong, a minor, son of
Hezekiah W. Strong, of said Amherst, may take the name of Henry Wright
Strong; both of the county of Hampshire; that Henry Hoyt, a minor, son
of Elihu Hoyt, Esq., of Deerfield, in the county of Franklin, may take the
name of Henry King Hoyt; that Sybil Hawk of West Stockbridge, in the
county of Berkshire, widow, may take the name of Sybil Niles; that Edward
Prescott, of Boston, aforesaid, may take the name of Edward G. Prescott;
that Catherine Francis, of Charlestown, in the county of Middlesex, may
take the name of her benefactor, Catharine Francis Eleanor Jackson; that
Joseph Frothingham, 3d, of Salem, may take the name of Joseph Augustus Frothingham.   And the several persons herein named, shall hereafter
be called and known by the names, which, by this act, they are respectively
allowed to assume as aforesaid, and the same shall be considered as their
only proper and legal names.   [*March 4, 1826.*

AN ACT to change the Names of the several Persons therein mentioned.
Be it enacted, etc., as follows:
    That Samuel Thompson, a minor, son of Alice Bently of Boston, may
take the name of Samuel Bently; that Samuel Brooks, late of Salem, scriv-
ener, may take the name of Samuel Mitchell Waring Brooks; that John
Cass, late of New Hampshire, may take the name of John Carr Cass; that
Samuel Conant may take the name of Samuel Williams Conant; that
Ebenezer Dyer may take the name of Ebenezer Elms Dyer; that Mabel C.
Ellis may take the name of Mary Ann Ellis; that Wendell Moreno may
take the name of George Wendell Lloyd; that Michael Myron, a minor,

may take the name of his father, William Myron; that Jacob Rogers may take the name of Jacob Abner Rogers; that Robert Steele, trader, may take the name of James Robert Steele; all of Boston in the county of Suffolk; that Judith Dole Bartlett, of West Newbury, may take the name of Caroline Judith Bartlett; that George Brown Very, of Salem, may take the name of George Brown; that Joseph Clements, of Newburyport, may take the name of Joseph Warren Clements; that John Fettyplace, of Salem, a minor, may take the name of Thomas John Fettyplace; that Richard Tink, of Manchester, master mariner, may take the name of Richard Trask; that Abigail his wife, may take the name of Abigail H. Trask; and also, that their three children, being minors, may take the name of Trask, viz.: that Richard T. Tink may take the name of Richard T. Trask; that Mary Abigail Tink may take the name of Mary Abigail Trask; and that Charles H. Tink may take the name of Charles H. Trask; that Hugh Judge Alley, of Lynn, may take the name of Elbridge D. Warren; all of the county of Essex; that William Howard Cades, of Charlestown, husbandman, may take the name of William Cades Howard; that Israel Newhall Peese, of South Reading, cordwainer, may take the name of Israel Newhall; that Greenleaf Henderson Pees, of said South Reading, may take the name of William Newhall; that Harriet Burnham, of South Reading, may take the name of Mary Rayner Burnham; all of the county of Middlesex; that Sylvester Sage Arnold, of Braintree, may take the name of George Washington Arnold; that Noah Fisk, of Dover, may take the name of Noah Allen Fiske; both of the county of Norfolk; that Jennings Bowen, of Leicester, tanner, may take the name of George Bowen; that Lois Whiting, of Barre, may take the name of Ann Louisa Whiting, both of the county of Worcester; that Betsey Caswell, of Middleborough, in the county of Plymouth, may take the name of Betsey Jones; and that her two children, being minors, may also take the name of Jones, viz., Ebenezer Jones Caswell may take the name of Ebenezer Jones, and that Paul Lewis Caswell may take the name of Paul Lewis Jones; that James Lawrence, a minor, of Sandwich, in the county of Barnstable, may take the name of James Lawrence Percival; and that Zadock Norton, of Edgartown, in the county of Dukes, tailor, may take the name of Francis Addlington. And the said several persons herein named shall hereafter be called and known by the names which, by this act, they are respectively allowed to assume as aforesaid, and the same shall be considered as their only proper and legal names. [*June 20, 1826.*

An Act to change the Names of the several Persons therein described. *Be it enacted, etc., as follows:*

That from and after the passing of this act, the several persons herein named, shall be known and called by the names they are hereby respectively allowed to assume, viz.: that Henry Adams, merchant, may take the name of Henry Fosdick Adams; that Dan Aldrich, may take the name of Lyman Dan Aldrich; that Thomas Bates, house carpenter, may take the name of Thomas Lathrop Bates; that John Blake, may take the name of John Harrison Blake; that Nancy Pierce Blanchard, may take the name of Ann Isabel Blanchard; that William H. Blanchard, may take the name of Henry Conyngham de Boies; that James Carney, may take the name of James George Carney; that Alvar Carter, may take the name of James Wilder

Carter; that Charles Coolidge, may take the name of Charles Leonard Coolidge; that Mary Crooker, may take the name of Mary Young; and that her son, Charles Turner Crooker, may take the name of Charles Turner Young; that Hatch Little, may take the name of Henry Hatch Little; that Henry Jones, may take the name of Henry Augustus Jones; that John Godfrey Schwab, may take the name of John Godfrey Stanville; that Enoch Silsby, jun., may take the name of George Enoch Silsby; that George Thomas, may take the name of George Priest Thomas; that Hugh Welsh, may take the name of Henry Welsh; that George West, may take the name of George Frederick West; that Albert Judd, may take the name of Albert Judd Wright; that Gardiner Chandler may take the name of his father, Gardiner Leonard Chandler; that Rufus Stillman Dodge, may take the name of Stillman Dodge, all of the city of Boston, in the county of Suffolk; that George Archer, 3d, may take the name of George Beckford Archer; that Edward Brooks, may take the name of Edward Howes Brooks; that Caroline Augusta Abbot, may take the name of Caroline Abbot Putnam; that David Putnam Abbot, may take the name of David Abbot Putnam; that Sarah Putnam Abbot, may take the name of Sarah Abbot Putnam; that Enoch Morris, may take the name of William Micklefield; that John Prince, 4th, merchant, may take the name of John G. Prince; that Samuel Knap, may take the name of Samuel Hooper Knap; that Andrew Morgan, jun., may take the name of Andrew Winslow Morgan, all of Salem; that Harriet Church Dodge, of Hamilton, may take the name of Phebe Ann Blanchard Faulkner; that Caroline Northend, of Newbury, may take the name of Caroline Soffrodini; that Henry Perkins, of Newburyport, may take the name of Henry Coit Perkins; that William Henry Jennis, of Rowley, may take the name of William Henry Kendal; that Ezra Worthen Gale, of Amesbury, may take the name of Ezra Worthen, all of the county of Essex; that Baxter B. Alcock, of Woburn, may take the name of Baxter B. Otis; that Alver Alcock, of Malden, may take the name of Alver Otis; that Mellen Chamberlain, of Hopkinton, may take the name of Henry Mellen Chamberlain; that Ben Dix, of Groton, may take the name of Benjamin Perkins Dix; that Calvin Dodge, of Groton, may take the name of Ira Thayer; that Phebe Rice Monson, of Framingham, may take the name of Susan Fiske Monson; that William Mellen, of Sherburne, may take the name of William Henry Mellen, all of the county of Middlesex; that Eunice Britton, of Western, may take the name of Eunice Allen; that Mary B. Cole, of Millbury, may take the name of Mary Ann Burnap; that James McQuin, of Leicester, may take the name of James Jackson; that Josiah Whitcomb, jun., of Leominster, may take the name of Alanson Josiah Whitcomb, all of the county of Worcester; that Vestus Haley, of Russell, may take the name of Vestus Parks; that Charles Oliver Cyrus Chapin, of Springfield, may take the name of Charles Chapin; that Pierpont Edwards Bottom, of Monson, may take the name of Pierpont Edwards Bates Botham, all of the county of Hampden; that Sylvanus White, of Chesterfield, in the county of Hampshire, may take the name of William Foot White; that Jane Strong, of Greenfield, in the county of Franklin, may take the name of Mary Jane Strong; that Homer O'Brien, of Great Barrington, may take the name of John Homer O'Brien; that Sarah Elizabeth Seymour, may take the name of Lucretia Elizabeth Newton; that Edward Newton Seymour, may take the name of Edward Seymour Newton, both of Pittsfield ; that Egbert French, of Great Barrington, may take the name of Henry Kirke Williams, all of the county of Berkshire ; that Sarah Chase, of Roxbury, in the county of Norfolk, may take the name of Sarah Ann Chase ; that Abby Green Norton, may take the name of Abby Adlington ; that Edmund Green Norton, may take the name of Edmund Green Adlington ; that Timothy Green Norton, may take the name of Timothy Green Adlington ; that Henry Osborn Norton, may take the name of Henry Osborn Adlington, all of Edgartown, in the county of Dukes' County ; and the several persons herein named shall hereafter be called and known by the names which, by this act, they are respectively allowed to assume as aforesaid, and the same shall be considered as their only proper and legal names.   [*March 10, 1827.*

An Act to change the Names of the several Persons therein described.
Be it enacted, etc., as follows:

That from and after the passing of this act, the several persons named herein shall be known and called by the names they are hereby respectively allowed to assume, viz.: that John Picket Pierce, of Newburyport, may take the name of John Bounds Pierce ; that Betsey Kerer Currier, of Rowley, may take the name of Eliza Matilda Currier ; that Winthrop Thing, of Boxford, may take the name of Winthrop Varnum ; that George Pike, of Rowley, may take the name of George Washington Pike ; that Austin Kilham, of Beverly, may take the name of Austin Daniel Kilham ; that Peter Lander, 3d, of Salem, may take the name of William P. Lander ; that David Hopkinson, of Bradford, may take the name of David Warren Hopkinson, all of the county of Essex ; that Susan Harrington may take the name of Susan Forbush ; that Mary Hall may take the name of Mary Doggett ; that Mary Ann Converse may take the name of Mary Ann Sylveira ; that James Harrison Flinn may take the name of James Flinn Harrison ; that Charles Hatstat may take the name of Charles Wade ; that George Wright may take the name of George Tyler Wright ; that Elisha Leighton Fogaty, may take the name of Elisha Perkins Leighton, all of Boston, in the county of Suffolk ; that Joshua Walter Hosley, of Pepperell, may take the name of Samuel Walter Hosley ; that Thomas Emerson, 3d, of South Reading, may take the name of Thomas Rayner Emerson, all of the county of Middlesex ; that Charles Heald, of Millbury may take the name of Charles Hale ; that Caleb Nanscawen, of Oxford, may take the name of Caleb Howe ; that Samuel Reed Puffer, of Westminster, may take the name of Samuel Puffer ; that Joseph Hildreth, jun., of Bolton, may take the name of Joseph Sullivan Hildreth, all of the county of Worcester ; that Ivory Colomey, of Dorchester, may take the name of Ivory Boylston ; that Edwards Park, of Stoughton, may take the name of Edwards Amasa Park, all of the county of Norfolk ; that James M. Tappan, of Hanover, in the county of Plymouth, may take the name of Morss Tappan ; that William Foote White, of Chesterfield, in the county of Hampshire, may take the name of Sylvanus White ; and that Joseph Sylvanus White, of the same Chesterfield, may take the name of William Foote White ; and the several persons herein named shall hereafter be called and known by the name which, by this act, they are respectively allowed to assume. [*June 16, 1827.*

An Act to change the Names of the several Persons therein described.
Be it enacted, etc., as follows:

That from and after the passing of this act, the several persons herein named shall be called and known by the names they are hereby respectively allowed to assume, and the same shall be deemed their only proper and legal names, viz. : That Joseph Dowding Bass Eaton may take the name of Joseph Bass Eaton ; that George Watson Patrick may take the name of George Watson ; that Henry Augustus Emery Humphrey, a minor son of George Humphrey, may take the name of Henry Smith Humphrey ; that Samuel Smith may take the name of Samuel James Hall Smith ; that William C. Johnson may take the name of William Johnson Cochrane ; that Nathaniel Russell Sturgis, jun., may take the name of Russell Sturgis ; that Elizabeth Palfrey may take the name of Elizabeth Cazneau Palfrey ; that George Dodd may take the name of George William Dodd ; that McCray Cutter may take the name of Thomas McCray Cutter ; that Prince Freeman, jun., may take the name of Henry Prince Freeman ; that Betsey Olivey Lane may take the name of Elizabeth Olivey Lane ; that Maxey Hall may take the name of Francis Maxey Hall ; that Theophilus Bradbury may take the name of Theophilus Washington Bradbury ; that Albent Smith may take the name of Albent William Smith ; that Thomas Ham may take the name of Thomas Ham Grenville ; that Francis Bigelow may take the name of Francis Rufus Bigelow ; and that Edwin Fullerton may take the name of James John Fullerton, all of the city of Boston, in the county of Suffolk ; that Amos Smith, jun., of Salem, may take the name of Amos F. Smith ; that William Balch, jun., of Bradford, may take the name of William Henry Balch ; that Sarah Tenny, of Bradford, may take the name of Sarah De Tenny ; that Hannah Ordway, of Bradford, may take the name of Hannah Dorothy Annis ; that John Nichols, of Salem, a minor son of George Nichols, may take the name of John H. Nichols ; that Jonathan Kimball, a minor son of John Kimball, of Andover, may take the name of Charles Kimball ; that John Richardson, jun., of Bradford, may take the name of John Pierce Richardson ; and that Timothy Abbot, of Andover, may take the name of Sereno Timothy Abbot, all of the county of Essex ; that William Hickox, of Weymouth, may take the name of William Harrington ; that Catharine Otis Farnsworth, of Weymouth, may take the name of Catharine Jane Delap Otis Farnsworth ; that James Barker, of Franklin, may take the name of James Adams ; that Abby Hayden Heath, of Brookline, may take the name of Abby Louisa Hayden Heath ; that Almira Penniman, of Brookline, may take the name of Almira Cornelia Penniman ; that Willis George Daniels, of Franklin, may take the name of George Willis Daniels ; and that George Peck, of Braintree, may take the name of George Batcheller Peck, all of the county of Norfolk ; that William Goddard Babcock, of Northborough, may take the name of William Goddard Emerson ; that Rufus Dodge, of Leicester, may take the name of Rufus Dexter ; that Sarah Dodge, wife of said Rufus, may take the name of Sarah Dexter ; that Lucy Gilbert Dodge, a minor daughter of said Rufus, may take the name of Lucy Gilbert Dexter ; that Lyman Cranch, of Bolton, may take the name of Charles Augustus Lyman ; that Joanna Allen, of Uxbridge, may take the name of Joanna Spring ; that John C. Allen, a minor son of said Joanna, may take the name of John C. Spring ; that Lavinia Ferguson, an adopted daughter of Benjamin Butman, of

Worcester, may take the name of Sally Lavinia Butman ; that Jedediah
Easterbrook, jun., of Rutland, may take the name of Joel Easterbrook ;
that Azubah Partridge Gardner, of Bolton, may take the name of Ellen
Partridge Gardner ; and that George Julius Dodge, an adopted son of Asa
Putnam, of Sutton, may take the name of George Julius Putnam, all of
the county of Worcester ; that Solomon S. Rice, of Cambridge, may take
the name of Henry Solomon Sibley Rice ; that Lovett Walker, of Holliston, may take the name of Charles Gibbs Walker ; that Mark Newcomb, of
Charlestown, may take the name of Mark Winchester ; that Isaac Austin,
of Charlestown, may take the name of Arthur Williams Austin ; that Suzan
Fiske Manson, of Framingham, may take the name of Susan Fiske Manson ;
that Sarah Hazen, of Shirley, may take the name of Sarah Hazen Parker ;
that William Francis Cotting, of West Cambridge, a minor son of William
Cotting, may take the name of William Wallace Cotting ; and that William
Hovey, of Cambridge, may take the name of William Bowles Hovey, all
of the county of Middlesex ; that James Sever, jun., of Kingston, may
take the name of James Nicholas Sever ; and that Zoroaster Edson, of
West Bridgewater, may take the name of Henry Edson, both of the
county of Plymouth ; that Job Cash Orchard, of Northampton, may take
the name of Josiah Curtis Orchard ; that Olcott Taylor, of Norwich, may
take the name of Charles Bizzell Taylor ; that Amasa Wade, of Northampton, may take the name of Amasa Dwight Wade ; that Patrick Slate,
of Northampton, may take the name of George Austin Slate ; and that
Royal Packard, of Cummington, may take the name of Royal Louis Packard, all of the county of Hampshire ; that George Appleton Gold, a
minor son of Thomas A. Gold, of Pittsfield, in the county of Berkshire,
may take the name of Nathan Appleton Gold ; that Joseph Smallidge,
jun., of Shutesbury, in the county of Franklin, may take the name of
Joseph Lucian Smallidge ; and that Gilbert Richmond Lawless, of New
Bedford, in the county of Bristol, may take the name of Gilbert Richmond.
[*March 11, 1828.*

AN ACT to change the Names of the Persons therein mentioned.
Be it enacted, etc., as follows :
    That from and after the passing of this act, Sarah Ballough, of Boston,
in the county of Suffolk, may take the name of Sarah Goodwin, that
Thomas Ballough may take the name of Franklin Goodwin, that Sarah Ann
Ballough may take the name of Sarah Elizabeth Goodwin, that Abigail
Lamb Ballough may take the name of Charlotte Augusta Goodwin, that
Samuel Ballough may take the name of Samuel Goodwin, and that George
Ballough may take the name of George P. Goodwin, all minor children of
said Sarah Ballough first named ; and the said persons, from and after the
passing of this act, shall be known and called by the names which they are
respectively allowed to assume as aforesaid.   [*March 11, 1828.*

AN ACT to change the Names of the several Persons therein described.
Be it enacted, etc., as follows :
    That from and after the passing of this act, the several persons herein
named shall be called and known by the names they are hereby respectively
allowed to assume, and the same shall be deemed their only proper and

legal names, viz. : That Nathaniel Johnson Robbins Sumner, of Rutland, in the county of Worcester, may take the name of Robbins Sumner ; that Jacob E. H. Richardson may take the name of Charles Elnathan Hammond Richardson ; that Ai Andrews may take the name of Alfred Ai Andrews ; that Thomas H. Bennett may take the name of Henry Joseph Pickering ; all of the city of Boston, in the county of Suffolk ; that Josiah Worcester, of Cambridge, may take the name of Frederick Augustus Worcester ; that Charles Parkhurst, of Framingham, may take the name of Charles Thurston Parkhurst ; that Martha Roulstone, of Charlestown, may take the name of Martha Teel, all of the county of Middlesex ; that Lydia Osgood of Salem, may take the name of Sarah Southwick Osgood ; that Lydia Stocker, of Salem, may take the name of Mary Stocker ; that Edward A. Lummus, of Lynn, physician, may take the name of Edward L. Coffin ; that Joseph Dagget, of Newburyport, may take the name of Joseph Brainerd ; that Ednah Dagget, wife of said Joseph, may take the name of Ednah Brainerd ; that Nathan Haskell Dagget, a minor son of said Joseph Dagget, may take the name of Edward Haskell Brainerd ; and that Samuel Dagget, Joseph Dagget, Charles Henry Dagget, Amos Hale Dagget, other minor sons of said Joseph Dagget, may severally take the surname of Brainerd ; that William Bodwell, jun., of Andover, may take the name of Hiram Bodwell ; that Caroline Swett, of Newburyport, may take the name of Caroline Rebecca Swett, all of the county of Essex ; that Justis F. Hawes, of Worcester, may take the name of Milton J. Adams ; that Asa Whitcomb, 2d, of Bolton, may take the name of Edwin A. Whitcomb ; that Prudence Barker Howe, of Bolton, may take the name of Ellen B. Howe ; all of the county of Worcester ; that Tryphena Trumbull, of South Hadley, may take the name of Mary Trumbull ; that Ezekiel Cheever Whitman, of Goshen, may take the name of Ezekiel Cheever ; both of the county of Hampshire ; that Brownell Little, of Westport, a minor son of Nichols Little, may take the name of John Brown Little ; that Warden Babcock, of Troy, may take the name of John Warden Adams ; and that the minor children of said Warden Babcock, viz. : Hiram Martin Babcock, John Quincy Babcock, and Mary Babcock, may take the surname of Adams, instead of Babcock, all of the county of Bristol ; and that Samuel Hudson Billings, of Roxbury, may take the name of Charles Henry Billings ; that Moses Tappan, of Hanover, in the county of Plymouth, may take the name of James Moss Tappan ; that George Barney, of Nantucket, in the county of Nantucket, may take the name of George H. Barney. [*June 12, 1828.*

AN ACT to change the Names of the several Persons therein mentioned. *Be it enacted, etc., as follows:*

That the several persons herein named shall hereafter be known and called by the names they are hereby respectively allowed to assume, viz. :

That John D. Pierce, minor son of Joseph H. Pierce, may take the name of John Pierce ; that William Brown may take the name of Augustus William Browne ; that Oliver Bliss may take the name of Oliver Henry Bliss ; that John Randall, minor son of Elizabeth Randall, may take the name of Otis Gray Randall ; that Bant Hawkes may take the name of George Washington Hawkes ; that Barnabas Reed may take the name of George Crosby Reed ; that Charles Ayer may take the name of Charles

Washington Ayers; that John Leighton Fogaty may take the name of John
Perkins Leighton; that John Roberts, book-binder, may take the name of
John Gray Roberts; that George Gray, minor son of Sally Gray, may take
the name of John Gray; that Mary Davis, wife of William Davis, may
take the name of Mary Jane Davis; that Ann T. Jones may take the name
of Anna T. Jones; that Caroline Maria Sumner may take the name of
Caroline Sumner Harris; that Abba Harris Sumner may take the name of
Abby Sumner Harris; that Susan Eastman, formerly the wife of Samuel
Eastman, may take the name of Susan Elizabeth Osborne; that Charles
Edward Eastman, minor son of the above named Susan, may take the
name of Charles Edward Osborne; and that Daniel Carney, jun., may
take the name of Daniel Williams Carney; all of the city of Boston;
that Moses Endicott, of Salem, may take the name of Charles M. Endicott;
that William Goodhue, jun., of Salem, may take the name of William
Penniman Goodhue; that Penn T. Richardson, of Salem, may take the
name of Penn Townsend; that Samuel Ober, 3d, of Beverly, may take the
name of Samuel Stuart Ober; that Henry Clement Chubuck, of Boxford,
may take the name of Henry Clement Sullivan; that Tristam Coffin Otis,
of Newburyport, may take the name of James Frederick Otis; that Theodore Norwood minor son of Eliza Rowe, of Gloucester, may take the name
of Gorham Norwood; that Sarah K. Jewett, of Ipswich, may take the name
of Sarah Kimball; that George Schaffer, minor son of Eliza Dexter, of
Gloucester, may take the name of George Vila; that John Vila Schaffer,
minor son of the above named Eliza, may take the name of John Vila;
that Elizabeth Robbins Schaffer, minor daughter of the before named Eliza,
may take the name of Elizabeth Robbins Vila; all of the county of Essex;
that Tilly Whitcomb Eames, minor son of Judith Eames, of Reading,
may take the name of Henry Ames; that Luther Sherman, jun., of East
Sudbury, may take the name of Luther Wheeler Sherman; that Sarah
Tarbell, of Lincoln, may take the name of Sarah Harding Tarbell; that
Abigail Fox Hoar, of Lincoln, may take the name of Abigail Fox; that
Sally Johnson, of Reading, may take the name of Sarah Ann Johnson;
that Angela Eaton Gould, of Reading, may take the name of Mersylna
Jane Johnson; all of the county of Middlesex; that Cornelius Fellows
Davis, of Roxbury, may take the name of Charles Davis; that Minot
Hickox, of Weymouth, may take the name of Minot Harrington; that
Anjenette Tinkham, daughter of Reuben Tinkham, jun., of Wrentham,
may take the name of Anjenette Blake; that Hiram Cary, of Medway, may
take the name of William H. Cary; all of the county of Norfolk; that
James Maccubbin Lingan Ward, minor son of Andrew H. Ward, of Shrews-
bury, may take the name of William Ward; that Samuel Cephas Williams,
of Shrewsbury, may take the name of Samuel Putnam Williams; that
Abijah Moore, of Lancaster, may take the name of Francis Merritt; that
David Holder, of Bolton, may take the name of David Green Holder; that
James Taylor, minor son of John Taylor, of Leominster, may take the name
of John James Taylor; that Dexter Whitney, of Westborough, may take
the name of Dexter Osborne Whitney; that Hannah Smith, infant daughter
of the late William Smith, of Mendon, may take the name of Maria Emeline
Barber Stone; that Sarah Larkin, of Bolton, may take the name of Sarah
Ann Haynes; that Sarah Boutelle, daughter of Sarah Boutelle, of Leominster, may take the name of Sarah Newton Boutelle; all of the county

of Worcester; that Charles Dwight, of Belchertown, may take the name
of Charles Hobart Dwight; that Hezekiah Watrous Davis, of Amherst,
may take the name of Hezekiah Davis; that Willard Nelson Taylor, of
Granby, may take the name of Willard Taylor; that Flavel Griswold, of
South Hadley, may take the name of John Flavel Griswold; all of the
county of Hampshire; that Jonathan Walker, of West Springfield, may
take the name of Jonathan Freeland; that Nathan David Hall, minor son
of Margaret Hall, of Granville, may take the name of Gordon Nathan
David Hall; all of the county of Hampden; that Madison Bowker, of
Savoy, may take the name of James Madison Bowker; that Curtis Mattoon,
minor son of Charles Mattoon, of Lenox, may take the name of Charles
Nash Mattoon; that Caroline Martin, daughter of Joel Martin, may take
the name of Caroline Martin Brown; all of the county of Berkshire;
that Archippus C. Hart, of New Bedford, may take the name of Charles
Hart; that Sion Seabury, of Westport, may take the name of Franklin P.
Seabury; that Lucy Leonard Richmond, of Taunton, may take the name
of Lucy Leonard Eaton; that Thankful Pierce Richmond, daughter of the
above named Lucy, may take the name of Maria Thankful Pierce Eaton;
all of the county of Bristol; that Morse Courtis Watson Hastings, of
Sandwich, may take the name of Watson Hastings; that Samuel Davis,
minor son of Wendell Davis, of Sandwich, may take the name of Samuel
H. Davis; that John Thornton Kirkland Davis, minor son of the above
named Wendell, may take the name of Wendell Thornton Davis; all of
the county of Barnstable; that George Coffin, of Nantucket, may take the
name of George Washington Coffin.   [*March 4, 1829.*

An Act to change the Names of the several Persons therein mentioned.
Be it enacted, etc., as follows:
   That Benjamin Crosby Horne, of Gloucester, may take the name of
Benjamin Crosby Orne; that Platts Phillips, of Danvers, may take the
name of Alonzo Platts Phillips; that Judith Dodge, of Danvers, may take
the name of Julia Therese Dodge; all of the county of Essex; that
Clarrisa Maria Butterfield, a minor, of Lowell, may take the name of Maria
Tyler; that Charlotte Susannah Dodge, a minor, of Newton, may take the
name of Charlotte Augusta Crehore, all of the county of Middlesex; that
Sterns Witt, of Oxford, may take the name of Sterns De Witt; that Alex-
ander C. Witt, of Oxford, may take the name of Alexander De Witt; that
Hollis Witt, of Leicester, may take the name of Hollis De Witt; that Mary
Walker Green, of Oakham, may take the name of Mary Walker Felton;
that Francis Merritt, of Lancaster, may take the name of Francis Merritt
Moore; that George Ferguson, a minor, of Worcester, may take the name
of George Ferguson Butman; that Joseph Morse, jun., of Leominster, may
take the name of Joseph George Morse; that Samuel Brooks, 4th, of
Ashburnham, may take the name of Ira Brooks, all of the county of
Worcester; that Harriot Andrews, of Ware, may take the name of Harriot
Francis Andrews; that James Waterman, of Ware, may take the name of
James Henry Waterman, all of the county of Hampshire; that Archibald
C. Witt, of Franklin, in the county of Norfolk, may take the name of
Archibald De Witt; that Lydia Damon, a minor, of Scituate, in the county
of Plymouth, may take the name of Lydia Thomas Jones Damon.

And the several persons herein named shall hereafter be called and known by the names which, by this act, they are respectively allowed to assume as aforesaid ; and the same shall be considered as their only proper and legal names. [*June 12, 1829.*

AN ACT to change the Names of the several Persons therein described.
Be it enacted, etc., as follows :
That Gustavus A. G. Robinson may take the name of Gustavus A. Robinson ; that Lorenzo Dow Smith may take the name of Lorenzo Gray Smith ; that Erastus Learned may take the name of William Wilkinson Learned ; that Nabby Callender, wife of William B. Callender, may take the name of Frances Callender ; that Thomas Davis Park, a minor son of Thomas Park, may take the name of Thomas Hammond Park ; that Thomas Brown may take the name of Thomas William Brown ; that Mary Perrin Harrington, a minor, may take the name of Mary Harrington Perrin ; that George Stearns may take the name of George B. Stearns ; that John H. Whittemore may take the name of William Whittemore ; that Ruth Binney may take the name of Anna Walker Binney ; that Samuel Sumner Wilton Barrett may take the name of Sumner Foster Barrett ; that Thomas Davis may take the name of Thomas Kemper Davis ; that Edward Sherburne Manning English, a minor son of Thomas Stanhope English, may take the name of Stanhope English ; that Sally Perkins Withington may take the name of Sarah Perkins Withington ; that Meriam Mason Phillips, a daughter of the widow Theresa H. Phillips, may take the name of Theresa Henshaw Phillips ; that Eunice Smith Boardman may take the name of Ellen Smith Boardman ; that Levi B. Fitts may take the name of Levi B. Witt ; that Samuel Vose may take the name of Charles Lightburn Vose, all of the city of Boston, in the county of Suffolk ; that Thomas Norwood Girdler, of Manchester, a minor son of John Girdler, may take the name of James Ingersoll ; that Ruth Choate, of Gloucester, may take the name of Helen Augusta Choate ; that John Felton, of Rowley, may take the name of John Grayham Milgrove ; that Samuel Cheney, of Bradford, may take the name of Samuel Wheeler Sawyer ; that William Winslow Mower, of Lynn, may take the name of Charles Winslow ; that William Kimball, 3d, of Bradford, may take the name of William N. Kimball ; that Lucy Brown, of Newbury, may take the name of Lucy Maria Brown ; that Moses Howe, of Rowley, may take the name of Moses Wood Howe ; that Nathaniel R. Dunphy, of Gloucester, may take the name of Nathaniel R. Webster ; that Nancy Dunphy, wife of said Nathaniel, may take the name of Nancy Webster ; that Elizabeth C. Dunphy, a minor daughter of said Nathaniel and Nancy, may take the name of Elizabeth C. Webster ; that their son, William Henry Dunphy, may take the name of William Henry Webster ; that Mary Ordway, of West Newbury, may take the name of Mary Melvina Ordway ; that Mary Pearson, of Rowley, may take the name of Mary Ethelinda Pearson ; that Noyes Pearson, of Rowley, may take the name of Charles Noyes Pearson ; that Charles Stevens, of Rowley, may take the name of Charles Mentraville Stevens ; that Gorham Jewett, of Rowley, may take the name of Gorham Laforace Miranda Jewett ; that James Bullock, of Salem, may take the name of James Ballard ; that Eliza Cotton Bullock, wife of said James, may take the name of Eliza Cotton Ballard ;

that Mary Eliza Bullock, a minor daughter of said James, may take the name of Mary Eliza Ballard ; that James Charles Bullock, a minor son of said James Bullock, may take the name of James Charles Ballard ; that Henry Archer Bullock, a minor son of said James Bullock, may take the name of Henry Archer Ballard ; that Susan Archer Bullock, a minor daughter of said James Bullock, may take the name of Susan Archer Ballard ; that Angeline Lenier Bullock, a minor daughter of said James Bullock, may take the name of Angeline Lenier Ballard ; that Roswell Augustus Bullock, a minor son of said James Bullock, may take the name of Roswell Augustus Ballard ; that Anstiss Williams Crowninshield, of Salem, may take the name of Anna Casper Crowninshield ; that Joshua Ward, jun., of Salem, may take the name of Joshua Holyoke Ward ; that William Stearns, a minor son of Joshua Bracket Stearns, of Salem, may take the name of William Bracket Stearns ; that David Holt Abbot, of Andover, a minor son of Stephen Abbot, may take the name of Stephen David Abbot ; that Pesanti Sanchez, of Salem, may take the name of George Leon ; that Nathan Berpee Jewett, of Newburyport, may take the name of Charles Augustus Warren ; that Joseph Batchelder, of Middleton, may take the name of Joseph Warren Batchelder ; that Sarah Howe, of Rowley, may take the name of Sarah Maria Howe, all of the county of Essex ; that Samuel Devens, son of David Devens, of Charlestown, may take the name of Samuel Adams Devens ; that Richard Devens, a minor son of David Devens of Charlestown, may take the name of Richard Goodwin Devens ; that Samuel Snow, of Reading, may take the name of Samuel Snow Rogers ; that Ruth Smith, of Woburn, lately the wife of Nathaniel Smith, may take the name of Ruth Cummings ; that Augustine Wellington, of Lexington, may take the name of Augustus Wellington ; that Jonathan Dix, of Charlestown, may take the name of Kimball W. Adams ; that John Wood, of Cambridge, may take the name of John Mason Wood ; that Charles Thurston Parkhurst, of Framingham, may take the name of Charles Ferdinand Wellington Parkhurst ; that Rebecca Richards Colburn, of Framingham, may take the name of Rebecca Florentina Augusta Colburn ; that Susan Parkhurst, of Framingham, may take the name of Susan Florentina Augusta Parkhurst, all of the county of Middlesex ; that Peyton Randolph Gay, of Dedham, in the county of Norfolk, may take the name of Edward Henry Gay ; that Francis White Howard, of Sutton, a minor, may take the name of Francis Howard Chamberlain ; that Lemuel Davis Montague, of Holden, may take the name of Lemuel Davis ; that Timothy Boutelle, a minor son of the widow Sarah Boutelle, of Leominster, may take the name of Timothy Loring Boutelle ; that Benedict Arnold, of Fitchburg, may take the name of George Benedict Arnold ; that David Augustus Hall Grosvenor, of Harvard, may take the name of Augustus Hall Grosvenor, all of the county of Worcester ; that Elizabeth Norton, of Hingham, may take the name of Elizabeth Cranch Norton ; that Beza Bisbee, of Plympton, may take the name of William Marshall Bisbee ; that Sarah Wade, of Scituate, may take the name of Sarah Totman, all of the county of Plymouth ; that Andrew Addison Everett, of Middlefield, may take the name of Addison Everett ; that Gulter Chapin Warner, of Granby, may take the name of Jeremiah C. Warner ; that Laisdell Abels, of Northampton, may take the name of Franklin Laisdel Abels ; that Artenatus Sweetser, of Amherst, may take the name of Joseph Artenatus Sweetser ;

that Peter Strong Burnell, of Chesterfield, may take the name of Strong Burnell; that William Gore, of Northampton, may take the name of William Dwight Gore; that Frederick Smith, of Northampton, may take the name of George Frederick Smith; that Elizabeth Sumner Wright, of Northampton, daughter of the widow Hannah Wright, may take the name of Elizabeth Mosely Wright; that Anna Clapp, of Easthampton, may take the name of Sarah Ann Clapp; that Moses Lafayette Clapp, of Easthampton, a minor son of Medad Clapp, may take the name of Lafayette Clapp; that Charles Lyman Bisbee, of Goshen, may take the name of Charles Augustus Lyman; that Asahel Abel, of Northampton, may take the name of Asahel Salmon Abels, all of the county of Hampshire; that William Howland, of New Bedford, may take the name of William P. Howland; that Ishbosheth Simmonds, of Taunton, may take the name of James Simmonds; that Gilbert Richmond, of Swansey, may take the name of Gilbert Richmond Lawless; that Elizabeth Hathaway Staples, daughter of William B. Staples, of Taunton, may take the name of Elizabeth Hathaway Williams, all of the county of Bristol; that Thomas Bates, of Charlemont, son of Stephen Bates, deceased, may take the name of Thomas Shaw Bates; that Lurena Elliott, of Leyden, may take the name of Lurena Chapin, all of the county of Franklin; that Squire Haskell Barrett, of Hinsdale, in the county of Berkshire, may take the name of Haskell Barrett; and that the several persons herein named shall hereafter be known and called by the names they are hereby respectively allowed to assume, as their only legal and proper names. [*March 12, 1830.*

AN ACT to change the Names of the Persons therein mentioned.
Be it enacted, etc., as follows:
　That Elizabeth Wyman may take the name of Elizabeth Sophia Adelaide Wyman; that John Wells may take the name of John B. Wells; that Arvada Reed may take the name of George Arvada Reed; that Asa Adams may take the name of Asa Perry Adams; that Ira Wormwood may take the name of Ira W. Allen; that John Osgood may take the name of John Hamilton Osgood; that John Oliver may take the name of John Putnam Oliver; that Joseph Evelith may take the name of Joseph G. Evelith; that Eleanor Stearns may take the name of Eleanor Georgiana Stearns; that William Brown may take the name of William Cowper Brown; that Wealthy G. Brown may take the name of Harriet G. Brown; that William Potter may take the name of William Potter Bishop; that Edward Warren, 2d, may take the name of Edward James Warren; that Emily West may take the name of Emily Georgiana West; that George Todd Dickinson may take the name of George Washington Dickinson; that Casper Adams, jun., may take the name of Henry Casper Adams; that Hubbard Newell may take the name of George Hubbard Newell; that Ross Dorety may take the name of George Ross; that Susan Jones may take the name Amanda Pelina Jones; that Alfred Hilton Bridge may take the name of Frederick William Bridge; that Andrew Griffin may take the name of George Williams Griffin; that David Jones may take the name of David Walter Jones; that Edward Holbrook may take the name of Ridgway Edward Holbrook; that Henry Eayres may take the name of Henry Clay Eayres; that John Chapman may take the name of John Brown Chapman;

that Michael Cassady may take the name of Adis Emmet Cassady; that Levi Haskell, of the firm of Whitney and Haskell, may take the name of Levi Boynton Haskell; that William Morgan Warriner may take the name of William Bostwic Warriner; that Leverett Clendennin, son of John Clendennin, may take the name of John Leverett Clendennin, all of the city of Boston, in the county of Suffolk; that Tryphosa Goldsberry, of Beverly, may take the name of Ann T. Goldsberry; that John I. Stanwood, of Ipswich, may take the name of John Lord Stanwood; that Mary Dennison Manton, of Gloucester, may take the name of Mary Manton Dennison; that William Wead, of Lynn, may take the name of William Winship; that Francis Low, jun., of Manchester, may take the name of Albert Everett Low; that Mercy Roche Vincent, of Salem, may take the name of Caroline Augusta Vincent; that Chloe Lawrence, of Salem, may take the name of Clarrissa C. Lawrence; that Charity Mason Johnson, of Danvers, may take the name of Elizabeth Mason Johnson; that Eunice Brown, of Salem, may take the name of Sarah Ellen Brown; that Daniel Chaplin, of Rowley, may take the name of Daniel West; that Elizabeth Pulsifer Mullen and John Mullen, minor children of John Mullen, of Newburyport, deceased, may take the respective names of Elizabeth Mellen and John James Mellen; that Offin Greenleaf Boardman, of Newburyport, may take the name of Offin Boardman; that Joshua Hills, 3d, of Newburyport, may take the name of Joshua Eliphalet Hills; that Samuel Thompson, of said Newburyport, may take the name of Samuel White Thompson; that Mary Elizabeth Frink, of Rowley, may take the name of Mary Elizabeth Osgood; that Sarah Lord, of Ipswich, may take the name of Sarah Elizabeth Lord; that Samuel Bell, of Andover, may take the name of Samuel B. Willis; that Rachel Mason Edmunds Barrett, of Newburyport, may take the name of Ann Mason; that Thomas Williams Monies, of Danvers, may take the name of Thomas Williams; that Eleazer Graves, of Marblehead, may take the name of Eleazer Trevett Graves; that Nelson Otis Chase, of Lynn, may take the name of Augustus Otis; and that Ann Eaton Chase, wife of the said Nelson Otis Chase, may take the name of Ann Maria Eaton Otis; that Linch Bott Goodhue, of Salem, may take the name of Charles Bott Goodhue; that Benjamin Stone, of Salem, may take the name of Benjamin Williams Stone; that Susan Lord, of Ipswich, may take the name of Susan Safford Lord; that Hannah Tenny, wife of John S. Tenny, of Ipswich, may take the name of Martha Hannah Dennis Tenny; that Edwin Jones Todd, a minor son of Francis Todd, of Newburyport, may take the name of Reuben Jones Todd; that Benjamin Manning, of Ipswich, may take the name of Benjamin Franklin Manning; that John Randlet Bean, of Rowley, may take the name of John P. Milton; that Munroe James Tuxbury, minor son of William Tuxbury, of Amesbury, may take the name of Munroe George Jewell Tuxbury; that William Joplin, jun., of Danvers, tailor, may take the name of William Dudley Joplin, all of the county of Essex; that Nancy Parker, of Reading, may take the name of Nancy Jane Parker; that George W. Verry, of said Reading, may take the name of George Washington Otis; that Joseph Hoar, of Lincoln, may take the name of Leonard Hoar; that Naomi Saunders, of said Reading, may take the name of Eliza Jane Saunders; that Edwin Pearson, of Reading, may take the name of Edwin Pierce; that Martha Prentice McFarland, a minor child of Archibald McFarland, of Lowell,

may take the name of Martha Prentice Adams; that Seneca Fay, of Framingham, may take the name of Thomas Seneca Fay; that Ela Fay, of
Framingham, may take the name of Edward Ela Fay, all in the county of
Middlesex; that John Sparhawk Baldwin, of Leicester, may take the
name John Rufus Baldwin; that Dexter Moor Chilson, a minor son of Eri
Chilson, of said Leicester, may take the name of John Dexter Chilson;
that Eurotis Graves, of Worcester, may take the name of Frederick Stratton Graves; that Festus Morgan, of Oxford, may take the name of William
Festus Morgan; that George Anson Plummer, of Barre, may take the
name of George Anson; that Jacob Bacon, of Bolton, may take the name
of Charles Wood; that Israel Waters Bacon, of Charlton, may take the
name of Berthier Bacon; that Elizabeth Waters Bacon, of Charlton, may
take the name of Elizabeth Adella Bacon; that Lucy Wiswall, of Westminster, may take the name of Philomela Hamilton; that Nelson Munroe,
of New Braintree, may take the name of Horatio Nelson Munroe; that Celia
Colton Burt, of Worcester, may take the name of Elizabeth Fay Burt, all in
the county of Worcester; that Samuel Hinkley Lyman, of Northampton,
may take the name of Samuel Lyman Hinkley; that Horatio Laurens Everett, of Worthington, may take the name of Horatio Everett; that Melinda
S. Russell, of Northampton, may take the name of Laura M. Russell; that
Daniel Gale, of Amherst, may take the name of Charles Daniel Gale; that
James Bull, jun., minor son of James Bull, of Northampton, may take
the name of James Perry Bull; that William Dexter Clapp, of Williamsburg, may take the name of William Horace Clapp; that Kinsley Underwood, jun., of Enfield, may take the name of Daniel Kinsley Underwood;
that Lewis James, of Goshen, may take the name of Lewis Lyman James,
all in the county of Hampshire; that John Wood, 2d, of Springfield,
may take the name of Homer John Wood; that Dixalana Clarke, of Blandford, may take the name of Mary Electa Clarke; that William Dwight,
2d, of Springfield, may take the name of William Courtland Dwight;
that Charles Eli Douglass, minor son of Henry Douglass, of Westfield,
may take the name of Darius Ely Douglass, all in the county of Hampden;
that Josiah Weeks Cannon, of Williamstown, may take the name of
Josiah Weeks Canning; and that Ebenezer Smith, Edward Weeks, Josiah
Deane, William Pitkin and Joseph Chauncy, all minor sons of the said
Josiah Weeks Cannon, may severally take the surname of Canning; that
Mandley Whiton, of Lee, may take the name of John Mandley Whiton, all
of the county of Berkshire; that Herman Curtis, of Roxbury, may take
the name of Joseph Herman Curtis; that William Swan, 3d, of Dorches-
ter, may take the name of William Draper Swan; that Jemima Aldana
Adams, of Medway, a minor child of William Adams, may take the name
Lorana Aldana Adams; that Mary Ann Bates Whitehouse, of Weymouth,
a minor child of Joseph H. Whitehouse, deceased, may take the name of
Mary Ann Bates, all in the county of Norfolk; that Elizabeth Hathaway
Staples, of Taunton, in the county of Bristol, daughter of Samuel B.
Staples, may take the name of Elizabeth Hathaway Williams; that Serenia
Curtis of Raynham, in said county of Bristol, may take the name of Serenia
Leonard; that John Baker, jun., of Brewster, a minor son of John
Baker, may take the name of John Peregrine Baker; that Nathan Hallett,
2d, of Yarmouth, may take the name of Franklin Hallett, both of the
county of Barnstable; that Lemuel Packard, of North Bridgewater, in the

county of Plymouth, a minor son of John Packard, may take the name of John L. Packard; that Edward Manning Saxton, a minor son of Jonathan Saxton, of Deerfield, may take the name of Edward Lowell Saxton; that Livonia Mehitabel Benton, of Bernardston, may take the name of Livonia Mehitabel Sanderson; that James Hervey Childs, a minor son of Sabra Childs, of Shelburne, may take the name of Asa Childs; that Amoret Graves, of Whately, a minor child, may take the name Amoret Morton, all in the county of Franklin; and the several persons before mentioned, from and after the passing of this act, shall be known and called by the names which by this act they are respectively allowed to assume as aforesaid, and said names shall forever hereafter be considered as their only proper and legal names to all intents and purposes. [*March 9, 1831.*]

AN ACT to change the Names of the Persons therein mentioned.
Be it enacted, etc., as follows:
That Samuel Gore of Boston, may take the name of Frederic S. Gore; that David Bradlee Eaton of Boston, may take the name of Albert Caspar Eaton; that Nehemiah Clap of Boston, may take the name of Charles Frederic William Clap; that Esther Rowe of Boston, a minor, and adopted daughter of Mary Harris, may take the name of Mary Esther Harris; that Joanna B. Berry of Boston, may take the name of Joanna B. Jewett; that Julia Lucretia Rogers of Boston, a minor, may take the name of Julia Leonora Rogers; that Antoinette Wright of Boston, a minor, daughter of Nathaniel Wright, may take the name of Anna Burlin Wright; that James Ivers Austin of Boston, may take the name of Ivers James Austin, all of the county of Suffolk; that Elijah Holt of Lynn, may take the name of Eli Holt; that Lucy Lovett of Beverly, a minor, daughter of Pyam Lovett, may take the name of Lucy Davis Lovett; that Stephen Sargent, 5th, of Amesbury, may take the name of Stephen N. Sargent; that Mary Ann Welch, of Newburyport, may take the name of Mary Ann Wingate; that Nathan Smith of Salem, and his wife, Martha I. Smith, may take the name of Nathan Pool and Martha T. Pool; that James Augustus Hodgkins, of Salem, a minor son of Elizabeth W. Hodgkins, may take the name of Augustus Hodgkins Lamson; that Ann Marston, a minor, of West Newbury, may take the name of Emma Ann Bailey, all of the county of Essex; that Benonia Boynton of Charlestown, in the county of Middlesex, may take the name of Benonia Boynton Buckingham; that William Wilder of Lancaster, may take the name of George Washington Wilder; that Daniel Rice of Leicester, may take the name of Daniel Tatman Rice; that Charles Austin Hunting of Barre, may take the name of Charles Austin, all of the county of Worcester; that Epaphroditus Williams, of Conway, in the county of Franklin, may take the name of Francis E. Williams; that Peter R. Bryant of Cummington, may take the name of Arthur Bryant; that Chileal Smith Douglass of Amherst, may take the name of Solomon Gilbert, all of the county of Hampshire; that Solomon Hoar, jun., of Brimfield, may take the name of Solomon Homer; that William P. Hoar of said Brimfield, may take the name of William P. Homer, and that Clarinda Hoar, wife of said William P., may take the name of Clarinda Homer, and that Martha Fullerton Hoar, Harriet Neal Hoar, and George Harding Hoar, minor children of said William P., and Clarinda Hoar, may take the

names respectively of Martha Fullerton Homer, Harriet Neal Homer and George Harding Homer, all of the county of Hampden ; that William Beale of Milton, may take the name of William Swift Beale ; that Isaac Adams of Brookline, may take the name of Isaac Mahtoa Wansongthi Adams ; that Charles Doggett of Brookline, may take the name of Charles Doggett Perry, all of the county of Norfolk ; that Nathaniel C. Towle of Norton, in the county of Bristol, may take the name of Nathaniel Towle Bowdoin ; that James Adams Mehuren, of Hingham in the county of Plymouth, may take the name of James Adams ; and the several persons herein mentioned are hereby allowed to take and hereafter be known by the respective names which by this act they severally are authorized to assume.
[*June 23, 1831.*

An Act to change the Names of the Persons therein mentioned.
Be it enacted, etc., as follows :
That Webber Ricker, of Boston, may take the name of George Webber Ricker ; that Orlando White, minor, son of Charles S. White, of Boston, may take the name of Henry Kirk White ; that Sampson Wilder Thurston, of Boston, may take the name of Wilder Stoddard Thurston ; that Petro Papathakes, of Boston, may take the name of Peter Patterson ; that William McManagil, of Boston, may take the name of William Pinkerton McKay ; that John McManagle, of Boston, may take the name of John McKay ; that Elizabeth McManagle wife of the said John McManagle, may take the name of Elizabeth McKay ; and that Mary Ann McManagle, daughter of the said John McManagle, may take the name of Mary Ann McKay ; and that his son, John Pinkerton McManagle, may take the name of John Pinkerton McKay : that Rebecca Waitt, of Chelsea, may take the name of Ann Rebecca Waitt ; that Thomas James Prince, of Boston, may take the name of James Prince ; that Lucius Augustus Hoar of Boston, may take the name of Lucius Augustus Horr ; that William Smith, of Boston, may take the name of William Otis Smith ; that Blowers Danforth, of Boston, may take the name of Bowers Danforth ; that Thomas Goddard, son of James Goddard, of Boston, may take the name of Thomas Austin Goddard ; that Nathaniel Thayer, minor, son of Susan F. Thayer, of Boston, may take the name of Nathaniel Frederick Thayer ; that Andrew Haskell, of Boston, may take the name of Andrew W. Haskell ; that William Eckley, minor, son of David Eckley, of Boston, may take the name of William Havard Eliot Eckley ; that Robert Lapish, of Boston, may take the name of Robert Hardison Dalton ; that James Lloyd Borland, son of John Borland, of Boston, may take the name of James Lloyd ; that William Richardson, of Boston, may take the name William Horatio Richardson, all of the county of Suffolk ; that Elizabeth Wendell, of Salem, may take the name of Mary Elizabeth Wendell ; that Samuel Becket Kehew, of Salem, may take the name of Samuel K. Appleton ; that Elhanan Winchester Knight, of Salisbury, may take the name of Winchester Knight ; that Josiah Cooper, of Newburyport, may take the name of Henry Franklin Benton ; that Caroline Chase, of Newburyport, may take the name of Caroline Boardman Chase ; that Harriet Chase, of Newburyport, may take the name of Harriet Augusta Chase ; that Peter Augustine Kimball, of Ipswich, may take the name of Augustine Phillips Kimball ; that William Micklefield, jun., minor, son of Mary Magrath, of Salem, may

take the name of Thomas Morris; that Daniel Putnam, jun., and William Putnam, 2d, sons of Daniel Putnam, Esq., of Danvers, may severally take the name of Daniel Franklin Putnam and William Richardson Putnam; that Timothy Dow Plumer, minor, son of Nathan Plumer, of Newburyport, may take the name of Charles Henry Plumer; that Helen Elizabeth Cook, and that Joseph Augustus Edwin Long Cook, minor children of John Cook, jun., of Newburyport, may take the respective names of Helen Mar Cook and Joseph Augustus Cook; that Pedro Blasina, of Beverly, may take the name of Edward Harrington; that Margaret Welman McMillan, of Salem, may take the name of Margaret Ann Maskall; that Cynthia Clarinda Dennis Young, minor, daughter of Levi Young, of Ipswich, may take the name of Cynthia Clarinda Young; that Nathaniel Rogers Lane, of Gloucester, may take the name of Fitz Henry Lane; that Daniel Jackson Doggett, of Ipswich, may take the name of Daniel Jackson Akerman; that Lucy Lord Doggett, wife of the said Daniel Jackson Doggett, may take the name of Lucy Lord Akerman; that Joseph L. Doggett, may take the name of Joseph Lord Akerman; that Sarah L. Doggett, may take the name of Sarah Lord Akerman; that Lucy M. Doggett, may take the name of Lucy Maria Akerman; that Susan L. Doggett, may take the name of Susan Lord Akerman; and that Walter P. Doggett, may take the name of Walter Phillips Akerman; the five above last named persons are minor children of the said Daniel Jackson Doggett; that Daniel Wardwell, 3d, of Andover, Mehitable Putnam Wardwell, wife of the said Daniel, that Susan Putnam Wardwell, minor daughter of the said Daniel Wardwell, may each respectively take the surname of Davenport, instead of Wardwell; that Morris Hern, of Rowley, may take the name of Morris Hersey; that Joseph Wormwood, of Lynn, that Susan Wormwood, wife of the said Joseph, and that Eliza Ellen Wormwood, daughter of the said Joseph, may each respectively take the surname of Everett, instead of Wormwood; — all of the county of Essex; that Charles Carter, minor son of Jacob Carter, of Leominster, may take the name of Charles Augustus Carter; that Stillman Hoar, of Sterling, may take the name of Stillman Haven; that Hannah Ward Hoar, wife of the said Stillman Hoar, may take the name of Hannah Ward Haven; that Oscar Dexter and Ward Knowlton, minor sons of 'said Stillman Hoar, may severally take the surname of Haven; that Jonathan Fairbanks, of Leominster, may take the name of Henry Fairbanks; that Samuel Granger, of New Braintree, may take the name of Edwin Granger; that Thomas Lawrence, 2d, of Leominster, may take the name of Thomas Edmunds; that John Babcock, of Fitchburg, may take the name of John B. Marshall; that Nathaniel Bradford, of Fitchburg, may take the name of Gustavus Lyman; that Ann Maria Keyes, of Ashburnham, may take the name of Almira Keyes; that Thomas Woodbury Gaffield, of Grafton, may take the name of George Woodbury Hale; that Oliver Goodridge, of Lunenburgh, may take the name of Oliver Newton Goodrich; that Abel Murdock, jun., of Leominster, may take the name of Thomas A. Murdock; that William Meriam, jun., of Ashburnham, may take the name of William Sanborn Meriam; that Nabby Willis, of Charlton, may take the name of Abigail Ellis Willis; that Mary L. B. Wiswall, of Westminster, may take the name of Mary Lyman; that Sarah Crouch, of Bolton, may take the name of Sarah Alvira Nelson; that Jefferson Beers, of Spencer, may take the name of Edward Beman; that Samuel Bullen, of Charlton, may take the name of Samuel Boyden; that Adams S. Bullen, of said Charlton, may take the name of Adams Boyden, all of the county of Worcester. That Moses C. Danforth, of Lowell, and that Pamelia Danforth, wife of the said Moses C. Danforth, may severally take the surname of Monroe, instead of Danforth; that John Henry Blasker, of Lowell, may take the name of John Henry Blake; that James Nichols, jun., of Reading, may take the name of James Churchill Nichols; that Vashti Brigham Barns, of Reading, may take the name of Mary Jane Barns; that Haslet Managle, of Marlboro', may take the name of Haslet McKay; that Nancy McManagle, wife of the said Haslet, that Ann, his daughter, and that William Pinkerton, his son, may respectively take the surname of McKay, instead of McManagle; that Ephraim Littlefield, of Holliston, minor, son of Oliver P. Littlefield, deceased, may take the name of Ephraim Oliver Prescott Littlefield; that Benjamin Thompson, of Charlestown, may take the name of Benjamin Lowell Thompson; that Samuel Matticks Ellen Kittle, of Townsend, may take the name of William Matticks Rogers; that James Kidder, minor child of James Kidder, jun., of Watertown, may take the name of James Hosmer Kidder; that Jason Chamberlain Smith, of Holliston, may take the name of Jason Smith; that Anna Damon, of Reading, may take the name of Anna Pratt; all of the county of Middlesex. That Isaac Mahtoa Wansongthi Adams, of Brookline, may take the name of Isaac Mahtra Wansongthi Adams; that Franklin Oakes, of Cohasset, minor son of Levi Oakes, may take the name of Benjamin Franklin Oakes; that Martin Spear, of Dedham, may take the name of Henry Forister Spear; all of the county of Norfolk. That Anna Mayo, of Eastham, may take the name of Anna Doane Mayo; that Lucy Knowles, of Eastham, may take the name of Lucy Harding Knowles; that Thankful Hallet Bray, of Yarmouth, may take the name of Susan Augusta Bray; all of the county of Barnstable. That Ignatious Loring, of Great Barrington, may take the name of Almon Ignatious Loring; that Grosvenor Curtis, of Egremont, may take the name of Harvey Grosvenor Curtis; both in the county of Berkshire. That John Foster, jun., of Scituate, may take the name of John Hatherly Foster; of the county of Plymouth. That Calvin Hoar, of Northampton; that Phebe Hoar, wife of the said Calvin; that William Patrick and Samuel Johnson, children of the said Calvin, may each respectively take the surname of Hoyt, instead of Hoar; all of the county of Hampshire. That Elisha Hunt, of Northfield, in the county of Franklin, may take the name of Elisha Watriss Hunt. That Martha Leavett Mayhew, an adopted daughter of Leavett Thaxter, of Edgartown, in the county of Dukes' county, may take the name of Martha Leavett Thaxter. That Nancy S. Covell, of New Bedford, may take the name of Nancy S. Blackmere; that Abigail Gifford, daughter of John Gifford, of Westport, may take the name of Abby Gifford; that Isaac Hathaway, of New Bedford, may take the name of Isaac Franklin Hathaway; all in the county of Bristol. And the several persons herein mentioned are hereby allowed to take and hereafter be known by the respective names which by this act they severally are authorized to assume. [*March 13, 1832.*

An Act to change the Names of Persons therein mentioned.
Be it enacted, etc., as follows:

That John Winslow Whitman, jun., of Boston, may take the name of George Henry Whitman; that Patrick Powers, of Boston, may take the name of John Patrick Powers; that Mary B. Murphy, of Boston, may take the name of Sarah Hunt; that Ebenezer W. Perry, of Boston, minor son of John B. Perry, may take the name of Ebenezer W. Townsend; that Joseph Buntin, of Boston, may take the name of Joseph Buntin Cornelius; that John Maky,.of Boston, may take the name of John Wirt May; that Mary Ann Maky, wife of the said John Maky, that his minor sons, viz., John James, Henry Rogers, William Thomas, Samuel Pearce, and also his minor daughter, Lucy Ann, may severally take the surname of May; that Ephraim Kendall Rogers, of Boston, may take the name of Edward Kendall Rogers; that Martha B. Waite, of Boston, may take the name of Martha B. Lawrence; that Hannah Sumner Cox, of Boston, may take the name of Hannah Sumner; that Nabby Phillips, of Boston, may take the name of Abigail Wales Phillips; that William Davis, of Boston, may take the name of William Guisby Davis; that Ralph Haskins, of Boston, may take the name of Ralph Thurston Haskins; that James Stackpole, of Boston, may take the name of James Wallace; that Delia Atwood, of Boston, minor daughter of Barnabas Atwood and Abigail Atwood, of Brewster, in the county of Barnstable, may take the name of Delia Atwood Thurston; that Penelope Green, of Boston, may take the name of Harriet Green; that James Boies Johnson, of Boston, may take the name of James Jeremiah Smith Boies; that Ann Dearing Johnson, wife of the said James, may take the name of Ann Dearing Boies; that James Theodore Johnson, may take the name of James Theodore Boies; that Ann Cordelia Johnson, may take the name of Cordelia Ann Boies; that William Rogers Johnson, may take the name of Ferdinand Augustus Boies; that William Octavius Johnson, may take the name of William Octavius Boies; that Charles Frederick Johnson, may take the name of Charles Frederick Boies; that Edward Alonzo Johnson, may take the name of Edward Alonzo Boies; all minor children of the said James Boies Johnson, first named; that John Bigelow, 2d, of Boston, may take the name of John Bradford Bigelow; that Bayard Rice, of Boston, may take the name of James Bayard Rice; that Smith Hills, of Boston, may take the name of Henry Smith Hills; that Ebenezer Leman, of Boston, cork-cutter, may take the name of Ebenezer C. Leman; that Elbridge Whitney, of Boston, may take the name of Elbridge Gerry Whitney; that Sarah Monk, of Boston, may take the name of Sarah M. Brown; that Benjamin Bates, of Boston, may take the name of Benjamin Edward Bates; that Benjamin Willard, of Boston, may take the name of Benjamin Franklin Willard; all of the county of Suffolk.

Essex county. That Edward Orne, of Salem, may take the name of Edward Osgood; that Charlotte Woodberry, minor daughter of David Woodbury, of Wenham, may take the name of Charlotte Woodberry Symons; that Charles William Peirce Crockett, of Newbury, may take the name of Charles Peirce Crocket; that Joseph James Galley Cuishing, a minor son of Joseph Cuishing, of Marblehead, may take the name of James Galley Cuishing; that John Hoyt Bean, of Lynn, may take the name of John Hoyt Henry; that Susan Lakeman, 3d, of Ipswich, may take the name of Susan Sarah Lakeman; that Sarah Stickney Hunt, of Newbury, may take the name of Sarah Jane Stickney; that Melancthon Elliot, of Newburyport, may take the name of Henry Melancthon Elliot; that Marcy Gidings Putnam, of Salem, may take the name of Maria Gidings Putnam; that Emily Bailey, of West Newbury, may take the name of Emily Mariketer Bailey; that Abraham Edwards, minor son of Abraham Edwards, of Beverly, may take the name of Abraham Franklin Edwards; that Daniel Bailey, 3d, of West Newbury, may take the name of Daniel Winslow Bailey; that Dudley Cross, jun., of Ipswich, may take the name of John Dudley Cross; that Lydia Little Dodge, of Salem, may take the name of Ellen Lydia Little Dodge; that Samuel Safford, a minor, of Salem, may take the name of Samuel Appleton Safford; that Samuel Whitefoot, of Danvers, may take the name of Samuel White; that Elizabeth, wife of the said Samuel Whitefoot, and that his minor son, Samuel Quince Whitefoot, may severally take the name of White; that John Hooper, jun., of Marblehead, may take the name of John Lee Hooper; that Ruth Moody Bradley, of Bradford, may take the name of Ruth Ann Moody Bradley; that Ruth Ingersoll Ladd, of Bradford, may take the name of Ellen Bradstreet Ladd; all of the county of Essex.

Middlesex county. That Lot Wiswall, of Cambridge, may take the name of William Daniels Wiswall; that Hiram Brown, of Lowell, may take the name of Hiram Alonzo Brown; that Polly Richardson, of Framingham, may take the name of Maria Antoinette Richardson; that William Paige, 1st, of Shirley, may take the name of William Weston Paige; that James Paul Crooks, of South Reading, may take the name of Paul Kruz; that Mary Crooks, his wife, may take the name of Mary Kruz; that Caleb Horace Pool Wakefield, of Reading, may take the name of Horace Pool Wakefield; that Ambrose Augustus Cole, of Charlestown, may take the name of Augustus Howard Cole; that Aira Kenny, of Reading, may take the name of Ellen Maria Kenny; that Loammi Kendall, jun., of Charlestown, may take the name of Arthur Kendall; that Samuel King, jun., of Cambridge, may take the name of Samuel Wilson King; that Fanny Tufts, of Medford, may take the name of Frances Emily Tufts; that William Searles, of Lowell, may take the name of William Coleman; that Alice Ann Fullerton, of Lowell, a minor, may take the name of Alice Ann Shattuck; that Edward Eels, jun., of Medford, may take the name of Edward Eels Nash; all of the county of Middlesex.

Norfolk county. That Benjamin Frost Cutter, of Brookline, may take the name of Benjamin Franklin Cutter; that Henry Peirce, and Edward Peirce, minor sons of Jesse Peirce, of Stoughton, may severally take the names of Henry Lillie Peirce, and Edward Lillie Peirce; that Joseph Kendall, of Dorchester, may take the name of Edward Joseph Kendall; all of the county of Norfolk.

Worcester county. That Jonadab Baker, of Ashburnham, may take the name of George Baker; that Boaz Moore Merrick, of West Brookfield, may take the name of Charles Augustus Merrick; that Anna Fitts, 2d, of Charlton, may take the name of Ann Maria Fitts; that Sally Bullen, of Charlton, may take the name of Sally Boyden; that Polly Bullen, of Charlton, may take the name of Mary Boyden; that Samuel Chandler Blake, of Worcester, may take the name of Francis Blake; that James Madison Cutter, of Fitchburg, may take the name of James Marshall Cutter; that Adam Hawks, of Ashburnham, may take the name of Henry Putnam

Hawks; that Sumner Smith, of Worcester, may take the name of Joseph Sumner Smith; that Mary G. Fisk, of Spencer, may take the name of Adelaide Mary Fisk; that Ebenezer Wilder, jun., of Lancaster, may take the name of Frederick William Wilder; that Emilia Dudley, minor daughter of Samuel Dudley, of Harvard, deceased, may take the name of Abba Willard Dudley; that John Davis, of Worcester, son of Joseph Davis, of Northboro', in said county, may take the name of John B. Davis; that William Sawyer of Berlin, may take the name of William Adison Sawyer; that William Henry Tower, a minor son of Asahel Tower, jun., of Lancaster, may take the name of Henry Ambrose Tower; that Emily Osgood, of Leominster, may take the name of Emily Rebecca Osgood; that Adeline Wheeler Stearns, of Oakham, minor daughter of Isaac Stearns, of Spencer, may take the name of Adeline Wheeler Ayres; that Asa Waters, jun., of Millbury, may take the name of Asa Holman Waters; all of the county of Worcester.

Plymouth county. That Nathaniel Fowle Bowdoin, of Hanson, may take the name of Nathaniel Towle Bowdoin; that his wife, Eunice, may take the name of Eunice Towle Bowdoin; that Harriet Newell Barker, of Halifax, may take the name of Harriet Jane Watterman; that Phebe Thompson, of Halifax, may take the name of Phebe Waterman Thompson; all of the county of Plymouth.

Hampshire county. That Emily Olds of Cummington, may take the name of Emily Read; that Experience Amanda Cooley, of Prescott, may take the name of Mary Jane Amanda Cooley; that Betsey Brewster, of Worthington, may take the name of Elizabeth M. Brewster; that James Dickson Benjamin, of Worthington, minor son of Alvah Benjamin, deceased, may take the name of Alvah Dickson Benjamin; that Calvin Mitchell, of Enfield, may take the name of Marcus Milton Mitchell; that George Mitchell, of Enfield, may take the name of George W. Mitchell; that Ashley Washington, of Amherst, may take the name of George Washington; all of the county of Hampshire.

Franklin county. That John Smith, of Sunderland, may take the name of John Rowe Smith; that Olive Cary, of Montague, may take the name of Olive Holton; both in the county of Franklin.

Hampden county. That George Francis Norcross, minor son of Erasmus Norcross, of Monson, may take the name of George Henry Norcross; of the county of Hampden.

Barnstable county. That Luke Baker, of Chatham, may take the name of Luke Clark Baker; of the county of Barnstable. And the several persons herein mentioned are hereby allowed to take and hereafter be known by the respective names, which by this act they severally are authorized to assume. [*March 27, 1833.*]

AN ACT to change the name of Charles Twining Tyler.
Be it enacted, etc., as follows:
That from and after the passing of this act, Charles Twining Tyler, of Boston, in the county of Suffolk, is hereby authorized to take the name of Royall Tyler. [*March 28, 1833.*]

AN ACT to change the Names of the Persons therein mentioned.

Be it enacted, etc., as follows:

That Luther Faulkner, 2d, of Boston, may take the name of Luther Winthrop Faulkner; that Ephraim Skerry, of Boston, may take the name of George Beals Hanover; that Francis Skerry, of Boston, may take the name of Samuel Blacklen Hanover; that Richard James Calley Prentiss, of Boston, may take the name of Henry James Prentiss; that Ann Rand More, of Boston, may take the name of Ann Louisa Callender; that Charles Bridge of Boston, a minor, may take the name of William Smith Rowson; that Alven Clement Gowell, of Boston, may take the name of Alven Clement Goell; that William Cunningham, of Boston, may take the name of Theodore William Cunningham; that Isaiah Atkins, of Boston, may take the name of Isaiah Malcolm Atkins; that John Joy, of Boston, may take the name of John Benjamin Joy; that Richard Roberts Skimmer, of Boston, may take the name of William Henry Otis; that John Temple Winthrop, of Boston, may take the name of John Temple James Bowdoin; that Thomas Vose, of Boston, may take the name of Thomas Baker Vose; that William Keith, of Boston, may take the name of William Henry Keith; that Simon Gillpatrick, of Boston, may take the name of Simon Gill; that Lucy Peterson, of Boston, may take the name of Lucy Adeliza Hewet Peterson; that Lucy McIntosh, of Boston, may take the name of Lucy Fiske McIntosh; that Daniel Fornis, a minor son of Sally Fornis, of Boston, may take the name of Daniel Thorndike Smith; that Simon P. Wiggin, of Boston, may take the name of James S. Wiggin; that Nathaniel Williams, of Boston, may take the name of Frederick G. Williams; that Marion Smith, of Boston, may take the name of Marion Smith Livermore; that Henry Smith, a minor son of the said Marion Smith, may take the name of Henry Smith Livermore; that John Clark, of Boston, may take the name of John Canque; that his two minor sons, viz., John and Francis, may severally take the surname of Canque; that Jonathan Champney, of Boston, may take the name of John Champney; and that Hezekiah Hartley Wright, of Boston, may take the name of Hartley Hezekiah Wright; all of the county of Suffolk.

That Catherine Judith Poor Tenney, of West Newbury, a minor, may take the name of Catharine Tenney Little; that Albert Rich, of Lynn, a minor, may take the name of Allen Smith Rich; that Eliza Treadwell, a minor daughter of Eliza Treadwell, of Ipswich, may take the name of Eliza White Treadwell; that Lydia Ann Farnum, a minor daughter of Jerre Farnum, of Andover, may take the name of Lydia Ann Lewis; that Lucy Tenney, of Rowley, may take the name of Lucy Harriet Tenney; that George Haycock, of Rowley, may take the name of George Cummins; that Eliza Haycock, wife of the said George Haycock, that his minor daughters, viz., Elizabeth Appleton and Martha Eliza, may severally take the surname of Cummins; also that Dolly Ann Palmer Haycock, a minor daughter of the said George Haycock, may take the name of Dolly Ann Palmer Cummins; that David Hood, of Topsfield, may take the name of Wesley de la Fletcher Hood; that Sally Chase Bailey Carr, of West Newbury, may take the name of Sarah Wyman Carr; that John March, of Newbury, may take the name of John Charles March; that William F. Vickery, of West Newbury, may take the name of William F. Loring; that Jane Veazey, of Newburyport, may take the name of Jane Lunt; that John Russell, of

Marblehead, may take the name of John Hickman Russell; that William Dove, of Marblehead, may take the name of William Curtis Anthony, and that Hannah Dove, the wife, of the said William Dove, may take the name of Hannah Anthony; that William Dodge, 3d, of Beverly, may take the name of William Franklin Dodge; and that Orlando Sargent, 3d, of Amesbury, may take the name of Orlando Howard Sargent; all of the county of Essex.

That James Gillpatrick, of Watertown, may take the name of James Gill; that Eliza Gillpatrick, the wife of the said James Gillpatrick, his minor daughter Mary Ann, and his minor son George, may severally take the surname of Gill; that Edmund Burpee, of Lowell, may take the name of Edmund Howes Kendall; that Henrietta Maria Sparhawk Burpee, wife of the said Edmund Burpee, and his minor son, Edmund Howes, may severally take the surname of Kendall; that Betsey Farnsworth, wife of William J. Farnsworth, of Charlestown, may take the name of Caroline Augusta Farnsworth; that Sarah Bradish Ayer, of Charlestown, a minor, may take the name of Sarah Eliza Ayer Jackson; that Elhanan Dean Bryant, a minor son of Ann Bryant, of Charlestown, may take the name of Dean Perham Bryant; that Edward Brown, of Charlestown, may take the name of Edward Wyer Brown; that Samuel Frost Arnold, of Framingham, may take the name of Samuel Frost; that John Smith, a minor son of Jesse Smith, of Chelmsford, may take the name of John Henry Smith; that Mitty Perry, of Framingham, may take the name of Elizabeth Ann Perry; that William McLane, of Cambridge, may take the name of William Sinclair Thompson; that Eben William Sage Stevens, a minor son of Thomas Holdup Stevens, of Charlestown, may take the name of Eben William Sage; all of the county of Middlesex.

That Lois Crouch, of Bolton, may take the name of Lois Elizabeth Nelson; that John Smith of West Boylston, may take the name of Austin Denney; that Milton J. Adams, of Worcester, may take the name of Sewel Hawes; that James P. Twitchell, of Westminster, may take the name of James P. Appleton; and that his wife, Emily C., may take the name of Emily C. Appleton; that Betsey Reed Joslin, of Leominster, may take the name of Elizabeth Marion Reed Joslin; that Lavinah Crouch, of Bolton, may take the name of Mary Lavinah Nelson; that Amos Pierce, of Sutton, may take the name of Charles Amos Pierce; that Mary W. Howe, of Grafton, may take the name of Mary W. Putnam; that James Henry Alexander Deland, of North Brookfield, may take the name of Henry Deland; that George Fornis, of Holden, a minor son of Sally Fornis, may take the name of George Howard Smith; that Enos Babcock, of Fitchburg, may take the name of Eneas Alson Marshall; that David Rice Babcock, of Fitchburg, a minor, may take the name of David Rice Marshall; that Alexander James Dallas Brown, of Southbridge, may take the name of Alexander James Dallas; that Sally Walker, of Hardwick, may take the name of Susan Walker; that Adelaide Mary Fisk, of Spencer, may take the name of Adelaide Mary Green; that Harlow Fisher Skinner, of Princeton, may take the name of Harlow Skinner; that Alden Briggs, of Grafton, may take the name of John Briggs; that Hezekiah Harris, of Princeton, may take the name of Charles Hamilton Davis; that Samuel Francis, of Lunenburg, may take the name of Franklin Samuel Francis; all of the county of Worcester.

That Marshall Comee Moody, of Granby, may take the name of Marshall Heman Moody ; that Chester Cowles, 2d, of Amherst, may take the name of Chester W. Cowles ; that Wright Dickinson, of Amherst, may take the name of Edward Wright Dickinson ; that Charles Sinkler Brakenridge, of Ware, may take the name of William Sinkler Brakenridge ; all of the county of Hampshire.

That Meshack Wilbur of Warwick, may take the name of Priest Wilbur ; that David Wood, of Hawley, may take the name of David Hough Wood ; that Sarah Ann Renough, of Hawley, a minor, may take the name of Sarah Ann King ; that Africa Gates, of Wendell, may take the name of Edmund Gates ; that Relief Wells, of Bernardstown, may take the name of Mary Gould ; that James Kilton, of Buckland, may take the name of James Carlton ; that Hannah Kilton, wife of the said James Kilton, that his minor son William Augustus Leverit, and his minor daughters, Mary Elizabeth, Sabra Willis and Jane Lurissa, may severally take the surname of Carlton ; that Norman Marsh, of Sunderland, may take the name of Norman Homer Marsh ; that Meroe Porter, of Leverett, may take the name of Lucy Meroe Porter ; that Harriet Shepard, a minor daughter of Amos Shepard, of Buckland, may take the name of Harriet Asenath Shepard ; all of the county of Franklin.

That Isaac Gray, of New Bedford, may take the name of Isaac Henderson Gray ; that John Fillebrown, of Taunton, may take the name of John Brown ; that Joanna Fillebrown, wife of the said John Fillebrown, and his minor daughter, Susan, and his minor sons, John, Calvin, and Seth Henry, may severally take the surname of Brown ; that Benjamin Weaver, of Fall River, may take the name of Charles Benjamin Weaver ; that William F. Jones, of Taunton, may take the name of William Jones ; that William Allen, of New Bedford, may take the name of William Marion Allen ; that James Foster, jun., of Attleborough, may take the name of James Sullivan Foster ; all of the county of Bristol.

That Nathaniel Webster, of Dorchester, may take the name of Nathaniel Francis Webster ; that Ichabod Holbrook, of Dorchester, may take the name of Clarendon Gorham Holbrook ; that St. Medard Holbrook, of Dorchester, may take the name of George Holbrook ; that Joanna Bates, of Cohasset, a minor daughter of Samuel Bates, may take the name of Joanna Nichols Bates ; that Charles George Glover, a minor son of Stephen Glover, of Roxbury, may take the name of George Stephen Glover ; all of the county of Norfolk.

That Polly Bardwell Nash, a minor daughter of Luke Nash, jun., of Abington, may take the name of Emeline Hamilton Nash ; that Dennis Snow, of Rochester, may take the name of Jackson Snow ; that Mercy Thompson, of Halifax, may take the name of Mercy Tillson ; all of the county of Plymouth.

That Hosea C. Bancroft, of Stockbridge, may take the name of George C. Bancroft ; that Partridge Snow, of Becket, may take the name of Seneca Lorenzo Snow ; all of the county of Berkshire.

That Moses Chapman Elliot, a minor son of Francis Elliot, of Springfield, may take name of William Henry Elliot ; that Wilson Hamilton Hoar, of Brimfield, may take the name of Wilson Homer ; that David Hoar, of Springfield, may take the name of David Hobart ; that his wife, Mabel

Maria, and his son David Parsons, may severally take the surname of Hobart; all of the county of Hampden.

That John Geyer, of Chilmark, may take the name of John Hayden; that Lucretia Geyer, wife of the said John Geyer, his minor daughters, Mary D., Sarah, Elizabeth, Lucretia and Caroline, and his minor son, John, may severally take the surname of Hayden; all of the county of Dukes County.

And the several persons herein mentioned are hereby authorized to take, and hereafter be known by the respective names, which by this act they severally are authorized to assume. [*March 22, 1834.*

AN ACT to change the Names of the Persons therein mentioned.
Be it enacted, etc., as follows:

That William Billings, of Boston, in the county of Suffolk, may take the name of William W. Billings; that Ninian Clark, jun , of Beverly may take the name of Augustus Ninian Clark; that Samuel Scott, of Andover, may take the name of Samuel Palmer Scott; and all of the county of Essex; that David Balcom, 3d, of Douglas, in the county of Worcester, may take the name of David Howard Balcom; that Achsah Ingram, of Amherst, in the county of Hampshire, may take the name of Ellen A. Ingram; that Nathaniel T. Bowdoin, of Hanson, in the county of Plymouth, may take the name of Nathaniel C. Towle; and that Eunice M., the wife of said Nathaniel T. Bowdoin, may take the surname of Towle. And the several persons herein mentioned are hereby allowed to take, and hereafter be known by the respective names which by this act they severally are authorized to assume. [*March 29, 1834.*

AN ACT to change the Names of Persons therein mentioned.
Be it enacted, etc., as follows:

That Stephen Chase, of Boston, may take the name of Stephen Chase Bent; that Julia Ann Chase, wife of said Stephen Chase, may take the name of Julia Chase Bent; that Frederick Wentworth, of Boston, may take the name of Frederick Augustus Wentworth; that Epafhias Kibby Brodhead, of Boston, may take the name of George Hamilton Brodhead; that Benjamin Callender, of Boston, may take the name of Benjamin Franklin Callender; that John Chandler, of Boston, may take the name of John Green Chandler; that Godfrey Cady, of Boston, may take the name of William Godfrey Cady; that James Leach, jun., of Boston, may take the name of James L. Duncan; that Jeremiah Fenno Holden, of Boston, may take the name of Edward Holden; that Simon Rowland Hart, of Boston, may take the name of Rowland St. Victor; that Philip Page, of Boston, may take the name of Philip Sidney Page; that Edward Augustus Hayman Rogers, of Boston, may take the name of Edward Hayman Rogers; that John Boies Broaders, of Boston, may take the name of John Dudley Richards; that James Smith, of Boston, may take the name of James Wiggin Smith; that Lydia Sprague, daughter of Samuel Sprague, of Boston, may take the name of Mary Chadwick Sprague; that Benaiah Spaulding, of Boston, may take the name of Benaiah Prescott Spaulding; that Fonzo White, of Boston, may take the name of William Fonzo White; that Alex-

ander Mair, of Boston, may take the name of Alexander Mair Williams ;
that George Washington Gorton, of Boston, may take the name of George
Washington Gorton Williams ; that Samuel Whiting, of Boston, may take
the name of Samuel Greenwood Whiting ; that Elisha E. Wellman, of Bos-
ton, may take the name of Samuel Ellenwood Wellman ; and that his
adopted daughter Sarah Jane Hamilton, may take the name of Sarah Ann
Wellman ; that Lyman Gaschall Reed, of Boston, minor son of Thomas and
Hannah Reed, may take the name of Elisha Smith Reed ; that Isabella
Parker, a minor, daughter of Isaac Parker, of Boston, may take the name
of Isabella Graham Parker ; and that Henry Parker, a minor son of said
Isaac Parker, may take the name of Henry Melville Parker ; that Hartford
Olney Claflin, of Boston, may take the name of Henry Claflin ; that John
Holker Welch, a minor son of Francis Welch, of Boston, may take the
name of Edward Holker Welch ; that John Boyd Wallace, of Boston, a
minor, may take the name of John Wallace Boyd ; that Alfred Bertershaw,
of Boston, may take the name of Alfred B. Shaw ; that Abigail Howe, of
Boston, a minor, may take the name of Abigail Howe Amee ; that Lewis
Wilder, of Boston, may take the name of Charles Lewis Wilder ; that
Abigail, daughter of Thomas Jackson, of Boston, may take the name of
Abigail Callender Jackson ; that James Adams, jun., of Boston, may take
the name of James Bartlett Adams ; that Thomas Bird Murphey, may take
the name of Thomas Murphey Bird ; that Henry Snook, of Boston, may
take the name of Henry Snook Bacon ; that William Eaton, of Boston,
a minor, may take the name of William Storer Eaton ; that James Harris,
of Boston, a minor, may take the name of James Watson Harris ; that
Lars Olsson, of Boston, may take the name of Lewis Olsson ; that Isaac
Wharff Smith, may take the name of Isaac William Smith ; all of the
county of Suffolk.

That John Felt, of Salem, may take the name of John G. Felt ; that
Jonas Loskey, of Salem, may take the name of George Loskey ; that Jona-
than Archer Ropes, of Salem, may take the name of Archer Ropes ; that
Royal Augustus Averell, of Middleton, may take the name of Albert
Augustus Averell ; that Samuel Christopher Kilby White, of Middleton,
may take the name of Henry Mansfield ; that Daniel Augustus Rogers, of
Gloucester, minor son of Betsey Rogers, may take the name of Daniel
Webster Rogers ; that William Pool, jun., of Gloucester, son of the late
William Pool, of Hallowell, state of Maine, may take the name of William
Grover Pool ; that Deborah Lambert Bridges, of Rowley, may take the
name of Deborah Hubbard Bridges ; that Charles Wilkins, of Salem, may
take the name of Charles Frederick Wilkins ; that Willard Harding, jun.,
of Lynn, may take the name of Willard Mason Harding ; that George
Creasey, of Rowley, may take the name of George W. Creasey ; that
Owen Eaton, of Andover, may take the name of Franklin Howard Eaton ;
that Daniel Hale Jaques, minor son of William Jaques, late of Newbury,
deceased, may take the name of William Jaques ; that Andrew Standley, 3d,
of Beverly, may take the name of Andrew Warren Standley ; that Mary
Lindsey, of Salem, may take the name of Mary Lindsey Putnam ; that
Joshua Eliphalet Hills, of Newburyport, may take the name of Eliphalet
Hills ; that John Patten Sargent, of Amesbury, may take the name of
Porter Sargent ; all of the county of Essex.

That Ezekiel Lysander Bascom Lamb, of Framingham, may take the

name of Lysander Wheelock; that Andrew Munroe, jun., of Reading, may
take the name of Andrew Brigham; that Jeremiah Paine, of Reading, may
take the name of Jeremiah Putnam; that Cheney Allen of Woburn, may
take the name of George Cheney Allen; that Samuel H. Newell, of Cambridge, may take the name of John Stark; that Joshua Barrett, of Westford,
a minor, may take the name of Joshua Payson Barrett; that Edward Woodcock, of Groton, may take the name of Charles Edwards Weston; that
David Woodcock, of Groton, may take the name of David Brainard
Weston; that Washington Woodcock, of Groton, may take the name of
George Washington Weston; that Charles Ensworth, of Cambridge, may
take the name of Charles Ward Tracy; that Joel Newton Onthank, of
Weston, may take the name of Joel Newton; that Edward Rogers and Edmund Rogers, of Groton, minors, sons of Willard Rogers, may severally
take the names of Edward Rogers Blood and Edmund Rogers Blood; that
Josiah Rider, of Lowell, may take the name of Josiah Lawrence; that
Robert L. Eells and Louisa H. Eells, of Medford, may severally take the
name of Robert L. Ells and Louisa H. Ells; that Mary Holden, of Waltham, may take the name of Mary Raymond Motley; that George Washington Falconer, of Newton, a minor, may take the name of Samuel Ad-
lam; that Olive Bean, of Holliston, may take the name of Elizabeth Olive
New; that Augustus Crossman, of Cambridge, a minor, may take the
name of Augustus Stedman; that John Williams, of Framingham, a minor,
may take the name of John Williams Turner; that Susan Rebecca Dame, of
Medford, may take the name of Susan Rebecca Steel; all of the county of
Middlesex.

That David B. Rider, of Hubbardston, may take the name of David B.
Makepeace; that Harriet F. Thompson, of Hubbardston, may take the
name of Harriet F. Phelps; that Metcalf C. Hardy, of Worcester, may
take the name of William Seth Hardy; that Samuel Hardy, of Worcester,
may take the name of Samuel Henderson Hardy; that Zacharius Reed, of
Warren, may take the name of Alden Reed; that Timothy S. Rice, of Leominster, may take the name of George Kendall; that Lawyer Stanford, of
Milford, may take the name of Joel L. Stanford; that Otis Sanford Billings, of Sutton, may take the name of Lysander Woodburn Henderson;
that Nicholas Cowper Moore, of Princeton, may take the name of Humphrey
Moore; that Minerva Morse, of Southbridge, may take the name of Oscar
Plimpton Morse; that Ivory Stackpole, of Athol, a minor, may take the
name of William Ebenezer Kelton Fowle; that Samuel Fiske, jun., of
Southbridge, a minor, may take the name of Samuel Lynn Fiske; that
Eunice Cronch, of Bolton, may take the name of Eunice Nelson; that Le-
ander Loring Ball, of Princeton, may take the name of Leander Loring;
that Luther L. Lackey, of Princeton, may take the name of Lurestan Chan-
velin; that Cyril Flint, of Barre, may take the name of Francis Allen; and
that Mary, his wife, as also their three children, minors, namely, John,
Georgiana and Moriah, may severally take the surname of Allen; that
Eliza Earl, of Hardwick, may take the name of Mary Eliza Earl; that
Martha Houghton, of Bolton, may take the name of Martha Stearns
Houghton; that Mary Gardner, of Bolton, may take the name of Mary
Louisa Gardner; that Betsey Osborn, of Bolton, may take the name of
Elizabeth Wyman Osborn; that Miranda Wheelock, of Winchendon, may
take the name of Miranda Elizabeth Wilder; that Henry Jackson Davis,

of Grafton, may take the name of Henry Davis; that Bostic Penniman Greenlief, of Dudley, may take the name of Thomas Bostic Penniman; all of the county of Worcester.

That Francis Witt, of South Hadley, may take the name of Francis De-Witt; that Lyman Nobles, jun., of Northampton, may take the name of Cyrus Dwight Nobles; that John Northum, jun., of Greenwich, may take the name of John Willcox Northum; that Harriet Graves, of Hatfield, may take the name of Harriet Cornelia Graves; that Zilpha Nutting, of Leverett, may take the name of Jane Celeste Nutting; that Orrin Blush Smith, of Middlefield, a minor, may take the name of Charles Smith; that Oliver Smith, of Middlefield, a minor, may take the name of Milton Smith; that Consider Scott, of Hatfield, may take the name of Consider Williams Scott; that Elijah Brass, of Southampton, may take the name of Elijah Brass Emerson; that Asahel Salmon Abels, of Northampton, may take the name of Asahel Salmon Abell; that James Stebbins, of Ware, a minor, may take the name of James Dexter Eddy; all of the county of Hampshire.

That David Needham, 2d, of Wales, may take the name of David Besse Needham; that Harriet Tillotson, of Granville, a minor, may take the name of Harriet Seymour; both of the county of Hampden.

That Julia Wait, of Whately, may take the name of Julia Angeline Wait; that Seth Washburn Willard, of Greenfield, a minor, may take the name of Washburn Willard Graves; that Lucy Mariah Whitney, of Warwick, may take the name of Lucy Whitney Pierce; that Esbon Elnathan Williams, of Wendell, a minor, may take the name of William Claggett Johnson; all of the county of Franklin.

That Mercy Turner, of Clarksburg, may take the name of Mercy Shipping; that Diana Huntington, of Becket, may take the name of Frances Diana Huntington; that George Turner, of Stockbridge, a minor, may take the name of George Nash Turner; that Douglass Turner, of Stockbridge, may take the name of Douglass Kellogg Turner; all of the county of Berkshire.

That Volley Swain Death, of Walpole, may take the name of Samuel Dickinson; that Aaron Stetson, of Quincy, may take the name of James Aaron Stetson; that Francis Antignola, of Weymouth, may take the name of Francis Hamilton; that Bathsheba H. Balch, of Medfield, may take the name of Ellen B. H. Balch; that Abigail Riley, of Dorchester, may take the name of Abigail Bartlett Ordway; and that her infant daughter, Sarah Hale Riley, may take the name of Sarah Hale Ordway; all of the county of Norfolk.

That Theodore Augustus Bigelow, of Taunton, a minor, may take the name of Theodore Stanwood Bigelow; that Greenleaf Orin Norice Bliss, of Seekonk, may take the name of Orin Norice Bliss; that William Gifford, of Dartmouth, may take the name of William Sisson Gifford; all of the county of Bristol.

That Prince William Snow, of Nantucket, a minor, may take the name of Aaron Prince Snow: and the several persons herein mentioned are hereby authorized to take, and hereafter be known by the respective names which by this act they severally are authorized to assume. [*April 8, 1835.*

An Act to change the Names of the several Persons therein mentioned. *Be it enacted, etc., as follows:*

Abram Babcock may take the name of George Williams Abram Babcock; William Hulin may take the name of William Hulin Clifton; John French may take the name of John Marshall French; Charles Robert Andrews, a minor son of Elizabeth Andrews, may take the name of John Dudley Andrews; Abel Munroe may take the name of Abel B. Munroe; Caroline Louisa Grosvenor may take the name of Louisa Grosvenor; John Calrow may take the name of John Glover Calrow; William Calrow, jun., may take the name of William Howard Calrow; Thomas Calrow may take the name of Thomas Baldwin Calrow; Patrick Cavanah may take the name of William Pollard Cavanah; John Hunting Capen, a minor, may take the name of John Capen; Charles Cunningham, a minor, may take the name of Charles West Cunningham; Lydia Emily Coffin, a minor, may take the name of Lydia Emily Coffin Morse; John Stoddard may take the name of John D. Stoddard; William Smith may take the name of Marcellus Judson Smith; Joseph Saunders Coffin, a minor, may take the name of Joseph Saunders; Percival Eaton Howe, a minor, may take the name of John Percival Howe; Gookin Parker may take the name of William Gookin Parker; all of the city of Boston, in the county of Suffolk. Peter Russell, of Lynnfield, may take the name of Helon Russell; William Burnham, 5th, of Essex, may take the name of William Haskell Burnham; Frederick Griffin, of Essex, a minor, may take the name of Frederick Perkins Gardiner; Susan Eliza Wood, of Gloucester, a minor, may take the name of Susan Bartlett Haskell; Ahira Putnam, of Danvers, may take the name of Ahira Herrick Putnam; Louisa Stickney, of Salem, may take the name of Louisa D. Kent; Nancy Collins Johnson, of Salem, may take the name of Emily Collins Johnson; Samuel Bartlett, of West Newbury, may take the name of Samuel Waldo Bartlett; John Currier, 4th, of Amesbury, may take the name of John Henry Currier; Israel Foster, 3d, of Beverly, may take the name of Israel Wallace Foster; Joseph Cole, of Ipswich, may take the name of Joseph D. Salisbury; Abigail Cole, of Ipswich, may take the name of Abigail L. Salisbury; Joseph Very, of Danvers, may take the name of Joseph Dempsey Very; Ansel Putnam, a minor, son of Daniel Putnam of Danvers, may take the name of Ansel Wallace Putnam; Mary Jane Morse, of Haverhill, a minor, may take the name of Mary Jane Smith; Charles Henry Kent, of Rowley, may take the name of Charles H. Webster; Sarah Merrill Kent, of Rowley, may take the name of Sarah Augusta Webster; Lavina Kimball, of Amesbury, a minor, may take the name of Lavina Kimball Pressey; Benjamin Foster, 4th, of Beverly, may take the name of Benjamin Lovett Foster; Mary Phillips Abbott, of Andover, may take the name of Mary Elizabeth Phillips Abbott; Moody Russell, of Middleton, may take the name of Samuel M. Russell; all of the county of Essex. Anthony Vaughn Baker, of Cambridge, may take the name of Anthony Vaughn Fletcher; Martha Baker, of Cambridge, may take the name of Martha Fletcher; Martha Elizabeth Baker, a minor daughter of Anthony Vaughn Baker, may take the name of Martha Elizabeth Fletcher; Benjamin Franklin Smith, a minor, of Woburn, may take the name of Benjamin Franklin Oakes Smith; Georgiana Reymond, of Malden, a minor, may take the name of Mary Ann Faulkner; Matthew Thomas Kidder Adams Griffin, of Westford, may take the name of George Adams Griffin; Sarah McIntire,

of Reading, may take the name of Sarah Flint; William Newell, of
Brighton, may take the name of William Whiting Wheaton Newell; Reu-
ben Seiders, of Cambridge, may take the name of Richard Thomas Austin;
Mary Jane Sanborn, of Lowell, may take the name of Mary Jane Rollins;
Ira Hodgman, of Ashby, may take the name of Charles Day; Nathan
Goodale, of Marlboro', may take the name of Nathan Munroe Goodale;
James Francis Smiley, of Groton, a minor, may take the name of James
Tarbell; Samuel Brown Stone, of Natick, may take the name of Warren
Stone; all of the county of Middlesex.   Jonathan Sawyer, of Harvard, a
minor, may take the name of Augustus Jonathan Sawyer; Royal C. Ches-
more, of Fitchburg, may take the name of Henry Otis Rockwell; Dolly Wil-
der, of Leominster, may take the name of Frances Hills Wilder; Jesse
Trickey, of Worcester, may take the name of Ivers R. Harvey; Elijah
Hitchcock, of Sturbridge, a minor, may take the name of William Henry
Hudson; Willard Billings, of Worcester, may take the name of John
Willard Billings; George Merriam Pride, of Fitchburg, may take the name
of George Henry Merriam; Gibson Colburn, of Northborough, may take
the name of Henry Gibson Colbourn; Samuel Adams Hitchcock, of Stur-
bridge, may take the name of Samuel Adams Hudson; Mehitable Rand, of
Westminster, may take the name of Ellen Mehitable Rand; Benjamin
Taft, jun., of Southbridge, may take the name of Merrick Luther Taft;
Jonathan Orcutt, jun., of Athol, may take the name of George Richardson
Orcutt; Jonah T. Houghton, of Berlin, may take the name of Henry Taylor Houghton; Jonathan C. Sloan, of Hardwick, may take the name of
Henry Clinton; Henry Taylor, of Leominster, may take the name of
George Henry Taylor; Moses Sawyer Hastings, of Berlin, may take the
name of Christopher Sawyer Hastings; John Crouch, of Brookfield, may
take the name of John Clayton; Benjamin Moon, of Charlton, may take
the name of Benjamin Brooks; Charlotte Moon, of Charlton, may take the
name of Charlotte Brooks; Stephen Moon, jun., of Charlton, may take the
name of Stephen Brooks; Eunice Moon, of Charlton, may take the name of
Eunice Brooks; Louisa and Laurenda, minor children of Stephen Moon,
may take the surname of Brooks; Samuel Lynn Fiske, of Southbridge,
may take the name of Samuel Lyon Fiske; Olerton Cushman Silvester, of
Leicester, may take the name of Oliver Cushman Silvester; William Clark,
of Spencer, may take the name of Orlendo Russell; Charles Augustus Munroe, of Shrewsbury, may take the name of Charles Augustus Harrington;
Aaron Lyon, jun., of Spencer, may take the name of Charles C. Pinckney;
Asa B. Howe, of Leominster, may take the name of Webster B. Randolph;
Cheney Hill, of Spencer, may take the name of Cheney Leander Mandell;
Lewis Trescott, of Lancaster, may take the name of Lewis Erastus Tres-
cott; Ballou Buffum, of Mendon, may take the name of David Ballou
Buffum; all of the county of Worcester.   Nehemiah Hoar, of Greenfield,
may take the name of Nehemiah Hunt; Charles Sawyer, of Colraine, may
take the name of Charles Carpenter; Lathrop Delano, of Montague, may
take the name of Edward Lathrop Delano; Leonard Chenery, of Montague,
may take the name of Edward Wells Chenery; Fanny Eliza Petton, of
Buckland, a minor, may take the name of Fanny Eliza Smith; Smith
Downing, of Sunderland, may take the name of Smith Downing Elliott; all
of the county of Franklin.   Clarinda Clark, of Granby, a minor, may take
the name of Sarah Clarinda Clark; Lewis Ford, of Cummington, a minor,

may take the name of Lewis Thayer Ford; Thomas James Quance, of
Hadley, may take the name of James Whitmarsh; Isaac Tubbs, Susan
Tubbs, Isaac N. Tubbs and Phebe Tubbs, of Cummington, may severally
take the surname of Allen; Daniel B. Tubbs and Henry M. Tubbs, of
Cummington, minors, may severally take the surname of Allen; Larry
Chapin, of South Hadley, a minor, may take the name of Joseph Corbin
Chapin; William Watson Witt, of South Hadley, a minor, may take the
name of William De Witt; Cornelia Dexter Bridges, of Ware, a minor, may
take the name of Cornelia Adeliza Gould; Philena Bates, of Cummington,
may take the name of Philena Ford; John Witt, jun., of Granby, may take
the name of John De Witt; Caroline Witt, of said Granby, may take the
name of Caroline De Witt; Charles Smith, of Northampton, may take the
name of Charles Pomeroy; all of the county of Hampshire. Joseph Bull,
jun., of Westfield, may take the name of Edward Joseph Bull; Alured B.
Hitchcock, of Brimfield, may take the name of John Boyden Austin;
Franklin K. Thrall, of Blandford, a minor, may take the name of Franklin
Knox Oatley; all of the county of Hampden. John Smith, of Williamstown,
may take the name of John Leddenhurst Smith; Benjamin Remington, jun.,
of Savoy, may take the name of Benjamin Franklin Remington; all of the
county of Berkshire. Allen Luther, jun., of Dighton, a minor, may take
the name of Allen Wardwell Luther; George Luther, of Somerset, a minor,
may take the name of George Bowers Luther; William Cole, of New Bedford, may take the name of William Bowen Cole; all of the county of Bristol. Amanda Cotton, of Yarmouth, a minor, may take the name of
Amanda Parker Cotton; Pinkham Baker, of Yarmouth, a minor, may take
the name of Frederick Pinkham Baker; Franklin Hallet, of Yarmouth, a
minor, may take the name of Joseph Franklin Hallet; all of the county of
Barnstable. Samuel Davis Heath, of Roxbury, may take the name of William Samuel Heath; William Patrick, of Roxbury, Elizabeth Mills Patrick,
wife of said William Patrick, William Barry Patrick and Rebecca Barry
Patrick, minor children of said William, may severally take the surname of
White; all of the county of Norfolk. Billa Bryant, of Rochester, may take
the name of William Bryant; William Clapp, of Scituate, may take the
name of Allen Clapp; all of the county of Plymouth. And the several persons before mentioned, from and after the passing of this act, shall be
known and called by the names, which by this act, they are respectively
allowed to assume as aforesaid; and said names shall hereafter be considered as their only proper and legal names, to all intents and purposes.
[*April 16, 1836.*

_____

An Act to change the Names of the several Persons therein mentioned.
Be it enacted, etc., as follows:
Elizabeth Sprague, a minor, may take the name of Helen Elizabeth
Sprague; John Quincy Adams Conkey may take the name of John Adams
Conkey; Luke George may take the name of Albert George; Charles Johnson
may take the name of Charles Borkley Johnson; William Hersey may take
the name of William Glover Hersey; Walter White may take the name of
Franklin John Walter White; Benjamin Tappan may take the name of
Edward Antill Tappan; Sarah W. Downey may take the name of Sarah
W. Johnson; William Hearsey may take the name of William Barron
Hersey; Matthew Tasker, a minor, may take the name of Matthew Calvert

Tasker; Charles Rhoades Lamson, a minor, may take the name of Charles Lamson; Robert Coe Burr may take the name of De Vere Burr; Jerushee Goodwin Hamilton may take the name of Melvina Jane Hamilton; Nancy Smith may take the name of Nancy Babcock; John Smith may take the name of John Clifton; Martha Ann Smith, a minor, may take the name of Martha Ann Babcock; Maria F. Smith may take the name of Maria F. Clifton; Joseph Dorr, merchant, may take the name of Joseph Goldthwait Dorr; Isaac Winslow Turn, a minor, may take the name of James W. Chilton; Henry John Stevenson Washburn may take the name of Henry Stevenson Washburn; all of the city of Boston, in the county of Suffolk. Daniel Verry, of Danvers, may take the name of Daniel Malcom Verry; Jacob Wiley, jun., of Lynnfield, may take the name of George William Wiley; Joseph Ober, 3d, of Beverly, may take the name of Joseph Edwards Ober; William Nichols, jun., of Amesbury, may take the name of William Howard Nichols; William Cox, of Lynnfield, may take the name of William Emerson Cox; Eliza Woodberry, of Beverly, may take the name of Eliza Augusta Woodberry; Hannah Elizabeth Batchelder, a minor, of Danvers, may take the name of Mary Jane Batchelder; Sarah Stanwood, of Ipswich, may take the name of Sarah Elizabeth Stanwood; Sarah Rand, of West Newbury, may take the name of Sarah Emery Rand; Grover Burnham Perkins, of Salem, may take the name of Edward Burnham Perkins; Mary Abbott, of Andover, may take the name of Mary James Abbott; Sarah Ashworth, of Amesbury, may take the name of Sarah Taylor; Dorothy Pearson Hills, of Rowley, may take the name of Laura Ann Hills; William Gardner Endicott, of Salem, may take the name of William Crowninshield Endicott; George Washington Read, of Salem, may take the name of George Fox Read; Daniel Sygestrom, of Danvers, a minor, may take the name of Daniel Sygestrom Henderson; Lois Peabody Spiller, of Rowley, may take the name of Martha Ann Webster; Charles Augustus Warren, of Amesbury, may take the name of Nathan Burpee Jewett; Mary Farrington Warren, of Amesbury, may take the name of Mary Farrington Jewett; Olwyn Jones, of Gloucester, a minor, may take the name of Olwyn Trask Jones; Charles Lewis Newball may take the name of Charles Lewis Delnow; Martha Jane Newhall may take the name of Martha Jane Delnow; Ellen Maria Newhall may take the name of Ellen Maria Delnow; Hubbard Mortimer Newhall may take the name of Hubbard Mortimer Delnow; and Charles Henry Newhall, of Lynn, may take the name of Charles Henry Delnow; John Clark, of Salem, may take the name of John Daniel Clark; all of the county of Essex. Francis Albert Leighton, of Westford, may take the name of Albert Leighton; Mary Ann Brown, of Lexington, a minor, may take the name of Mary Ann Gleason; Caleb Symmes, 3d, of Charlestown, may take the name of Caleb Trowbridge Symmes; Albert Lawrence Bull, of Concord, may take the name of Albert Chester Lawrence; Rhoda Ann Bull, of Concord, may take the name of Rhoda Ann Lawrence; Albert Lawrence Bull, of Concord, a minor, may take the name of Albert Chester Lawrence; Caroline Matilda Thayer, of Cambridge, may take the name of Caroline Thayer Penniman; Susan A. Raymond, of Malden, may take the name of Susan Ann Barrett; George Cook, of Cambridge, may take the name of George Lincoln Cook; Mary Adams Ferrell, of Framingham, may take the name of Mary Barnes Adams; Thomas Hovey, of Cambridge, may take the name of Thomas

Green Hovey; Allen Blood, of Medford, may take the name of George Washington Allen; Sarah Bancroft, of Townsend, may take the name of Sarah Proctor; Caroline Clark, of Framingham, a minor, may take the name of Caroline Buckminster Clark; Charles Brown, of Woburn, may take the name of Charles William Stevens; William Greenough Blood, of Woburn, may take the name of William Townsend Perry; Fanny Vickers, of Natick, may take the name of Fanny Wheeler; all of the county of Middlesex. Matthew Davenport, of Boylston, may take the name of James Davenport; Eunice Tainter, of Leominster, may take the name of Elizabeth Eunice Tainter; John Emery Marsh, of North Brookfield, may take the name of John Edward Marshall; Jarvis Hunting, of Hubbardston, may take the name of William Jarvis Parker; Joseph Park, of Millbury, may take the name of Asa Lewis Park; Isaac Smith, 2d, of Leominster, may take the name of Isaac Warren Smith; John Park, 2d, of Millbury, may take the name of John William Park; Elizabeth Maria Keyes, of Leominster, may take the name of Maria Caroline Richardson; William Peck, of Royalston, a minor, may take the name of James W. Peck; Silas Holman, 2d, of Bolton, may take the name of Silas W. Holman; Salome Fay, of Northborough, may take the name of Mary Salome Fay; William Houghton, of Berlin, may take the name of William Addison Houghton; George Hitchcock, of Sturbridge, a minor, may take the name of George Hitchcock Hudson; John Gleason, 3d, of Worcester, may take the name of John Fiske Gleason; Charles C. Pinckney, of Spencer, may take the name of Francis Aaron Lyon; Edwin Norcross, of Shrewsbury, may take the name of Henry Wilson; Roger Phelps, of Northborough, may take the name of Henry Rogers Phelps; all of the county of Worcester. Maria Cowles, daughter of Eleazer Cowles, of Amherst, may take the name of Maria Harriet Cowles; Washington Everleth, George Everleth and Lucy Hinsdale Everleth, of Belchertown, may respectively take the surname of Eliot; Zimri Everleth, of the same Belchertown, may take the name of Charles Eliot; Relief Russell, of Hadley, may take the name of Jane Russell; Henry Fay, of Ware, may take the name of Charles Brakenridge Fay; Climene Clapp, of Westhampton, a minor, may take the name of Climene Clapp Lyman; all of the county of Hampshire. Dorcas W. Fisk, of Ludlow, may take the name of Elizabeth W. Fisk; Foster Newell Hitchcock, of Brimfield, a minor, may take the name of Foster Newell; Phineas Crouch, of Brimfield, may take the name of James Munroe Clayton; Ozni Underwood, of Springfield, may take the name of Henry Robert Vaille; all of the county of Hampden. Emily Field, of Gill, may take the name of Emily Gratia Field; Ferona Drusilla Field, of Gill, may take the name of Ferona Dwight Field; Reuel Coller, of Northfield, may take the name of Reuel Collier; John Nash, of Northfield, may take the name of John Farnsworth; Mercy Allen, of Gill, may take the name of Sarah M. Allen; Abel Bullock, of Montague, may take the name of Abel Carpenter Adams; George Kentfield, of Montague, may take the name of George Lee Horton; Rhoda Kentfield, of Montague, may take the name of Jane Horton; Phineas Hemenway, jun., of Leverett, may take the name of James Phineas Hemenway; Jonah Ball, jun., of Shutesbury, may take the name of Jonah Rudolph Ball; all of the county of Franklin. Nial Bentley, of Pittsfield, in the county of Berkshire, may take the name of James Henry Bentley; Hannah S. Whittemore, of Weymouth, may take the name of Augusta

Whittemore ; Alfred Tupper, of Roxbury, may take the name of Alfred Tupper Gray ; Mary Woodward Tupper, wife of said Alfred, may take the name of Mary Woodward Gray ; Mary Woodward Tupper, minor, and daughter of said Alfred and Mary, may take the name of Mary Woodward Gray ; Augusta Greenleaf Tupper, daughter of said Alfred and Mary, may take the name of Augusta Greenleaf Gray ; Alfred Greenleaf Tupper, son of said Alfred and Mary, may take the name of Alfred Greenleaf Gray ; Helen Matilda Tupper, minor, daughter of said Alfred and Mary, may take the name of Helen Matild Gray ; Edward Gray Tupper, minor, son of said Alfred and Mary, may take the name of Edward Tupper Gray ; M. Edward Hunt, of Braintree, may take the name of Edward Hunt ; James Trickey, of Dedham, may take the name of James Lyman ; George Curtis, of Roxbury, may take the name of George Scarborough Curtis ; Bezer Keith, of Braintree, a minor, may take the name of Bezer Richmond Keith ; all of the county of Norfolk.   Hanan Hack Skinner, of Taunton, may take the name of Hanan Hack ; William Blackmer, jun., of New Bedford, may take the name of William Tisdale Blackmer ; George Frederick Wing, of Dartmouth, may take the name of George Wing Slocum ; all of the county of Bristol.   Louiza Beck, of Duxbury, in the county of Plymouth, may take the name of Louisa B. Drew.   Mayo Bassett, of Yarmouth, in the county of Barnstable, may take the name of Isaac Mayo Bassett ; Michael Cook, of Provincetown, may take the name of Harvey Cook ; Charles Thacher, minor, of Yarmouth, may take the name of Henry Charles Thacher :   And the several persons before mentioned, from and after the passing of this act, shall be known and called by the names which, by this act, they are respectively allowed to assume as aforesaid ; and said names shall hereafter be considered as their only proper and legal names, to all intents and purposes.   [*April 19, 1837.*

An ACT to change the Names of the several Persons therein mentioned.
Be it enacted, etc., as follows:
 John Bailey may take the name of John Adams Bailey ; Elizabeth Lewis may take the name of Frances Elizabeth Dunnells ; Henry Andrews may take the name of Henry Richmond Andrews ; Lendol Enoch W. Freeman Witham, Delania T. Witham, and Dorcas Witham, may severally take the surname of Freeman ; William King may take the name of William Taubert King ; Albert Richardson may take the name of Albert Louis Richardson ; Mary Catherine Fitzgerald may take the name of Mary Ellen Byrant ; Mary Goddard may take the name of Mary Jane Goddard ; Anna Carpenter may take the name of Anna Swinerton ; Margery Tirrill may take the name of Mary Tirrill ; Charles Rice may take the name of Charles Brooks Rice ; Samuel Langmaid may take the name of Samuel Prentis Langmaid ; Sarah Merrill may take the name of Sarah Jane Winship ; Isaac Crockett may take the name of Daniel Wright ; Elbridge West may take the name of Elbridge Gerry West ; Francis Hatstat may take the name of Francis Wade ; Mary Chadwick Sprague may take the name of Mary Elizabeth Sprague ; Abner Shelley, Belinda Shelley, and Daniel H. Shelley, may severally take the surname of Shirley ; James Browne may take the name of James Henry Browne ; all of the city of Boston, in the county of Suffolk.   Peter Russell, of Lynn, may take the name of Orin Russell ; Ebenezer Hart, jun., of Lynnfield, may take the name of Charles

Henry Granville; John Barnard, 3d, of Andover, may take the name of
John Clark; Joseph Tiplady, of Salem, may take the name of Joseph
Taylor; Hannah Sewell Riley, a minor, of Newburyport, may take the
name of Hannah Sewell Dimmick; Oliver William Philpot, of Methuen,
may take the name of William Freeman; Thomas Philpot, of Methuen,
may take the name of Thomas Freeman; Ann Peat, of Manchester, may
take the name of Ann Hardy Smith; Daniel Wheeler Tuttle, jun., of
Gloucester, may take the name of Daniel Wheeler; Addison Rust, of
Manchester, may take the name of Addison Clarendon; Billy Patch, of
Beverly, may take the name of William Amma Patch; John Graham Mil-
grove, of Rowley, may take the name of John Felton; Benjamin Pickett of
Rowley, may take the name of Benjamin Franklin Pickett; Polly Eaton
Parker, of Bradford, may take the name of Mary Hathorne Parker; George
Henry Eye, of Lynn, a minor, may take the name of George Henry
Brackett; Lucy Mary Jewett, of Ipswich, may take the name of Lucy Mary
Woodbury; Mary Gould, of Ipswich, may take the name of Mary Jane
Gould; Harriet Caldwell, of Ipswich, may take the name of Harriet Frances
Caldwell; Mary Harris, of Ipswich, may take the name of Mary Elizabeth
Harris; Elizabeth Hiddon Harris, of Ipswich, may take the name of Sarah
Elizabeth Harris; Samuel Heath, of Bradford, may take the name of
Samuel S. Heath; Harriet B. Smith, of Bradford, may take the name of
Sarah Jane Smith; John Kinsman, of Ipswich, may take the name of John
C. Kinsman; all of the county of Essex.   Alden Winn, a minor, of Con-
cord, may take the name of Alden Bradford Winn; Elmira Coombs, of
Charlestown, may take the name of Helen Amanda Herbert; Jackson Ames,
of Pepperell, may take the name of Asa Jackson Ames; Simeon Blanchard,
of Cambridge, may take the name of Simeon Tenney Blanchard; Charlotte
Pamelia Pike, of Charlestown, may take the name of Charlotte Pamelia
Cutter; Van Rensellaeir Osborn Jewell, of Marlborough, may take the
name of Lewis Rensellaier Jewell; Joseph Skinner, of Holliston, may take
the name of Joseph Oberlin Skinner; Jonathan Edward Gay, of Weston,
may take the name of Edward Austin Gay; Michael Gay Brackett, of
Weston, may take the name of Henry Gay Brackett; Mary Ann Bettis, of
Charlestown, may take the name of Mary Ann Eaton Campbell; all of
the county of Middlesex.   James S. Gilbert, of West Brookfield, may take
the name of James Snow Sherman; George Henry Beebe, of Auburn, a
minor, may take the name of George Henry Banner; Henry Nind, of Harvard, may take the name of Charles Henry; Margaret Pollard, of Harvard,
may take the name of Margaret Elizabeth Franklin Pollard; Minerva
Chamberlain, of Southborough, may take the name of Minerva Wilder
Chamberlain; Ezra Kendall, of Templeton, may take the name of Ezra
Clay Kendall; James Toole, and Julia Ann Toole, of Auburn, may severally
take the surname of Thompson; Silas Wood Smith, of Holden, may take
the name of Silas Smith Hall; Samuel Witt, of Shrewsbury, may take the
name of Samuel De Witt; Sarah Elizabeth Dwight Witt, of Shrewsbury,
may take the name of Sarah Elizabeth Dwight De Witt; Harriet D. Flagg,
of Boylston, a minor, may take the name of Caroline Flagg; Paul Wheelock,
of Charlton, may take the name of John Adams Wheeler; Elisha Dorance,
of Spencer, may take the name of Elisha D. Clark; James C. Clapp, of
Petersham, may take the name of Ai Wood; Manasseh Sawyer Gerry, of
Harvard, may take the name of Henry Albert Gerry; Oliver Burgess, of

Harvard, may take the name of Oliver Warren Whitcomb ; Dolly Wheeler, 2d, of Bolton, a minor, may take the name of Dolly Marion Wheeler ; Moses Chase, jun., of Sterling, may take the name of Mervine Wilbur Chase ; Edwin M. Cutler, of Shrewsbury, may take the name of Edwin Miranda Garfield ; Eliza Jane Sibley, of Spencer, a minor, may take the name of Ruth Eliza Sibley ; Joseph Faxon Seaver, of Northborough, may take the name of Joseph Napoleon Seaver ; George Ordway, of Fitchburg, may take the name of George Henry ; Alfred Ordway, of Fitchburg, may take the name of Alfred Rufus ; Joshua Kendall, of Boylston, may take the name of Sanford Mason Kendall ; Hyram Smith, of Oxford, may take the name of Brigham Hyram Smith ; Imena W. Frost, of West Boylston, may take the name of Almira W. Frost ; Henry De Wolf Handy, of Uxbridge, may take the name of Henry De Wolf ; Lydia H. Wheeler, of Rutland, may take the name of Juliaetta Lydia Hall Wheeler ; all of the county of Worcester. Arthur Phelps, of Hadley, may take the name of Arthur Davenport Phelps ; Benjamin Fowler Witt, of Greenwich, may take the name of Fowler Pomeroy Taylor ; Hiram Cowan, Sophronia Cowan, Hiram Munroe Cowan, and Harriet Maria Cowan, of Belchertown, may severally take the surname of French ; Benoni Coleman, 2d, of Southampton, may take the name of William Washington Coleman ; Consider McFarland, of Amherst, may take the name of Charles McFarland ; all of the county of Hampshire. Norris Hoar, Mary Hoar, Mary Woodworth Hoar, Laura Hoar, Edwin Norris Hoar, and Elizabeth Joanna Hoar, of Brimfield, may severally take the surname of Hale ; David Hoar, Pamelia Cook Hoar, Solomon Hoar, Lucina Hoar, Linus Hoar, Betsy Bond Hoar, Ruth Bliss Hoar, Alured Hoar, Lucia Hoar, Abigail Goodell Hoar, Susan Bond Hoar, Mehetabel Hoar, Mary Ann Brown Hoar, Ellen Edgell Hoar, Harriet Eunecia Hoar, George Carroll Hoar, Charles Alured Hoar, and Charlotte Ann Amanda Hoar, may severally take the surname of Homer ; and Betsey Hoar, may take the name of Elizabeth Homer, all of Brimfield ; Henry Stebbins, 2d, of Springfield, may take the name of Henry Willcox Stebbins ; Charles H. Frost, of Springfield, may take the name of Charles H. Warren ; Haskell C. Paine, of Springfield, may take the name of Haskell C. Goodman ; Phineas Lyman Tinker, of Granville, may take the name of Phineas Lyman Buell ; Martin Buell Tinker, of Granville, may take the name of Martin Buell ; all of the county of Hampden. David Wait, senior, of Deerfield, may take the name of David Reed Wait ; William Thayer Chapin, of Buckland, a minor, may take the name of William Chapin Porter ; Sarah Field, of Northfield, may take the name of Sarah Callender Field ; Sylvester Bangs, may take the name of Sylvester Woodbury Bangs ; Charles Kellogg may take the name of Charles Carroll Kellogg ; Martha Adams Kentfield, a minor, may take the name of Martha Adams Horton, all of Montague ; Orramel Cooley, of Hawley, may take the name of Orramel Wellington Cooley ; all of the county of Franklin. Woodhouse Francis, of Pittsfield, may take the name of Charles Milton Francis ; Jerusha P. Parish, of Adams, may take the name of Jerusha Phillips, and her minor children, Catharine A. Parish, may take the name of Catharine Phillips ; Samuel C. Parish, may take the name of Samuel C. Phillips ; and John Parish, may take the name of John Phillips ; all of the county of Berkshire. Thomas White, of Braintree, may take the name of Thomas Alexander White ; Elizabeth White Tilden, a minor, of Weymouth, may take the name of Mary Elizabeth White

Tilden ; all of the county of Norfolk.   Edward Stowers Clapp, of Pawtucket, may take the name of Edward Stowers ; John Chace, of New Bedford, may take the name of John Anthony Chace ; all of the county of Bristol. Artimirisia Bryant, of Bridgewater, may take the name of Abigail Bryant ; of the county of Plymouth.   William Chipman, a minor, of Sandwich, may take the name of William Churchill Chipman ; Kimball Chipman, a minor, of Sandwich, may take the name of Isaac Kimball Chipman ; James Smalley, and his minor children, Joshua P. Smalley, Betsy C. Smalley, James H. Smalley, Mary T. Smalley, and Benjamin F. Smalley ; Samuel Smalley, jun., and Ruth S. Smalley, his minor child ; Samuel Smalley, and his minor children, Lot Smalley, Sally Smalley, and Peggy H. Smalley ; Nathaniel H. Smalley, and his minor children, Esther T. Smalley, Uriah Smalley, and Mary S. Smalley ; Taylor Smalley, and his minor children, Jonah G. Smalley, Benjamin T. Smalley, Alexander Smalley, and Abigail Smalley ; Abraham Smalley, jun., and his minor children, Norman S. K. Smalley, Jane C. Smalley, and Abraham Smalley, 3d ; John Smalley, and his minor children, Arnold Smalley, John Smalley, Rebeckah H. Smalley, and Pamela H. Smalley ; Abraham Smalley, Isaac Smalley, 2d, Heman Smalley, Nathan Smalley, Isaac Smalley, 3d, Thomas R. Smalley, Leonard Smalley, and Benjamin Smalley, all of Provincetown, may severally take the surname of Small ; all of Barnstable county.   And the several persons before mentioned, from and after the passing of this act, shall be known and called by the names, which, by this act, they are respectively allowed to assume as aforesaid, and said names shall hereafter be considered as their only proper and legal names, to all intents and purposes.   [*April 25, 1838.*

AN ACT to change the Names of the several Persons therein mentioned. *Be it enacted, etc., as follows:*

Joshua Leach may take the name of John Colburn Leach ; Abijah Adams Hill, a minor, may take the name of Adams Sherman Hill ; Sarah Blynn may take the name of Sarah Sherman ; James Henry Brewer may take the name of James Henry Beal ; Eliza Beal Brewer may take the name of Eliza Beal ; Adela Julia Ann Stitz, a minor, may take the name of Adela Julia Ann Bogardus ; Sarah Vose may take the name of Sarah Baxter Vose ; Nathan Kingsley may take the name of Nathan Phinney Kingsley ; Amelia Giraud Laponte may take the name of Amelia Giraud ; George Samuel Eldridge may take the name of George Miller ; Edward Darley Jones Boit may take the name of Edward Darley Boit ; Patrick Monks may take the name of John P. Monks ; James Barnard may take the name of James Munson Barnard ; Harrison Latham may take the name of Harrison Whitman Latham ; John Collins may take the name of John H. Collins ; Dolly Richardson may take the name of Eliza Richardson ; Matilda Dockum may take the name of Matilda Mason ; Louisa Dockum may take the name of Louisa Mason ; Tabitha Read Nolen may take the name of Elizabeth Read Nolen ; Mary Elizabeth Varney Mickell may take the name of Mary Elizabeth Varney Granville ; Lovet Stimson, jun., may take the name of Alexander Lovet Stimson ; Henry Murphy, of Chelsea, may take the name of Henry James Adams ; Samuel Nathan Moore, a minor, of Boston, may take the name of Orrin Samuel Nathan Moore ; Elizabeth Minot may take the name of Elizabeth Augusta Minot ; Hannah Tirrell may take the name

of Hannah Snell Tirrell ; William Wheeler, of Boston, may take the name
of William Zenas Wheeler ; all of the county of Suffolk.   Daniel Fortesque
Currier, of Georgetown, may take the name of Edward Fortesque Currier ;
Emerson Gould, of Topsfield, may take the name of Emerson Prescott
Gould ; Alexander Hamilton Jordan, his wife Mary Ann Jordan, and their
infant child Mary Ann Jordan, may severally take the surname of Ham-
ilton ; Alfred Davis, of Lynn, may take the name of Henry Alfred Davis ;
Moses Bachelor, of Lynn, may take the name of William Frederick Bachelor ;
Blaney Ingalls, of said Lynn, may take the name of Augustus B. Ingalls ;
Andrew Jackson Morrill, a minor, of Salisbury, may take the name of
Albert Morrill ; Eliza Ellen Hazeltine, of Lynn, a minor, may take the
name of Eliza Ellen Hilton ; Elizabeth Ann Mardin, a minor, of Danvers,
may take the name of Elizabeth Jane Bomer ; Eliza White, of Newburyport,
may take the name of Elizabeth White ; Deborah Ramsdell, of Lynn, may
take the name of Deborah Burnell Ramsdell ; Margaret Rogers, a minor,
of Ipswich, may take the name of Margaret Brown Rogers ; Sarah Sargent
may take the name of Sarah Louisa Sargent ; Dolly Sargent may take the
name of Dolly Greeley Sargent ; Caroline Sargent may take the name of
Caroline Pilsbury Sargent, severally of Amesbury ; Albert Williams Bridge,
of Andover, a minor, may take the name of John Albert Bridge ; George
William Entwistle, of Lynn, may take the name of George William Fuller ;
Warner Choate Burroughs, and his wife Nancy Burroughs, and their
daughter Charlotte Augusta, may severally take the surname of Choate, all
of Beverly ; Bradstreet Emerson Davis, of Boxford, may take the name of
Willard Hubbard Davis ; an adopted child of Andrew Howarth, bearing
the surname of Johnson, of Salisbury, may take the name of Helen Elizabeth
Howarth ; Adna Bailey, of Danvers, may take the name of Edward Forrest
Bailey ; Abijah Mason, of Andover, may take the name of Horace Mason ;
William Herrick, 5th, of Beverly, may take the name of William Lovett
Herrick ; Barnard Lunaway, of Gloucester, may take the name of Barnard
Stanwood ; Edith Swinerton Goodale, of Danvers, may take the name of
Caroline Augusta Goodale ; Charles Adamas Lowell, of Georgetown, may
take the name of Charles Mason ; Charles Osgood Frink, of Newbury, may
take the name of Charles Osgood Morrill ; Isaac Crampesy, of Beverly,
may take the name of Isaac Standley Crampesy ; William Jennings, of
Georgetown, may take the name of William Adams Munroe ; Elizabeth
Huntoon, of Georgetown, may take the name of Elizabeth Sleeper ; Polly
Latime Burdett, of Lynn, may take the name of Mary Elizabeth Burdett ;
William Adams, of Georgetown, may take the name of George Washington
Adams ; William Putnam, of Danvers, may take the name of William
Newton Putnam ; Sarah Emerson Folansbee, of Newburyport, may take
the name of Sarah Folansbee Emerson ; Mercy Dodge Foster, of Rowley,
may take the name of Eliza Caldwell Foster ; all of the county of Essex.
Timothy Carter, jun., of Wilmington, may take the name of Timothy Jaques
Carter ; William McConihe, of Lowell, may take the name of William
Conihe ; Charles Edward Sisson, of Charlestown, a minor, may take the
name of Walter Jefferds Sisson ; Mary Fletcher, of Westford, may take
the name of Mary Elizabeth Fletcher ; William Leland, of Sherburne, may
take the name of William Wallace Leland ; Samuel Parker Shattuck, of
Pepperell, may take the name of Samuel Pepperell Shattuck ; all of the
county of Middlesex.   Abigail H. Edwards, and Parnal M. Edwards, minor

children of Philip Edwards, deceased, may severally take the surname of
Crosby, severally of the town of Holden; Dolly A. Greene, of Lancaster,
may take the name of Elizabeth Foster Greene; Isaac Pierce Damon, of
Holden, may take the name of Isaac Damon; Paul Wheelock, of Charlton,
may take the name of John Adams Wheelock; William W. Collier, of
Rutland, may take the name of Warren Collier; William Henry Scott
Greenleaf, of Worcester, may take the name of William Greenleaf; Charles
R. Houghton, of Princeton, may take the name of Charles H. Allen; Jesse
D. Partridge, of Princeton, may take the name of Edward Merrick; Jona-
than Allen, of Princeton, may take the name of Jonathan Moses Allen;
Albee C. Guillow, of Worcester, may take the name of Albee C. Wright;
Aaron Hogaboom, of Brookfield, his wife Susanna, and their son Charles
Henry Hogaboom, may severally take the surname of Parker; Hector
Jackson, of Southbridge, may take the name of Vernon Heman Jackson;
Altamont Rice, of Northborough, may take the name of Dennis Rice;
Eliza Knight, of Dudley, may take the name of Eliza Alzada Upham;
Patience Bancroft Brown, of Templeton, may take the name of Maria Jane
Bancroft Brown; Alothina Bartlett Howe, a minor, of Northborough, may
take the name of Ellen Frances Gertrude Howe; Benjamin House, of
Fitchburg, may take the name of Benjamin Julius House; James McFar-
land Barnes, of Rutland, and his wife Mary Ann D. C. Barnes, may take
the surname of Haynes; Ira Barton, of Worcester, may take the name of
Ira Moore Barton; Horace Tarbell, of Leominster, may take the name of
Horace Wilson Tarbell; Frances Asenath Swan, of Westminster, a minor,
may take the name of Frances Swan Ames; Elbridge G. Smith, of Douglas,
may take the name of Elbridge G. Wallace; all of the county of Worcester.   Lewis Ingraham, of South Hadley, may take the name of Lewis
Burnett Ingraham; Ezekiel Brown, of Greenwich, may take the name of
Harrison Richard Brown; William Smith, 3d, of Hadley, may take the
name of William Austin Smith; Phineas Franklin Everett, of Worthington, may take the name of Franklin Everett; Jonas Petingell, of Belchertown, may take the name of Jonas Melville; Zebina Montague, of Amherst,
may take the name of Zebina Clinton Montague; Russell Searl, of Southampton, may take the name of Josiah Russell Searl; all of the county of
Hampshire.   Hawley Russell, a minor, of Russell, may take the name of
Hawley Stimson; Augustus Russell, a minor, of Russell, may take the
name of Augustus Lyman Dimmock; John Smith, of Granville, may take
the name of John Phelps; Eli Hoar, Hannah H. Hoar, and their minor
children, George Milton Hoar, Jane Frances Hoar, and Ames Hunn Hoar,
all of Springfield, may severally take the surname of Hobart; John Carle
Cranska, Abigail Cranska, and their children, Mary Ann Cranska, John
Clark Cranska, Samuel Fiske Cranska, and Abigail Cranska, all of Brimfield, may severally take the surname of Draper; Hannah Parker, of Brimfield, a minor, may take the name of Hannah Holmes; Lucy Ann Belden,
of Montgomery, may take the name of Lucy Ann Baker; all of the county
of Hampden.   Charlotte Clark, of Whately, may take the name of Charlotte
Maynard Clark; Franklin Severance, of Shelburne, may take the name of
John Franklin Severance; George Gould, of Heath, may take the name of
George Adams; Polly Priscilla Belden, of Sunderland, may take the name
of Polly Baker; Lucy Ann Belden, of Sunderland, may take the name of
Lucy Ann Baker; Philander Root Death, of Deerfield, may take the name

of Philander Root Dickenson; Josiah Puffer, of Sunderland, may take the
name of Josiah Osgood Puffer; Parisatis Scott, of Whately, may take the
name of Maria Scott; all of the county of Franklin. William Jarvis
Babbitt, a minor, of Savoy, may take the name of William Snellem Bab-
bitt; Luther Patch, of North Adams, may take the name of Luther Corydon
Homer; all of the county of Berkshire. Irene Rhodes, a minor, of Wal-
pole, may take the name of Irene Rhodes Harding; Patrick Glynn, jun., of
Roxbury, may take the name of Henry Glynn; Amaziah Atkins Cooke, of
Quincy, may take the name of Henry Atkins Cooke; all of the county of
Norfolk. Albert A. Cornell, of New Bedford, may take the name of Albert
A. Brownell; Sarah B. Chase, a minor, of Somerset, may take the name
of Sarah B. Slade; Susannah Chase, of Somerset, may take the name of
Susan Chase; Otis Little, of New Bedford, may take the name of Otis
Laforest Little; all of the county of Bristol. Elisha Freeman, 3d, of
Middleborough, may take the name of Elisha Eddy Freeman; Thomas
Rogers, 3d, of Marshfield, may take the name of Thomas William
Rogers; Albegence Lee, of Bridgewater, may take the name of Albert Lee;
all of the county of Plymouth. Joshua H. Crowell, of Dennis, a minor,
may take the name of Nathan Crowell; Orpha Gage, of Yarmouth, may
take the name of Olive Gage; Leander Crowell Furnell, of Yarmouth, may
take the name of Leander Crowell; Patty Crowell, a minor, of Yarmouth,
may take the name of Martha Crowell; John Thomas Bourne, of Falmouth,
a minor, may take the name of John Barachiah Bourne; Mary Alexander
Baker, a minor, of Yarmouth, may take the name of Abby Kelley Baker;
all of the county of Barnstable. And the several persons before mentioned, from and after the passing of this act, shall be known and called by
the names, which, by this act, they are respectively allowed to assume as
aforesaid, and said names shall hereafter be considered as their only proper
and legal names, to all intents and purposes. [*April 9, 1839.*

An Act to change the Names of the Persons therein mentioned.
Be it enacted, etc., as follows:
Augustus Newman Blake may take the name of Francis Gillman Wheeler
Blake; Thomas F. Grimes may take the name of Thomas F. Graham;
Elizabeth G. Grimes may take the name of Elizabeth G. Graham; Elisha
Allen Upton may take the name of Eugene Allen Upton; William F. H.
Weld may take the name of William Howland Weld; Elias Keyes may take
the name of Edward L. Keyes; Charles Suton Mead may take the name
of Charles Suton Brigham; Edward Colman Wheelock Glover may take
the name of Edward Colman Wheelock; Reuben William Gerry may take
the name of William Gerry; Charles J. T. French may take the name of
Charles Otis French; David Child may take the name of David Weld
Child; Joseph Morse may take the name of Joseph Henry Morse; John
Dole may take the name of John State; Edward Augustus Howard, a
minor, may take the name of Abraham Howard; Huldah Howes Crowell, a
minor, may take the name of Caroline Frances Crowell; Alexander W.
Price may take the name of Alexander Pope; Anne Price may take the
name of Anne Pope; Benjamin Price may take the name of Benjamin Pope;
Mary Price may take the name of Mary Pope; Alexander Price, jun., may
take the name of Alexander Pope, jun.; Hubert Price may take the name of

Hubert Pope; Edward Courtenay Price may take the name of Edward
Courtenay Pope; Abel Barbadoes Howard may take the name of Alfred
Gardner Howard; all of Boston, in the county of Suffolk. Moses George,
4th, of Haverhill, may take the name of Moses D. George; Moses Hoyt,
jun., of Amesbury, may take the name of Moses B. Hoyt; Nathaniel M.
Grimes, of Haverhill, may take the name of Nathaniel M. Graham; Charles
G. Grimes, of Haverhill, may take the name of Charles G. Graham; Mary
F. Grimes, of Haverhill, may take the name of Mary F. Graham; Rufus
K. Grimes, of Salem,, may take the name of Rufus K. Graham; Sarah A.
Grimes, of Salem, may take the name of Sarah A. Graham; William
Knowlton, of Salem, may take the name of William Cummings Knowlton;
Jonathan Ropes, a minor, of Salem, may take the name of John Felt Ropes;
Caroline Olivia Deland, a minor, of Salem, may take the name of Caroline
Olivia Quarles; Sarah Elizabeth Holmes, of Salem, may take the name of
Sarah Elizabeth Bruce; Sarah Herrick Holmes, of Salem, may take the
name of Sarah Herrick Bruce; Dean Babcock, of Manchester, may take
the name of Dean Nelson Kimball; Debby Hooper Broughton, a minor, of
Marblehead, may take the name of Mary Hooper Broughton; George
Prime Smith, of Andover, may take the name of George Phillips Smith;
Achsah Dinsmore, of Methuen, may take the name of Achsah Hemphill;
Isaac Standley Crampsey, of Beverly, may take the name of Isaac Standley;
Israel Trask, jun., of Beverly, may take the name of Israel Wallis Trask;
George D. Chapman, of Beverly, may take the name of George Chapman;
Samuel Herrick, of Beverly, may take the name of Samuel Dinsmore Her-
rick; Joseph Chapman, of Ipswich, may take the name of Joseph Warren
Chapman; Joseph Knight Noyes, of Ipswich, a minor, may take the name
of James William Noyes; Isaac Crockett, of Newburyport, may take the
name of Daniel Wright; Caroline Elizabeth Thurston, of Newburyport, a
minor, may take the name of Caroline Elizabeth Perkins; Susan Louis
Tarbox, of Lynn, may take the name of Susan Louis Peirce; Sally Anne
Tarbox, of Lynn, may take the name of Sarah Anne Peirce; Samuel Tar-
box, of Lynn, may take the name of Charles Elbridge Peirce; Jonathan
Kenrick, of Lynn, may take the name of Charles Gustavus Rodman; Mary
H. Kenrick, of Lynn, may take the name of Mary H. Rodman; Rufus
Newhall, 3d, of Lynn, may take the name of Rufus F. Newhall; Elijah
Thwing, jun., of Lynn, may take the name of Harrison Thwing; Ira A.
Poland, of Lynnfield, may take the name of Ira A. Meriam; Benaiah Tit-
comb, of Newburyport, may take the name of Benaiah B. Titcomb; Caro-
line Racroft, of Salem, may take the name of Caroline Ann Howard;
William Brophy, of Gloucester, may take the name of William Benton;
Mary Brophy, of Gloucester, may take the name of Mary Benton; Elijah
Merrill, of Haverhill, may take the name of George Merrill; Abner Libbey,
of Danvers, may take the name of Fervin Abner Fenwood; all of the
county of Essex. Thomas Osborn Southwick, of Marlborough, may take
the name of Ai Roe; Samuel Robinson Oliver, of Cambridge, may take
the name of Andrew Oliver; John Colburn, of Charlestown, may take the
name of John Coburn; Nathan Harding Praro, of Westford, may take the
name of Nathan Harding; Paulina Grover, of West Cambridge, may take
the name of Paulina Carrol; Amasa Hayes, of Natick, may take the name
of George Blake; Rufus Fisk, of Cambridge, may take the name of Eugene
Rufus Fisk; Francis Blacker, of South Reading, may take the name of

Francis Williams; Louisa Luther Rice, of Marlborough, may take the name of Louisa Malvina Rice; all of the county of Middlesex. Levi Flagg Thing, of Worcester, may take the name of Levi Flagg; Jonathan Lovejoy, of Harvard, may take the name of Jonathan Wyman Lovejoy; Andros Peirce, of Sutton, may take the name of John Andrew Peirce; Joseph Wilder, of Lancaster, may take the name of Joseph Masket Wilder; Amos Waite, of Hubbardston, may take the name of Warren Cutler Waite; Henry Goodspeed, a minor, of Hubbardston, may take the name of Thomas Henry Goodspeed; Cyrus Cowl, jun., of Worcester, may take the name of Cyrus Cole; Josiah Sawyer, 2d, of Berlin, may take the name of Josiah Ellsworth Sawyer; George Elliot Cutting, a minor, of Boylston, may take the name of George Elliot Fawcett; Lois C. Rice, of Northborough, may take the name of Louisa C. Rice; Winthrop Bailey Sawyer, of Berlin, may take the name of Winthrop Bailey; Thomas Edward Valentine, of Northborough, may take the name of Thomas Weston Valentine; Stephen Crouch, of Harvard, may take the name of Stephen Gardner; Harvey Hitchcock, of Sturbridge, may take the name of Harrison Hudson; Sally Eager, of Northborough, may take the name of Sarah J. Eager; Eber Cutter, of Warren, may take the name of Ebenezer Cutler; Franklin Cutter, Adaline Cutter, and Hiram Briggs Cutter, minors, of Warren, may severally take the surname of Cutler; Abel Wilder, 2d, of Leominster, may take the name of Abel Carter Wilder; Margaret Stoddard Taft, of Uxbridge, may take the name of Margaret Louisa Taft; Nancy Pollard, of Lancaster, may take the name of Anna Gertrude Pollard; all of the county of Worcester. Benjamin Taylor, of Chesterfield, may take the name of Elisha Benjamin Taylor; Fanny Smith, a minor, of Middlefield, may take the name of Miranda Smith; Ansel Abell, of Northampton, may take the name of Ansel George Abell; Josiah A. Orcutt, of Goshen, may take the name of Josiah Orcutt Armes; all of the county of Hampshire. Hezekiah Fisk, of Ludlow, may take the name of William H. Fisk; of the county of Hampden. Frederick Parker, of Buckland, may take the name of Franklin Frederick Parker; Peter Cheney, jun., of Orange, may take the name of Edward P. Cheney; Ruby Crosby, of Hawley, may take the name of Charlotte Ruby Crosby; Cephas Gunn, of Montague, may take the name of Cephas Sherwood; Diadema Mack Gunn, of Montague, may take the name of Diadema Maria Sherwood; Noadiah Gunn, of Montague, may take the name of Charles Julius Sherwood; John Bartlet, of Shutesbury, may take the name of John Henry Bartlet; Edwin Eaton, of Shutesbury, may take the name of Edwin Mason Eaton; Daniel Wood, jun., of Shutesbury, may take the name of Daniel Edwin Wood; Reuel Spear, of Shutesbury, may take the name of James Reuel Spear; all of the county of Franklin. Harriet Pierce Shepard, a minor, of Dorchester, may take the name of Sarah Pope Shepard; Henry Reed, of Canton, may take the name of Henry Matthews; Joseph Foster Taft, a minor, of Dedham, may take the name of Josiah Foster Flagg; all of the county of Norfolk. Erial Allen Cobb, of Middleborough, may take the name of Allen Cobb; Charles Peirce, of Middleborough, may take the name of Charles Frederick Peirce; Joseph Cushman, 2d, of Kingston, may take the name of Joseph Tilson Cushman; Jonathan Wilson Cobb, of Middleborough, may take the name of Wilson Cobb; Francis Dana Bumpus, of Wareham, may take the name of Francis Dana; Eliza Bumpus, of Wareham, may take the name of Eliza Dana;

Seth S. Loring, of Duxbury, may take the name of Seth L. Sprague; all of the county of Plymouth. Joseph Martin, of Truro, may take the name of Joseph Lee; Charles Breen, of Barnstable, may take the name of Charles Green; David Cook, 2d, of Provincetown, may take the name of Winthrop David Cook; all of the county of Barnstable. And the several persons before mentioned, from and after the passing of this act, shall be known and called by the names, which, by this act, they are respectively allowed to assume as aforesaid, and said names shall hereafter be considered as their only proper and legal names, to all intents and purposes. [*March 23, 1840.*

An Act to change the Names of the several Persons therein mentioned. *Be it enacted, etc., as follows:*

George Adams may take the name of George Edward Adams; James Adams may take the name of James Henry Adams; Thomas Womersly may take the name of Thomas Womersly Melbun; William French may take the name of William Estabrooks French; James Blake, jun., may take the name of James Gorham Blake; Albert Parker may take the name of Charles Albert Parker; George Williams may take the name of George Frederic Williams; Henry Matthews may take the name of Henry Matthews Reed; Patrick Kenny may take the name of Lewis Kenny; James Long, jun., may take the name of James Henry Long; Nathaniel Shaw may take the name of Nathaniel Burrill Shaw; Leonard Stearns Payson may take the name of Edward Webster Payson; Oliver C. Guptill may take the name of Oliver C. Gardiner; Adelaide Bangs, minor daughter of George P. Bangs, may take the name of Elizabeth Simpkins Bangs; Mary Jane Reed Gooch, a minor, may take the name of Mary Jane Reed; Mary Pell Grigg may take the name of Mary Josephine Faxon; Oliver Sawyer Nichols may take the name of Prince Edward Nichols; George B. Farwell, a minor, an adopted child of Amasa Harrington, may take the name of George B. Harrington; William Townsend Perry may take the name of William Blood, and his minor son, William Cutler Perry, may take the name of William Cutler Blood; Dorothy Harris may take the name of Mary Dorothy Harris; John Smith Mudget may take the name of John Smith, and his wife, Elvira Pricilla Mudget, may take the name of Elvira Pricilla Smith, and Elvira Martha, Amanda Fitzland, Lucy Ann, Mary Jane, Adeline, Lewis William, and George Edward, children of the said John Smith and Elvira Pricilla Mudget, may severally take the surname of Smith; Phillip Augustus Trafford Moshier may take the name of Joseph Augustus Noble; Rhoda Luvina Hosmer may take the name of Elizabeth Hosmer; and Elizabeth Tarbox may take the name of Elizabeth Augusta Stanley; all of the city of Boston, in the county of Suffolk. Judith Ann Stickney, of Salem, may take the name of Harriet Fowler Stickney; Betsey Brown, 2d, of Manchester, may take the name of Eliza Tappan Brown; Frederick Daniel Hoyt Huntington, minor son of Moses Huntington, jun., of Amesbury, may take the name of Daniel Hoyt Huntington; Mary Bradbury, of Newburyport, may take the name of Mary Louisa Bradbury; Sally Forster Allen, of Manchester, may take the name of Sarah Forster Tappan; Ambros Martin, jun., of Salem, may take the name of Albert Ambros Martin; Adoniram Wentworth, of Lynn, may take the name of George Wentworth; Sally Hooper Tappan, 2d, of Manchester, may take the name

of Sarah Hooper Tappan; Henry Edmund Titcomb, minor son of Sarah
L. Titcomb, of Newburyport, may take the name of Henry Titcomb;
William Merrill, jun., minor son of William J. Merrill, of Amesbury, may
take the name of William Thomas Merrill; Mary Hood, of Georgetown,
may take the name of Mary Elizabeth Hood; Silas Ross, of Georgetown,
may take the name of Silas Cushing Everett; William Bachellor, and
Rebecca Carleton Bachellor, wife of said William, and George Kendall
Bachellor, all of Georgetown, may severally take the name of William Ken-
dall, Rebecca Carleton Kendall, and George Kendall; John Evans, 3d, of
Newburyport, may take the name of Ferdinand Evans; Humphrey Green,
of Lynn, may take the name of Otis Humphrey Green; William Lovett
Copeland, of Haverhill, may take the name of William McClary Holman
Copeland; Ferren A. Fenwood, of Danvers, may take the name of Irville
Leslie; Elbridge Mansfield, of Lynn, may take the name of Elbridge Gerry
Mansfield; Joseph Whitworth Roberts Millet, of Lynn, may take the name
of Joseph Millet; Olivia Kinsman Staple, daughter of Mark and Elizabeth
S. Staple, of Lynn, may take the name of Lois Atkinson Staple; William
C. W. Quimby, of Salisbury, may take the name of William Currier; Lydia
McFarland, of Salem, may take the name of Lydia Farland; Thomas
Lefavour, 4th, minor son of Thomas Lefavour, of Beverly, may take the
name of Thomas Augustus Lefavour; Abigail Parsons, of Ipswich, may
take the name of Caroline Augusta Parsons; Martha Steele Lord, minor
daughter of Levi Lord, of Ipswich, may take the name of Martha Ann
Lord; Joseph Lord, of Ipswich, may take the name of Joseph Harrison
Lord; Joseph Bird, of Salem, may take the name of Joseph Stephen
Mason; Lucinda Jane Phillips, of Lynn, may take the name of Laura Ann
Rodman; Sylvester P. Flint, of Lynn, may take the name of Charles P.
Flint; Abigail C. Jackson, of Beverly, may take the name of Abigail Car-
rico Boardman; Adeline Smith Richards, minor daughter of Hix Richards,
of Danvers, may take the name of Martha Smith Richards; James Grimes,
and Caroline Grimes, wife of the said James Grimes, and Area Grimes, all
of Haverhill, may severally take the name of James W. Graham, Caroline
Graham, and Area S. Graham; William P. Brega, of Salem, may take the
name of William Brega Davis; Lois Parsons Stone, minor daughter of
Jacob Stone, of Newbury, may take the name of Louisa Parsons Stone;
Josiah Thing, jun., of Newburyport, may take the name of Josiah Bradlee;
his wife Eliza may take the name of Eliza Bradlee; their children, Paul
Bailey, Charles Augustus, Josiah Warren, James Henry, George William,
Lucy Ann, Maria Jane, and Caroline Louisa, may severally take the name
of Paul Bailey Bradlee, Charles Augustus Bradlee, Warren Bradlee, James
Henry Bradlee, George William Bradlee, Lucy Ann Bradlee, Maria Jane
Bradlee, and Caroline Louisa Bradlee; Francis Henley Osgood, minor son
of Joseph Osgood, of Haverhill, may take the name of John Francis Full-
ington; all of the county of Essex.   Major Brown, of Worcester, may
take the name of Henry Brown; Orrin Slayton, of Brookfield, may take
the name of John Slayton; William Henry Darling, an adopted child of
John G. Woodward, of Ashburnham, may take the name of William Henry
Woodward; Walter Sibley, of Spencer, may take the name of Walter
Livermore Sibley; Olive Brewer, minor daughter of Thomas Brewer, of
Boylston, may take the name of Lucy Ann Brewer; Daniel Carter, 2d, of
Berlin, may take the name of Daniel Henry Carter; Emeline Chapin Willard,

of Uxbridge, may take the name of Emma Chapin Willard; Zeruiah Whitcomb, of Bolton, may take the name of Louisa Frances Whitcomb; Daniel
F. Mason, of Petersham, may take the name of Daniel Mason Fales;
Alonzo Hoar, of Bolton, may take the name of Henry Lincoln; George
Hoar, of Bolton, may take the name of George Lincoln; George Green, a
minor, and an adopted son of Francis W. Maynard, of Oakham, may take
the name of George Francis Maynard; Leonard Kenney, of Spencer, may
take the name of Leonard Knights; James Hollingworth, of Southbridge,
may take the name of James Milton Hollingworth; Jonah S. Bancroft, of
Auburn, minor son of Peter M. Bancroft, of Worcester, may take the name
of Charles S. Bancroft; Barnabas Stiles, of Shrewsbury, may take the
name of Alonzo Stiles; Windsor Rice, of Warren, may take the name of
Windsor Drewry; Theodore Lyman Washburn, of Warren, may take the
name of Theodore Lyman, and Clarissa Washburn, his wife, may take the
name of Clarissa Lyman; Julia Cheney, of Milford, may take the name of
Julia Nelson; all of the county of Worcester. Patrick McElroy, of
Charlestown, may take the name of Charles McElroy; Angeline C. Hatch,
of Lowell, may take the name of Angeline C. Brown; Clarissa Page, of
Lowell, may take the name of Clarissa Hatch; Samuel Chipman, jun., of
Marlborough, may take the name of Samuel Adams Chipman; Alcimus
Fairbanks, of Marlborough, may take the name of George Fairbanks;
Joseph S. Trowbridge, of Marlborough, may take the name of Joseph S.
Bradley; Lucy Minerva Stearns Preston, of Bedford, may take the name
of Lucy Minerva Stearns, and her minor son, George Warren Preston, may
take the name of Sherman Stearns Preston; Oliver Mead, minor son of
Nathaniel Mead, of Boxborough, may take the name of Oliver Warren
Mead; Edward Clary, of Lowell, may take the name of Edward Warren
Clary; all of the county of Middlesex. Edward L. Death, of Northamp-
ton, may take the name of Edward L. Dexter; Jeremiah Bartlett, of Ware,
may take the name of John Bartlett; Oliver Smith, jun., of Hadley, may
take the name of Oliver Eastman Smith; Jesse Holton, of Northampton,
may take the name of Jesse Duren Holton; Joseph Hoar Patrick, of Green-
wich, may take the name of Joseph Homer Patrick; all of the county of
Hampshire. Ellis Draper, of Brimfield, may take the name of Charles
Cole Graves; Sparrow Howes Bangs, of Springfield, may take the name of
Edward Dwight Bangs; William C. McLehose, of Westfield, formerly of
Scotland, may take the name of William Lonsdale; all of the county of
Hampden. George Field, of Sunderland, may take the name of George
Rochester Field; Emerson Merrifield, of Shelburne, may take the name of
George Emerson Merrifield; Benjamin Montague, of Shelburne, may take
the name of Benjamin Franklin Montague; Bushrod Washington Johnson,
of Orange, may take the name of George Washington Johnson; Harriet
Wood Gage, of New Salem, may take the name of Harriet Wood Sanderson,
and her minor son, Matthew Wood Gage, may take the name of Matthew
Wood Sanderson; Caleb Cooley Wells, of Whately, may take the name of
Clifford Carlton Wells; John Guilford, 2d, of Ashfield, may take the name
of Charles Samuel Guilford; Dickman Rowe, of Ashfield, may take the
name of William Henry Rowe; all of the county of Franklin. Bartholo-
mew Chapman, of Stockbridge, may take the name of George Chapman;
and Sarah Sophia Shelden, of Adams, a minor, and an adopted child of
Harvey Arnold, may take the name of Sarah Sophia Arnold; both of the

county of Berkshire. Pepperill Frost Scammon, of Canton, may take the name of John Frost Scammon; Zephaniah Spurr Williams, a minor son of Joshua Howard Williams, of Roxbury, may take the name of Howard Spurr Williams; Joseph Maynard, jun., of Needham, may take the name of Joseph Warren Maynard; Lucy Campbell Lillie, minor daughter of John Lillie, of Milton, may take the name of Elizabeth Baker Lillie; William E. Ayers, of Dedham, may take the name of William E. Andrew; all of the county of Norfolk. Elizabeth Ann Endley, of New Bedford, in the county of Bristol, may take the name of Elizabeth Endley Gibbs. James Ingham, minor son of Mary Otis, of Scituate, may take the name of James Otis; Thomas G. Drinkwater, of Abington, may take the name of George Thomas; Zilpha Stetson Rogers, of Hanover, may take the name of Zilpha Stetson; Cyrus Dyer, of Abington, may take the name of Cyrus Aurelius Dyer; Dolly Wood Savary, of North Bridgewater, may take the name of Ellen Maria Savary; all of the county of Plymouth. Edwin Keith, of Sandwich, may take the name of Edwin Aberdeen Keith; Jonathan French Baker, minor son of Isaac Baker, of Wellfleet, may take the name of Isaac French Baker; Edward Whilden, jun., of Yarmouth, may take the name of Silvanus Whilden; all of the county of Barnstable. Moses Barnard, of Nantucket, may take the name of Moses J. Barnard; and Rebecca R. Eldridge, of Nantucket, may take the name of Heromine Angeline Melville, both of the county of Nantucket. And the several persons before mentioned, from and after the passing of this act, shall be known and called by the names which by this act they are respectively allowed to assume as aforesaid, and the same shall hereafter be considered as their only proper and legal names. [*March 17, 1841.*

An Act to change the Names of the several Persons therein mentioned.
Be it enacted, etc., as follows:
Anne Kaniffle may take the name of Ann Maria Williams; Charles Little may take the name of Charles Henry Little; Susan P. McCurdy may take the name of Susan P. Stoddard; Charles Cook may take the name of Charles Edward Cook; Edwin Bray Nichols may take the name of Edwin William Bray; Anna Channing Woodbridge may take the name of Lucy Ann Woodbridge; Charles Plander LeCain, a minor, may take the name of Charles Lamont LeCain; Levi Whitcomb, may take the name of Levi Lincoln Whitcomb; Elkanah Bates may take the name of Elkanah Gerry Bates; Daniel Kimball may take the name of Daniel B. Kimball; Maria Percival Weeks, a minor, may take the name of Maria Weeks Percival; Henry Williams may take the name of Henry Lewellynn Williams; all of the county of Suffolk. Amasa Ham, of Danvers, may take the name of George Clinton Claiborne; Mary Jane Fisher, a minor, of Amesbury, may take the name of Louisa Jane Hadley; Joseph Treadwell Grafton, a minor, may take the name of Joseph Grafton Treadwell; Martha Johonnot Treadwell, a minor, may take the name of Martha Treadwell; George Johonnot Treadwell, a minor, may take the name of George Treadwell; severally of Salem; Sarah Withey, of Georgetown, may take the name of Sarah Augusta Stanley; Eliza Willet Cheney, of Georgetown, may take the name of Mary Willet Cheney; Samuel French Steele, a minor, of Gloucester, may take the name of Samuel Steele French; Dolly Jayne, of Lynn, may take the

name of Augusta Jayne ; John Dial, a minor of Lynn, may take the name
of Charles Warren Foster ; Lydia Alley, of Lynn, may take the name of
Lydia Maria Alley ; George Augustus Smith, of Salem, may take the name
of George Augustus Pousland ; John Rich, a minor, of Lynn, may take the
name of John Tyler Ingalls ; John Pierpont Bailey, a minor, of Hamilton,
may take the name of Ebenezer Pierpont Bailey ; all of the county of
Essex.   Lydia Symmes, of Charlestown, may take the name of Lydia
Maria Symmes ; Alexander E. Pope, of Marlborough, may take the name
of Franklin Mancer Pope ; Charles Henry Benjamin, a minor, of Waltham,
may take the name of Charles Henry Haven ; Nahum Allen Dalrymple, of
Marlborough, may take the name of Nahum Allen Gay ; Dolly Ann Francina Butterfield, a minor, of Pepperell, may take the name of Francina Ann
Bolles ; Sarah White, of Charlestown, may take the name of Sarah White
Dalrymple ; Harrison Thwing, of South Reading, may take the name of
Charles Harrison Thwing ; Kendall Bailey Shedd, of Charlestown, may
take the name of Kendall Bailey ; Elizabeth Shedd, of Charlestown, may
take the name of Elizabeth Bailey ; an infant child of the said Elizabeth
may take the name of Kendall Bailey ; Josiah Crosby Whitman, a minor,
of Waltham, may take the name of Bernard Whitman ; Cornelius Roswell
Richardson, of Woburn, may take the name of Albert Richardson ; Mary
Elizabeth Emerson, a minor, of Concord, may take the name of Mary Elizabeth Emerson Kimball ; Susan H. Blood, of Acton, a minor, may take the
name of Susan B. Hayward ; Adaline Parker, of Lowell, may take the
name of Adaline Amanda Parker ; Joshua Augustus West, of Stow, may
take the name of Joshua Augustus Severance ; John Wolcott, of Natick,
may take the name of John Benjamin Wolcott ; Charles Haynes, 2d, of
Charlestown, may take the name of Charles Haynes Haselton ; Rufus Lee,
of Waltham, may take the name of Rufus Seymour Lee ; all in the county
of Middlesex.   Squire Butterfield Wood, of Westborough, may take the
name of Charles Butterfield Wood ; Climena Roxlana Wood, of Westborough, may take the name of Frances Climena Wood ; David Allen, jun ,
of Leominster, may take the name of David C. Allen ; Hiram Harrington
Crosby, a minor, of Northborough, may take the name of Hiram Webster
Crosby ; Patrick Hunt, of Northbridge, may take the name of William
Hunt ; William Upham, 2d, of Sturbridge, may take the name of William
Henry Upham ; Frances Abigail Morse, a minor, of Upton, may take the
name of Frances Abigail Walker ; Mary Gerrish Colburn, of Leicester, may
take the name of Mary Greenough Colburn ; Dorcas Farnsworth, of Lan-
caster, may take the name of Dorcas Eliza Farnsworth ; Thomas Miles
Manard may take the name of Thomas Manard Miles ; his wife, Lydia
Merriam Manard, may take the name of Lydia Merriam Miles ; both of
Warren ; Oreemus Perington Clark, a minor, of Upton, may take the name
of Oliver Clark Haven ; Sarah Ingraham, a minor, of Ashburnham, may
take the name of Sarah Ingraham Watkins ; all of the county of Worces-
ter.   Orrick Willis, of Belchertown, may take the name of William Holmes
Willis ; William Brown, a minor, of Pelham, may take the name of William
Lyman Mirick ; Orrigen Johnson, of Amherst, may take the name of Orren
Johnson ; all of the county of Hampshire.   Ozias Hoar, Leonard Russell
Hoar, Eley Barney Hoar, Celia Hoar, Armenia Knowlton Hoar, Lamira
Ophelia Hoar, Cornelia Luretta Hoar, and Leonard Sikes Hoar, all of
Palmer, may severally take the surname of Hudson ; all of the county of

Hampden. Jane Steele Mansfield, of Conway, may take the name of Lucy Jane Steele ; Martha Moody, a minor, of Northfield, may take the name of Martha Nevers ; Sarah Cornelia Day, of Hawley, a minor, may take the name of Sarah Cornelia Crosby ; Lovina Streeter, of Bernardston, may take the name of Lovina Gould ; Henry Dwight Peirce, of Shutesbury, may take the name of Henry Peirce ; all of the county of Franklin. Charles A. Woodford, of Quincy, may take the name of Charles A. Woodward ; Cynthia Maynard Gay, of Needham, may take the name of Helen Wheeler ; Charles Peirce, of Dorchester, may take the name of Charles Bates ; all of the county of Norfolk. James Lobdell Holmes, of Plympton, may take the name of Pelham Holmes ; John Morse, of Plymouth, may take the name of John Atwood Morse ; both of the county of Plymouth. George Hall, a minor, of Dennis, may take the name of George Henry Hall ; John Smith, jun., a minor, of Truro, may take the name of John Wesley Smith ; Josiah H. Howes, a minor, of Dennis, may take the name of Edward Howes ; all of the county of Barnstable. And the several persons before mentioned, from and after the passing of this act, shall be known and called by the names which by this act they are respectively allowed to assume as aforesaid, and the same shall hereafter be considered as their only proper and legal names. [*March 3, 1842.*

An Act to change the Names of the several Persons therein mentioned.
Be it enacted, etc., as follows :
  Harriot Clarke may take the name of Harriot Pomroy Clarke ; Delia Clarke may take the name of Sarah Delia Clarke, of the county of Suffolk. Henry Wetherbee Chase may take the name of Charles Henry Wharton, in the county of Middlesex. Martha McHard may take the name of Martha H. Maynard ; Alphonso W. McHard may take the name of Charles Maynard ; Martha A. McHard may take the name of Martha A. Maynard ; Lucy H. McHard may take the name of Lucy H. Maynard ; Mary E. McHard may take the name of Mary E. Maynard ; John L. McHard may take the name of John L. Maynard ; William H. McHard may take the name of William H. Maynard, of the county of Franklin. And the several persons before mentioned, from and after the passing of this act, shall be known and called by the names which by this act they are respectively allowed to assume as aforesaid, and the same shall hereafter be considered as their only proper and legal names. [*September 16, 1842.*

An Act to change the Names of the Persons therein mentioned.
Be it enacted, etc., as follows :
  Joseph Eames may take the name of Joseph Ames ; John Cunningham may take the name of John Adams Cunningham ; Antonio Jacinth may take the name of Antonio Jacinth Francis ; Desire Jacinth may take the name of Desire Francis ; Hannah Jacinth may take the name of Hannah Francis ; Margaret Rebecca Vaugh may take the name of Margaret Rebecca Henry ; James Carlton may take the name of John D. Roach ; Horace Gardner Smith may take the name of Horace Gardner Berry Smith ; Dorothy Harris Faxon may take the name of Mary Harris Faxon ; Eliza White may take the name of Eliza Stodder ; Betsy Davis may take the name of

Betsy Alds ; William Tolman may take the name of William George Tolman ; John Rogers may take the name of John Webster Rogers ; Charles Veazie, jun., may take the name of Charles Stewart Veazie ; Elizabeth Veazie may take the name of Mary Elizabeth Veazie ; Edward Darley Baker may take the name of Darley Baker ; Charles Augustus Munroe may take the name of Charles Augustus Bartlett ; John Harleston Parker may take the name of Harleston Parker ; Susan Lane may take the name of Susan Douglas ; David C. Pearson may take the name of Edward Sewall Pearson ; Elizabeth Hewes, of Chelsea, may take the name of Elizabeth Brown Hewes ; Abigal Elizabeth Lunt may take the name of Abby Lunt Tewksbury ; Roger McGowan may take the name of William Roger McGowan ; Tryphena Van Buskirk may take the name of Frances Elizabeth Coffin ; Ephraim Baker McLaughlin may take the name of Ephraim Baker Mason ; Mary Thomas McLaughlin may take the name of Mary Thomas Mason ; Henry Wainwright McLaughlin may take the name of Henry Wainwright Mason ; Mary Elizabeth McLaughlin may take the name of Mary Elizabeth Mason ; Joseph Hastings McLaughlin may take the name of Joseph Hastings Mason ; Ephraim Baker McLaughlin, jun., may take the name of Ephraim Baker Mason, jun. ; William Hague McLaughlin may take the name of William Hague Mason ; Sarah Wilson may take the name of Sarah Caroline Morse ; Philander C. Jacobs may take the name of Philander Jacobs Forrestall ; John Moffett Robinson may take the name of John Holton Moffett ; Benjamin Field may take the name of Benjamin Franklin Field ; Charles Brown may take the name of Charles H. Brown ; Jonathan Houghton may take the name of John Coolidge Houghton ; Ossian Doolittle may take the name of Ossian Doolittle Ashley ; Cristy Gregg may take the name of Charles C. Gregg ; Henry Rice may take the name of Henry Marshall Rice ; all of the county of Suffolk.   Nathan Eames, of Saugus, may take the name of Nathan Ames ; Jeremiah Sawyer, jun., of Salisbury, may take the name of Jeremiah Hayden Sawyer ; Joseph Blake Prescott, of Rowley, may take the name of Joseph Warren Prescott ; John Pickard, of Rowley, may take the name of Daniel Webster ; Caleb Brown, of Newburyport, may take the name of John Caleb Brown ; Betsey Gould, of Topsfield, may take the name of Elizabeth Maria Gould ; George F. Hawkes, of Lynn, may take the name of William Warren Hawkes ; Rachel Hawkes, of Lynn, may take the name of Almira Aurelia Hawkes ; Daniel Millett, of Salem, may take the name of Daniel Caldwell Millett ; John Goodwin, of Marblehead, may take the name of Samuel John Goodwin ; Horace Fish, his wife Ruhamah Fish, and their children, Eliza Dutton Fish and Julia Anna Fish, of Amesbury, may severally take the surname of Tremont ; Ira Beckford, of Lynn, may take the name of William Ira Beckford ; Anthony Leon, of Ipswich, may take the name of Charles Leon Willcomb ; William Straw may take the name of William Niles ; his wife, Hannah Straw, may take the name of Hannah Niles ; Hannah Maria Straw may take the name of Hannah Maria Niles ; Charles Otis Kimball Straw may take the name of Charles Niles ; William Eustis Straw may take the name of William Eustis Niles ; John Calvin Straw may take the name of John Niles ; George Dighton Straw may take the name of George Niles ; Cynthia Sophila Straw may take the name of Sophila Niles ; Orestus Herbert Straw may take the name of Orestus Niles ; all of Georgetown ; Joseph Smith, 4th, of Salem, may take the name of Joseph Augustus

Smith ; Warren Hartwell Johnson, of Lynn, may take the name of Charles Warren Johnson ; Junius Augustus Noble, of Salem, may take the name of Augustus Noble ; Enoch Chase, of Newbury, may take the name of Enoch Pilsbury Chase ; Elizabeth Ann Long, of Andover, may take the name of Elizabeth Ann McNamara ; Joseph Page, of Bradford, may take the name of Rufus Holmes Page ; Charity Dennis, of Gloucester, may take the name of Mary Frances Dennis ; Samuel Osgood Baker may take the name of Samuel B. Osgood ; Sarah B. Baker may take the name of Sarah R. Osgood ; Sarah Ellen Baker may take the name of Sarah Ellen Osgood ; Josephine Augusta Baker may take the name of Josephine Augusta Osgood ; and Anna Elizabeth Baker may take the name of Anna Elizabeth Osgood ; severally of Salem ; Levi Hutchinson, jun., of Danvers, may take the name of Levi Hutchinson Russell ; Nathan Fellows, jun., of Ipswich, may take the name of Nathan Warren Fellows ; John Hoyt Henry, his wife, Margaret Henry, and their children, Mary Jane Henry and John William Henry, of Danvers, may take the surname of Bean ; Jeduthan C. Calden, of Amesbury, may take the name of Albert Nelson Edwards ; James Kimball, of Boxford, may take the name of James K. Henry ; Samuel Noyes Coker, of Newburyport, may take the name of George Edward Byron ; all of the county of Essex.   John Boyd, jun., of Marlborough, may take the name of John Merrick Boyd ; Thomas Colley, of Marlborough, may take the name of Thomas Corey ; Josiah Kemp, of Westford, may take the name of Greenville Pike ; Nathaniel Mead, jun., of Boxborough, may take the name of Adelbert Mead ; Charles Hartwell may take the name of Charles Belknap Hartwell ; and Catharine Hartwell may take the name of Catharine Adair Hartwell, both of Framingham ; Jonathan Nelson, of Woburn, may take the name of John Nelson ; Jonathan Brigham Cunningham, Sarah Cunningham, Lydia Ann Cunningham, and Sarah Cunningham, jun., all of Marlborough, may severally take the surname of Brigham ; Maria Antoinette Gavazone of Charlestown, may take the name of Maria Antoinette Gavazone Doyle ; Charles Courtsworth Babcock, of Marlborough, may take the name of Charles Dana Elliot ; William Helstone of Lowell, may take the name of William Elston ; Mercy Doane, of Charlestown, may take the name of Elizabeth Freeman Doane ; Andrew Clark may take the name of Andrew Jackson Clark ; Levi Clark may take the name of Levi Flint Clark ; Sarah Clark may take the name of Sarah Brooks Clark ; Rebecca Clark may take the name of Rebecca Lydia Clark ; severally of Concord ; all of the county of Middlesex.   Semanthia Adams, of Northborough, may take the name of Abba Maria Adams ; Dolly Wheelock Oakes, of Southbridge, may take the name of Catharine Wheelock Oakes ; Silas Pierce, of Sutton, may take the name of Silas Austin Pierce ; Abel Houghton, of Bolton, may take the name of Edward Elliot Houghton ; Joseph Burley, of Northbridge, may take the name of Joseph Crocker ; Ann Walkins, of Warren, may take the name of Ann Elizabeth Watson ; Hannah Hacket, of Douglas, may take the name of Hannah Aldrich ; Lewis McIntyre, of Charlton, may take the name of Lewis Trumbull Mason ; James Bailey, jun., of Holden, may take the name of James Hamilton Bailey ; Joseph Eaton, of Fitchburg, may take the name of Joseph Myron Rensselaer Eaton ; Charles Robbins, of Millbury, may take the name of Charles Birney Robbins ; Alvira Hubbard, of Millbury, may take the name of Elvira Calista Hubbard ; John Lawrence, 2d, of West Boylston, may take the name of Jacob George Washington ;

Coridon Marsh, of Spencer, may take the name of George Brigham Marsh; Israel Wheeler, of Milford, may take the name of George Israel Evelyn Wheeler; George Edward Knowles Bancroft, of Auburn, may take the name of George Bancroft; Albertson Watkins, of Warren, may take the name of Albert Watson; his wife, Mary E. Watkins, and their daughter, Mary I. Watkins, may severally take the surname of Watson; all of the county of Worcester. Lyman Dwight Marshall, of Enfield, may take the name of Lyman Dwight Walker; Harvey Holland, of Northampton, may take the name of James Harvey Holland; William Warren Lee, of Northampton, may take the name of Samuel Warren Lee; Abner Kingsley Burnell, of Northampton, may take the name of Kingsley Abner Burnell; John Taft, of Ware, may take the name of John Edward Taft; Eunice Ramsdell, of Belchertown, may take the name of Eunice Smith; Chrissa Smith, of Granby, may take the name of Chrissa Kinsley Moody; all of the county of Hampshire. Nancy Tarbox may take the name of Nancy Taber; Eliza Ann Tarbox may take the name of Eliza Ann Taber; Almeda Tarbox may take the name of Almeda Taber; Julia Abby Tarbox may take the name of Julia Abby Taber, severally, of Springfield; Franklin Andrews Whipple, of Monson, may take the name of Franklin Whipple; all of the county of Hampden. Frederick Curtis Squires, of Sunderland, may take the name of Samuel Pomroy Montague; George Allen, of Sunderland, may take the name of George Allen Morse; David Manson Daniels, of Montague, may take the name of Manson Wells Braynard; John Bangs, of Montague, may take the name of John Cushman Bangs; Sylvia Johnson Goddard, of Orange, may take the name of Sarah Johnson Goddard; Elvira Wrisley, of Gill, may take the name of Elvira Jackson; Levi Goodnow, of Charlemont, may take the name of Joseph Watson Goodnow; Diana Goddard, of Orange, may take the name of Amelia Elizabeth Goddard; all of the county of Franklin. Rufus Temple, 2d, of Williamstown, may take the name of Munroe Temple; Harriett Atwood White, of Williamstown, may take the name of Harriett White Young; John Wesley Haxford and Sarah Watson Haxford, of Lenox, may severally take the surname of Butler; all of the county of Berkshire. Hannah Foster, of Dorchester, may take the name of Anna Elizabeth Foster; Eliza Clapp Thayer, of Dorchester, may take the name of Eliza Thayer Clapp; Charles Bates, of Dorchester, may take the name of Charles Bates Pierce; Benaiah Prescott Spaulding, of Randolph, may take the name of Benjamin Prescott Spaulding; Sarah Howard Wales Curtis, of Stoughton, may take the name of Martha Mary Worcester Curtis; George Washington Bull may take the name of George Washington Webster; his wife, Hannah Leach Bull, may take the name of Hannah Leach Webster; Frances Ann Bull may take the name of Frances Ann Webster; George Henry Bull may take the name of George Henry Webster; Charlotte Louisa Bull may take the name of Charlotte Louisa Webster; all of Roxbury; James Henry Hodgkins, of Weymouth, may take the name of George Brooks; Albert Stoddard, of Weymouth, may take the name of Albert Austin Stoddard; all of the county of Norfolk. Harriet Isabel Crocker, of Taunton, may take the name of Harriet Burling Crocker; George Bedon, of Dartmouth, may take the name of George Butts; Julia Marvin Coggeshall, of New Bedford, may take the name of Julia Marvin Parker; Rebecca Pierce Selee, of Easton, may take the name of Catharine Rebecca Pierce Selee; Harriet G. Parks, of Taunton, may

take the name of Harriet G. Richmond; all of the county of Bristol.
Joseph Warren Maglathlin, of Pembroke, may take the name of Joseph
Warren Way; Calvin Shaw, 2d, of Abington, may take the name of Calvin
Holmes Shaw; Brackley Shaw, 4th, of Abington, may take the name of
Brackley White Shaw; Betsey Dyer, of Abington, may take the name of
Elizabeth Lavinia Dyer; Mary Ann Hollis, of Halifax, may take the name
of Eliza Jane Waterman; all of the county of Plymouth. Zoheth Smith,
2d, of Truro, may take the name of Zoheth Manlius Smith; Alvan Cobb,
of Truro, may take the name of Richard Alvan Cobb; Edward S. Howes,
of Dennis, may take the name of Jotham Howes; Joshua D. Knowles, of
Truro, may take the name of Daniel A. Knowles; Ermina Townley Phinney,
of Falmouth, may take the name of Sophronia Wicks Phinney; Zenas
Eldridge, of Harwich, may take the name of Zenas D. Eldridge; Patty
Myric, of Harwich, may take the name of Lucy Myrick; all of the county
of Barnstable. And the several persons before mentioned, from and after the
passing of this act, shall be known and called by the names which, by this
act, they are respectively allowed to assume as aforesaid, and the same shall
hereafter be considered as their only and proper and legal names. [*March
24, 1843.*

An Act to change the Name of A. Macon Bolling.
Be it enacted, etc., as follows:
SECT. 1. A. Macon Bolling, of the city of Boston, in the county of Suffolk, may take the name of Macon Bolling Allen, and shall be hereafter
known and called by that name, as his only proper and legal name, to all
intents and purposes.
SECT. 2. This act shall take effect from and after its passage. [*January
20, 1844.*

An Act to change the Names of the Persons therein mentioned.
Be it enacted, etc., as follows:
County of Suffolk: — Benjamin Gilbert, a minor, may take the name of
Benjamin Williams Gilbert; Amaziah Atwood, jun., may take the name of
Francis Amaziah Atwood; Charles Parker may take the name of Charles
Sargent Parker; John Mason may take the name of John Warren Mason;
Rebecca Locke may take the name of Louisa Rebecca Locke; James Col-
bert may take the name of Caleb Colbert Mortimer; Ruthy Low Colbert
may take the name of Sarah Lynch Mortimer; Caleb Cushing Woodman
may take the name of Caleb Cushing Emerson Mortimer; William Storer
Wormwood may take the name of William Storer; Jonathan Kimball
Rogers may take the name of John Kimball Rogers; Alphonso Horatio
Foster may take the name of Franklin Henry Foster; Louisa Cody Palmer,
a minor, may take the name of Louisa Caldwell Palmer; Prince Edward
Nichols may take the name of Ferdinand Almy Nichols; Francis Moore
may take the name of Francis Clifford Moore; Charles Augustus Bartlett
may take the name of Charles Augustus Bartlett Munroe; Dominicus
Scammans Lewis may take the name of Alfred Scammons Lewis; Jonathan
Ingersol Kendall may take the name of Henry Ingersol Kendall; Mary
Doughty may take the name of Mary Jane Cutter; Jeremiah Bean Moulton
may take the name of Charles Bean Moulton; Richard Hazen Fitz may
take the name of Richard Hazen Wellington; William Pynchon Oliver

may take the name of Peter Oliver; Ephraim N. Buyn may take the name
of Ephraim N. Bowen; Sarah Livermore Coburn, a minor, may take the
name of Anna Livermore Coburn; Charles Appleton Burzeil may take the
name of Charles Appleton; Benjamin Franklin Cowdin, a minor, may take
the name of Franklin Cowdin Merriam; Sarah Robbins Whitehouse may
take the name of Adelaide Austin; William Henry Cowen, a minor, may
take the name of Eleazer Porter Wells; Charles Holbrook, may take the
name of Charles Augustus Holbrook; Eunice Fellows may take the name
of Eunice Caroline Fellows; Joseph Wood Whiting may take the name of
Joseph Whiting Wood; Sarah Starr Lombard may take the name of Emily
Livingston Lombard; Harriet Morton Bull may take the name of Harriet
Morton Lawrence; Samuel Gooch may take the name of Samuel Henfield
Gooch, severally of the city of Boston; Edmund Bowker, of Chelsea, may
take the name of Jacob Henry Bowker; all of the county of Suffolk.
John Lewis Rowe, of Gloucester, may take the name of Lewis Rowe;
Moses Marsh, 2d, of Haverhill, may take the name of Moses Chandler
Marsh; Proctor Perley Batchelor, of Georgetown, may take the name of
Morrison Proctor; Joseph Bradley, 3d, of Haverhill, may take the name of
Joseph Hildreth Bradley; Judith Bray, of Newbury, may take the name of
Maria Bray; Ann Maria Bean, a minor, of Hamilton, may take the name
of Eliza Symonds Patch; Sewell Barrett, a minor, of Lynn, may take the
name of Nicholas Bowler; John Tarbox Kimball, a minor, of Methuen, may
take the name of John Tarbox; Christian Nelson, of Salem, may take the
name of Charles Nelson; George Washington Cook, a minor, of Salem,
may take the name of George Washington Emerson; Gustavus Nourse, of
Lynn, may take the name of Gustavus Frelinghuysen Nourse; Isaac Burley
Horn, of Topsfield, may take the name of Burley Orne; William Groves
Millett, a minor, of Beverly, may take the name of William Groves; Jona-
than Rundlett, jun., of Newburyport, may take the name of Jonathan D.
Rundlett; James Smith may take the name of James Albert Smith;
Edward H. Brooks may take the name of John Brooks Edwards; Stephen
Phippen Hill may take the name of Stephen Prescott Hill, severally of
Salem; Eliza and Lucy Townsend, minors, of Lynn, may take the names of
Eliza Malvina and Lucy Maria Townsend; Valeria Pew, a minor, of
Gloucester, may take the name of Mary Pew; John Jumper, of Gloucester,
may take the name of John Edward Mason; Sereneth Chamberlain Good-
rich, a minor, of Andover, may take the name of Mary Elizabeth French;
Henry French Goodrich, a minor, of Andover, may take the name of Peter
Henry French; John Hamilton Brown, of Lynn, may take the name of
Hamilton Brown; John Boardman Cheney, of Georgetown, may take the
name of John Oseola Brown; Michael Milkiey, of Danvers, a minor, may
take the name of Warren Emerson; Harriet Newell Brookings, of Newbury,
may take the name of Harriet Newell Bartlett; Hadassah Chase Bragdon,
of Newbury, may take the name of Ellen Chase Bragdon; Lucy Maria
Cloutman, a minor, of Lynn, may take the name of Lucy Maria Wheeler;
Abigail M. Hall may take the name of Abigail Barton; and her children,
Mary S. Hall, Abby M. Hall, Susan C. Hall, Frances E. Hall, Emily F.
Hall, and Maria B. Hall, of Salisbury, may severally take the surname of
Barton; Daniel Adams Emes may take the name of Daniel Adams Ames;
Lura Emes may take the name of Lura Ames; Lovey Emes may take the
name of Lovey A. Ames; Martha Emes may take the name of Martha

Sabrina Ames, severally of Saugus; all of the county of Essex. Sally
Prescott, of Groton, may take the name of Phidelia Prescott; Lucretia
Barnes, of Marlborough, may take the name of Lucretia Felton; Samuel
Bowman Nelson, of Waltham, may take the name of Samuel Nelson;
Richard Stone, of Sherburne, may take the name of Richard Cecil Stone;
Earl H. Southwick, of Marlborough, may take the name of George Houghton; Huldah Copeland Tribon, of Cambridge, may take the name of Amelia
Copeland Tribon; David Porter Fuller, a minor, of Natick, may take the
name of David F. Fiske; John Richard C. Brown, of Charlestown, may
take the name of John C. Brown; S. W. Palmer, of Newton, may take the
name of Hazlitt Arvine; Mary A. Palmer, of Newton, may take the name
of Mary A. Arvine; Charlotte Reed Gipson, of Burlington, may take the
name of Charlotte Louisa Reed; Ingebor Janson, a minor, of Lowell, may
take the name of Ingebor Janson Anderson; Clarissa Coburn, of Dracut,
may take the name of Clarissa Fox; Edward Richardson, of Dracut, may
take the name of Edward Everett Richardson; Andrew Blanchard, 3d, a
minor, of Medford, may take the name of Andrew Delaval Blanchard;
Benjamin Thorp Henderson, of Woburn, may take the name of Benjamin
Thorp Henderson Porter; James Russell MacCurdy, of South Reading,
may take the name of James Russell; Benjamin F. Breding, of Cambridge,
may take the name of Benjamin F. Bridden; Patrick Frederick Hewes, of
Groton, may take the name of William Frederick Hewes; Clara Frink, of
Lowell, may take the name of Clara Wilson; Elizabeth Fletcher Henderson,
of Littleton, may take the name of Elizabeth Fletcher Grimes; Rebecca
Grimes Henderson, her daughter, may take the name of Rebecca Whitcomb
Grimes; Polly M. Woodcock, of Lowell, may take the name of Mary M.
Wood; Thomas Womersley Melbon, of Lowell, may take the name of
Thomas Womersley; Barzillai Birdet Williams, of Groton, may take the
name of John Birdet Williams; all of the county of Middlesex.   Sarah
Rebecca Fletcher, a minor, of Leominster, may take the name of Sarah
Rebecca Adams; Thomas Smith, of Sterling, may take the name of George
Richard Smith; Dorothy Allen, of Leominster, may take the name of
Dorothy Helen Allen; Miranda Heywood, of Lunenburg, may take the
name of Miranda Priest Heywood; Lois Brigham Nourse, a minor, of
Northborough, may take the name of Louisa Brigham Nourse; Lydia
Wallis McIntire, of Charlton, may take the name of Vanda Lydia Wallis
Kilburn; William H. Carlton, of Sutton, may take the name of Augustus
Carlton; Benjamin David Perkins, a minor, of Royalston, may take the
name of Benjamin Conant Perkins; Mary Elizabeth Florence, a minor, of
Northborough, may take the name of Mary Arravilla Carter; John Cotton,
a minor, of Leominster, may take the name of John Atwood Cotton;
Thomas Brewer, 2d, of Boylston, may take the name of Leander Watson
Brewer; Sarah Elizabeth Flagg, a minor, of Boylston, may take the name
of Sarah Theresa Flagg; Asa Goodnow Howe, of Northborough, may take
the name of John Calhoun Howe; Charles Albert Babbitt, of Athol, may
take the name of Charles Babbitt Albert; Alexander Hamilton, of Worcester, may take the name of Edward Hamilton; all of the county of Worcester.   Mary Ingram, of Amherst, may take the name of Mary Boltwood
Ingram; Abigail Davis, of Granby, may take the name of Abby Martha
Davis; Abner Witt and Eliza T. Witt, minors, of South Hadley, may take
the names of Abner DeWitt and Eliza T. DeWitt; Milton Coates, of

Middlefield, may take the name of Milton Henry Coates; Franklin B. Leonard, of Middlefield, may take the name of Franklin B. Ely; Joseph William Strong may take the name of James William Strong; Silas Cook may take the name of Silas Dwight Cook; Francis James Pepper may take the name of Francis James Pepper Beaumont; Albert Ingram may take the name of Albert Barnes Ingram, severally of Northampton; Ansel Edwards Durant, of Westhampton, may take the name of Ansel Edwards; Harriet Melvina Sears, a minor, of Williamsburgh, may take the name of Harriet Eliza Sears; David McClintock, of Ware, may take the name of David Woods; Samuel Train, of Northampton, may take the name of Orson Eates Train; Lyman Cook, a minor, of Pelham, may take the name of Lyman Van Buren Cook; all of the county of Hampshire. Sylva Bissel, a minor, of Ludlow, may take the name of Sylva B. Alden; Maria Crosby, a minor, of Springfield, may take the name of Sarah Maria Crosby; Thomas Ainsworth Wedge may take the name of Thomas Ainsworth Bradford; Sophronia Ruth Wedge, his wife, may take the name of Sophronia Ruth Bradford; Sarah Adeline Wedge, their daughter, may take the name of Sarah Adeline Bradford; Eliza Ann Wedge, their daughter, may take the name of Eliza Ann Bradford; Thomas Waterman Wedge, their son, may take the name of Thomas Waterman Bradford; Lucy Mariah Wedge, their daughter, may take the name of Lucy Mariah Bradford; Ellen Frances Wedge, their daughter, may take the name of Ellen Frances Bradford, all of Brimfield; John Fostick, of Brimfield, may take the name of John Lyman; Betsey M. Crooks, of Blandford, a minor, may take the name of Betsey Crooks Morton; Timothy Leary, of Springfield, may take the name of Theodore Lyman; all of the county of Hampden. John Death and Eunice Death, his wife, may take the names of John Dickinson and Eunice Dickinson; Asahel G. Death, Jotham P. Death, and Abel S. Death, their minor children, may severally take the surname of Dickinson; John G. Death and Mary Ann Death, his wife, may take the surname of Dickinson, all of Deerfield; Abby Craw, of Greenfield, may take the name of Abigail Sawtell; Nathaniel Macomber, 2d, of Shutesbury, may take the name of Nathaniel Dwight Macomber; Charlotte P. Peabody, of Wendell, may take the name of Charlotte P. Stone; George W. Hotchkiss, a minor, of Montague, may take the name of George W. Puffer; Frederick Ross, of Deerfield, may take the name of Frederick Clapp Ross; William Harrison Hanks, a minor, of Shutesbury, may take the name of William Hanks Spear; Jacob Quackenbush, of Bernardston, may take the name of Jacob Bush; all of the county of Franklin. Thomas Crode Cushing, of Lenox, may take the name of Edward Cushing, of the county of Berkshire. Martha Mary Worcester Curtis, a minor, of Stoughton, may take the name of Martha Mary Crane Worcester; Joseph S. Mutchmore, of Braintree, may take the name of Joseph S. Pratt; Joseph Henry Jackson and his wife, Susan Hatch Jackson, of Braintree, may take the surname of Thayer, in addition to their present names; Sarah Adams, of Quincy, may take the name of Sarah Hardwick Adams; Sally Wilkinson Lewis, of Walpole, may take the name of Sarah Wilkinson Lewis; William Dudley Wells, of Roxbury, a minor, may take the name of George William Wells; all of the county of Norfolk. Ann Elizabeth Nichols, of New Bedford, may take the name of Ann Elizabeth Nichols Eddy; Caroline H. Jenney, of New Bedford, may take the name of Caroline Bartlett Hall: of the county of

Bristol.   Mason McLauthlin may take the name of Henry Mason ; Hannah McLauthlin, his wife, may take the name of Hannah Mason ; George Mason McLauthlin, their minor son, may take the name of George Mason, all of Duxbury ; Albert Torrey, a minor, of Scituate, may take the name of Henry Albert Torrey ; Return Tilden, of Marshfield, may take the name of Elliot Return Tilden ; Jacob Stetson, of Abington, may take the name of Jacob Shaw ; Merrill Whitmarsh, of East Bridgewater, may take the name of Mary Livingston Whitmarsh ; all of the county of Plymouth.   Warren Fish Baker, of Falmouth, may take the name of Henry Baker ; Nathaniel Hopkins, a minor, of Truro, may take the name of Sylvanus Rich Hopkins ; John Cogswell, a minor, of Yarmouth, may take the name of John Bear Doane Cogswell ; Albert Dunbar, jun., a minor, of Yarmouth, may take the name of Albert Henry Dunbar ; Daniel A. Rich, of Truro, a minor, may take the name of Henry Holmes Rich ; Horace C. Davis, of Barnstable, a minor, may take the name of Daniel Davis ; all of the county of Barnstable.   And the several persons before mentioned, from and after the passing of this act, shall be known and called by the names which, by this act, they are respectively allowed to assume as aforesaid, and the same shall hereafter be considered as their only proper and legal names.   [*March 16, 1844.*

An Act to change the Names of the Persons therein mentioned.
Be it enacted, etc., as follows :
William Winthrop Andrews, now United States Consul at the Island of Malta, may take the name of William Winthrop ; Moses Fisher may take the name of Moses Everett Fisher ; Daniel Warren Amasa Davis Cowdin may take the name of Warren Davis ; Henry Ballard, a minor, may take the name of Henry Ballard Dyer ; Sarah Elizabeth Hooper, a minor, may take the name of Sarah Elizabeth King ; Joachim Gervasio may take the name of Joseph Gervasio Oakes ; Francis Harrison Blanchard may take the name of Francis Harrison Clay Blanchard ; Oliver Ayres may take the name of Oliver Emmons Ayres ; Joseph McCollum, and Thurza McCollum, his wife, and William B. McCollum, their minor son, may severally take the surname of Chandler, instead of McCollum ; Moses Bullen may take the name of Moses Burlen ; Horace H. Whitmore may take the name of Horace Hersey Vinton ; Ann Maria Robson, a minor, may take the name of Ann Maria Armstrong ; Elizabeth Robson, a minor, may take the name of Elizabeth Lydia Armstrong ; Willard Feachem, a minor, may take the name of Willard Danforth ; Theodore Ashley Doolittle may take the name of Theodore Ashley ; Antoney Pairar may take the name of Charles Almeder Perry ; John Knight Smith may take the name of John Prince Knight ; Lucy Maria Faxon, an adopted daughter of Daniel Bartlett, jun., may take the name of Lucy Faxon Bartlett ; Hiram Fogg may take the name of Hiram Edwards Fogg ; Mary Vose may take the name of Mary Newell ; Horace Cutter may take the name of Horace Frederick Cutter ; William E. Cox may take the name of William E. Warren ; Charles O. Cox, a minor, may [take] the name of Charles O. Warren ; Chester Peeler may take the name of Chester Peeler Marshall ; Sarah E. Seaman may take the name of Sarah E. Saymore ; Lucinda Porter Bean may take the name of Lucinda Porter Whitman ; also her minor children, Stephen Bean, may take the name of Stephen Whitman ; Helen Maria Bean, may take the

name of Helen Maria Whitman ; Rufus Henry Bean, may take the name of
Rufus Henry Whitman ; Hannah Emily Bean, may take the name of Han-
nah Emily Whitman ; Louisa Almira Bean, may take the name of Louisa
Almira Whitman, and Ephraim Whitman Bean, may take the name of
Ephraim Parks Whitman ; Oliver Bicknell Wedge, a minor, may take the
name of Oliver Bicknell Lothrop ; Everard Wesley, a minor, and an adopted
son of Oliver Dyer, may take the name of Everard Wesley Dyer ; Temper-
ance Ann Bickford may take the name of Georgiana Brackett ; Jasper
Ferdinand Way may take the name of Jasper Franklin Ferdinand ; Mary
Atwood may take the name of Mary Clifford ; Charles Norlando Tentorni
may take the name of Charles Norlando Sibley ; Stephen F. Harding may
take the name of Stephen F. Hoogs ; Abel Wright Conant may take the
name of Arnold William Conant ; Simon Johnson Blanchard may take the
name of Edgar Johnson Blanchard ; Moses Brackett may take the name of
Walter M. Brackett, all of the city of Boston. Jacob Henry Bowker, of
Chelsea, may take the name of Edmund Bowker ; Warren Bowker, a minor
of Chelsea, may take the name of Henry Jacob Bowker ; Ellery Eldridge,
a minor of Chelsea, may take the name of Ellery Watson Eldridge ; all of
the county of Suffolk. Joseph E. Killam, of Bradford, may take the name
of Joseph E. Bartlett ; Jonathan E. Eastland, of Marblehead, may take
the name of George Eastland ; Deborah Morse, of Marblehead, may take
the name of Caroline Morse ; Foster Smith, jun., of Newburyport, may
take the name of Foster Waldo Smith ; Marie Antoinette Bliss, of Newburyport, may take the name of Marie Adelaide Otis ; also, her minor son,
William Starkie Bliss, may take the name of Joseph William Otis ; Joseph
Augustus Peabody, a minor, of Salem, may take the name of George
Augustus Peabody ; Mary Putnam, of Saugus, may take the name of Mary
Emery ; Hitte Cave Porter, of Lynn, may take the name of Ellen Maria
Porter ; James Bachelder French, a minor, and an adopted son of Harrison
B. Fowler, of Salisbury, may take the name of Henry Harrison Fowler ;
Edward Payson Stimson and Sarephina Cass, minors, and adopted children
of Daniel C. Bagley, of Amesbury, may take the names of Edward Stimson
Bagley and Abby Bayley Bagley ; Margaret Elizabeth Carmady, a minor
of Andover, may take the name of Margaret Elizabeth Gray ; Seabury
Treadwell Witt, of Lynn, may take the name of George Seabury De Witt ;
Jonathan Crosby Allen, of Salem, may take the name of Charles Crosby
Allen ; Asa Osgood, of Danvers, may take the name of Charles Asa Osgood ;
Moses A. Styles, of South Andover, may take the name of Charles D.
Willoughby ; Samuel Wadleigh, an adopted son of Moses Town of Andover,
may take the name of Samuel Town ; Barachias Hartwell Abbott, of
Andover, may take the name of Hartwell B. Abbott ; Ellen M. Kimball, a
minor, of Bradford, may take the name of Ellen Berry Kimball ; William
Wallace Hinkson, a minor, of Bradford, may take the name of William
Wallace Holmes ; Joseph Buntin Cornelius, of Newburyport, may take the
name of Joseph Buntin ; and his wife, Margaret Cornelius, may take
the name of Margaret Buntin ; also, their children, James Hervey Cornelius,
Ann Eliza Cornelius, and Rebecca Cornelius, may severally take the surname of Buntin instead of Cornelius ; Warren Hedding Currier, of Lynn,
may take the name of Warren Holbrook Currier ; William Tarbox, Lydia
Tarbox, and Martha Ellen Tarbox, of Lynn, may severally take the surname of Appleton instead of Tarbox ; Andrew Jackson McCrate, of Salem,

may take the name of William Hale ; Thomas Magee, of Lynn, may take
the name of Thomas Reed ; William Henry Berdge, of Newburyport, may
take the name of William Henry Barton, and Sarah Berdge, his wife, may
take the name of Sarah Louisa Barton ; also their child, Mary Adelaide
Berdge, may take the name of Mary Goodrich Barton ; John Bullough, and
his wife, Catharine Bullough, of Newburyport, may take the surname of
Bullou, instead of Bullough ; and Eliza Bancroft Bullough, Catharine
Moore Bullough, Nancy Kingsbury Bullough, Henry Willard Bullough, and
Adaline Frances Bullough, may severally take the surname of Bullou,
instead of Bullough ; Liberty Bullough, of Newburyport, may take the
name of Liberty Clement Bullou ; Joseph Bullough, of Newburyport, may
take the name of Joseph Warren Bullou ; Harriet Bullough, of Newbury-
port, may take the name of Harriet Ann Bullou ; Henrietta Bullough, of
Newburyport, may take the name of Henrietta Maria Bullou ; Robert Barr
McClintock, of Salem, may take the name of Robert Putnam Barr ; Charles
Addison Noyes, of Newburyport, may take the name of Charles Albert ;
and Nancy Osgood Noyes, his wife, may take the name of Nancy Albert.;
Daniel Adams, of Newburyport, may take the name of Daniel Palmer
Adams ; Ruth Ann Pinkham, a minor, of Saugus, may take the name of
Anna Pinkham ; all of the county of Essex.   William Blacker, of Lowell,
may take the name of William Francis Blake ; James Gilman Piper, Daniel
Caldwell Piper, Artemas Woodbury Piper, and Malinda Caldwell Piper,
minor children of Malinda C. P. Taylor, of Newton, may severally take
the surname of Taylor, instead of Piper ; Ichabod Eugene Norton, a minor,
of Charlestown, may take the name of Eugene Lindsey Norton ; Joel Gan-
nett, a minor, and an adopted son of William D. Eastman, of Lowell, may
take the name of Joel Albert Eastman ; Ruthy Ann Barrett, of Lowell, may
take the name of Sarah Ann Mortimer Barrett ; William Toombs and Ruth
F. Toombs, his wife, of Marlborough, may take the names of William
Edward Wood and Ruth Fry Wood ; also, their three minor children,
Louisa Elizabeth Toombs, Martha Toombs, and Mary Toombs, may take
the surname of Wood instead of Toombs ; Frederic Grimes, Jane Amanda
Grimes, and Caroline Grimes, of Lowell, may severally take the surname of
Graham instead of Grimes ; Abraham Rice, of Marlborough, may take the
name of Abraham Winfield Rice ; Lydia Ann Brigham, an adopted daughter
of William Coolidge, of Natick, may take the name of Sarah Ann Coolidge ;
Thomas Joyce, of Cambridge, may take the name of Thomas Joyce White ;
and his wife, Sally Joyce, may take the name of Sarah White ; also their
minor children, Charles White Joyce, and Sarah Joyce, may take the names
of Charles Joyce White, and Sarah White ; Calvin Richardson, 3d, of
Woburn, may take the name of Calvin Baldwin Richardson ; Henry Cain,
of Woburn, may take the name of Henry Wendall ; Zachariah Hill, of Concord, may take the name of William Adolphus Hill ; Augustus Williams, of
Charlestown, may take the name of Augustus Peirce ; Samuel H. Linikin,
of Cambridge, may take the name of Samuel L. Willard ; Charles Bullough,
of Newton, may take the name of Charles Nelson Bullou ; Mary Abigail
Temple, a minor, and an adopted daughter of Jesse Wright, of Littleton,
may take the name of Mary Abigail Wright ; Albert Wellington, of Medford, may take the name of Albert Kirk Wellington ; all of the county of
Middlesex.   Parker Howe, of Boylston, may take the name of George
Parker Howe ; George Washington Hodgerny, of Grafton, may take the

name of George Washington Lincoln ; Mary Abigail Upham, and John
William Upham, of Millbury, minors, may take the surname of Copeland
instead of Upham ; Joseph Leland, of Northbridge, may take the name of
Joseph Warren Leland ; William Robinson, of Spencer, may take the name
of George Robinson ; Amanda Dickey, of Southbridge, may take the name
of Amanda Hall ; Ellen Pray Denton, an adopted minor daughter of Thomas
W. Butterfield, of Worcester, may take the name of Ellen Louisa Butter-
field ; Allen Beaman, of Worcester, may take the name of Allen Conant
Beaman ; Francis D. Wheeler, of Westminster, may take the name of
Clinton D. Wheeler ; Charles Whitney, 2d, and George Whitney, minors,
of Westminster, may take the names of Charles Hubbard Whitney, and
George Edwin Whitney ; Ebenezer White Sawtell, a minor, of Westminster,
may take the name of Walter Hubbard Farnsworth Sawtell ; Abigail Larned
Davis, a minor, of Oxford, may take the name of Abby Larned Davis ;
Martha Ann Mason, of Worcester, may take the name of Martha Pierson
Mason ; John Pratt, of Worcester, may take the name of John Bush Pratt ;
George Aspinwall, of Brookfield, may take the name of George Gray ;
Gamaliel Beaman, jun., of Princeton, may take the name of Gamaliel Sawyer Beaman ; Sarah Ann Channing Robinson, of Northbridge, may take
the name of Martha Channing Robinson ; Simeon Dwinell, of Millbury,
may take the name of Simeon Du Nel ; Reuben M. Hoar, of Worcester,
may take the name of Reuben M. Hudson ; Philo A. Wheeler, of Bolton,
may take the name of Harriet Wheeler ; Lyman Brooks Macullar, of Worcester, may take the name of Lyman Brooks ; Clarinda Maria Legg Thayer,
a minor, of Milford, may take the name of Clarinda Maria Thayer Legg ;
Lurestan Chauvelin, of Princeton, may take the name of Luther Luton
Lakey ; and his wife, Asenath Chauvelin, may take the name of Asenath
Lakey ; also their minor children, George Augustus Chauvelin and Charles
Henry Chauvelin, may take the surname of Lakey, instead of Chauvelin ;
Samuel Hoar and Elizabeth Hoar, his wife, of North Brookfield, may take
the surname of Homer, instead of Hoar ; also their children, Adin Hoar,
Samuel Hoar, jun., and Rodolphus Wilber Hoar, may severally take the
names of Adin Alonzo Homer, Samuel Hoar Homer, and Rodolphus Wilber
Homer ; Franklin Hamant, of Sturbridge, may take the name of Benjamin
Franklin ; Samuel Wood, of Northborough, may take the name of Samuel
Lees Wood ; all of the county of Worcester.   William Quance, of South
Hadley, may take the name of William Ransom ; Frederick Plummer Tracy,
of Williamsburg, may take the name of Frederick Palmer Tracy ; Samuel
Nash, of South Hadley, may take the name of Samuel Adams Nash ; all
of the county of Hampshire.   Allen Look and Harriet Look, of Springfield,
may take the names of Allen Guild Lincoln and Harriet Guild Lincoln ;
Albert Clark, a minor, and an adopted son of Jonathan Steele, of Spring-
field, may take the name of Henry Albert Steele ; Fanny Hoar, of Spring-
field, widow, may take the name of Fanny Homer ; also, her three children,
Adaline, Elvira, and John Harvey Hoar, may severally take the surname
of Homer instead of Hoar ; Elias Bean, of Palmer, may take the name of
Elias Bean Whitman ; all of the county of Hampden.   Edwin Ward, of
Orange, may take the name of Edwin Daniel Ward ; Porter Snow, of
Whately, may take the name of Porter Howard Snow ; Eunice Hibbard, of
Rowe, may take the name of Eunice Emerson Hibbard ; Rebecca Sears
Crosby, a minor, of Hawley, may take the name of Ellen Sears Crosby ;

all of the county of Franklin. Mary Elizabeth Upton, a minor, and an adopted daughter of Oliver Arnold, of Adams, may take the name of Mary Elizabeth Arnold ; Joab Brace, jun., of Lanesboro', may take the name of Edward Joab Brace ; all of the county of Berkshire. William Hartwell Johnson, of Dorchester, may take the name of Willis Hartwell Johnson Renville ; James Cunningham, jun., a minor, of Dorchester, may take the name of James Swan Cunningham ; George Stearns, of Roxbury, may take the name of George Osborne Stearns ; Alfred Showell Marsh, of Milton, may take the name of Alfred Showell ; William Oscar Whittington, of Dorchester, a minor, may take the name of William Whittington Brooks ; Mary Ann Amanda Whittington, of Dorchester, a minor, may take the name of Amanda Whittington Brooks ; George Driver, of Quincy, may take the name of George W. Churchill ; George Sutherland, of Quincy, may take the name of George Churchill ; Dearborn Moses, of Quincy, may take the name of Moses Churchill ; Antoinette S. Moffatt, of Roxbury, may take the name of Antoinette S. Jones ; George T. Moffatt, a minor, of Roxbury, may take the name of George Alexander Jones ; all of the county of Norfolk. Abigail Jucket, of Freetown, may take the name of Julia Palmer ; George James Moore, a minor, and an adopted son of Samuel O. Dunbar, of Taunton, may take the name of George James Dunbar ; Stephen Cornell, of Westport, may take the name of Stephen B. Cornell ; Emily Pullen, Andrew R. Pullen, Bethany B. Pullen, David B. Pullen, and Eliza I. Pullen, of Mansfield, minors, may severally take the surname of Hyer, instead of Pullen ; Caroline Wilson Smith, of Taunton, may take the name of Caroline Wilson Farnham ; Josiah Gardner Johnson, a minor, and an adopted son of William Samuel Cobb, of New Bedford, may take the name of William Samuel Cobb ; Hannah Elizabeth Freeman, of New Bedford, may take the name of Eliza F. Tallman ; all of the county of Bristol. Joseph Thomas Sylvester, of Hanover, may take the name of William Thomas Sylvester ; James Horace Hammond, a minor, of Rochester, may take the name of John Wilks Hammond ; Charles Fayette Loomis, of North Bridgewater, may take the name of La Fayette Charles Loomis ; Henry Packard, of North Bridgewater, may take the name of Henry Howe Packard ; George Leonard, 3d, of Middleborough, may take the name of George Savery Leonard ; James Lloyd Keith, of Plymouth, may take the name of Lloyd Keith ; James Otis, of Scituate, may take the name of James Ingham ; all of the county of Plymouth. Hannah S. Crocker, a minor, of Barnstable, may take the name of Persis S. Crocker ; Joseph Baker, of Dennis, may take the name of Joseph Kelly Baker ; Joseph Kelly, of Dennis, may take the name of Joseph Baker Kelly ; Henry Milton Gifford, a minor, of Falmouth, may take the name of Watson Hatch Gifford ; Lucy Freeman, of Provincetown, may take the name of Lucy Freeman Cook ; Davis Crowell Baker, of Yarmouth, a minor, may take the name of Elihu Davis Baker ; Mary Crowell, of Yarmouth, a minor, may take the name of Mary Parker Crowell ; Atwood Rich, a minor, of Truro, may take the name of Atwood Franklin Rich ; all of the county of Barnstable. And the several persons before mentioned, from and after the passing of this act, shall be known and called by the names which, by this act, they are respectively allowed to assume as aforesaid, and the same shall hereafter be considered as their only proper and legal names. [*March 25, 1845.*

An Act to change the Name of Daniel Hitchcock.
Be it enacted, etc., as follows:
SECT. 1. Daniel Hitchcock, second of that name, of the town of Warren, in the county of Worcester, may take the name of Daniel Townsley Hitchcock, and shall be hereafter known and called by that name, as his only proper and legal name, to all intents and purposes.
SECT. 2. This act shall take effect from and after its passage. [*March 23, 1846.*

An Act to change the Names of the Persons therein mentioned.
Be it enacted, etc., as follows:
Ruth Castles may take the name of Ruth Cobb; Henry Castles may take the name of Charles Henry Cobb; Thomas Coffin Amory may take the name of Thomas C. Amory; Sylvia Fellows Mudget may take the name of Sylvia Fellows Thomas; George B. Kehew may take the name of George B. Appleton; Nathaniel Baker may take the name of Henry Smith Baker; Albert Callender may take the name of Charles Albert Callender; William Sewall Murphy, minor son of widow Sarah L. Pool, may take the name of William Sewall; Samuel Hutchinson Parkhurst may take the name of Julius Thorn Parkhurst; George Vincer may take the name of Edwin Vincer Welch; Mary Whitten may take the name of Mary Wilbur; Caroline Maria Haynes, minor, may take the name of Caroline Maria Crane; Joseph Joost may take the name of Joseph Joost Hewes; William Gray may take the name of William Chandler Gray; Josiah Battes may take the name of Josiah Winslow Battes; Stephen Briant Stephenson may take the name of Briant Stephenson; Lewis Clark may take the name of George Lewis Clark; Dolly Miller may take the name of Eliza May Miller; Henry Foster may take the name of Henry Haven Foster; William Cowen Alexander Gault may take the name of William Gault; Maria Cloutman may take the name of Maria Brown; Eliza Daws Cloutman may take the name of Eliza Daws Brown; Joseph Henry Towne may take the name of Joseph Hardy Towne; Thomas Sawyer may take the name of Oliver Thomas Sawyer; John Bottum may take the name of John Botume, also, John Bottum, jun., minor son of John Bottum, may take the name of John Botume, jun., Elizabeth Hale Rowell may take the name of Elizabeth Hale, also, that her minor children, Elizabeth Christiana, Mena Douglas, Gertrude Corriana, and Howard Augustus, may severally take the surname of Hale; Caroline S. Thwing may take the name of Elizabeth Barnes Thwing; William Rice may take the name of William Adams Rice; Elizabeth Cushing may take the name of Elizabeth Lane Cushing; Abby Tryphenia Knox, adopted daughter of George A. Parish, may take the name of Abby Tryphenia Parish; Peter Pearce Hutchinson may take the name of Pearce Huchins; Almira Gilpatrick may take the name of Almira Gill; William Davenport Irish may take the name of William Davenport, also, his family, Deborah, Sarah Frances, William, George Edward, John Henry, Benjamin Franklin, may severally take the surname of Davenport; Jesse Ross Rhodes may take the name of Jesse Rhodes Mayo; severally of the city of Boston, all of the county of Suffolk.
James Hambleton Hill may take the name of Horace Lane Hill; Francis Ashton Monarch may take the name of Francis Monarch Ashton; Theodore Monarch may take the name of Theodore Ashton; Harriot Webb may take

the name of Harriot Northey Webb, severally of the city of Salem. George
Gordon Murphy may take the name of George Gordon Mosely; Lydia
Gordon Murphy may take the name of Lydia Amanda Mosely; Mary
Elizabeth Murphy, minor, may take the name of Mary Elizabeth Susannah
Mosely; George Francis Murphy, minor, may take the name of George
Francis Mosely; James Blackey may take the name of James Blackey
Dennison; Edward Newell Gilson may take the name of Edward Sylvanus
Newhall; Anna G. Shove, minor, may take the name of Anna S. Johnson;
Gilbert Boyce, jun., may take the name of Gilbert Russell Boyce; Elijah
Hedding Alley may take the name of Freeman Alley, severally of the town
of Lynn. William McConnell, of Georgetown, may take the name of Wil-
liam Corliss; Thomas L. Lucy may take the name of George Hudson;
Elizabeth P. Lucy, his wife, may take the name of Lucy Hudson; John
W. Lucy, Helen L. Lucy, Martha J. Lucy, and Charles T. Lucy, their
minor children, may take the surname of Hudson; Samuel Miller Somes
may take the name of Alvan Moroni Monteirth, severally of the town of
Bradford. Adeline Mears Brown, of Ipswich, may take the name of Abby
Ann Brown; Hipsabeth P. Wiggin, of the town of Danvers, may take the
name of Elizabeth P. Wiggin; William Pousland may take the name of
William Pousland Friend; Nancy Stephens Pousland may take the name
of Nancy Stephens Friend; William Stephens Pousland, minor, may take
the name of William Stephens Friend; James Hill Pousland, minor, may
take the name of James Hill Friend, severally of the town of Beverly.
Polly Smith, of Salisbury, may take the name of Mary Jane Smith; Charles
Morris Chace, of Newburyport, minor, may take the name of Edwin Bayley
Chace; Jonathan Andrew, of Salem, may take the name of John Andrew;
Benjamin Harris Saunders, of Rowley, a minor, may take the name of
Amos Joseph Saunders; Abigal Pike, a minor, daughter of True Pike, of
Salisbury, may take the name of Mary Abigal Pike; Jeremiah Farnham,
a minor, of Andover, may take the name of Charles Farnham, all of the
county of Essex.
    Augustus Fitzaubut Richards, of Natick, minor, may take the name of
George Fuller; John Franklin Nealy, of Wayland, may take the name of
Franklin Foster; Mary S. Nealy of Wayland, may take the name of Mary
Foster; John Ingalls Wiley, of South Reading, minor, may take the name
of Elmer Alonzo Willis; Henry McIntire, of Reading, may take the name
of Henry Clay; Elizabeth Jane Donahoe, of Lowell, minor, may take the
name of Lydia Anna Nealy; Leander Shelton, of Cambridge, may take the
name of Leander Lincoln; Mary C. Shelton, of Cambridge, may take the
name of Mary C. Lincoln; also, Sarah E. Shelton, John L. Shelton, Martha
J. Shelton, Henry C. Shelton, Mary E. R. Shelton, and Angeline C. Shelton,
may severally take the surname of Lincoln; Roxanna B. Davis, of Cambridge, may take the name of Ann B. Davis; James Western Babcock, of
Framingham, may take the name of James Austin Elliot; Caroline Lucinda
Beck, adopted daughter of James M. Beal, of Natick, may take the name
of Caroline Lucinda Beal; Oliver Rice, of Sudbury, may take the name of
Oliver Richard Rice; James Whiting, of Charlestown, may take the name
of James Henry Whiting; Comfort Harriet Corson, of Lowell, may take
the name of Hellen Marr Corson; Phillip Coverly, of Brighton, may take
the name of Edward Marshall Abbott; Frederick Buckingham, minor, of
Cambridge, may take the name of Frederick Alexander Buckingham;

George Washington Aiken, of Watertown, may take the name of Certus
Imus Aiken; George Fuller, of Newton, may take the name of Charles
Jeremiah Fuller; Eliza Jane Nickerson, minor, adopted daughter of Wil-
liam and Caroline M. Howe, of Lowell, may take the name of Eliza Auburn
Howe; Gamaliel Bradford, of Charlestown, may take the name of Alden
Howard Bradford; Mary Miller, of Holliston, minor, may take the name of
Mary Jones Miller; Julia Ann Caine, (the wife of Henry Caine, of Woburn,
who has taken the surname of Wendall,) may now take the surname of
Wendall; also, his daughter, Luella Bell Caine, may take the name of
Julia Ann Wendall; Mary Cornell, of Framingham, may take the name of
Mary Clara Hemenway; Charles Watkins, adopted son of William Wight,
of Holliston, may take the name of Charles Winthrop Wight; Adolphus C.
Sebalt of Lowell, may take the name of Charles Thompson; Lydia Rich-
ardson of Chelmsford, may take the name of Lydia Richardson Warren;
Anna S. Green, of Holliston, may take the name of Ann Smith; Theoph-
ilus Bigelow, of Holliston, may take the name of Richard Bigelow; George
L. Avery, of Malden, may take the name of James Conant Austin; Guy
Slade Burroughs, of Sudbury, may take the name of George Burroughs;
Dolly D. Brown, of Stoneham, may take the name of Mary Davis Brown;
John Aloysius Hanner, of Somerville, a minor, adopted son of George W.
Beck, may take the name of John Aloysius Beck; Daniel Forbes, of
Charlestown, may take the name of Daniel H. Forbes; Emily Amelia Win-
ship, a minor, daughter of Jonathan Winship, of Brighton, may take the
name of Amelia Meriam Winship; Levi Bartlett Thyng, of Lowell, may
take the name of Levi Bartlett Tyng; all of the county of Middlesex.

Eleazer Allen Battell, of the town of Worcester, may take the name of
Allen E. Battell; Lemuel Newton, of Hardwick, may take the name of
Stephen Eleazer Newton; Samuel Allen, of Grafton, may take the name of
Samuel Home Allen; John Wetherell, jun., of Oxford, may take the name
of John Wolcott Wetherell; Mahala Hoit, of Milford, may take the name
of Mahala Hoit Cook; Desire Goddard, wife of Elisha Goddard, of the
town of Princeton, may take the name of Sarah Desire Goddard; Amanda
Zurriah Stewart, of Upton, may take the name of Amanda Zurriah Webster;
Eliza Ann Pratt, of Worcester, may take the name of Eliza Ann Brewer;
David Sylvester Clark, of Royalston, minor, may take the name of David
Sylvester Brown; Harvey Allen, of Princeton, may take the name of Harvey Wilbur Allen; Persis Elizabeth Weld, of Charlton, may take the name
of Elizabeth Weld; Antoinette G. York, of Upton, may take the name of
Jane Maria Walker; Charles Smith Straw, of Worcester, may take the
name of Charles Smith Lee; John Waldo Lincoln, of Worcester, counsellor
at law, may take the name of Edward Winslow Lincoln; Algernon S.
Crawford, of Barre, may take the name of Algernon S. Butler; Julia
Sophronia Ruble, adopted daughter of Simon Hubbard, of Holden, may
take the name of Julia Caroline Hubbard; Joshua L. Knight, of Leicester,
may take the name of Charles S. Knight; all of the county of Worcester.

Henry Graves, of Northampton, may take the name of Henry Graves
Moore; Cyrus M. Bartlett, of Worthington, may take the name of Cyrus
M. Parsons; Sedate Manly Thayer, of Northampton, may take the name of
Manly Sedate Thayer; Edward McIntire, of Springfield, may take the
name of Edward West; Sarah Burnell, of Northampton, may take the name
of Sarah Burnell Breck; Medad Russell Wright, of Easthampton, may take

the name of Russell Medad Wright; John Smith, of Amherst, may take the name of Hervey John Smith; Lewis Joy of Amherst, may take the name of Lewis Everet Joy; all of the county of Hampshire.

Mary Taft, of Springfield, county of Hampden, adopted daughter of Edward M. Joy, may take the name of Lillian Almeria Joy; Elizabeth Antoinette Chase, adopted daughter of Henry R. Vaille, of Springfield, may take the name of Elizabeth Pitman Vaille; Alonzo Stearns, of Williamsburg, may take the name of Alonzo Lysander Stearns; all of the county of Hampden.

Oliver Death, of Wendell, may take the name of Oliver Davis; Sally Death, of Wendell, may take the name of Sally Davis; also their children, viz.: William S., Eliza, Oliver, Mary E., Benjamin, Royal Francis, Hannah Jane, Sarah Ann, Eliza Sophronia, may severally take the surname of Davis; John Sumner Mudge, of Northfield, may take the name of John Green Mudge; Sabra Willis Carlton, of Buckland, minor, may take the name of Sabra Maranca Carlton; William Dwight Monk, of Deerfield, may take the name of William Dwight; Candace M. Master, of Buckland, may take the name of Candace Carr Howard; Daniel Sweetland, of Bernardston, adopted son of Richard Montague, may take the name of Daniel Richard Montague; Wealthy Minerva Roxana Trask, of Leverett, may take the name of Wealthy Roxana Cowles; also her two minor children, Sarah Maria, and George Evens, may severally take the surname of Cowles; Leander Morton, of Whately, may take the name of Leander Lincoln Morton; all of the county of Franklin.

King Williams, of Stockbridge, to take the name of King Sacket Williams; Charity Johnson, of Becket, may take the name of Charity Whitemore; all of the county of Berkshire.

William Leland, of Roxbury, may take the name of William Sherman Leland; Edward Gill, of Quincy, may take the name of Edward Howard Gill; Lafayette Whitney, of Braintree, may take the name of Lewis Lafayette Whitney; Mary T. Fisher, of Franklin, may take the name of Mary Thurston; Harlows Whitney, jun., of Wrentham, may take the name of Gustavus H. Whitney; Augustine Joshua Bryant, of Milton, may take the name of Augustus Bryant; Ferdinand Clark, of Roxbury, may take the name of Ferdinand Nimrod Clark; Josephine Friedham Wright, adopted daughter of J. W. Parkhurst, of Dedham, may take the name of Mary Josephine Parkhurst; Margaret Howe Brown, of Dorchester, may take the name of Margaret Howe; all of the county of Norfolk.

John Wilson, of Fall River, may take the name of John Yates Wilson; Jonathan Soule, of Westport, may take the name of Jonathan P. Soule; Orin Bassett, of Taunton, may take the name of Orin Larnard Bassett; Sarah Brown, of Norton, minor, may take the name of Sarah Hunt; William Armstrong Dobson, of Taunton, may take the name of William Armstrong; Eliphalet Robbins, 2d, of New Bedford, minor, may take the name of Eliphalet Howe Robbins; Mary Maccomber, of Westport, may take the name of Mary G. Macomber; Richard F. Marchant, of New Bedford, may take the name of Richard F. Merchent; Oliver Perry Coggshall, of Pawtucket, a minor and adopted son of David R. Sprague, may take the name of Oliver Coggshall Sprague; all of the county of Bristol.

Nathan Chandler McLauthlen, of Kingston, may take the name of Nathan Chandler; Elijah Lamb, of Abington, may take the name of Elijah Gay

Morris ; Rosella Ford Hatch, of Marshfield, minor daughter of David P. Hatch, may take the name of Mary Dyke Ames Hatch ; Ellis P. Richards, of North Bridgewater, adopted child of Lyman Clark, may take the name of William Ellis Clark ; also, Sarah A. Richards, adopted child of Lyman Clark, may take the name of Caroline Augusta Clark ; Olive W. Faunce, of North Bridgewater, may take the name of Ellen Maria Faunce ; Ebenezer D. Trickey, of Chatham, may take the name of Ebenezer D. Trakez ; Patience Jane Trickey, his wife, may take the name of Patience Jane Trakez ; Hester Ann R. Trickey, a minor daughter, may take the name of Hester Ann R. Trakez ; Charles Henry Hall, of Marshfield, may take the name of Charles Henry Austin ; all of the county of Plymouth.

Ruthy Chase, wife of Lysander Chase, of Yarmouth, may take the name of Ruth Chase ; Jonathan Franch Whorf, of Provincetown, may take the name of Charles Francis Whorf ; Polly Bassett Fairfield, of Yarmouth, may take the name of Mary Bassett Fairfield ; Tabitha Atwood, of Brewster, may take the name of Abby Atwood ; Marshal Underwood, of Dennis, may take the name of Marshall Sears Underwood ; Mary Helan Wixson, of Dennis, minor, may take the name of Susan Helan Wixson ; Joseph Baker, a minor, of Dennis, may take the name of Joseph Kelley Baker ; all of the county of Barnstable.

Moses Starbuck, a minor son of widow Mary Ann Starbuck of Nantucket, may take the name of Albert Wilson Starbuck, county of Nantucket. And the several persons before named, from and after the passing of this act, shall be known and called by the names which, by this act, they are respectively allowed to assume as aforesaid, and the same shall hereafter be considered as their only proper and legal names. [*April 16, 1846.*

An Act to change the Names of the Persons therein mentioned.
Be it enacted, etc., as follows :

John C. McRoberts may take the name of John C. Roberts ; Henry Smith, minor, may take the name of Henry Farnam Smith ; Charles Bean Moulton may take the name of Charles Jeremiah Bean Moulton ; William Hunt may take the name of William Morris Hunt ; Alexander Wheeler may take the name of Alexander Balch Wheeler ; James Pedder may take the name of James Sumner ; Sarah Ann Pratt Perkins may take the name of Sarah Ann Pratt Cummings ; her minor daughter, Sarah Ann Porter Perkins, may take the name of Sarah Ann Pratt Cummings ; Forrester Pelby Anderson, minor, may take the name of Forrester Anderson Pelby ; Samuel French may take the name of Samuel Albert French ; William H. Call may take the name of William H. Mackintosh ; James Lewis, minor, son of Winslow Lewis, jun., may take the name of Winslow Lewis, 3d ; Diederick Elderman may take the name of Charles Batchelder ; John Williams may take the name of John Earl Williams ; Allen Bangs may take the name of Allen E. Bangs ; George Lawrence Corporal may take the name of George Corporal Lawrence ; his wife, Martha Corporal, may take the name of Martha Lawrence ; and their three minor children, to wit, George Lawrence Corporal, Joshua Thorp Corporal, and Martha Amelia Corporal, may severally take the names of George Corporal Lawrence, Joshua Thorp Lawrence, and Martha Amelia Lawrence ; Mary Eliza Stowell Hurley may take the name of Mary Eliza Leeds ; Sophronia Perry may take the name of Sophronia White ; Lucretia E. Beers may take the name of Lucretia E. Pierce ; and her two minor sons, George Henry Beers and Allen Augustus Beers, may take the names of George Henry Pierce and Allen Augustus Pierce ; Catharine Matilda Wheelock, minor, may take the name of Catharine Brattle Wheelock ; Christiana K. Richmond may take the name of Christiana K. Sargent ; Ebenezer Ball may take the name of Ebenezer Wallis Ball ; Hiram Parker may take the name of Hiram Munroe Parker ; Joseph Lee, minor, may take the name of Thomas Joseph Lee ; Davis Estis may take the name of David Estis ; Lucius Doolittle, jun., may take the name of Lucius Doolittle Ashley ; Samuel Gerrish Barrett, a minor, may take the name of Samuel Eddy Barrett ; Jonathan Wade may take the name of John Wade ; John Mulligan may take the name of John Warren Atkins ; Lyman Vose, minor, may take the name of Lyman Tucker Vose ; Charles Parker may take the name of Charles Maverick Parker ; Joseph Bunnell Coy may take the name of Joseph Coy Chickering ; George W. March may take the name of George W. Wilson ; Peter Shumway, jun., may take the name of Franklin P. Shumway ; Nathan Heard, jun., may take the name of Nathan Ferdinand Heard ; James Ryan may take the name of James Walker Ryan ; George W. Porter may take the name of George W. Eustis ; Patrick Fitzpatrick may take the name of William Fitz ; D. Warren Malony may take the name of Dexter Warren ; Nathan Kimball may take the name of Nathan Ralph Kimball ; Samuel Stratton may take the name of Joy Hamlet Stratton ; James Johnson, jun., may take the name of James Chauncey Johnson ; severally of the city of Boston, all of the county of Suffolk.

Lydia S. Cook, of Salem, may take the name of Anna Emerson ; Ann Augusta Sumner Lewis, minor, of Lynn, may take the name of Ann Augusta Sumner Marsh ; Mary P. Gould, of Danvers, may take the name of Mary P. Cheever ; Julia Valentine Ames, minor, of Salem, may take the name of Julia Barnard ; William K. Hobson, of Rowley, may take the name of William Kimball ; his wife, Drusilla H. Hobson, may take the name of Drusilla H. Kimball ; Morgiana Scott, minor, of Lynn, may take the name of Anna Scott Johnson ; Enos True Curtis, of Bradford, may take the name of Edwin Taylor Curtis ; Moses B. Somes, of Bradford, may take the name of Charles B. Somes ; Thomas Frothingham Hopping, of Salem, may take the name of Thomas Hopping Frothingham ; James S. Kimball, jun., of Salem, may take the name of James Walter Kimball ; Martha Henderson, minor, of Danvers, may take the name of Mary R. Henderson ; Samuel Franklin Tarbox, of Lynn, may take the name of Samuel Franklin Appleton ; Benjamin Washington Tarbox, of Lynn, may take the name of Benjamin Washington Appleton ; his wife, Sarah Adeline, together with their two minor children, Ellen Augusta, and Frances Washington, may severally take the names of Sarah Adeline Appleton, Ellen Augusta Appleton, and Frances Washington Appleton ; Henry O. Neill, of Lynn, may take the name of Henry Neill ; his wife, Priscilla Cloutman, together with their three minor children, Helen Amanda, William Henry, and Charles Frederick, may severally take the names of Priscilla Cloutman Neill, Helen Amanda Neill, William Henry Neill, and Charles Frederick Neill ; Niles Richardson Hardy, minor, of Bradford, may take the name of Niles Gardner Parker ; Darius Johnson, of Haverhill, may take the name of Darius W. Johnson ; Mehitable Stickney Peabody, a minor, of Boxford,

may take the name of Mary Stickney Peabody ; Samuel Tucker, of Salem,
may take the name of Samuel Dudley Tucker ; Eliza Foster Haskell, of
Beverly, a minor, may take the name of Eliza Foster Lefavour ; Joseph
Swasey, of Salem, may take the name of Charles Warren Swasey ; Deborah
Elizabeth Wiggin Killam, wife of William E. Killam, of Boxford, may take
the name of Elizabeth Wiggin Killam ; all of the county of Essex.

Martha Ann Page, of Lunenburg, may take the name of Martha Ann
Robinson ; her minor son, Henry Morton Page, may take the name of
Henry Morton Robinson ; Austin Hoar, of West Boylston, may take the
name of Austin Wilbur Sidney ; his wife, Esther Whitaker Hoar, may take
the name of Esther Whitaker Sidney ; Emma E. Gould, a minor, of Lancaster, may take the name of Emily E. Pratt ; John Young, of Shrewsbury,
may take the name of John Williams Young ; Edwin Bigelow, of Lancaster,
may take the name of Edwin Samuel Bigelow ; Marcellus Emerson, minor,
adopted by Warren Fay, of Southborough, may take the name of Marcellus
Emerson Fay ; Harriot D. Pidge, minor, adopted by Samuel and Nancy F.
Rich, of West Sutton, may take the name of Harriot P. Rich ; Albert
Henry Richardson, minor, of Brookfield, may take the name of Albert
Henry Bartlett ; Pliny Litchfield, minor, may take the name of Pliny
Thurston Litchfield, of Southbridge ; Isaac Cuttar Snow, of Leicester, may
take the name of William Cuttar Snow ; Leonard Mowry, of Douglas, may
take the name of Daniel Mowry ; Esther Ann Bancroft, minor, of Auburn,
may take the name of Anna Eudora Esther Bancroft ; Charles Dwight
Eager, of Northborough, may take the name of Charles Henry Eager ;
Mary Ellen Sawyer, minor, of Fitchburg, may take the name of Mary Ellen
Peirce ; Jacob Addison Bemis, of Southborough, may take the name of
Addison Jacob Bemis ; Morris Taft Judd, of Upton, minor, may take the
name of Lysander Morris Perham ; Samuel Preston, of Worcester, may
take the name of Samuel Hildrith Preston ; Charles Walker, of Westborough, may take the name of Charles Wellington Walker ; Ezra Staples,
of Uxbridge, may take the name of Ezra Freeman Staples ; Anne Devillers
Lincoln, minor daughter of Nancy H. Lincoln, of Worcester, may take the
name of Georgiana Devillers Lincoln ; Mary Sigourney Towne Miller, of
Worcester, may take the name of Mary Sigourney Towne ; all of the county
of Worcester.

John Smith, of Hadley, minor, may take the name of John Porter Smith ;
Carlo Howe, of Granby, may take the name of Carlos Howe ; Sarah Cleaveland, minor, of Williamsburg, may take the name of Sarah Luann Cleaveland ; Charles Ferry, of Granby, may take the name of Charles Sherman
Ferry ; Melancton Hamilton Hyde, of Ware, may take the name of Hamilton Hyde ; Alvan A. Garside, of South Hadley, may take the name of
Alvan White Alvord ; Laura Bacon, a minor, of Ware, may take the name
of Amelia Salome Eddy ; Diantha C. Lee, a minor, of Northampton, may
take the name of Cornelia Frances Lee ; all of the county of Hampshire.

Reuben Amasa Doolittle Palmer, of West Springfield, may take the name
of Amasa Reuben Palmer ; Joseph Brown, of Springfield, may take the
name of Joseph Charles Brown ; Matthew Willard, of Wilbraham, may take
the name of Charles M. Willard ; Dolly Miller, of Springfield, may take the
name of Eliza May Miller ; Levi Tower, of Springfield, may take the name
of Levi Howard Tower ; all of the county of Hampden.

Rachel Jane Wheelock, of Shutesbury, may take the name of Rachel

Jane Spear; Lucinda Hodgkins, of Montague, may take the name of
Lucinda Pike; David Boynton Gage, of Wendell, may take the name of
David Boynton Harris; Albert Shaw, of New Salem, may take the name
of Albert Edward Shaw; Martha M. Buel, minor, of Leverett, may take
the name of Martha M. Woodward; all of the county of Franklin.

James Wheeler Hayden, of Boxborough, may take the name of James
Rule Hayden; Joseph Pulsifer, of Charlestown, may take the name of
Edgar Pulsifer; Sarah Bruce, of Marlborough, may take the name of Sarah
Elizabeth Bruce; Jonathan Brooks Nichols, of South Reading, may take
the name of John Brooks Nichols; Johnson Green, of South Reading, may
take the name of Robert Green; William Penn Thompson, of Woburn, may
take the name of George Thompson; Obadiah Richardson Varnum, of
Lowell, may take the name of George Noel Varnum; John Doyle, of Bil-
lerica, may take the name of John George Oliver; Mary Annette Huntoon,
minor, of Lowell, may take the name of Mary Annette Johnson; William
Underwood, of Billerica, may take the name of William Henry Crosby;
Phebe Atkinson, minor, of Lowell, may take the name of Henrietta Phebe
Atkinson; Mary Grace Hunkins, of Lowell, minor, may take the name of
Sarah Jane Farmer; Ithamar Winship, of Lowell, may take the name of
Charles Henry Winship; Abram S. McLaughlin, of Framingham, may
take the name of Abram S. Mack; his wife, Dilly Ann, together with their
two children, James C., and Hester Ann J., may severally take the names
of Dilly Ann Mack, James C. Mack, and Hester Ann J. Mack; Henry
Davis, of Charlestown, may take the name of Henry Turner Davis; Howard
Whitney, of Waltham, may take the name of Warren Howard; Horace
Bacon, of West Cambridge, may take the name of Horace Clinton Bacon;
William Henry Smith, of Lowell, may take the name of William Henry
Leland Smith; Sarah Margaret Newhall, minor, of Reading, may take the
name of Sarah Margaret Weston; Osiander Carter, of Wilmington, may
take the name of Osgood Allen Carter; Philo Fisher Sanford, a minor, of
Lowell, may take the name of Lewis Philo Sanford; Cyrus Houghton
Heywood, of Lowell, may take the name of Charles Houghton Heywood;
all of the county of Middlesex.

Joseph Crosier Gallub, of Adams, may take the name of Joseph Crosier
Marsdale; his wife, Laura Jane, and their four minor children, Edwin
Ruthven, Althine Idalia, Francelia Blandina, and Gerald Embert, may
severally take the names of Laura Jane Marsdale, Edwin Ruthven Marsdale,
Althine Idalia Marsdale, Francelia Blandina Marsdale, and Gerald Embert
Marsdale; Henry Bliss, of Adams, may take the name of Henry Clay
Bliss; James Willow Cotton, a minor, of Hancock, may take the name of
James Porter White; all of the county of Berkshire.

Harlows Whiting, jun., of Wrentham, may take the name of Gustavus
H. Whiting; Susan Maria Carney, of Quincy, minor, may take the name
of Susan Maria Richardson; Peter Cushing, of Weymouth, may take the
name of William Pomroy Cushing; Elizabeth Baxter, minor, of Quincy,
may take the name of Elizabeth Lydia Baxter; Roby Lydston, of Roxbury,
may take the name of Alfred Henry Lydston; all of the county of Norfolk.

John Palmer Perry, 2d, of Dighton, may take the name of George Byron
Perry; Hamblin Tillson, jun., of New Bedford, may take the name of
Henry Hamblin Tillson; Frederick Briggs, jun., of Dighton, may take the
name of Frederic Caro Briggs; Joseph A. Allen, a minor, of Attleborough,

may take the name of Eugene Hervey Richards ; all of the county of Bristol.

Francis Berthier, minor, of Rochester, may take the name of Francis Berthier Pitcher ; of the county of Plymouth.

Ebenezer Davis, jun., of Truro, minor, may take the name of Ebenezer Lester Davis ; Caroline Howes, of Dennis, a minor, may take the name of Eunice Bartlett Howes ; Thankful Winslow Nealus, minor, of Dennis, may take the name of Mary Ellen Nealus ; Mary Ellen Bassett, minor, of Yarmouth, may take the name of Mary Marie Bassett ; William Managan, minor, of Truro, may take the name of William Henry Harrison ; William James Donahoe, a minor, of Truro, may take the name of William James Davis ; all of the county of Barnstable.

John Minot West, a minor, of Nantucket, may take the name of Paul West ; of the county of Nantucket.

And the several persons before named, from and after the passing of this act, shall be known and called by the names which, by this act, they are respectively allowed to assume, as aforesaid, and the same shall hereafter be considered as their only proper and legal names. [*April 26, 1847.*

An Act to repeal a portion of " An Act to change the Names of the Persons therein mentioned," passed in the year one thousand eight hundred and forty-seven.

Be it enacted, etc., as follows:

So much of the act, entitled " an act to change the names of the persons therein mentioned," passed on the twenty-sixth day of April, in the year one thousand eight hundred and forty-seven, as provides that Joseph Bunnell Coy may take the name of Joseph Coy Chickering, and shall be known and called thereby, and that the same shall be considered as his only proper and legal name, is hereby repealed. [*May 3, 1848.*

An Act to change the Names of the Persons therein mentioned.

Be it enacted, etc., as follows:

Winthrop Sears may take the name of Knyvet Winthrop Sears ; James Foster may take the name of James Rolf Foster ; Isaac Bradford, a minor, may take the name of Isaac Buckminster Bradford ; William Brookings, a minor, may take the name of William Adams ; Francis Joseph Nursptill may take the name of Francis Joseph Nourse ; his wife, Mary Elizabeth, and their minor children, Mary Elizabeth, Francis Joseph, Sophrona and Jacob Gilmore, may severally take the surname of Nourse ; Jacob Nursptill may take the name of Jacob Nourse ; Caroline, his wife, and George Henry, their minor son, may each take the surname of Nourse ; Charles Miller Reed may take the name of Gardner Kinsell Reed ; Mehitable Eastman may take the name of Maria Mehitable Eastman ; Roswell Dunnakin may take the name of Roswell Brooks ; Roswell Munroe and Frederic Justus, his minor sons, may each take the surname of Brooks ; Joseph Warren Appleton may take the name of William Appleton ; Isaac De St. Croix Woodbury may take the name of Isaac De Woodbury ; George Washington Jenks Furness, may take the name of George Jenks Furness ; George Henry Snelling may take the name of George Lester Snelling ;

Jonathan Robbins may take the name of John Robbins; David G. McMurphy may take the name of David G. Merrill; Isaac Stevens Parker may take the name of W. Stevens Parker; Charles Rice Sherman, a minor, may take the name of Charles Bowler Sherman; Christopher List may take the name of Charles List; severally of the city of Boston, all of the county of Suffolk.

Caroline Elizabeth Chaplin, of Rowley, a minor, may take the name of Caroline Louisa Chaplin; Michael Hoyt Morse, of Newburyport, a minor, may take the name of Edward Hoyt Morse; George Kimball, of Bradford, may take the name of George M. Kimball; Charles Kimball, a minor, of Bradford, may take the name of Charles B. Kimball; Jeremiah Staniford Harris, of Salem, may take the name of George Harris; Jonathan Cass Whippen, of Lynn, may take the name of Henry Cass Whippen; Samuel Dickinson Bartlett, of Newburyport, may take the name of Samuel Waldo Bartlett; Enoch Thurlow Bartlett, of Newburyport, may take the name of Henry Thurlow Bartlett; Horace Bailey Balch, of Bradford, may take the name of Horace Morse Balch; Charles Scott, of Hamilton, minor, may take the name of Charles Aaron Dodge; Albert Pitman Allen, of Manchester, may take the name of John Woodberry Allen; Sarah Ellen Varnum, of Lynn, minor, may take the name of Sarah Ellen Alley; Ira D. Ricker, of Beverly, may take the name of Ira Davis; Elias Endicott Putnam, of Danvers, may take the name of Elias Putnam; George Honeycomb, of Salem, may take the name of George Henry Peirson; Sampson Cummings, of Lynn, may take the name of Thomas Clarkson Cummings; Betsey Potter Allen, a minor, of Lynn, may take the name of Helena Potter Allen; Joseph Waters, of Salem, may take the name of Joseph Linton Waters; George Moody, of Rowley, may take the name of Latimer George Moody; Perley Goodale King, of Danvers, may take the name of Perley King; John Pearson, 3d, of Newburyport, may take the name of John Perley Pearson; John W. Rogers, of Newbury, may take the name of John Roger Williams; Andrew W. Abbott, of Salem, may take the name of Andrew Abbott Ward; all of the county of Essex.

Angelina Elizabeth Chapman, of Lowell, may take the name of Dianna Elizabeth Phelps; William Coffern Gilman Nutting, of Dracut, may take the name of Coffern Nutting; Thomas Baldwin Brown, of South Reading, may take the name of Thomas Baldwin Burnap Brown; America Perkins Bonney, of Lowell, may take the name of Arthur Perkins Bonney; Calvin Nichols, of Reading, may take the name of John Calvin Nichols; William Edes, of Natick, a minor, may take the name of William Francis Newhall; William Henry Trigger and John Trigger, of Newton, may each take the surname of Phillips instead of Trigger; William Thurston Powers, of Reading, may take the name of William Thurston; Stephen Brooks Hoar and Timothy Hoar, of Brighton, may each take the surname of Brooks instead of Hoar; Rice Kendall, of Sherburne, may take the name of Charles Rice Kendall; Susan E. Amidown, a minor, of Lowell, may take the name of Susan E. Walker; Hannah S. Converse, of Woburn, minor, may take the name of Hannah S. Thompson; Alvan Phillis, of Concord, may take the name of Alvan Phillis Parker; Mary Maria Felton, of Stow, may take the name of Mary Maria Withington; Herod Collins, of Charlestown, may take the name of Edwin Collins; Samuel Leighton, of Newton, may take the name of Samuel Stillman Leighton; Mary Underwood, of Chelmsford, may take the name of Mary Farr; Rhoda Fullerton, of Lowell, may take the name of Frances Fullerton; Roger Vose, of Lowell, may take the name of Roger Vance; Benjamin Rice Davison, of Lexington, may take the name of William Henry Davison; Lucinda Frost of Natick, may take the name of Clara Howard; all of the county of Middlesex.

George Lyman Chilson, of Leicester, may take the name of George Dexter Chilson; Daniel Mowry, of Douglas, may take the name of David Mowry; Foster Death of Rutland, and his wife, Hepsibeth Death, and their minor children, Charles and Henry, may each take the surname of Dana instead of Death; Elizabeth D. Shackford, of Shrewsbury, may take the name of Elizabeth Davis; and her minor children, John J. Sylvester and George L., may severally take the surname of Davis instead of Shackford; Joseph Hoar may take the name of Joseph H. Heywood; Samuel R. Hoar may take the name of Samuel R. Heywood; Dorcas K. Hoar may take the name of Dorcas K. Heywood; Dwight Hoar may take the name of Dwight H. Heywood; Mary R. Hoar may take the name of Mary R. Heywood; Ezra H. Hoar may take the name of Ezra H. Heywood; Fidelia M. Hoar may take the name of Fidelia M. Heywood; Lyman B. Hoar may take the name of Lyman B. Heywood; Alonzo P. Hoar may take the name of Alonzo P. Heywood; all of Princeton. Isaac Merrill Wheeler, of Rutland, may take the name of Merrill Wheeler; John Allyn Weston, of Worcester, may take the name of Allyn Weston; Vina Newton, of Worcester, may take the name of Levinia Pierce Robbins; Jared Curtis Delany, of Southbridge, a minor, may take the name of Jared Curtis Healy; Henry Adin Stone, of Shrewsbury, may take the name of Isaac Hubbard Stone; Levi Carruth, of Templeton, may take the name of Levi W. Carruth; Paschal Peola Deming Weld, of Charlton, may take the name of Vernon Weld; Joseph Knowlton Mann, of Petersham, a minor, may take the name of Joseph Mann Jackson; William Everett Dalrymple, a minor, of Northborough, may take the name of William Everett Warren; Franklin Bradford Metcalf, of Leicester, may take the name of Franklin Bradford King; Mary Davis Goodspeed, of Hubbardston, a minor, may take the name of Mary Alma Goodspeed; Abraham Vest, of Grafton, may take the name of John Negus Wilson; Sally Vest, wife of the said Abraham Vest, and Walter Vest, and Mary Elizabeth Vest, their minor children, may take the surname of Wilson, instead of Vest; Willard Sherman, of North Brookfield, may take the name of Harrison Willard Sherman; Ephraim Warren Fuller, of Worcester, may take the name of Warren Fuller; Michael Herne, and John Herne, of Lancaster, may each take the surname of Kelley, instead of Herne; all of the county of Worcester.

Reuben Pierce, of Northampton, may take the name of Henry Reuben Pierce; Charles Judd Bridgman, of Northampton, a minor, may take the name of Charles Judson Bridgman; all of the county of Hampshire.

Reuben Benjamin Crosier, of Heath, a minor, may take the name of Lemuel Sanford Churchill; Eliza H. Ball, of Northfield, may take the name of Eliza H. Wright; William D. Watton, of Gill, may take the name of William Burrows; Martha Brown, of Whately, a minor, may take the name of Martha Cummings Brown; Frederick Mason Richards Brown, a minor. of Whately, may take the name of Frederick Richards Brown; Warren Marsh, of Montague, may take the name of Warren Bryant Marsh; Henry Dickinson, of Deerfield, may take the name of Henry Whipple Dickinson;

Katharine A. Crafts, of Whately, may take the name of Caroline A. Crafts; Remembrance Smith, of Whately, may take the name of Justin Remembrance Smith; Preserved Smith Guellow, of Greenfield, may take the name of Albert Preserved Wright; Araunah Ide, of Shelburne, may take the name of John A. Ide; Martin Severance, of Shelburne, may take the name of Martin Juan Severance; all of the county of Franklin.

Charity Whittemore, of Becket, may take the name of Charity Whittemore Johnson; John Abbott, 2d, of Hinsdale, may take the name of John Hubbard Abbott; Thalia Maria Abbott, of Hinsdale, may take the name of Mary Maria Abbott; Stephen McCrea, of Williamstown, a minor, may take the name of Stephen Southworth; Julia Andrews, of New Marlborough, may take the name of Julia Bullard; all of the county of Berkshire.

Harriet Jane Morey, of Bellingham, a minor, may take the name of Harriet Jane Cook; Julia Ann Potter, of Franklin, a minor, may take the name of Ann Olivia Potter Whiting; Ellen Augusta Bragg, of Medfield, a minor, may take the name of Ellen Augusta Fales; Hubert Gaumond, of Canton, may take the name of Hubert G. Woodbury; Greenleaf Sanger, of Dover, may take the name of Simon Greenleaf Sanger; all of the county of Norfolk.

William Lemma, of North Bridgewater, may take the name of William Lemmar; Sarah Elisabeth Ames, of Marshfield, a minor, may take the name of Sarah Dering Thomas Ames; Françoise Berthier, of Rochester, a minor, may take the name of Frances Berthier Pitcher; Sherman Allen Sturtevant, of Plymouth, may take the name of Sherman Allen; John Quincy Adams Faunce, of Kingston, may take the name of Quincy Adams Faunce; Nathaniel Faunce, jun., of Kingston, may take the name of Nathaniel Arthur Faunce; Sarah Kinney, of Rochester, may take the name of Sarah Dunham; all of the county of Plymouth.

Noah Erastus Fillebrown, of Easton, may take the name of Erastus Brown; Eliza Adeline Fillebrown, of Easton, may take the name of Eliza Adeline Brown; Margaret Myer, of New Bedford, a minor, may take the name of Margaret Myer Wood; Martha A. Holmes, of Mansfield, a minor, may take the name of Martha A. Gordon; Laban Mitchel Wheaton Wild, of Norton, a minor, may take the name of Laban Mitchel Wheaton; all of the county of Bristol.

Charles Bray, of Yarmouth, a minor, may take the name of Charles Matthews Bray; Joseph Baker, of Harwich, may take the name of Joseph Otis Baker; Lydia Matthews Bassett, of Yarmouth, may take the name of Lydia Matthews Sherman; Frederick U. Small, a minor, may take the name of James Henry Small; Benjamin F. Small, a minor, may take the name of Joshua D. P. Small, both of Provincetown; Bethiah Crowell Matthews, of Yarmouth, may take the name of Fanny Bethiah Matthews; Eunice Hallett Matthews, of Yarmouth, a minor, may take the name of Rebekah Hallett Matthews; all of the county of Barnstable. And the several persons before named, from and after the passing of this act, shall be known and called by the names which by this act they are respectively allowed to assume as aforesaid, and the same shall hereafter be considered as their own proper and legal names. [*May 10, 1848.*

An Act to change the Name of Nathaniel Merril Leathers.
Be it enacted, etc., as follows:
From and after the passing of this act, Nathaniel Merril Leathers, of
Danvers, in the county of Essex, may take the name of Nathaniel Merril
Warren, and he shall thereafter be known and called by that name, and the
same shall thereafter be considered as his only legal and proper name.
[*March 24, 1849.*

An Act to change the Names of the Persons therein mentioned.
Be it enacted, etc., as follows:
Thomas Vaughan Baron may take the name of Thomas Barry; Lydia
Bradford Orcutt may take the name of Lydia Bradford; George Colburn, a
minor, may take the name of George Colburn Cabot; John Cutts Smith
may take the name of John Smith Cutts; Charles Gillpatrick may take the
name of Charles Gill; Catharine Coolidge Gates may take the name of
Catharine Gates Thaxter; James Morss Williams may take the name of
James Morss William Williams; Virginia Albina Williams, a minor, may
take the name of Virginia Albina Fullick; Charles Rollins Torrey, a
minor, may take the name of Rollins Torrey; Jeremiah Buxton Favor may
take the name of Frank Favor; Elijah Baldwin may take the name of Eli-
jah Shirman Baldwin; George Hastings may take the name of George
Russel Hastings; George Hoogs may take the name of George H. Fran-
cis; his minor son, George A. Hoogs, may take the name of George
A. H. Francis; Alfred White Chamberlain may take the name of Alfred
White Sprague; William McNaught may take the name of William
Henry Thomas; Naomi Porter Shaw, a minor, may take the name of
Naomi Porter Mace; Arabella N. Livingston may take the name of
Imogene De Errence, and her minor son, Alfred Maitland Livingston, may
take the name of Ivan Marion De Errence; Michael Collins may take the
name of Michael Henry Collins; Thomas M. Center, George F. Center,
and Emma L. Center, minors, may assume the surname of Dickinson;
William Gordon may take the name of William George Gordon; Mary
Rhoades Josselyn may take the name of Mary Rhoades Darling; all of
the county of Suffolk.
Nathaniel Conant, 2d, of Danvers, may take the name of Nathaniel P.
Conant; Elizabeth E. Swan, a minor, of Newburyport, may take the name
of Elizabeth Esther Page; Ayer Spofford, of Bradford, may take the name
of Mary Ayer Spofford; Abby Faltch, of Salisbury, may take the name of
Abby Phenietta Dennitt; Richard Wilson, of Newbury, may take the name
of Richard Burritt Wilson; Marcus Marcellus Danforth, of Bradford, may
take the name of George Edwin Danforth; Joseph Warren Smith of Brad-
ford, may take the name of Austin F. Smith; Gorham Parsons, 3d, of
Gloucester, may take the name of Gorham M. Parsons; John Ober, of
Beverly, may take the name of John Thissell Ober: Matilda Wardwell, of
Andover, minor, may take the name of Eliza Dodge Wardwell; Mary
Elizabeth Boody, of Danvers, may take the name of Mary E. B. Gillion;
Emeline Eliza Hill, of Danvers, may take the name of Emily Eliza Hill;
James McBride, of Lawrence, may take the name of James Brooks; John
Albree Downie, of Salem, a minor, may take name of John Albree;
Harriet Nowell, of Salem, may take the name of Harriet Nowell Howard;
James Mooney, of Lynn, may take the name of James Forrest; Benjamin

Franklin Newhall, jun., of Saugus, may take the name of Benjamin
Newhall; Lydia Eveline Wyman, of Danvers, may take the name of Lydia
Eveline Peirce; Henry Phillips, of Salem, may take the name of Edward
B. Phillips; Ruby Mellen Moore, of Salem, minor, may take the name of
Abby Moore Kimball; Edwin Moody Burbank, of Bradford, may take the
name of George Byron Sanford; Charles Dearborn Nowell, of Salem, may
take the name of Charles Dearborn Howard; Gideon Barstow Monarch, of
Salem, may take the name of Gideon B. Moore; his minor children,
Charles James Monarch, may take the name of Charles James Moore;
Gideon B. Moore Monarch may take the name of Gideon B. Moore;
Frederick Moore Monarch may take the name of Frederick Moore; and
John Moore Monarch may take the name of John Moore; John Abbott
Johnson, of Danvers, may take the name of Abbott Johnson; Timothy
Ross, of Ipswich, may take the name of Timothy Burnham Ross; all of the
county of Essex.

Charles Pratt Houghton, of Cambridge, minor, may take the name of
Charles Houghton Pratt; Charles McElroy, of Charlestown, may take the
name of Charles Leroy; Samuel William Wyman, of Medford, may take
the name of Frank Peirce; Ann Elizabeth Perley, of Lowell, minor, may
take the name of Ann Elizabeth Wright; Abraham Rand Thompson, of
Charlestown, minor, may take the name of Abraham Warren Thompson;
William Parsons, of Charlestown, may take the name of William Alfred
Parsons; Frances Ann Huggins, of Dracut, minor, may take the name of
Frances Ann Stearns; Lucinda Frost, of Natick, minor, may take the
name of Isadore Edwards; Walter Hayes, of Tyngsborough, minor, may
take the name of Walter Hayes Farwell; William Brown Chase, of Marl-
borough, may take the name of William Chase; Frances Wright Faulkner
Jones, of Acton, may take the name of Frances Jones; Silas Proctor
Pingrey, of Marlborough, may take the name of Proctor Pingrey; William
Higgins, of Charlestown, may take the name of William Franklin Higgins;
John Beasley, of Cambridge, may take the name of Peter Manning; Henry
Ward Hitchcock, of Charlestown, a minor, may take the name of Henry
Ward Johns; all of the county of Middlesex.

Joseph Badger, of Leominster, may take the name of Joseph Badger
Brown; Samuel F. Hill, of Sturbridge, may take the name of Samuel
Fairbanks; his wife Mary Ann Hill, may take the name of Mary Ann
Fairbanks; and their minor children, viz.: Elizabeth, Loring H., and John
A., may severally take the surname of Fairbanks; Victoria Keith, of
Shrewsbury, minor, may take the name of Jane Maria Allen; Sarah Ann
Hair, of Hubbardston, minor, may take the name of Sarah Ann Lucy
Hunting; John Laughna, of Hubbardston, minor, may take the name of
Charles Lawrence Laughna; Nancy Hunstable Hosmer, of Worcester, may
take the name of Anna Hunstable Hosmer; Marion Eneri Allen, of
Shrewsbury, minor, may take the name of Marion Irene Hemenway
Allen; George F. Hoar, of Worcester, may take the name of George F.
Baker; Ziba Bass Cary Dunham, of Leominster, may take the name of
Howard Cary Dunham; Edward N. Divoll, of North Brookfield, may take
the name of Edward Newell; Solomon B. J. Howe, of New Braintree, may
take the name of Bolivar J. Howe; Lydia Lucebia Bartlett, of Berlin,
minor, may take the name of Selucia Ann Bartlett; Milton Morse, of

Worcester, may take the name of Milton M. Morse; all of the county of Worcester.

Wealthy Healy, of Worthington, may take the name of Wealthy Deborah Howard; Mary Ann Moody Ferry, of Belchertown, minor, may take the name of Mary Ann Ferry; Henry White, of South Hadley, may take the name of Henry Kirk White; Polly Garside, of South Hadley, may take the name of Mary Alvord; Merrick Orson Graves, of Williamsburg, minor, may take the name of Orson Merrick Graves; Ella Warner Smith, of Enfield, minor, may take the name of Ella Frances Gross; Emily Evelina Bement, of Easthampton, minor, may take the name of Emily Bement Smith; Harriet Clark Hawks, of Easthampton, minor, may take the name of Eliza Hawks Smith; Ellen M. H. Paine, of Greenwich, minor, may take the name of Ellen M. H. Johnson; all of the county of Hampshire.

Chander Brown, of Ashfield, minor, may take the name of Chander Eugene Smith; Ellen Streeter, of Montague, a minor, may take the name of Ellen Elvira Horton; Ellen Eliza Leonard, of Conway, minor, may take the name of Ellen Leonard Childs; Anna Eloisa Field, of Northfield, minor, may take the name of Anna Eloisa Mary Field; all of the county of Franklin.

George Sidebottom, of Adams, may take the name of George Nottingham; and his wife, Sarah Sidebottom, may take the name of Sarah Nottingham; George William Sidebottom, of Adams, may take the name of George William Nottingham; and his wife, Sarah Walbridge, and his minor son, may severally take the surname of Nottingham; John Race, of Great Barrington, may take the name of John Franklin Race; all of the county of Berkshire.

Daniel Houghton Goodspeed, of West Springfield, may take the name of Daniel Houghton; Julia Ann Harger, of West Springfield, may take the name of Julia Ann Moore; all of the county of Hampden.

Phillip Pear, of Roxbury, may take the name of Phillip Montague Pier; Eliza Charles Davis Parker, of Dedham, may take the name of Eliza Davis Parker; Israel Putnam Richardson, of Medway, minor, may take the name of Putnam Richardson Clark; John Bullough, jun., of Needham, may take the name of John Ballou; and his wife Sarah, and their minor children, John Warren, Sarah Eliza, William Henry, and Joseph Willard Bullough, may severally take the surname of Ballou; all of the county of Norfolk.

Eliot Benjamin Sheffield, of Rochester, minor, may take the name of Stafford Benjamin Brownell; Daniel Howard, 2d, of North Bridgewater, may take the name of Daniel S. Howard; Joshua Crooker, 3d, of North Bridgewater, may take the name of Allen Jay Crooker; Martha Proctor Ball, of Hingham, minor, may take the name of Martha Ball Corthell; Charles Seaver Burt, of West Bridgewater, may take the name of Charles Seaver; and his wife, Celinda Taylor Burt, may take the name of Celinda Taylor Seaver; and their minor son, Charles, may take the surname of Seaver; Charles Henry Lovett, of Hingham, minor, may take the name of Charles Augustine Lovett; all of the county of Plymouth.

Alfred Heyer, of New Bedford, minor, may take the name of Alfred H. Perry; Almira Frances Reed, of New Bedford, may take the name of Almira Frances White; Arthur Donley, of Berkley, may take the name of George Burt; Peter Stewart, his wife, Anna C., and their children,

Caroline Amelia, Catharine Gibbs, and Henry Ridgway, of Attleborough, may severally take the surname of Bishop ; all of the county of Bristol.

Michael Angelo Nuzze, of Provincetown, may take the name of William Gale ; Elizabeth Taylor, of Yarmouth, may take the name of Elizabeth Joice Taylor ; Vinson Cahoon, jun., of Harwich, may take the name of Vinson Franklin Cahoon ; Polly Hallett Berry, of Yarmouth, may take the name of Mary Hallett Berry ; Reuben Cahoon, of Harwich, may take the name of Reuben Calhoon ; Flora Augustine Childs, of Barnstable, may take the name of Adulsa Nickerson Childs ; Isaiah Nickerson Handy, of Barnstable, may take the name of Robert Childs Handy ; Lewis Thacher Crowell, of Barnstable, minor, may take the name of Timothy Baker Crowell ; Jesse Hall, of Dennis, minor, may take the name of Jesse Sumner Hall ; all of the county of Barnstable.

And the several persons before mentioned, from and after the passage of this act, shall be known and called by the names which, by this act they are respectively allowed to assume as aforesaid, and said names shall hereafter be considered as their only proper and legal names, to all intents and purposes. [*May 2, 1849.*

AN ACT to change the Names of the Persons therein mentioned.
Be it enacted, etc., as follows :

Richard Howes may take the name of Richard Arthur Howes ; Caroline Elizabeth Pierce, a minor, may take the name of Ella Pierce ; Henry Dennie may take the name of Charles Henry Dennie ; Joshua Chandler may take the name of Joshua Herbert Chandler ; Charles Henry Brown may take the name of Ariel Brown ; William Churchill may take the name of William B. Churchill ; Almira Georgiana Murphy and William Henry Harrison Murphy, minors, may take the names of Almira Georgiana Vose, and William Henry Harrison Vose ; Peter Jest may take the name of Frederick Adolphus Miller ; Daniel and Joseph Trickey may severally take the names of Daniel Warren and Joseph Warren ; Edward Perry Twitchell may take the name of Edward Twitchell Perry ; Priscilla Ward Blake may take the name of Ella Blake ; Caroline D. Jackson may take the name of Caroline D. Waldron ; Samuel Smith Tuckerman may take the name of Samuel Tuckerman ; Rodney H. Paresh may take the name of Rodney H. Powers ; the hereafter named family may take the following names : Lewis Clark may take the name of Louis Bieral, Mary A. Clark may take the name of Ada Maria Bieral, Ada Carmelita Clark may take the name of Ada Carmelita Bieral ; George Francis Oliver Train may take the name of George Francis Train ; Charles Noakes may take the name of Charles Noakes Leavitt ; Henry J. Holt may take the name of Henry W. Holbrook ; John Milton Hervey Palton Partridge, of Boston, may take the name of Hervey Milton Palmantridge ; Emily Baxter, of Boston, may take the name of Emily Robinson Baxter ; all of the county of Suffolk.

Fanny Blake Furber, of Lynn, may take the name of Fanny Blake Rich, and her minor son may take the name of Samuel Edwin Rich ; George Noyes, of Newburyport, may take the name of George Washington Noyes ; Antonio Knight, of Rowley, may take the name of Antonio E. Knight ; Edward Skinner, of Lynn, may take the name of Edward Augustus Skinner ; John Spiller, of Georgetown, may take the name of John Preston ; Mary Danforth, of Salem, may take the name of Mary

Russell; Edward Hammond, jun., of Haverhill, may take the name of Edward Hanover Hammond; John Ober, jun., of Beverly, may take the name of John Richard Ober; Anna Maria Verrey, of Danvers, may take the name of Anna Maria Wallis; Ichabod Randall Hoyt, jun., of Salem, may take the name of George Randall Hoyt; Noble Pye, of Lynn, a minor, may take the name of Charles Noble Robinson; Michael Connors, of Gloucester, may take the name of Michael Poland; Bridget Farrell, of Salem, may take the name of Helen Farrell; David Perkins, jun., of Topsfield, may take the name of David Granville Perkins; Christopher Columbus Hawkes, of Lynn, may take the name of Charles Maurice Maudant; Almaretta Turner, of Danvers, may take name of Charlotte Elizabeth Turner; Henry Francis Kimball, of Bradford, may take the name of Frank Henry Kimball; John Albert Emerton, of Lynn, a minor, may take the name of John Albert Makepeace; all of the county of Essex.

Mary A. Pierce, of Lowell, may take the name of Mary Ames Beard, and her minor daughter may take the name of Abigail Ames Beard; Lucius Emmett Clary Paige, of Cambridge, may take the name of Lucius Robinson Paige; Ledry Cooledge Wright, a minor, of Marlborough, may take the name of Charles Wright; Jerome Buonaparte Morse, of Natick, may take the name of Joseph Spencer Bigelow; Rebekah F. Cooper, of Framingham, may take the name of Rebekah Brown Fuller; Jonathan Otis Howard, of Tyngsborough, may take the name of Otis Jonathan Howard; Charlotte Elizabeth Hunt, a minor, of Natick, may take the name of Abby Charlotte Hunt; all of the county of Middlesex.

Melvina Bristol, of Fitchburg, may take the name of Flora Melvina Cutter; Joel Hartwell, of Fitchburg, may take the name of Joel Willoughby Hartwell; Ephraim Chamberlain, of Southborough, may take the name of Ephraim Hale Chamberlain; Louisa M. Allen, of Mendon, may take the name of Louise Maria Aldrich; Wyman Goodell, a minor, of Athol, may take the name of Jonathan Wyman Goodell; Frederick Emery Blakeley, of Barre, may take the name of Frederick Emery Hastings; Leonard Brigham, of Worcester, may take the name of Edward Leonard Brigham; the hereafter named family, all of Worcester, may take the following names: Luther Gunn may take the name of Edward Luther Holman; Mary Sophia Gunn may take the name of Mary Sophia Holman; Edwin Howe Gunn may take the name of Edwin Howe Holman; Agnes Louisa Gunn may take the name of Agnes Louisa Holman; Almira Wood Gunn may take the name of Almira Wood Holman; Jonathan Pierce Holt, of Northbridge, may take the name of John Peirce Holt; Carlo Waite, of Hubbardston, may take the name of Charles Munroe Waite; Abigail K. Partridge, of Worcester, may take the name of Abigail G. Knowlton; Frederick Gates, a minor, of Holden, may take the name of Frederick Gates Chaffin; Leona Malvina Whitney, a minor, of Upton, may take the name of Leonah Melvenah Lesure; Rebecca Palmer, of Paxton, may take the name of Rebecca Farnsworth Palmer; Hannah Howe Hastings Hayward, of Mendon, may take the name of Anna Howe Hastings Hayward; Edmund Rice Greenwood, jun., of Hubbardston, may take the name of Edmund Greenwood; Benjamin Thales Cooley, of Worcester, may take the name of Benjamin Franklin Cooley; all of the county of Worcester.

Galusha Ford Bates, of Williamsburg, may take the name of Galusha Ford Miller; William Field, of Northampton, may take the name of

William Edward Field; Philip Ridgway Vining, of Williamsburg, may take the name of Seignior Jokenne Hillman; the hereafter named family, all of Granby, may take the following names: Benjamin Witt may take the name of Benjamin De Witt; Polly Witt may take the name of Mary De Witt; Benjamin Hollis Witt may take the name of Benjamin Hollis De Witt; Mary Ann Witt may take the name of Mary Ann De Witt; Sarah Jane Witt may take the name of Sarah Jane De Witt; Louisa Sanford Witt may take the name of Louisa Sanford De Witt; Henry Witt, of Granby, may take the name of Henry De Witt; William Pomeroy Clapp, of Williamsburg, may take the name of William Clapp Pomeroy; all of the county of Hampshire.

William Jonas Brown Colburn, a minor, of Amherst, may take the name of William Brown Colburn; the hereafter named family, all of Chicopee, may take the following names: Milton Hoar to take the name of Milton Woodville; Fanny Worthington Hoar to take the name of Fanny Worthington Woodville; Robert Worthington Hoar may take the name of Robert Worthington Woodville; Maria Hoar to take the name of Maria Lorene Woodville; Emily Hoar to take the name of Emily Amelia Woodville; Mary Frances Hoar to take the name of Mary Frances Woodville; Susan Phelps Hoar to take the name of Susan Phelps Woodville; Roderick Milton Hoar to take the name of Roderick Milton Woodville; Lucy Morely Hoar to take the name of Lucy Morely Woodville; Nelson Stratton, of Springfield, may take the name of Nelson Pitkin Stratton; all of the county of Hampden.

Cyrus Ball Mack, of Sunderland, may take the name of Cyrus Mack Hubbard; Otis Gunn, jun., of Montague, may take the name of Otis Berthoud Gunn; George P. Wood, of Orange, a minor, may take the name of George P. Whitney; Alanson Ward, of Buckland, may take the name of Alanson Wendell Ward; Celia Maria Stratton, and her minor children, of Northfield, may take the following names: Celia Maria Stratton, to take the name of Celia Maria Herbert; Henry Augustus Stratton to take the name of William Henry Herbert; Sarah Florence Stratton to take the name of Sarah Florence Herbert; Jane Clark, of Conway, may take the name of Minerva Jane Gunn; all of the county of Franklin.

Mira H. Spencer, of Hinsdale, may take the name of Mira Hinsdale; Charles Hinsdale Spencer, minor, of Hinsdale, may take the name of Charles Franklin Hinsdale; Lorenzo Elliott Dole, of Peru, may take the name of Lorenzo Lyman; Ann C. Ford, of Windsor, a minor, may take the name of Hester Ann Ford; Sarah Adaline Baker, a minor, of Peru, may take the name of Sarah Adaline Miner; Dorah Frissell, of Peru, may take the name of Emily Frissell; all of the county of Berkshire.

Harriet Elliot Cobb, of Dorchester, a minor, may take the name of Harriet Elliot Peake; Emma Louisa Reed, of Roxbury, may take the name of Emma Elizabeth Palmer; Harriet Augusta Sumner, of Medfield, minor, may take the name of Henrietta Augusta Robinson; James Lynch, of Medway, may take the name of James Lewis Pond; Julia A. Hartshorn, an adopted child, of Walpole, may take the name of Julia Howard; Caroline Fellows Johnson, of Roxbury, an adopted child, may take the name of Elsey Susan Lewis; Alfred Hunt, 2d, of Weymouth, may take the name of Alfred Harper; all of the county of Norfolk.

Cornelia E. Caswell, of Taunton, may take the name of Cornelia E. Allen; Mary Silas Presbrey, of Taunton, may take the name of Mary Presbrey Ellis; Deborah Turner Bodfish, of New Bedford, single woman, may take the name of Deborah Frances Bodfish; Melvin Bates, of Taunton, may take the name of William Leonard Eddy; Samuel L. Paull, of Taunton, may take the name of John Henry Richmond; all of the county of Bristol.

Grenville Marsh Tappan, a minor, of Marshfield, to take the name of William Brigham Tappan; Harriet D. Swift, a minor, of Middleborough, may take the name of Harriet D. Reed; Arthur L. Gould, of Hingham, a minor, may take the name of Josiah L. Gould; Elisha C. Bubier, of Abington, may take the name of Elisha C. Davis; all of the county of Plymouth.

James Mac Quire, of Truro, may take the name of James Henry Lee; John Mac Quire, of Truro, may take the name of John Quincy Myrick; Ellen A. Phillips, a minor, of Yarmouth, may take the name of Ellen A. Matthews; all of the county of Barnstable.

Rebecca West, a minor, of Chilmark, may take the name of William Valentine Worth; of the county of Dukes.

And the several persons before mentioned, from and after the passage of this act, shall be known and called by the names which by this act they are respectively allowed to assume, as aforesaid, and said names shall hereafter be considered as their only proper and legal names to all intents and purposes. [*April 29, 1850.*

AN ACT in addition to "AN ACT to change the Names of Persons therein mentioned."

Be it enacted, etc., as follows:

Laura Todd, of Lynn, may take the name of Laura Maria Walden; Samuel Capen Bancroft, of Salem, may take the name of Sidney Chapin Bancroft; Cyrus Killam, of Boxford, may take the name of Cyrus K. Bartlett; the hereafter named family of Lynn, may take the following names: Joseph T. Guilford may take the name of Torry Peabody; Matilda Hartland Guilford may take the name of Matilda Hartland Peabody; Joseph Guilford may take the name of Torry Peabody, jun.; Almiria Guilford may take the name of Almiria Newhall Peabody; Frances Peabody Guilford may take the name of Frances Peabody; Abby Ann Guilford may take the name of Abby Ann Peabody, all of Essex county. Hopestill Davis Baker, of Athol, may take the name of Mary Hopestill Baker, of Worcester county. Charles Richard Gallup, of Roxbury, may take the name of Charles Henry Eversdyk Gallup, of Norfolk county. Stephen Macy, of New Bedford, may take the name of Franklin Macy, of Bristol county. William H. Hill, of Abington, may take the name of Eugene Bray, of Plymouth county. Ebenezer Holway, of Provincetown, may take the name of Ebenezer Wing Holway, of Barnstable county. And the several persons before named, from and after the passage of this act, shall be known and called by the names which by this act they are respectively allowed to assume as aforesaid, and the same shall hereafter be considered as their own proper and legal names. [*May 3, 1850.*

An Act to change the Names of the Persons therein mentioned.
Be it enacted, etc., as follows:

Henry Cushing may take the name of Henry Howard Cushing; George W. Trickey may take the name of George Bruce Milton; Henry Bradlee Gutterson may take the name of Henry Eaton Bradlee; Robert Green may take the name of John Green; Edward Dana Greene may take the name of Edward Dana Erving Greene; Josiah Quincy, 3d, may take the name of Josiah Phillips Quincy; James Bates may take the name of James Warren Bates; Caroline S. Spencer may take the name of Caroline S. Hartford; George Hartford Spencer may take the name of George Edward Hartford; Emeline F. Ames may take the name of Emma Frost; Frederick W. McKoy may take the name of Frederick William Mozart; Edmund Doe may take the name of Edmund Doe Spear; James Mitchell may take the name of James Munroe Mitchell; Ebenezer Cutter may take the name of Eben Cutter; George Payne, a minor, may take the name of George Vose Payne; Joseph Coolidge Swett may take the name of Joseph Swett Coolidge; all of Boston, in the county of Suffolk.

James Francis Brown, of Danvers, may take the name of Charles Francis Brown; Charles E. Spinney, of Haverhill, may take the name of Edwin S. Milton; Anna Lane, of Newbury, may take the name of Lucy Anna Lane; Morrison Proctor, of Georgetown, may take the name of Maurice Henrie Proctor; Ezra Upton, of Salem, may take the name of Warren Augustus Upton; Orlando D. Hogan, of Salem, may take the name of Orlando D. Chandler; William Cockett, of Lynn, may take the name of William Wallace Wilson; John Luffin, of Beverly, may take the name of Joel Sheldon; Patrick Smith, of Lynn, may take the name of Patrick H. Smith; Moses Brown, of Lynn, a minor, may take the name of Frank Bridge Brown; David Dornican, of Beverly, may take the name of David Shepard; Mary Maria Carlton, of Salisbury, a minor, may take the name of Mary Abby Dow; Charles Harris Fisher, of Salisbury, a minor, may take the name of Charles William Dow; James Feathern, of Lynn, may take the name of James F. Howard; Lucy Ann Feathern, of Lynn, may take the name of Lucy Ann Howard; Orin Ross Maddox, of Lynn, may take the name of Orin M. Howard; Harriet Symonds Verry, of Danvers, may take the name of Harriet Symonds Hutchinson; John Hallowell Mansfield Nourse, of Lynn, may take the name of John Nourse; Eliza Clarke, of Methuen, may take the name of Eliza Adelaide Clarke; Elizabeth D. Heywood, of Salem, may take the name of Elizabeth D. Page; George F. Osterhold, of Newburyport, may take the name of George Frederick Wilbur; Silas Adams Cook, of Newburyport, may take the name of John Adams Cook; Caroline F. Esty, of Salem, may take the name of Caroline F. Symmes; Gideon W. Hunt, of Newburyport, may take the name of Gideon W. Waring; Mary W. Hunt, of Newburyport, may take the name of Mary W. Waring; Hartly Holt Hunt, of Newburyport, may take the name of Charles H. Waring; Seraphina D. M. Hunt, of Newburyport, may take the name of Seraphina D. M. Waring; Elizabeth Ann Lee, of Manchester, may take the name of Lizzie Lee; Patience Ivers Whippen, of Lynn, may take the name of Caroline Ivers Whippen; Benjamin Howard, of Salem, may take the name of Benjamin Cheever Howard; Henry Perry, of Danvers, may take the name of Henry Wallace Perry; Mary Frances Willy, of Groveland, a minor, may take the name of Mary Frances Emery;

Elizabeth Willy, of Groveland, a minor, may take the name of Elizabeth
Reed ; Abby Moore Kimball, of Salem, may take the name of Ruby Mellen
Moore ; Abraham Lummus, jun., of Ipswich, may take the name of Henry
Abraham Lummus ; all of the county of Essex.

Porter Woodbury, of Acton, may take the name of George Porter
Woodbury ; Nelson Wood, of Framingham, may take the name of Nelson
Wood Richardson ; Nancy Remond Lenox, of Watertown, may take the
name of Sybil Remond Lenox ; Edward Lawrence, of Acton, may take the
name of Edward Hobart Lawrence ; Emma Allen, of Charlestown, may
take the name of Emma Lucy Allen ; Patrick Collins, of Waltham, may
take the name of Albert James ; Mary Ann Maynard, of Charlestown, may
take the name of Mary Ann Averill ; Samantha Altana Pasco, of South
Reading, a minor, may take the name of Samantha Althea Sabine ; Caroline
Matilda Pratt, of Charlestown, a minor, may take the name of Caroline
Pratt Emerson ; Richard Potter, of Groton, may take the name of Richard
Bulkley Potter ; Henry Gowing, of Worcester, a minor, may take the name
of Henry Augustus Gowing ; Maria Bolles, of Littleton, may take the name
of Maria Altoinne Bolles ; Thomas Miller Croocker, of Charlestown, may
take the name of Thomas Miller Crocker ; Warren Payson, of Holliston,
may take the name of Warren Lindley Payson ; Orlando Blanchard, of
Framingham, may take the name of William Fisk Smith ; Luther Rice, of
Marlborough, may take the name of Luther Melville Rice ; Michael Fanning, of Ashland, may take the name of Edmund Judson Fanning ; Bridget
McDonald, of Charlestown, may take the name of Mary McDonald ;
Sophronia Weston Lowe, of Charlestown, may take the name of Sophia
Abby Weston Lowe ; Amos Hartwell Hodgman, of Carlisle, may take the
name of Celius Melbourne Hodgman ; John Samuel Trickey, of Charlestown, may take the name of John Samuel Milton ; Francis Louis Ringold,
a minor, of Cambridge, may take the name of Francis Louis Lander ; all
of the county of Middlesex.

Ephraim Kingsbury Weatherbee, of Gardner, may take the name of
Ephraim Weatherbee ; Mary Adaline Putnam, of Hubbardston, may take
the name of Mary Putnam Clark ; Simon Ephraim Willard Peck, of Hard-
wick, may take the name of Willard Peck ; Josiah Richardson, of Leomin-
ster, may take the name of Josiah Carter Richardson ; Silas Smith Hall, of
Northbridge, a minor, may take the name of Silas Wood Smith ; Ralph
Patch, jun., of Leominster, may take the name of William Ralph Patch ;
Almon Whittemore, of Leominster, may take the name of George Almon
Whittemore ; Charles Clarence Valentine Hyde, of Southborough, a minor,
may take the name of Charles Clarence Hobart ; John Henry Capron, of
Uxbridge, may take the name of Henry Capron ; Susan M. Blood, of
Worcester, may take the name of Susan M. Thompson ; Foster Walker, of
North Brookfield, may take the name of Lyman Walker ; Perez French,
jun., of Hubbardston, may take the name of Charles Willis Ashley ; Mary
Maley, of Upton, may take the name of Mary Jane Hall ; Benjamin Mun-
joy, of Westminster, may take the name of Benjamin Blake ; Dolly Munjoy,
of Westminster, may take the name of Dolly Blake ; Francis Munjoy, of
Westminster, may take the name of Francis Blake ; Calvin Munjoy, of
Westminster, may take the name of Calvin Blake ; Sarah E. Munjoy, of
Westminster, may take the name of Sarah E. Blake ; Harriet E. Munjoy,
of Westminster, may take the name of Harriet Eliza Blake ; Franklin

Webster Adams, of Douglas, may take the name of Franklin Adams Fairbanks; William Jackson Davis, of Southbridge, may take the name of Andrew Jackson Davis; Lucy Woodward Harrington, of Paxton, may take the name of Lucy Alona Harrington; Edwin Munjoy, of Westminster, may take the name of Edwin Blake; all of the county of Worcester.

Jared Smith Bement may take the name of Henry Smith Nash; Abby Sophia Hawks may take the name of Abby Hawks Nash; both of Granby, in the county of Hampshire.

Moses Eustis Hamilton, of Chester, may take the name of William Eustis Hamilton; Adams Hamilton, of Chester, may take the name of Edward Everett Hamilton; Chauncey R. Gross, of Westfield, may take the name of Chauncey R. Chauncey; Elias Smith Cook, of Wilbraham, may take the name of Ansel Wright; Jane Ann Cook, of Wilbraham, may take the name of Jane Wright; Ira Hinckley Cook, of Wilbraham, a minor, may take the name of Ira Hinckley Wright; Laura Jane Cook, of Wilbraham, a minor, may take the name of Laura Jane Wright; Austin Smith Cook, of Wilbraham, a minor, may take the name of Austin Smith Wright; Lucy Ann Cook, of Wilbraham, a minor, may take the name of Lucy Ann Wright; Mary Elizabeth Cook, of Wilbraham, a minor, may take the name of Mary Elizabeth Wright; John Rollin Alden, of Wilbraham, may take the name of Charles Harrey Gay; Mary Alden, of Wilbraham, may take the name of Emma Lucy Gay; Ella Maria Alden, of Wilbraham, may take the name of Ella Maria Gay; Jonathan Hoar, of Monson, may take the name of Jonathan Homer; Rodolphus Hoar, of Monson, may take the name of Rodolphus Homer; Pamelia Graves Hoar, of Monson, may take the name of Pamelia Graves Homer; Louisa Adelaide Hoar, of Monson, may take the name of Louisa Adelaide Homer; Martha A. Sumner, of Palmer, may take the name of Martha A. Converse; Caroline King Hoar, of Monson, may take the name of Caroline King Homer; Mary Robbins Hoar, of Monson, may take the name of Mary Robbins Homer; Albert King Hoar, of Monson, may take the name of Albert King Homer; George Adams Hoar, of Monson, may take the name of George Adams Homer; Lucinda Graves, of Springfield, may take the name of Mariah Luella Graves; all of the county of Hampden.

David Allen Graves, of Ashfield, a minor, may take the name of Addison Graves; Charles Henry Fairbanks, of Rowe, a minor, may take the name of Myron Corbet Blodgett; Mercy Mayhew Hawkes, of Charlemont, may take the name of Clara Isadore Hawkes; Benjamin Dunkley, of Sunderland, may take the name of Benjamin Franklin Dunkley; Younglove Bixby, of Leverett, may take the name of John Younglove Bixby; Sophronia Augusta Smith, of Sunderland, may take the name of Helen Maria Wright; Edwin Blakeslee, of Heath, may take the name of Edwin Louis Blakeslee; all of the county of Franklin.

Josiah Hamilton Leonard, of Peru, a minor, may take the name of Josiah Hamilton Butts; James Munroe Wilcox, of Sandisfield, may take the name of Munroe Wilcox; Lucy Wilder, of Peru, may take the name of Lucy Ide Cone; Silas Bingham Bottom, of Hinsdale, may take the name of Silas Bingham; Mary Charlotte Bottom, of Hinsdale, may take the name of Mary Charlotte Bingham; Marion Bottom, of Hinsdale, may take the name of Julia Marion Bingham; Elizabeth Nelson Bottom, of Hinsdale, may take the name of Elizabeth Nelson Bingham; George S. Moulton, of

Lee, may take the name of George Moulton Bradley; Margaret Joy, of Hinsdale, may take the name of Margaret Loomise; all of the county of Berkshire.

John King, of Roxbury, may take the name of John Crookshanks King; Eliza Boyden Bullard, of Walpole, may take the name of Adaliza Maria Curtis; Calvin Cutler, of Dorchester, a minor, may take the name of John Calvin Cutler; George Sampson, of Dorchester, a minor, may take the name of George Alfred Sampson; Martha Ann Batchelder, of Quincy, may take the name of Martha Ann Brown; Hannah Maria Shepherd, of Milton, may take the name of Hannah Josephine Shepherd; Lucy Ann Ambler, of Dedham, may take the name of Lucy Ann Priest; Matthew H. Stanley, of Cohasset, may take the name of Charles H. Stanley; Emma Josephine Weeks, of Quincy, a minor, may take the name of Emma Josephine Cole; Charles William Miles, of Roxbury, a minor, may take the name of Charles Appleton Miles; Theodore Dunn, jun., a minor, of Roxbury, may take the name of Theodore Leonard Dunn; Richard White, of Roxbury, may take the name of Richard Guilford White; Charles Francis Atkinson, of Brookline, a minor, may take the name of Charles Follen Atkinson; James M. Tucker, of Roxbury, may take the name of James Tucker Dudley; all of the county of Norfolk.

Gideon Tripp, of Westport, may take the name of Gideon Wait Tripp; John Wood, of New Bedford, may take the name of John Franklin Wood; Bathsheba Dean, of Fall River, may take the name of Annie B. Dean; all of the county of Bristol.

William Brigham Tappan, of Marshfield, may take the name of William Bingham Tappan; John Perkins, of Middleborough, a minor, may take the name of John Jasper Perkins; Eugene Bray, of Abington, may take the name of Henry Warren Hill; Eliza Vaughan Harvey, of Plymouth, a minor, may take the name of Eliza Sutton Vaughan Harvey; Martin Packard, of North Bridgewater, may take the name of Martin T. Packard; Martin Sumner Orcutt, of East Bridgewater, may take the name of Martin Sumner; Susan Orcutt, of East Bridgewater, may take the name of Susan Sumner; Newton Sumner Orcutt, of East Bridgewater, may take the name of Newton Sumner; Susan Mercy Orcutt, of East Bridgewater, may take the name of Susan Mercy Sumner; all of the county of Plymouth.

Sukey Crosby Sparrow, of Orleans, may take the name of Susan Maria Sparrow; Ella Theodora Crowell, of Yarmouth, minor, may take the name of Abigail Hedge Crowell; Edward Hallet, 2d, of Yarmouth, may take the name of Edward Bangs Hallet; David Smith, 3d, of Provincetown, may take the name of David Augustus Smith; Thankful C. Foster, of Brewster, may take the name of Emily C. Foster; Thaddeus F. Young, of Brewster, may take the name of Charles F. Young; Edward McLaughlin, of Chatham, may take the name of Edward Howard; Emily McLaughlin, of Chatham, may take the name of Emily Howard; Emma Augusta McLaughlin, a minor, of Chatham, may take the name of Emma Augusta Howard; Marcus William McLaughlin, a minor, of Chatham, may take the name of Marcus William Howard; Agnes Ann McLaughlin, a minor, of Chatham may take the name of Agnes Ann Howard; all of the county of Barnstable.

Edwin Coffin, a minor, of Edgartown, in the county of Dukes County, may take the name of Edwin Russell Coffin.

And the several persons before named, from and after the passing of this act, shall be known and called by the names which by this act they are respectively allowed to assume as aforesaid, and the same shall hereafter be considered as their only proper and legal names. [*May 23, 1851.*]

An Act to change the Names of the Persons therein mentioned.
Be it enacted, etc., as follows :

Wiliam Seaton may take the name of William Harrison Ainsworth; John Henry Bright may take the name of Henry Bright; Franklin John Walter White may take the name of Benjamin Franklin White; Robert Lane Colby may take the name of Robert Colby; George Bradford may take the name of George Royal Bradford; all of Boston, in the county of Suffolk.

Catherine McMahan, of Danvers, may take the name of Catherine Wilson; Asa Loring Breed, of Lynn, may take the name of Asa Breed; John Atkinson, of Newburyport, may take the name of John Moses Atkinson; all in the county of Essex.

George Monroe may take the name of Luther A. Reed; George Henry Monroe, a minor, may take the name of George Henry Reed; Mary Frances Monroe may take the name of Mary Frances Reed, all of Charlestown; Ann McCarthy may take the name of Ann Miles; Mary Jane McCarthy may take the name of Mary Jane Miles; Elizabeth Howard McCarthy may take the name of Elizabeth Howard Miles; Thomas McCarthy may take the name of Thomas Miles; Ellen McCarthy may take the name of Ellen Miles; Miles McCarthy may take the name of Francis Miles, all of Waltham; Jerome Bonaparte Lord may take the name of Jerome Bonaparte Lawton; Solomon Fletcher may take the name of Solomon Lawrence Fletcher, both of Winchester; all in the county of Middlesex.

Owen Wilson, of Leominster, may take the name of Owen Augustus Wilson; Alden Woodcock, of Leominster, may take the name of Alden Augustus Woodman; Daniel Webster Gilbert, of West Brookfield, may take the name of De Witt Gilbert; Jacob Henry Paige, of Berlin, may take the name of William Henry Paige; Susan Gideon Warner, of Boylston, may take the name of Mary Sophia Hastings; Sarah Ann J. French, of Hubbardston, may take the name of Sarah Jane Ashley; Daniel P. Munjoy, of Westminster, may take the name of Daniel P. Blake; all in the county of Worcester.

Grant Powers Stafford, of Cummington, in the county of Hampshire, may take the name of Lewis Grant Stafford.

Hannah Mellen Lyman may take the name of Annie Lyman; Abel Chapin may take the name of Abel Dexter Chapin, both of Springfield, in the county of Hampden.

Charles Gay, a minor, of Roxbury, in the county of Norfolk, may take the name of Henry Phillips.

Celinda J. Hammond may take the name of Isabella J. Hammond; Betsy F. Goss may take the name of Lizzie F. Goss; both of Middleborough, in the county of Plymouth.

And the several persons before mentioned, from and after the passage of this act, shall be known and called by the names which by this act they are respectively allowed to assume as aforesaid, and the same shall hereafter be considered as their only proper and legal names. [*May 24, 1851.*]

In COMPLIANCE with the requirements of chap. 256 of the Acts of the year 1851, and of chap. 148, sect. 14, of the Public Statutes, returns of the following changes of names have been received at the department of the Secretary of the Commonwealth, as decreed by the several judges of the probate courts in their respective counties : —

SUFFOLK COUNTY.

Date of Decree.	Original Name.	Name Decreed.	Residence.
1851.			
Aug. 25,	Edwin Hatstat, *a* . . .	Edwin Clinton, . . .	Boston.
25,	Ellen S. Hatstat, *a* . . .	Ellen Clinton, ...	Boston.
Nov. 24,	Henry Welles Smith, *a* .	Henry Fowle Durant, .	Boston.
Dec. 29,	Patrick Coady, *a* . . .	Edward Johnson Coady, .	Boston.

ESSEX COUNTY.

Nov. 4,	Joseph McQuid, *a* . . .	Joseph Walton, . . .	Amesbury.

WORCESTER COUNTY.

Dec. 23,	Julia Ardelia Thurston, *a* .	Julia Ardelia Thurston Allen,	Southwick.

NORFOLK COUNTY.

Oct. 25,	William Henry Magrath, *a* .	William Gray, . . .	Roxbury.

SUFFOLK COUNTY.

1852.			
Jan. 12,	James Lougheed, *a* . . .	James Loheed, . .	Boston.
Mar. 1,	Bridget Potter, *a* . . .	Catharine Mineva Potter,	Boston.
22,	Sophia Agnes Murphoy, *a* .	Sophia Agnes Hill, . .	Boston.
April 19,	David C. Cobb, *a* . . .	David Williams, . .	Boston.
19,	Martha Ann Chase, *a* . .	Martha Ann Hill, . .	Boston.
May 3,	Hannah Weld Merry, *a* .	Anna Weld Merry, . .	Boston.
17,	Lydia Barrus, *a* . . .	Lydia Barrows, . .	Boston.
17,	Horace Granville Barrus, *a*	Horace G. Barrows, . .	Boston.
17,	Emmeline Milton Barrus, *a*	Emmeline M. Barrows, .	Boston.
17,	Thaddeus Milton Barrus, *a*	Thaddeus M. Barrows, .	Boston.
17,	Lydianna Barrus, *a* . .	Lydianna Barrows, . .	Boston.
17,	Fanny Forrester Barrus, *a*	Fanny F. Barrows, . .	Boston.
17,	Frank Lewis Barrus, *a* .	Frank L. Barrows, . .	Boston.
31,	Jonas Davis, *a* . . .	John Davis, . . .	North Chelsea.
Aug. 9,	Sybel Maria Moors, *alias* Lorilla Maria Moore, *a* . . .	Maria Lorilla More, . .	Boston.
Oct. 11,	Emma Cecelia Campion, *a* .	Louisa Simes, . . .	Boston.
11,	Charles Campion, *a* . .	George Simes, . . .	Boston.

a See Blue Book edition of the laws of 1883.

ESSEX COUNTY.

Date of Decree.	Original Name.	Name Decreed.	Residence.
1852.			
Mar. 30,	David Brown, . . .	David Fellows Brown, . .	Newburyport.
May 4,	Moses Monarch, . . .	Charles Augustus Averill, .	Salem.
18,	Philander Basford, . . .	Philander Randolph Basford,	Danvers.
18,	Winthrop Brown, . . .	Henry Ward Brown, . .	Ipswich.
June 8,	Michael D Hart, . . .	Michael Desmond Hart, .	Lawrence.
Aug. 17,	Patrick McGinley, . . .	Joseph Boynton, . . .	Lynn.
17,	Susan Seeley, ...	Susan Samson, . . .	Lynn.
Dec. 7,	William S. Babcock, . .	William Babcock Sturgis, .	Manchester.

MIDDLESEX COUNTY.

May 17,	Charles Smith, ...	Charles Skippins, . . .	Charlestown.
17,	Louisa Smith, ...	Louisa Skippins, . . .	Charlestown.
Oct. 12,	Consider Glass Davis, . .	Sydney Glass Davis, . .	———.

WORCESTER COUNTY.

–	George W. Rice, . . .	George Edward Rice, . .	———.
–	Wolf Humes, . . .	William Humes, . . .	———.
–	Horace De Witt Smith, .	Horace Smith De Witt, . .	———.
–	Arthur Stillman, . . .	Arthur Stillman Whitney, .	———.
–	George Elbridge Fisher, .	George Woolsey Elbridge Fisher, ...	———.

HAMPSHIRE COUNTY.

July 6,	Ellen Matilda Flinn, . . .	Ellen Matilda Draper, . .	Pelham.

HAMPDEN COUNTY.

Feb. 3,	Jonathan Hoar, . . .	Jonathan Homer, . . .	Monson.
3,	Caroline Hoar, . . .	Caroline Homer, . . .	Monson.
3,	Mary Robbins Hoar, . .	Mary Robbins Homer, . .	Monson.
3,	Albert King Hoar, . . .	Albert King Homer, . .	Monson.
3,	George Adams Hoar, . .	George Adams Homer, . .	Monson.
3,	Rodolphus Hoar, . . .	Rodolphus Homer, . . .	Monson.
3,	Pamelia Hoar, ...	Pamelia Homer, . . .	Monson.
3,	Louisa Adelaide Hoar, . .	Louisa Adelaide Homer, . .	Monson.

FRANKLIN COUNTY.

Mar. 9,	Henry Joy, a	Henry Clay Joy, . . .	Hawley.
Dec. 21,	Almira Laura Chapin, * a .	Almira L. Bemis, . . .	Orange.

a See Blue Book edition of the laws of 1883.   * Changed by reason of adoption.

NORFOLK COUNTY.

Date of Decree.	Original Name.	Name Decreed.	Residence.
1852.			
July 17,	Elizabeth Jane Clapp, . .	Elizabeth Jane Jenkins, .	Dorchester.
Sept. 18,	Mary E. Davis, ...	Eveline Augusta Noyes, .	Dedham.
Oct. 5,	Florence Corbett, . . .	Florence Thompson, .	Dedham.

PLYMOUTH COUNTY.

May 4,	George Henry John Ahrenholtz,	George Henry John Arnold, .	Middleborough.
4,	Elizabeth Ahrenholtz, . .	Elizabeth Arnold, . . .	Middleborough.
4,	Henry Herman, ...	Henry Arnold, . . .	Middleborough.
4,	Patrick Murray, . . .	James Murray, . . .	East Bridgewater.

BARNSTABLE COUNTY.

Aug. 10,	Joseph Mash, ...	Joseph Marsh, . . .	Sandwich.
10,	Mary Ann Mash, . . .	Mary Ann Marsh, . . .	Sandwich.
10,	Joseph E. Mash, . . .	Joseph E. Marsh, . . .	Sandwich.
10,	George H. Mash, . . .	George H. Marsh, . .	Sandwich.
10,	Jane E. Mash, ...	Jane E. Marsh, . .	Sandwich.
10,	Charles W. Mash, . . .	Charles W. Marsh, . .	Sandwich.
10,	Edith M. Mash, ...	Edith M. Marsh, . . .	Sandwich.
10,	Mary L. Mash, ...	Mary L. Marsh, . . .	Sandwich.
10,	William J. S. Mash, . . .	William J. S. Marsh, . .	Sandwich.
10,	Victoria Mash, ...	Victoria Marsh, . . .	Sandwich.
10,	Josephine Mash, . . .	Josephine Marsh, . . .	Sandwich.

NANTUCKET COUNTY.

–	Henry J. Defrees, . . .	Henry J. Defriez, . . .	———.

SUFFOLK COUNTY.

1853.			
Feb. 7,	John Mason Good Parker, *a* .	Mason Good Parker, .	Boston.
28,	Lucy Peabody Greenlaw, *a*	Lucy Peabody De Maine, .	Boston.
28,	Volta Maurice Greenlaw, *a*	Volta Maurice De Maine, .	Boston.
28,	George Festus Greenlaw, *a*	George Festus De Maine, .	Boston.
Mar. 7,	Bill Tewksbury, Jr , *a* .	Hermon Bill Tewksbury, .	Winthrop.
28,	John C. Gillooley, *a* . .	John C. Williams, . .	Boston.
April 11,	Seneca Hill, *a*	James Seneca Hill, .	Boston.
18,	James McCann, *a* . .	James Bartlett, . .	Boston.
18,	Carlos Milton McNabb, *a* .	Carlos Milton Duncan, .	Boston.
18,	Frances Juliette McNabb, *a*	Frances Juliette Duncan, .	Boston.
18,	Mary McNabb, *a* . .	Mary Duncan, . .	Boston.
June 20,	Charles Weyman Smith, *a*	Charles Smith Weyman, .	Boston.
20,	Robert Greer, *a* . . .	John Greer, ...	Boston.
July 18,	Michael Coburn, *a* . .	Alonzo Walter Coburn, .	Boston.
Aug. 22,	Ansel Smith Maxham, *a* .	Andrew Maxham Smith, .	Boston.
29,	Franklin Cowdin Meriam, *a*	Benjamin Franklin Cowdin, .	Boston.
29,	Thomas O'Brien, *a* . .	Thomas Charles Brown, .	Boston.
Sept. 19,	James Morrissey, *a* . .	James Herbert, . .	Boston.
Oct. 17,	Dennis John McGillycuddy, *a* .	John Dennis McGill, .	Boston.
Dec. 14,	Patrick Lawler, *a* . . .	William Edson Lawler, .	Boston.

a See Blue Book edition of the laws of 1883.

ESSEX COUNTY.

Date of Decree.	Original Name.	Name Decreed.	Residence.
1853.			
Feb. 1,	Jane E. Danforth, . . .	Jane E. Niles, . . .	Danvers.
May 17,	Charles Albert Solarris, . .	Charles Albert Lawrence, .	Danvers.
June 7,	William Pool, ...	William Choate Pool, . .	Rockport.
Nov. 1,	Mary Ann Griffin, . . .	Susan Swan Griffin, . .	Salem.
1,	William Henry Hicer, . .	William Henry Parker, .	Salem.

MIDDLESEX COUNTY.

Jan. 11,	Emerson Pepper, . . .	Frederick Emerson Willis, .	Lowell.
May 17,	Margaret Grace French, . .	Margaret Grace Hastings, .	Cambridge.
Nov. 1,	Walter Powers, . . .	Thomas Walter Powers, .	Reading.
1,	John McCarty, ...	John Mack, ...	Lowell.
1,	Ann McCarty, ...	Ann Mack, ...	Lowell.
1,	Charles McCarty, . . .	Charles Mack, . . .	Lowell.
1,	Andrew McCarty, . . .	Andrew Mack, . . .	Lowell.
1,	John McCarty, ...	John Mack, ...	Lowell.
1,	Mary Frances McCarty, . .	Mary Frances Mack, . .	Lowell.

WORCESTER COUNTY.

Jan. 4,	Windsor Adams, . . .	Windsor Adams Bowen, .	Brookfield.
July 5,	Major Chamberlin, . . .	Andrew M. Chamberlin, .	Southbridge.
5,	Emily Todd, ...	Emily S. Walden. . . .	Worcester.
5,	Emily Barber,* . . .	Emily Barber Richardson, .	Winchendon.
Aug. 2,	Mary Davis,* . . .	Mary Davis Cheney, .	Holden.
2,	Nancy Ann Temple,* . .	Nancy Ann Harrington, .	Worcester.
Oct. 4,	James Williams Randles,* .	James Williams Hagan, .	Upton.
4,	Jane Head,*	Jane Barrows, . . .	Clinton.
Dec. 6,	Eugene F. Brigham Swan,* .	Eugene Brigham Fuller, .	Holden.
6,	Finette Louisa Miller,* .	Finette Louisa Bryant, .	———.
6,	Silas Andrew Freeman, . .	Andrew Silas Freeman, .	Millbury.

HAMPSHIRE COUNTY.

Jan. 4,	Frances Laura Miller, .	Sarah Jane Miller, . . .	Northampton.
May 3,	Albert Henry Saunders, . .	John Henry Damon, . .	Middlefield.
3,	Nancy Haydon, ...	Nancy Hannum, . . .	Williamsburg.
Sept. 6,	Perrin Mathews, . . .	Charles Perrin Mathews, .	South Hadley.

HAMPDEN COUNTY.

–	Michael Corbett, . . .	Charles Corbett, . . .	Palmer.
–	Moses Chapin, 2d, . . .	Moses Whitman Chapin, .	Chicopee.

BERKSHIRE COUNTY.

Jan. 4,	Lois I. Rogers, *a* . . .	Mary Lois Drake, . . .	Lee.
Oct. 12,	Lovain Patridge, *a* . . .	Leonard Lovain Rider, . .	Cheshire.

* Changed by reason of adoption.   *a* See Blue Book edition of the laws of 1883.

NORFOLK COUNTY.

Date of Decree.	Original Name.	Name Decreed.	Residence.
1853.			
Feb. 26,	Anderson Hollingsworth, . .	Ellis Anderson Hollingsworth,	Braintree.
May 7,	Frederick Graham Howard, .	Benjamin Chandler Howard,	Brookline.

PLYMOUTH COUNTY.

Nov. 1,	Michael Marea, ...	Shearman T. Marea, . .	N'th Bridgewater.

BRISTOL COUNTY.

–	Pardon A. Sisson, . . .	Edward R. Sisson, . .	New Bedford.
–	John Wood, ...	John Franklin Wood, . .	New Bedford.
–	Cornelius Mahoney, . . .	Cornelius Allen White, . .	Raynham.

BARNSTABLE COUNTY.

Jan. 11,	Emma Adelaide Ward, . .	Kezia Adelaide Ward, . .	Chatham.
Feb. 8,	Robert Austin Lovell, . .	Austin Lovell, . . .	Barnstable.
8,	Forbes Douns, ...	Isaac Downs, ...	Dennis.
April 18,	Isaac Smith, 2d, . . .	Isaac Harvey Smith, . .	Harwich.
May 17,	Alvin W. Rich, ...	Michael A. Rich, . . .	Truro.
17,	Henry Phineas Shaw, . .	Cornelius Henry Shaw, . .	Truro.
Aug. 9,	Julia Nye Loring, . . .	Julia Annette Loring, . .	Barnstable.

SUFFOLK COUNTY.

1854.			
–	Anna Maria Downs Lord, . .	Anna Maria Downs, . .	Boston.
–	Danforth Eri Newcomb, . .	Sylvanus Judkins, . . .	Boston.
–	James Sylvester Morphey, .	James Sylvester Norman, .	Boston.
–	John Paine, ...	John Shearer Paine, . .	Boston.
–	Leonard Lamperts-dörfer, . .	Leonard Lamperts, . .	Boston.
–	George W. Dunnaway, . .	George W. Jones, . . .	Boston.
–	Daniel L. McGear, . .	Daniel L. Gear, . . .	Boston.
–	Edward William Burrows Thompson, ...	Edward Thompson, . .	Boston.
–	Francis Boott Brooks, . .	Francis Brooks, . . .	Boston.
–	Philip Keating, ...	Philip Keating Holbrook, .	Boston.

ESSEX COUNTY.

Jan. 3,	John Cronin, ...	John Byron Howard, . .	Salem.
Mar. 7,	Catherine Murray, . . .	Adelaide Herbert Robinson, .	Lynn.
June 6,	Clara E. Richmond, . . .	Bessie Richmond, . . .	Marblehead.
July 4,	George Hunkins, ...	George Warren, . . .	Haverhill.
4,	Maria E. Hunkins, . . .	Maria E. Warren, . . .	Haverhill.
4,	Emma F. Hunkins, . . .	Emma F. Warren, . . .	Haverhill.
4,	Helena A. Hunkins, . . .	Helena A. Warren, . .	Haverhill.
–	Charles Henry Tiplady, .	Charles Henry Pierce, . .	Salem.

ESSEX COUNTY — *Concluded.*

Date of Decree.	Original Name.	Name Decreed.	Residence.
1854.			
Oct. 3,	Michael L. Whidden, . .	Henry L. Whidden, . .	Danvers.
17,	Caroline Cheswell Story, .	Caroline Ireland Story, .	Salisbury.
Nov. 7,	Patrick Welsh, . . .	William Welsh, . . .	Salem.
21,	Nathaniel Hooper, . .	Nathaniel Leach Hooper, .	Marblehead.

MIDDLESEX COUNTY.

May 2,	Cyrus Frederick Smith, .	Cyrus Frederick Knight, .	Brighton.
Aug. 8,	Augustus P. Murray,* .	Charles Fairbanks Morse, .	Hopkinton.
15,	Dorcas Maria Chaffin, .	Maria Dorcas Chaffin, .	Newton.
Sept. 19,	Elizabeth Blood,* . .	Katy Josephine Morrill, .	Lowell.
19,	Silva Ann Elliott,* . .	Mary Eliza Townsend, .	Lowell.
19,	Abby Ann Ness,* . .	Abby Ann Blake, . .	Lowell.
Oct. 10,	Thomas Stone,* . . .	Frank Stone Emerson, .	Melrose.
Nov. 14,	Laura Wheeler,* . .	Laura Chapman Wetherbee, .	Concord.
21,	Thomas Francis Maguire,*	Thomas Francis Murray, .	Somerville.

WORCESTER COUNTY.

Jan. 3,	George S. Wicker, . .	George Sherman Wesson, .	Oxford.
Feb. 7,	Ferdinand Holbrook, .	Emory Holbrook, . .	Grafton.
7,	James Merritt Leverett,* .	James Leverett Merritt, .	Fitchburg.
Mar. 7,	Joel Haggett, . . .	Joel Hudson, . . .	Paxton.
7,	George Muzzy, . . .	George M. Gallup, . .	Brookfield.
7,	Jane Lemira Barrus,* .	Jane Lemira Bigelow, .	West Boylston.
7,	Nancy Levina Barton, .	Harriet Nancy Barton, .	Fitchburg.
7,	Abby Carolin Lawrence,* .	Abby Carolin Hastings, .	West Boylston.
May 3,	Eldora Leonora Rawson,*	Eldora Rawson Hannum, .	Douglas.
18,	Estus Smith Fay,* . .	Estus Smith Russell, .	Gardner.
18,	Ella Eliza Fay,* . .	Ella Eliza Russell, .	Gardner.
June 6,	Marion Chapin,* . .	Marion Chapin Thayer, .	Milford.
6,	Emily Mentoria Brizzee,* .	Emily Elizabeth Hyde, .	Hubbardston.
Sept. 5,	Lilla Maria Staples,* . .	Lilla Maria Hastings, .	Hubbardston.
5,	Cynthia Augusta Seley,* .	Clara Seley Houghton, .	Leominster.
Dec. 5,	Georgianna Summers,* .	Georgianna Bridge, .	Gardner.

HAMPSHIRE COUNTY.

Nov. 7,	Silvia Montague Marsh,* .	Silvia Marsh Montague, .	Westhampton.
Dec. 5,	Eliphaz Elbridge Dickinson,	Henry Anderson Dickinson, .	Granby.

HAMPDEN COUNTY.

Jan. 3,	Edward Warren Osgood, .	Edward Sherburne Osgood, .	Springfield.
Aug. 22,	Louisa Rebecca Eno, .	Louisa Eno Gillette, .	Westfield.
22,	Royal Greenwood, . .	Royal Greenwood Clifton, .	Westfield.
Sept. 26,	Mary Fidelia Sikes, . .	Mary Fidelia Palmer, .	West Springfield.

* Changed by reason of adoption.

FRANKLIN COUNTY.

Date of Decree.	Original Name.	Name Decreed.	Residence.
1854.			
Mar. 14,	John Dwight Coy,* . . .	George Dutton Snow, . .	Bernardston.
Aug. 22,	Lucy Maria Locke,* . .	Lucy Maria Smith, . .	Buckland.
22,	Martha Laurens Locke,* . .	Martha Laurens Smith, .	Buckland.
Oct. 18,	Alexander Browne,* . . .	Charles Alexander Smith, .	Buckland.
18,	George W. Browne,* . . .	George Alfred White Smith, .	Buckland.

BERKSHIRE COUNTY.

–	Thomas Demoranville, . .	Thomas Ranville, . . .	———.
–	Esther Demoranville, . .	Esther Ranville, . . .	———.
–	Chester L. Demoranville, .	Chester L. Ranville, . .	———.
–	Adeline E. Demoranville, .	Adeline E. Ranville, . .	———.
–	Albert T. Demoranville, .	Albert T. Ranville, . .	———.
–	Lucy I. Demoranville, . .	Lucy I. Ranville, . . .	———.
–	John H. Demoranville, . .	John H. Ranville, . . .	———.

NORFOLK COUNTY.

Mar. 25,	John Humphrey, . . .	John Humphrey Kelley, .	Stoughton.
April 4,	Abby Jane Calder, . . .	Abby Jane Colburn, . .	Dedham.
8,	Jonathan Franklin Woodside, .	Franklin Woodside, . .	Roxbury.
May 6,	Eliza Ann Fowler, . . .	Mary Louisa Boyden, . .	Dedham.
13,	Manly Fowler, ...	Manly Fowler Cutter, . .	Roxbury.
June 24,	Emma Lavinia Fales, . .	Emma May Mann, . .	Canton.
Nov. 25,	Michael Grace Read, . . .	Alton Grace Read, . .	Roxbury.
Dec. 2,	Samuel Knowles Scott, . .	Samuel Scott Knowles, .	Roxbury.
–	Joseph Monasses, . . .	Joseph Silva, ...	Cohasset.

BRISTOL COUNTY.

Jan. 6,	Frances Ruth Snow, . . .	Frances Ruth Maria Snow, .	Taunton.

PLYMOUTH COUNTY.

Mar. 7,	William Henry McCarthey, .	William Henry Harrison, .	Hingham.
May 2,	Isabella Frances Drew, .	Isabella Frances Holmes, .	Bridgewater.
15,	Deborah Alden Ford, . .	Deborah Alden Tolman, .	Pembroke.
15,	Bethia Harrington Ford, .	Bethia Harrington Cobb, .	Pembroke.
Oct. 3,	Elizabeth Williams Lee, .	Susan Elizabeth Frost, .	Abington.

BARNSTABLE COUNTY.

June 20,	Eleazer Atwood, Jr., . . .	Eleazer Higgins Atwood, .	Wellfleet.
Oct. 30,	Ida Davis,*	Ida Davis Pitcher, . .	Barnstable.

* Changed by reason of adoption.

SUFFOLK COUNTY.

Date of Decree.	Original Name.	Name Decreed.	Residence.
1855.			
–	George Barnard, . . .	George Barnard Brown, .	———.
–	William Piggot Casey, . .	William Piggot, . . .	———.
–	James Gilleland, . . .	James Gillingham, . .	———.
–	Warren Gookin, . . .	Warren Plummer Wilder, .	———.
–	Nellie Howe, ...	Emma Frances Colburn, .	———.
–	Susan Dillaway Irish, .	Susan Dillaway Taylor, .	———.
–	Edwin Augustus Irish, .	Edwin Augustus Taylor, .	———.
–	James Franklin Irish, .	Frank Berry Taylor, . .	———.
–	Samuel Keep, ...	Samuel Hamilton Keep, .	———.
–	Uriah Thomas Ling, . .	Uriah Thomas Stone, .	———.
–	John McCarter, . . .	John Mason Carter, . .	———.
–	Martha A. Morrow, . .	Martha A. Morse, . .	———.
–	William Roddin, . . .	William Brown Adams, .	———.
–	Mary Ann Robinson, .	Frances Ella Butts, . .	———.
–	Henrietta A. Smith, . .	Henrietta A. Reed, . .	———.
–	Mary Ann Tancock, . .	Mary Ann Sharland, . .	———.
–	William Brown Adams, .	William Roddin, . . .	———.
–	Matilda Allen Fearing, .	Matilda Fearing Allen, .	———.
–	Mary Elizabeth Fuller, .	Mary Frances Williams, .	———.
–	John Gilligan, ...	John Gilligan Adams, .	———.

ESSEX COUNTY.

Date of Decree.	Original Name.	Name Decreed.	Residence.
April 3,	Mary Snethen, ...	Mary Snethen Abbott, . .	Salem.
May 15,	James Gott, 3d, ...	James Jabez Gott, . . .	Rockport.
15,	Franklin Putnam Fish, . .	Franklin Putnam, . . .	Andover.

MIDDLESEX COUNTY.

Date of Decree.	Original Name.	Name Decreed.	Residence.
Jan. 9,	Thomas Saunders, . . .	Thomas Edward Saunders, .	Lowell.
Feb. 20,	Jackson McCartee, . . .	Loring Mason Jackson, .	Burlington.
Mar 6,	James Alfred Loker, . .	Alfred J. Livingston, . .	Tewksbury.
6,	Mary Savory Price, . .	Mary Price Savory, . .	Lowell.
20,	Mehitable S. Benson, .	Sarah Benson Green, . .	South Reading
20,	Frances Ellen Sawyer, .	Frances Ellen Wright, .	Lowell.
April 10,	Charles Dearth, ...	Charles Howe, . . .	Sherborn.
10,	The wife and three children of the above, ...	——— Howe, ...	Sherborn.
10,	Henry Dearth, ...	Henry Howe, ...	Sherborn.
10,	The wife and two children of the above, ...	——— Howe, ...	Sherborn.
10,	John Brown, ...	John Manson Brown, . .	Charlestown.
10,	Mary Jane Mosman, . .	Mary Jane Smith, . . .	Sudbury.
10,	Michael Powell, ...	Martin Powell, . . .	Cambridge.
May 15,	Mazelli Augustus Benson, .	Ellen Benson Baldwin, .	Reading.
June 5,	Idaetta Towne, ...	Idaetta Thompson, . .	Lowell.
12,	George Washington Robinson,	George Dexter Robinson, .	Lexington.
26,	Ellen Euseba Montague, .	Ella Euseba Sherman, . .	Ashland.
Aug. 21,	Malcom Holden, . . .	Howard Malcom Holden, .	Malden.
Sept. 4,	Josiah Cooledge McKenney, .	Josiah Cooledge Hadley, .	Waltham.
18,	Patrick Driscoll, . . .	Frederick Driscoll, . .	Groton.
Nov. 13,	George Michali, ...	George Hayden, . . .	Lincoln.
Dec. 4,	Charlotte Louisa Hubbard, .	Ella Frances Gooding, .	Somerville.
18,	Nathaniel Palmer, . . .	Nathaniel Palmer Leach, .	Charlestown.
18,	Elizabeth P. Palmer, . .	Elizabeth Perkins Leach, .	Charlestown.

WORCESTER COUNTY.

Date of Decree.	Original Name.	Name Decreed	Residence.
1855.			
April 3,	Frances Everline Livermore,* .	Frances Everline Day, . .	Millbury.
May 1,	Caleb Warren Dalrymple, .	Caleb Warren, . . .	Shrewsbury.
8,	Ezra Batcheller, 2d, . .	Ezra Daniel Batcheller, . .	North Brookfield.
June 5,	Edward Perkins,* . .	Edward Chalmers Haynes, .	Leominster.
July 3,	Charles Marvin Cleveland,* .	Charles Cleveland Wheelock,	Worcester.
3,	Edward Alonzo Howe, . .	Alonzo Edward Gibson, .	Barre.
Aug. 7,	Mary Ann Delon,* . . .	Laura Mehitable Chamberlain,	Southborough.

HAMPSHIRE COUNTY.

Date of Decree.	Original Name.	Name Decreed	Residence.
April 3,	Patrick Falvey, . . .	Henry S. Falvey, . . .	Hadley.
May 1,	Emma Cordelia Snow,* . .	Emma Cordelia Hubbard, .	Williamsburg.
July 3,	George Edgar Stowell,* . .	George Stowell Temple, . .	Northampton.
Aug. 7,	Susan E. Cook, ...	Susan E. Babbit, . . .	Pelham.
Sept. 4,	Eliza Maria Gorman,* . .	Eliza Maria Tower, . .	Northampton.

HAMPDEN COUNTY.

Date of Decree.	Original Name.	Name Decreed	Residence.
Jan. –	James Rodolphus Hoar, . .	James Rodolphus Homer, .	Monson.
Feb. –	Abner Post Langdon, . .	Abner Post, ...	Westfield.
Mar. –	Elmira Ann Bond, . . .	Almira Ann Dean, . . .	———.
June –	Joseph W. Boot, . . .	Joseph W. Wright, . . .	———.
Aug. –	Jennette Marsh, ...	Jennette Gilmore, . . .	Springfield.
–	Eliza Ann Goodell, . . .	Mary Ella Street, . . .	Springfield.
Nov. –	Phineas Clark, ...	Charles Henry Smith, . .	Chicopee.

FRANKLIN COUNTY.

Date of Decree.	Original Name.	Name Decreed	Residence.
Feb. 13,	Charles D. Deth, . . .	Charles D. Gilmore, . .	Erving.
Dec. 18,	Sumner Lincoln, . . .	Increase Sumner Lincoln, .	Rowe.

BERKSHIRE COUNTY.

Date of Decree.	Original Name.	Name Decreed	Residence.
June 5,	Frederick C Shumway, . .	Frederick Shumway Ford, .	———.

NORFOLK COUNTY.

Date of Decree.	Original Name.	Name Decreed	Residence.
Jan. 6,	Ella Medora French, . . .	Ella Medora French Parker, .	Quincy.
April 14,	Alonzo Howard, . . .	Alonzo Potter Howard, . .	Brookline.
May 3,	Mary A. Westcott, . . .	Mary A. Dascomb, . .	West Roxbury.
3,	Annette W. Wyman, . .	Annette W. Cobb, . . .	Wrentham.
26,	Ella Josephine Dowe, . .	Ella Josephine Watson, . .	Quincy.
July 1,	Lewis G. Seaver, . . .	Lewis Seaver Dixon, . .	Dedham.
Oct. 13,	Alice Clayton Stoddard, . .	Alice Clayton Baker, . .	Hull.
Nov. 17,	Charles Everett Chase, . .	Charles Everett Martin, . .	Foxborough.
Dec. 8,	Emeline Gowell, . . .	Emeline Gurney, . . .	Weymouth.

* Changed by reason of adoption.

BRISTOL COUNTY.

Date of Decree.	Original Name.	Name Decreed.	Residence.
1855. Jan. 5,	Michael Mulliken, . . .	Thomas Edward Mulliken White, ...	New Bedford.

PLYMOUTH COUNTY.

Feb. 27,	Betsey Maria Pittsley,* . .	Betsey Maria Cahoon, . .	Wareham.
June 5,	John Dubbs, ...	John Deering, . . .	Hingham.
5,	Grace Lawrence,* . . .	Abby Grace Bracket, . .	Marshfield.
July 3,	Lemira Jenness Morrow,* . .	Mary Jenness Perry, . .	Pembroke.
Aug. 28,	Henrietta Lewis,* . . .	Annette Webster Sawyer, .	Taunton.
Sept. 24,	Peleg Sprague Ellison, . .	William Peleg Ellison, . .	Duxbury.

BARNSTABLE COUNTY.

Mar. 13,	Julia Maria Gervassio, .	Julia Maria Gervassio Oakes,	Barnstable.
13,	Mary Augusta Crocker, .	Martha Ann Crocker, . .	Brewster.
13,	Elizabeth Nealus, .	Elizabeth Rogers, . .	Dennis.
13,	Inis W. Bearse,* . .	Inis W. Bacon, . .	Barnstable.
13,	Prince Albert Hinckley,* .	Prince Albert Fuller, .	Barnstable.
June 19,	Sophia Wilson Hinckley,*	Sophia Wilson Hallett, .	Barnstable.
19,	William R. Vredenburgh,*	William R. Robbins, .	Harwich.
July 17,	Margaret Lyons,* . .	Ellanora Stiff, . .	Barnstable.
Sept. 11,	Gorham Brackett, . .	Gorham Brackett Knowles, .	Yarmouth.
11,	Catharine Martin,* . .	Louisa Maria Sears, . .	Dennis.

NANTUCKET COUNTY.

Oct. 6,	Sarah Briggs, . . .	Sarah H. Briggs, . . .	———.
Nov. 15,	Franklin B. Chase, . .	Benjamin Franklin Chase, .	———.

SUFFOLK COUNTY.

1856. —	Phebe Baker, . . .	Ida Estella Germain, .	———.
—	Eva Barnard Chase, . .	Mary Eloise Edmands, . .	———.
—	Sarah Ann Drown, . .	Sarah Ann Battell, . .	———.
—	Delia Doherty, . . .	Delia Willson, . .	———.
—	Annie Ladd, . . .	Gertrude Straw, . .	———.
—	Albert F. Murphy, . .	Albert Freeman, . .	———.
—	Mary E. Murphy, . .	Mary Elizabeth Freeman, .	———.
—	Nathaniel L. Murphy, .	Nathaniel Murphy Lowe, .	———.
—	James H. Murphy, . .	James Murphy Hurd, .	———.
—	Elizabeth McAdams, . .	Elizabeth Adolphus Piercy, .	———.
—	Oriana Lucetta Marston, .	Ann Eliza Robbins, .	———.
—	John James O'Halloran, .	John James Vallelly, .	———.
—	Parmelia Parker, . .	Mary Ann Young, .	———.
—	Anne Maria Porter, . .	Annie Bourne, . .	———.
—	Abby Robinson, . .	Sarah Gertrude Babb, .	———.
—	Wallah Redding, . .	Wallah Redding,† . .	———.
—	Laurette Tibbetts, . .	Laura Ann Winchester, .	———.
—	John Williams, . . .	John Russell Williams, . .	———.

* Changed by reason of adoption.
† The real name of the child was unknown to the petitioners. She is the only survivor of the massacre in the Wallah Wallah Valley, in California. Her white friends found her, and saved her, giving her the name of Wallah Redding, which name the probate court decreed that she should be known by hereafter. Her parents were murdered with the other Indians, at the time above alluded to, and the child was found lying across the mother's breast after the massacre.

ESSEX COUNTY.

Date of Decree.	Original Name.	Name Decreed.	Residence.
1856.			
Jan. 15,	John Garrety, ...	John Henry Burnham, . .	Ipswich.
Mar. 4,	William Ensign Sargent, . .	William Parrott Sargent,	Lynn.
4,	William Clark, ...	William R. Clark, . .	Lynn.
25,	Francis Brown,* . . .	George Francis Carr, .	Newburyport.
25,	Almira Ellen Corson,* . .	Emma Judson Cropley, .	Newburyport.
May 6,	Abigail F. Jenkins, . .	Abby F. Jenkins, . . .	North Andover.
6,	Jens Rasmussen, . . .	James R. Hamilton, . .	Gloucester.
June 10,	Eliza C. Turnbull,* . . .	Mary Frances Dockum, .	Newburyport.
July 1,	John Johnson, ...	John George Johnson, .	Andover.
Sept. 2,	Henrietta C Janes, . . .	Henrietta C. Choate, . .	Lynn.
2,	Samuel J. B. Currier, . .	Samuel J. Brown, . . .	Salisbury.
Oct. 7,	Charles Warren Johnson, . .	Charles Benjamin Johnson, .	Nahant.

MIDDLESEX COUNTY.

Date of Decree.	Original Name.	Name Decreed.	Residence.
Jan. 8,	Francis Harvey Batchelder, .	George Francis Harvey Batchelder, ...	Charlestown.
8,	Mary Augusta Walker Page, .	Mary Page Snow, . . .	Cambridge.
Feb. 19,	Laura Elizabeth Bradford, .	Lizzie Ann Fay, . . .	Lowell.
April 11,	Abba Frances Colby, . .	Anna Josephine Blanchard, .	Lowell.
24,	Josephine Elizabeth Wigginton,	Josephine Elizabeth Brown, .	Stoneham.
Aug. 19,	Isabella Anthony, . . .	Isabella Anthony Gordon, .	Malden.
19,	Mary Eliza Anthony, . .	Mary Eliza Wait, . . .	Malden.
19,	Fanny Clark Goddard, . .	Fanny Clark Bigelow, . .	Medford.
Sept. 16,	Evangeline Hobbs, . . .	Alice Allen Hosmer, . .	Lowell.
Oct. 28,	Elizabeth M. McEuen, . .	Elizabeth Baker, . . .	Framingham.
Dec. 16,	Clara Jane Hunt, . . .	Clara Jane Orcutt, . . .	Cambridge.

WORCESTER COUNTY.

Date of Decree.	Original Name.	Name Decreed.	Residence.
Jan. 1,	Hannah Adaline Winslow,* .	Hannah Adaline Cutler, .	———.
Feb. 5,	Eunice Augusta Drury,* . .	Carrie Augusta Ballard, .	———.
5,	William Wendell Drury,* . .	William Drury Wight, . .	Worcester.
5,	Helen Isabella Howland,* .	Helen Isabella Chapin, . .	Worcester.
5,	Mary Jane Waite,* . . .	Jennie Waite Whipple, . .	Worcester.
Mar. 4,	Andrew H. Ham, . . .	Andrew H. Hammond, . .	Worcester.
April 1,	Sarah Amarett Cleveland,* .	Sarah Maria Wheelock, . .	Worcester.
1,	Frances Ada Hanenstock,* .	Ada Isabella Brown, . .	Worcester.
1,	William Edwin Rogers, . .	William Edwin Gilbert, . .	West Brookfield.
May 22,	George Orville Ford,* . . .	George Ford Foskett, . .	Gardner.
June 3,	———,*	Abbie Frances Fisk, . .	Webster.
Sept. 2,	Eliza Leighton Randall,* . .	Annie Thayer Chapin, . .	Worcester.

HAMPSHIRE COUNTY.

Date of Decree.	Original Name.	Name Decreed.	Residence.
May 6,	George Sawyer Tracy, . .	George Sawyer, . . .	Belchertown.
6,	George Andrew Sawyer Tracy,	George Andrew Sawyer, .	Belchertown.
June 3,	John Eddy Dunbar Lamberton,	John Lamberton, . . .	Ware.
Oct. 7,	Charles Braman Herrick,* .	Charles Frank Cole, . .	Huntington.
Dec. 2,	Martha Riden,*	Mary Eva Lamb, . . .	Williamsburg.

* Changed by reason of adoption.

HAMPDEN COUNTY.

Date of Decree.	Original Name.	Name Decreed.	Residence.
1856. Jan. 1,	Sarah Jane Moore, . . .	Sarah Jane Orswell, . .	——.

FRANKLIN COUNTY.

Feb. 12,	Sarah Ida Brown,* . . .	Sarah Ida Hawks, . . .	Heath.
12,	Asahel Hawks Coats,* . .	Asahel Coats Hawks, . .	Heath.
Mar. 11,	Lucy Maria Harris,* . . .	Harriet Ella Goodwin, . .	Charlemont.
Oct. 14,	——,*	Charles Sumner Park, . .	Greenfield.
14,	Amos Deth, ...	Amos Dexter, ...	——.
14,	Hannah Deth, ...	Hannah Dexter, . . .	——.
14,	Hiram Deth, ...	Hiram Dexter, . . .	——.
21,	Michael Barden,* . . .	Willis Thomas Crosby, . .	Hawley.
21,	Mary Ann Barden,* . . .	Mary Ann Crosby, . . .	Hawley.

BERKSHIRE COUNTY.

Dec. 2,	William Wells Doolittle, . .	William Wells Smith, . .	——.
2,	Mary Elizabeth Doolittle, .	Mary Elizabeth Smith, . .	——.
2,	Cynthia Jane Crouch, . .	Cynthia Jane Wheeler, . .	——.

NORFOLK COUNTY.

Jan. 12,	Royal Lincoln Carsley, . .	Royal Lincoln, . . .	Roxbury.
19,	Maria Marinda Bicknell, . .	Marinda Dorr Bicknell, . .	Weymouth.
Mar. 15,	Sarah E. T. Burrage. . .	Sarah Burrage Palmer, . .	Roxbury.
Apr. 19,	David Webber Gridley, . .	Daniel John Webber, . .	Roxbury.
June 21,	Bridget Kenny, ...	Delia Shine, ...	Quincy.
21,	Mary A. Morris, . . .	Mary Ann Page, . . .	Stoughton.
Sept. 27,	Henry Dewey Cain, . . .	Henry Dewey Wilson, . .	Cohasset.
Oct. 11,	Mary Augusta Wyman, . .	Augusta Clapp, . . .	Dorchester.

BRISTOL COUNTY.

Aug. 5,	Humphrey Smith, . . .	Humphrey Howland Henry Crapo Smith, . . .	New Bedford.

PLYMOUTH COUNTY.

Mar. 4,	Peter Sprague, ...	Peter N. Sprague, . . .	Hingham.
Dec. 1,	Mary Ann Fuller,* . . .	Annie Isabel Lane, . . .	Charlestown.

BARNSTABLE COUNTY.

July 15,	Frances Oceana Gifford,* . .	Alice Frances Gifford, . .	Falmouth.
15,	Augustus Forest Smith, . .	John Forest Smith, . .	Truro.
Aug. 12,	John Peroney, ...	John Peroney Eldridge, . .	Barnstable.
12,	Ebenezer Hallet, jun., . .	Ebenezer Alger Hallet, . .	Yarmouth.

* Changed by reason of adoption.

DUKES COUNTY.

Date of Decree.	Original Name.	Name Decreed.	Residence.
1856.			
–	William Ross Merrills, . .	William Ross Pease, . .	Edgartown.
–	William Buckley Norton, . .	William Robert Norton, .	Tisbury.

NANTUCKET COUNTY.

–	Sarah Briggs, ...	Sarah H. Briggs, . . .	——.
–	Franklin B. Chase, . . .	Benjamin Franklin Chase, .	——.

SUFFOLK COUNTY.

1857.			
–	Chares C. Amory, . . .	Charles Amory, . . .	——.
–	George Barnard, . . .	George B. Oliver, . . .	——.
–	Chester G. Brown, . . .	Gilbert C. Brown, . . .	——.
–	Mary Biggins, ...	Martha Ella Teear, . . .	——.
–	Richmond Doyne, . . .	Charles R. Doane, . . .	——.
–	John Dean, ...	John Ward Dean, . . .	——.
–	Elizabeth Doherty, . . .	Elizabeth Ulmar, . . .	——.
–	Mary M. Donovan, . . .	Jenny Brown, . . .	——.
–	Phebe Ann Eldredge, . .	Anna Eldredge, . . .	——.
–	William Henry Gray, . .	William Wallis Jenkins, .	——.
–	Mary E. Haden, . . .	Eliza Frances French, . .	——.
–	Manoah Meade Livingston, .	Montgomery Meade Livingston	——.
–	James O'Connor, . . .	James Connor, . . .	——.
–	Ernest H. Ruggles, . . .	George Washington Farr, .	——.
–	Mary E. Skelsey, . . .	Albertina Renocia Gardner, .	——.
–	Mary J. Salisbury, . . .	Mary Jane Felton, . . .	——.
–	Mary Sonnenberg, . . .	Hannah Marilla Belcher, .	——.
–	Charles Sawyer, . . .	Charles Alfred Sawyer, . .	——.
–	Jessie Turner, . . .	Elizabeth Piercy, . . .	——.
–	Eva Louisa Thomas, . .	Ella Louisa Fullerton, . .	——.
–	Ellen Worthen, ...	Ellen Turel Jackson, . .	——.
–	Henry Augustus Whitney, .	Henry Austin Whitney, . .	——.
–	Eliphalet G. Williams, . .	Edward Gordon Williams, .	——.
–	Almira E. Watson, . . .	Elizabeth Watson Cheney, .	——.
–	Howard A. Watson, . . .	Howard Clifton Watson, .	——.

ESSEX COUNTY.

May 5,	Martha Rafferty, . . .	Martha Rogers, . . .	Salem.
5,	The five children of the above, .	—— Rogers, . . .	Salem.
5,	John Torr, 2d, ...	John Stevens Torr, . .	South Danvers.
June 9,	Sarah Jane Frink, . . .	Sarah Jane Bentley, . .	Haverhill.
Sept. 1,	William Tarbox, . . .	William Wallingford, . .	Lynn.
1,	The wife and two children of the above, ...	—— Wallingford, . .	Lynn.
Dec. 1,	Joseph Henry Chandler, . .	Joseph Chandler, jun., . .	Andover.

MIDDLESEX COUNTY.

Jan. 13,	Ellar F. Atkinson,* . . .	Frances A. McNeill, . .	Lowell.
13,	Charles Edwin Morrison, . .	Miles Morse, ...	Hopkinton.
13,	Abner Thurston Linnikin, .	Abner Thurston Linnikin Weston, ...	Malden.
13,	The wife and son of the above, .	—— Weston, . . .	Malden.

* Changed by reason of adoption.

MIDDLESEX COUNTY — *Concluded.*

Date of Decree.	Original Name.	Name Decreed.	Residence.
1857.			
Feb. 17,	Rebecca Kilby Eaton, . .	Rebecca Eaton Parker, . .	Cambridge.
17,	Sarah Ann Eaton, . . .	Sarah Ann Eaton Parker, .	Cambridge.
Mar. 3,	Emma J. Durant,* . . .	Emma Frances Gregory, .	Waltham.
3,	Lizzie Ann Fay,* . . .	Lizzie Ann Stevens, . .	Lowell.
May 19,	Mary Frances Willett,* . .	Mary Frances Hall, . .	Concord.
June 3,	Catherine Floyd Clifton,* .	Ellen Elizabeth Hine, . .	Woburn.
30,	Zipporah Belcher,* . . .	Martha Eugenie Leland, .	Natick.
Aug. 11,	Michael Gorman,* . . .	Charles Francis, . . .	Marlborough.
Sept. 1,	Michael Kavanagh, . . .	Edward Kavanagh, . .	Lowell.
8,	Mary Jane Moore,* . . .	Mary Jane Smith, . . .	Cambridge.
22,	Annie Hall,*	Nellie Homer, . . .	Cambridge.
Oct. 13,	Oliver Clough Moore,* . .	Oliver Clough Moore Smith, .	Somerville.
13,	Lizzie Whitten,* . . .	Emma Whitten Flanders, .	Lowell.
27,	Benjamin Gallighan,* . .	Willie Fletcher Robbins, .	Holliston.
27,	Delia Maria Starrott,* . .	Emma Maria Phinney, . .	Melrose.
27,	Emma Althea Daniels,* . .	Emma Daniels Ware, . .	Sherborn.
Nov. 10,	Mary Gallagher, . . .	Mary E. Walcott, . . .	Waltham.

WORCESTER COUNTY.

Jan. 6,	Charles E. Jones,* . . .	Charles E. Whitney, . .	——.
Feb. 3,	Adaline Augusta White,* .	Emma Banister, . . .	——.
Mar. 3,	Mary Louisa Flint, . .	Julia Daniels Flint, . .	Southborough.
May 20,	Herbert Stearns White,* .	Herbert Stearns Lesure, .	West Boylston.
June 2,	Martha Rogers, ...	Martha Bachelor Edwards, .	West Brookfield.
July 7,	Jonathan Austin Davis, .	Austin Davis, ...	Oxford.
7,	Timothy Ide Nicholas, .	Timothy N. Ide, . . .	Milford.
Aug. 4,	—— Pond,* . . .	Charles Wallace Bliss, .	——.
4,	Frances Ada Havenstock,*	Ada Isabella Gale, . . .	Millbury.
Sept. 29,	William B. Chesmore,* .	Herbert Gay Fairbanks, .	Westborough.
Oct. 6,	Emily Jane Farwell, . .	Emily Jane Upton, . .	Fitchburg.

HAMPSHIRE COUNTY.

Feb. 3,	William Wilcomb Bennett, .	William Bell, ...	Belchertown.
Apr. 7,	Joseph P. Walker,* . . .	Joseph Walker Field, . .	Northampton.
July 7,	Sophronia Smith Cummings, .	Sophronia Granger Cummings,	Ware.
Oct. 6,	Louisa J. Nichols,* . . .	Louisa J. Patten, . . .	Williamsburg.

HAMPDEN COUNTY.

Feb. 3,	John H. Smith, ...	William J. Burt, . . .	——.
Nov. 24,	Sarah Bond, ...	Emely Clark, ...	——.

FRANKLIN COUNTY.

Feb. 10,	Mary E. Warner, . . .	Mary Elizabeth Churchill, .	Colrain.
Mar. 10,	Alma Seaver, ...	Alma Clap, ...	Gill.
10,	Abby Seaver, ...	Abby Clap, ...	Gill.
Oct. 13,	Fanny M. Stimpson, . .	Ida Streeter, ...	Northfield.
13,	Caroline Hibbard, . . .	Caroline Wunsch, . . .	Greenfield.
Dec. 15,	Marriam Sophia Belden, .	Marriam Sophia Nash, . .	Whately.

* Changed by reason of adoption.

BERKSHIRE COUNTY.

Date of Decree.	Original Name.	Name Decreed.	Residence.
1857.			
Apr. 7,	Nancy E. Lane, . . .	Cynthia E. Davis, . . .	——.
29,	Lovaine Patridge, . . .	Leonard Lovaine Ryder, .	——.

NORFOLK COUNTY.

Jan. 17,	Mary Isabella Phillips, . .	Mary Isabella Sumner, . .	Dorchester.
May 30,	George Luther Clapp, . .	George Fisher Gay, . .	Sharon.
June 6,	Francis Edgar Packard, .	Frank Edgar Packard, . .	Quincy.
Aug. 11,	Lewis A. Packard, . . .	Elisha Fackard, . . .	Quincy.
15,	Sarah Dorr, ...	Grace Ada Howard, . .	Canton.

PLYMOUTH COUNTY.

Jan. 12,	Josphine Corbett,* . . .	Flora Webster Chamberlain, .	Abington.
May 18,	Helen M. Muirhead, . .	Helen M. Gray, . . .	Kingston.
July 7,	William Henry Cowenskiff, .	William Henry Cowen, .	Rochester.
Aug. 4,	Henry Alden Humphrey, .	Henry Peirce Alden, .	Bridgewater.
10,	Ann Goodell,*	Ann Goodell Hatch, . .	Middleborough.
10,	Edward Wadsworth, . .	William W. Holmes, . .	Duxbury.

BARNSTABLE COUNTY.

May 14,	Eliza B. Drody, . . .	Eliza B. Crowell, . . .	Barnstable.
14,	George C. Drody, . . .	George Crowell, . . .	Barnstable.
19,	Mary Allen Knowles, . .	Mary Rowe Knowles, . .	Yarmouth.
June 16,	Mary Green,*	Alice Josephine Cobb, . .	Barnstable.
Dec. 14,	Joshua Francis Small, . .	Daniel Francis Small, . .	Provincetown.

SUFFOLK COUNTY.

1858.			
–	George R. Curran, . .	Stukely S. Wescott, . .	——.
–	Caroline Tinkham Grinnell, .	Caroline Grinnell Smith, .	——.
–	Michael Gibbs, jun , . .	Melville Shields Gibbs, .	——.
–	George Thomas Gillett, .	George Thomas Phinney, .	——.
–	Mary McGregor, . . .	Gertrude Eleanor Baker, .	——.
–	Newell Campbell Rogers, .	Newell Rogers Campbell, .	——.
–	Hinman Stevens, . . .	Hiram Stevens, . . .	——.
–	Minnie Stall, . . .	Nellie Florine Barton, . .	——.
–	Celia Maria Sawyer, . .	Celia Maria Hamilton, . .	——.
–	Harriet Ann Webber, . .	Hattie Tarbox, . . .	——.
–	Charles Forbush Warren, .	Jonathan Charles Warren, .	——.

ESSEX COUNTY.

Feb. 2,	Mary Noonan,*	Ella Dole, ...	Rowley.
2,	Albert Knight,* . . .	Eli Vickery Bartlett, . .	Marblehead.
Mar. 6,	Amos Abbott, 2d, . . .	Amos Chandler Abbott, .	Andover.

* Changed by reason of adoption.

ESSEX COUNTY — *Concluded.*

Date of Decree.	Original Name.	Name Decreed.	Residence.
1858.			
Mar. 30,	Conrad Henser, ...	Conrad Henser Brooks, . .	Ipswich.
April 6,	Charles Dunn, ...	Charles Wilson, . . .	Marblehead.
6,	Margery Dunn, ...	Margery Wilson, . . .	Marblehead.
6,	Alexander W. Dunn, . .	Alexander W. Wilson, . .	Marblehead.
6,	Henrietta C. Dunn, . .	Henrietta C. Wilson, . .	Marblehead.
6,	Thomas W. Dunn, . . .	Thomas W. Wilson, . .	Marblehead.
6,	Mary Ellen Dunn, . . .	Mary Ellen Wilson, . .	Marblehead.
June 8,	Matthew E. MacDaniel, .	Matthew E. Daniel, . .	——.
8,	Mary Elizabeth MacDaniel, .	Mary Elizabeth Daniel, . .	——.
8,	George Emery MacDaniel,	George Emery Daniel, . .	——.
8,	Charles Frank MacDaniel,	Charles Frank Daniel, . .	——.
8,	Elinor J. Brown,* . . .	Nellie J Danforth, . .	Bradford.
July 20,	Ellen Kemble Oliver, . .	Ellen Wendell Oliver, . .	Lawrence.
Nov. 2,	Mary Ann Meagher,* . .	Arietta Brown, . . .	Lynn.
16,	Horace L. Connolly, . .	Horace Ingersoll, . .	Salem.

MIDDLESEX COUNTY.

Jan. 5,	James Richardson,* . .	George Wight, . . .	Wayland.
26,	Eleanor White,* . . .	Ellen Metcalf Adams, . .	Melrose.
Feb. 23,	Priscilla Alley,* . . .	Priscilla Augusta Leathe, .	Reading.
23,	George Harris Thompson,*	George Harris Welch, . .	Charlestown.
Mar. 23,	George Albert Hayward,* .	George Albert Hayward Richardson, ...	Dracut.
April 6,	William Edward Tuckerman, .	Edward Gustavus Tuckerman,	Lowell.
13,	Sarah Elizabeth Fletcher,*	Sarah Elizabeth Dutton, .	Carlisle.
13,	Angelia Leighton,* . .	Annie Leighton Fairbanks, .	Somerville.
May 11,	Mary Josephine Thomas,*	Mary Josephine Pearsons, .	Lowell.
June 8,	Lizzie Sophia Watts,* .	Lizzie Sophia Raymond, .	Lowell.
22,	Evangeline Farrington,* .	Julia Maria Robbins, . .	Holliston.
22,	Arethusa Jameson, . .	Zilla Weatherbee, . . .	Newton.
22,	Henry Bigelow Somes,* .	Lewis Henry Whitney, . .	Woburn.
Aug. 10,	Mary Grace Moore,* . .	Mary Grace Goodnough, .	Sudbury.
Oct. 5,	Emma Loheed, ...	Hattie Twing, . . .	Lincoln.
26,	Ella Faxon,*	Ella Jane Pierce, . . .	Holliston.
Nov. 9,	Frances Ellen Wight,* .	Frances Ellen Sawyer, . .	Lowell.
23,	Eliza Stratton, . . .	Eliza Tufts, ...	Charlestown.
23,	Catherine Clinton Porter,* .	Catherine Porter Simonds, .	Cambridge.
23,	Gustav Ernst Friedrich Regen,*	Gustav Ernst Friedrich Regen Birnstill, ...	Newton.
Dec. 7,	Mary Elizabeth Robinson.* .	Mary Elizabeth Butterfield, .	Lowell.
28,	Elizabeth Locke,* . . .	Elizabeth Merkle, . . .	Cambridge.

WORCESTER COUNTY.

Jan. 5,	Willie Fairbanks Hubbard,* .	Willie Fairbanks Knowlton, .	Holden.
5,	Frances L. Simpson,* .	Fanny Louisa Ballard, . .	Worcester.
Mar. 2,	Ella Girtrude Jewett.* .	Ella Girtrude Houghton, .	Harvard.
April 6,	Mary Frances Cunliffe,* .	Mary Frances Walkden, .	Worcester.
6,	Thomas Conroy,* . . .	Thomas Conroy Welch, . .	Worcester.
6,	Dianna Maria Lurena Wood,* .	Dianna Maria Lurena Johnson,	Upton.
June 1,	Silas Holt,*	Henry Isaac Hilton Mundell, .	Hubbardston.
1,	Ann Eliza Jones,* . . .	Ann Jones Estey, . . .	Worcester.
Aug. 3,	Sarah B. Jackman, . .	Sarah B. Whipple, . . .	Warren.
Oct. 5,	Henrietta Evelyn Morse,* .	Henrietta Evelyn Morse Hall,	Worcester.

* Changed by reason of adoption.

WORCESTER COUNTY — *Concluded.*

Date of Decree.	Original Name.	Name Decreed.	Residence.
1858.			
Oct. 5,	Jane Elizabeth Rice,*	Jane Elizabeth Pierce,	Worcester.
5,	Genette Rosella Rice,*	Genette Rosella Pierce,	Worcester.
5,	Grace Thatcher,*	Minnie Idella Folger,	Milford.
Dec. 7,	Almirah B. Davenport,	Almirah B. Cummings,	Mendon.

HAMPSHIRE COUNTY.

Jan. 5,	Thomas Cogan,	Thomas Raymond,	Ware.
Feb. 2,	Willie Duane Ward,*	Willie Duane Selman,	Northampton.
April 6,	Dwight Thomas Robbins,*	Thomas Dwight Woods,	Ware.
May 4,	Isabella Fowler,*	Lida Belle Hawes,	Middlefield.
Aug. 3,	Mary Ann Savary,*	Helen Burleigh,	Huntington.
Dec. 7,	George Franklin,	George Franklin Amidon,	Belchertown.

FRANKLIN COUNTY.

April 27,	Clarence Alburtus Taylor,*	Clarence Alburtus Wheaton,	Wendell.
May 11,	Frances S. Stebbins,*	Fannie Stebbins Ware,	Deerfield.
11,	William Garrotte, jun.,	Edwin Max Wilhelmi,	Deerfield.

BERKSHIRE COUNTY.

Jan. 5,	Lucy Jane Sparks,*	Lucy J. Cornell,	———.
5,	George Wilson,*	David W. Gamble,	———.
13,	Charity Adelia Brennin,	Adelia Brown,	———.
Mar. 2,	Jonathan Gross Barnard,	John Gross Barnard,	———.
April 6,	Juliette Neal,*	Juliette Stilson,	———.
May 24,	Michael Flannagan,	Charles Pitt Frissell,	———.
July 27,	Sarah Jane Fleming,*	Sarah J. Proctor,	———.
Oct. 13,	George Stillman Hart,*	George Stillman Clark,	———.
13,	Elliot Eugene Childs,*	Elliot Eugene Clark,	———.

NORFOLK COUNTY.

May 8,	Theodore Hooton,	Walter Henry Brock,	Dorchester.
June 5,	Mary Louisa Walker,	Mary Louisa Chase,	Canton.
July 6,	John Henry Brightman,	Albert Davis Kingsbury,	Medfield.

PLYMOUTH COUNTY.

–	Sidney T. Ford,	Elijah T. Ford,	Duxbury.

* Changed by reason of adoption.

BARNSTABLE COUNTY.

Date of Decree.	Original Name.	Name Decreed.	Residence.
1858.			
–	Charles H. Haskell, . . .	Charles H. Swift, . . .	Dennis.
–	Cyreno Franklin Pierce, .	Israel Franklin Pierce, .	Truro.
–	Freeman Ryder, 2d, . .	Freeman Gage, . . .	Harwich.
–	Willis G. Hallet, . . .	Simeon Hallet, . . .	Yarmouth.
–	Henry Baker, ...	Henry H. Baker, . . .	Barnstable.
–	Mary Caroline Whelden, .	Mary Caroline Bursley, .	Barnstable.

SUFFOLK COUNTY.

Date of Decree.	Original Name.	Name Decreed.	Residence.
1859.			
–	Nellie Frances Bartlett, .	Nellie Frances Wright, .	——.
–	Williamina Arrabella Crolius, .	Williamina Arabella Potter, .	——.
–	Caroline F. Eaton, . . .	Betsey Watson Eaton, . .	——.
–	John Finegan, ...	John Dillon, ...	——.
–	Mary Elizabeth Goodwin, .	Mary Elizabeth Johnson, .	——.
–	Anna Cordelia Adelaide Hanson, ...	Anna Cordelia Adelaide Johnson, ...	——.
–	Heilda Hanson, ...	Sarah Eliza Swasey, . .	——.
–	John Munroe Little, . .	John Mason Little, . . .	——.
–	Henrietta Stewart Robinson,	Marietta Stewart Foster, .	——.
–	Elizabeth Schrader, . .	Lizzie Paige, ...	——.
–	Charlotte A. Snelling, .	Charlotte A. Pratt, . . .	——.
–	William Mathew Smith, .	William Smith Phillipson, .	——.
–	Mary Elizabeth Walker, .	Minnie Cecilia Hatchman, .	——.

ESSEX COUNTY.

Date of Decree.	Original Name.	Name Decreed.	Residence.
Apr. 5,	Josiah Dearborn Clark, .	George Merrill Clark, . .	Methuen.
5,	Ella Meady,*	Ella Florence Meady Bailey, .	Salem.
19,	Lucy E. Goodhue,* . .	Emma L. Johnson, .	West Amesbury.
May 3,	Lewis Tappan, . . .	Lewis Northey Tappan, .	Manchester.
3,	Annah Frame,* . . .	Myra Anna Lane, . . .	Gloucester.
June 7,	Alexander Cobban, . .	George Albert Cobban, . .	Groveland.
7,	Aquilla R. Baker, . .	William Rich Baker, . .	Marblehead.
July 5,	Orrin Ross Maddox, . .	Orrin Maddox Ross, .	Lynn.
5,	Michael O'Brien,* . .	Michael Hayes, . . .	Georgetown.
Oct. 4,	William Otis Dearborn,* .	William Otis Cheever, .	Lynn.
4,	Eva Mathews,* . . .	Evalyne Snow, . . .	Methuen.
18,	George Tucker,* . . .	William Gale, . . .	Haverhill.
Dec. 6,	Victoria Stone,* . . .	Sarah Livonia Longley, .	Rockport.
6,	George W. Bennett,* . .	William C. W. Page, . .	Newburyport.
27,	William L. Jones,* . . .	Albert Sumner Merrill, .	Amesbury.

MIDDLESEX COUNTY.

Date of Decree.	Original Name.	Name Decreed.	Residence.
Jan. 4,	——,*	Ida Frances Hartwell, .	Littleton.
4,	——,*	Annie Augusta Peirce, .	Lowell.
Mar. 8,	Samuel M. P. Hersey, .	Samuel M. Plummer, .	Charlestown.
8,	Emma Fairbarn,* . .	Emma Lucy Bourne, .	Charlestown.
8,	Amelia West,* . . .	Carrie Amelia Wing, .	Newton.

* Changed by reason of adoption.

MIDDLESEX COUNTY — *Concluded.*

Date of Decree.	Original Name.	Name Decreed.	Residence.
1859.			
April 26,	William Richard M a r s h a l l Goodall,*	William Richard Dinsmoor,	Cambridge.
May 10,	Mary Elizabeth Churchill,*	Mary Elizabeth Watson,	Lowell.
June 7,	Ellen Quinn,*	Mary Ellen Hamblet,	Dracut.
14,	John Knight, 3d,	John Gould Knight,	Woburn.
14,	John Mirrorgen,	John Forrest,	South Reading.
28,	Emma Frances Gregory,*	Emma Frances Hurd,	Waltham.
Aug. 9,	John Barrett Brewster,	John Calvin Brewster,	Malden.
Sept. 6,	Sarah Jane Card,*	Sarah Jane Parker,	Woburn
Oct. 11,	Emma Gertrude ——,*	Emma Gertrude Lufkin,	Cambridge.
11,	Clara Lavinia Spalding,*	Mary Lavinia Tufts,	West Cambridge.
25,	Mary Jane McElmurry,*	Mary Frances Turner,	Newton.
Nov. 8,	Jennie Taylor,*	Jennie Augusta Pickering,	Waltham.
22,	Evalyn Maria Brown,*	Matilda Fairbanks,	Melrose.
Dec. 13,	John Stewart,*	Franklin Wesley Gardner,	Cambridge.

WORCESTER COUNTY.

–	Cyrus Angell,	Cyrus Locke,	——.
–	William A. Frinke,	William Augustus Mandell,	——.
–	Sarah Anna Leonard,	Sarah Anna Leonard Howe,	——.
–	Wilbur Fiske,	William Arthur Loud,	——.
–	Georgiana Salisbury,	Georgiana Eliza Rugg,	——.
–	Martha Ann Peirce,	Ann Eliza Wood,	——.
–	George Harrison Sherwin,	George Sherwin,	——.
–	Craft Eastman,	Edward Craft Eastman,	——.
–	John Carey,	John Carey Wood,	——.
–	Charles Sylvester Hoar,	Charles Sylvester Brooks,	——.
–	Patrick Duffy,	John Duffy,	——.
–	Hartwell B. Staples,	Thomas Benton Staples,	——.
–	Mary Elizabeth Clapp,	Mary Elizabeth Clapp Watson,	——.
–	Charles Follen Blood,	Charles Follen Blake,	——.
–	Helen B. Fish,	Emma Eldredge,	——.
–	Artemas Brigham,	Andrew Densmore,	——.
–	Jennie Rice,	Jennie Rice Eaton,	——.
–	Frank Wilder Messer,	Frank Wilder Gibson,	——.
–	Jessie F. Watson,	Jessie Watson Clark,	——.
–	Elizabeth Colon,	Elizabeth Greenwood,	——.
–	George W. A. Lane,	George W. Johnson,	——.
–	Elizabeth Reynolds,	Agnes Aldanah Billings,	——.
–	George Jones Gage,	George Tufts Brackett,	——.

HAMPSHIRE COUNTY.

June 7,	Willie Albro Mellen,*	Willie Albro Curtis,	Worthington.
July 5,	Clarence H. Williams,*	Clarence H. Langdon,	Westhampton.

HAMPDEN COUNTY.

Mar. 1,	Isabel Julia Smith,*	Isabel Julia Shaw,	——.
July 5,	Lizzie Pitman Vaille,	Lizzie Chase,	——.
Sept. 13,	Elizabeth Francis Bracket,*	Elizabeth Frances Tainter,	——.

* Changed by reason of adoption.

FRANKLIN COUNTY.

Date of Decree.	Original Name.	Name Decreed.	Residence.
1859.			
Feb. 8,	Ellen E. Carpenter,* . . .	Ellen E. Hovey, . . .	Greenfield.
Oct. 11,	Mary Ellen Hawks,*. . .	Mary Ellen Upton, . .	Charlemont.
Nov. 1,	Fanny M. Wells,* . . .	Fanny B. Dutton, . . .	Colrain.
1,	Ida Mary Roberts,* . . .	Ida Mary Bardwell, . .	Shelburne.

BERKSHIRE COUNTY.

May 3,	Edward Homer England,* .	Edward Homer Rath, . .	Hinsdale.

NORFOLK COUNTY.

–	Anne Smith,*	Florence Eliza Brooks, . .	Quincy.
–	John Chisholm,* . . .	Ernest Laighton, . . .	Stoughton.
–	Beulah Wadsworth Sprague Joyce,*	Beulah Josephine Hitchcock,	Sharon.
–	Mary Damon,*	Cora Ann Daniels, . . .	Stoughton.
–	Frances Louisa Hendrick,* .	Frances Louisa Field, . .	Brookline.
–	Elizabeth B. Sanderson,* .	Liza Studley, ...	Cohasset.
–	Maria Antoinette Hill, .	Maria Antoinette Perry, .	Foxborough.
–	Frank Ellis Hill, . . .	Frank Ellis Perry, . . .	Foxborough.

BRISTOL COUNTY.

Jan. 4,	Joseph Lawton, ...	Joseph Lawton Mosher, .	———.
June 7,	Emeline A. Rounds, . . .	Emeline A. Hathaway, . .	———.
July 8,	Walter Hollis, ...	Ernest Albert Guild, . .	———.

PLYMOUTH COUNTY.

–	Juliet C. Morton, . . .	Hannah H. Morton, . .	Middleborough.

BARNSTABLE COUNTY.

–	Addie Maria Crowell, .	Olivia James Crowell, . .	———.
–	Henry Ebenezer Crosby, .	Henry Ebenezer Atkins, °	———.
–	Eunice Clark Swift, . .	Eunice Catharine Swift, .	———.

SUFFOLK COUNTY.

1860.			
–	Joel Barber, ...	Joel Dwight Barber, . .	———.
–	George William Buchanan,	George William Buchanan Cains, ...	———.
–	Edward Crowninshield, .	Edward Augustus Crowninshield, ...	———.
–	Miriam Goodwin Copp, .	Miriam Copp Sanderson, .	———.

* Changed by reason of adoption.

SUFFOLK COUNTY — *Concluded.*

Date of Decree.	Original Name.	Name Decreed.	Residence.
1860.			
—	John Carson,	Charles Stebbins,	——.
—	Lizzie Crane,	Lizzie Crane Staples,	——.
—	Ellen Carroll, jun ,	Jennie Frances Oliver,	——.
—	Frances Collins,	Martha Saunders Thompson,	——.
—	Emma Melissa Davis,	Emma Melissa Pratt,	——.
—	Thomas Johnson Entwisle,	Thomas Johnson.	——.
—	Ellen Fitzgerald,	Emma Judson Gullefer,	——.
—	Michael Greene, .	George Leslie Greene,	——.
—	Martha Earl Hughes,	Martha Avise Earl,	——.
—	Mary Kingston, .	Angenora Barber, .	——.
—	William Russell Lane,	Russell Lane, .	——.
—	Alexander Lane,	Alexander McLane,	——.
—	Edis Henrietta Nichols,	Edis Henrietta Metcalf,	——.
—	Elizabeth Rogers,	Elizabeth Smith,	——.
—	Margaret Ellen Simpson,	Margaret Ellen Stark,	——.
—	James Munroe Stevens,	Munroe Stevens,	——.
—	William Ellery Albert Thomas,	William Ellery Cotton,	——.
—	George A'Court Webb,	George Webb A'Court,	——.
—	Henry Clarence Wright,	Haynes Henry Wright,	——.

ESSEX COUNTY.

Date of Decree.	Original Name.	Name Decreed.	Residence.
Feb. 7,	Edward Augustus Baker,	Edward Augustus Webber,	Beverly.
Mar. 13,	Alonzo Eliphalet Hardy,*	Alonzo Hardy Humphrey,	Lawrence.
27,	—— Goodrich,*	Ruth Ann Bartlett,	Haverhill.
27,	Jeremiah Morris Spofford,	Morris Spofford,	Groveland.
May 1,	Richard Mead,	Richard C. Hale,	Rowley.
July 3,	Lucinda Marshall,	Lucinda Lyford,	Andover.
3,	Alexander Peckham, jun.,	Charles Edwin Peckham,	Lynn.
17,	Alice Maude Mary Cook,*.	Alice Maude Williams,	Amesbury.
Sept. 18,	Lois Perry Woolley,*	Ella Mariah Bagley,	Amesbury.

MIDDLESEX COUNTY.

Date of Decree.	Original Name.	Name Decreed.	Residence.
Jan. 3,	Robert Chaffin Conant,*	Robert Conant Chaffin.	Acton.
3,	Susannah Chaffin Conant,*	Susannah Conant Chaffin,	Acton.
10,	Julia Barnes,*	Etta Hull,	Charlestown.
10,	Grace Atkins,*	Grace Atkins Hull,	Charlestown.
24,	Anna V. Barnard,*	Anna V. B. Sanborn,	Lowell.
Feb. 14,	——,*	Leo Schnepf,	Cambridge.
Mar. 13,	Mary Augusta Richards,*	Minnie Williams,	Holliston.
27,	Frederick Kent,*	Frederick Kent McKenzie,	Charlestown.
Apr. 3,	Mary Marden,*	Ella Francis Martin,	Lowell.
3,	Matilda Goddard Holmes,*	Matilda Goddard Allen,	Lowell.
May 8,	Mary Kate Bowen,*	Mary Catherine Bowen Sullivan,	Cambridge.
June 5,	Sarah Annah Scarlett,	Sarah Annah Gray,	Tewksbury.
12,	Elizabeth Smith,*	Lizzie Ann Raymore,	Hopkinton.
26,	William Apel,*	Herbert William Duxbury,	Cambridge.
Aug. 14,	Annie Abbott Gibson,*	Annie Abbott Smith,	Lexington.
28,	Abraham Paul,*	Abraham Paul Belmore,	Marlborough.
Sept. 11,	Caroline Effeda Greene,*	Effie Locke,	West Cambridge.
25,	Herbert William Duxbury,*	William Herbert Apel,	Cambridge.
Oct. 9,	Rufus Fuller Smith,*	Harlow Rufus Foster,	Ashby.
Nov. 13,	Willie Walsh,*	Willie Walsh Monroe,	Charlestown.
13,	Maria Louise Wainwright,	Maria Louise Hayward,	——.

* Changed by reason of adoption.

WORCESTER COUNTY.

Date of Decree.	Original Name.	Name Decreed.	Residence.
1860.			
–	Eliza Ann Barnes, . . .	Lizzie Anna Gibson, .	——.
–	Annette M. Covell, . .	Frances Maria Stockwell, .	——.
–	James Albert Carpenter, .	James Albert Sadler, . .	——.
–	George Jonas Gage, . .	George Tufts Brackett, .	——.
–	George W. Green, . .	George Henry Wilder, .	——.
–	Peter Labadore, . . .	Peter Marron, . . .	——.
–	Jennette Louise Parker, .	Jennie Louise Parker, .	——.
–	Ida Maria Woodward, .	Ida Maria Hoppin, .	——.
–	Charles Albee, . . .	Charles Albee Chickering, .	——.
–	Cora Bradbury, . . .	Cora S. Howland, . .	——.
–	Harriet Alice Ward, . .	Harriet Alice Putnam, .	——.
–	Edmond John McMannus,	Edmond John Morton, .	——.

HAMPSHIRE COUNTY.

Date of Decree.	Original Name.	Name Decreed.	Residence.
Jan. 3,	Emma Virginia Wheeler,* .	Emma Virginia Burke, .	Ware.
Dec. 4,	Henrietta Josephine Cole,* .	Henrietta Josephine Stevens, .	Worthington.
–	Phoebe Amanda Pierce,* .	Emma Amanda Ashley, .	Prescott.

HAMPDEN COUNTY.

Date of Decree.	Original Name.	Name Decreed.	Residence.
Jan. 3,	Fanny Jane Hawks,* .	Fanny Jane Jennings, .	Springfield.
Feb. 7,	Flora Emergene Stodard,* .	Flora Emergene Hubbard, .	Montpelier, Vt.
April 11,	Joseph W. Babcock, . .	Joseph E. Webster, .	Chester.
24,	Charles Henry Speakman,*	Charles Henry Lee, .	Monson.
May 22,	Linnie Maud Collins,* .	Minnie Harriet Watrous, .	Palmer.
June 5,	Ida Mason,* . . .	Josephine Ida Clark, .	Springfield.
12,	Henry Nelson,* . . .	Henry Nelson Thompson, .	Wales.
19,	Samuel J. Harris,* . .	Aaron William Rising, . .	——.
July 3,	Nellie A. Sheldon,* . .	Nellie Louisa Shaw, .	Chicopee.
Aug. 28,	Anna Maria Pierce,* . .	Anna Maria Pease, .	Westfield.
Dec. 18,	Francis McCan, . . .	Francis Fuller, .	Springfield.
–	Caroline E. McCan, . .	Caroline E. Fuller, .	Springfield.
–	Jerome E. McCan, . .	Jerome E. Fuller, . .	Springfield.

FRANKLIN COUNTY.

Date of Decree.	Original Name.	Name Decreed.	Residence.
–	Mary Schneider,* . . .	Mary Schneider Whitney, .	Buckland.
–	John Ferroth,* . . .	Christian Hawser. . .	Greenfield.
–	Nina Estella Wright,* .	Catharine Wells Ford, .	Charlemont.
–	Mary J. Seavery,* . .	Mary Jane Barrus, . .	Conway.

BERKSHIRE COUNTY.

Date of Decree.	Original Name.	Name Decreed.	Residence.
Jan. 1,	Ann Doud, ...	Eva Ann Johnson, . .	——.
3,	D. Lyon Davidge, . .	Charles Bray Davidge, .	——.
April 25,	Amy Merilla Williams, .	Amy Merilla Wright, .	——.
May 1,	Franklin Secor, . . .	Franklin Potter, . .	——.
July 18,	Ellen Maria Potter, . .	Ellen Maria Wood, .	——.
25,	Ida Muller, ...	Ida Keach, . . .	——.
25,	Harriet Lois Palmer, .	Elizabeth Annett, . .	——.
25,	Charles J. Ferguson, . .	Charles J. Stowell, . .	——.

* Changed by reason of adoption.

NORFOLK COUNTY.

Date of Decree.	Original Name.	Name Decreed.	Residence.
1860.			
–	Aurelia Jane Angier,	Aurelia Jane Hunt,	——.
–	Francis Balch,	Francis Vergines Balch,	——.
–	William Duncan Foster,	William Foster Duncan,	——.
–	Emma Sawin,	Emma Sawin Patten,	——.
–	Eva L. Smith,	Addie Ellis Richardson,	——.
–	Benie Potter,	Flora Ann Reed,	——.
–	Amelia Hannah Willis,	Amelia Hannah Lesuer,	——.
–	Charles Sumner Stevens,	Charles Stevens Ayer,	——.
–	Martha Jane McAndrews,	Martha Jane Grace,	——.
–	Sarah E. Honey,	Amy Elizabeth Pettee,	——.
–	Harriet Amanda Pond,	Harriet Ella Gay,	——.
–	Mary Ann Maddock,	Mary Ann Gay,	——.

BRISTOL COUNTY.

Date of Decree.	Original Name.	Name Decreed.	Residence.
Oct. 2,	Anne Frances Baker,	Annie Frances Davis,	——.
Nov. 9,	Harriet Upham,	Harriet Upham Andrews,	——.
Dec. 4,	Sarah McGurk,	Sarah McGurk Reed,	——.
4,	Frances Borden,	Frances Borden Vincent,	——.
4,	Hannah V. D. Robinson,	Hannah Valentine Durfee,	——.
4,	Fidelia Durfee Robinson,	Fidelia Durfee,	——.
4,	George Durfee Robinson,	George Durfee,	——.

BARNSTABLE COUNTY.

Date of Decree.	Original Name.	Name Decreed.	Residence.
–	Harry Wallen,	Harry Franklin Clark,	——.
–	Emma Thompson,	Emma Nelson Hallet,	——.
–	Huldah Thompson,	Addie William Loring,	——.
–	Harriet Augustus Bartlett,	Harriet Bartlett Robinson,	——.
–	Josephine Hallett Sturgis,	Muriel Mary Rogers,	——.
–	Ellen Jane Sullivan,	Hannah Nye,	——.
–	Atkins Dyer Paine,	Elisha Lewis Lombard Paine,	——.
–	Marshal E. Paine,	Marshal Paine Snow,	——.
–	Henry T. Hallett,	Henry T. Coombs.	——.
–	Alice Maria Osgood,	Fanny Maria Hoxie,	——.
–	Eliza Jones Collins,	Eliza Jones Nickerson,	——.

SUFFOLK COUNTY.

Date of Decree.	Original Name.	Name Decreed.	Residence.
1861.			
–	Armond Christian Armondson,	Thomas Benson,	——.
–	Sarah Gertrude Babb,	Sarah Babb Hobart,	——.
–	Dora Betzner,	Lizzie Davis Harding,	——.
–	Blanche Lillian Brown,	Blanche Lillian Blake,	——.
–	Eva Brown,	Eva Maria Briggs,	——.
–	Frederick Augustus Case,	Frederick Augustus Taft,	——.
–	Fanny Cutter,	Fannie Starkey,	——.
–	Sarah Griffiths,	Ella Melissa Wentworth,	——.
–	Frederick Hannah,	Charles Frederick Stevens,	——.
–	Carrie Lee Hardy,	Carrie Oakman Gardner,	——.
–	George Washington Heard, jun ,	George Farley Heard,	——.

SUFFOLK COUNTY — *Concluded.*

Date of Decree.	Original Name.	Name Decreed.	Residence.
1861.			
–	Annie Hitchcock, . . .	Caroline Elizabeth Spalding, .	———.
–	Mary Louisa Hudson, .	Ella Louisa Scudder, . .	———.
–	Matilda Irvin, . . .	Maria Osborne, . .	———.
–	Isaac H. McCartee, . .	Isaac H. Carter, . . .	———.
–	Patrick Mahoney, . .	George Henry Miller, . .	———.
–	Anna Elizabeth Maiers, .	Annie Elizabeth Humphrey, .	———.
–	Edward F. Milliken. . .	Edward Milliken Rumery, .	———.
–	Anna Geraldine O'Shahan,	Anna Geraldine de Bonneville, ...	———.
–	Charles Henry Preston, .	Charles Frank Hardcastle, .	———.
–	John Turner Welles Sargent,	Turner Sargent, . .	———.
–	Cecelia Susan Ward, . .	Cecelia Susan Woods, .	———.
–	Walter Weston, . . .	James Russell Spalding, .	———.
–	Harriet B— Whitaker, .	Harriet Burr Whitaker, .	———.

ESSEX COUNTY.

Date of Decree.	Original Name.	Name Decreed.	Residence.
Mar. 19,	Nancy Norwood Lull, .	Kate Norwood Lull, . .	Manchester.
May 7,	Hattie P. Mayhew.* . .	Hattie Mayhew Perry, .	Danvers.
7,	Emeline Augusta Teague,*	Emeline Augusta Reith, .	South Danvers.
17,	Mary Jane Tullock,* . .	Mary Jane Demsey, .	Danvers.
June 11,	John Taylor, . . .	John Zach Taylor, . .	Haverhill.
11,	Elizabeth Bixby,* . .	Elizabeth Frances Ashton, .	Lawrence.
July 2,	Esther Alice Hicks,* . .	Alice Hilliard, . . .	Newburyport.
16,	Jonas S. Sinclair,* . .	John Symonds Dorman, .	Boxford.
Aug. 6,	William S. Dalton,* . .	George William Winn, .	Salem.
Oct. 1,	Emma Jane Getchell,* .	Emma Florence French, .	Lynn.
Dec. 18,	Stephen Wendell Abbott,*	Wendell Phillips Kenney, .	Lawrence.

MIDDLESEX COUNTY.

Date of Decree.	Original Name.	Name Decreed.	Residence.
Jan. 22,	Chester Bradshaw Guild, .	Robert Bradshaw Guild, .	Charlestown.
Feb. 26,	Robert Dunn,* . . .	Albion Robert Clapp, .	Malden.
Mar. 5,	Lucy Ellen Merrill,* . .	Lucy Merrill Eaton, .	Cambridge.
April 2,	Cabot Hoes Whitaker, .	George Cabot Whitaker, .	Lowell.
2,	Abby Frances Eastman,* .	Abby Frances Morrison, .	Lowell.
9,	Thomas Peachy Tukey, .	Frederick Sumner Tukey, .	Lowell.
9,	George Brackett, . .	George Callender Brackett, .	Somerville.
9,	Ann Foley,* . . .	Ann Reynolds, . .	Cambridge.
9,	Carrie Wood Hitchcock,* .	Carrie Abby Wood, .	West Cambridge.
9,	Willie Stone,* . . .	Jonathan Huse Brown, .	Tewksbury.
23,	Grace Porter,* . . .	Grace Porter Simonds, .	Cambridge.
May 7,	Charlotte L. Coburn,* .	Annette Nicholas, . .	Lowell.
28,	Louisa Emerline Bixby,* .	Hattie Alsie Randall, .	Groton.
June 25,	Mary Jane Eginton,* .	Mary Jane Walker, .	Newton.
Aug. 13,	Dudley C. Boynton, .	Dudley Chace Mumford, .	Medford.
Sept. 10,	William Gaw,* . . .	William Stinson, . .	Cambridge.
10,	Hatty Jane Rice,* . .	Hattie Jane Marsh, .	Medford.
Oct. 1,	George Marshall,* . .	George Gardner Brown, .	Lowell.
Nov. 26,	Charles Curtis,* . .	Charles Cook, . .	Cambridge.
Dec. 10,	Hattie L. Rand,* . .	Hattie Adel Packard, .	Cambridge.
10,	Eliza Jane Mayo,* . .	Eliza Jane Pike, . .	Waltham.

* Changed by reason of adoption.

WORCESTER COUNTY.

Date of Decree.	Original Name.	Name Decreed.	Residence.
1861.			
–	Annetta E. Dodge,	Annetta Elizabeth Taft,	———.
–	Elizabeth S. Williams,	Minerva Florence Balcome,	———.
–	Charles Lyman Chickering,	Charles Lyman Williams,	———.
–	Caroline Louisa Chickering,	Caroline Louisa Williams,	———.
–	Clara Shepherd,	Clara Etta Shepherd,	———.
–	James Henry Penney,	William Henry Gardner,	———.
–	Herbert Scovell,	George Herbert Nichols,	———.
–	Alexander De Witt Scovell,	De Witt Clinton Nichols,	———.
–	Ella Maria Spooner,	Ella Maria Cleveland,	———.
–	Harriet Augusta Jones,	Hattie Augusta Taylor,	———.
–	Almira H. Rockwood,	Almira H. Wood,	———.
–	Clarissa Augusta Patch,	Clarissa Augusta Brigham,	———.
–	Nellie Phebe Goodman,	Nellie Phebe Blood,	———.
–	Carrie May Thompson,	Carrie May Gould,	———.
–	Eliza Jane Morse,	Eliza Jane Rogers,	———.
–	Benjamin Lee,	Benjamin Lee O'Callaghan,	———.
–	Hattie Fitzgerald,	Lucy Hill,	———.

HAMPSHIRE COUNTY.

Date of Decree.	Original Name.	Name Decreed.	Residence.
Jan. 5,	Caroline J. Hendrichson,*	Carrie J. Whitehouse,	Boston.
Feb. 5,	Emily Sarah Cole,*	Emily Sarah Packard,	Cummington.
May 14,	Frederick Lyman Pittsinger,*	Frederick Lyman Kimball,	Enfield.
June 4,	Margrette Kearney,*	Louisa Margrette Macomber,	Northampton.
Aug. 13,	Mary Elizabeth Gleason,*	Lillie Sarah Barnard,	Athol.
Oct. 1,	Ida Allen,*	Ida Hatch,	Holyoke.

HAMPDEN COUNTY.

Date of Decree.	Original Name.	Name Decreed.	Residence.
Mar. –	Ira H. Clagstone,*	Ira H. Cain,	Holyoke.
–	William Speakman,*	William Everett Nichols,	———.
April –	Monroe Fox,*	Monroe Stevens Rising,	Granville.
June –	Nellie Eliza Dailey,*	Nellie Eliza Willard,	Holyoke.
–	Fannie Estel Dailey,	Fannie Estella Loomis,	Holyoke.
–	Nellie Blake,*	Minnie E. Taylor,	———.
–	George Woodbury Fiske,*	George Woodbury Rogers,	Holyoke.
July –	Kate S. H. Thompson,*	Kate Thompson,	———.
Sept. –	Nellie May Hosford,*	Nellie May Clark,	Springfield.

FRANKLIN COUNTY.

Date of Decree.	Original Name.	Name Decreed.	Residence.
Jan. 1,	Charles Robert Bolton,*	Charles Frederic Clap,	Boston.
Feb. 5,	Harlekin S. Cross,*	Harley Cross Amidon,	Rowe.
Mar. 2,	Sarah J. Gleason,*	Lizzie Field Cushing,	Athol.
2,	Eva Maria Gleason,*	Eva Maria Reed,	Athol.
2,	Oscar D. Fisk,*	Oscar D. Hapgood,	Warwick.
28,	Eugene Thaxter Gurney,*	Eugene Thaxter Williams,	Hawley.
Aug. 6,	Mary Emma Denslow,*	Mary Emma Vincent,	Shelburne.
Dec. 3,	Sarah Lizzie Geer,*	Lizzie Maria Blake,	Ashfield.

* Changed by reason of adoption.

BERKSHIRE COUNTY.

Date of Decree.	Original Name.	Name Decreed.	Residence.
1861.			
Jan. 1,	Ann Doud,*	Eva Ann Johnson, . . .	Washington.
June 4,	Sarah Sprong,*	Sarah Leffingroell, . . .	Pittsfield.
July 17,	Cora Mambert,* . . .	Cora Gibson, ...	Sheffield.
24,	Charles E. Williams,* . .	Charles E. Sherman, . .	Adams.

NORFOLK COUNTY.

Date of Decree.	Original Name.	Name Decreed.	Residence.
–	Virginia Bird, ...	Mary Elizabeth Drake, . .	——.
–	Charles Bird, ...	Charles Bird Wade, . .	——.
–	Frederick Knox Wait, . .	Frederic Wait Foster, . .	——.
–	Charles Hall Thing, . .	Charles Hall Thwing, . .	——.
–	Benjamin F. Cooke, . .	Benjamin F. Cook Cressey, .	——.
–	Horatio Davis, ...	Charles Davis, jun , . .	——.
–	Charles May Livingston, .	Charles Henry Pierce, . .	——.

BRISTOL COUNTY.

Date of Decree.	Original Name.	Name Decreed.	Residence.
Oct. 1,	Annie Elizabeth Taggard, .	Annie Elizabeth Hoar, . .	——.
Dec. 3,	Ann Eliza Fish, . . .	Ann Eliza Gibbs, . . .	——.
3,	Nellie Frances Trafton Collins,	Nellie Frances Trafton Tripp,	——.

SUFFOLK COUNTY.

Date of Decree.	Original Name.	Name Decreed.	Residence.
1862.			
Jan. 13,	Einor Hanson, ...	George Einor Swasey, . .	Boston.
Feb. 10,	Caroline Nichols Leach, . .	Caroline Leach Smith, . .	Boston.
Apr. 7,	Michael Crosby, . . .	Frank Michael Crosby, . .	Boston.
14,	Abby Amelia Wright, . .	Nellie Gertrude Emery, . .	Boston.
28,	Mary Tweed, ...	Mary Ahrend, . . .	Boston.
May 12,	Jacob Corman, . . .	Jacob Corman Bopp, . .	Boston.
June 16,	Thomas Henry Woodell, .	Willie Chellis Rowe, . .	Boston.
Oct. 20,	Paulina Roney, . . .	Sarah Lind Littlefield, . .	Boston.
Nov. 3,	Edgar C. Wainwright, . .	Edward Roberts, . . .	Boston.
Dec. 15,	Annie Murphy, . . .	Annie Maria Lincoln, . .	Boston.

ESSEX COUNTY.

Date of Decree.	Original Name.	Name Decreed.	Residence.
April 1,	Emma Dodge, ...	Emma Florence Adams, .	Topsfield.
May 20,	Mary E. Cross, . . .	Mary Emma Delnow, . .	Middleton.
July 1,	Olive Durell Stickney, . .	Olive Durell Little, . .	Newbury.
Oct. 7,	William Webb, ...	William Webb Russell, . .	Marblehead.

MIDDLESEX COUNTY.

Date of Decree.	Original Name.	Name Decreed.	Residence.
Feb. 11,	Ida Peterson, ...	Ida Augusta Kidder, . .	Newton.
11,	James Robbins, ...	James Arthur Robbins, . .	Watertown.
25,	Charles Edward Parker, . .	Charles Parker Spalding, .	Lowell.
25,	Frederick Augustus Parker, .	Frederick Parker Spalding, .	Lowell.
25,	Walter Hillier, ...	Frederick Arthur Wildes, .	Charlestown.

* Changed by reason of adoption.

MIDDLESEX COUNTY — *Concluded.*

Date of Decree.	Original Name.	Name Decreed.	Residence.
1862.			
Mar. 11,	Charles Gallagher, . . .	Charles Henry Reed, . .	Somerville.
25,	Harriet Haynes, . . .	Hattie Lambert Osgood, .	Hopkinton.
Apr. 1,	Francis Donavan, . . .	George Francis Parsons, .	Lowell.
May 6,	Minnie E. Atchinson, .	Minnie Eveline Packard, .	Lowell.
Sept. 9,	Adelia B. Black, . . .	Adelia Black Williams, .	Reading.
Oct. 14,	Josiah Gould, ...	Josiah Gould Chapman, .	Woburn.
28,	Jenny Deloes, ...	Jenny Delves Gibby, . .	Lowell.
Nov. 11,	Abbie Frances Ann Libbey, .	Abbie Frances Ann Coburn, .	Cambridge.
11,	Mary E. Bailey, . . .	Mary Ellen Danforth, . .	Lowell
11,	John Henry Sowersby, . .	John Henry Nichols, . .	Somerville.
Dec. 23,	Emily Isabella De Blois, . .	Emma Bertha Wilson, . .	Framingham.

WORCESTER COUNTY.

Jan. 1,	Louisa Adams, ...	Lillie Louise Page, . . .	Southborough.
Feb. 4,	Lizzie Adele Cowdrey, .	Lizzie Adele Cowdrey Warren,	Lancaster.
Mar. 4,	Alfred Augustus Hitchcock, .	Alfred Orsen Hitchcock, .	Fitchburg.
4,	Edward Wellman Hitchcock, .	Edward Wyman Hitchcock, .	Fitchburg.
4,	James Wellman Hitchcock, .	James Ripley Wellman Hitchcock, ...	Fitchburg.
4,	Peter W. Chamberlain, .	Frank Wheeler, . . .	Petersham.
4,	Harriet W. Chamberlain, .	Harriet M. Wheeler, . .	Petersham.
4,	Arthur Chamberlain, .	Arthur Wheeler, . . .	Petersham.
April 1,	Ellathyna P. Muzzey, .	Ellathyna Lavinia Prouty, .	Spencer.
1,	Frances Helen Griggs Pond, .	Frances Helen Griggs, .	Grafton.
May 6,	Jennie Elouise Stearns, .	Jennie Hill Munroe, . .	Worcester.
June 3,	Albert Augustus Moore, .	Albert Augustus Kidder, .	Oxford.
3,	George D. Mason, . .	George William Cole, .	Clinton.
July 1,	Laura Belle Bartlett, . .	Laura Belle Arnold, . .	Fitchburg.
1,	Clifford Holman Smith, .	Clifford Holman Batchellor, .	Worcester.
Aug. 5,	Allen Richard Bennett, .	George Channing Holt, . .	Royalston.
5,	Francis Littlefield, . .	Francis Roper, . . .	Princeton.
Sept. 2,	George Perry Phillips, .	George Perry Clark, . .	Spencer.
2,	Mary Lizzie Byrnes, . .	Nellie Frances Ide, . . .	Milford.
Oct. 23,	Cora Adams, ...	Cora A. Crocker, . . .	Templeton.
Nov. 4,	Mary Ward, ...	Mary Ward Whitney, . .	Ashburnham.
4,	George Lampson Stone, .	George Lampson Stone Knowlton, ...	Gardner.
Dec. 2,	Annie Laura McNally, .	Annie Laura Wood, . .	Leominster.
2,	Annie Harrigidon, . .	Lizzie Alice Sanders, . .	Worcester.
2,	Lizzie Hubbard Ellis, . .	Lizzie Ellis Hubbard, . .	Milford.
2,	Alfred Merriam, . . .	Charles Alfred Merriam, .	Worcester.
2,	Abby Ann Stearns, . .	Abby Ann Waite, . . .	Fitchburg.

HAMPSHIRE COUNTY.

Jan. 7,	Isabella P. Webster, . .	Isabella P. Clapp, . . .	Easthampton.
Feb. 4,	Martha E. Stebbins, . .	Martha Antoinette Morton, .	Hatfield.
April 1,	Cornelia Powers, . . .	Mary Elizabeth Powers, .	Westfield.

HAMPDEN COUNTY.

Feb. 4,	—— Stickney,* . . .	Charles Stickney, . . .	Westfield.
Mar. 4,	Julena Powers, . . .	Julena Julian, . . .	Springfield.
June 17,	Edward Adams Briggs, .	Edward Adams Bishop, .	Russell.
Nov. 5,	Adelbert Allyn, ...	Albert Allyn, ...	Holyoke.

* Changed by reason of adoption.

FRANKLIN COUNTY.

Date of Decree.	Original Name.	Name Decreed.	Residence.
1862.			
Aug. 5,	Catharina Pfwsirh (or Phersy),	Catharina Niter, . . .	Shelburne.
Sept. 9,	Mary Conners, ...	Mary Rosella Lyman, .	Northfield.
9,	Georgiana Ripley,	Lessie Abigail Moore, .	Northfield.
Oct. 7,	Mary A. Pratt, ...	Mary Nettie Alden, .	Montague.
Jan. 7,	Harriet Severance, . . .	Pearl Maxwell, . . .	Charlemont.
Feb. 11,	Helen Nunny, ...	Nellie Nanny Thompson, .	Buckland.

BERKSHIRE COUNTY.

Mar. 4,	Louisa Williams, . . .	Louisa Parker, . . .	Adams.
April 1,	Gurdon Joyner, ...	Gurdon Hollenbeck, .	Pittsfield.
May 6,	Elizabeth Hamlin, . . .	Ida M. Rodgers, . .	Becket.
Dec. 2,	Bird W. Powell, ...	Bird W. Gorham, . .	Sheffield.

NORFOLK COUNTY.

May 10,	Mary Elbridge Higgins, .	Mary Livermore Stanton, .	Roxbury.
Aug. 16,	George Sumner Joy, . .	George Sumner Goldthwait, .	Weymouth.
Sept. 20,	Hannah Adelaide French, .	Annie Adelaide French,	Quincy.

BRISTOL COUNTY.

Jan. 7,	Lavinia Case, ...	Lavinia Knapp, . .	Taunton.
21,	Rachel Wilson, ...	Kate Mundell Jones, .	Taunton.
April 4,	Unknown, ...	Lizzie B. Eddy, . .	Swanzey.
Aug. 1,	Alfred H. Potter, . . .	Alfred H. Fisher, . .	New Bedford.
Sept. 5,	George Clinton, . . .	George Clinton Bliss, .	New Bedford.
5,	Hattie Farrell, . . .	Mary Elizabeth Newcomb, .	Taunton.

PLYMOUTH COUNTY.

April 1,	Julia A. Moore, . . .	Julia A. Sylvester, . .	Hanover.
Aug. 11,	Mabel W. Leathers, . .	Mabel W. Lowell, . .	Abington.
Oct. 28,	Hannah C. Sears, . .	Hannah Sears West, .	Rochester.

BARNSTABLE COUNTY.

May 20,	Samuel Young, . . .	Edward Francis Young, .	Chatham.
20,	Samuel Young, jun., .	Edward Francis Young, jun.,	Chatham.
June 17,	Amanda M. Baker, . .	Amanda Maria Skinner, .	Dennis.
17,	Ida Ann Smithurst, . .	Ida Mary Fuller, . .	Lynn.
17,	John Smith, 2d, . .	John Smith Kemp, . .	Wellfleet.
17,	John Vira Williams, .	George Vira Williams, .	Wellfleet.

SUFFOLK COUNTY.

Date of Decree.	Original Name.	Name Decreed.	Residence.
1863.			
Jan. 26,	Silvia Dana Eaton, . . .	Grace Dana Homer, . .	Boston.
Feb. 16,	Bridget Ann O'Brien, . .	Bridget Ann Kehoe, . .	Boston.
Mar. 9,	Mary Josephine Pearsons, .	Mary Josephine Thomas, .	Boston.
16,	Maria J. Harris, . . .	Edith Jane Chase, . .	Boston.
April 6,	Eliot Guild, . . .	Samuel Eliot Guild, . .	Boston.
13,	Georgianna Marion Watson, .	Georgianna Marion Thompson,	Boston.
27,	George Winfield Young, .	George Winfield Siegrist, .	Boston.
27,	Leander Sebastian Streeter, .	Lee Streeter, . . .	Boston.
May 11,	Carrie Louisa Marshall, .	Carrie Louisa Pycott, .	Boston.
June 8,	John Josephs, . . .	John Cooper, . . .	Boston.
22,	Elena Hatch Keenan, .	Harriet Maria Johnson, .	Boston.
29,	John Henry Burbeck, . .	Francis Herbert Short, .	Boston.
Aug. 10,	Fanny Lincoln, . . .	Fanny Lincoln Bowdlear, .	Boston.
Nov. 30,	Catharine Fitzgibbon, . .	Catharine Sullivan, . .	Boston.
Dec. 14,	Charles Augustus Ferdinand Weuskowsky, . . .	Charles Ferdinand Bowers, .	Chelsea.
14,	Sarah Weuskowsky, . . .	Sarah Bowers, . . .	Chelsea.
14,	Caroline Louisa Weuskowsky, .	Caroline Louisa Bowers, .	Chelsea.

ESSEX COUNTY.

Jan. 6,	Hattie Newell Card, . . .	Hattie Newell Sanborn, . .	Groveland.
Feb. 3,	—— Decatur, ...	Clara W. Carey, . . .	Lynn.
Mar. 17,	Eddie Higgins, ...	Edward D. Smith, . . .	Danvers.
April 7,	Susan Davis, ...	Susan Eliza Meader, . .	Newburyport.
7,	Martha Goodwin, . . .	Ellen Buffinton Kehew, .	Salem.
May 5,	Charles Edward Wilson, .	Charles Edward Burrill, .	Swampscott.
Sept. 8,	Ida Watts, ...	Mary Ida Waterhouse Smith, .	Andover.
Oct. 6,	Ruth N. Leavitt, . .	Lizzie Leavitt Main, . .	Marblehead.
6,	Eliza Gilbert Pearce, . .	Eliza Pearce Peabody, . .	South Danvers.
Nov. 3,	John Mowry, ...	John Welsh, ...	Amesbury.

MIDDLESEX COUNTY.

Mar. 24,	Charles Callahan, . .	Charles Edwards Hall, . .	Somerville.
April 14,	Mary Frances Brigham, .	Mary Frances Barnard, .	Marlborough.
14,	Francis E. Symmes, . .	Francis Edward Clark, . .	Newton.
June 9,	Lucy Angelia Law, . .	Lucy Angelia Stone, . .	Framingham.
9,	Nancy M. Conant, . .	Annie M. Conant, . .	Stow.
9,	Louise Prentiss Warren, .	Helen Talcott Warren, . .	Charlestown.
Sept. 1,	William Henry Clough, .	William Henry Peabody, .	Dracut.
1,	Martin Peabody Clough, .	Martin Peabody, . .	Dracut.
Jan. 27,	Sylvanus Judkins,* . .	Danforth E. Newcomb, .	Medford.
Feb. 3,	Marietta Montgomery,* .	Marietta Sherman, . .	Lowell.
10,	Lillie Catharine Shattuck,*	Lillie Catharine Bass, . .	Lowell.
10,	Mary Ellen Copperthorn,*	Minnie Treat Allen, . .	Newton.
24,	Mary Ann Lindsay,* .	Mary Lindsay Patten, . .	Billerica.
Mar. 10,	Angelina Gibson,* . .	Annie Proctor Weston, .	Cambridge.
10,	John A. Gibson,* . .	Edward Henry Weston, .	Cambridge.
10,	Mary Ella Huntress,* . .	Mary Ella Fall, . . .	Malden.
24,	Jennie Paul,* . . .	Jennie Laura Hardy, . .	Natick.
April 28,	Jennie Elliot Coolidge,* .	Jennie Elliot Cotting, .	Marlborough.
May 26,	——,* . . .	Clara Frances Woods, . .	Shirley.
26,	Marble Jennie Adams,* .	Elizabeth Ann Robertson, .	Lowell.
June 2,	Annie Little Eaton,* . .	Annie Little Emerson, .	Lowell.

* Changed by reason of adoption.

MIDDLESEX COUNTY — *Concluded.*

Date of Decree.	Original Name.	Name Decreed.	Residence.
1863.			
June 9,	Charles Laush*, . . .	Charles Wilde, . . .	Malden.
23,	Florence Evalina Mead,* . .	Minnie Ferris Cottle, . .	Belmont.
Aug. 11,	William Turner,* . . .	William Turner Maxwell, .	Ashby.
Sept. 1,	Alice Severns,*	Alice Parker, ...	Lowell.
8,	Cornelius Beeden,* . . .	Cornelius Kain, . . .	Brighton.
22,	Emma Esther Withy,* . .	Rosa Emma Stinehart, .	Weston.
Oct. 27,	John Henry Moore,* . . .	John Henry Shorey, .	Cambridge.
Nov. 24,	Adie Foster,*	Adie Florence Putnam, .	Charlestown.
Dec. 8,	Susan Elizabeth Kidder,* .	Susie Belle Bemis, . . .	Waltham.

WORCESTER COUNTY.

Date of Decree.	Original Name.	Name Decreed.	Residence.
Jan. 6,	Francis Walter Haynes, . .	Charles Francis Wight, . .	Hopkinton.
April 7,	Amelia Andi Mahan, .	Caroline Amelia Burbank, .	Worcester.
7,	Luke Cram, ...	Luke Remington, . .	Fitchburg.
7,	Sarah Abigail Cram, .	Sarah Abigail Remington, .	Fitchburg.
7,	Charles Ansel Cram, .	Charles Ansel Remington, .	Fitchburg.
7,	George Luke Cram, . .	George Luke Remington, .	Fitchburg.
7,	Walter Davis Cram, . .	Walter Davis Remington, .	Fitchburg.
May 20,	Fannie L. Taylor, . .	Fannie Taylor Stratton, .	Athol.
July 7,	Margaret Elizabeth Rogers, .	Helen Henrietta Davis, .	Templeton.
Sept. 1,	Charles E. Sawyer, . .	Charles Sawyer Barrows, .	Worcester.
Oct. 20,	Louisa Gaede, ...	Paulina Kencher, . . .	Clinton.
Dec. 1,	Hannah Flora May Gill, .	Flora May Jones, . . .	Worcester.

HAMPSHIRE COUNTY.

Date of Decree.	Original Name.	Name Decreed.	Residence.
Jan. 6,	Nellie Parsons, ...	Nellie Parsons Bray, . .	Northampton.
6,	Robert Brennan, . . .	Clarence Dewey Ogden, .	Northampton.
13,	Delilah Nichols, . . .	Ida Frances Arnold, .	Pelham.
13,	Mary Ann Devine, . .	Mary Ann Rigley, . . .	Amherst.
April 7,	Freddie Stanley, . .	Freddie Sawyer, . . .	South Hadley.
July 7,	Julia Almeda Newman, .	Julia Almeda Newman Dickinson, ...	Hatfield.
Oct. 6,	Helen M. Upton, . .	Helen M. Taylor, . . .	Amherst.
Nov. 3,	Mary Campbell, . . .	Nellie M. Thayer, . . .	Williamsburg.
3,	Mully Flanagan, . . .	Henry Clinton Frissel, . .	Northampton.

HAMPDEN COUNTY.

Date of Decree.	Original Name.	Name Decreed.	Residence.
Jan. 6,	Ella Dora Young,* . . .	Ella Dora Bartlett, . . .	Springfield.
Feb. 3,	Jason Theodore Morse,† . .	Jason Morse, ...	Brimfield.
3,	Jane M. Hosley,† . . .	Jane M. Phelps, . . .	Springfield.
3,	Joel N. Clark,†	Joel Norton, . . .	Blandford
April 28,	Lydia Jane Bishop,* . .	Jennie Elva Palmer, . .	Palmer.
Sept. 22,	Lewis P. Knight,* . . .	Lewis P. Watson, . . .	Holyoke.
Nov. 4,	Corinna Josephine Davidson,* .	Corinna Josephine Chase, .	Springfield.
4,	Ada Clark,*	Ada Chase, ...	Springfield.
Dec. 1,	Jason C Case,*	Jason C. Hathaway, . .	Chicopee.
1,	Elnora Violetta Thayer,* . .	Ella Viola Comins, . .	Palmer.
1,	Joel N. Clark, ...	Joel Norton, ...	Blandford.

* Changed by reason of adoption.
† Decree has been made for change of name, but notice of decree not having been yet proved, no certificate has been issued.

FRANKLIN COUNTY.

Date of Decree.	Original Name.	Name Decreed.	Residence.
1863.			
Feb. 10,	George Hall, . . .	George Hall Baker, . .	Hawley.
May 26,	Stillman Clark Turner, .	Stillman Clark Carter, . .	Hawley.
Aug. 4,	Abbie Maria Kenney, .	Abbie Maria Jones, . .	Deerfield.
4,	Nancy Ellen Death, . .	Ellen Anderson, . .	Montague.
4,	———, ...	Willie Bush, . . .	Greenfield.
Sept. 1,	Emma Boswell, . .	Emma Melinda Bardwell, .	Shelburne.
Oct. 27,	Mary Elizabeth Clark, .	Mary Elizabeth Sanderson, .	Whately.

BERKSHIRE COUNTY.

Date of Decree.	Original Name.	Name Decreed.	Residence.
June 2,	Alice Johnson, ...	Alice Hannah Bacon, . .	Adams.
July 22,	Willie Gilbert, ...	Willie Thomas Comstock, .	Great Barrington.

NORFOLK COUNTY.

Date of Decree.	Original Name.	Name Decreed.	Residence.
Jan. 17,	Nancy Gordon, ...	Nancy Maria Dow, . .	Quincy.
Mar. 28,	Anna Cora Bower, . .	Anna Bower Hibbard, . .	Roxbury.
Apr. 4,	Elizabeth F. Wilbur, .	Elizabeth F. Grover, . .	Foxborough.
7,	Jennie Brown, . . .	Florence Evylyn Snell, .	Dedham.
Aug. 15,	Henry Packard, . . .	Henry Thomas Packard, .	Quincy.
Sept. 1,	Clarance B. Clark, . .	George W. Wilcox, . .	Wrentham.

BRISTOL COUNTY.

Date of Decree.	Original Name.	Name Decreed.	Residence.
Jan. 2,	John B. Vandenhough, . .	John Bowers, ...	Somerset.
2,	William Lyman Vandenhough,	William Lyman Bowers, .	Somerset.
Feb. 6,	Emma S. Upham, . . .	Emma S Monroe, . .	New Bedford.
6,	Emma Peyser, . . .	Emma Peyser Hyman, .	New Bedford.
June 5,	James L. S. Russell, . .	James Russell Tracy, .	Raynham.
July 10,	Adeline F. Cole, . . .	Adeline F. Slade, . .	New Bedford.
Aug. 21,	George Heighlints, . .	George Haworth, . .	Taunton.
Nov. 6,	Mary Ellen McKim, . .	Nellie Delano, . . .	New Bedford.
Dec. 4,	Mabel Alice Hall, . . .	Annie Mabel Maxham, .	Taunton.

PLYMOUTH COUNTY.

Date of Decree.	Original Name.	Name Decreed.	Residence.
Feb. 24,	Adeline L. Coots,* . . .	Hattie Tyler Cobb, . . .	N'th Bridgewater.
24,	Helen P. Wood,* . . .	Helen Pierpont Cobb, . .	N'th Bridgewater.
July 13,	Lizzie F. Griffith,* . . .	Florence W. Harris, . .	Wareham.
Oct. 26,	Fannie Frisbie,* . . .	Fannie Frisbie Gibbs, . .	Wareham.
Nov. 23,	Harry M. Packard,* . . .	Isaac M. P. Brett, . .	N'th Bridgewater.
23,	Sarah J. Nye,*	Emma Sarah Lane, . .	Abington.

BARNSTABLE COUNTY.

Date of Decree.	Original Name.	Name Decreed.	Residence.
Feb. 10,	Isaac Hall, 2d, ...	Isaac Freeman Hall, . .	Dennis.
Aug. 11,	Muriel May Rogers, . .	Muriel May Downs, . .	Dennis.
Sept. 8,	Agnes Whitmore Simmons, .	Mary Lewis Simmons, . .	Barnstable.
Dec. 8,	Betsey Ann Kelley, . .	Betsey Ann Kelley Hamblin,	Yarmouth.

* Changed by reason of adoption.

DUKES COUNTY.

Date of Decree.	Original Name.	Name Decreed.	Residence.
1863.			
Jan. 19,	Tristram Ripley,* . . .	Tristram R. Holley, . .	Edgartown.

SUFFOLK COUNTY.

1864.			
Jan. 4,	Maria Fitzgibbon, . . .	Maria Havey, . . .	Boston.
Mar. 21,	Louis Paul Otis, . . .	Alfred Lewis Baury, . .	Boston.
28,	Robert Miller Slater, . . .	Howard Randolph Bowers, .	Boston.
April 11,	Isaac Davenport Fisher, . .	Davenport Fisher, . . .	Boston.
11,	Charles William Brown, . .	Gardner Charles Brown, .	Boston.
May 9,	Ella Walsh, ...	Carrie Ella Judkins, . .	Boston.
16,	Lillian Cornis, ...	Lillian Webster Brown, .	Boston.
June 6,	Arthur Latham Rowell, . .	Arthur Latham Clough, .	Boston.
27,	James Henry Very, . . .	James Henry Wakefield, .	Boston.
Oct. 3,	William Thomas Ashton, . .	William Thomas Bancroft, .	Boston.
Nov. 14,	Richard Godfrey, . . .	Richard Irwin, . . .	Boston.
Dec. 5,	Mary P. Nye, ...	Bertha Lincoln Putnam, .	Boston.
5,	Abigail Libby Coverley, . .	Abby Libby Lunt, . . .	Boston.
19,	Gracie Emma Thomas, . .	Gracie Emma Kelley, . .	Boston.
19,	Sophia Beck, ...	Gertrude Hatchman, . .	Boston.

ESSEX COUNTY.

Feb. 2,	William E. Fisher,* . . .	William E. Prentiss, . .	Marblehead.
Mar. 1,	Mary Jane Fremont,* . .	Alice Fremont Willey, . .	South Danvers.
June 7,	Annie Elizabeth King, . .	Annie Fabens King, . .	Salem.
7,	Mary Jane Howe,* . . .	Mary Jane Bridges, . .	Newburyport.
14,	Harry Dow, ...	Harry Dow Moray, . .	Lawrence.
14,	Mary Emma Bean,* . . .	Emma Bean Chase, . .	Lawrence.
July 5,	William Fitzgibbon,* . .	William Fitzgibbon Erwin, .	Gloucester.
Aug. 2,	Maria Emma Ingalls, . .	Emma Williston Ingalls, .	Andover.
2,	Elizabeth D. Howe, . . .	Elizabeth Howe Richards, .	Lynn.
Oct. 4,	Emma Frances Cheneworth,* .	Emma Frances Burns, . .	Lynn.
11,	Eva Adelaide DeWolf,* . .	Eva Adelaide Smith, . .	Gloucester.
18,	William Carr Moreau,* . .	William Charles Anderson, .	Groveland.
Dec. 13,	Lizzie Maria Withey,* . .	Lizzie Maria Higgins, . .	Lawrence.

MIDDLESEX COUNTY.

Jan. 26,	Susan Elizabeth Ames,* . .	Susan Elizabeth Sparhawk, .	Brighton.
26,	Rhoda Jane Ames,* . . .	Rhoda Jane Sparhawk, . .	Brighton.
Feb. 5,	Fanny M. Hunt,* . . .	Fanny Hamilton Flint, . .	Cambridge.
Mar. 22,	John Alexander Jennison,* .	John Alexander Holmes, .	Wayland.
April 5,	Charles Fremont Chapman,* .	Charles Henry Pierson, . .	Wilmington.
5,	William P. L. Chapman,* . .	William Justin Damon, . .	Reading.
12,	Eugene Hall,*	William Henry Gurney, . .	Natick.
26,	Anne Stewart,*	Anne Crowley, . . .	Malden.
May 10,	William Parker Lewis,* . .	Samuel William Fowler, . .	Malden.
June 14,	Sarah Jane Carroll,* . .	Sarah Jane Twitchell, . .	Hopkinton.
14,	Annie A. Cushman,* . . .	Annie Augusta Hastings, .	Natick.
28,	Horace Joseph Butterworth,* .	Horace Joseph Allen, . .	Woburn.
Aug. 9,	Kenneth John Brown, . .	Kenneth John Ware, . .	Medford.

* Changed by reason of adoption.

MIDDLESEX COUNTY — *Concluded.*

Date of Decree.	Original Name.	Name Decreed.	Residence.
1864.			
Sept. 6,	Charles Henry Pratt,*	Charles Henry Lovett,	Lowell.
6,	Clara W. Weeks,*	Clara W. Smith,	Lowell.
13,	George Fred. Mortimer Nowlan,*	Fred. Mortimer Bell,	Malden.
27,	Nellie Hoyet,*	Hattie Mills,	Groton.
Oct. 4,	Mary Catharine Houghton,*	Mary Catharine Beath,	Cambridge.
11,	Mary Elizabeth Kenedy,*	Merriam Farrington,	Holliston.
Nov. 22,	Horatio Griffin,*	Horace James,	Medford.
Dec. 13,	Harry Ellison Chase,*	Harry Ellison Seaver,	Charlestown.
13,	Emma Jane Parker,*	Emma Mehitable Morse,	Marlborough.
13,	Leslie Frances Martin,*	Leslie Frances Adams,	Lowell.
27,	Lida Cecelia Pearl,*	Ida Webb,	Waltham.

WORCESTER COUNTY.

Mar. 1,	Evelyn E. Tidd,	Evelyn E. Plummer,	Warren.
Feb. 2,	Edwin Tyson Townsend,	Edward Townsend,	Spencer.
April 5,	Sarah Maria Farnum,	Sarah Maria Taft,	Uxbridge.
5,	Mary Ann Dowd,	Mary Ann Darney,	Worcester.
5,	Catharine Dowd,	Catharine Gernhard,	Worcester.
May 3,	Nellie Brown,	Nellie Wakefield,	Worcester.
3,	Arthur W. Conant,	Arthur Warren Conant Loverwell,	Gardner.
June 7,	Cassie Vernon Miller,	Cassie Vernon Miller Long,	Westborough.
7,	Annie Dowd,	Annie Vail,	Worcester.
7,	Nettie Maria Norcross,	Nettie Maria Martin,	Worcester.
7,	Susie Adams,	Susie A. Dodd,	Paxton.
July 5,	Margaret Josephine Perry,	Margaret Louise Humphrey,	Milford.
Aug. 2,	Georgie E. Smith,	Ella Maria Sibley,	Westborough.
2,	Hattie Ann Spooner,	Hattie Ann Brown,	Leicester.
Sept. 6,	Stephen Edward McGann,	Stephen Edward McGann Finnesty,	Milford.
6,	Clara Etta Gould,	Nellie Elizabeth Hatch,	Leicester.
6,	Joseph Washington Estabrook Lindsay,	Joseph Ira Lindsay,	Grafton.
29,	Cora M. Gould,	Cora M. Wheaton,	Leicester.
Nov. 1,	Lucy Caroline Brooks,	Lucy Caroline Warner,	Harvard.
1,	Eva Kendall,	Eva Merton Clemence,	Worcester.
1,	George Fabian Dupsey,	George Carr,	Worcester.
1,	William Arthur Cummings,	William Arthur Eager,	Leominster.
1,	Ernest Buck,	Ernest Clapper,	Millbury.
Dec. 6,	Lizie E. Hubbard,	Lizie H. Ellis,	Milford.

HAMPSHIRE COUNTY.

Jan. 5,	Frank Fiske,	Frank Fiske Brown,	South Hadley.
5,	William A. Turner,	Leon Ellsworth Beals,	Northampton.
Mar. 1,	Emily Adelaide Livingston,	Katie Emma King,	Plainfield.
April 14,	Joseph W. Porter,	Wellington Joseph Patterson,	Huntington.
Sept. 6,	Curtis R. Graves,	Curtis R. Smith,	Amherst.
Oct. 11,	Lucy Ellen King,	Lucy King Dikeman,	Northampton.
Nov. 1,	Ella J. Bushnell,	Ella J. Warner,	Williamsburg.

* Changed by reason of adoption.

HAMPDEN COUNTY — *Concluded.*

Date of Decree.	Original Name.	Name Decreed.	Residence.
1864.			
Feb. 2,	George Sidney Brown, . .	George Sidney Hamilton, .	Blandford.
Mar. 15,	Frederick B. Winchell, . .	Frederick B. Rogers, . .	Chester.
April 5,	Charles Bates, ...	Charles Weaver, . . .	Chicopee.
5,	Clara Eva Harvey, . .	Clara Eva Easton, . . .	Southwick.
June 7,	Mary Butler, . . .	Minnie W. Pinkham, . .	Springfield.
7,	Mary M. Simons, . . .	Mary M. Burt, . . .	Longmeadow.
July 5,	Mary Ida Simons, . . .	Cora Bell Clark, . . .	Chester.
5,	Alia Eveline Thompson, .	Alia Eveline Kendall, . .	Chicopee.
5,	John Neal, ...	John N. Capen, . . .	Springfield.
17,	Charles Dinkle, ...	Frederick Briggs Converse, .	Monson.

FRANKLIN COUNTY.

Date of Decree.	Original Name.	Name Decreed.	Residence.
Feb. 2,	Alice F. Dunbar, . . .	Alice F. Munson, . . .	Greenfield.
9,	Franklin E. Turner, . . .	Lyman F. Griggs, . . .	Ashfield.
9,	James Hicks, ...	James Hicks Hunt, . .	Rowe.
May 3,	Henrietta E. Smith, . .	Henrietta Emeline Wilson, .	Shutesbury.
3,	Minnie Maria Hall, . .	Minnie Maria Pierce, . .	Buckland.
June 7,	Abigail Thomas, . .	Abbie Maria Willis, . .	Buckland.
July 5,	Sarah Nunney, ...	Sarah Sprague, . . .	Buckland.
Aug. 2,	Elizabeth A. Dawson, . .	Mary Ella King, . . .	Buckland.
2,	Emily Nunney, ...	Emily Nunney Brown, .	Buckland.
Sept. 6,	William E. Martin, . .	William Arthur Cook, . .	Heath.
Oct. 25,	Ada Johnson, ...	Ada Johnson Powers, . .	Shelburne.
25,	Daniel P. Johnson, . .	Daniel Johnson Powers, .	Shelburne.
25,	Lucinda Melessa Payne, .	Beadie Melessa Payne, .	Buckland.
Dec. 6,	Carrie B. Vose, ...	Carrie Belle Harris, . .	Charlemont.

BERKSHIRE COUNTY.

Date of Decree.	Original Name.	Name Decreed.	Residence.
Mar. 18,	Laura Ellen Shattuck, . .	Ellen Jane Ballou, . ○ .	Adams.

NORFOLK COUNTY.

Date of Decree.	Original Name.	Name Decreed.	Residence.
Feb. 13,	William Sherman Elliot, . .	William Sherman Fellows, .	Milton.
27,	Frank W. Slater, . . .	John Franklin Bowling, .	Foxborough.
April 2,	Charles Mansfield, . . .	Charles Henry Mansfield, .	Needham.
16,	Nellie Baker Spring, . . .	Helen Amelia Shaw, . .	——.
July 2,	Esther H. P. Stevens, . .	Esther H. P. Sumner, . .	Foxborough.
Aug. 20,	Frank Ellis Perry. . .	Frank Ellis Hill, . . .	Foxborough.
27,	Henry Ambrose Heeling, .	Henry Lomasney Kirby, .	Roxbury.
Nov. 5,	Margaret Cunningham, . .	Mary Ella Burroughs, . .	——.

BRISTOL COUNTY.

Date of Decree.	Original Name.	Name Decreed.	Residence.
Feb. 5,	Emma Louisa Caneau, . .	Emma Louisa Dean, . .	Taunton.
15,	Hannah Louisa Pratt, . .	Hannah Louisa Stanley, .	Taunton.
19,	Mary Ella Black, . .	Mary Ella Hunt, . . .	Taunton.
Mar. 16,	Caroline Elizabeth Cheatham, .	Caroline Elizabeth Bosworth,	Attleborough.
July 8,	Alice Almy Davol, . . .	Almy Cartwright, . . .	Somerset.
Aug. 19,	Hester Henrietta Pratt, .	Hester Henrietta Fuller, .	Rehoboth.
Sept. 16,	Emma Theresa Harriman,	Emma Allen Battelle, . .	Taunton.

PLYMOUTH COUNTY.

Date of Decree.	Original Name.	Name Decreed.	Residence.
1864. June 12,	Irene Allen Taylor,* . . .	Irene Allen White, . . .	Duxbury.

BARNSTABLE COUNTY.

June 21,	Charles Ellis, ...	Charles Sears, ...	Dennis.
21,	Frederick Joseph Crocker, .	Frederick William Crocker, .	Barnstable.
Nov. 3,	Minnie Fletcher Howe, . .	Minnie Fletcher Luscombe, .	Provincetown.

NANTUCKET COUNTY.

Sept. –,	James Ross Gardner, . .	James Ross, ...	Nantucket.

SUFFOLK COUNTY.

1865. Jan. 9,	Abby Jennette Smith, . .	Emma Jennette Ford, . .	Stow.
16,	Henrietta Clapp, . . .	Henrietta Beckwith, . .	Boston.
30,	Anna Livingston, . . .	Annie Blanche Twombly, .	Cambridge.
Feb. 20,	Clara Blanchard, . . .	Clara Paddleford Holden, .	Charlestown.
27,	Margaret Curry, . . .	Margaret Ellen Cotter, .	Framingham.
Mar. 13,	Sarah Louise Craig, . .	Sarah Louise Craig Hale, .	Springfield.
20,	William Henry Farren, . .	William Henry Winslow, .	Boston.
April 17,	Anna Maria Bennett, . .	Anna Maria Naylor, . .	Boston.
May 1,	Julia George, ...	Julia George Kilpatrick, .	Lawrence.
29,	Charles Wragg, *alias* Charles Wray, ...	Henry Dale, ...	Boston.
June 5,	Louis Powers, otherwise called Louis Sawyer, . .	Louis Sawyer Whitcomb, .	Litchfield, Me.
12,	Hannah Elizabeth Donovan, .	Hannah Elizabeth Pratt, .	St. John, N. B.
12,	Agnes Riona Smith, . .	Clara Morse, ...	Boston.
12,	Almira Susan Teed, . .	Nellie Hunter Morrison, .	Rovingstown, Me.
12,	Margaret Elizabeth Reynolds, .	Margaret Wendell Reynolds, .	Boston.
26,	Ellen Dwight Parkman, .	Ellen Twisleton Parkman, .	Boston.
Aug. 7,	Hubert Kent Sutton, . .	Hubert Kent Reynolds, .	Boston.
7,	Estella Louisa Penney, .	Estella Young, . . .	Malden.
14,	Edward Moses, . . .	Edward Heath Spooner, .	Boston.
28,	Isabelle Smith, . . .	Helen Louisa Bailey, .	Boston.
Sept. 4,	Sarah Elizabeth Williams, .	Sarah Elizabeth Brown, .	Boston.
18,	Elizabeth Mulhearn, . .	Elizabeth Murphy, . .	Boston.
25,	Robert Carr Tubbs, . .	Robert Carr Dunham, .	Boston.
Oct. 9,	Henry Boynton, . . .	Joseph Henry Binney, .	Somerville.
9,	Frederic Myers, . . .	Frederic Manson Brooks, .	Boston.
16,	Edward Stanley Tubbs, . .	Edward Stanley Dunham, .	Boston.
23,	Osgood Harriman, . .	Osgood Harriman Sewall, .	Chatham, N. H.
30,	Feridoon J. R. Wood, . .	Feridoon Wood Parents, .	Boston.
Nov. 6,	Josiah Carr Tubbs, . .	Josiah Carr Dunham, .	Boston.

* Changed by reason of adoption.

ESSEX COUNTY.

Date of Decree.	Original Name.	Name Decreed.	Residence.
1865.			
Jan. 10,	Mary Ellen Gingras,*	Mary Ellen Firth,	Methuen.
Feb. 7,	Francis Prentis Blaney,	Stephen Francis Blaney,	South Danvers.
Mar. 9,	Jesse Goodnow,	Jesse Gardner Gould,	Lawrence.
21,	Luella Johnson,*	Anna Lenora Burrill,	Newbury.
June 6,	Florence L. Worthen,	Florence Louise Greene,.	Haverhill.
13,	Ada Augusta Lord,*	Ada Augusta Hodgman,	Lawrence.
July 5,	Isabell Jane Gilson,*	Isabell Jane Smith,	Bradford.
Aug. 1,	Frank William Chase,*	Frank William Chase Folsom,	Georgetown.
Sept. 5,	Daniel Collins,*	Daniel Collins Smyth,	Lynn.
Oct. 3,	Sarah Elizabeth Frederic,*	Elizabeth Goddard Stone,	Marblehead.
3,	George Dudley Abbott,	Stephen Woodbury Abbott,	Beverly.
10,	George Scarth,*	George Fanton,	Gloucester.
Nov. 7,	Leonora Williams,*	Leonora Brice,	Lynn.
7,	Anna Janett Williams,*	Anna Janett Brice,	Lynn.
14,	Georgianna Scott,*	Georgianna Scott French,	Lawrence.
Dec. 5,	Emeline W Stannard,*	Emeline Stannard Laroch,	Gloucester.
5,	Jennie L. Stannard,*	Jennie Stannard Estabrook,	Gloucester.
12,	George B. Tubbs,	George B. Dunham,	Lynn.
12,	Christianna S. Tubbs,	Christianna S. Dunham,	Lynn.

MIDDLESEX COUNTY.

Jan. 10,	John Hannibal Augustus Rollins,	John Augustus Rollins,	Charlestown.
10,	Susan Ann Senior,*	Anna Jane Shackley,	Cambridge.
24,	Helen Grey Trask,*	Helen Maria Grey,	Tewksbury.
Feb. 14,	Darius Messer,	Darius Morton Messer,	Stoneham.
April 11,	Ella Frances Stevens,*	Emma Louisa Shory,	Cambridge.
11,	Ida Louisa Waterman,*	Ida Louisa Whitney,	Medford.
May 23,	Sarah E. Poor,	Sarah E. Hartshorn,	Reading.
23,	Ella Augusta Poor,*	Ella Augusta Hartshorn,	Reading.
23,	Benjamin Richmond,*	Benjamin Roundy,	Medford.
June 13,	Benjamin Pinkus,*	George Rafalgen Stimpson,	Somerville.
13,	Addie Maria Bennett,*	Amy Eager Gates,	Medford.
Aug. 22,	Bertha Hankin,*	Bertha Tucker,	Newton.
Sept. 12,	Grace Hankin,*	Grace Plummer,	Brighton.
Oct. 10,	George Haven Dugan,	George Dugan Haven,	Somerville.
24,	Thomas Frederick Carr,*	Thomas Frederick Eames,	Framingham.
Nov. 14,	Lottie Louisa Green,*	Lottie Louisa Garfield,	Groton.
14,	Nellie E. Rideout,*	Nellie Emogene Flood,	Lowell.
Dec. 12,	Mabel Ada Brown,*	Mabel Alden,	Ashfield.
26,	Alexis Dufresne,*	Alexis Rivard Lavigne, Jr.,	Woburn.

WORCESTER COUNTY.

Jan. 3,	Frank Lincoln Marshall,	Frank Marshall Kendall,	Leominster.
Feb. 7,	Fannie Maria Dadmun,	Fannie Maria Phillips,	Fitchburg.
7,	Hattie Frances Brockway,	Hattie Frances Coolidge,	Berlin.
Mar. 7,	William Harrison Webber,	William Harrison Carlton,	Brookfield.
7,	Willard Clark,	Charles Willard Clark,	Milford.
7,	Maria Brown Pettis,	Emeretta Frances Farwell,	Boylston.
April 4,	Perez O'Hearn,	Charles Henry Brown,	Upton.
4,	Richard O'Hearn,	William Rawson,	Upton.
4,	Ellen Parker,	Ellen Butler,	Mendon.

* Changed by reason of adoption.

WORCESTER COUNTY — *Concluded.*

Date of Decree.	Original Name.	Name Decreed.	Residence.
1865.			
May 2,	Michael McKenzie, . . .	Charles Elmer McKenzie, .	Northbridge.
2,	Anna Nickerson Baker, . .	Anna Elizabeth Warren, .	Upton.
2,	Mary Jane Morgan, . . .	Mary Jane Mellen, . . .	Fitchburg.
23,	Frederick Seaver, . . .	Frederick Seaver Madden, .	Milford.
June 6,	Hiram Samson, ...	Hiram Elwin Piper, o	Charlestown.
July 5,	Andrew Belcher, . . .	Edwin Vincent Lilley, . .	Milford.
Sept. 5,	Lura May Stearns, . . .	Lura Jane Amidon, . .	Holden.
5,	Charles Henry Russell, . .	Charles Henry Hawes, . .	Oxford.
5,	Freddie Duncan Putnam, .	Freddie Duncan Loring, .	Worcester.
5,	—— Russell, ...	Nellie Mabel Weaver, . .	Boston.
Oct. 10,	Edward Everett Smith, . .	Edward Potter Newell, . .	Northbridge.
10,	Ella Nora Smith, . . .	Ella Nora Newell, . . .	Northbridge.
18,	Alice E. Findell, . . .	Alice Emma Marble, . .	Ashburnham.
20,	Sarah Frances Harrington, .	Sarah Harrington Goddard, .	Barre.
Dec. 5,	Anna Francelia Coots, . .	Anna Francelia Howe, . .	N'th Bridgewater.
5,	Tearney McMurry, . . .	Tearney Cryne, . . .	Milford.

HAMPSHIRE COUNTY.

Jan. 3,	Clara Eliza Baker, . . .	Clara Eliza Weeks, . .	Worthington.
3,	John Smith, ...	John S. Cooke, . . .	South Hadley.
June 6,	George M. Boice, . . .	George M. Gaylord, . .	Hadley.
6,	Cora D. Boice, ...	Cora D. Spooner, . .	Hadley.
Aug. 1,	Carrie E. Harwood, . . .	Carrie Amelia Harwood, .	Northampton.
1,	Levi G. Bliss, ...	George C. Montague, . .	Granby.
1,	Cyrene J. Bliss, ...	Cyrene J. Montague, . .	Granby.
1,	Lillie M. Damon, . . .	Lillie M. Brown, . . .	Goshen.
Oct. 3,	Jennie Sinclair, ...	Jennie L. Field, . . .	Northampton.
Dec. 5,	Sarah Jane Judd, . . .	Sada Jane Judd, . . .	South Hadley.

HAMPDEN COUNTY.

Jan. 3,	Frederick Hart,* . . .	Frederick Henry Moore, .	Granville.
Feb. 7,	Hattie Maria Bancroft,* . .	Hattie Maria Chamberlain, .	Granville.
7,	Henry Clarence Bancroft,* .	Henry Clarence Chamberlain, .	Granville.
21,	Frances Ruthella Gott,* . .	Frances Ruthella Dewey, .	Agawam.
Mar. 7,	Ida May Owen,* . . .	Ida May Allen, . . .	Springfield.
7,	Nettie Owen,*	Nettie Owen Allen, . .	Springfield.
11,	Winnifred Grant,* . . .	Winnifred Grant Plummer, .	Springfield.
April 4,	Oscar Newton Warriner,* .	Oscar Newton Allen, . .	West Springfield.
July 11,	Eva A. Squires,* . . .	Eva Amelia Chandler, . .	Springfield.
Oct. 3,	Jennie Elva Palmer,* . .	Jennie Elva Davis, . . .	Palmer.
17,	Frank A. Hills,* . . .	Frank Lewis Day, . . .	Springfield.
17,	Minnie Elvira Madison,* .	Minnie Elvira Cook, . .	Westfield.
Dec. 5,	Ernest L. Paine,* . . .	Albert Henry Brierly, . .	Springfield.

FRANKLIN COUNTY.

Mar. 7,	Clara Isabella Sweetser, . .	Clara Isabella Armstrong, .	Sunderland.
June 6,	William Arthur Cook, . .	William Earford Martin, .	Rowe.
Sept. 5,	Eva Stella Howard, . . .	Eva Stella Lyman, . . .	Montague.

* Changed by reason of adoption.

FRANKLIN COUNTY — *Concluded.*

Date of Decree.	Original Name.	Name Decreed.	Residence.
1865.			
Sept. 5,	George N. Butler, . . .	George Lincoln, . . .	Sunderland.
Oct. 3,	Maggie L. Murphy, . . .	Maggie L. Clapp, . . .	Montague.
3,	George William Cimter, . .	George William King, . .	Greenfield.
24,	Emma A. Clark, . . .	Emma Adelade Carpenter, .	Rowe.
Dec. 11,	Oscar S. Cole, ...	Oscar Stephen Ripley, . .	Leverett.
12,	Martha E. Williams, . . .	Martha Emogene Haskell, .	New Salem.

BERKSHIRE COUNTY.

April 4,	Mary Murphy, ...	Mary Toban, ...	Hinsdale.
26,	Hubert T. Trowbridge, . .	Hubert T. Haradon, . .	Savoy.
26,	Fanny E. Trowbridge, . .	Sarah Eudora Haradon, . .	Savoy.
Sept. 5,	Franklin Potter, ...	Franklin Secor, . . .	W. Stockbridge.

NORFOLK COUNTY.

Jan. 28,	Mabel Georgianna Burrill,* .	Georgianna Clinton Burrill, .	Brookline.
Mar. 4,	Harriet Hitchborn, . . .	Harriet Louisa Hitchborn, .	Brookline.
11,	Evelyn Lucinda Kerr,* . .	Evelyn Lucinda Bullard, .	Canton.
11,	Sarah Maria Beless,* . .	Sarah Maria King, . .	Needham.
April 1,	Ada Parker,*	Ada Parker Roberts, . .	Fitzwilliam, N. H.
May 13,	Juliet Mann,*	Eliza Ella Goldthwait, . .	Randolph.
16,	Outis Fisk,*	Elona V. Fisk, . . .	Medway.
27,	Eben Wheeler Onion, . .	Eben Wheeler Warren, .	Brookline.
27,	Alice Jane Onion, . . .	Alice Jane Warren, . .	Brookline.
27,	Willard Douglass Onion, . .	William Douglass Warren, .	Brookline.
27,	George Onion, ...	George Warren, . . .	Roxbury.
27,	Isabel Onion, ...	Isabel Warren, . . .	Dorchester.
27,	Rebecca Winslow Onion, . .	Rebecca Winslow Warren, .	Roxbury.
27,	Willard Onion, Jr., . .	Willard Warren, . . .	Brookline.
27,	Mary Pollard Onion, . .	Mary Allisson Warren, . .	Brookline.
27,	Ella Frances Onion, . .	Ella Frances Warren, . .	Brookline.
June 3,	Mary Louisa Yeaton,* . .	Mary Louisa White, . .	Paris, Me.
6,	Harriet Coy,*	Harriet Brewster, . . .	Oxford, Me.
July 1,	Mary Jane Dearing,* . .	Mary Jane Jenkins Dearing, .	Boston.
Aug. 26,	Abba Louisa Russell,* . .	Abba Louisa Ward, . .	Cambridge.
Sept. 23,	Reuben Hill Gilbert, . .	Richelieu Hill Gilbert, .	Roxbury.
Oct. 21,	Joseph Robertson Hodge, . .	Joseph Robertson, . . .	Quincy.
Nov. 11,	Frances Adelaide Thayer,* .	Frances Adelaide Dyer, . .	Bridgewater.

BRISTOL COUNTY.

Jan. 20,	Betsey B. Cummings, . .	Betsey Bradley Allen, . .	Dartmouth.
Feb. 3,	George William Joseph, . .	George William Joseph Moulton, ...	New Bedford.
15,	Abram L. Allen Percival,* .	Abram L. Allen, . . .	Late Providence, R. I., now New Bedford.
17,	Nellie Josephine Hill,* . .	Nellie Josephine Craig, . .	Late Foxborough, now Attleborough.
May 5,	Abby Harriet Sherman,* . .	Abby Harriet Pratt, . . .	New Bedford.

* Changed by reason of adoption.

BRISTOL COUNTY — *Concluded.*

Date of Decree.	Original Name.	Name Decreed.	Residence.
1865.			
May 19,	Edward L. Hathaway,*	Edward L. Smith,	Late Berkley, now Taunton.
June 2,	Lilian Frances Hathaway,*	Lilian Francis Clapp,'	Taunton.
June 13,	Annie E. Marston,	Annie E. Crosby,	Taunton.
21,	Emma P. Baldwin,*	Emma P. Tobey,	New Bedford.
Aug. 16,	Sophronia R. Crocker,*	Annie B. Dunham,	New Bedford.
Oct. 20,	Mary Anna Leydon,	Mary Anna Dean,	Taunton.
Dec. 1,	Mary Elizabeth Duncan,*	Eliza Francis Kerrigan,	Late Boston, now Taunton.
1,	Francis Edward Tucker,*	Francis Edward Bowring,	Late Norton, now Taunton.
Dec. 15,	John Otis Drake,*	Charles Henry Jenkins,	Taunton.

PLYMOUTH COUNTY.

April 10,	Mary Lizzie Thayer,	Lizzie Lena Ellis,	Duxbury.
June 26,	John Hannum,	John H. Burrell,	Abington.
Sept. 11,	Lizzie E. Rogers,	Lizzie E. Pittee,	Plymouth.

DUKES COUNTY.

Jan. 16,	Nettie Packard,*	Nettie Louisa Packard,	Edgartown.
June 5,	Harry H. Ferguson,	Harry Adams Norton,	Edgartown.

SUFFOLK COUNTY.

1866.			
Jan. 1,	Emma Giles Merrill,	Emma Giles Cormier,	Boston.
29,	Nancy Anna Harriman,	Anna Norris Philbrook Drake,	Boston.
29,	Winfield Scott Harriman,	Winfield Scott Drake,	Boston.
Feb. 26,	Frederica Howes Briggs,	Lilian Frederica Briggs,	Boston.
Mar. 5,	Carrie Thacher Briggs,	Carrie Briggs Sargent,	Boston.
12,	Nelson Hollis Fisher,	Nelson Edgar Hollis,	Boston.
April 9,	Marietta Flaherty,	Marietta Martis,	Bridgewater.
9,	Laura Amelia Hathaway,	Carrie Amelia Fairfield,	Taunton.
23,	Mary Ellen Webb,	Mary Ellen Dinsmore,	Portland, Me.
May 21,	Mary Jessie Tubbs,	Mary Jessie Allison,	Boston.
21,	Charlotte Elizabeth Tubbs,	Charlotte Elizabeth Allison,	Boston.
June 4,	James Molony,	James William Taylor,	Boston.
4,	Mary Louisa Molony,	Mary Louisa Taylor,	Boston.
18,	Frances Alice Bacon,	Alice Frances Anna Murch,	Cambridge.
Aug. 6,	Samuel M. Druif,	Samuel Whitebone,	Boston.
6,	Eunice Fry Mineard,	Annie Tyler,	Chelsea.
20,	Zillah Marina Stacy,	Zillah Marina Andrews,	Boston.
Oct. 1,	Charles Chase,	Frederick William Herchenroder,	Boston.
1,	Sarah Elizabeth Williams,	Lizzie Wood Allyn,	Danvers.
Nov. 5,	Chas. Henry Wheelwright Chamberlain,	Charles Wheelwright Chamberlin,	Boston.
26,	Eliza Marshall,	Amice Belle Hinckley,	Boston.
Dec. 17,	Susan Elizabeth Clark,	Elizabeth Tyler Clark,	Boston.
24,	Isaac Humphrey Houston,	Frank Key Houston,	Boston.

* Changed by reason of adoption.

ESSEX COUNTY.

Date of Decree.	Original Name.	Name Decreed.	Residence.
1866.			
Jan. 9,	Margaret Carr,*	Winnie Margaret Burns, .	Lawrence.
9,	Lottie Clark,* . . .	Lizzie Lord Perkins, .	Andover.
Feb. 6,	Jonathan Waldo, jun., .	John Waldo, . . .	Andover.
6,	——— Leavitt,* . . .	Carrie Augusta Swett, .	Swampscott.
April 3,	Francis Crohan, . . .	Francis Dixie, . .	Marblehead.
3,	Franklin Porter Currier Cole,* .	William Henry Lovell, .	Newburyport.
3,	Andrew Ward Spence, .	Andrew Ward, . .	Salem.
May 15,	Mary Ann Lloyd,* . . .	Mary Ann Bickerton, .	Lynn.
June 5,	Ema Frances Burnham,* .	Emily Burnham Agge, .	Haverhill.
5,	Annie Laura Martin,* .	Annie Laura Taylor, .	Lynn.
12,	Harry Lawrence Millett,* .	Harry Millett Eames, .	Andover.
July 3,	Mary Ward Burchmore, .	Mary Ward Rowell, .	Salem.
3,	Sarah Clifton Burchmore Ross,	Sarah Clifton Whitmore, .	Salem.
3,	Anna White Kimball,* .	Anna Kimball Copeland, .	Haverhill.
Aug. 7,	Martha McGovern, . .	Martha Dana, . . .	Saugus.
7,	William Edward Smith,* .	John Albert Smith, .	Ipswich.
Oct. 9,	George Alphonso Coffin,* .	George Albert Graffan, .	Salem.
Nov. 6,	Warren Ayres Fisk,*	Warren Fowler, .	Lynn.
Dec. 4,	Edward Poole Stevens, .	James Edward Poole Stevens, ...	Andover.

MIDDLESEX COUNTY.

Date of Decree.	Original Name.	Name Decreed.	Residence.
Feb. 13,	Margaret Hegarty,* .	Annie Margaret Floyd, .	Weston.
13,	(A male infant), .	James Durno Maitland, .	Cambridge.
Mar. 13,	Florence M. Mansur,* .	Nellie Florence Whittemore, .	Groton.
13,	Joseph W. Morrison,* .	Joseph Morrison Wilson, .	Dracut.
April 10,	Laura Belle Arnold,* .	Laura Belle Bartlett, .	Groton.
10,	Oliver Hazard Benson,* .	Charles Calvin Leland, .	Natick.
10,	Lucy Frances Benson,* .	Jennie Wolcott Leland, .	Natick.
May 22,	Louisa Ann Howe, .	Annie Louisa Howe, .	Marlborough.
June 5,	Joseph H. D. Hayes,* .	Joseph Henry Douglass Hayes, . . .	Lowell.
5,	Helen E. Clarke, .	Helen Eliza Cowdrey, .	Acton.
26,	Dudley Taylor Kidder, .	Dudley Cotton Redpath, .	Malden.
26,	Charles Wellington, .	Charles Wellington Cragin, .	Ashby.
26,	Francis Evans,* .	Frank Bean, . .	Marlborough.
Aug. 14,	Minnie Brennan,* .	Lillian Louisa Lancey, .	Newton.
14,	Mary Emma Sleeper,* .	Mary Emma Brooks, .	Cambridge.
14,	George Edward Sleeper,* .	Edward Brooks, . .	Cambridge.
14,	Evelina Sleeper,* .	Evelina Brooks, . .	Cambridge.
14,	Angus Horn Morrow,* .	Arthur Horn Bradford, .	Boxborough.
14,	George Young Morrow,* .	George Young Hutchins, .	Acton.
14,	William Trow Morrow,* .	William Trow Mason, .	Acton.
14,	Mary Frances Mansfield,* .	Mary Mansfield Morse, .	Natick.
Sept. 4,	Sally W. Wetherbee, .	Sally Whitcomb Green, .	Ashby.
11,	Robert Conant Chaffin, .	Robert Chaffin Conant, .	Lowell.
11,	Charles Ira Eaton,* .	Charles Ira Ellis, .	Stoneham.
11,	Carrie Chandler Fish,* .	Carrie Chandler Paul, .	Newton.
25,	Julia Lucius,* . . .	Julia Abbott, . .	Lowell.
Oct. 9,	Agnes Isabella Meldrum, .	Susan Cooke Meldrum, .	Cambridge.
Nov. 27,	Elmira Gillespie, .	Elmira Morse, . .	Waltham.
27,	Emily Louisa Gillespie, .	Emily Louisa Morse, .	Waltham.
27,	George Washington Gillespie,	George Washington Morse, .	Waltham.
27,	Carrie Augusta Gillespie, .	Carrie Augusta Morse, .	Waltham.

* Changed by reason of adoption.

WORCESTER COUNTY.

Date of Decree.	Original Name.	Name Decreed.	Residence.
1866.			
Jan. 2,	Hannah C. Stratford,	Hannah C. Holbrook,	Blackstone.
Feb. 6,	James Morrow,	George Damon Parker,	Phillipston.
6,	Emma Frances Frary,	Ida Mabel Thompson,	Holden.
6,	William Henry Frary,	Charles P. Leavitt,	Holden.
Mar. 6,	Etta Woodcock,	Etta Elizabeth King,	Phillipston.
6,	(Unknown),	Clara Winnie Gates,	Fitchburg.
April 3,	Lewis Mills Larned,	Lewis Mills Learned,	Worcester.
3,	John Joseph Rutherford,	John Joseph McDonald,	Worcester.
May 1,	Daniel Bliss,	Daniel J. Bliss,	Warren.
1,	Sarah Nellie Hodgden,	Sarah Nellie Holbrook,	Leicester.
1,	Ellen M. McLaughlin,	Nellie A. Rice,	Westminster.
23,	Frederick Seaver,	Frederick Seaver Madden,	Milford.
June 5,	Lizzie C. Dunton,	Lizzie C. Wyman,	Phillipston.
May 17,	Nellie J. Dunton,	Nellie Jennette Ward,	Athol.
Aug. 7,	Lillian Grace Collins,	Nellie Fisher,	Milford.
7,	Stella Isabell Wetherbee,	Stella Isabell Cooley,	Holden.
7,	Cora F. Woodcock,	Cora Florence Haskins,	Worcester.
April 3,	Mary Spencer,	Hattie May Ruggles,	Upton.
Sept. 4,	Grace Leland Gleason,	Mabel Caroline Knox,	Worcester.
Oct. 2,	Elisabeth Lavinia Flagg,	Lizzie Lavinia Parker,	Templeton.
16,	Harriet F. Pratt,	Harriet Frances Johnson,	Milford.
18,	Charlie Levi Byam,	Charlie Edward Levi Cross,	Royalston.
Nov. 6,	Ida S. Sutherly,	Ida Elizabeth Heredeen,	Charlton.
Dec. 4,	J. Elisabeth Lyon,	J. Lizzie Potter,	Southbridge.
4,	Sarah Helen Webster,	Flora Italia Young,	Templeton.
4,	(Unknown),	John Eddie Thomas,	Holden.
4,	Ella Maria Gates,	Ella Maria Foshay,	Spencer.
4,	Nettie Houghton,	Nettie Houghton Hale,	Fitchburg.
4,	Mary Elisabeth Bergen,	Mary Elisabeth Newhall,	Leicester.

HAMPSHIRE COUNTY.

Date of Decree.	Original Name.	Name Decreed.	Residence.
May 1,	Martha L. Clapp,	Martha Louisa Abell,	Northampton.
1,	George Alanson Cushman,	George Alanson Kelley,	Worthington.
1,	William Eugene Robbins,	William Eugene Canterbury,	Belchertown.
June 5,	Clarence Merton Chamberlain,	Clarence Merton Russell,	Hadley.
5,	Johnnie Francis Chamberlain,	John Francis Marshall,	Amherst.
July 3,	Eveline E. Lovett,	Eveline E. Fish,	Amherst.
May 8,	Anna Lee Bishop,	Anna Lee Clark,	Belchertown.
Aug. 7,	Anna W. Taylor,	Anna W. Robinson,	Ware.
Sept. 4,	Lula Orpha Hanson,	Emma Frances Burley,	Williamsburg.
Oct. 2,	Emma L. Crandall,	Emma Luella Smith,	Belchertown.
9,	Gilbert Damon,	Louis Fabacher Bridgman,	Belchertown.
Nov. 7,	Charles Hanks,	Charles Church,	Granby.
9,	Ada Augusta Fuller,	Ada Augusta Montague,	Amherst.
9,	Charles Frederic Fuller,	Charles Frederic Montague,	Amherst.

HAMPDEN COUNTY.

Date of Decree.	Original Name.	Name Decreed.	Residence.
June 5,	Arthur Hale,	Arthur Milo Nye,	Blandford.
July 3,	Emma Fry,	Emma Sabine Leppens,	Chicopee.
Aug. 7,	Armadilla Holcomb,	Martha Jane Buttles,	Granville.
Nov. 7,	Anton J. Andersen,	John Frederick Almquist,	Springfield.
7,	Freddie Woodford Tinker,	William Edson Fiske,	Chester.
Dec. 4,	Emma N. Towne,	Clara Bell Merrill,	Springfield.
8,	Louis Maynard Manning,	Oliver Louis Wolcott,	Longmeadow.

FRANKLIN COUNTY.

Date of Decree.	Original Name.	Name Decreed.	Residence.
1866.			
Feb. 13,	Minnie M. Warner, . . .	Minnie M. Whitney, . .	Buckland.
May 15,	Cora Lincoln Blodgett, . .	Cora Lincoln Lee, . . .	Conway.
July 10,	Sarah Eliza White, . . .	Sarah Eliza Kenney, . .	Northfield.
10,	Alonzo P. Wales, . . .	Alonzo Granger, . . .	Charlemont.
Aug. 7,	Emma Estella Phillips, . .	Hattie Estella Woods, . .	Whately.
Sept. 4,	Emory Pike, ...	Emory White, ...	New Salem.
4,	Ellen E. Johnson, . . .	Ellen E. White, . . .	New Salem.
Dec. 4,	Charles Sumner Crosby, . .	Charles Cutler Smith, . .	Whately.
14,	Frank Hosmer, ...	Frank Dunbar Harrington, .	Orange.

BERKSHIRE COUNTY.

April 25,	John Benjamin, ...	Hugh M. Briggs, . . .	Clarksburg.
July 17,	Charles A. Robbins, . . .	Charles A. Weatherly, . .	Pittsfield.
17,	Margaret Mohanna, . . .	Alice Maggie Brown, . .	Williamstown.

NORFOLK COUNTY.

Jan. 2,	Newell Francis Onion, . .	Newell Francis Ashton, . .	Medway.
2,	Susan Margaret Onion, . .	Susan Margaret Ashton, .	Medway.
2,	Florence Hastings Onion, .	Florence Hastings Ashton, .	Medway.
2,	Ella Stanley Onion, . .	Ella Stanley Ashton, . .	Medway.
2,	Alfred Onion, . . .	Alfred Ashton, . . .	Medway.
Feb. 3,	John Welch, ...	John Eldredge Welch, . .	Needham.
April 14,	Capitola Connell,* . .	Capitola Maria Belcher, .	Randolph.
14,	Edmund Connell,* . .	Edmund Belcher, . . .	Randolph.
May 12,	Jesse Robertson,* . . .	Jesse Robertson Humphrey, .	Weymouth.
June 16,	Charles Heber MacBurney, .	Charles MacBurney, . .	Roxbury.
Aug. 18,	Mary Caroline Barrett,* . .	Carrie Mabel Swett, . .	Roxbury.
18,	Adelaide Harwood Mineaid,* .	Addie Florilla Beal, . .	Cohasset.
18,	Susan Augusta Mineaid,* .	Susie Almena Beal, . .	Cohasset.
25,	Mary Madock Mineaid,* .	Mary Emma Leseur, . .	Milton.
Dec. 22,	Henry Hitch Johnson, . .	Laurence Henry Hitch Johnson, ...	West Roxbury.

BRISTOL COUNTY.

Feb. 21,	Mary Jenkins Fisher, . .	Mary Jenkins Hyers, . .	Charlestown.
Mar. 2,	George Franklin Perry, . .	George Parker Jordan, . .	Taunton.
April 6,	Alice M. Hatch. . . .	Alice M. Cotton, . . .	Fall River.
20,	Arabella H. Wharton, . .	Arabella Wharton Barrows, .	Taunton.
July 3,	Thomas Warring, . . .	Thomas Briggs Warring, .	Fall River.
Nov. 16,	Louisa Adelaide Briggs, . .	Louisa Adelaide Wade, . .	Taunton.
Dec. 21,	Hannah Attante Field, . .	Hannah Wilbur, . . .	Raynham.

PLYMOUTH COUNTY.

Jan. 8,	Thomas Herrick Wadsworth, .	Thomas Wadsworth Herrick,	Duxbury.
Mar. 12,	Irene Allen White, . . .	Irene Allen Estes, . . .	Duxbury.
April 9,	Albert E. Darling, . . .	Albert Elmer Caswell, . .	Plymouth.

* Changed by reason of adoption.

PLYMOUTH COUNTY — *Concluded.*

Date of Decree.	Original Name.	Name Decreed.	Residence.
1866.			
April 9,	Mary Lizzie Thayer, . . .	Lizzie Lena Ellis, . . .	Duxbury.
June 11,	Robert Matthews, . . .	Robert Richardson, . .	Plymouth.
25,	Sarah J. Lucas, ...	Nettie Reed, ...	Duxbury.
Aug. 27,	Albert Webster Sprague, . .	Arthur Loring Jacobs, . .	Hingham.
Oct. 8,	Anna Maria Pearson, . .	Annie Maria Thrasher, . .	Plymouth.
Dec. 24,	Lucy Ann Hersey, . . .	Lucy Ann Field, . . .	East Bridgewater.

BARNSTABLE COUNTY.

Jan. 9,	Albert C. Smith, . . .	Albert C. Vincent, . . .	Dennis.
May 15,	Clara B. Fisher, ...	Clara B. Blackington, . .	Sandwich.
Aug. 14,	Flora H. Crowell, . . .	Flora H. Nickerson, . .	Harwich.

NANTUCKET COUNTY.

Sept. 13,	William Henry Rogers, . .	Wm. Henry Jones, . . .	Nantucket.

SUFFOLK COUNTY.

1867.			
Jan. 21,	Susannah Odessa Benedict,* .	Susannah Odessa Tune, . .	Boston.
21,	Addie Maria Eldridge,* . .	Agnes Lee Calder, . . .	Plymouth, N. H.
Feb. 4,	William Henry Chase,* . .	William Henry Nutter, . .	Boston.
4,	Matthew Lynch, . . .	Matthew Leeds, . . .	Boston.
11,	James Henry Sutherland, .	William Henry Bartholomew, ...	Durham, C. E.
25,	Mary Donovan,* . . .	Idia Olivia McCurdy, . .	Boston.
25,	Nellie Maria Huntress,* . .	Nellie Everett Perkins, . .	Haverhill.
Mar. 18,	Hiram Bingham Chamberlain, .	Frank Hiram Chamberlain, .	Boston.
25,	Willie Edwin Loomis,* . .	Willie Edwin Harding, . .	Chelsea.
April 15,	Adelaide Russell,* . . .	Mildred Miers Fox, . .	Chelsea.
29,	John Norris Page, . . .	John Paige Prescott, . .	Boston.
May 13,	Emma Allen Battelle,* . .	Emma Theresa Harriman, .	Taunton.
June 10,	George Washington Murphy, .	George Washington Freeman, ...	Boston.
10,	Henry Augustus Smith, . .	Henry Smith Waldron, . .	Boston.
17,	Miriam White Cary, . .	Miriam White Priest, . .	Boston.
26,	Albert Burroughs Short, . .	Albert Burroughs, . .	Boston.
Aug. 12,	Carrie Susannah Savage,* . .	Elizabeth Davis Stowell, .	Danvers.
12,	Mary Ellen Thorp,* . . .	Mary Ellen Martin, . .	Boston.
26,	Edward Francis Blaisdell, . .	Frank Blaisdell Wilder, . .	Boston.
26,	Euphemia Fenno Tudor, . .	Fenno Tudor, ...	Boston.
26,	Charles Frederic Young,* . .	William Henry Haley, . .	Boston.
Sept. 2,	John Prince Larkin Thorndike,	John Larkin Thorndike, .	Boston.
9,	Mary Alice Croker, . . .	Elizabeth Kennedy, . . .	Boston.
Oct. 8,	Mary Adams Blancher,* . .	Mary Blancher Kingsbury, .	Cambridge.
8,	Samuel Hinckley, . . .	Samuel Parker Hinckley, .	Boston.
8,	Eva Jackson,*	Eva Andrews, . . .	Montreal, Can'da.
8,	Abby Maria Smith, . . .	Caroline Maria Smith, . .	Boston.
Nov. 11,	Ellen Watson,*	Ellen Watson Johnson, . .	Boston.
Dec. 30,	Walter Charles Nickerson,* .	Walter Charles Johnson, .	Boston.

* Changed by reason of adoption.

ESSEX COUNTY.

Date of Decree.	Original Name.	Name Decreed.	Residence.
1867.			
Mar. 5,	Frank Reed,* . . .	Frank Carr Stearns, . .	Lynn.
April 9,	Mary B. Hinkley,* . .	Mary B. Burgess, . . .	Gloucester.
16,	Nellie Chapman, . .	Nellie M. Roundey, . .	Marblehead.
May 11,	Easter Ellen McGraw,* .	Easter Ellen Parker, . .	Lawrence.
11,	Sarah Jane McGraw,* .	Sarah Stevenson, . . .	Lawrence.
11,	Samuel McGraw,* . .	Samuel Battye, . . .	Lawrence.
21,	Kingsley G. Norton,* . .	Evander Sherman Brummitt,	Danvers.
June 4,	Linette Adams,* . . .	Susan Williamenor Smith Thomas, ...	Lynn.
4,	Jane Theresa Weeks,* .	Mary Marshall, . . .	Rockport.
July 16,	Edgar Warren Barrett,* .	Charles Henry Vincent, .	Lynn.
16,	Sarah Elvina Migreault,* .	Sarah Alvina Charon, . .	Lawrence.
Aug. 6,	Sarah Maria Adams,* .	Sarah Alley Aborn, . .	Lynn.
6,	—— Lufkin,* . . .	James Frederic Haskell, .	Essex.
6,	Walter S. Noyes,* . .	Walter S. Buxton, . . .	Salem.
Sept. 17,	Lizzie Howard Chase, .	Lizzie Howard Chase Folsom, ...	Georgetown.
17,	Amanda Welch, . . .	Amanda Gertrude Smiley, .	Lynn.

MIDDLESEX COUNTY.

Jan. 8,	Alice Dascomb,* . . .	Alice Maria Cleland, . .	Natick.
Feb. 12,	Charles Greenough Lincoln,* .	Greenough Lincoln Bill, .	Framingham.
12,	George Edward Lincoln,* . .	George Edwin Parmenter, .	Waltham.
12,	Oliver Craven Phillips,* .	Oliver Craven Parker, .	Woburn.
26,	Joseph Allen Smith,* .	William Jason Tolman, .	Newton.
26,	Ada F. Williams,* . .	Myrtle Madaline Bullard, .	Hudson.
Mar. 12,	Fred W. Jenness,* . .	Fred Wellman Jenness, .	Lowell.
26,	Walter Aiken,* . . .	Frederick Willis Patterson, .	Charlestown.
26,	George Rice, . . .	George Elhanan Rice, .	Lexington.
April 2,	Maria A. Burns, . .	Maria Arnold French, .	Lowell.
23,	Margaret Jane Woods,* .	Margaret Jane Hodge, .	Lowell.
23,	Susie Carr,* . . .	Nellie Eliza Morse, .	Lowell.
May 14,	Ellen Bean,* . . .	Edna Gertrude Parker, .	Lowell.
14,	Sarah E. Rogers, . .	Sarah Evelyn Atkins, .	Cambridge.
June 4,	John Keenan,* . . .	John Birkenhead, .	Lowell.
25,	James Thomas Penn,* .	James Thomas Lord, .	Chelmsford.
25,	Arthur Bemis,* . . .	Arthur Greenwood, .	Marlborough.
Aug. 13,	Edgar Ames Dean,* . .	William Edgar Holmes, .	Holliston.
13,	George Edward Dixon,* .	Joseph Dixon Lane, jun., .	Lowell.
13,	Annette E. Wallace,* . .	Nettie Jennie Gibson, .	Marlborough.
13,	Mary Elizabeth Belcher Patten, ...	Mary Florence Patten, . .	Waltham.
13,	William Durant Bullard, .	William Bullard Durant, .	Cambridge.
27,	Mary Ann Flavin,* . .	Mary Ann Flynn, . .	Marlborough.
Sept. 10,	Albert Heidenrich,* . .	Herbert Reed Brigham, .	Marlborough.
10,	Freddie Heidenrich,* . .	Feddie Ellsworth Wilkins, .	Marlborough.
10,	Flora Holt,* . . .	Annie Florence Whitney, .	Natick.
Oct. 1,	Ella Jane Hemphill,* .	Ella Hemphill Perry, . .	Marlborough.
8,	Chastina Cullis Gould,* .	Chastina Cullis Holbrook, .	Charlestown.
22,	Benjamin Roundy,* . .	Benjamin Richmond, . .	Melrose.
22,	Cora E. Whittemore,* .	Cora Maria Newhall, .	Malden.
Nov. 12,	Bessie Lena Robbins,* .	Harriet Folsom, . . .	Somerville.
Dec. 10,	Mary Heald Underhill,* .	Mary Heald Dix, . . .	Woburn.
24,	Franklin Augustus Keene,* .	Franklin Augustus Young, .	Cambridge.
24,	Nellie Fairbank,* . .	Nellie Hammond, . . .	Wayland.

* Changed by reason of adoption.

WORCESTER COUNTY.

Date of Decree.	Original Name.	Name Decreed.	Residence.
1867.			
Jan. 1,	Frances Taylor,	Addie La Francies Sessions,	Worcester.
Feb. 5,	Julia Emma Sullivan,	Emma Julia Meriam,	Worcester.
5,	Frederic Tatman Sullivan,	Frederic Tatman Meriam,	Worcester.
5,	Sarah Ellen Browning,	Sarah Ellen Boyce,	Spencer.
5,	Mary Lizzie Hymes,	Mary Lizzie Jaquith,	Ashburnham.
Mar. 5,	(Name unknown),	Helen Eliece Flint,	Ashburnham.
5,	(Name unknown),	Anna Frances Hubbard,	Holden.
5,	Sarah G. Kittredge,	Sarah G. Osborn,	Harvard.
5,	Cora Luella Thresher,	Cora Luella Harwood,	Barre.
5,	Mary Lizzie Nichols,	Lillie Estelle Sheldon,	Worcester.
5,	George Henry Sanger,	George Henry Lackey,	Milford.
April 2,	Charles W. O. Bailey,	Charles William Cook,	Lunenburg.
May 7,	(Name unknown),	Flora Estella Lakin,	Paxton.
21,	Mary Blake,	Ella Josephine Haskell,	Harvard.
23,	Delia Ellsworth Lane,	Delia Mary Lane,	Ashburnham.
June 4,	Cora Ella Holbrook,	Cora Ella Hunt,	Milford.
4,	Minnietta May Hymes,	Minnietta May Bean,	Ashburnham.
4,	Agnes Arabella Aldrich,	Agnes Aldrich Barry,	Worcester.
4,	Cynthia Rosella Bartlett,	Cynthia Rosella Page,	Lunenburg.
11,	Mary Ella Ainsworth,	Ella M. Bowker,	Athol.
July 2,	Eva Arabella Randall,	Eva Arabella Lord,	Templeton.
2,	Alice Eldora Randall,	Alice Eldora Lord,	Templeton.
2,	Frederick Howard Randall,	Frederick Howard Lord,	Templeton.
Sept. 3,	Fidelle Asenath Edwards,	Fidella Asenath Temple,	Worcester.
3,	Ella Slate Edwards,	Ella Slate Woodruff,	Worcester.
Oct. 1,	Joseph Malbeuf,	Joseph Bonneville,	Worcester.
Nov. 5,	Frank T. Miller,	Frank T. Little,	Phillipston.
5,	Josephine Rich,	Nellie Maria Johnson,	Templeton.
5,	Anna Mabel ——,	Anna Mabel Sly,	Worcester.
Dec. 3,	Rose Alma Worthing,	Mina Florence Revere,	Worcester.
3,	Caroline A. Hiscox,	Caroline A. Grayson,	Worcester.
3,	Harriet Elizabeth Swain,	Harriet Elsie Warner,	Harvard.

HAMPSHIRE COUNTY.

Jan. 1,	Nettie Grace Dodge,*	Nettie Grace Searle,	Northampton.
Feb. 5,	Luther Eaton,*	Frederick Arthur Crouch,	Southampton.
April 2,	Nellie P. Bray,*	Nellie Parsons,	Northampton.
June 4,	Edward Whiting Harris,	Edward Harris Bell,	Southampton.
July 2,	Mertie Frances,*	Mertie Frances Hall,	Northampton.
Aug. 20,	Clara R. Watson,*	Clara R. Bardwell,	Granby.

HAMPDEN COUNTY.

Mar. 5,	Sarah Ella Roberts,*	Sarah Ella Hendrick,	Holyoke.
5,	Francis P. Miles,*	Francis Plimpton Keyes,	Springfield.
May 7,	Ellen Clifford,*	Nellie Emma Moore,	Springfield.
7,	Willie A. Knox,*	Willie A. Burdick,	Blandford.
July 2,	Joseph Loveglen,*	Joseph Francis Runell,	Holyoke.
Nov. 5,	Mary Celinda Roberts,*	Annie Elizabeth Nevers,	Springfield.
5,	Nameless,*	Cora Taylor Smith,	West Springfield.
Dec. 14,	Hattie Annie Bailey,*	Hattie Annie Lyman,	Chester.

* Changed by reason of adoption.

FRANKLIN COUNTY.

Date of Decree.	Original Name.	Name Decreed.	Residence.
1867.			
Feb. 12,	Matthew Nunney,*	Matthew Nunney Barlow,	Buckland.
Aug. 6,	Henry Bryan,*	Wm. Henry Smith,	Whately.

BERKSHIRE COUNTY.

Date of Decree.	Original Name.	Name Decreed.	Residence.
Mar. 5,	Martha Elliott,	Carrie Elliott Warner,	Pittsfield.
June 4,	Lillie M. Brown,	Lillie May Harder,	Williamstown.
Nov. 12,	Emma Louisa Savage,	Emma Louisa Chickering,	Pittsfield.
Dec. 3,	Carrie Bell,	Carrie Bell Deming,	Hinsdale.

NORFOLK COUNTY.

Date of Decree.	Original Name.	Name Decreed.	Residence.
Feb. 9,	—— Tripp,	Flora Estella Pond,	Foxborough.
April 13,	Francis Cragin,	Francis Henry Fullerton Cragin,	Roxbury.
May 25,	Almira B. Noyes,	Almira B. Allen,	Roxbury.
June 29,	Job Ramsbottom,	Job Wilson,	Walpole.
29,	Mary Elizabeth Ramsbottom,	Mary Elizabeth Wilson,	Walpole.
29,	John Arthur Ramsbottom,	John Arthur Wilson,	Walpole.
29,	Anna Florence Ramsbottom,	Anna Florence Wilson,	Walpole.
29,	Eleanor Ramsbottom,	Eleanor Wilson,	Walpole.
Aug. 20,	Sada Hall,	Lillia Reeves,	Walpole.
24,	Frederick Ellis Simpson,	Frederick Ellis Broad,	Milton.
31,	Mary Ellen Lines,	Mary Ellen Shaw,	Braintree.
Oct. 1,	Lottie L. Clapp,	Lottie C. Beal,	Cohasset.
5,	Etta M. Loomis,	Gertrude Maria Bruce,	Franklin.
19,	William James Todd,	William James Wright,	Brookline.
19,	Charles Francis Todd,	Charles Frances Wright,	Brookline.
19,	John Wright Todd,	John Russell Wright,	Brookline.
Nov. 9,	William Everett Wortman,	William Everett Morton,	Randolph.
16,	Samuel Maddock,	Thomas Blanchard,	Canton.
23,	Mary Elizabeth Todd,	Mary Elizabeth Wright,	Brookline.
23,	—— Daniels,	Mary Ann Metcalf,	Franklin.
Dec. 14,	Frances L. Mansfield,	Mary Louisa Austin,	Roxbury.
14,	Mary Celia Conlan,	Emily Clara Bainard,	Roxbury.

BRISTOL COUNTY.

Date of Decree.	Original Name.	Name Decreed.	Residence.
Jan. 4,	Edward Richardson,	George Edward Richardson,	Easton.
Feb. 1,	Clarence M. Allen,	Clarence M. Allen,	New Bedford.
April 5,	Mary Elizabeth Tucker,	Mary Elizabeth Compton,	New Bedford.
June 7,	Alexander Bathurst Fuentes Wood,	Alexander Bathurst Wood,	New Bedford.
Sept. 6,	Anna Handy,	Anna Otis Bunn,	Fall River.
6,	Cora Evelin Tripp,	Cora Evelin Remington,	Taunton.
Oct. 18,	Ida Haskell,	Winifred Jane Newcomb,	Taunton.
18,	Adela Francis Sherry,	Adela Francis Porter,	Taunton.
Dec. 6,	William Donney,	Aloysius Rooney,	Taunton.

* Changed by reason of adoption.

PLYMOUTH COUNTY.

Date of Decree.	Original Name.	Name Decreed.	Residence.
1867.			
Jan. 14,	Carrie Holmes,* . . .	Carrie Holmes Paty, . .	Plymouth.
28,	Eliza Roach,*	Eliza Jane Rowe, . . .	N'th Bridgewater.
Mar. 11,	Addie Augusta Henderson,* .	Marcia Ripley Cobb, . .	Kingston.
11,	Hattie A. Whitcomb,* . .	Hattie Whitcomb Peterson, .	Duxbury.
25,	Harriet Frances Perry,* . .	Clara Maud St. Clair, . .	N'th Bridgewater.
April 8,	Noah Torrey Hathaway, .	Walter Lloyd Hathaway, .	Abington.
Dec. 9,	Annie C. Peirce,* . . .	Annie P. Raymond, . .	Plymouth.

BARNSTABLE COUNTY.

April 19,	Millie Freenan, ...	Millie Washburn Young, ..	Orleans.
May 21,	Matilda Adelaide Lavendar, .	Sophronia Adelaide Lecount,	Provincetown.
21,	John Thompson, . .	John Thompson Gage, . .	Harwich.
Oct. 16,	Rosalia King, ...	Angie Thomas Whelden, .	Provincetown.

NANTUCKET COUNTY.

Mar. 14,	Benjamin M. Hussey, . .	James S. Hussey, . . .	Nantucket.
Aug. 26,	Ida Cora Dupung, . . .	Alice Cushman, . . .	Nantucket.

SUFFOLK COUNTY.

Date of Decree.	Original Name.	Name Decreed.	Residence.
1868.			
Jan. 13,	Sarah Jane Jameson,* .	Sarah Jane McGinnis, . .	Boston.
Feb. 3,	James Freeman, . .	James Goldthwaite Freeman,	Boston.
3,	Willie Hammond Kenney,	Willie Hammond Hosmer, .	Boston.
3,	George Washington Thaxter,* .	Warren Everton Chase, .	Boston.
17,	Chessman Field Pollard,* .	Chessman Pollard Vinson, .	Boston.
24,	Martin Timothy Flanagan,	Timothy James Martin, .	Boston.
Mar. 2,	Corrilla Evadne Hansom,* .	Corrilla Frances Kittredge, .	Boston.
2,	Ellen McKinney,* . .	Ellen Gannon, . . .	Boston.
16,	Frances Louisa Snaith, .	Louisa Calkins Francis, .	Boston.
16,	Corydon Porter Stockman, .	Charles Porter Stockman, .	Boston.
23,	Elizabeth Oliver, . .	Carrie Elizabeth Stone, .	Boston.
23,	Mabel Vickery,* . .	Mabel Linnell, . . .	Boston.
30,	Samuel Allen Gilpatrick, .	Samuel Allen Gilbert, . .	Boston.
30,	Nellie Gertrude Luxton,* .	Alice Luella Martin, . .	Boston.
April 13,	Julia Bissell LeCain,* .	Julia Bissell Kendall, . .	Boston.
13,	Mary Catherine LeCain,* .	Mary Catharine Kendall, .	Boston.
May 18,	Charles Henry Dugan, .	Charles Oliver Parker, . .	Boston.
June 8,	John Edward Brown,* .	William John Driscoll, . .	Boston.
8,	Walter Rockwood,* . .	Walter Rockwood Stedman, .	Boston.
22,	Patrick Barry, . . .	George Marshall Barry, . .	Boston.
22,	Benjamin Franklin Coke,* .	Samuel Henry Wood, . .	Boston.
29,	Roland Barnard Murphy, .	Roland Murphy Barnard, .	Boston.
Aug. 10,	Caroline Frances Yallalee,* .	Carrie Frances Harding, .	Boston.
17,	Lilian Gertrude Hooper,* .	Helen Gertrude Whiting, .	Boston.
24,	Lillie Gertrude Steele,* .	Lillie Gertrude Pease, . .	Boston.
31,	William Joseph Shorts,* .	William Joseph Alexander, .	Boston.
Sept. 7,	George Washington Colomy, .	George Washington Chesley, .	Boston.
7,	Ida Etta Foote,* . .	Gertrude Scolley, . . .	Boston.

* Changed by reason of adoption,

SUFFOLK COUNTY — *Concluded.*

Date of Decree.	Original Name.	Name Decreed.	Residence.
1868.			
Sept. 14,	George Wilson Vinal, . .	George Odiorne Wilson, .	Boston.
21,	Henry Augustus Meiring, .	Henry Augustus Eiler, .	Boston.
Oct. 5,	Edward A. Sly, . . .	Edward A. Stevens, .	Boston.
5,	John Amory Lowell Putnam,	John Pickering Putnam,	Boston.
12,	Emma Frances Burns,* .	Emma Frances Chenoweth, .	Lynn.
12,	Mansfield Haskins, . .	Thomas Mansfield Haskins, .	Boston.
Nov. 2,	Edward Hamilton Osgood,	Hamilton Osgood, . .	Chelsea.
Dec. 7,	Ida May Smith,* . .	Melvina Eunie Chapman, .	Topsfield.
28,	Louis May,* sometimes called Louis Shales, . . .	Louis Shales, . . .	Boston.

ESSEX COUNTY.

Jan. 14,	Mary L. Goodwin,* . .	Gertrude Plumer, . .	Lynn.
Mar. 3,	Frank Morse Morrison,* .	Frank Philip Morse, .	Boston.
3,	Richard Walden,* . .	Charles Henry Colby, .	Lynn.
3,	Annetta Robinson Sargent,*	Annie Florence Cressey, .	Lynn.
April 14,	George Batchelder,* . .	George Eliphalet Patterson, .	Beverly.
May 5,	John Francis LeBaron Patch,	John Francis LeBaron, .	Ipswich.
June 16,	Eliza Ellen Willey,* . .	Harriet Ellen Wiley Russ, .	Salem.
July 7,	Iva Teresa Bartlett,* . .	Iva Teresa Holley, . .	Salem.
7,	Amos Warren Dorman, .	Warren Dorman, . .	Lynn.
21,	Georgianna Welch,* . .	Georgianna Welch Poland, .	Danvers.
Sept. 1,	John George Murray,* .	George Murray Foster, .	Peabody.
1,	William Henry Lombard, .	William Henry Ilsley, .	Georgetown.
Oct. 13,	Laura Brown,* . . .	Carrie May Ingersoll, .	Manchester.
20,	Edwin Little, . . .	Edwin Colman Little, .	Newbury.
20,	Arthur Stickney, . .	George Arthur Stickney, .	Newbury.
Nov. 10,	Hannah Woodbridge, .	Anna Woodbridge, . .	Andover.
Dec. 8,	Elliott Howard Stevens,* .	Elliott Howard Weston, .	Lawrence
8,	George L. Young,* . .	Charles G. Trueworthy, .	North Andover.
15,	Ruth C. Bullard, . .	Ruth C. Ware, . .	Andover.

MIDDLESEX COUNTY.

Jan. 7,	Fred Peter Haggerty,* . .	Fred Prince Crane, . .	Lowell.
14,	Elizabeth F. Wilson,* .	Elizabeth Burbank Smith, .	Charlestown.
Feb. 25,	Emmaetta S. Coburn,* .	Emma Coburn Davis, .	Lowell.
Mar. 10,	Stephen Dustin Carey, .	Albert Dustin Haynes, .	Charlestown.
24,	Catharine Sheaha,* . .	Arabella Call, . . .	Charlestown.
24,	Joanna Batchelder Rackliff,*	Joanna Batchelder Chadbourn, ...	Brighton.
April 14,	Sarah Ann Umpleby,* .	Sarah Ann Hyde, . .	Lowell.
28,	Eva Robins Taylor,* . .	Eva Marian Bullock, .	Cambridge.
May 12,	Nellie McNally,* . .	Nellie Bartlett Snow, .	Newton.
June 2,	Mary Lizzie Ellis,* . .	Mary Lizzie Whitaker, .	Ashland.
9,	Addie Drew,* . . .	Addie Lyford, . . .	Lowell.
23,	Nancy Grace Stevens,* .	Nancy Grace Thompson, .	Lowell.
23,	George Bradley Hobbs, .	George Butcher, . .	Cambridge.
Sept. 1,	John Clifford,* . . .	George Kelly, . . .	Cambridge.
1,	Anna Ednah Whitney Phipps,*	Emma Lizzie Tighlman Barker, ...	Cambridge.
1,	Emily May Hayes,* . .	Emma Theresa Currie, .	Melrose.
8,	Georgianna Floyd,* . .	Georgianna Garfield, .	Waltham.

* Changed by reason of adoption.

MIDDLESEX COUNTY — *Concluded.*

Date of Decree.	Original Name.	Name Decreed.	Residence.
1868.			
Sept. 8,	Mary Collins,*	Mary Collins Merrill,	Hopkinton.
22,	Annie Lee.*	Sarah Annie Allen,	Charlestown.
Oct. 6,	John Green,*	George Washington Fogg,	Medford.
13,	Anna White Warren,*	Anna White Draper,	Marlborough.
Nov. 17,	John Henry Greenhalgh,*	John Henry Harrison,	Lowell.
17,	Isaac Fletcher Greenlaw,	Cyrus Fletcher Nasson,	Lowell.
17,	Emma Merrill Spear,*	Lilian Emma Starbird,	Malden.
17,	George Hamilton,*	George Hamilton Stimson,	Lowell.
Dec. 1,	Minard Stygles,	Daniel Minard Webber,	Woburn.
8,	Francis Levi Page,*	Willis Luther Gould,	Woburn.
22,	Patrick Flanagan,	Daniel Howell Brown,	Wayland.

WORCESTER COUNTY.

Date	Original Name.	Name Decreed.	Residence.
Jan. 7,	Alice Theresa Willard,	Alice Theresa Willard Warren,	Worcester.
7,	Emma Estella Balou,	Emma Estella Lyons,	Milford.
Feb. 4,	Betsey Adams,	Sarah Betsey Lemon,	Webster.
Mar. 3,	Mary Eliza Smith,	Mary Eliza Henry,	Holden.
3,	John Thomas White,	Leon Ira Temple,	Southborough.
3,	Susan Horton Spooner,	Susie Spooner Temple,	Southborough.
3,	Ellen Lucinda Nurss,	Ellen Lucinda Haskell,	Oakham.
May 5,	Sidney Lynmore Heywood,	Sidney Lynmore Winch,	Winchendon.
5,	Edward Alexander Gates,	Edward Alexander Bragg,	Grafton.
12,	Thomas Dumphy,	Thomas Michael Dumphy,	Sturbridge.
19,	Peter McGowan,	Emerson Peter McGowan,	Worcester.
20,	Forest Verr Peck,	Clarence Reno Marshall,	Fitchburg.
June 2,	Ella L. Whittemore,	Ella L. Butler,	Worcester.
9,	Sarah Martina Clough,	Mattie Sarah Newman,	Winchendon.
July 7,	William Henry Dow,	William Henry Bigelow,	Westminster.
Aug. 4,	Francis Lefaivre,	Francis Dragon,	Webster.
Sept. 1,	Lilla May Nimms,	Lillian Belle Reynolds,	Worcester.
1,	Elmer Rogene Thresher,	Elmer Rogene Allen,	Oakham.
Oct. 1,	Nellie Elizabeth Bolton,	Nellie Elizabeth Brigham,	Fitchburg.
Nov. 3,	Lottie L. Moore,	Lottie L. Leslie,	Leominster.
Dec. 1,	Grace Maria Haggerty,	Grace Maria Whitin,	Northbridge.
1,	Julia Taft Dingwell,	Julia Taft Parker,	Worcester.
1,	Ida Mabel Thompson,	Emma Frances Frary,	Holden.
1,	John Jay Mackenzie,	John Jay Kensington,	Worcester.
1,	Milo Leonard Mackenzie,	Milo Leonard Kensington,	Worcester

HAMPSHIRE COUNTY.

Date	Original Name.	Name Decreed.	Residence.
Jan. 7,	Lula Maria Gates,*	Lula Maria Parsons,	Northampton.
Feb. 4,	Laura J. Grant,*	Jane Laura Miller,	Williamsburg.
April 7,	William A. Brewster,*	William Augustus Reed,	Northampton.
7,	Charlotte Bryant,*	Charlotte Rose Clay,	Northampton.
Oct. 5,	George Kingman,*	George Kingman Clarke,	Northampton.
5,	Sarah E. Smith,*	Sarah Emily Porter,	Hatfield.
Nov. 4,	Eliza Wood,*	Eliza Potter,	Easthampton.
4,	Abby Jane Roberts,*.	Abby Jane Augevine,	Northampton.
4,	Mary Clementine Chapin,*	Mary Eastman Marshali,	Amherst.
Dec. 1,	Frederick A. Latham,*	Frederick Arthur Cooley,	Amherst.

* Changed by reason of adoption.

HAMPDEN COUNTY.

Date of Decree.	Original Name.	Name Decreed.	Residence.
1868.			
Jan. 28,	Justine Emma. White,*	Justine Emma Bailey,	Springfield.
Mar. 3,	Anna Winchell,*	Anna J. B. Pomeroy,	Springfield.
May 5,	John Roland Colby,*	John Roland Colby Browning,	Chicopee.
5,	Edwin Moulton,*	Herbert Samuel Brown,	Palmer.
June 2,	Jenny Handyside,*	Jennie Grace Douglas,	Springfield.
Oct. 6,	Ella Mabel Eaton,*	Ella Mabel Carter,	Springfield.
Nov. 4,	William W. Handyside,*	Luther Wallace Bruner,	Wilbraham.
Dec. 1,	George Franklin Wolcott,*	" Name remains same,"	Agawam.

FRANKLIN COUNTY.

Mar. 3,	—— Bryan,*	Manna A. Powers,	Whately.
June 2,	Anne E. Gibson,*	Anne Elizabeth Coburn,	Greenfield.
16,	Mary Lyons,*	Mary Isabel Orcutt,	Orange.
Oct. 27,	Mary Adeline Hawks,*	Mary Adeline Green,	Ashfield.
27,	Emma Maria Hawks,*	Emma Maria Stetson,	Ashfield.
27,	Henry Francis Pike,*	Henry Francis Latham,	Shelburne Falls.
27,	Charles ——,	Charles Sylvester Whitney,	Shelburne Falls.
Dec. 1,	Fanny R. G. Streeter,	Fanny R. G. Bowen,	Colrain.

BERKSHIRE COUNTY.

Mar. 3,	Delancy Glasscut,	Delancy Glasscut Burbank,	Pittsfield.
April 7,	" A foundling child,"	Minnie E. Van Bramer,	Pittsfield.
7,	Homer Williams, Jr.,	George Henry McDermott,	Pittsfield.
July 29,	Alfred Kingsbury,	Alfred Morton,	Adams.
29,	Charles H. Miner,	Charles Julius Holman,	Windsor.
Oct. 6,	Thomas W. Clapp,	Warren Thomas Clapp Colt,	Pittsfield.

NORFOLK COUNTY.

Feb. 25,	Emma E. Dole,*	Emma E. Hawes,	Stoughton.
May 5,	Eva Clara Adams,*	Eva Clara Dix,	Dorchester.
June 2,	Lydia Sherwin Higgins,*	Lydia Higgins Sherwin,	Brookline.
2,	Sarah B. Goodrich,	Sarah B. Doolittle,	Foxborough.
10,	Eleanor F. Mott,*	Nellie F. Brown,	Cohasset.
24,	Mary Winslow,*	Margaret Reed Derry,	Quincy.
Sept. 30,	Drusilla Ware,*	Hellaxer Colson,	Milton.
Nov. 3,	Georgianna Perry,*	Georgianna Lake,	Dedham.
4,	Harriet N. Storer,	Harriet Newell,	Weymouth.
4,	Charles Edward Storer,	Charles Edward Newell,	Weymouth.

BRISTOL COUNTY.

Jan. 17,	Edgenora Augusta Potter,	Edgenora Augusta Leonard,	Taunton.
Mar. 18,	Catherine R. Hobbs,	Catherine R. Borden,	New Bedford.
18,	Mary E. Hobbs,	Mary E. Borden,	New Bedford.
18,	Caroline Hobbs,	Caroline Borden,	New Bedford.

* Changed by reason of adoption.

BRISTOL COUNTY — *Concluded.*

Date of Decree.	Original Name.	Name Decreed.	Residence.
1868.			
Mar. 18,	Asa James Sherman Lippard, .	Asa James Sherman, . .	New Bedford.
18,	Sarah Tucker Lippard, . .	Sarah Tucker Sherman, . .	New Bedford.
April 3,	Josephine Fitspatrick, . .	Josephine Fitspatrick Porter, .	Fall River.
3,	Walter S. Bumpus, . .	Walter S. Tillson, . . .	New Bedford.
June 17,	Ida Marion Swain, . .	Ida Marion Martin, . .	New Bedford.
Sept. 4,	Jerusha G. Nichols, . .	Jessie G. Nichols, . .	Berkley.
16,	Elisa Emma Morriss, . .	Elisa Emma Gent, . .	Taunton.
Nov. 6,	Henry A. Thing, . . .	Henry A. Caldwell, . .	New Bedford.
6,	Jane H. N. Burk, . .	Jane H. Newhall, . .	Berkley.
6,	Parentage unknown, . . .	Alfred D. Watson, . .	New Bedford.
6,	Parentage unknown, . . .	Lenora A. Parker, . .	New Bedford.

PLYMOUTH COUNTY.

Jan. 27,	Patrick Kily, ...	Alvin Andrew Kily, . .	Hanson.
Oct. 12,	Ida J. Channell,* . . .	Ida Cheney Wood, . .	Plymouth.
Nov. 9,	George W. Worthen,* . .	George Henry Bourne, . .	Marshfield.
23,	—— Marsh,*	Sarah Margaret Briggs, . .	Scituate.

SUFFOLK COUNTY.

1869.			
Jan. 4,	Alfred Gibbons,* . . .	Edward Abner Joseph, . .	Newton.
11,	Lydia Ann Mason,* . . .	Lydia Ann Chase, . . .	Stratton, N. H.
25,	Anna Orr, ...	Annie Hillborn, . .	Boston.
Feb. 1,	Bertha Eastman,* . . .	Mary Eloise Coates, . .	Charlestown.
1,	Charles Henry O'Brine, .	Charles Henry Doolin, . .	Boston.
8,	Emma Augusta Maxwell, .	Emma Augusta Tirrill, .	Boston.
8,	Julia Edwina Maxwell, .	Julia Edwina Tirrill, .	Boston.
8,	Virginia Randall, . .	Alice Brockway, . .	Boston.
15,	Mary Brennan, . . .	Mary Raftery, . .	Boston.
15,	Fannie Isadore Frye, .	Fannie Leighton, . .	Boston.
Mar. 1,	Theresa Althea Lynch, .	Theresa Althea Hull, . .	Boston.
1,	Francis Stockwell Dam, .	Franklin Bernard Ingalls, .	Boston.
1,	Albert Dickinson, . .	Albert Edward Dickinson, .	Boston.
22,	Mary Delia Harris, . .	Mary Azelia Lesur, . .	Boston.
29,	Eugene Herbert Dam, .	Eugene Herbert Ingalls, .	Boston.
29,	Isabella Cornelia Dam, .	Isabella Cornelia Ingalls, .	Boston.
29,	Sarah Eaton Dam, . .	Sarah Eaton Ingalls, . .	Boston.
29,	Mary Louise Dam, . .	Mary Louise Ingalls. . .	Boston.
April 5,	John Donovan, . . .	John Franklin Dearington, .	Boston.
May 24,	Mary Ann Holland,* . .	Ann Mary Doherty, . .	Fall River.
31,	Margaret Theresa Stanley,*	Margaret O'Connor, . .	Malden.
Aug. 16,	Lizzie Maria Oliver, . .	Lizzie Maria Stone, . .	Boston.
23,	Mary Brown, . . .	Mary McCann, . .	Boston.
30,	Annie Goodnow,* . .	Grace Somes Welch, . .	Concord.
30,	William Henry Kernachan,	William Henry Kenyon, .	Boston.
Sept. 6,	Elizabeth L. Hastings,* .	Elizabeth L. Parmelee, . .	Chicago, Ill.
20,	Elizabeth Koebe, . .	Elizabeth Luttmann, . .	Boston.
27,	Sherman Leland, . .	William Sherman Leland, .	Boston.
Oct. 11,	Agnes Dorsey, ...	Agnes Sylvester, . .	Boston.
18,	Elizabeth Ann Edwards,* .	Mary Eva Adams, . .	Newport, R. I.

* Changed by reason of adoption.

SUFFOLK COUNTY — *Concluded.*

Date of Decree.	Original Name.	Name Decreed.	Residence.
1869.			
Oct. 18,	Leonora Isabel Silva, . .	Leonara Martin, . . .	Boston.
25,	Julius Everett Jongenell, . .	Julius Everett Jongenell Bechthold, ...	Boston.
Nov. 29,	Edward Livingston Dana, .	Edward Livingston Underwood, ...	Boston.
29,	Betsey Fuller, otherwise called Betsey Blair,*	Gertrude Gwynne, . . .	Brookline.
30,	Carrie Sullivan, ...	Carrie Lincoln Jenness, .	Boston.
Dec. 4,	Mary Louise Rose,* . . .	Mary Louise Eyssen, .	Charlestown.
13,	Annie Rose Delony,* . . .	Annie Rose Townsend, .	Athens, Ga.
13,	Roberto Willard, . . .	Rupert Foye, ...	Boston.
27,	Charles Augustus Newman White, ...	Charles Newman White, .	Winthrop.

ESSEX COUNTY.

Date of Decree.	Original Name.	Name Decreed.	Residence.
Jan. 5,	Elizabeth Ann Coblents,* . .	Elizabeth Cheever, . . .	Beverly.
5,	Etta Frances Coblents,* . .	Henrietta Stanwood Heron, .	Beverly.
Feb. 16,	Ellen Augusta Haskins,* . .	Ellen Augusta Sanborn, .	Rockport.
Mar. 9,	Nellie L. Jack,* . . .	Nellie L. Nickerson, .	Haverhill.
April 13,	Martha A. Gray,* . . .	Martha A. Doe, . .	Rockport.
13,	John Shaw,*	John Daniel Jacobs, .	Gloucester.
May 18,	Frederic Hoyt,* . . .	Frederic E. Blye, . .	Haverhill.
18,	George Louisa Messer,* . .	Carrie Louisa Bott, .	Peabody.
July 6,	Bailey Brown,* . . .	Frank Bailey Currier, .	Amesbury.
Aug. 2,	Emily Josephine Sanborn, .	Sarah Emily Sanborn, .	Lynn.
3,	Orlando Eugene Holmes,* .	William Orlando Dufreme, .	Haverhill.
20,	Martha Gray Fabens, . .	Martha Webster Fabens, .	Salem.
Sept. 14,	Annie J. Smith,* . . ' .	Annie S. Knox, . . .	Lawrence.
17,	Anna Cogswell Brown,* . .	Anna Cogswell Gardiner, .	Essex.
21,	William Janes,* . . .	William Webster Spofford, .	Georgetown.
Oct. 5,	Etta Frances Moore.* . .	Etta Moore Fowler, .	Salem.
18,	William Franklin Cloon,* . .	William Franklin Millett, .	Marblehead.
Dec. 16,	Ellen Frances Cheever,* . .	Ellen Frances Ramsdell, .	Stoneham.
27,	Willie B. Atkins,* . . .	Willie B. Butman, . .	Marblehead.

MIDDLESEX COUNTY.

Date of Decree.	Original Name.	Name Decreed.	Residence.
Feb. 23,	Cora Elizabeth Drew,* . .	Cora Elizabeth Pebbles, .	Natick.
23,	Anna E. Mott,*	Anie Elizabeth Roberts, .	Malden.
Mar. 9,	Thomas Wallace,* . . .	Thomas Dunn, . .	Marlborough.
16,	A female child,* . . .	Nettie Blanche Wright, .	Lowell.
April 6,	Margaret Logue,* . . .	Annette Fracker, . .	Cambridge
6,	Cora May Boynton,* . . .	Mabel Perry, . . .	Natick.
6,	Helen Catherine Campbell, .	Helen Catherine Baldwin, .	Charlestown.
13,	A female child,* . . .	Annie Mansfield Stott, .	Lowell.
13,	Calvin George Pratt,* . .	George Calvin Sawyer, .	Concord.
13,	Minnie J. Atwood,* . . .	Minnie J. Farnham, .	Lowell.
27,	Rufus Schwartz Fenerty,* .	Frederic Southgate Beck, .	Somerville.
27,	A female child,* . . .	Adah Emerson Bates, .	Cambridge.
May 11,	John Harrold,*	John Harrold Connolly, .	Lowell.
18,	Frank Ward Smith,* . . .	Frank Smith Gerard, .	Cambridge.
25,	John Edwards.* . . .	John Parker Edwards, .	Cambridge.
25,	Emilie A. Jackson,* . . .	Emilie Adeline Hunt, .	Reading.

* Changed by reason of adoption.

MIDDLESEX COUNTY — *Concluded.*

Date of Decree.	Original Name.	Name Decreed.	Residence.
1869.			
June 8,	Lorena Kitchen,* . .	Lorena Campbell, . . .	Lowell.
22,	Augusta Gardner,* . .	Addie Sophia Berry, . .	Charlestown.
22,	Norman Stygles, . .	George Henry Webber, .	Woburn.
July 6,	William Knapp,* . .	William Ellery Savage, .	Lowell.
13,	Benjamin F. Hoar, .	Benjamin Franklin Wellington, ...	Lincoln.
27,	Delmena Hill,* . .	Ida Minnie Foster, . .	Charlestown.
27,	Edmund Taylor, . .	Edmund Morton Taylor, .	Hudson.
27,	Charles Damon Welsh, .	Charles Damon Weld, .	Wakefield.
27,	Stephen Peirce Welsh, .	Stephen Peirce Weld, .	Wakefield.
27,	William Franklin Welsh, .	William Franklin Weld, .	Wakefield.
Sept. 7,	A female child,* . .	Alice Story Hatch, . .	Newton.
28,	Edward A. Allbright,* .	Edward Augustus Walton, .	Pepperell.
28,	Augustus Henry Goupee, .	Augustus Goupille Wesley, .	Cambridge.
Oct. 5,	Eva Alice Howard,* . .	Eva Alice Colburn, .	Lowell.
12,	Frederick Alanson Ricker,*	Frederick Alanson McCausland, ...	Brighton.
12,	William Henry McMichael,	William Henry Reed, .	Charlestown.
12,	Christina McMichael, .	Christina Reed, . .	Charlestown.
12,	Henry Wilbur McMichael,	Henry Wilbur Reed, .	Charlestown.
26,	Mary Ellen Regan,* . .	Albena Nailer, . .	Malden.
Nov. 23,	Lillie P. Eginton,* .	Lillie Taylor Eginton Warren, ...	Waltham.
23,	Susan Simonds Monroe, .	Susan Simonds Barnard, .	Woburn.
23,	Ira Tuttle Gates, . .	Ira George Bates, . .	Cambridge.
Dec. 7,	Harry Edgar Martin,* .	Harry Edgar Putney, .	Cambridge.
7,	Emma Louisa Davis,* .	Emma Louisa Walker. .	Natick.
7,	Clara Jane Greenwood,* .	Clara Jane Greenwood Coolidge, ...	Cambridge.
14,	Harriet H. Hill,* . .	Hattie Henrietta Evans, .	Ashland.
14,	Jane Louisa Hill,* . .	Jennie Louisa Evans, .	Ashland.
28,	Mary McLaughlin,* . .	Margaret Ann Hartness, .	Cambridge.

WORCESTER COUNTY.

Jan. 5,	George Irving Baily, . .	George Irving Leland, .	Upton.
5,	Phebe Josephine Wright, .	Josephine Elizabeth Remington, . . .	Northbridge.
Feb. 2,	———, ...	Addison Miller Moores, .	Hubbardston.
Mar. 2,	Nettie Gibson, . .	Nettie Electa Wallis, .	Ashburnham.
2,	Joshua A. Lane, . .	Frank A. Hadley, . .	Ashburnham.
2,	Rachel Sarah Cold, .	Lucy Sarah Goddard, .	Westborough.
April 6,	Eloise Jane Leithead, .	Lucinda Howe Houghton, .	Berlin.
May 18,	Sarah Ann Fisher, .	Sarah Ann Fay, . .	Clinton.
25,	Mark Wm. Loui Tucker, .	Mark William Loui Phillips, .	Grafton.
June 15,	George Bryant, . . .	Frank W. Bradford, .	Worcester.
July 6,	Bessie Taylor, . .	Lillie Bessie Houghton, .	Worcester.
Sept. 7,	Mary A. Goodenough, .	Mary Alice Hutchinson, .	Fitchburg.
7,	Frederick Justin Byrne, .	Frederick Justin Byrne Adams,	Worcester.
7,	Annie Warren Stewart, .	Annie Warren Kennedy, .	Worcester.
28,	Laura S. Snow, . .	Laura Sophia Snow Woods, .	Leominster.
28,	Ann Lillie Haskell, .	Ann Lillie Dixon, . .	Webster.
Oct. 5,	Lillian M. Hobson, . .	Lillian May Hildreth, . ' .	West Boylston.
13,	Elizabeth Kelly, . .	Bessie Agnes Brown, .	Barre.
19,	Patrick McQue, . .	Patrick Colman, . .	Fitchburg.
19,	Catherine Griffin, . .	Catherine Griffin Carney, .	Spencer.
Nov. 2,	Lottie Hawes, . . .	Lottie McFarland, . .	Worcester.

* Changed by reason of adoption.

WORCESTER COUNTY — *Concluded.*

Date of Decree.	Original Name.	Name Decreed.	Residence.
1869.			
Dec. 7,	Mabel A. Hawes, . . .	Ellen Mabel Wheeler, . .	New Braintree.
21,	Hattie E. Lovewell, . . .	Hattie Eliza Lovewell Whitney, ...	Gardner.
21,	Clara Hale, ...	Clara Alice Jones, . . .	Worcester.
21,	George Aaron Parmenter, .	Charles William Ross, . .	Leominster.
21,	Addie Wood, ...	Addie C. Lamb, . . .	Auburn.

HAMPSHIRE COUNTY.

Jan. 5,	Charles A. Killany, . . .	Charles A. Lilly, . . .	Huntington.
Feb. 2,	Jennie E. Baldwin, . . .	Jennie E. Manchester, . .	Northampton.
April 13,	Emma Maria Holmes, . .	Emma Ida Humphrey, . .	Northampton.
June 1,	Willie Bemis, ...	Willie Bisbee, ...	Easthampton.
1,	Albert D. Reed, ...	Albert D. Sanders, . . .	Northampton.
Dec. 7,	Mary Augusta Weeks, . .	Ada Louisa Russell, . .	Northampton.

HAMPDEN COUNTY.

Mar. 2,	Lizzie E. Noble,* . . .	Nellie Eggleston, . . .	Westfield.
May 4,	Lydia Melvina Warner,* . .	Lydia Melvina Warner Shaw,	Palmer.
July 6,	Sarah Nellie Sands,* . .	Ellen Sands Bridgman, . .	Springfield.
Sept. 7,	Carrie A. Clark,* . . .	Carrie Isabella Bush, . .	Springfield.
20,	Annie Cora Wells,* . . .	Annie Cora Higgins, . .	Chicopee.
Oct. 18,	Mary McKeever,* . . .	Mary McKechnie, . . .	Springfield.
Nov. 3,	Jane Charlesworth,* . .	Jennie Edith Clapp, . .	Holyoke.
3,	Hattie Adella Potter,* . .	Hattie Adella Wheeler, .	Holyoke.

FRANKLIN COUNTY.

Jan. 5,	James H. Hunt, ...	James Hicks, ...	Rowe.
9,	Edmund B. Hawkes, . . .	Edwin Bement Meekins, .	Buckland.
May 4,	Kate D. Duval, ...	Stella Angie Hobart, . .	Sunderland.
4,	Nellie Hortense Baldwin Smedley, ...	Nellie Mary Haman, . .	Shelburne.
Aug. 3,	Rhoda Rosanna Chloe Harris, .	Rosie Chloe Pike, . . .	Wendell.
Sept. 7,	Hattie Emma Wrisley, . .	Hattie Wrisley Waterman, .	Shutesbury.
Oct. 27,	Mary B. Harris, . . .	Mary Estella Reniff, . .	Buckland.

BERKSHIRE COUNTY.

Feb. 2,	Dele Prudom, ...	Julia Tromble, . . .	Pittsfield.
April 6,	A foundling child with no known name, ...	Belle Inez Wood, . . .	Lanesborough.
May 4,	Carrie Stone, ...	Carrie Howard, . . .	Adams.

* Changed by reason of adoption.

CHANGE OF NAMES.

NORFOLK COUNTY.

Date of Decree.	Original Name.	Name Decreed.	Residence.
1869.			
Jan. 13,	Nellie McLane,*	Carrie Ada Derry, . . .	Quincy.
Feb. 10,	Neilette F. Jackson,* . . .	Nellie Florence Partridge, .	Bellingham.
Mar. 3,	Betsey Spear,*	Caroline Frances Newcomb, .	Quincy.
9,	John B. Brady,* . . .	John B. Leddy, . . .	Canton.
10,	Anna M. Gilmore,* . . .	Anna M. White, . . .	Medway.
31,	A foundling,*	Myrtilla Geneva Fisk, . .	Medway.
June 23,	Catharine Barrett,* . . .	Catharine Farrelly, .• .	West Roxbury.
July 6,	Willie Kimball,* . . .	Albert C. Davis, . . .	Dorchester.
Sept. 8,	Mary H. Newhall,* . . .	Mary Harriet Holmes, . .	Canton.
22,	Maud Claverie,*	Maud Claverie O'Niel, . .	Dorchester.
Nov. 17,	Charles Simeon Fisher,* . .	Albert Jarvis Hastings, . .	Medway.
17,	Margaret K. Mixer,* . . .	Margaret Kimball, . . .	Stoughton.
24,	Mary Ann Metcalf,* . . .	Harriet Mary Ann Metcalf Gay, ...	Franklin.
24,	Maud E. Page, ...	Mary Elizabeth Page, . .	Dorchester.
Dec. 1,	Benjamin Clark Cutler Hard-wick, ...	Benjamin Cutler Hardwick, .	Quincy.

BRISTOL COUNTY.

Feb. 5,	Thomas J. Backus, . . .	Thomas J. Taylor, . . .	New Bedford.
19,	Adelaide E. Francis, . . .	Annie Louisa Lincoln, . .	Mansfield.
Mar. 5,	Sarah J. Francis, . . .	Jennie Augusta Lincoln, .	Mansfield.
May 7,	Gertrude A. Aliff, . . .	Gertrude A. Paine, . .	Taunton.
21,	Ruth Ann Milne, . . .	Mary Lee Horton, . . .	Taunton.
21,	Pardon G. Booth, . . .	Pardon Booth Gifford, . .	Easton.
June 4,	Nameless child, ...	Mary Emily Perry, . .	Somerset.
July 9,	George T. Dwelly, . . .	George Dwelly, . . .	New Bedford.
Aug. 6,	Laura J. Brightman, . . .	Laura A. Sisson, . . .	Westport.
Sept. 3,	Adrianna Frances Hinds, . .	Adrianna Frances Strange, .	Taunton.
3,	Nameless child, ...	Walter L. Weaver, . . .	New Bedford.
Nov. 5,	Gustave Bouffanais, . . .	Gustave Tripp, . . .	Taunton.

PLYMOUTH COUNTY.

Jan. 11,	Antoinette Thomas Smith,* .	Antoinette Thomas Brett, .	Bridgewater.
Mar. 8,	Unknown,*	Lydia Cushing, . . .	Kingston.
June 28,	Patrick Casey, ...	Henry Casey, ...	East Bridgewater.
Nov. 8,	Sarah M. Clapp,* . . .	Eliza Warren Tilden, . .	Marshfield.

DUKES COUNTY.

July 19,	Andrew R. Luce,* . . .	Charles L. Wicks, . . .	Tisbury.

* Changed by reason of adoption.

SUFFOLK COUNTY.

Date of Decree.	Original Name.	Name Decreed.	Residence.
1870.			
Jan. 10,	Edith Badger Kennedy,* . .	Gertrude Goddard Davis, .	Boston.
17,	Percy Elizabeth Scarborough,*.	Percy Scarborough Thaxter, .	Brooklyn, Conn.
31,	Ella Frances Caine,*	Ella Frances Haven, . .	Quincy.
31,	Charles Homer Lengille,* .	Charles Howard Wood, .	Nova Scotia.
31,	Sarah Jane McLearn,* . .	Daisy Rebecca Jones, . .	Rawdon, N. S.
Feb. 7,	Mabel Forrest,* . . .	Mabel Forrest Peck, .	Boston.
21,	Frank Hartley Turner,* . .	Franklin Henry Walker, .	Boston.
Mar. 7,	Anna Freeland, ...	Anna Freeland Robinson, .	Boston.
21,	Martin Atwood Burbank, .	John Burbank Smith, .	Chelsea.
21,	Peter Schmidt,* . . .	Charles Fries, . . .	Wilkesbarre, Pa.
April 11,	Emma Frances Bray,* .	Emma Frances Coleman, .	Gloucester.
May 2,	Harriet Cordelia Tuttle, .	Harriet Cordelia Hawley, .	Boston.
9,	Albert Warren Murphy, .	Albert Warren, . . .	Boston.
9,	Elizabeth Wentworth Thompson, ...	Elizabeth Wentworth Stevens,	Boston.
23,	Frank Martin,* . . .	Frank Martin Scott, . .	Brooklyn, N. Y.
June 13,	August W. Frenzel,*. . .	Wilfred August French,. .	Boston.
Aug. 1,	Sarah Erving Hudson,*	Sarah Hudson Murray, .	Boston.
8,	Mary Ellen Thayer,*. . .	Mary Ellen Vale, . .	Boston.
29,	Charles Orville Gibson, .	Charles David Page Gibson, .	Boston.
Sept. 5,	Nellie Laura Gerrit,* .	Nellie Laura Bemis, .	Arlington.
12,	Jennie Frances Barr,*	Jennie Frances Gallagher, .	Boston.
26,	May Tinker,* . . .	Mary Josephine Whitmore, .	Burrillville, R. I.
Oct. 10,	Maria O'Byrne,* . . .	Fannie Augusta Blake, .	Boston.
24,	Flora Stewart,*	Lucy Flora Dieterich, .	Lowell.
Dec. 19,	William McGowen,* . . .	Robert William Hogg, .	New York City.
19,	Gracie McGowen,* . . .	Jessie Ingalls Hogg, . .	New York City.

ESSEX COUNTY.

Feb. 1,	Pyam L. Johnson, . .	Frank L Johnson, . .	Lynn.
1,	Ellen E. Mitchell, . .	Ellen E. Burns, . .	Lynn.
Mar. 19,	Mary Herrigan, . . .	Emma Frances Hanson, .	
April 5,	Laura Wilkins Toohey, .	Laura Wilkins, . .	Salem.
5,	Wendell Phillips Toohey, .	Wendell Phillips Wilkins, .	Salem.
5,	Ellen Wilkins Toohey, .	Ellen Wilkins, . .	Salem.
5,	Mary Jane Parshley,. .	Elizabeth Knight Cloutman, .	Salem.
June 7,	James William Colwell, .	Henry Weston Pierce, .	Boston.
7,	Hermon Goodrich, . .	Hermon H. Campbell, .	Boston.
7,	George A Lefavour, . .	Ralph A. Hussey, . .	Beverly.
7,	Phebe Ann Maxner, . .	Phebe Ann Nason,. .	Lunenburg, N. S.
14,	Caroline Olive Staples, .	Caroline Olive Coolidge, .	Lawrence.
14,	Anna Morse Webster, .	Anna Morse Bailey, .	Lawrence.
23,	Lizzie Blanchard, . .	Lizzie Ruth Porter, .	Danvers.
July 5,	John Edson, . . .	Lyman Howe Perley, .	Ipswich.
19,	Susie W. Ross, . . .	Susie W. Baker, . .	Newburyport.
Aug. 2,	Thomas Batchelder Simonds, .	Thomas Stanley Simonds, .	Beverly.
2,	Charles Saunders Turpin, .	Charles Turpin Smith, .	Gloucester.
Sept. 6,	Leon De Gardonez Rideout, .	Leon Rideout,. .	Lynn.
Oct. 4,	Martha A. Doe, . . .	Martha A. Gray, . .	Rockport.
4,	Alice Elizabeth Johnson, .	Alice Elizabeth Johnson Robinson, ...	Lynn.
18,	Frances E. Bayley, . .	Frances E. Goodwin, .	Newburyport.
Nov. 15,	Angennetta Sargent, . .	Nettie Medbury, . .	Lynn.
15,	Caroline P. Tebbetts (wife of Hall W. Tebbetts), . .	Kate P. Tebbetts, . .	Lynn.
Dec. 13,	Ida May Dresser, . . .	Ida May Morse, . .	Haverhill.

* Changed by reason of adoption.

MIDDLESEX COUNTY.

Date of Decree.	Original Name.	Name Decreed.	Residence.
1870.			
Jan. 4,	Hiram McKinnon,*	Clarence Stanley Elder,	Chelmsford.
25,	George Dana Winch,	George Dana Mansfield,	Marlborough.
Feb. 1,	Harriett Estes,*	Viola Greenwood Marston,	Cambridge.
8,	Emma Louise Pratt,*	Emma Louise Tyler,	Newton.
8,	Rena Sherwood Pratt,*	Rena Sherwood Tyler,	Newton.
Mar. 1,	Patrick Foley,*	Patrick Gillon,	Cambridge.
8,	Philip Badger,*	Frederic Watson Badger,	Lowell.
22,	Ira Franklin Johnson,*	Ira Franklin Mason,	Malden.
April 5,	Mary Stephenson Washburn,	Mary Stephen Breed,	Medford.
26,	Flora Ella Chapman,*	Flora Ella Bond,	Shirley.
May 3,	Mary Alice Morris,*	Mary Alice Gragg,	Bedford.
10,	Hattie Wallace,*	Helen Elizabeth Almy,	Somerville.
24,	Ella Frances Smyth,*	Florence May Hamlin,	Cambridge.
June 7,	Mary Elizabeth Carver,*	Martha Bigley Rider,	Cambridge.
7,	Mary Elvira Catlin,*	Mary Elvira Marrett,	Cambridge.
14,	Georgianna Wilson,*	Elma Florence Gilson,	Pepperell.
14,	Horatio N. Williams, Jr.,	Horace Percy Howard,	Everett.
28,	Minnie DeLong,*	Minnie Whitcomb Hartwell,	Littleton.
July 19,	Mary Kelly,*	Mary Deede,	Charlestown.
Sept. 6,	Abraham Paul Belmore,*	Abraham Paul,	Marlborough.
6,	Mary Lizzie King.*	Mary Lizzie Caban,	Charlestown.
13,	Minnie Edna Spiller,*	Minnie Edner Thimme,	Natick.
13,	Sarah Elizabeth Fletcher,*	Sarah Elizabeth Ingles,	Littleton.
13,	Herbert Norton Oliver,	Herbert Fairfield Oliver,	Wakefield.
27,	Laura Louise Morse,*	Laura Louise Hall,	Lowell.
Oct. 4,	Frank Everett White,*	Frank Everett Turner,	Lowell.
Nov. 1,	Alice Putnam.*	Cora Alice Fisher,	Woburn.
1,	Abbie Bright Fisk,	Abbie Bright Tufts,	Charlestown.
8,	George Henry Butterworth,*	George Henry Scott,	Lowell.
8,	Margaret Moynihan.*	Margaret Devine,	Sudbury.
8,	William Henry Madden,*	William Henry Marden,	Stoneham.
Dec. 13,	Anna Drew Smith,*	Ella Swett Philpot,	Wakefield.
27,	Alice Durant,*	Alice Bartlett,	Winchester.
27,	Fred William McMaster,	Fred William Masters,	Watertown.
27,	Adelaide A. Wentworth,	Adelaide A. Byrns,	Somerville.

WORCESTER COUNTY.

Date of Decree.	Original Name.	Name Decreed.	Residence.
Feb. 1,	Kate Morris,	Gertrude Bailey Whipple,	Worcester.
1,	Ida D. M. Gates,	Ida Gates Burnham,	Bolton.
15,	Frederick J. Hare,	Frederick J. Kendall,	Phillipston.
Mar. 1,	Frederick A. J. Higgins,	Frederick A. J. Richardson,	Worcester.
April 5,	Lura Estelle Wight,	Lura Wight Nelson,	Upton.
5,	Jane Maria Thompson,	Jane Della Burt,	Northbridge.
19,	Lizzie Dahlman,	Lizzie Doyle,	Worcester.
May 3,	Mary McGrath,	Mary Elizabeth Hyde,	Worcester.
3,	Frances A. O'Brine,	Frances A. Bryant,	Paxton.
June 7,	Frederick Herbert Connor,	Frederick Herbert Leary,	Rutland.
21,	George Ford Foskett,	George Orville Forde,	Gardner.
Sept. 6,	Michael Carney,	Henry Carlton,	Worcester.
6,	Mary L. Carney,	Mary L. Carlton,	Worcester.
20,	Eliza Melinda White,	Lizzie Jennie Brigham,	Grafton.
Oct. 5,	Elmire St. Cyr,	Almira Defoe,	Shrewsbury.
5,	Nazè St. Cyr,	Charles Defoe,	Shrewsbury.
Nov. 15,	Fred Winn,	Fred Winn Parker,	Worcester.
15,	Myron Edson Newell,	Myron Newell Ayers,	Petersham.
Dec. 20,	Emeline Howe,	Emeline Bardwell,	Southbridge.

* Changed by reason of adoption.

HAMPSHIRE COUNTY.

Date of Decree.	Original Name.	Name Decreed	Residence.
1870.			
Jan. 4,	Herbert S. King,* . . .	Herbert S. Ring, . . .	Huntington.
Mar. 8,	Foundling, no name,* . .	Charles Frederick Peck, .	Hatfield.
April 5,	Walter Frederick Winslow,* .	Frederick Eugene Beston, .	Enfield.
May 3,	Francis S. Pike, ...	Francis S. Thayer, . .	Amherst.
21,	Elizabeth Pursey,* . . .	Mary Louisa Baker, . .	Amherst.
Oct. 11,	Edna Gibbs,*	Edna Elizabeth Snow, . .	Enfield.
Nov. 1,	Fanny Harthorn,* . . .	Fanny Agnes Russell, . .	Hatfield.
Dec. 15,	Bridget Ryan,*	Catherine Bridget Kearns, .	Easthampton.

HAMPDEN COUNTY.

Feb. 1,	John M. McKennon,* . .	John Cochrane, . . .	Holyoke.
May 3,	Samuel Judson Whaley, . .	Judson William Avery, .	Holyoke.
Sept. 6,	Thomas Crane, ...	Thomas Wallace, . . .	Westfield.
6,	Mary McMaster,* . . .	Mary McMaster Spencer, .	Chicopee.
Dec. 6,	Caroline M. Kellogg, . .	Caroline M. Fisk, . . .	Westfield.

FRANKLIN COUNTY.

Feb. 1,	Cincinnatus Shepardson, . .	Edmund Cincinnatus Shepardson, ...	Orange.
9,	Freddie C. Hitchcock,* . .	Freddie Converse Allen, .	Buckland.
April 5,	Sarah Lucretia Ward, . .	Emma Tyler Ward, . .	Greenfield.
May 24,	Nettie Gertrude Field,* . .	Nettie Lemira Goodwin, .	Ashfield.
24,	William Ellery,* . . .	Lutie Lucien Purinton, .	Buckland.
June 7,	Emma ———,* . . .	Emma Field Smith, . .	Sunderland.
Sept. 7,	Jessie Flora Damon,* . .	Laura Flora Morton, . .	Whately.
Oct. 4,	Hattie Maria Sawyer,* . .	Hattie Maria Starkey, . .	Orange.
Dec. 6,	Mary Ellen Winslow,* . .	Mary Ellen Smith, . .	Sunderland.
6,	Harriet Robinson,* . . .	Harriet Robinson Migrath, .	Greenfield.
6,	Julia A. Stearns,* . . .	Julia A. Webster, . .	Northfield.
6,	Edith Gertrude Hubbard,* .	Gertrude Hubbard Smead, .	Shelburne.
13,	Charles Levere Hall,* . .	Charles Henry Haskell, . .	Wendell.

BERKSHIRE COUNTY.

April 8,	James T. Curry,* . . .	Charles Lorin Temple, . .	Adams.
May 3,	Mary Lizzie Hart, . . .	Mary Lizzie Pratt, . . .	Lanesborough.
June 7,	Achsah B. Searl, . . .	Achsah B. Clark, . . .	Adams.
July 21,	Grove Van Horn,* . . .	Grove Crocker, . . .	W. Stockbridge.
21,	David Henry Penlony,* . .	David Henry Wager, . .	Adams.
Oct. 6,	Mary Frances Lampman,* .	Mary Frances Connolly, .	Adams.
6,	Lewis Everett Jobin,* . .	Lewis Everett Goodell, . .	Adams.

NORFOLK COUNTY.

Jan. 4,	John Hair, ...	John I. Kemp, . . .	Quincy.
Mar. 1,	Edwena J. Sturtevant, . .	Josephine Wales, . . .	Randolph.
April 5,	John Hawley, ...	John Lyons, ...	Medway.
May 3,	Adolphus P. Raymond, . .	Adolphus P. Pool, . . .	Weymouth.
3,	Amie Ann McCannah, . .	Amie Ann Allen, . . .	Wrentham.

* Changed by reason of adoption.

BRISTOL COUNTY.

Date of Decree.	Original Name.	Name Decreed.	Residence.
1870.			
Jan. 7,	Frances Everett Warren, . .	Frances Everett Pope, . .	Fall River.
7,	Lydia Jane Alden, . . .	Annie Millard, . . .	Fall River.
Mar. 6,	———, ...	Helen Worthing Tripp, .	New Bedford.
April 15,	Flora F. Walker, . . .	Flora F. Mason, . . .	Taunton.
May 6,	Robert Wood, ...	Robert Castle, . . .	New Bedford.
6,	Joseph C. Valdans, . . .	William C. Murray, . .	New Bedford.
Oct. 7,	Edwin G. Kay, ...	Edwin G. Davol, . . .	Fall River.
Nov. 18,	Alice Louisa Sherman, . .	Alice Louisa Hack, . . .	Taunton.

PLYMOUTH COUNTY.

Date of Decree.	Original Name.	Name Decreed.	Residence.
Jan. 10,	Alice Isabel Boyd,* . . .	Carrie Elizabeth Barrell, .	Abington.
24,	Mary Frances Walker,* . .	Mary Frances Poole, . .	Plymouth.
Feb. 14,	Addie Pettingail,* . . .	Addie Antoinette Upman Brett, ...	Bridgewater.
April 11,	Elizabeth Frances Hayden,* .	Elizabeth Frances Clark, .	East Bridgewater.
11,	Isabella Meechan,* . . .	Isabella Sheldon, . . .	Duxbury.
11,	Samuel W. Meechan,* . .	Samuel W. Sheldon, . .	Duxbury.
May 9,	Mary R. Marshall,* . . .	Mary R. Lincoln, . . .	Middleborough.
9,	Leila M. Marshall,* . . .	Leila M. Lincoln, . . .	Middleborough.
June 13,	Carrie Elizabeth Cudworth,* .	Carrie Josephine Nickerson, .	Rochester.
Oct. 17,	Clara S. Jones,*	Clara S. Packard, . . .	N'th Bridgewater.

DUKES COUNTY.

Date of Decree.	Original Name.	Name Decreed.	Residence.
Jan. 6,	Mary E. Skidmore,* . . .	Fanny A. Lewis, . . .	Tisbury.
Sept. 5,	Martha A. M. Bell,* . . .	Annie L. Thomas, . . .	Tisbury.
Oct. 17,	Sarah Edith Hatch,* . . .	Ava J. S. Athearn, . .· .	Tisbury.

SUFFOLK COUNTY.

Date of Decree.	Original Name.	Name Decreed.	Residence.
1871.			
Jan. 2,	Bertha Coleman,* . . .	Bertha Coleman Richardson,	Boston.
16,	An unnamed infant,* . . .	Annie Gray Richardson, .	Braintree.
Feb. 6,	Susan Adelaide Phillips,* . .	Susan Adelaide Low, . .	Boston.
20,	Evelyn Lawrence Taylor,* .	Evelyn Pettingill, . .	Boston.
21,	Ormonde Macbrien, . . .	Ormonde Macbrien Reid, .	Boston.
27,	Emma Hunt,*	Emma Hunt Varney, . .	Chelsea.
27,	Minnie Maud Stewart,* . .	Minnie Maud Stackpole, .	Boston.
Mar. 6,	Minnie Carrol Cooley,* . .	Minnie Carrol Dow, . .	Boston.
10,	Reliance Freeman Crosby, .	Gertrude Freeman Crosby, .	Chelsea.
13,	George Byron Chapin,* . .	George Byron Adams, . .	Chelsea.
13,	Alberti Christy,* . . .	Grace Irving Whiting, . .	Philadelphia.
April 3,	——— Round,* . . .	Sarah Louise Knapp, . .	Boston.
3,	Grace Maud Belknap,* . .	Grace Belknap Winch, . .	Boston.
May 3,	Edward Flood Smith, . .	Edward Flood, . . .	Boston.
8,	Joseph Henry Ridlon Kendall,*	Joseph Henry Ridlon, . .	Charlestown.
22,	Alice Lee Gookin,* . . .	Alice Lee, ...	Hampton, N. H.
June 12,	Frank Cornin,*	Harry Henderson Piper, .	Boston.
26,	Francis Davis Baker, . .	Francis Woods Baker, . .	Boston.
July 17,	Rosa Sherburne,* . . .	Jennie May Aldrich, . .	Boston.

* Changed by reason of adoption.

SUFFOLK COUNTY — *Concluded.*

Date of Decree.	Original Name.	Name Decreed.	Residence.
1871.			
July 18,	Fanny Elizabeth Crory, . .	Fanny Elizabeth Benedict, .	Boston.
Aug. 14,	George Franklin Marshall,*	George Franklin Marshall Ricketson, ...	New York City.
21,	Margaret Josephine Wakefield,*	Margaret Josephine Maguire,	Needham.
25,	James Edward Savage, . .	James Edward Pollo, . .	Boston.
Sept. 11,	Mary Vincent,*	Mabel Louise Simmons, . .	——.
Oct. 23,	Anna Vinton Wilde,* . .	Anna Virginia Wilde, . .	Randolph.
23,	Nelly Porter Childs, . .	Helen Porter Childs, . .	Boston.
Nov. 20,	Lucy West Coffin,* . . .	Louise West Pray, . . .	New Bedford.
27,	Georgie Hill Marks,* . .	Georgie Hill Emery, . .	Ship Harbor, N. S.
27,	Henrietta Razour,* . .	Alice Ella Rugg, . . .	Chelsea.
Dec. 4,	Theodore Razour,* . . .	Theodore Fowle, . .	Chelsea.
4,	Minnie Angeline Sawtelle, .	Minnie Angeline Holmes, .	Boston.

ESSEX COUNTY.

Jan. 3,	Amelia Beane,*	Amelia Butts, ...	Gloucester.
3,	Cynthia Elvira Watts,* .	Cynthia Anna Nichols, .	Lynn.
Feb. 14,	Jane Rendle Hainsworth,*	Jane Rendle, ...	Lawrence.
Mar. 7,	Annie Florence Elwell,* .	Florence Merlina Bridge,	Rockport.
7,	Henrietta Frances Trask,*	Henrietta Frances Standley, .	Beverly.
April 4,	Carrie Emma McIntire,* .	Carrie Emma Dearborn,	Salem.
4,	George Washington Thomes,	George Washington Stanton,	Lynn.
4,	Emma Frances Trask, .	Emma Frances Standley,	Beverly.
May 2,	Maria L. Chester,* . .	Maria L. Bates, . . .	Marblehead.
2,	Oscar Watson,* . . .	Oscar W. Clark, . . .	Wenham.
June 13,	Aggie S. Brown,* . .	Aggie S. Colson, . . .	Lynn.
Sept. 5,	Ella Essulia Sleeper,* .	Ella Essulia Roberts, . .	Lynn.
12,	Charles Francis Dresser,* .	Frank Gurley, . . .	Haverhill.
Oct. 3,	Jennie L. Durgin,* . .	Jennie Lucy Langley, . .	Lynn.
Nov. 7,	John Hurley, ...	John Francis Hurley, . .	Salem.

MIDDLESEX COUNTY.

Jan. 3,	Greenough Lincoln Bill,* . .	Charles Greenough Lincoln, .	Cambridge.
10,	Mary Ann Riley,* . . .	Mary Ann Lynch, . . .	Woburn.
10,	Emma Amanda McCleary,*	Gertrude Eloise Drew, .	Charlestown.
17,	Charles W. Parsons,* . .	Adelbert Wellington Hay, .	Lowell.
24,	Minnie Edna Thimme,* .	Minnie Edna Carter, .	Ashland.
Feb. 7,	Charlie Glyde,* . . .	Charles Edward Lincoln,	Natick.
28,	Mary Elizabeth Arnold,* .	Mary Arnold Tufts, .	Newton.
Mar. 28,	Arthur Wellesley Newell, .	Arthur Henry Newell, .	Cambridge.
April 11,	John Carney,*	John Francis Mack, . .	Charlestown.
May 2,	Edward Ward Hinks,* . .	Edward Winslow Hincks, .	Cambridge.
16,	Catharine Coughlin,* .	Catherine Coughlin Robinson,	Woburn.
23,	Silas Edmund Reed, . .	Burkner Franklin Burlington,	Wakefield.
23,	Gracie Getchell,* . .	Gracie Lincoln Harding, .	Charlestown.
23,	A female child,* . .	Lillie Mary Stinehart, . .	Somerville.
June 6,	Charles Sullivan,* . .	Charles Timothy Mahoney, .	Woburn.
6,	Winifred Constantine,*	Winnifred Mitchell, .	Lowell.
July 11,	Peter Christmas, . .	Peter Noel, ...	Marlborough.
25,	Minnie Hart,* . . .	Minnie Clark, . . .	Lowell.
Sept. 5,	Hattie Heather,* . .	Kittie Mary Newman Sawyer,	Newton.
5,	A female child,* . . .	Nettie Blanche Wright, .	Lowell.

* Changed by reason of adoption.

MIDDLESEX COUNTY — *Concluded.*

Date of Decree.	Original Name.	Name Decreed.	Residence.
1871.			
Sept. 19,	Edgar DeWitt Livingston,*	Edgar Robert Champlin,	Cambridge.
26,	George Albert Penn,*	George Albert Barnes,	Lowell.
Nov. 7,	Arthur Clinton Shaw,*	Wesley Frederick Howard,	Ashland.
7,	James Moroney,	James Murray,	Waltham.
7,	Eliza Moroney,	Eliza Murray,	Waltham.
14,	Nellie Gertrude Haynes,*	Nellie Gertrude Hayward,	Ashby.
14,	Frank Erastus Miller,*	Frank Gould Proctor,	Ashland.
Dec. 5,	Mary Lizette Drake,*	Mary Lizette Boyd,	Somerville.
12,	Franklin Henry Walker,*.	Frank Albert Mansfield,	New York.
26,	Mary A. Reynolds,*	Mary Eva Conant,	Lowell.

WORCESTER COUNTY.

Date of Decree.	Original Name.	Name Decreed.	Residence.
Jan. 3,	Sarah Cogans,	Sarah Jane Cogans Kelley,	Gardner.
17,	Clara Belle Davis,	Clara Belle Withington,	Fitchburg.
Feb. 7,	John Chicoine,	John Bedard,	Northbridge.
21,	——,	Stella Viola Partridge,	Royalston.
21,	George Hoseman,	George Washington Samson,	Worcester.
21,	Sarah A. Cooley,	Nellie Gleason.	Webster
Mar. 7,	Lillie E. Sheldon,	Lillie E Nichols,	Templeton.
April 4,	Armet Powers,	Frank Arthur Miller,	Brookfield.
18,	Ellen Slimonds,	Ellen Slimonds Potts,	Clinton.
May 2,	—— Walker,	Charles Henry Ellis,	Worcester.
2,	Joanna B. Chadbourn,	Joanna B. Radcliffe,	Fitchburg.
10,	James W. Thresher,	James W. Potter,	Barre.
10,	Clara Jones,	Clara Silvers,	Worcester.
10,	Cora Louise Weaver,	Cora Louise Stone,	Leicester.
16,	Zula E. Evans,	Lizzie Luella Rugg.	Sterling.
July 18,	Franklin Campbell,	Franklin Campbell Schultz,	Rutland.
Sept. 5,	—— Andrews,	Sarah Jane Vizina,	Spencer.
5,	Jennie L. Pierce,	Jennie L. Ware,	Spencer.
5,	Mary Ann Drenning,	Mary Drenning Temple,	Gardner.
19,	Alice Hussey,	Alice Hussey Moran,	Athol.
19,	Minnie L. Laverty,	Minnie Locke Jones,	Worcester.
Oct. 11,	Elizabeth Marsh Everett,	Elizabeth March Reed,	Brookfield.
11,	Sumner Haynes Everett,	Sumner Haynes Reed,	Brookfield.
Nov. 7,	Clarence C. Prouty,	Clarence Austin Humes,	Worcester.
21,	Mary Chamberlain,	Mabel Marian Ballou,	Winchendon.
Dec. 5,	Henry N. Hunting,	Henry Nelson Rice,	Hubbardston.
19,	Frances A. Lewis,	Caro. Frances Goulding,	Worcester.

HAMPSHIRE COUNTY.

Date of Decree.	Original Name.	Name Decreed.	Residence.
July 5,	Maria Estelle Woods,	Maria Estelle Dearborn,	Belchertown.
Nov. 8,	Eddie Hawks,	Eddie Hawks Goodale,	Amherst.

HAMPDEN COUNTY.

Date of Decree.	Original Name.	Name Decreed.	Residence.
Mar. 21,	Elma A. Holcomb,*	Elma A. Pratt,	Granville.
June 6,	Pamelia Witt,	Pamelia De Witt,	Springfield.
6,	Edmund Dickinson Witt,	Edmund Dickinson De Witt,	Springfield
6,	Jennette Sophia Witt,	Jennette Sophia De Witt,	Springfield.

* Changed by reason of adoption.

HAMPDEN COUNTY — *Concluded.*

Date of Decree.	Original Name.	Name Decreed.	Residence.
1871.			
June 6,	Timothy Edward McMasters, .	Timothy Edward Masters, .	Holyoke.
July 6,	William Doyle,* . . .	William Thomas Farrington,	Holyoke.
Sept. 5,	Mary Harris,*	Mary Barney, ...	Holyoke.
Nov. 8,	Edward C. Dallgster, alias Edward C. Keeper, . . .	Edward Charles Allen, . .	Westfield.
Dec. 5,	William Sullivan,* . . .	William Matthews, . .	Springfield.

FRANKLIN COUNTY.

May 2,	Freddie D. Reynolds,* . .	Freddie D. Freeman, . .	Leverett.
9,	Eva M. Allen,*	Eva M. Bass, ...	Warwick.
23,	Gertie May Hitchcock,* . .	Gertie May Thwing, . .	Hawley.
June 6,	Mary Estelle Bortney, . .	Mary Estella Gunn, . .	Sunderland.
6,	Arthur William Morse,* . .	Willie Arthur Wright, . .	Northfield.
Aug. 14,	Infant child of C. M. Howland,*	Herbert Russell Lee, . .	Conway.
Sept. 5,	Jessie Watson,*	Alice Georgie Rand, . .	Orange.
Dec. 12,	Abie Augusta Adams,* . .	Lula Augusta Tenney, . .	Orange.

BERKSHIRE COUNTY.

Jan. 3,	Hattie Flemming, . . .	Hattie Maria Bentley, . .	Savoy.
Feb. 7,	Dora Gray, ...	Dora Gray Fuller, . . .	Pittsfield.
7,	Julia Clark Jenkins, . .	Louisa Jenkins Stebbins, .	Adams.
Mar. 7,	Evelina B. Hicks, . . .	Evelina B. Cleghorn, . .	Adams.
April 4,	Nellie Bard, ...	Nellie Kaley, ...	Cheshire.
May 3,	Julia Evans, ...	Julia Lawrence, . . .	Lee.
June 6,	Harriet Augusta Avery, .	Harriet Augusta Hawley, .	Windsor.
6,	Lillian M. Hudson, . . .	Lillian M. Seymour, . .	Stockbridge.
July 20,	Caroline E. Haynes, . .	Caroline E. Ballou, . .	Adams.
Sept. 5,	Jennie Etta Butterfield, .	Jennie Etta Mallery, . .	New Ashford.
5,	Mary E. Mead, ...	Mary E. Doherty, . . .	Pittsfield.
5,	Margarett Mead, . . .	Margarett Doherty, . .	Pittsfield.

NORFOLK COUNTY.

Feb. 15,	Ebenezer Prince Burgess, .	Ebenezer George Burgess, .	Dedham.
Mar. 8,	Ada Ellen Beasley,* . .	Ida Helen Sanborn, . .	Quincy.
May 3,	Sarah Maria King,* . .	Alice Poyner, ...	Needham.
3,	Hannah Augusta Hixon, .	Anna Augusta Hixon, .	Medway.
June 21,	Angeline Turner,* . . .	Angeline Toon, . . .	Needham.
28,	William Everett Morton,*. .	William Everett Wortman, .	Randolph.
-,	Almira Frances Stearns, .	Almira Frances Daniels, .	Foxborough.
July 26,	Francis Welch, ...	Francis Sargent, . . .	Medway.
-,	James E. Welch, . . .	James E. Sargent, . . .	Medway.
Sept. 27,	Lucy Ann Wellington,* . .	Florence Louisa Carter, .	Quincy.
Oct. 4,	Charles Henry Aldrich,* .	Charles Henry Fisher, . .	Norfolk.

BRISTOL COUNTY.

Jan. 6,	Weston E. De Moranville, .	Weston L. Cook, . . .	Westport.
18,	William Henry Tallman, .	William Henry Gifford, .	Dartmouth.
Mar. 3,	Charles D. West, . . .	Charles S. Morse, . . .	New Bedford.

* Changed by reason of adoption.

BRISTOL COUNTY — *Concluded.*

Date of Decree.	Original Name.	Name Decreed.	Residence.
1871.			
April 7,	Name unknown,	William H. C. Snow,	New Bedford.
21,	Elizabeth Eveline Hervey,	Name unchanged,	Attleborough.
June 2,	James Michael Kaniry,	James Michael Noonan,	Taunton.
21,	Horace C. Hull,	James Collins Rockwell,	New Bedford.
July 14,	William Waring,	William J. Waring,	Fall River.
14,	Martin R. Chace,	Martin R. Wallace,	Fall River.
Aug. 4,	Name unknown,	Ada Allen,	New Bedford.
Oct. 20,	William Manchester,	William Durfee,	Fall River.
Nov. 17,	Anna Bragdon,	Anna Bragdon Chaffin,	Easton.
17,	Robert W. McBurney,	Robert Chaffin Randall,	Easton.

PLYMOUTH COUNTY.

Mar. 13,	Delphenia W. Shaw,*	Delphenia Laustein Wade,	Carver.
May 8,	Emma F. Paine,*	Mary Emma Bourne,	Marshfield.
Oct. 23,	Emma C. Bolles,*	Emma C. Tripp,	Marion.
Nov. 13,	John E. Robinson,	John Washburn,	Plymouth.
27,	Unnamed child,*	William Leonard White,	Bridgewater.

BARNSTABLE COUNTY.

April 20,	Abby N. Clark,	Abby Frank Nye,	Sandwich.
May 18,	Charles P. Valentine,	Charles P. Jacint,	Provincetown.
18,	Manuel Valentine,	Manuel Pevear,	Provincetown.
Sept. 12,	Ada Hubert Baxter,	Ada Baxter,	Dennis.

DUKES COUNTY.

June 5,	Frederick A. Quinnell,*	Frederick O. Luce,	Edgartown.

SUFFOLK COUNTY.

1872.			
Jan. 1,	Ann Elizabeth Johnson,*	Martha Robinson,	Boston.
1,	William Henry Parsons,*	William Henry Simpson,	Sudbury.
1,	Josephine Swain,*	Josephine Swain Osgood,	Guilford, N. H.
15,	Minnie Hill Myrick,*	Minnie Hill Myrick Burke,	Lewiston, Me.
29,	Child of Anna McKinnan,*	Gracie Evelyn Blaisdell,	Newton.
Feb. 19,	Annie Bregan,*	Annie Connor,	Boston.
19,	Mary Jane Bregan,*	Mary Jane Connor,	Boston.
19,	Sarah Bregan,*	Sarah Connor,	Boston.
26,	Annie Nelvena Grant,	Anne Nellie Beaman,	Boston.
26,	Mary Estella Lewis,*	Mary Stella Came,	Brunswick, Me.
Mar. 4,	Evelyn Louis Menni Bonn,*	Evelyn Bonn Goodsell,	Taunton.
18,	Child of Catharine Kerrigan,*	William Jacobs,	Boston.
April 29,	Frederick Franklin Allen,*	Frederick Franklin Beaman,	Canton, Me.
June 3,	Adelaide Johnston,*	Ada Fisher,	Boston.
10,	Nicolay Tysland Johnson,*	Nicolay Tysland Legranger,	Boston.

* Changed by reason of adoption.

SUFFOLK COUNTY — *Concluded.*

Date of Decree.	Original Name.	Name Decreed.	Residence.
1872.			
Aug. 5,	Ann Elizabeth Fay,*	Ann Elizabeth Wilson,	Boston.
12,	Annie Cavanagh,*	Annie Bell,	Boston.
12,	Emma Elizabeth Hudson,*	Emma Elizabeth Jenkins,	Boston.
19,	Edward Hill Judkins,	Edward Judkins Hill,	Boston.
Oct. 7,	William Soule,*	William Regal,	Duxbury.
14,	Rosa Dunn,*	Catharine Esther Beecher,	Boston.
14,	Catherine Coughlan Robinson,*	Catherine Coughlin,	Boston.
14,	Lucy Gardner,*	Lucy Jane Sanborn,	Boston.
28,	Charlotte Augusta Betcher,*	Lottie Betcher Drew,	Boston.
28,	Annie Cleopatria Howard,*	Annie Cleopatria Jones,	Lynn.
Nov. 4,	Mary Elizabeth Leonard,*	Gertrude Maud Melville,	Boston.
Dec. 2,	Charles Wayland Edwards,	Charles Willard Carter,	Boston.
2,	Lucy Ella Howe Edwards,	Lucy Ella Howe Carter,	Boston.
2,	James Melvin Edwards,	James Melvin Carter,	Boston.
30,	Jane Brewer,*	Emma Anna Cash Hogan,	Cambridge.
30,	Katie Dana,*	Katie Neale Dana,	Scituate.
30,	Elizabeth Dury,*	Annie Proctor,	Bridgewater.

ESSEX COUNTY.

Date of Decree.	Original Name.	Name Decreed.	Residence.
Feb. 6,	Frank Herbert Frye,*	Frank Frye Buxton,	Salem.
6,	Fred L Frye,*	Fred Frye Getchell,	Salem.
6,	Lula A Frye,*	Lula Frye Symonds,	Salem.
6,	William H. Gilson,	Samuel H. Gilson,	Gloucester.
6,	Laura Antoinette Maben,*	Laura Antoinette Maben Kinney,	Saugus.
20,	Alphonsus Hallowell,*	Alphonsus Bowes,	Methuen.
20,	Florence Hammond,*	Florence Allen,	Lynn.
20,	Maggie S. Winston,*	Maggie S. Gray,	Newburyport.
Mar. 5,	Arthur I. Lovett,*	Arthur Willis Edwards,	Beverly.
12,	Mary Jones,*	Nellie B. Giles,	Lawrence.
19,	Richard Conway,	John Charles Fowler,	Lynn.
19,	Josie Emma Ross,*	Josie Emma Badger,	Boxford.
19,	Lizzie Ellen Ross,*	Lizzie Ellen Badger,	Boxford.
April 2,	Ellen Driscoll,*	Ellen Moore,	Salisbury.
May 21,	Daniel Burns,*	Daniel Carr, 3d,	Lawrence.
21,	Lydia Amey Hoag,	Amy Breed Hoag,	Lynn.
June 4,	Nellie Bailey,*	Ida Ella Johnson,	Lynn.
11,	Mina Florence Revere,*	Mina Florence Worthing,	Lawrence.
18,	Betsy Jackman Cheney,	Maria Hale Cheney,	Newburyport.
Sept. 3,	Ernest Allen,*	William Henry Cripps,	Saugus.
10,	Annie Osgood Stickney,*	Annie Osgood Saunders,	Lawrence.
Nov. 5,	Joseph Martin Plaice,*	Joseph Martin Jones,	Lynn.
5,	Luella Stone,*	Luella Rich,	Lynn.
12,	Mariah Doe Cann,*	Lillian Mabel Couch,	Lawrence.
19,	Jennie A. Tilton,	Jennie A. Ordway,	Bradford.
Dec. 17,	Joseph Albert Corey,*	Joseph Albert Roberts,	Salisbury.

MIDDLESEX COUNTY.

Date of Decree.	Original Name.	Name Decreed.	Residence.
Jan. 2,	Eveline Coe.*	Maud Draper Downs,	Ashland.
23,	Herbert Gillis,*	Herbert Boynton Sanger,	Natick.
23,	Emma Addie Ryan,*	Emma Addie Clayton,	Charlestown.
Feb. 13,	Mary Ellen Moynihan,*	Mary Ellen Grimes,	Acton.

* Changed by reason of adoption.

MIDDLESEX COUNTY — *Concluded.*

Date of Decree.	Original Name.	Name Decreed.	Residence.
1872.			
Feb. 13,	Flora Ann Temple, . .	Florence Eugenie Temple, .	Marlborough.
27,	Kate Keenan,* . . .	Kate McFarlin, . . .	Lowell.
27,	Elmer Ellsworth Rollins,*	George Elmer Barnard, .	Lowell.
Mar. 12,	William Brown,* . .	William Edwin Rogers,.	Charlestown.
12,	Mary Emma Brown,* .	Mary Emma Lewis, .	Lowell.
12,	Helena Coke,* . . .	Mabel Grace Foster, .	Malden.
12,	John Francis Mears,* .	Manfred Marshall, . .	Melrose.
26,	Michael Ball,* . . .	Francis Maley, . .	Stoneham.
April 2,	Georgie Gertrude Rogers,* .	Georgie Gertrude Burbank, .	Charlestown.
23,	Georgie Mabel Streeter,* .	Georgie Mabel Jacobs, .	Marlborough.
May 7,	Mary Chesman,* . .	Mary Evaline Hutchinson, .	Cambridge.
7,	Axie L Comey,* . .	Axie Comey Palmer. .	Hopkinton.
7,	Mary Lucinda Clark,* .	Mary Lucinda Paddleford, .	Holliston.
14,	Thomas G. Collins, . .	Thomas George Otte, .	Waltham.
June 11,	Frederick Ward,* . .	Freddie A. Morse, .	Hopkinton.
July 9,	George S. Morrison,*. .	George Young Allen, .	Cambridge.
16,	Edward B. McFarland,* .	Edward Brewer Martin, .	Lowell.
23,	Alfred B. Morse,* . .	Willie Henry Edson, .	Charlestown.
Sept. 3,	Jane Hinman, . . .	Jane Damon, . . .	North Reading.
3,	Mary Jane Hinman, .	Mary Jane Damon, .	North Reading.
3,	Frederick Damon Hinman,	Frederick Damon, .	North Reading.
3,	Eva Hannah Hinman, .	Eva Hannah Damon, .	North Reading.
17,	An infant,*	Abby P. Waldo, . .	Lowell.
24,	Mary Elizabeth Goulette,* .	Mary Lester McKey, .	Everett.
Oct. 22,	Benjamin Baldwin, . .	Benjamin Chase Baldwin, .	Lowell.
22,	Jane Mahoney, . .	Jane Manning, . .	Waltham.
Nov. 12,	Annie Kanns,* . . .	Winifred Glover, . .	Cambridge.
12,	Lizzie A. McBaine,* . .	Lizzie Woodworth, .	Lowell.
Dec. 10,	Mary Tyler Peabody, .	Mary Cranch Peabody, .	Concord.

WORCESTER COUNTY.

Jan. 2,	Frances A. Lewis, . . .	Caro Frances Goulding, .	Worcester.
Feb. 20,	Margaret Rosalla McCormic, .	Margaret Rosalla Howe, .	Spencer.
20,	Gertrude Amey Jackson, .	Gertrude Amey Knight, .	Douglas.
20,	Edwin Ames Herrick, .	Edwin Herrick Ames, .	Worcester.
Mar. 5,	Mary Williams Russell, .	Lizzie Mary Walker, .	Leominster.
5,	Mary R. Haworth, . .	Mary Louise Davis, .	Leominster.
5,	Alfred Fuller Smith, .	Alfred Wadsworth Dana, .	Worcester.
5,	Daniel Wilbur Morse, .	Wilbur Francis Morse, .	Worcester.
19,	Clarence Arthur Warren, .	Silas Gleason Warren, .	Leicester.
19,	Charles Henshaw Smith, .	Charles Henshaw Dana, .	Worcester.
19,	Charles Frederic Archer, .	Charles Frederic Waldo Archer, . . .	Worcester.
April 2,	Ada Wilson, . . .	Lillian Mabel Magoun, .	Worcester.
2,	Julia Sullivan, . .	Julia Collins, . . .	Worcester.
2,	Annie Sullivan, . .	Annie Collins, . . .	Worcester.
2,	Lena Elizabeth Thomas, .	Lena Elizabeth Farwell, .	Fitchburg.
2,	Abbie Bullard Boardman, .	Abbie Bullard Drury, .	Spencer.
2,	Martha E. Dyer, . .	Martha E. Felton. .	Clinton.
16,	Willie Gilmore Sargent, .	Willie Gilmore Clark, .	Hubbardston.
16,	Georgianna S. Warren, .	Georgianna Seager Parks, .	Shrewsbury.
16,	James Harrigan, . .	James Harrington, .	West Boylston.
23,	Frances Aldrich, . .	Grace Mabelle Carter, .	Leominster.
23,	Fannie S. Martain, . .	Fannie Martain Pitts, .	Leominster.
June 4,	Harriet Adelaide Macomber, .	Harriet Addie Richardson, .	Royalston.
Sept. 3,	Mary Ann McGill, . .	Mary Ann Oakes, . .	Harvard.

* Changed by reason of adoption.

WORCESTER COUNTY — *Concluded.*

Date of Decree.	Original Name.	Name Decreed.	Residence.
1872.			
Sept. 10,	William O'Donnell, . . .	William Barlow, . . .	Milford.
17,	Emma Crapo, ...	Jessie Willard Freeman, .	Westborough.
Oct. 15,	Alice Reed, ...	Gracie Alice Lagard, .	Worcester.
15,	Pasquale Anastace, . .	Joseph Ansello, . . .	Worcester.
Nov. 5,	Eliza Ann Converse, . .	Eliza Ann Lamson, .	Worcester.
19,	Unknown, ...	Bertha Josephine Hopkins, .	Worcester.
Dec. 17,	Linda Burt, ...	Nellie Jane Emmons, .	Douglas.

HAMPSHIRE COUNTY.

Date of Decree.	Original Name.	Name Decreed.	Residence.
Jan. 2,	Susie Grout,*	Minnie M. Childs, . .	Williamsburg.
2,	Henry Gray,* . . .	Henry Surrell, . .	Williamsburg.
April 2,	Hattie McIntire,* . .	Mary Frances Baker, .	Northampton.
2,	John Elgin Pike, . .	John Elgin Williams, .	Amherst.
2,	James Harbottle, . .	James Edmonds, . .	Ware.
2,	Sarah Helen Harbottle, .	Sarah Helen Edmonds, .	Ware.
2,	Charles Frederick Harbottle, .	Charles Frederick Edmonds, .	Ware.
2,	Albert William Harbottle,	Albert William Edmonds, .	Ware.
2,	Mary Florence Harbottle, .	Mary Florence Edmonds, .	Ware.
June 4,	Katie Russell,* . . .	Katie Russell Fairchild, .	Easthampton.
4,	Emma Dell,* . . .	Emma Dell Dewey, .	Huntington.
July 2,	Albert Gardner,* . .	Henry Silas Morgan, .	Greenwich.
Nov. 6,	Mary Eugenia Bradley,* .	Mary Eugenia Dawes, .	Cummington.
Dec. 3,	Roxana Voilette,* . .	Roxana Lafleur, . .	Northampton.

HAMPDEN COUNTY.

Date of Decree.	Original Name.	Name Decreed.	Residence.
Feb. 6,	Mary Ann Doyle, . . .	Mary Ann Kelly, . .	Holyoke.
Mar. 5,	Jesse M. Edwards, . . .	Frank Edwards Gibson, .	Holyoke.
April 2,	Louisa Smith, . . .	Anna Louisa Barton, .	Springfield.
June 18,	Hattie Cady, ...	Hattie Williams, . .	Westfield.
Dec. 17,	Lewis Forron, . . .	Frank Lewis Holcomb, .	Southwick.

FRANKLIN COUNTY.

Date of Decree.	Original Name.	Name Decreed.	Residence.
Feb. 6,	Everett Newell,* . .	Everett Newell Dickinson, .	Bernardston.
6,	Rosaline Estella Cole,* .	Rosaline Estella Abell, .	Conway.
13,	James S. Clark,* . .	George Everett Taylor, .	Shelburne.
Mar. 5,	Henry Culver Bigelow,* .	Henry Allen Steele, .	Shelburne.
12,	Mary Jane Turner,* . .	Clara Jennie Wright, .	Ashfield.
April 2,	Merrill Austin Moore,* .	Merrill Austin Holton, .	Montague.
2,	Caroline Elizabeth Moore,* .	Caroline Elizabeth Holton, .	Montague.
2,	Parthenia Porter,* . .	Mattie Culver, . .	Shelburne.
May 28,	Clarance Windsor Woodward,* .	Clarance Windsor Ward, .	Buckland.
28,	Wesley L. Bigelow,* . .	Wesley L. Culver, . .	Shelburne.
28,	Mary E. Bigelow,* . .	Mary E. Culver, . .	Shelburne.
July 2,	Emma Tyler Ward,* . .	Emma Willard Tyler, .	Greenfield.
Aug. 6,	Ida J. Shannon,* . .	Ida J. Richardson, . .	Deerfield.

* Changed by reason of adoption.

BERKSHIRE COUNTY.

Date of Decree.	Original Name.	Name Decreed.	Residence.
1872.			
April 5,	Clara J. Montgomery, . .	Clara J. Brown, . . .	Adams.
May 7,	James Melville Anthony, .	James Melville Davis, . .	Pittsfield.
8,	Olive C. Scott, . . .	Olive C. Palmer, . . .	Alford
July 16,	Edgar Preston, . . .	Edgar Preston Fairbanks, .	Pittsfield.
16,	William J. Muff, . .	William J. Meleer, . .	Adams.
Nov. 6,	Mary Angeline Bishop, .	Mary Bishop Curtis, . .	Stockbridge.
Dec. 3,	Thomas Henry Keating, .	Thomas Henry Gordon, .	Peru.

NORFOLK COUNTY.

Date of Decree.	Original Name.	Name Decreed.	Residence.
Jan. 10,	George Terrell,* . . .	George Edwin Coleman, .	Burlington, Vt.
Feb. 14,	Frances Lincoln Parrott,* .	Anna Frances Comey, . .	Quincy.
14,	—— —— Ware,* . .	George Wallaston Walker, .	Boston.
21,	Catharine Flanagan, . .	Catharine Frances Swan, .	Brookline.
28,	Margaret McClellan,* .	Marnie Vinal Brooks, . .	Lawrence.
Mar. 6,	George Winslow Hardwick, .	George Henry Hardwick, .	Quincy.
April 10,	Fannie Gertrude Swears,* .	Fannie Gertrude Pierce, .	Weymouth.
July 3,	Frank Fuller Saul, . .	Frank Edward Fuller, . .	Quincy.
Sept. 11,	Edwin E. Young,* . .	Edwin S. Morrill, . .	Boston.
Oct. 2,	Silas William Henry How,*	Harry Marriot, . . .	Needham.
2,	Rosa Lena How,* . .	Lena Foster, ...	Needham.

BRISTOL COUNTY.

Date of Decree.	Original Name.	Name Decreed.	Residence.
Jan. 19,	Ada May Palmer, . .	Ada May Hodgson, . .	Mansfield.
Feb. 2,	Susan Maria Chase, . .	Maria Louise Taber, . .	Acushnet.
Mar. 1,	Charles S. C. Pierce, . .	Charles Stephen Chace, .	Swansey.
April 5,	Melissa Gifford, . . .	Melissa Gifford Lawton, .	Dartmouth.
19,	Nameless, ...	Jennie May Fuller, . .	Attleborough.
June 7,	Nameless, ...	Lena Clark Bliss, . .	New Bedford.
Aug. 2,	Charles Franklin Chace, .	Charles Franklin Gifford, .	New Bedford.
Sept. 6,	Caroline Brewer, . .	Olive J. Hadwin, . .	Fall River.
6,	Hannah Reagan, . .	Hannah R. O'Neil, . .	Fall River.
6,	Arthur Almy Pickering, .	Arthur Pickering Almy, .	Fall River.
Oct. 4,	Felix Chaquette, . .	Felix Donelson, . . .	Fall River.
Nov. 1,	Sarah A. Chace, . .	Sarah Candace French, .	New Bedford.
1,	Susan Leonora Townsend, .	Susan Worcester Alden, .	Fall River.
Dec. 6,	Georgianna W. Clark, .	Georgianna W. Vaughn, .	Taunton.

PLYMOUTH COUNTY.

Date of Decree.	Original Name.	Name Decreed.	Residence.
Jan. 22,	Annie McDonald,* . .	Anne Conry, ...	Abington.
Feb. 12,	William Bullen,* . .	Frank Souther, . . .	Hingham.
12,	Lottie M. Hersey,* . .	Annie Louise Shedd, . .	Bridgewater.
Mar. 11,	Eliza W. Skiff, . . .	Eliza W. Cowen, . .	Rochester.
25,	Mary R. Lincoln,* . .	Mary Rebecca Shephard, .	Middleborough.
April 8,	Mary Elizabeth Haley,* .	Mary Elizabeth Thompson, .	Marshfield.
Nov. 25,	Euphenia Hector,* . .	Nellie Josephine Gardner, .	Bridgewater.
25,	Georgianna F. Reynolds,*	Georgianna F. Packard, .	N'th Bridgewater.

* Changed by reason of adoption.

DUKES COUNTY.

Date of Decree.	Original Name.	Name Decreed.	Residence.
1872.			
Jan. 15,	Agusta Lewis, ...	Agusta Heft, ...	Tisbury.
Dec. 2,	Willie F. Simpson, . . .	Willie F. Saunders, . .	Tisbury.
2,	Eliza Ann Simpson, . . .	Eliza Ann Spencer, . .	Tisbury.

NANTUCKET COUNTY.

Sept. 12,	Charles Macy, ...	Charles H. Macy, . . .	Nantucket.

SUFFOLK COUNTY.

1873.			
Jan. 13,	Lucy Hayden,*	Blanche Hamilton Booth, .	Boston.
20,	George Witham,* . . .	Henry Leon Noyes, .	Boston.
27,	Mary Augusta Hyland,* .	Mary Augusta Ashcroft, .	Boston.
27,	Louis Nachmann, . .	Louis Newman, .	Boston.
Feb. 3,	Frances Clara Martin,* .	Frances Clara Hastings, .	Boston.
Mar. 10,	Albert Gaston,* . . .	Albert Ghastin, . .	Boston.
10,	Albert Millard King, .	Albert Millard Wiley, .	Boston.
10,	Calvin Bradford King, .	Bradford King Wiley, .	Boston.
24,	Maud Blanch Cary,* . .	Ella Louise Chase, . .	Boston.
24,	Emma Dumpson,* . .	Ardonia Grey, . .	Boston.
24,	Abby Augusta Dow,* .	Jean Edson Perkins, .	Boston.
31,	Mary Lemist Hanson, .	Mary Lemist Clarke, .	Boston.
31,	Rebecca Haswell Hanson, .	Rebecca Haswell Clarke, .	Boston.
31,	George Lemist Hanson, .	George Lemist Clarke, .	Boston.
31,	Ellen Montresor Hanson, .	Ellen Montresor Clarke, .	Boston.
April 7,	James William McKenne, .	James William Hale, .	Boston.
14,	Jeremiah Shea, · . .	James Farrell, . .	Boston.
28,	Clarence Abbott Ruggles, .	Abbott Lawrence Ruggles, .	Boston.
May 5,	Sarah Louise Newhall.* .	Sarah Louise Hicks, .	Boston.
5,	Frank Russell Mundell,* .	Frank Russell Sargent, .	Boston.
5,	Ida May,*	Susie Ella Spaulding, .	Boston.
June 16,	Helen Francis Wellington,*	Helen Guardenier, .	West Roxbury.
Aug. 25,	Joseph Francis Reed, .	Joseph Francis Stanton, .	West Roxbury.
Sept. 1,	John Joseph Currie.* .	John Joseph Kennedy, .	Boston.
29,	Hermann Constantin Lagreze,*	Hermann Lagreze Strack, .	Marburg, Pruss.
29,	Anna Conway,* . .	Anna Maud Beal, .	Boston.
29,	Catherine O'Brien,* . .	Ellen Catherine Welch, .	Boston.
Oct. 6,	Margaret Forbes,* . .	Margaret Glass, . .	Charlestown.
Nov. 3,	Edward Bishop,* . .	George Warner Harris, .	Bedford.
24,	John Long,* . . .	John Daley, . . .	Boston.
24,	George Anson Bennett, .	George Anson Williams, .	Boston.
Dec. 15,	Charles W. Pratt,* . .	Charles Delphin, . .	Lynn.
22,	Susan Lynch,* . . .	Minnie Louisa McKenzie, .	Boston.

ESSEX COUNTY.

Feb. 4,	Mary Jane Fields, . .	Mary Jane McClosky, .	Peabody.
4,	Elizabeth Maria Tarbox, .	Alice Mary Stuart, . .	Lynn.
18,	Alice May Larrabee, .	Alice May Richardson, .	Lynn.

* Changed by reason of adoption.

ESSEX COUNTY — *Concluded.*

Date of Decree.	Original Name.	Name Decreed.	Residence.
1873.			
April 1,	Edward Griffin, . . .	Edward Warren Babcock, .	Keene, N. H.
15,	Hannah Maria Sweeney, .	Hannah Maria McCarthy, .	Peabody.
15,	Margaret Sweeney, . .	Margaret McCarthy, . .	Peabody.
June 3,	Lizzie Webb Dean, . .	Elizabeth Dean Webb, .	Beverly.
10,	Frederick S. Stone, . .	Frederick S. Wilson, . .	Lawrence.
July 1,	Josephine F. Brown, . .	Josephine F. Hurd, . .	Ipswich.
Sept. 9,	Ella Martha Johnson, .	Ella Martha Hale, . . .	Lawrence.
Oct. 7,	—— Bryant, . . .	James Howard Gregory, .	Marblehead.
Nov. 4,	Melinda Bell Whittier, .	Minnie Belle Littlefield, .	Gloucester.
11,	Flora L. Symonds, . .	Florence Pierce Symonds Buffum, ...	Salem.

MIDDLESEX COUNTY.

Jan. 7,	Mary Eva Conant, . .	Ethel Blanch Aldrich, . .	Lowell.
14,	Lizzie Cronin, . . .	Edith Eliza Leach, . . .	Brighton.
28,	Arthur Chester Russell, .	Arthur Marshall Cheney, .	Weston.
28,	Benjamin P. Roberts, .	Benjamin Payson Palmer, .	Somerville.
28,	Martha C. Roberts, . .	Martha Clarissa Palmer, .	Somerville.
28,	Harry P. Roberts, . .	Harry Payson Palmer, . .	Somerville.
Feb. 4,	Susan Ann McMullen, .	Susan Ann Ordway, . .	Lowell.
11,	Luella Frances Colby, .	Luella Frances Curtis, . .	Lowell.
11,	Bertram Pierce, . . .	Thomas Herbert Shepard, .	Winchester.
Mar. 4,	Joseph Bond Blanchard, .	Joseph Bond, jun , . .	Cambridge.
4,	Walter Henderson Merriam,	Walter Henderson, . .	Everett.
11,	George Alexander McIntyre,	George Winslow Southworth,	Medford.
11,	Maud Mary Sawtell, . .	Maud Isabella Hayward, .	Ashby.
25,	Ella Prudence Brown, .	Ella Cora Baker, . . .	Marlborough.
25,	Emma Louise Umberhend,	Emma Louise Tarbox, . .	Charlestown.
April 1,	John Albert Hufstadder, .	John Albert Jones, . . .	Malden.
8,	Lizzie Eldora Nichols, .	Lizzie Eldora Simonds, .	Charlestown.
22,	George Ford, . . .	George Quinn, . . .	Dracut.
May 13,	Elmina Charlotte Hunting,	Elmina Charlotte Chase, .	Cambridge.
20,	Anna Butler, . . .	Anna Goodwin, . . .	Medford.
20,	Rachel Hibbert, . . .	May Bell Rachel Potter, .	Lowell.
20,	Charles Henry Andrews, .	Charles Henry Whitney, .	Lowell.
27,	Mary Ellen Wiley, . .	Minnie Ayer, ...	Conway, N. H.
27,	Fannie Gertrude Foster, .	Fannie Gertrude Tompkins, .	Somerville.
June 10,	Frank E. Gay, . . .	Frank Lovejoy, . . .	Wayland.
10,	Mary Ida O'Reilly, . .	Mary Ida McDonald, . .	Charlestown.
24,	Susan A. Gerry, . . .	Susan Augusta Hovey, . .	Cambridge.
24,	Charles Edward Logan, .	Walter Scott Campbell, .	North Reading.
July 1,	George Moulton, . .	George Moulton Coggeshall, .	Lowell.
8,	Ella Josephine Harding, .	Josephine Harding Batchelder, ...	Holliston.
Sept. 2,	Alfred Thibeault, . .	Herbert Andrews Cox, . .	Everett.
2,	William Dodge, . . .	Robert Stanley Sanderson, .	Newton.
9,	Marietta Hasling, . .	Bertha Walker, . . .	Lowell.
Oct. 7,	Mary Ann Clarke, . .	Mary Lamson Clarke, . .	Natick.
7,	Elizabeth Mahan, . .	Lydia Frederika Mahan, .	Natick.
14,	Lilla Eddy, ...	Lillie Maria Dolliver, .	San Fr'ciso. Cal.
14,	Mary Lois Bushey, . .	Alice Towle, ...	Brentwood, N. H.
28,	Eleanor Coleman, . .	Eleanor Bibrim, . . .	Charlestown.
28,	Annie Belle Lund, . .	Annie Belle Harding, . .	Lowell.
Nov. 25,	Mary Jane Fletcher, . .	Mary Jane Farrier, . .	Stoneham.
Dec. 9,	Lizzie Maud McDonald, .	Gracy Kemmick, . . .	Natick.
23,	William Alexander Kirk Nevers,	George Hardy Duncan, .	Watertown.

WORCESTER COUNTY.

Date of Decree.	Original Name.	Name Decreed.	Residence.
1873.			
Jan. 7,	Georgie Desire Daniels,* . .	Georgie Desire Ford, . .	Grafton.
21,	Josephine Graceau,* . . .	Josephine Cormier, . .	Southbridge.
21,	Pauline Bailey,*. . . .	Pauline Estabrook, . .	Milford.
Mar. 18,	Winnie Abbie Baldwin,* .	Winnie Abbie Sawin, . .	Templeton.
18,	Catharine O'Donnell,* . .	Catharine Sheran, . . .	Milford.
18,	Leslie Reynolds,* . . .	Leslie Hemenway. . . .	Worcester.
April 1,	Frank E. Holbrook,*. . .	Frank Edward Whitman, .	Uxbridge.
1,	Maud Hussey,*	Gertrude Mabel Carter, .	Leominster.
15,	Virginia Stols,*	Virginia Dumas, . . .	Webster.
May 6,	John Warren Ramsdell,* .	John Warren Tower, . .	Athol.
20,	Franklin Campbell Schultz,*	Franklin Campbell, . .	Worcester.
20,	Maud Stuart,*	Jennie Maud Tyler, . .	Leominster.
June 17,	Mary Brown,*	Cora Isabella Walker, . .	Brookfield.
July 15,	Mary Amanda Moore,* .	Carrie May Dodge,. . .	Sutton.
15,	Leona Isabel Stone,* . .	Leona Isabel Dugar, . .	Charlton.
Sept. 2,	—— Dayton,*	Grace Hasley,. . . .	Fitchburg.
2,	Fannie Hamilton Trumbull,*	Fannie Hamilton Trumbull Cross, ...	Worcester.
Oct. 7,	Walter Edward Richardson,* .	Walter Edward Stearns, .	Worcester.
21,	Georgiana M. Andrews,* . .	Annie Maria Andrews, .	Leicester.
Nov. 4,	George Levi Whitaker,* .	Bertie Herbert Phelps, . .	Ashburnham.
Dec. 2,	Caroline Mable Hartwell,* .	Caroline Hartwell Goodell, .	Worcester.
16,	Alice Amelia Seaborne,* . .	Mary Alice Hill, . . .	Sutton.

HAMPSHIRE COUNTY.

Date of Decree.	Original Name.	Name Decreed.	Residence.
June 3,	Mary Belle McFarland,* . .	Mabel Porter, ...	Williamsburg.
July 2,	Grace Louisa Morley,* . .	Grace Marion Rockwell, .	Middlefield.
2,	Martha Annette Farnham,* .	Mattie Anneta Redding, .	Amherst.
Sept. 2,	Mertie E. Wells,* . . .	Mertie E. Strong, . .	Easthampton.
Oct. 14,	Orilla J. Shearn,* . . .	Orilla J. Wright, . . .	Belchertown.
Dec. 3,	Aldoras Sefton Ornell,* . .	Aldoras Sefton Hendrick, .	Easthampton.

HAMPDEN COUNTY.

Date of Decree.	Original Name.	Name Decreed.	Residence.
Feb. 4,	Melville S. Harvey,* . . .	Bertie Melville Harvey, . .	Palmer.
Mar. 4,	Rosetta Maria Converse, . .	Rose Standish Converse, .	Monson.
May 6,	Carrie M. Pierce,* . . .	Carrie Boyden, . . .	Chicopee.
8,	Marshall Wilson Bacon, . .	Marshall Wilson Newton, .	Palmer
June 3,	Mary Elizabeth Phelon,* . .	Mary Elizabeth Phelon, .	Westfield.
3,	Mary E. Riley,*	Mary Ellen Kearns, . .	Holyoke.
Sept. 2,	Helen Olive Rogers,*. . .	Helen Olive Howe, . .	Chicopee Falls.
Nov. 4,	Ella G. Smith,*. . . .	Ella G. Johnson, . .	Chicopee.
4,	Benjamin Spear Bryant,* .	Benjamin Spear, . . .	Springfield.
4,	Robert Henry Smith, . .	Robert Bemis Smith, . .	Holyoke.
5,	Annie Bell Gustella Wilbur,* .	Annie Bell Cook, . . .	Springfield.

FRANKLIN COUNTY.

Date of Decree.	Original Name.	Name Decreed.	Residence.
Feb. 11,	Charles Pratt Wood,* . . .	Charles Pratt Stockwell, .	Buckland.
April 8,	Mary Frances Kisor,* . . .	Minnie Eliza Alexander, .	Northfield.
May 27,	Wayne W. Woodward,* . .	Wayne C. Wheeler, . .	Charlemont.

* Changed by reason of adoption.

FRANKLIN COUNTY — *Concluded.*

Date of Decree.	Original Name.	Name Decreed.	Residence.
1873.			
June 3,	Mattie C. Franklin,* . . .	Mattie Logan Smith, . .	Montague.
Sept. 2,	Clara T. Whedden,* . . .	Clara T. Mowry, . . .	Greenfield.
Oct. 7,	Charles S. Beach,* . . .	Charles S. Porter, . . .	Greenfield.

BERKSHIRE COUNTY.

Date	Original Name.	Name Decreed.	Residence.
Feb. 4,	Hattie Estella Flouton, . .	Hattie Estella Burnett, . .	W. Stockbridge.
4,	Francis Carpenter, . . .	Francis Varren, . . .	Adams.
April 3,	Ernest Goodrich, . . .	Ernest Towers Goodrich Holwell, ...	Pittsfield.
May 6,	Fannie Shepherd, . . .	Fannie Porter Bailey, . .	Pittsfield.
6,	Fred. Temple, ...	Fred. Horton, . . .	Cheshire.
July 15,	Alice Hoose, ...	Alice Martin, ...	Pittsfield.
Sept. 2,	James Melville Davis, . .	James Melville Anthony, .	Pittsfield.
2,	Grace Maria Hamilton, . .	Grace Maria Hoose, . .	Pittsfield.
3,	Herbert White, ...	Herbert Harmon, . . .	New Ashford.
Oct. 7,	Thomas Connolly, . . .	Thomas Butler, . . .	Hinsdale.
7,	Margaret Ellen Connolly, .	Margaret Ellen Obey, . .	Hinsdale.
7,	Nellie Hinckley, . . .	Nellie Margaret Griffin, .	Lanesborough.
8,	William Ham, ...	Allen Munroe Sheldon, .	Great Barrington.
Nov. 5,	Ida Shelter, ...	Ida Amelia Lang, . . .	Pittsfield.

NORFOLK COUNTY.

Date	Original Name.	Name Decreed.	Residence.
Feb. 5,	Isabella Theldal Campbell,* .	Annie Maria Thomas, . .	Weymouth.
5,	Fanny Gunning,* . . .	Amy Greene, ...	Milton.
5,	Mary Alice Munroe,* . .	Mary Ellen Fay, . . .	West Roxbury.
5,	Samuel Otis,*	Samuel Cooper, . . .	Boston.
May 21,	Charles A. Loring, . . .	Charles Edwin Wood, . .	Dedham.
July 2,	Peter Charden Brooks Adams, .	Brooks Adams, . . .	Quincy.
Sept. 3,	William Atherton Hewins, .	William Peters Hewins, .	Medfield.
3,	Francis R. Richardson,* .	Caleb Francis Craft, . .	Stoughton.
Oct. 8,	Swan Miller,*	Joseph Roberts, . . .	Quincy.
Dec. 10,	Annie Lorena Ford,* . .	Annie Ford Richardson, .	Foxborough.

BRISTOL COUNTY.

Date	Original Name.	Name Decreed.	Residence.
Jan. 3,	James Britton, ...	James Britton Wilbar, . .	New Bedford.
3,	Catherine Klure, . . .	Catherine Dempsey, . .	Fall River.
3,	John Mullaney, ...	John Shaugnessy, . . .	Fall River.
3,	Mary E. Mullaney, . . .	Esther Tyrell, ...	Fall River.
Feb. 7,	Abby Grafton, ...	Abby D. Kempton, . .	New Bedford.
7,	Clara Josephine Gifford, .	Clara Josephine Munroe, .	Mansfield.
7,	John McCarty, ...	John Carter Emery, . .	New Bedford.
Mar. 7,	Mary Ellen Sale, . . .	Name unchanged, . . .	Fall River.
7,	Ellen and Sarah Ann Granger, .	Ellen and Sarah Ann Wilkinson, ...	Attleborough.
21,	Evelyn A. Horr, . . .	Evelyn A. Blake, . . .	Mansfield.
April 18,	Helena Sands, ...	Alice Weaver, ...	Taunton.
18,	Nameless, ...	Elisha Bassett, . . .	Freetown.
June 6,	Nameless, ...	Kate Josepha Bartlett, . .	New Bedford.
6,	Carrie Hayes, ...	Maud Sherwood Boyce, .	Attleborough.

* Changed by reason of adoption.

BRISTOL COUNTY — *Concluded.*

Date of Decree.	Original Name.	Name Decreed.	Residence.
1873.			
July 11,	Maria L. Gill, ...	Maria L. Meade, . . .	Taunton.
Aug. 1,	Anna Henderson Moore, . .	Anna Maria Gainsville, . .	New Bedford.
Sept. 5,	Horace Perry Howard, . .	Clarence Howard Montgomery, ...	Attleborough.

PLYMOUTH COUNTY.

Mar. 10,	Sophronia L. Sampson,* . .	Lilian Sampson Shaw, . .	Hanson.
10,	Frank Poland,*	William Francis Davis, . .	Middleborough.
April 14,	Grace Eleanor Carbone,* .	Grace Eleanor Sivorich, . .	Hull.
14,	Lizzie May Staples,* . . .	Lizzie Staples Holmes, . .	Plymouth.
May 26,	Anna Dyke Washburn, . .	Anna Washburn Burnham, .	Bridgewater.
June 23,	Mary Carlton Howland,* . .	Mary Carlton Reed, . .	Pembroke.
July 8,	Francis Bartlett Hervey, . .	David Bartlett Hervey, . .	N'th Bridgewater.
Sept. 8,	Catharine Irwin.* . . .	Clara Elizabeth Sinclair, .	Hingham.
8,	Elmer E. Jones,* . . .	Elmer E. Enos, . . .	Plymouth.
Oct. 20,	Sarah E. Carr,*	Mary E. Reach, . . .	N'th Bridgewater.

BARNSTABLE COUNTY.

April 15,	Lydia Ford Backus, . . .	Lydia Ford Wood, . . .	Barnstable.
15,	Esther Louisa Sparrow, . .	Esther Louisa Cammett, . .	Barnstable.
Aug. 12,	Elizabeth W. Nightingale, .	Elizabeth Nightingale Marston, ...	Barnstable.

DUKES COUNTY.

Mar. 3,	Hannah Rose Crosby, . .	Aleta Thomas Robinson, .	Tisbury.
June 2,	Essie G. Thaxter, . . .	Essie G. Wilbur, . . .	Edgartown.
Dec. 1,	Elizabeth Elnora White, . .	Elizabeth Elnora Cleveland, .	Tisbury.

NANTUCKET COUNTY.

June 12,	Lydia W. Francis, . . .	Lydia W. Chappel, . .	Nantucket.
12,	Isabelle A. Kingsbury, . .	Isabelle A. Orr, . . .	Nantucket.

SUFFOLK COUNTY.

1874.			
Jan. 5,	Robert Bulling, ...	Robert Burlen, . . .	Boston.
5,	Frances Elizabeth Bulling, .	Frances Elizabeth Burlen, .	Boston.
5,	Alfred Henry Bulling, . .	Alfred Henry Burlen, . .	Boston.
5,	Edith Frances Bulling, . .	Edith Frances Burlen, . .	Boston.
5,	Estella Boynton,* . . .	Sarah Humphrey Buck, .	New Haven, Ct.

* Changed by reason of adoption.

SUFFOLK COUNTY — *Concluded.*

Date of Decree.	Original Name.	Name Decreed.	Residence.
1874.			
Jan. 12,	Maud May Guptill,* . . .	Carrie Green Barnes, . .	Boston.
19,	Patrick Henry Horan,* . .	Henry Horan McCann, . .	Boston.
26,	Nathan Boenstein,* . . .	Nathan Smith, . . .	Boston.
Feb. 2,	Elizabeth Kearney,* . . .	Abby Harriet Furber, . .	Boston.
2,	Frank Swett, ...	Frank Sweet, . . .	Chelsea.
9,	Mary Ellen Maguire,* . .	Minna Trabandt, . . .	Boston.
9,	Charles Pottsdamer,* . .	Charles Jefferson Hatch, .	Boston.
16,	Mary Moore Walker,* . .	Mary Moore Dean, . .	Boston.
16,	Abbie Hedge Crowell, . .	Abbie Hedge Hills, . .	Boston.
Mar. 2,	Minnie Etta Smith,* . .	Ada Louise Burroughs, . .	Boston.
23,	Willie Edmund Kirk,* . .	Willie Kirk Tirrell, . .	Chelsea.
23,	Gilbert Edward Frazier,* . .	Charles Fazier Raymond, .	Boston.
30,	George Quinn,* . . .	Moses Myers, ...	Boston.
30,	Fanny Blake,*	Fanny Maria Cartwright, .	Boston.
April 6,	Bessie Ann Christie,* . .	Bessie Ann George, . .	Boston.
13,	Belle Wallace Thorndike,*	Belle Wallace Brown, . .	Camden, Me.
13,	Millie Louisa Robinson,* .	Millie Louisa Wentworth, .	Boston.
20,	Grace Darling McAbee,* .	Grace McAbee Perham, . .	Zanesville, Ohio.
20,	George Prescott Tay,* . .	George Clinton Clark, . .	West Springfield.
20,	Patrick Lynch,* . . .	Francis Louis Monjet, . .	Chelsea.
27,	John Murphy, ...	John Downing Murphy, .	Boston.
May 11,	Alice Mason Sumner, . .	Alice Mason, ...	Boston.
11,	Mary Eliza Russell,* . .	Florence Ring, . . .	Boston.
25,	Francis Eldorus Dwyer,* .	Francis Eldorus Heminway, .	Boston.
25,	Jane Broderick,* . . .	Menagh Jane Clarke, . .	Boston.
June 15,	Joseph Paysant Bull, . .	Joseph Payzant Bullard, .	Boston.
15,	Charles Thompson,* . .	Charles Collins, . . .	Boston.
15,	Clara Bell,*	Ora F. Buck, ...	Boston.
22,	Nellie May Eaton,* . . .	Phebe Johnson Woodman, .	Boston.
22,	Sarah Ellen McQuade,* . .	Sarah Gertrude Sullivan, .	Lawrence.
29,	Albert Frederick Walsh,* .	Albert Frederick Hennessey, ...	Biddeford, Me.
29,	Joseph Geo. Lewis Nelson,* .	Joseph George Fitzmorris, .	Boston.
July 6,	David Cunningham,* . .	David O'Hanlon, . . .	Boston.
6,	Margaret Cunningham, . .	Margaret O'Hanlon, . .	Boston.
20,	Martha Ellen Warner,* . .	Grace Ellen Dunklee, . .	Boston.
27,	Margaret Warner,* . . .	Lucy Ashcroft, . . .	Gr'd Menan, Me.
27,	George Jepson Smith,* . .	George Jepson, . . .	Boston.
Aug. 17,	Leonora Chamberlin,* . .	Leonora May Walker, . .	Boston.
24,	Ida Marsh,*	Ada Brewster Richardson, .	Boston.
Sept. 7,	Mary R. Belden,* . . .	Mary Belden Wells, . .	Boston.
7,	George Bohring,* . . .	George Thomas Ritchie, .	Boston.
7,	Emma Dora Thayer,* . .	Emma Dora Gray, . . .	Boston.
14,	Hannah Brown,* . . .	Hannah Stone, . . .	Boston.
14,	Susan A. Murray,* . . .	Susan A. Libby, . . .	Boston.
21,	William Hudson Parshley, .	William Hudson, . . .	Boston.
Oct. 26,	Eliza Bartlett, ...	Eliza Bartlett Seymour, .	Boston.
26,	Mabel Campbell,* . . .	Mabel C. Goodwin, . .	Boston.
26,	John Golding,*	Charles Wallace, . . .	Bridgewater.
26,	Fanny Davis,*	Bessie Lockwood Tucker, .	Boston.
26,	William Otis Booth,* . .	Williard Otis Barnes, .	Boston.
26,	Samuel James Staples,* . .	Karl Adolp Spangenberg, .	Boston.
26,	Viola Estella Whittier,* .	Viola Estella McDonald, .	Boston.
Nov. 16,	Ottmar Kammerar, . .	Edward Kammerer, . .	Boston.
16,	Emma Petis,*	Emma Seamon, . . .	Boston.
30,	Anna M. A. Matson,* . .	Cornelia Lee Munson, . .	Boston.
Dec. 7,	Charlotte Elizabeth Taylor,* .	Charlotte Elizabeth Morrison, ...	Boston.
7,	Charles Smith Osborn,* . .	James Richards Williams, .	Boston.
14,	Mary Waicott Almon, . .	Mary Elizabeth Almon, . .	Boston.
14,	Cora Lawrence,* . . .	Ada Seymour, . . .	Boston.

* Changed by reason of adoption.

ESSEX COUNTY.

Date of Decree.	Original Name.	Name Decreed.	Residence.
1874.			
Jan. 6,	Richard Trask Eaton, . .	Allen Leach Eaton, . .	Beverly.
20,	Charles Martins, . . .	Clarimundo Martins, . .	Salem.
20,	Benjamin Franklin Vollor, .	Benjamin Franklin Buffum, .	Salem.
Feb. 3,	Eddie Reed Flint, . . .	Eddie Flint Leach, . . .	Manchester.
10,	Minnie A. Mitchell, . .	Maud Adelphia Gilbert, .	Gloucester.
Mar. 10,	Frank Graham, . . .	Frank Godin, . . • .	Haverhill.
17,	Ella Lee Trask, . . .	Ella Lee Wilson, . . .	Beverly.
April 7,	Charles Steele, . . .	Charles Wallis Steele, .	Salem.
7,	Warren Horne, . . .	Joseph Warren Caldwell, .	Ipswich.
7,	James Trimble, . . .	James May, ...	Lawrence.
7,	Sarah C. Tuller, . . .	Sarah C. Pulsifer, . .	Gloucester.
14,	Ernest Hawkins, . . .	Ernest H. Winson, . .	Salem.
14,	Mary Edith Griffin, . .	Mary Edith Knight, . .	Gloucester.
21,	Hattie Isabel Waldron, .	Hattie Isabel Towne, .	Topsfield.
21,	Charles Horace Dixon, .	Charles Horace Coppen, .	West Newbury.
21,	Jessie Dixon, ...	Jessie Coskery, . . .	West Newbury.
May 5,	Charles Gibson, . . .	James P. Clark, . . .	Gloucester.
5,	Katie Strickland, . . .	Katie S. Plummer, . .	Swampscott.
July 7,	Alice A. Mason, . . .	Alice Mason North, . .	Lawrence.
Oct. 5,	Sarah Ellen A. Winkley, .	Sarah Ellen A. Chadwick, .	Rockport.
Nov. 2,	Anna Elizabeth Currier, .	Anna Elizabeth Proctor, .	Manchester.
9,	Frank Dolliver, ...	Frank Orison Freethy, .	Lawrence.
9,	Mary Myrtle, ...	Mary Myrtle Pierce, . .	Lawrence.

MIDDLESEX COUNTY.

Jan. 6,	Lucy Ann Rahr, . . .	Lucy Rahr Emerson, . .	Wakefield.
20,	Albert Sibley, ...	Albert Sidney Lyon, . .	Wayland.
27,	Etta Childs, ...	Etta Childs Madigan, . .	Natick.
27,	Lucy Ann Gould, . . .	Annie Black, ...	Cambridge.
Mar. 10,	Minnie Corcoran, . . .	Marion Lulu Stanley, . .	Malden.
17,	Lizzie Jane Frasier, . .	Lizzie Jane Hubert, . .	Malden.
17,	Mary Jane Louisa Dooley, .	Mary Jane Louisa Johnson, .	Lowell.
April 7,	Sarah Ann Hyde, . . .	Sarah Ann Umpleby, . .	Lowell.
10,	Charles Benjamin Connor, .	Charles Bradley Manning, .	Cambridge.
May 20,	Catharine Riley, . . .	Catharine Rick, . . .	Dracut.
June 2,	William P. Small, . .	William S Richards, . .	Cambridge.
9,	Arthur H. Russell, . .	Arthur Walker, . . .	Marlborough.
July 7,	Mary Gray, ...	Caroline Elizabeth Brooks, .	Concord.
7,	Marshia Magee, . . .	Marshia Bachelder, . .	Cambridge.
14,	Isabel Beedem, . . .	Lena Blanch Slack, . .	Malden.
14,	Anthony Lamb, . . .	Samuel Treat Lamb, . .	Cambridge.
28,	Ellen Kearney, . . .	Ellen Stephens, . . .	Medford.
Sept. 1,	Emeline C. Lock, . . .	Martha Hildreth, . . .	Natick.
1,	John Riley, ...	John Rick, ...	Dracut.
22,	Evalina Wier, ...	Evalina Wier French, . .	Tewksbury.
Oct. 13,	Ann Elizabeth Rush, . .	Ann Elizabeth Edds, . .	Lowell.
27,	Flora Mabel Place, . .	Flora Mabel Fuller, . .	Natick.
27,	Edith Blanchard Saunders, .	Bessie Nichols, . . .	Natick.
27,	Agnes Garrison Freeman, .	Eleanor Isabella Anderson, .	Cambridge.
27,	Ida May Anderson, . .	Ida May Fatal, . . .	Cambridge.
27,	Ellen Stewart, . . .	Nellie May Miller, . .	Cambridge.
Nov. 10,	Margaret C. O'Hare, . .	Margaret Catharine Grimes, .	Lowell.
10,	Albert Rodney Drake, . .	Albert Rodney Parker, . .	Malden.
10,	Mary Louisa Cowdry, . .	Mary Louisa Tilton, . .	Lowell.
17,	William Badger West, . .	William Badger Lawrence, .	Medford.
24,	Alvin Drake Moonie, . .	Alvin Moonie Wyman, . .	Arlington.
Dec. 8,	Lilla Frances Avery, . .	Lilla Frances Brooks, . .	Lowell.

WORCESTER COUNTY.

Date of Decree.	Original Name.	Name Decreed.	Residence.
1874.			
Jan. 6,	—— ——— . . .	Mary Edna Wakefield, . .	Millbury.
20,	Francis Agan, . . .	Francis Willis Brown, . .	Uxbridge.
Feb. 3,	Nellie Delia Deane, . .	Nellie Delia Plimpton, . .	Dudley.
3,	Lewis Harlan Gilman, .	Lewis Harlan Gale, . .	Worcester.
3,	William T. Flint, . .	William Flint Smith, . .	Phillipston.
3,	Fanny Maria Flint, . .	Fanny Maria Smith, . .	Phillipston.
17,	Belle Marium Baldwin, .	Belle Marium Bailey, . .	Athol.
Mar. 3,	Anne Elizabeth Widdup, .	Anne Elizabeth Bray, . .	Worcester.
17,	Mary McGauran, . .	Emma Addie Ellsworth. .	Boston.
April 7,	William Henry Swan, .	Theodore William Aldrich, .	Mendon.
7,	Elizabeth C. Swan, . .	Elizabeth C. Aldrich, . .	Mendon.
7,	——— Owens, . .	Ruth Whittemore, . . .	Worcester.
7,	Johanna Crowley, . .	Johanna Murphy, . . .	Worcester.
7,	John Wilson Welch, . .	John Lincoln Harris, . .	Worcester.
21,	Nellie Bonner, . . .	May Violet Montreuil, . .	Worcester.
May 5,	Joseph Chaffin, . . .	Eugene Richard McCoy, . .	Worcester.
12,	Alice Lilian Bowen, . .	Alice Lillian Fisher, . .	Royalston.
12,	Minnie Gertrude Knapp, .	Minnie Gertrude Fisher, .	Royalston.
13,	Lizzie Sherburne, . .	Elizabeth Maria Ayres, .	Petersham.
13,	Lucy Edith Howe, . .	Edith Wetherell Howe, .	Petersham.
19,	Ella A. Baker, . . .	Ella A. B. Tenney, . .	Worcester.
June 2,	Augustus Hector, . .	Richard Augustus Ford, .	Worcester.
16,	Edith Annette Fuller, .	Edith Annette Fuller Lemoine,	Webster.
July 7,	David Alexander Allen, .	James Cook Allen, . .	Worcester.
21,	Hannah Read Tilden, .	Anna Read Allen, . .	Milford.
21,	Ida Lizzie Hapgood, . .	Mabel Hapgood Holden, .	Barre.
21,	William Edward Conkling,	William Edward Lovell, .	Worcester.
Sept. 1,	Alice Bell, ...	Alice Bell Proctor, . .	Bolton.
1,	Charles F. Safford, . .	Charles Hermon Sawyer, .	Lancaster.
Oct. 6,	Mary Olive Given Rankin,	Minnie Olive Given Wasson, .	Boston.
Nov. 3,	Emily Morris, ...	Lula Agnes Vinton, . .	Southbridge.
17,	Margaret Klane, . .	Margaret Allen, . . .	Charlton.
17,	Albert Curtis Maynard, .	Albert Maynard Rood, . .	Worcester.
Dec. 1,	Mabel Wallace Veazie, .	Mabel May, ...	North Brookfield.
1,	Nancy T. Stone, . .	Nancy T. Stevens, . .	Northborough.
15,	——— Wheelock, . . .	Arthur Willis Newell, . .	Gardner.

HAMPSHIRE COUNTY.

Feb. 3,	Nellie Luden, ...	Mary Eastman Buckman, .	Northampton.
June 9,	Lola Frances Kennard, .	Frances L. Bridgman, . .	Belchertown.
July 7,	Francis Albert Hawkes, .	Frank Herbert Witherell, .	Pelham.

HAMPDEN COUNTY.

Mar. 3,	Henry Francoeur,* . .	Henry Fountaine, . .	Northampton.
April 7,	Minnie Roberts,* . .	Lucy Agnes Reed, . . .	Hartford, Ct.
7,	Grace Emma Larkins,* .	Grace Emma Larkins Webber,	Minneapolis,Minn.
May 5,	John Frederick Gruendler,*	John Frederic Buschman, .	Westfield.
5,	Grace Taylor,* . . .	Grace Hunt Dawes, . .	Northampton.
June 2,	Lucy Jane Orcutt,* . .	Lucy Josephine Ames, . .	Washington,Mass.
July 7,	Mary Eleanor Emritch,* .	Grace Evelyn Perry, . .	Westfield.
Sept. 1,	Louis Laplant, Jr.,* . .	Louis Cummings, . .	Springfield.
1,	Annie Laplant,* . . .	Annie Cummings, . .	Springfield.

* Changed by reason of adoption.

HAMPDEN COUNTY — *Concluded.*

Date of Decree.	Original Name.	Name Decreed.	Residence.
1874.			
15,	Mary Abbie Ingraham,* . .	Mary Abbie Miles, . . .	Greenwich, N. Y.
Oct. 6,	Cora Etta Coleman,* .	Cora Etta Howe, . . .	Springfield.
Dec. 1,	Martha W Blackwell,* . .	Martha B. Blackstone, . .	Lake City, Minn.
15,	Sulena Grover,*	Sulena Washington, . .	Westfield.

FRANKLIN COUNTY.

Feb. 10,	Cora F Wilcox,* . . .	Cora F. Gilman, . . .	Shelburne.
Mar. 3,	Charles Whitney,* . . .	Charles Andrew Moore, .	New Salem.
3,	Mary E. Watson,* . . .	May E. Haynes, . . .	Charlemont.
3,	Emma J. Ellor,* . . .	Alice J. Dodge, . . .	Greenfield.
10,	George M. Moore,* . . .	George M. Mayo, . . .	Orange.
May 26,	Amelia M. Streeter,* . . .	Cora May Bond, . . .	Buckland.
June 2,	Caroline Gould,* . . .	Caroline Emon, . . .	Montague.
2,	Mary J Gould,* . . .	Mary J. Saro, . . .	Montague.
2,	Margaret Gould.* . . .	Margaret Levielle, . .	Montague.
2,	Willie Grant Wilcox,* . .	Willie G. Underwood, .	Heath.
July 7,	(Infant) Clark,*. . . .	Lottie Graves Purrinton, .	Buckland.
7,	(Infant) Clark,*. . . .	Lula Salinia King, . .	Buckland.
Sept. 8,	Horace A. Dewey,* . . .	William Frederick Hough, .	Colrain.

BERKSHIRE COUNTY.

Jan. 6,	Marvin Dole, ...	William Worth, . . .	Clarksburg.
8,	Alice M. Clark, . . .	Alice M. Baker, . . .	North Adams.
May 5,	Katie Jane Campbell, .	Katie Campbell Southwick, .	Adams.
6,	Fanny E. Ingraham, . .	Fanny E. Orton, . . .	Great Barrington.
June 2,	Hannah Dickinson, . .	Annie Dickinson Newton, .	Lanesborough.
July 23,	William Hills, . . .	William Howard, . . .	Adams.

NORFOLK COUNTY.

Jan. 7,	William Percy Austin, .	Percy Austin, ...	West Roxbury.
7,	Gracie Carlson, . . .	Gracie Whiting, . . .	Hyde Park.
Feb. 25,	Sarah Ann Lumb, . . .	Lillian Louise Bronsdon, .	Milton.
25,	Agnes May, . . .	Mary Agnes O'Neil, .	Hyde Park.
April 15,	Asa Ansel Jones, . .	Asa Jones Adams, . .	Hyde Park.
15,	Lewis Herbert Skinner, .	Lewis Herbert Hammond, .	Norfolk.
June 17,	Ellery B. Polsey, .	Ellery B. Clark, . .	Wrentham.
17,	Elizabeth A. Polsey, .	Elizabeth A. Clark, .	Wrentham.
July 8,	Effie Mabel Benson, .	Mabel Cooper Snow, .	Hyde Park.
22,	Charles Francis Pero, .	Charles Pero Niles, .	Randolph.
Dec. 2,	Annette Baldwin, . .	Jennie Garside, . . .	———
23,	Alice Maud Kaynes, .	Alice Maud Newton, .	Cambridge.

BRISTOL COUNTY.

Jan. 2,	John William Bradly, . .	John William France, . .	Fall River.
Feb. 6,	Edith E. Dodge, . . .	Edith E. Cole, . . .	Nova Scotia.
6,	Jenny Buffinton, . . .	Jennie Buffinton Ball, . .	Fall River.

* Changed by reason of adoption.

BRISTOL COUNTY — *Concluded.*

Date of Decree.	Original Name.	Name Decreed.	Residence.
1874.			
Mar. 6,	Sarah Frances Gidley, . .	Sarah Frances Royce, . .	Dartmouth.
April 17,	Alice Maud Thompson, . .	Mary Jane Day, . . .	Chesterfield, N. H.
July 10,	Nameless, ...	Sarah E. Cook, . . .	Fall River.
10,	Annie A. Andrews, . .	Annie A. Robinson, . .	Tiverton.
10,	Harriet S. Motsler, . .	Harriet S. Ginnodo, . .	Attleborough.
10,	John G. Motsler, . .	John G. Ginnodo, . . .	Attleborough.
10,	Emma A. Washburn, . .	Emma Sumner Green, . .	Attleborough.
Sept. 4,	Nameless, ...	Jane E. Read, ...	Dartmouth.
4,	William Edward Coffin, .	Edward William Gifford, .	New Bedford.
Nov. 6,	Nameless, ...	Mabel Frances Gurney, .	Fairhaven.
6,	Eugene Herbert Albro, .	Eugene Herbert Cornell, .	New Bedford.
6,	Nameless, ...	Elisa Annie Butts, . . .	Fall River.
Dec. 4,	Betsey Ann Maria Carr, .	Annie Maria Carr Rounds, .	Fall River.

PLYMOUTH COUNTY.

Date of Decree.	Original Name.	Name Decreed.	Residence.
Jan. 10,	Lizzie S. Holmes,* . . .	Fanny L. Hodge, . . .	Plymouth.
Feb. 9,	Delbert E. Thompson,* .	George D. Deane, . . .	Marion.
April 13,	Isaac M. Rashkowsky, .	Isaac Marks, ...	Rockland.
May 25,	Abby Fisher,* . . .	Katie L. Drew, . . .	Kingston.
25,	Zina Cochran,*	Zina Cannaway, . . .	Rockland.
25,	—— Roper,*	William F. Meserve, . .	Abington.
Dec. 14,	Edith H. Lincoln,* . . .	Edith H. L. Hersey, . .	Hingham.
14,	Sarah E. Whitney,* . .	Sarah E. Denham, . . .	Mattapoisett.
14,	Etta Hiller,*	Etta Norveil, . . .	Middleborough.
28,	Albert Kurz,*	Albert O. Nichols, . . .	Plymouth.

BARNSTABLE COUNTY.

Date of Decree.	Original Name.	Name Decreed.	Residence.
June 16,	Lucy P. Bangs, ...	Lizzie Gertrude Myrick, .	Provincetown.
Oct. 29,	Nehemiah Harding Fisher,	Irving Harrison Fisher, .	Provincetown.

NANTUCKET COUNTY.

Date of Decree.	Original Name.	Name Decreed.	Residence.
Mar. 12,	Cora Francis, ...	Cora M. Sandsbury, . .	Nantucket.

SUFFOLK COUNTY.

Date of Decree.	Original Name.	Name Decreed.	Residence.
1875.			
Jan. 18,	Daisie Marion Penn,* . .	Dasie Marion Burrows, .	Liverpool, Eng.
18,	William Penn,*	William Burrows, . . .	Liverpool, Eng.
18,	Jennie Sargent, . . .	Jennie Ricker, . . .	Boston.
25,	Mary Nagle,* . . .	Mary Lemoine, . . .	Woburn.
Feb. 15,	Emma Jane Bell,* . .	Emma Jane Pulsifer, . .	Cambridge.
15,	Mary Ann McGurdy,* .	Mary Ann Bird, . . .	Cambridge.
15,	Margaret McGurdy,* . .	Margaret Bird, . . .	Cambridge.
23,	Anna F. Mahoney,* . .	Anna F. Dunn, . . .	Boston.
Mar. 1,	Mary Jane Curtis,* . .	Mary Jane Grant, . . .	Troy, N. Y.

* Changed by reason of adoption.

SUFFOLK COUNTY — *Concluded.*

Date of Decree.	Original Name.	Name Decreed.	Residence.
1875.			
Mar. 22,	Jessie E. Kirkpatrick,* . .	Jessie Elizabeth Gates, . .	Boston.
April 5,	Waldo Clarence Haynes,* .	Joseph Rollins De Castro French, ...	Boston.
5,	Walter Edward Welch,* .	Fredie Walter Emerton, .	Boston.
12,	Elizabeth Ruddick,* . .	Eliza Watson, . . .	Boston.
May 3,	Loammi Crosby, . .	Lew Crosby, . . .	Boston.
17,	Edith Augusta Smith,* .	Edith Augusta Ham, .	Boston.
17,	Andrew Hall Ferdinand, .	Andrew Ferdinand Hall,	Boston.
June 14,	Lucy Brackett Wadleigh,* .	Lucy Brackett Chase, .	Brooklyn, N. Y.
21,	Martha Thain,* . . .	Carrie Wilson Carpenter,	Boston.
21,	Imogene Russell Harding,	Gena Russell Harding, .	Boston.
21,	Odelia Baltz,* . . .	Matilda Bach, . . .	Boston.
June 28,	Charlotte White,* . .	Mabel Angel Carter, .	Dedham.
28,	Annie Sullivan,* . .	Annie C. Randall, . .	Boston.
July 6,	Charles McClellan Murphy,	Charles McClellan Ballard,	Boston.
26,	Harry G. Collins, . .	Alberton Deshorne Breding,	Boston.
Aug. 9,	John Boyce, . . .	John Fitzgibbon, . .	Boston.
16,	Herman Bowers, . .	Herman Wenskowski, .	Boston.
28,	Nathaniel William Curtis, .	Nathaniel Curtis, . .	Boston.
Oct. 11,	Marie Koehling,* . .	Marie Saalwaechter, .	Boston.
11,	Friedrick Koehling,* . .	Friedrick Saalwaechter, .	Boston.
18,	Grace Williams,* . .	Grace Nourse, . .	Cambridge.
Nov. 15,	Leonard Marshall Prescott,*	Leonard Prescott Hilton,	Somersw'th, N. H.
Dec. 6,	Saida Gray,* . . .	Saida Baker, . . .	Boston.
13,	Thomas Vinton Young, .	Richard Randolph Shaw,	Boston.
27,	Marvin Sumner,* . .	Mervin Sumner Johnson,	Boston.
27,	Mary Flatley,* . . .	Nettie Harris Smith, .	Boston.
27,	Ida May Costello,* . .	Alice Goodridge, . .	Cambridge.

ESSEX COUNTY.

Jan. 18,	Blanche Augusta Lawrence,	Blanche Lawrence Cummings,	Andover.
25,	Pauline Carr, . . .	Pauline Wadleigh, . .	Salisbury.
25,	Claudia Lee Horne, . .	Fannie Spencer Littlefield,	Haverhill.
Mar. 1,	Frank R. Smith, . .	Frank R. Frost, . .	Haverhill.
8,	Katie Jane Carter, . .	Katie Jane Robinson, .	Lawrence.
8,	Mary Ann Fuller, . .	Maria Annie Dawson, .	Lawrence.
22,	Paulina Chambers, . .	Annie Peabody True, .	Salisbury.
22,	Arthur Webster Johnson, .	Arthur Webster Ballard,	Salem.
April 12,	Hattie Margenson, . .	Hattie Denby, . . .	Newark, N. J.
19,	Hannah Tinker, . . .	Hannah Butterworth, .	Salisbury.
June 14,	Ellen Maria Fuller, . .	Nellie Fuller Manning, .	Rockport.
21,	Clarence Elmer Bailey, .	Clarence Elmer Wirth, .	Peabody.
21,	Frank Bailey, . . .	Edward Oscar Wirth, .	Peabody.
21,	Joseph Walter Bailey, .	Joseph Walter Wirth, .	Peabody.
Aug. 2,	Alice Ruth Legro, . .	Alice Reynolds Hood, .	Beverly.
Sept. 6,	Ada Ingalls Gaskill, . .	Ada Joseph Young, . .	Salisbury.
13,	Frank Bent, . . .	Frank William Holt, .	Lawrence.
13,	Anna Maria Corser, . .	Annie Maria Baker, .	Amesbury.
20,	Lewis Thorndike Lee, .	Alfred Thorndike Lee, .	Lynn.
Oct. 18,	Frederick C. Trefethen, .	Frederick C. Joslyn, .	Lynn.
25,	Charlotte Ann Saunders, .	Charlotte Ann Taylor, .	Lynn.
Dec. 6,	Ida F. Twiss, . . .	Ida Twiss Bragdon, .	Danvers.
20,	William M. Coffin, jun., .	William M. Gray, . .	Milford, N. H.
20,	Florence Etta Twiss, . .	Florence Etta Melden, .	Lynn.

* Changed by reason of adoption.

MIDDLESEX COUNTY.

Date of Decree.	Original Name.	Name Decreed.	Residence.
1875.			
Jan. 5,	Viola Fletcher, ...	Alice Maud Jacobs, . .	Marlborough.
5,	Clara Robinson, . . .	Clara Wakefield, . . .	Hopkinton.
19,	William Walters Whitten, .	William Burr Plunkett, . .	Lowell.
19,	Frances Gertrude Valentine Sylvester, ...	Frances Gertrude Valentine, .	Newton.
19,	Mabel Hedwig Valentine Sylvester, ...	Mabel Hedwig Valentine, .	Newton.
26,	Helena Josephine Dick, . .	Helena Josephine Goldsmith,	Lowell.
Feb. 9,	Joanna McCarron, . . .	Josephine Agnes Barnes, .	Marlborough.
Mar. 9,	Cora Mabel Gould, . . .	Cora Mabel Hapgood, . .	Ashby.
April 6,	Etta Frances Taylor, . .	Etta Frances Palmer, . .	Lowell.
6,	Lottie Agnes Howe, . .	Charlotta Agnes Holbrook, .	Ashland.
13,	Samuel Mitchell, . .	Samuel O'Kelly, . . .	Marlborough.
13,	Ida Lucy Morehouse, .	Ida Lucy Wells, . .	Lowell.
May 11,	Amy Polland, ...	Amy Maier, ...	Cambridge.
18,	Carrie Isabella Ackerman, .	Carrie Isabella Hibbard, .	Hopkinton.
25,	Ella Frances Collins, . .	Annie Gertrude Hicks, . .	Somerville.
June 22,	Matilda Ann Gregory, .	Elizabeth Stephens Latimer, .	Newton.
July 6,	Cynthia Louisa Hoffer, .	Lulu Cox, ...	Cambridge.
27,	Nellie F. Brigham, . .	Nellie Fay Brigham Belknap,	Marlborough.
Sept. 7,	Ida Ella Wilson, . .	Clara Ella Page, . . .	Ayer.
14,	Emma Keziah Page, . .	Nellie Keziah Farrington, .	Lowell.
28,	Jessie Anna Brooks, . .	Jessie Anna Spaulding, . .	Groton.
Oct. 12,	George Levi Morse, . .	Joseph Warren Adams, . .	Somerville.
12,	Herbert William Prouty, .	Herbert William Estabrook, .	Natick.
26,	George Wiley, ...	George Wiley Higgins, . .	Holliston.
26,	Emma Cutting Bent, . .	Emma Cutting Bent Gray, .	Framingham.
Nov. –,	Anne Max, ...	Anne Max Murphy, . .	Stoneham.
23,	Ida L. Haven, . . .	Ida Lillian Hutchinson, .	Burlington.
23,	Mary McNaught, . .	Mary Hutchinson, . .	Burlington.
23,	John S. McNaught, . .	John Stuart Hutchinson, .	Burlington.
Dec. 14,	Ella Maud Johnson, . . .	Maud Ellene Noyes, . .	Somerville.

WORCESTER COUNTY.

Jan. 5,	Anna Maria Lamb, . . .	Anna Maria Wilson, . .	Leicester.
5,	Charles H. Baylies, . .	Charles H. Warren, . .	Templeton.
19,	John Carter, ...	John Albion Carter, . .	Petersham.
Mar. 2,	Nellie Dascomb Lovejoy, .	Nellie Dascomb Temple, .	Gardner.
2,	Mabel H. Ball, . . .	Mabel Stevens Ball, . .	Worcester.
April 6,	Frances Maria Eaton, .	Frances Maria Chase, . .	Milford.
20,	James Edward White, .	James Edward Mowry, . .	Douglas.
27,	———, ...	Emmie Clinton Smith, .	Athol.
June 15,	George K. Warner, . .	George W. Lawrence, . .	Fitchburg.
July 6,	Harriet Higgins Merrill, .	Harriet Merrill Marcy, . .	Southbridge.
20,	Frederick D. Gassett, .	Frederick Hildreth, . .	Milford.
20,	Ella Frances Jones, . .	Ella Frances Hale, . . .	Leominster.
Sept. 7,	Frances Eliza Young, . .	Edna Eliza Morse, . .	Webster.
7,	Cora Augusta Shaw, . .	Cora Augusta Davies, . .	Winchendon.
7,	Eugene Manning, . .	Eugene Ames, . . .	Royalston.
28,	Bertha Alace Carlton, .	Carrie Emeline Young, . .	Templeton.
Oct. 5,	Effie Gibson, . . .	Alice Effie Kimball, . .	Fitchburg.
5,	Caro Frances Goulding, .	Caro Frances Wetherbee, .	Worcester.
Nov. 2,	Willie Henry Akins, . .	Willie Henry Wilson, . .	Leicester.
2,	Ida M. Davenport, . .	Madge Davenport Ballou, .	Grafton.
16,	William Henry Brown, .	William Henry Sherman, .	West Brookfield.
Dec. 7,	Cora Ella Bradford, . .	Cora Ella Remington, . .	Northbridge.

HAMPSHIRE COUNTY.

Date of Decree.	Original Name.	Name Decreed.	Residence.
1875.			
Jan. 5,	Edward Ericsson,* . . .	Frank Edward Main, . .	Northampton.
Mar. 2,	Hattie Munn,*	Eliza Bennett, . . .	Middlefield.
May 4,	Mary Lueser Beaman,* . .	Mary Lueser Lovell, . .	Amherst.
4,	Charlie Rhood,* . . .	Frederic A Bryant, . .	Chesterfield.
4,	Frank Wilbur Rhood,* . .	Frank Wilbur Clark, . .	Huntington.
July 6,	Edwin J. Beaman,* . . .	Edwin J. Ingram, . . .	South Hadley.
Sept. 7,	Inez Eudora Park,* . . .	Inez Eudora Park Butterfield,	South Hadley.
Nov. 3,	Clarance W. Hunt,* . . .	Clarance W. Spooner, . .	Granby.
3,	George N. Hunt,* . . .	Geo. N. Goldthwait, . .	Granby.
9,	Clara Bell Truesdell Kendall,* .	Clara Bell Kendall Thayer, .	Amherst.

HAMPDEN COUNTY.

Date of Decree.	Original Name.	Name Decreed.	Residence.
Jan. 5,	Mary Emma Hodge, . . .	Josephine Allen Burton, .	West Springfield.
Feb. 2,	Arabella Horton, . . .	Bella Horton Stevens, . .	Westfield.
Mar. 2,	Edward Maurer, . . .	Edson Bradford Turpin, .	Springfield.
April 14,	Isabella Brown, ...	Bertha Arabel Cook, . .	Springfield.
May 4,	John Work, ...	John Dudley Colton, . .	Longmeadow.
4,	Gertrude Welden Hastings Barrett, ...	Edith Gertrude Johnson, .	Chicopee.
July 6,	Addie Martin, ...	Addie Lupin, ...	Palmer.
9,	Laura Barney, ...	Laura Barney Wakefield, .	Wales.
Oct. 16,	Nellie Brennan, . . .	Nellie Josephine Marvin, .	Springfield.
Nov. 23,	Walter Albert Crowell, . .	Walter Albert Reed, . .	West Springfield.
Dec. 7,	Franklin Brown, . . .	Frank Watson Halladay, .	Agawam.

FRANKLIN COUNTY.

Date of Decree.	Original Name.	Name Decreed.	Residence.
Feb. 9,	Luther O. Root,* . . .	Charles L. Bullock, . .	Bernardston.
9,	Geneva L. Searle,* . . .	Geneva L. Morse, . . .	Montague.
Mar. 9,	Jennie L. Rhood,* . . .	Jennie L. Lawrance, . .	Conway.
June 1,	John McCarty, ...	John Barber, ...	Northfield.
1,	Etta E. Parker,* . . .	Etta E. Bond, ...	Buckland.
July 6,	Mary Moore,*	Bertha A. Chamberlain, .	Orange.
6,	Frank B. Farlin,* . . .	Frank B. Graves, . . .	Greenfield.
Sept. 7,	Flora M. Reynolds, . . .	Flora M. Freeman, . .	Shutesbury.
7,	—— Seley (infant),* . .	John G. L. Quinton, . .	Greenfield.
Nov. 3,	Geo. W. Loveland,* . . .	Geo. W. Gunn, . . .	Montague.
3,	Effie A. Loveland,* . . .	Effie A. Gunn, . . .	Montague.
Dec. 7,	Lula L. Brown,*	Lula L. Temple, . . .	Heath.
7,	Sadie R. Brown,* . . .	Sadie R. Maxwell, . .	Heath.
7,	—— Weston (infant),* . .	Lillian E. Morton, . .	Whately.
7,	—— Cutler (infant),* . .	Eva M. Parker, . . .	Greenfield.
7,	Oscar S. Ripley,* . . .	Oscar S. Williams, . .	Sunderland.
14,	Daisy Clark, ...	Daisy J. Leland, . . .	Orange.

BERKSHIRE COUNTY.

Date of Decree.	Original Name.	Name Decreed.	Residence.
Jan. 5,	Agnes Connover, . . .	Florence Agnes Butler, . .	Adams.
Feb. 2,	David Munn, ...	David Larmary, . . .	Becket.
Mar. 2,	Thomas Hopper, . . .	Thomas Fortune, . . .	Hinsdale.

* Changed by reason of adoption.

BERKSHIRE COUNTY — *Concluded.*

Date of Decree.	Original Name.	Name Decreed.	Residence.
1875.			
May 4,	Louisa Le Barnes,	Annie V. Babcock,	Pittsfield.
July 20,	Lydia Amanda Le Barnes,	Lydia Amanda Proper,	Pittsfield.
Nov. 3,	Ettie Irene Bicknell,	Ettie Irene Converse,	Dalton.
Dec. 7,	Joseph Alexander Marsh,	Joseph Alexander Strong,	Adams.

NORFOLK COUNTY.

Date of Decree.	Original Name.	Name Decreed.	Residence.
Jan. 6,	Etta Estelle Knowles,*	Etta Estelle Wilbur,	Randolph.
6,	Patrick Treacy,*	Patrick Meaney,	Brookline
July 21,	Annie F. Richardson,*	Annie Lorena Ford Reed,	Foxborough.
21,	Frederick U. Smith,*.	Frederick Henry Barker,	Quincy.
Sept. 1,	Mary Rollins,*	Mary Malinda Mac Kenzie,	Hyde Park.
Dec. 15,	McKean Clifford Churchill,	McKean Gardner Churchill,	Milton.

BRISTOL COUNTY.

Date of Decree.	Original Name.	Name Decreed.	Residence.
Jan. 1,	Lissie Maria Leslie,	Lissie Maria Briggs,	New Bedford.
April 2,	Earnest A. Brown,	Charles Armstrong Cole,	New Bedford.
June 4,	George Gates,	Edward Livingston Baker,	New Bedford.
4,	Mary Lydia Orvis,	Mary Lydia Weston,	Fall River.
July 9,	Addie E. Provost,	Emma Etoily Peirce,	Rehoboth.
Aug. 6,	Ladora I. Howland,	Dora Elizabeth Shores,	Dartmouth.
6,	Frank H. Stetson,	Frank H. Harrison,	Fall River.
6,	Louisa Cook,	Louisa Cook Spellman,	Taunton.
Sept. 3,	Susan Abby Jones,	Alice Draper Brown,	Woonsocket.
3,	Margaret Boland,	Margaret Galligan,	Norton.
Nov. 19,	Bertha Frances Briggs,	Bertha Frances Wilbar,	Taunton.
19,	Sarah Maria Briggs,	Sarah Maria Walker,	Taunton.
Dec. 17,	Anna Mildred Hall,	Millie Kennedy,	Easton.

PLYMOUTH COUNTY.

Date of Decree.	Original Name.	Name Decreed.	Residence.
Jan. 11,	Flora Staples,*	Flora Nichols,	Plymouth.
April 12,	Margaret E. Hamilton,*	Florence M. Holmes,	Plymouth.
May 10,	Julia Bennett,*	Ida May Whittier,	Brockton.
June 14,	Francis Harrington,*.	Francis Keough,	Brockton.
July 12,	Annie Bohring,*	Gracie L. Otis,	Scituate.
Sept. 27,	Myron L. Bryant,*	Myron L. Hartwell,	Bridgewater.
Nov. 8,	Edward J. Maloy,*	Edward M. Thomas,	Middleborough.
8,	Frances R. Shaw,*	Frances E. Atwood,	Plymouth.
Dec. 13,	Nathan C. Freeman,*	Nathan F. Cook,	South Abington.
27,	Frederic B. Goldsborough,*	Albert Raymond,	Plymouth.

BARNSTABLE COUNTY.

Date of Decree.	Original Name.	Name Decreed.	Residence.
Mar. 9,	Mary Ellen Wilson,	Mary Stuart Ellen Wilson,	Barnstable.
May 20,	Nehemiah Harding Fisher,	Irving Harrison Fisher,	Provincetown.
Aug. 10,	Emma Gage Crowell,	Emma Gordon Crowell,	Barnstable.

* Changed by reason of adoption.

DUKES COUNTY.

Date of Decree.	Original Name.	Name Decreed.	Residence.
1875.			
June 7,	Josephine Anderson, . . .	Josephine Sylva, . . .	Edgartown.
July 9,	Samuel Smith Daggett Esau, .	Samuel Smith Daggett, . .	Edgartown.

SUFFOLK COUNTY.

Date of Decree.	Original Name.	Name Decreed.	Residence.
1876.			
Jan. 10,	May Rose Carlton,* . . .	Florence May Pike, . .	Boston.
10,	Josephine Spain,* . . .	Josephine Pagani, . . .	Boston.
17,	Edward Everett Balch,* . .	Edward Everett Kidney, .	Manchester, N. H.
24,	Elizabeth W. Work, . . .	Elizabeth W. Cushing, . .	Boston.
31,	Martha Elizabeth Keith, . .	Martha Elizabeth Dickinson,	Boston.
Feb. 21,	Clarence Henry Foster,* . .	Clarence Henry Orth, . .	Boston.
28,	Solomon McNeal Dickey, . .	Neal Solomon Dickey, . .	Boston.
28,	Lawrence Conway,* . . .	Edward Lawrence Boss, .	Boston.
Mar. 6,	Rosa Lewis Warren,* . .	Mary Elizabeth Hildreth, .	Boston.
13,	Minnie Frasier,* . . .	Jennie A. Stuart, . . .	Chelsea.
April 10,	John Joseph Brennan,* . .	John Joseph Donahoe, . .	Boston.
May 8,	Charles Upham, . . .	Charles James Upham, . .	Boston.
15,	Herbert Whiting Mahoney, .	Herbert Merrill Whiting, .	Boston.
29,	Frank Willard Seabury, . .	Frank Seabury, . . .	Boston.
29,	Ida May Morrison,* . . .	Lydia Ann Stewart, . .	Boston.
29,	Katie Fullington Shields,* .	Katie Fullington Higgins, .	Boston.
June 12,	Isaac Taylor Hoague, . .	Isaac Theodore Hoague, . .	Boston.
19,	Mary Ann McGowan,* . .	Mary Ann McLaren, . .	Boston.
19,	Henry Palmer,*. . . .	Henry Johnson, . . .	Boston.
26,	Mabel Bray, ...	Mabel Winslow, . . .	Boston.
26,	Clevenger Allston Powers,* .	Clevenger Allston Eastman, .	Boston.
26,	Charles Parker Smith,* . .	Charles Parker Simmons, .	Boston.
July 17,	Mabel Dunbar Warren,* . .	Mabel Sumner Power, . .	Boston.
Aug 7,	Geneva Chase,*	Mary Leavitt Mallon, . .	Taunton.
Sept. 18,	Jane E. Parker,* . . .	Elizabeth Loudon, . . .	Monson.
Oct. 9,	Ellen Cleora Hartwell,* . .	Ellen Cleora Gamage, . .	Harvard.
16,	Frederick Judd Smith,* . .	Frederick Judd Robinson, .	Boston.
23,	William Murphy,* . . .	Tony William Washburn, .	Boston.
Nov. 6,	Daisy Dudley Le Seur,* . .	Helen Bessie Rothwell Fernald, ...	Milford.
13,	Jeannette Eastman.* . . .	Gertrude Viana Byam, . .	Boston.
Dec. 4,	Ellen Elizabeth Littlefield,* .	Nellie Kezar Littlefield, . .	Boston.
11,	Lucette Brown Rogers, . .	Lucette Webster, . . .	Boston.
11,	Clarence Greenlaw,* . . .	Clarence Libby, . . .	Boston.
18,	Imogene Bailey,* . . .	Florence Imogene Crosby, .	Marblehead.

ESSEX COUNTY.

Date of Decree.	Original Name.	Name Decreed.	Residence.
Jan. 10,	Sarah E. Thurston,* . . .	Sarah T. Osgood, . . .	Haverhill.
10,	Georgiana Colburn Ward,* .	Georgiana Colburn Soper, .	Lawrence.
24,	Henry Emerson Raymond,* .	Henry C. Emerson, . .	Salem.
Feb. 21,	Grace A. Woodbridge,* . .	Grace Maria Gray, . . .	North Andover.
Mar. 13,	Octavia Grace Brown,* . .	Grace Brown Noyes, . .	Haverhill.
27,	Charles Leslie Ordway, . .	Charles Leslie Currier, . .	Newbury.
April 3,	Charles Steele, ...	Charles Wallis Steele, . .	Salem.
17,	Alma Maria Raddin,* . .	Alice Upton King, . . .	Peabody.
24,	George Winchester Smith,† .	Winchester Smith, . . .	Salem.
May 1,	Sarah Anna Sophia Bonnell,* .	Annie Bubier Gregory, . .	Marblehead.

* Changed by reason of adoption.   † No return of notice.

ESSEX COUNTY — *Concluded.*

Date of Decree.	Original Name.	Name Decreed.	Residence.
1876.			
1,	William Edgar Gammel,* .	Edgar Gregory, . . .	Marblehead.
8,	Mabel Allard,*	Flora Mabel Woodman, .	Lynn.
15,	Nellie H. Cushing,* . .	Nellie H Williams, . .	Gloucester.
15,	Estella Perkins,* . . .	Estella Clemons Kemp, .	Lynn.
Aug. 7,	Stepto C. Bridges,† . .	Stephen Burger, . . .	Salem.
7,	Alice Hews,*	Carrie Grata Haynes, .	Marblehead.
7,	—— Towle,*	Fanny Woodbury Towle Foster, ...	Salem.
7,	Alice Maria Barnard,* .	Alice Maria Lewis, . .	Lynn.
Sept. 2,	Eli Everett Boynton, . .	Everett Boynton, . . .	Swampscott.
11,	Katie Bogen,*	Katie O'Brien, . . .	North Andover.
Oct. 16,	Harry P. Collins,* . .	Harry P. Abbott, . . .	Andover.
16,	Sarah O'Brien,* . . .	Sarah Ella Lakeman, . .	Lynn.
16,	Mary Otis,*	Emma Jane Halsted, - .	Rockport.
Nov. 6,	Gertie Elvira Lee,* . .	Gertie Elvira Lee Cook, .	Saugus.
15,	George William Douglass Strout,	George William Douglass,	Salem.
20,	Laura Ann Harwood,* . .	Laura Harwood Gregory, .	Marblehead.
20,	Grace Williams,* . . .	Grace Nevada Jellerson, .	Lynn.
27,	Willie Haight,* . . .	William Daniel McCarn, .	Salem.
27,	Mary Augusta Lowell, .	Agnes Augusta Lowell, .	Salisbury.
Dec. 4,	Mary Robbarts, *alias* Mary Reynolds Robinson,* .	Anna Monroe Warren, . .	Gloucester.
4,	Julia Augusta Bartlett,* .	Julia Augusta Halsted, .	Rockport.
16,	Arthur Oren Neal, . .	Arthur George Neal, .	Lawrence.
16,	Austin Parker Orren Neal,	Austin Parker Neal, .	Lawrence.
18,	Nellie Edna Goldsmith,* .	Nellie Edna Purbeck, .	Salem.
28,	Mary Ellen Moore, . .	Mary Seccomb Moore, .	Salem.

MIDDLESEX COUNTY.

Jan. 11,	Edward Everett Hunt, .	Edward Harlow Duston, .	Lowell.
11,	Dillian Emmagene Rowe, .	Emmagene Rowe Cochran, .	Hudson.
18,	Maud Williams, . . .	Maud Edna Kenerson, .	Cambridge.
25,	William Bridges, . .	William James Gafney, .	Cambridge.
Feb. 1,	Lizzie Jane Hubert, . .	Lizzie Jannette Raymond, .	Malden.
8,	Onslow Leroy Moody, .	Winslow Leroy Leadbetter, .	Weston.
Mar. 23,	Alice Gordon Campbell, .	Alice Gordon Hayes, .	Lowell.
28,	Herbert Eugene Conant, .	Herbert Eugene Pebbles, .	Natick.
28,	Lucy Perry Conant, . .	Lucy Perry Pebbles, .	Natick.
28,	Clara Amelia White, . .	Clara Amelia Parker, .	Woburn.
April 11,	Georgia E. Eggleston, .	Georgia Eggleston Duane, .	Springfield.
25,	Hattie Jones, . . .	Hattie Pinkham, . .	Lowell.
25,	Kate Farr Blodgett, . .	Kate Blodgett Farr, .	Lowell.
25,	Richard Yapp, . . .	Richard Yapp Nelson, .	Boxborough.
May 2,	Carrie Hallet Norton, .	Carrie Norton Turnbull, .	Stoneham.
2,	Bianch Smith, . . .	Lillian Blanch Bunker, .	Cambridge.
2,	Patrick Callahan, . .	John Patrick Callahan, . .	Cambridge.
16,	Edwin Barclay, . . .	Edwin Sanderson, . .	Lowell.
23,	Charles Edwin Booth, .	Charles Edwin Ramsdell, .	Cambridge.
June 13,	Nancy Jane Cook, . .	Nancy Jane May, . .	Groton.
13,	Margaret O'Hare, . .	Margaret Magoun, . .	Medford.
27,	Charles Eben Williamson, .	Harvey Whitney Wilder, .	Somerville.
27,	Franklin Webster Hardy, .	Franklin Webster Seavey, .	Natick.
27,	Charles Everett Hoar, .	Charles Everett Wright, .	Cambridge.
July 18,	Claud Augustus Davis, .	Claud Augustus Swasey, .	Lowell.
25,	Robertine Geoffrion, .	Tiny Marin, ...	Lowell.
27,	John Kane, ...	John Kane Currier, .	Malden.

* Changed by reason of adoption.   † No return of notice.

MIDDLESEX COUNTY — *Concluded.*

Date of Decree.	Original Name.	Name Decreed.	Residence.
1876.			
Sept. 5,	Joseph Story, ...	Warren Clark Potter, . .	Cambridge.
19,	Kate May Dyer, ...	Kate May Usher, . . .	Lowell.
Nov. 14,	Grace Susan Horton, . . .	Grace Horton McClary, . .	Waltham.
21,	Catharine Manning, . . .	Minnie Electra Pettigrew, .	Lowell.
Dec. 12,	Mindora Fisher Daggett, . .	Maud Fanny Dyar, . .	Marlborough.

WORCESTER COUNTY.

Jan. 4,	Lefe Maria Hall, . . .	Minnie Pray, ...	Webster.
Feb. 1,	Hattie Orinda Smith, .	Harriet Oriana Wood, . .	Millbury.
15,	George Henry Thomas, .	John Whitefield Griswoold, .	Ashburnham.
15,	Catherine Kenney, . .	Mary Catherine Brewer, .	Clinton.
April 4,	Roxa Temple Stone, . .	Rose Tennyson Stone, .	Princeton.
June 20,	Ida M. Cambridge, . .	Ida M. Bliss, . . .	Worcester.
20,	———. . . .	William Henry Larhna, .	Ashburnham.
July 5,	Emily F. Pettet, .	Emily F. Remington, .	Southbridge.
16,	Cora Augusta Davis, .	Cora Augusta Commeau, .	Winchendon.
18,	Alice Maud Conant, . .	Alice Maud Conant Buck, .	Warren.
18,	Charles Enzas Patrick, .	Charles Enzas Frenney, .	Gardner.
Sept. 5,	Etta Florence Smith, .	Florence May Peck, .	West Boylston.
5,	Fred Ransom Taylor, .	Ransom Fred Taylor, .	Worcester.
19,	William White, . .	Paul Clifton Wheeler, .	North Brookfield.
19,	Charles Sawyer Barrows, .	Charles Edward Sawyer, .	Worcester.
19,	Emma R. Howard, . .	Isabella Thurston Barrett, .	Fitchburg.
19,	Etta Coffin, . .	Helen Louise Utley, .	New Braintree.
Nov. 7,	Bertha May Brigham, .	Agnes Helen Aldrich, .	Mendon.
Dec. 5,	Nellie Baldwin, . .	Mabel Lucretia Prouty, .	Spencer.
5,	Ethel F. Davis, . .	Ethel Frances Montgomery, .	Leominster.
19,	Robert McKenna, . .	Harry Robert Lovell, . .	Worcester.

HAMPSHIRE COUNTY.

Jan. 4,	Robert Allen Vandalinda,* .	Robert Allen Burnham, . .	Easthampton.
4,	Fred A. Boynton,* . .	Fred A. McMaster, .	Amherst.
Feb. 1,	Caroline Emon,* . .	Caroline Milo, . .	Hadley.
Mar. 7,	Joseph Alden Packard, .	Joseph Alden, . .	Plainfie.d.
May 2,	Ada Adell Smith,* .	Ada Adell Tower, . .	Chesterfield.
2,	Alice Bertha Smith,* .	Alice Bertha Keith, .	Granby.
9,	Winnona A. Blair,* .	Winonna A. Bruce, .	Belchertown.
Dec. 5,	Kate Mauren,* . .	Kate M. Guernesey, .	Amherst.
5,	Amasa D. Skinner,* .	Amasa D. Nelson, . .	Amherst.

HAMPDEN COUNTY.

Feb. 1,	George Herbert Tuck, .	George Herbert Wright, .	Holyoke.
1,	Thomas Allen Macnamara, .	Thomas Arthur Allen, . .	Springfield.
Mar. 7,	Catherine Reilly, . .	Fayolin Julia Hyde, . .	———.
7,	Frank Collins, . . .	Frank Gates Merriam, .	Springfield.
7,	Anna L. Barton, . .	Anna L. Randall, . .	West Springfield.
May 2,	Louise Fay Kelley, . .	Louise Fay, . . .	Westfield
June 6,	Clarence Van Deusen Fansler, .	Clarence Van Deusen, .	Westfield.
July 5,	Iza Dritte Dixon, . .	Iza Dritte Abbey, . .	Palmer.

* Changed by reason of adoption.

HAMPDEN COUNTY — *Concluded.*

Date of Decree.	Original Name.	Name Decreed.	Residence.
1876.			
Sept. 5,	Mary Jane Lagney, . . .	Mary Jane Beauchamp, . .	Holyoke.
12,	Jennie E. Hastings, . . .	Jennie E. Brainard, . .	Palmer.
19,	Lyman Root Harris, . . .	Lyman Root, ...	Westfield.
Oct. 3,	Grace Chenery Brown,	Grace Chenery Foote, . .	Newton.
3,	Esther Maria Hood, . . .	Esther Maria Angus, . .	Springfield.
3,	Winfred Luther Howard, . .	Winfred Howard Churchill, .	Springfield.
3,	Mabel Anna Howard,	Mabel Anna Churchill, . .	Springfield.
Nov. 8,	Mattie Laura Graves, . .	Caroline Estella Chapin, .	Springfield.
8,	Jessie May Pepperell, . .	Jessie Mary Parker, . .	Tewksbury.
28,	Lillian Lestina Foster, . .	Lillian Lestina Shamp, . .	Springfield.

FRANKLIN COUNTY.

Feb. 1,	(Infant) Walker,* . . .	Frank Adelbert Peck, . .	Shelburne.
Mar. 14,	(Infant) Wilby,* . . .	Jennie Lillian Jacobs, . .	Brattleboro', Vt.
June 24,	Estella Haley,*	Estella H. Knapp, . . .	Warwick.
24,	Annie Lewis Sampson,* . .	Anna Lewis Carpenter, . .	New Salem.
July 5,	Mabel A. Blakslee,* . . .	Mabel A. Dexter, . . .	New Salem.

BERKSHIRE COUNTY.

Jan. 4,	Lillie B Haydon, . . .	Lillie Bell Lee, . . .	Becket.
6,	Emma J. Shattuck, . . .	Emma Josephine Haley, .	Adams.
April 4,	Mary Adeline Veats, . .	Adaline Jacobs, . . .	Dalton.
June 6,	Eva May Hemenway, . .	Eva May Corbit, . . .	Pittsfield.
July 20,	Carrie Alice Towle, . . .	Delight E. Lindsey, . .	Adams.
Sept. 5,	Hattie Augusta Murray, .	Hattie Augusta French, . .	Pittsfield.
5,	Harriet Eliza Batey, . . .	Hattie Augusta Carpenter, .	Richmond.
Dec. 5,	William B. Boss, . . .	William B. Boss Arnold, .	Adams.

NORFOLK COUNTY.

April 19,	Violet Leonora Brooks,* .	Violet Brooks Pond, . .	Norwood.
July 5,	Ella Hattie Cobb,* . . .	Ella Hattie Blake, . . .	Wrentham.
Nov. 8,	Patrick Mullen, ...	Henry Mullen, . . .	Quincy.
Dec. 6,	James Wadsworth Sampson,* .	Arthur Ashley Sprague, .	Quincy.

BRISTOL COUNTY.

Jan. 21,	Hannah W. Borden, . . .	Annie W. B. Baker, . .	Fall River.
Feb. 18,	Elisabeth Heunt, . . .	Cecilia Gertrude Heinich, .	Fall River.
Mar. 17,	John Valentine, ...	George J. Leonard, . . .	Taunton.
April 7,	Luella F. Davis, . . .	Luella F Winslow, . . .	Fall River.
7,	Mary Anne Hasey, . . .	Mary Anne Duffy, . . .	Fall River.
7,	Teresa Hasey, ...	Teresa Duffy, ...	Fall River.
21,	Margaret M. Miles, . . .	Lillie M. Holmes, . . .	Taunton.
May 5,	Elmer Atwood, ...	Melvin Ellis Butler, . .	Everett.
5,	Frederick Augustus Sampson, .	Frederick Augustus Haskell, .	Taunton.
5,	Clarence Johnson, . . .	Clarence Crapo, . . .	New Bedford.

* Changed by reason of adoption.

BRISTOL COUNTY — *Concluded.*

Date of Decree.	Original Name.	Name Decreed.	Residence.
1876.			
Sept. 1,	Josie E. Wetherell, . . .	Minnie Josie Robbins, . .	Attleborough.
Nov. 3,	Joanna Louise Saarat, . .	Joanna Louise Hansen, . . .	Attleborough.
3,	Moses Russell, ...	George Taber Fuller, . .	New Bedford.
Dec. 1,	Charles Leslie Fairbanks, .	Charles Leslie Fairbanks	
		Paull, ...	Somerset.
15,	Ernest Armstrong Cole, . .	Ernest Armstrong Brown, .	New Bedford.

PLYMOUTH COUNTY.

Date of Decree.	Original Name.	Name Decreed.	Residence.
Jan. 24,	Mary Gunn,*	Mary McMinamy, . . .	Brockton.
Feb. 28,	George H. Barden,* . . .	George H Meserve, . .	Abington.
April 17,	Rebecca C. Thompson, . .	Rebecca C. Silsby, . . .	Brockton.
June 12,	Sarah J. Evans,* . . .	Sadie M. Swift, . . .	Plymouth.
Oct. 23,	Perly L. Horn,*	Perly L. Perry, . . .	Hanover.

BARNSTABLE COUNTY.

Date of Decree.	Original Name.	Name Decreed.	Residence.
Mar. 14,	Matilda F. Cahoon, . . .	Matilda F. Simpson, . .	Harwich.
July 18,	Almira Wilson, ...	Almira Hallet, . . .	Yarmouth.
Aug. 8,	Everett Kendall Wilson, . .	Everett Kendall Hallet, . .	Yarmouth.
8,	Alice Maud Wilson, . . .	Alice Maud Hallet, . . .	Yarmouth.

DUKES COUNTY.

Date of Decree.	Original Name.	Name Decreed.	Residence.
Sept. 4,	Alonzo Manual,* . . .	Alonzo Mason Ripley, . .	Edgartown.

SUFFOLK COUNTY.

Date of Decree.	Original Name.	Name Decreed.	Residence.
1877.			
Jan. 8,	Cora Estella Carter,* . . .	Cora Estella Powers, . .	No. Conway, N. H.
8,	Willie Wallace Lewis, . .	Willie Wallace Lunt, . .	Boston.
22,	Marcia Harris Clarke,* . .	Nellie May Sunbury, . .	Portland, Me.
22,	Alice Dunbar Coe,* . . .	Alice Dunbar Heustis, . .	Boston.
22,	Nettie Maria Ferrell,* . .	Nettie Maria Battelle, . .	Chelsea.
27,	Georgina Scott Page,* . .	Jessie Anna Prescott, . .	Boston.
29,	Florence Royle Smith,* . .	Florence Delano Howland, .	Boston.
Feb. 19,	Daniel P. Walker,* . . .	Daniel Walker Brintnall, .	E. Wakef'ld, N. H.
26,	James Quinn,*	Jerome Buonaparte Look, .	Athol.
Mar. 5,	Joseph Riley,*	Joseph Dolan, ...	Boston.
5,	Thomas Riley,*	Thomas Dolan, ...	Boston.
5,	Edward Riley,*	Edward John McCauley, .	Boston.
19,	Frank Wright,*	Frank Wright Hawes, . .	Abington.
26,	John Francis Walch, . . .	John Francis Martin, . .	Boston.
April 2,	———,*	Jennie May Twiss, . . .	Chelsea.
2,	Mary Jane McNabb, . . .	Mary Wright, ...	Boston.
9,	Edward Walter Allen,* . .	Edward Walter Kitchen, .	Boston.
23,	Ada Fisher,*	Ada Fisher Laurence, . .	Boston.
23,	George Augustus Piper, . .	George Augustus Raymond, .	Boston.
30,	Frank A. Smith, ...	Frank A. Locke, . . .	Boston.

* Changed by reason of adoption.

SUFFOLK COUNTY — *Concluded.*

Date of Decree.	Original Name.	Name Decreed.	Residence.
1877.			
April 30,	James Stewart Kibbey,	James Stewart King,	Boston.
May 21,	John O'Neal,	John Neal,	Boston.
28,	Joseph John Liever,	Joseph John Todd,	Boston.
June 25,	Mabelle Louise Frye,*	Mabelle Louise Southwick,	Boston.
July 2,	Maria Frances Welch,*	Maria Frances Emerson,	Swampscott.
9,	Clara Angeline Murphy,*	Clara Angeline Hadley,	Lynn.
9,	Frederick Weeks,*	Frederick Joseph Shields,	Boston.
16,	Elizabeth Mason,*	Theresa Pauline Smith,	Boston.
30,	Emily Kronenwirth.*	Emily Schuth,	Somerville.
Aug. 6,	Frederick S. Howard,*	Frederick S. Fowler,	Boston.
Sept. 3,	Henry Wallace Green,*	Henry Wallace Sargent,	Cotuit.
10,	Charles Wheeler Clark,*	Frederick Henry Weld,	Boston.
Oct. 8,	Elizabeth McNulty,	Elizabeth Burns,	Boston.
8,	James McNulty.*	James Burns,	Boston.
8,	Mary T. McNulty,*	Mary T. Burns,	Boston.
8,	Ellen McNulty,*	Ellen Burns,	Boston.
8,	Charlotte Hartshorn,*	Elizabeth Gray Cabot,	Germantown, Pa.
8,	Ellen Maud Mallon,*	Harriet Maud Day,	Boston.
29,	——,*	Florence Pearl Garland,	Boston.
29,	Jessie Agnes McGregor,*	Mabel Parkington,	Boston.
29,	John Morgan,*	Frederick Douglas Hall,	Boston.
29,	William Roche,	Charles Christopher Grover,	Boston.
Nov. 5,	George Frellick,*	Arthur Lane Sampson,	Boston.
5,	Henry Byron Means,*	Henry Means Bowles,	Boston.
5,	Francis Joseph McWill,*	Francis Henry Blair,	Boston.
12,	Frank Mack,*	Frank Washington Barrows,	Boston.
12,	Rollin Thorne Hayden,	John Ellerton Vassall Hayden,	Boston.
19,	Susie Laura Tucker,*	Susie Caroline Nason,	Lawrence.
26,	Anna Laura Staple *	Laura Elliot Cunningham,	Boston.
26,	Charles Henry Hall.*	Charles Frederic Gustin,	Boston.
26,	Emma Corliss Partlow,*	Emma Isabella Nichols,	Boston.
Dec. 3,	Maria Gertrude MacDonald,*	Blanche Emily Moulton,	Boston.
3,	Mary Tolles Edgerton,*	Adelia Landon,	Boston.
10,	Bradford Gibbs,	Franklin Bradford Gibbs,	Boston.
17,	John Henry Bohaker,	John Henry Bowker,	Boston.
31,	Abby Budson,*	Mabel St. Armand Stone,	Boston.
31,	Caroline Amelia Wait,*	Lottie McLean,	Boston.
31,	Julia Wood,*	Ida Gertrude Norton,	Boston.

ESSEX COUNTY.

Date	Original Name.	Name Decreed.	Residence.
Feb. 5,	Nellie Flynn,*	Nellie Flynn Quarters,	Lynn.
5,	George McVane,*	Frank Malcolm Vella,	Lynn.
Mar. 19,	Annie Ellen Connors,*	Annie Ellen Wilkinson,	Lawrence.
21,	Aaron Hill Ethridge.	Walter Hill Ethridge,	Salem.
April 30,	Clarence Eugene Ramsden,	Clarence Eugene Robinson,	Lawrence.
May 8,	Clarence Waters Jenkins,	Lawrence Waters Jenkins,	Salem.
28,	Sarah Thurston Osgood,*	Sarah Elizabeth Thurston,	Amesbury.
June 11,	Alfred Thorndike Lee,*	Lewis Thorndike Armstrong,	Lynn.
25,	—— Alden,*	Charles Melvin Hoyt,	Newburyport.
July 9,	James Henry Smith,*	James Henry Loflin,	Salem.
9,	Eva Maud Wildes.*	Eva Maud Hubbard,	Georgetown.
9,	John Joseph Withy,	John Withy Bell,	Andover.
11,	Lydia Thompson,	Lydia Messervey,	Marblehead.
16,	Ida May Jones,*	Ida May Butterfield,	Lawrence.
23,	Charles Augustus Robinson,*	Charles Augustus Lanzey,	Lynn.
Sept. 10,	Frederick Coveney,*	Charles Frederick Greenleaf,	Lawrence.

* Changed by reason of adoption.

ESSEX COUNTY — *Concluded.*

Date of Decree.	Original Name.	Name Decreed.	Residence.
1877.			
Sept. 15,	Eva Dalrymple,	Evaline Creesy,	Salem.
Oct. 22,	Sadie Victoria Squires,*	Gertrude Clifton Austin,	Gloucester.
Nov. 12,	Florence Mabel Smith,*	Alice Sargent Haskill,	Beverly.
12,	Enoch Howard Stacy,*	Enoch Hall Russell,	Bradford.
Dec. 3,	Herbert S. Palmer,*	Herbert S. Cushman,	Somerville.
17,	Catherine Connelly,*	Catherine Healey,	Lynn.
17,	Laura May Hunt,*	Laura May Hunt Deland,	Salem.

MIDDLESEX COUNTY.

Date	Original Name.	Name Decreed.	Residence.
Jan. 9,	Mary Elizabeth Cragen,	Bertha Crane Stone,	Newton.
16,	Mary Etta O'Niel,	Mary Etta Harris,	Lowell.
16,	Carrie Edna Jones,	Carrie Edna Russell,	Lowell.
16,	Dora Bell Jones,	Dora Bell Russell,	Lowell.
16,	George Hall Jones,	George Hall Russell,	Lowell.
23,	Abbie Frances Hall,	Abbie Frances Dennison,	Cambridge.
Feb. 27,	Carlotta Mann,	Carlotta Thompson,	Lowell.
Mar. 13,	Elizabeth Mary Tully,	Elizabeth Mary Crosby,	Billerica.
27,	Gertrude Ellis,	Clara Rebecca Robinson,	Lexington.
27,	Katie E. Felch,	Evelyn Katie Waters,	Newton.
27,	Rachel Scott,	Rachel Wagner,	Maynard.
April 3,	Nellie Anderson,	Ella Moulton,	Cambridge.
3,	Minnie May Bodwell,	Daisy Affelhoy,	Malden.
3,	Sarah Lee Bartlett Ryan,	Sarah Lee Bartlett,	Cambridge.
10,	Annie E. Connor,	Annie Elizabeth Connor Baker,	Malden.
10,	Charles Dexter Boutelle,	Charles Dexter Appleton,	Cambridge.
24,	Augustus Bernard Carter Berg,	Edgar Francis Viles,	Waltham.
May 1,	Mary E. Young,	Mary Elizabeth Bickford,	Sherborn.
8,	Emma Louise Ashton,	Emma Louise Blood,	Natick.
June 5,	Carrie Alger,	Carrie Shattuck,	Townsend.
26,	Walter Clark Macy,	Walter Emerson,	Melrose.
July 24,	Effie Abbie Cross,	Effie Abbie Bailey,	Cambridge.
24,	Florence Sibyl Wyman,	Ina Florence Wiggin,	Stoneham.
Sept. 25,	Grace Horton McCleary,	Susan Grace Horton,	Chelsea.
Oct. 2,	Charles Henry Belgea,	Charles Henry Bemis,	Stow.
9,	Margaret Sears,	Maud Berdine Hodgdon,	Somerville.
9,	Bertha Grace,	Jennie Kimball Jewett,	Malden.
9,	James Arthur Bradshaw,	James Arthur Doyle,	Cambridge.
23,	Susan Maria Chamberlain,	Nettie Coffin,	Winchester.
23,	Marnie Burns,	Marnie Lincoln,	Somerville.
23,	Stella E. Beaman,	Stella E. Reed,	Westford.
Nov. 6,	Adeline Hackett,	Edith Helen Poole,	Waltham.
6,	Grace Johanson,	Grace Buzzell,	Everett.
6,	Chevletta Francis Thomas,	Mabel Blanch Atwood,	Lowell.
13,	Annie Cunningham,	Gracie Edna Chapin,	Lowell.
20,	Edith Marion Wetherbee,	Edith Marion Wetherbee Spaulding,	Dunstable.
20,	Grace Welch,	Gracie Annie Felch,	Lowell.
20,	Alice Blodgett,	Gertrude Boynton Hayward,	Somerville.
27,	Robert Henry Hannah,	Robert George Simmons,	Woburn.
Dec. 4,	Estha Valentine Wiggin,	Helen Maria Eastman,	Melrose.
4,	Emma Florence Davis,	Gertrude May Davis,	Lowell.
11,	Woodbury Wallace Sweeney,	Woodbury Wallace Smith,	Wakefield.
11,	Francenia H. Pratt,	Francenia H. Jackson,	Waltham.
11,	William Albert Pratt,	William Albert Jackson,	Waltham.
11,	Ama Francenia Pratt,	Ama Francenia Jackson,	Waltham.
11,	Ida May Pratt,	Ida May Jackson,	Waltham.

* Changed by reason of adoption.

WORCESTER COUNTY.

Date of Decree.	Original Name.	Name Decreed.	Residence.
1877.			
Jan. 16,	——, ...	Maud Eliza Wilder, . .	Sterling.
16,	——, ...	Ernest Warren Howe, . .	West Boylston.
16,	Emma E. Hastings, . .	Emma Hastings Gladwin, .	Worcester.
16,	Charles Edwin Chamberlain,	Charles Edwin Chamberlain Marble, ...	Sutton.
Feb. 6,	Walter Henry Barrell, .	Walter Henry Wallace, .	Winchendon.
6,	Mary Jane Rivers, . .	Mary Jane Blair, . . .	West Boylston.
Mar. 20,	H. Norman Grover, . .	Norman Grover Smith, .	Westborough.
20,	Maud Clary, . . .	Emily Louisa Harper, .	Dudley.
20,	John Herbert Whitney, .	John Herbert Hapgood, .	Leominster.
20,	Oscar Paine Ellison, . .	Oscar Paine Chase, . .	Northbridge.
April 17,	George W. Wright. . .	Oscar Frederick Ball, .	Holden.
17,	Lydia Adelaide Robinson,	Bertha Adelaide Willard, .	Harvard.
May 1,	George Edgar, . . .	George Edgar Heald, .	Southbridge.
1,	Rosa E. Elliott, . . .	Rosa Elmiria Elliott Aldrich,	Oxford.
June 5,	Hattie Francena Clemans, .	Alice Maria Holman, .	Westborough.
5,	Joseph H. Whalon, . .	Joseph Henry Lashna, .	Ashburnham.
5,	Charles M. Whalon, . .	Charles Moses Stainbridge, .	Fitchburg.
5,	Harriet Louisa Landers, .	Harriet Louise Landers Jefferds, ...	Milford.
19,	Flora Augusta Sherman, .	Flora Augusta Johnson, .	Worcester.
July 17,	William Dyer, . . .	William Dyer Sullivan, .	Leominster.
17,	Minnie Adams, . . .	Lillie Adams Rand, .	Clinton.
Sept. 4,	Lillie Adams Rand, . .	Susan Permelia Smith, .	Clinton.
4,	Charlotte Amanda Landers,	Charlotte Amanda Mackowen,	Milford.
18,	Cyrus Bertram Combs, .	Cyrus Bertram Black, .	Princeton.
Oct. 2,	Gertrude M. Farrar, .	Gertrude M. Fletcher, .	Lancaster.
Nov. 6,	Agnes P. Bohonan, . .	Lillian Agnes Willard, .	Fitchburg.
20,	Arlon Jason Moore, . .	Arlon Jason Jeffers, .	Northbridge.
20,	Emma L. Farwell, . .	Gracie Emma Hutchinson, .	Fitchburg.

HAMPSHIRE COUNTY.

Jan. 9,	Bertha H Maurer,* . .	Bertha H. Baker, . .	Amherst.
9,	Herbert Holden,* . .	Herbert P. Bardwell, .	Northampton.
Feb. 6,	Walter S. Hodge,* . .	Walter F. Gaylord, .	Amherst.
July 3,	Annie O. Donnell,* . .	Annie Fahey, . . .	Northampton.
Dec. 5,	Grace E. Chester,* . .	Grace Evelyn Dyer, .	Plainfield.
5,	Mabel Scott,* . . .	Jennie Mabel Sears, .	Plainfield.

HAMPDEN COUNTY.

Jan. 2,	Minnie Elizabeth Goodrich,*	Minnie Estelle Henry, .	Wales.
Feb. 6,	Carl M. Townsend,* . .	Carl Standish Meacham, .	Chicopee.
June 5,	Lewis Raymond Bucklin,*	Louis Raymond Miller, .	Springfield.
Sept. 4,	Kate Fitzgerald,* . .	Kate Hayes, . . .	Springfield.
4,	George Avery Burbank,* .	George Avery Butterfield, .	Springfield.
4,	Emily Etta Miller,* . .	Etta Miller Kelly, . .	Chicopee.
21,	Ella Louisa Freeborn,* .	Edith Ella Abbott, . .	Holyoke.
Oct. 2,	Lillie A. Frohlick,* . .	Lillie A. Miller, . .	Westfield.
Nov. 7,	Susie Aloney Benson,* .	Susie Aloney Wilbur, .	Springfield.
22,	Dennis Mahoney, . .	William Dennis Mahoney, .	Palmer.
Dec. 4,	Henry Taylor,* . . .	Henry Taylor Moran, .	Wilbraham.

* Changed by reason of adoption.

FRANKLIN COUNTY.

Date of Decree.	Original Name.	Name Decreed.	Residence.
1877.			
May 22,	George Weaver,* . . .	Charles W. Amidon, . .	Montague.
Dec. 4,	James M. Sweeney, . . .	James M. Duncan, . . .	Shelburne.

BERKSHIRE COUNTY.

Jan. 4,	Clarence Daniels, . . .	Clarence Daniels Mallery, .	New Ashford.
Mar. 13,	Maud Elizabeth Mullins, . .	Maud Elizabeth Farrar, .	Lee.
May 1,	George Benoit, ...	George Benoit Gordon, . .	Washington.
1,	Nicholas Paddock, . . .	Nicholas Carpenter, . .	Stockbridge.
1,	Lizzie Mason, ...	Lizzie Carpenter, . . .	Stockbridge.
June 5,	William Henry Sanders, . .	William Henry Sanford, .	Pittsfield.
Sept. 4,	Bertha Watson, ...	Bertha Watson Young, . .	Lee.
4,	Theodore Pomeroy Whittelsey,	Theodore Pomeroy Whittlesey Power, ...	Pittsfield.
4,	Charles Whittelsey, . . .	Charles Whittlesey Power, .	Pittsfield.
Oct. 2,	Adelia Sarah Dickinson, . .	Sarah Emily McCarthy, .	Pittsfield.
Nov. 7,	Lettie Bell Lewis, . . .	Lettie Bell Carpenter, .	Pittsfield.
7,	Thomas Kidd, ...	Thomas Charles Hahneman, .	Pittsfield.
Dec. 5,	Grace Mason, ...	Grace Yale, ...	Stockbridge.

NORFOLK COUNTY.

Jan. 24,	Anna H Fisher,* . . .	Anna H. Ware, . . .	Wrentham.
Feb. 28,	Mary Alice Thomas Roach,* .	Carrie Milton Tucker, . .	Milton.
28,	Roy Sumner Smith,* . . .	Roy Sumner Paine, . .	Foxborough.
April 11,	Walter John Welsh,* . . .	Walter John Hade. . .	Quincy.
May 16,	Mary Elizabeth Pierce,* . .	Sadie Frances Dodge, . .	Medfield.
June 20,	—— —— Snell,* . . .	Ellis Gilbert Simpson, . .	Needham.
20,	Grace Howell Smith, . . .	Grace Howell Pond, . .	Norwood.
July 25,	Clara Amelia Howard,* . .	Clara Amelia Johnston, . .	Hyde Park.
Nov. 7,	Lillian Bryant,*	Hope Beatrice Hayes, . .	Brookline.
14,	Nellie Hutchinson,* . . .	Nellie Webb Allen, . .	Braintree.
Oct. 3,	Caroline Elizabeth Cheetham,* .	Caroline Elizabeth Southwick,	Needham.
Dec. 19,	Johanna Bates Bramble,* .	Mabel Bates Burt, . .	Milton.

BRISTOL COUNTY.

Jan. 5,	Rachel Cartledge, . . .	Rachel Crighton, . . .	Fall River.
12,	Ada Medora Carrier, . . .	Ada Medora Leonard, . .	Taunton.
Feb. 2,	William Mitchell, . . .	William Mitchell Briggs, .	Fall River.
Mar. 30,	Eldo Alden Hackett, . .	Eldora Alden Hathaway, .	Taunton.
April 6,	Sarah Crowther, ...	Lena J. Peircy, . . .	Fall River.
20,	Jennie Geagan alias Galligan, .	Ella Jane Mattison, . .	Fall River.
May 11,	Mary S. S. Robinson, . .	Mary S. S. Thomas, . .	New Bedford.
25,	Mary Ann McIntyre, . .	Cornelia Swift Aiken, . .	Westport.
June 15,	Sarah Maria Walker, . .	Sarah Maria Cooley, . .	Taunton.
July 13,	Welcome Square Leonard, .	Welcome Square Borden, .	Westport.
Aug. 3,	Catherine Lowe Hankerson, .	Elizabeth Lowe, . . .	New Bedford.
Nov. 2,	James E. Crowther, . . .	Alfred E. Rainford, . .	New Bedford.
2,	Mary Hannah Crowther, . .	Mary Hannah Higham, . .	New Bedford.
2,	Charles Delano, . . .	Charles Ezra Potter Delano, .	New Bedford.
23,	Margaret Ann McKenzie, .	Margaret Ann McPhee, . .	Attleborough.
30,	Nellie A. Hall, ...	Nellie A. Hopkins, . .	Norton.

* Changed by reason of adoption.

PLYMOUTH COUNTY.

Date of Decree.	Original Name.	Name Decreed.	Residence.
1877.			
Jan. 8,	Mary I. Costello,*	Mary Isabella Clifford,	Kingston.
22,	Estella W Pratt,*	Ella Pratt Stone,	Carver.
Feb. 12,	Samuel Bibley,*.	George Heance,	Plymouth.
April 9,	Etta Brown,*	Ellen Thayer Bourne,	Marshfield.
June 25,	——,*	Marion Whiton Sprague,	Hingham.
Sept. 10,	Lucy F. Vail,*	Sarah Palmer Stone,	Carver.
Oct. 15,	Selina Seldin,*	Selina Haldin,	Brockton.
15,	Barnabas Clark Ellis,	Clark Ellis,	Plymouth.
Nov. 12,	Ira F. Hackett,*.	Ira F. Hathaway,	Wareham.
26,	Moritz Krame,* .	Warren N. Landers,	Brockton.
Dec. 10,	Anna E. Lucas,*	Anna E. Dunham,	Plymouth.
10,	Idella Dean Almy,*	Grace Idella Robbins,	Carver.
24,	Lillian Adelaide Patterson,*	Lillian Adelaide Gayner,	Brockton.

BARNSTABLE COUNTY.

Feb. 13,	Clarence Austin Smith,	Clarence Austin Cook,	Provincetown.
May 14,	Edward Grant Wixon,	Remark E. Wixon,	Dennis.
June 19,	Thomas W. Easterbrooks,	Thomas Smith Easterbrooks,	Barnstable.
Oct. 22,	Otis E. Hawes, .	Otis E. Kelley,	Dennis.

SUFFOLK COUNTY.

1878.			
Jan. 7,	Henry Malone,* .	Charles Howard Lombard,	Boston.
7,	Lillian Eva Tucker,* .	Lillian Eva Brickett,	Lawrence.
7,	Lily O'Rourke,*.	Eva Minerva Smith,	Boston.
14,	Gertrude Maud Williams,*	Gertrude Susan Sherwin,	Boston.
14,	Annie Dillminard,*	Alberta Waters,	New York City.
14,	M. Stanislaus Ochs,	Stanislaus Xavier Boswin,	Boston.
21,	Ellen Judge,*	Nellie Judge Harrison,	Boston.
21,	Allie Jeanette Austin,*	Allie Jeanette Squire,	Boston.
21,	Alna Jane Austin,*	Alna Jane Squire,	Boston.
21,	Edith Elizabeth Leach, formerly Lizzie Cronin,*	Nellie McLaud,	Boston.
21,	Joseph Jacob Hoffert,	Joseph Homer,	Boston.
Feb. 4,	Mary Moore Dean,*	Mary Moore Walker,	Boston.
4,	William McDonald,*	George Edmond Dunham,	Boston.
11,	Colestia Mary Smith,*	Marabell Ruth Mason,	Boston.
18,	Alice Richardson,*	Lina Gertrude Hanson,	Boston.
18,	Lizzie Mabel Norcross.*	Hattie Mabel Tate,	Boston.
18,	Elizabeth Augusta Elliott,*	Elizabth Elliott Reed,	Boston.
18,	Louis Roberts Whitehouse,*	Lou Allen Whitehouse Browne,	Boston.
25,	Arthur Adams,*	Arthur Howard Whitney,	Boston.
25,	Ellen Frances Hews,*	Emma Nickerson,	Boston.
25,	Mary Elizabeth Hoffer,*	Mary Lizzie Sprague,	Boston.
Mar. 4,	Lizzie Wood Marple,*	Lizzie Wood Thompson,	Boston.
4,	Emma Celia Whittemore,*	Pamelia Dana Whitney,.	Boston.
4,	Francis Henry Mattrass,* .	Francis Henry Cowin,	Boston.
4,	Edward Everett Kidney,* .	Edward Everett Balch,	Boston.
4,	Maud ——*	Olla Maud Blackwood,	Boston.
11,	Emma Marshall,*	Gertie May Wainwright,	Boston.
11,	Frankie Brown,*	Frank Walter Bishop,	Boston.
11,	Marietta Wallace,*	Alice Frances Raymond,	Boston.

* Changed by reason of adoption.

SUFFOLK COUNTY — *Continued.*

Date of Decree.	Original Name.	Name Decreed.	Residence.
1878.			
Mar. 18,	Mary Jane Gercett,* . . .	Adrith Hoyt, ...	Boston.
18,	James Albert Fletcher,* . .	James Albert Hanscom, . .	Boston.
25,	Gertrude Musso Purrington,* .	Josie Ella Silsby, . . .	Boston.
April 1,	Mary Brown Noyes,* . .	Harriet Allen Bedlington, .	Boston.
15,	Mary Donovan,* . . .	Mary Emma Whiteside, .	Boston.
15,	Mary Stewart,*	Cora Edith Burnham, . .	Boston.
22,	Oscar Alexis Simmerström, .	Oscar Alexis Norman, . .	Boston.
29,	Isabella Graham,* . . .	Isabella Frances Belcher, .	Boston.
29,	Mary Elizabeth Hayes,* . .	Rebecca Eunice Hill, . .	Boston.
29,	Blanche May Howe,*. . .	Blanche May Gerrish, . .	Boston.
May 6,	Dora Bachelder,* . . .	Dora Smith, ...	Wakefield.
6,	Leland Peters,*	Leland Weeks, . . .	Boston.
6,	Francis James Peters,* . .	Francis James Weeks, . .	Boston.
6,	John Wood Goldthwait,* . .	Frank Ayres Daggett, . .	Boston.
6,	Eugene Sanborn,* . . .	Asa Howard Emery, . .	Boston.
13,	Leroy Owens,*	Cuthbert Parkhurst Redder, .	Boston.
13,	Edwin Bliss Wright,* . .	George Otis Eaton, . . .	Boston.
20,	Willy Curley,*	Willie Weeks, ...	Boston.
20,	Jennie Marzynski, . . .	Jennie Mason, ...	Boston.
20,	Waldo Henry Marzynski, . .	Waldo Henry Marzynski Mason, ...	Boston.
20,	Henry Marzynski, . . .	Henry Marzynski Mason, .	Boston.
20,	William Myers,* . . .	Frederick Mercer, . . .	Boston.
20,	Alice Loring,*	Florence Isabelle Garrett, .	Boston.
20,	Richard Tuttle Bradlee,* . .	Willy Charles Erras, . .	Boston.
27,	Rollin Allain Goodenough, .	Stanislas Allain Farley, . .	Boston.
27,	Alfred O'Connor, *alias* Grant,*	Frederick Grant Young, . .	Boston.
27,	Frank Henry Dewey,* . .	Frank Dewey Hodgkins, .	Boston.
27,	Wendell Jones Faber,* . .	Ernest McGauley, . . .	Boston.
27,	Henry Frank Dewey,* . .	Henry Dewey Hodgkins, .	Boston.
27,	Eleanor Shattuck Goodenough, .	Eleanor Shattuck Farley, .	Boston.
June 3,	John Thomas Tyman,* . .	George Herbert Cameron, .	Boston.
3,	Eva Hyde,*	Ella Frances Pierce, . .	Boston.
3,	Grace Richards Hitt, . .	Grace Richards Drake, . .	Boston.
3,	Fred Crouse Piper, . . .	Fred Crouse Raymond, . .	Boston.
3,	Josiah Fletcher Osgood, . .	Fletcher Osgood, . . .	Chelsea.
10,	George Peterson,* . . .	Thomas Charles Robertson, .	Boston.
10,	Carrie May Hurley,* . . .	Carrie May Dodge, . . .	Boston.
17,	Ruth Preston,*	Ida May Clifford, . . .	Boston.
17,	William Williams,* . . .	Frank Crane, ...	Boston.
17,	Eva Adeline Brown,* . .	Eva Adeline Black, . .	Boston.
24,	Arthur Henry Crompton,* .	Arthur Henry Wright, . .	Boston.
July 22,	Lillian Wilkinson Spellman,* .	Lillian Wilkinson Potter, .	Boston.
22,	Gertrude Fuller,* . . .	Rae Blanche Silsby, . .	Boston.
29,	Mary C. Clark, ...	Mary C. Reynolds, . . .	Chelsea.
29,	Agnes Gardner,* . . .	May Marcy Henderson, . .	Boston.
Aug. 19,	Lucy Evans,*	Jennie Alice Bovyer, . .	Boston.
19,	Grace Gouldrop,* . . .	Bertha Viola Grindle, . .	Boston.
Sept. 16,	Lillian Bell Lyon,* . . . ‘.	Ethel Elmira Ford, . . .	Boston.
23,	John Christopher Brickley, .	John Christopher Brickley Bryant, ...	Boston.
23,	Bertha Elsasser,* . . .	Bertha Elsasser Ryan, . .	Boston.
23,	Catherine Elsasser,* . . .	Catherine Elsasser Russell Laforme, ...	Boston.
30,	Frank Chapman,* . . .	William Howard Hill, . .	Boston.
30,	Augusta Frederika Moses,* .	Augusta Frederika Reuter, .	Boston.
Oct. 7,	Laura Louise Hall,* . . .	Laura Louise Vore, . .	Lowell.
7,	Grace Lillian Partridge,* . .	Grace Helen Clifford, . .	Boston.
7,	Lizzie Florence Partridge,* .	Angie May Robinson, . .	Boston.
28,	Child of Annie E. Newell,* .	Ethlyn Gertrude Wood, . .	Boston.
28,	Katie Alma West,* . . .	Kathleen Hamilton Malloch, .	Boston.

* Changed by reason of adoption.

SUFFOLK COUNTY — *Concluded.*

Date of Decree.	Original Name.	Name Decreed.	Residence.
1878.			
Oct. 28,	Mary Eliza Lee,* . . .	Ethel Mary Cheney, . .	Boston.
Nov. 4,	Mary Jane Gordon, otherwise Mary Hines,*	Ellen Maria Murphy, . .	Boston.
Dec. 9,	Patrick Francis Flaherty, .	Patrick Flaherty Ferris, . .	Boston.
16,	Grace Elizabeth Madden,* .	Florence Agnes Humphrey, .	Boston.
23,	Flora Fleming,*	Ruth Ruby Frost, . . .	Boston.
23,	Lucius Clark Edwards, jun.,* .	Louis Shirley Chase, . .	Boston.
23,	Minnie Engel Schemmel,* . .	Georgianna Williams, . .	Boston.
30,	Minnie Smith,*	Lillian Pierce Howard, . .	Boston.

ESSEX COUNTY.

Jan. 7,	Emma Bohring,* . . .	Emma Brown, . . .	Salisbury.
19,	Susan Myrtle,*	Susan Gardner, . . .	Methuen.
28,	Caroline Goldie,* . . .	Eva Maud Emlyn, . . .	Lynn.
Feb. 4,	Arthur P. Lincoln,* . . .	Arthur P. Poor, . . .	Danvers.
18,	Josephine Rollins,* . . .	Josephine Beaver, . . .	Salem.
27,	Eva Louisa Dalrymple, . .	Eva Louisa Creesy, . . .	Salem.
April 1,	Paul Sieber, *alias* Jacob Sieber,*	Willie Everett Hollis, . .	Lynn.
1,	Elizabeth Adelaide Stevens,* .	Elizabeth Florence Potter, .	Boxford.
8,	Charles A. Kent,* . . .	Charles A. Clark, . . .	Beverly.
15,	Frank Perry,*	Frank Hoyt, ...	Newburyport.
15,	Hattie Childs,*	Helen Adelaide Butler, . .	Lynn.
22,	Margaret Florence Charlotte Olson,*	Ann Allison Crawford, . .	Lawrence.
May 6,	Frederick Norman Sherwood,* .	Frederick Sherwood Webb, .	Salem.
13,	Eleanor May,*	Gertrude May Banks, . .	Haverhill.
27,	Mary E. O'Brine, . .	Mary E. Emerson, . . .	Haverhill.
June 10,	James Goodhue,* . . .	James Goodhue Tuttle, . .	Salem.
24,	Elizabeth W. Soule, . . .	Elizabeth W. Pike, . . .	Salisbury.
Oct. 7,	Jessie M. Noyes,* . . .	Jessie Malcalm Hutchins, .	Lynn.
Dec. 15,	Charles Walter Allston, . .	Charles Walter Allston Thurston, ...	Lynn.

MIDDLESEX COUNTY.

Jan. 1,	Susan Parsons, ...	Miniola Landry, . . .	Lowell.
1,	Lilly Abbott, *alias* Lilly Edinborough, ...	Eva Carrie Wright, . .	Medford.
15,	Frederick H. Hathaway, . .	George Melvin Wascott, . .	Newton.
22,	Hattie Livingstone, . .	Hattie Jane Buchanan, . .	Lowell.
Feb. 5,	Charles Frederick Gifford, .	Charles Frederick Raymond,	Cambridge.
5,	Emma Anderson, . . .	Anna Maria Newhall Clough,	Cambridge.
5,	Herbert Lincoln Crawford, .	Lincoln Crawford Heywood, .	Belmont.
5,	Clara Forbush Cutler, . .	Clara Adelaid Forbush, . .	Natick.
12,	Marion Marks, . . .	Harriet Hartwell Knowlton, .	Lowell.
Mar. 5,	Esther Ann Roberts, . .	Mary Etta Kimball, . .	Wakefield.
5,	William T. Pierson, . .	Harrie Elton Ward, . .	Somerville.
12,	Emma Axtell, . . .	Emma Louisa Hinckley, . .	Malden.
19,	Susan E. Chase, . . .	Susan Everline Wheeler, . .	Somerville.
26,	Mary Jones, ...	Grace Emily Cooper, . .	Natick.
April 9,	Maude Florence McInnes, .	Maude Florence Collins, . .	Medford.
23,	Harold Moore, ...	Harold Woodbury Davis, . .	Waltham.
23,	Albert James Fisher Kelley, .	Ralph Ernest Mayhew, . .	Cambridge.
May 7,	Charles Miller, ...	Henry Parks Sherman, . .	Wayland.

* Changed by reason of adoption

MIDDLESEX COUNTY — *Concluded.*

Date of Decree.	Original Name.		Name Decreed.		Residence.
1878.					
May 14,	Grace Abbie Colburn,	. .	Grace Abbie Gates,	. .	Framingham.
21,	Gertrude Ball, . .	. .	Gertrude Fairchild,	. .	Stoneham.
28,	Frank P. Burgin,	. .	Frank Penly Briggs,	. .	Ayer.
28,	Fred B. Burgin, .	. .	Fred Byron Briggs,	. .	Ayer.
June 4,	May A. Colburn,	. .	Maud Coburn,	. .	Hopkinton.
25,	Lydia Lincoln Choate,	. .	Lydia Lincoln Choate Wright,	.	Sudbury.
July 16,	Louis James Munroe,	. .	Louis James McDonnell,	.	Lowell.
16,	Jennette Lizzie James,	. .	Jennette Lizzie Stratton,	.	Lincoln.
23,	Mary Adellah Thayer,	. .	Mary Adellah Howorth,	.	Malden.
Aug. 6,	Isabella White, . .	. .	Isabella Stephenson,	. .	Cambridge.
6,	Harriet Thompson, .	. .	Harriet Louise Symmes,	.	Arlington.
Sept. 3,	——, . .	. .	Charlotte Maria Therese Wieland, . . .	. .	Medford.
17,	Jennie E. Clifton,	. .	Mabel Jane Trombley,	. .	Lowell.
24,	Arthur W. Richardson,	. .	Arthur Warren Richardson,	.	Woburn.
Oct. 22,	Susie McGonigle,	. .	Susie Doherty,	. .	Stoneham.
22,	Mabel Jane Trombley,	. .	Maud Clifton Pinkham,	.	Lowell.
Nov. 19,	Nellie E. Freeman, .	. .	Nellie Endora Booby,	.	Lowell.
19,	Edith White, . .	. .	Edith Brookings White Sanborn, . . .	. .	Somerville.
19,	Gertrude Black, . .	. .	Gertrude Beatrice Gregg,	.	Watertown.
26,	Evangeline Longfellow,	. .	Grace Morrill Teele,	. .	Somerville.

WORCESTER COUNTY.

Jan. 1,	Mary Robinson,	. .	Lizzie Scott Buckley,	. .	Northbridge.
1,	Lizzie Bohring, .	. .	Lizzie Jeannette Perry, .	.	Athol.
1,	Willie Ethan Allen, .	. .	William Ethan Allen,	. .	Worcester.
15,	Maria Leahey, .	. .	Maud Anne Kelley,	. .	Oxford.
Feb. 5,	Katie Baldwin, .	. .	Florence May Litchfield,	.	Lunenburg.
5,	——, . .	. .	Freddie Gilbert Hale,	. .	Royalston.
5,	Elizabeth A. Patrick,	. .	Elizabeth Adelaide Potter,	.	Worcester.
19,	Caroline Callon, .	. .	Ellen Caroline Gleason, .	.	Sturbridge.
Mar. 5,	Michael Harrigan,	. .	Frank Webster Allen,	. .	Warren.
19,	Isabella Gould, .	. .	Mary Bell Harris, .	. .	Worcester.
19,	Mabel Pierson Percy,	. .	Alice Mabel Talbot,	. .	Hubbardston.
19,	Blanche Pigeon, ,	. .	Jennie Blanche Thompson,	.	Worcester.
April 2,	Addie Laura Foster, .	. .	Addie May Willoughby,	.	Fitchburg.
2,	Eugene Brigham Fuller,	. .	Frank Eugene Brigham,	.	Oakham.
9,	Sarah Jaques, . .	. .	Sarah Elizabeth Bradbury,	.	Millbury.
May 7,	Edward Bassett, *alias* Edward Hoxie, . . .	.	Charles Sumner Whitney Wright, . . .	.	Harvard.
7,	Carl Klinschuster,	. .	Carl Mohr, . .	.	Worcester.
21,	Sylvia Ann Byam,	. .	Sylvia Sabry Bemis,	.	Royalston.
21,	Wallace L. Lane,	. .	Wallace L. Sargent,	.	Lancaster.
Sept. 3,	Samuel Parkinson,	. .	Minot Volney Bastian,	.	Clinton.
3,	Bessie Maria Acres, .	. .	Bessie Elizabeth Parmenter,	.	Princeton.
17,	Susie Lewis,	. .	Lizzie Mabel Austin,	. .	Oakham.
Nov. 7,	Sarah J. Woodward, .	. .	Sarah J. Billings, .	. .	Athol.
19,	George Washington Onthank,	.	George Washington Rice,	.	Southborough.
26,	Kate Boyle, . .	. .	Maud Rena Walker,	. .	Fitchburg.
Dec. 17,	——, . .	. .	Frances Louisa Doane,	.	Warren.
17,	Mabel Arbing, . .	. .	Ethel Marion Lillie,	. .	Milford.

HAMPSHIRE COUNTY.

Mar. 6,	Charles Washington, .	. .	Charles Arthur Cole,	. .	Northampton.
April 3,	Mary Hannah Fitzgerald, .	.	Mary Hannah Eager,	. .	Northampton.

HAMPSHIRE COUNTY — *Concluded.*

Date of Decree.	Original Name.	Name Decreed.	Residence.
1878.			
June 4,	Agnes Bolton, ...	Agnes Bolton Howard, . .	Amherst.
July 2,	Florence Ann Frizello, . .	Hattie Mary Redding, . .	Amherst.
Dec. 17,	Emma Louisa Barton, . .	Emma M. Sprague, . .	Ware.

HAMPDEN COUNTY.

Feb. 5,	Lottie Annie Estella Lee, . .	Lottie Annie Estella Manegin,	Longmeadow.
Mar. 11,	Foundling, ...	Gertrude May Smith, . .	Holyoke.
April 2,	Gracie Miellez, ...	Grace Judson Root, . .	Hartford, Ct.
May 7,	Dwight Varnum Dixon, . .	Harry Dwight Tuttle, . .	Holyoke.
June 4,	Ralph Howard Farrington, .	Ralph Howard Nevins, . .	Holyoke.
July 3,	Desmond Annis Taisey, .	Bertha Augusta Smith, . .	Holyoke.
3,	Frederick Lapworth Eastman, .	George Gilbert Tucker, . .	Westfield.
Aug. 1,	Annie May Ross, . . .	Annie May Coomes, . .	Springfield.
Sept. 4,	Henry Powell Hughes, . .	Henry Powell Tye, . . .	Chicopee.
Nov. 6,	Mabel Chandler, . . .	Lucy Augusta Barton, . .	West Springfield.
Dec. 3,	Lena Davis, ...	Lena Jones, ...	Chicopee.

FRANKLIN COUNTY.

Jan. 15,	—— ——*	Nettie L. Hale, . . .	Gill.
Mar. 5,	Isaletta B. Smith,* . .	Isaletta B. Thompson, . .	New Salem.
May 7,	Mary A. Burnham,* . .	Eva Turner, ...	Greenfield.
21,	Ella A. Anthoine,* . . .	Ella O. Holman, . . .	Montague.
June 4,	Emma F. Smith, . . .	Emma F. Clifford, . . .	Northfield.
4,	Lucinda A. Hore,* . . .	Angeline Freeman, . . .	Conway.
Sept. 3,	Bela A. Wilds,* . . .	George N. Bryant, . . .	Ashfield.
3,	Ellen L. Flagg,* . . .	Ellen L. Mack, . . .	Orange.
Dec. 3,	Walter H. Saxton,* . . .	William M. Fisher, . .	Montague.
10,	James E. Bliss,* . . .	James E. Luisea, . . .	Orange.

BERKSHIRE COUNTY.

Feb. 5,	Alton Wesley Fielding, .	Alton Wesley Rouse, . .	Tyringham.
6,	Elizabeth Peterson, . .	Mary Elizabeth Olds, . .	Pittsfield.
April 3,	Willard Bainbridge Brown, .	Charles William Ackerson, .	Lee.
June 4,	Gratia A. Burr, . . .	Gratia A. Chamberlin, . .	Dalton.
4,	Hattie Maria Degothard, .	Hattie Maria Hall, . . .	W. Stockbridge.
July 16,	Gertrude Horan, . . .	Gertrude Eaton. . . .	Pittsfield.
16,	Evyline Cadwell, . . .	Evyline Cadwell Shaw, . .	W. Stockbridge.
16,	Ellen A. Welch, . . .	Ellen A. Dwyre, . . .	Hinsdale.
16,	Thomas John Francis Welch, .	Thomas Francis O'Connor, .	Dalton.
18,	Fred Darwin Mosher, . .	Fred Darwin Field, . .	Adams.
Sept. 3,	Charles P. Welch, . .	Charles P. Ryan, . . .	Hinsdale.
Nov. 6,	Charles Henry Schultz, .	George Herman Knapp, .	Pittsfield.

NORFOLK COUNTY.

Mar. 6,	Sarah Alice Hoyt, . . .	Grace Lillian Bill, . . .	Chelsea.
20,	John Isaac Willett, . . .	John Lewis Caldwell, . .	Hanson.

* Changed by reason of adoption.

NORFOLK COUNTY — *Concluded.*

Date of Decree.	Original Name.	Name Decreed.	Residence.
1878.			
April 17,	Mary Dodge, ...	Mary Ella Newton, . .	Boston.
May 22,	Marian Chester Flynn, . .	Marian Chester Deane, . .	Machiasport, Me.
July 17,	Mary Elizabeth Anderson, .	Marian Lewis Pierce, . .	Boston.
Nov. 20,	William Francis Rourke, . .	Frank Long, ...	Medfield.

BRISTOL COUNTY.

Feb. 8,	James B. T. Robinson, . .	James B. Thomas, . . .	New Bedford.
Mar. 15,	Fernando Franklin Hart, .	Frank Hart Gifford, . .	Dartmouth.
22,	Anne Sophia Swain, . .	Edith Gray Silva, . . .	New Bedford.
April 5,	Sarah Elizabeth Harding, .	Sarah Elizabeth Burgess Harding, ...	Somerset.
5,	Mary A. H. Shepherd, . .	Mary A. H. Clark, . .	New Bedford.
May 3,	Annie Bismore, . . .	Annie Bismore Barrett, . .	Dartmouth.
3,	Isabel Swain Bismore, . .	Isabel Swain Barrett, . .	Dartmouth.
3,	William Henry Peck, .	James Butler Sanford, . .	New Bedford.
17,	Arthur Herbert Wordell, . .	Arthur Herbert Hack, . .	New Bedford.
24,	William Goodwin, . . .	William Goodwin Jenney, .	Foxborough.
24,	Elle Perett, ...	Minnie Kinghorn Crossley, .	Fall River.
July 5,	Charles Sandford Almy, . .	Charles Sandford Remington,	Mattapoisett.
Aug. 2,	Edmund Baylies, . . .	Edmund Lincoln Baylies, .	Taunton.
Sept. 6,	Alvin H Mills, ...	Alvin H. Young, . . .	Westport.
20,	Lizzie Terry, ...	Lizzie Terry Williston, . .	New Bedford.
Oct. 11,	Bertha Leavett Jackson, . .	Bertha Scott Frink, . .	Attleborough.
Nov. 7,	Eliza J. Luscomb, . . .	Eliza J. Culver, . . .	New Bedford.
Dec. 6,	Mary Ellen Sullivan, .	Mary Ellen Cavanaugh, .	Fall River.
6,	Nellie Clifton Gifford, .	Nellie Clifton Devoll, . .	New Bedford.
17,	Willie Carlton Sherman, .	Willie Carlton Cook, . .	Mansfield.

PLYMOUTH COUNTY.

Jan. 14,	Joanna O'Donnell,* . . .	Isabel Maria Damon, . .	Scituate.
April 15,	———,*	Arthur S. Studley, . . .	South Scituate.
May 13,	John F. Callahan,* . .	Edgar S. Hills, . . .	Scituate.
13,	Mabel A. Blankenship,* . .	Mabel Augusta Curtis, . .	South Scituate.
13,	Charles E. Glass,* . . .	Charles E. Soule, . . .	Duxbury.
13,	Jeremiah Sullivan, . .	Walter Pierce, . . .	Hanover.
Aug. 26,	Laura A. Walker,* . . .	Bertha M. Dobson, . .	South Abington.
Sept. 26,	Mary Shefford,* . . .	Charlotte Kierstead, .	Plymouth.
Nov. 11,	———,*	Ella Frances Kenerson, .	Hingham.
25,	Gertrude B. Gray,* . . .	Gertrude Borden Otis, .	South Scituate.
Dec. 9,	Annie Warren,*	Annie Warren Bartlett, . .	Kingston.

BARNSTABLE COUNTY.

Aug. 13,	David Look Hallet, . . .	Leander Lothrop Hallet, .	Dennis.

* Changed by reason of adoption.

SUFFOLK COUNTY.

Date of Decree.	Original Name.	Name Decreed.	Residence.
1879.			
Jan. 13,	Alfred Spurr,*	Frank Leon Phelps,	Boston.
13,	Julia Sabbatee,*.	Julia Addie Pike,	Boston.
Feb. 3,	Julia Viola Pike,	Viola Jay Merrill,	Boston.
3,	Grace Flowers,*.	Helen Edith Aldrich,	Boston.
3,	Jennie Richards,*	Grace Phelps Woodbridge,	Boston.
17,	Daniel Graham,*	William Elmer Clark,	Boston.
17,	Hannah Hallason,*	Annie Gwynne Applebee,	Boston.
17,	Frances Farrell,*	Effie May Buffum,	Boston.
Mar. 3,	Helen Allen,*	Helen Lydia Frost,	Boston.
3,	Louia Thomas Chase,*	Louia Chase Dennett,	Boston.
3,	William Cody,* .	William Boyd Roberts,	Boston.
3,	Ina Rosabel Marshfield,*	Ina Rosabel Bond,	Boston.
10,	Josephine A. Murphy,	Josephine A. Ayers,	Boston.
10,	Henry Grunbaum,	Henry Green,	Boston.
10,	Julia Grunbaum,	Julia Green,	Boston.
10,	Warren Drew,*	Warren Abbot Smith,	Boston.
17,	Minnie Haynes,*	Minnie Abbott Hewett,	Boston.
April 7,	George Sidney Wheelock,	Sidney Wheelock,	Boston.
14,	Mary Ann Berdens,* .	Anne Platt Kitching,	Boston.
May 5,	Tina Brown,*	Anne McGlinn,	Boston.
12,	Henry F. Schnück,	Henry F. Shaneck,	Boston.
12,	Herman G. Schnück, .	Herman G. Shaneck,	Boston.
12,	Frank Burchard,*	Frank Campbell,	Boston.
12,	Herbert Walton,*	Robert Warren Dill,	Boston.
19,	Mabel Boyd,*	Mabel Boykin,	Boston.
19,	Isadora Haley, .	Isadora Leavitt,	Boston.
26,	Jacob Backhaus,	Jacob Becker,	Boston.
June 2,	Charles Backhaus,	Charles Becker,	Boston.
9,	Alice Gertrude Patten,	Alice Gertrude Patten Laurie,	Boston.
9,	Herbert Sawyer Patten,	Herbert Sawyer Patten Laurie,	Boston.
16,	Benjamin McKinstry Willis,	Hamilton Willis,	Boston.
16,	John Holland,* .	John Holland Driscoll,	Cambridge.
16,	Michael Holland,*	Michael Holland Driscoll,	Cambridge.
30,	Sarah Ann Mabel Kendrick,*	Sarah Ann Mabel Hurie,	Boston.
30,	Emily Mary Kendrick.*	Emily Mary Kendrick Hurie,	Boston.
30,	John William Kendrick,* .	John William Kendrick Hurie,	Boston.
July 7,	—— ——,* .	Mabel Kaulbach Balch,	Boston.
14,	Earl Moody,*	William Edmund Leggett,	Boston.
14,	Grace McDonald,*	Grace Belle Dodds,	Boston.
21,	Marietta ——,* .	Marietta Guardenier,	Boston.
28,	Lizzie May Darrell,* .	Elsie Dinsmore Keniston,	Boston.
28,	Samuel Manning,*	Henry Samuel Dodds,	Boston.
Sept. 1,	Henry Dubelle,*	Henry Willard Starkey,	Boston.
Oct. 6,	Mary Brennan,* .	Mary Sullivan,	New York City.
6,	George Brennan,*	George Sullivan,	New York City.
13,	Thomas Prudent Yuertein,	Thomas Prudent Brown,	Boston.
27,	Emma Justine Cleveland,*	Emma Justine Mitchell,	Chelsea.
27,	Mary Wilson,* .	Nellie Mehitable Davis,	Boston.
Nov. 17,	Mary Carlan,*	Mary Elizabeth McCann,	Chelsea.
17,	Maud Hersey,* .	Lottie Wheeler Clark,	Boston.
17,	Charles Blanchard.* .	Charles Blanchard Eaton,	Boston.
17,	George Lewis Trott,* .	George Lewis Smith,	Boston.
24,	Catherine Hughes,* .	Mabel Elsie Mochmore,	Boston.
Dec. 1,	Samuel Tilden,* .	Joseph Brett Dennison,	Boston.
8,	Ellen Louisa Trott,	Ellen Louisa Smith,	Boston.
8,	Mary Dyer.*	Cora Ann Harris,	Boston.
22,	Anthony Wayne Strouss, .	Anthony Wayne Strauss,	Boston.
22,	Alice Gertrude Choate,* .	Eleanor Howard Dean,	Boston.
22,	John Graham or John Grames,	John Graham,	Boston.

* Changed by reason of adoption.

ESSEX COUNTY.

Date of Decree.	Original Name.	Name Decreed.	Residence.
1879.			
Jan. 13,	Mary Wilson,*	Annie Rose Crocker,	Woodstock, N. B.
Feb. 17,	Katie Cummings,*	Kate Blanchard Hill,	Jersey City, N. J.
Mar. 10,	Stephen Francis Mullin,*	Stephen Francis Metcalf,	Lawrence.
17,	Esther A. Bowden,*	Alice Atwood Morgan,	Topsfield.
17,	Michael Thomas McDermott,	Thomas Riley McDermott,	Danvers.
April 7,	Thomas Gould, 2d,	Thomas Franklin Gould,	Topsfield.
14,	Lewis Brewster Cobb,*	Lewis Brewster Cobb Dolloff,	Manchester, N. H.
14,	Maud Estelle McConihe,*	Maud Estelle Kimball,	Haverhill.
28,	Mabel Story,*	Mildred Suratt,	Rockport.
May 19,	Katie Corbett,*	Katie Corbett Cahill,	Boston.
19,	John Franklin Fall,	John Franklin Moulton,.	Haverhill.
July 7,	Florence Ruth Snow,*	Mabel Blanche Fogg,	New Hampshire.
7,	Philip Vergnies Learoyd,	Francis Vergnies Learoyd,	Saugus.
14,	Henry L. Kenney,*	Lyall Henry Coulie,	New Bedford.
Sept. 1,	Susan McPhee,*.	Susan Hodgkins,	Rockport.
1,	Ella F. McDuffie,	Ella F. Eaton,	Salem.
Oct. 20,	Carrie Bush,*	Carrie Bush Tappan,	Ulster, Pa.
Nov. 3,	Maud Dyer,*	Myra F. Sherman,	Lynn.
17,	Ella Louisa Middlebrook,*	Ella Maud Millward,	Providence, R. I.
Dec. 15,	Mabel Lucretia Hadley,*	Jesse Eva Jellison,	Cambridge.

MIDDLESEX COUNTY.

Date of Decree.	Original Name.	Name Decreed.	Residence.
Jan. 7,	Ann Maria Girdlestone,*	Anna Maria Dimond,	Newton.
14,	Grace May Wainwright,*	Grace May Gooding,	Somerville.
28,	Nettie Smart,*	Maud Evelyn Doore,	Lowell.
28,	Mary Alice Preston,*	Mary Alice Hasey,	Lowell.
Feb. 4,	George H. Lang,*	Samuel William Cushing,	Waltham.
25,	Frederick Wellington,	Albert Elbridge Wellington,	Somerville.
Mar. 4,	Anne Sullivan,*	Anne Bell Caverly,	Lowell.
4,	Flora Bell Glynn,*	Flora Bell Stinehart,	Somerville.
18,	Anne Baker,*	Mabel Annie McCoy,	Lowell.
25,	Edward Freeman,*	Fred Freeman Underwood,	Framingham.
April 1,	Beatriss Kildruff,*	Luella Florence McIntire,	Somerville.
8,	Manuel Marcaut,*	Wendell Phillips Patterson,	Newton.
22,	George Alfred Washburne,*	George Alfred Williams,	Lowell.
May 6,	Mary Reily,	Mary Reily Scully,.	Malden.
6,	Albert E. Emery,*	Albert Edward Hutchins,	Lexington.
6,	George Willard Brown,	Willard Brown,	Lowell.
13,	Catharine Ensign Henry,*	Catharine Ensign Bigelow,	Melrose.
20,	Mary Ellen Eagan,*	Mary Ellen Shephard,	Lowell.
20,	Guy Lester Smart,*	Albert Henry Briggs,	Lowell.
20,	Mabel Conley,*	Mabel May Skiff,	Marlborough.
27,	Gertrude Harrington,*	Gertrude May Weeks,	Melrose.
27,	Joseph George Dugnay,*	Joseph George Le Blanc,	Lowell.
June 10,	Alice Drew,*	Alice Drew Proper,	Lowell.
10,	William R. Gibbins,*	Henry Alexander Brosseau,	Cambridge.
24,	Mary Carroll,*	Mary Burns,	Cambridge.
July 1,	Lettie Jane Anderson,*	Lettie Jane Burgin,	Waltham.
8,	Mary Belle Henderson,*	May Belle Brooks,	Somerville.
8,	Ida Foster Henderson,*	Ida Frances Brooks,	Somerville.
15,	Viva Idella Smart,*	Viva Idella Perry,	Chelmsford.
15,	Luther Leland,*.	Luther Taylor,	Hopkinton.
Aug. 19,	Josephine Fuller,*	Josephine Martin,	Cambridge.
19,	Lewis Center Clark,	Edward Lewis Center Clark,.	Cambridge.
23,	Frederick Montgomery McKay,*	Frederick McKay Montgomery,	Cambridge.
Sept. 23,	Nancy Locke Richmond,	Annie Locke Richmond,	Lowell.

* Changed by reason of adoption.

MIDDLESEX COUNTY — *Concluded.*

Date of Decree.	Original Name.	Name Decreed.	Residence.
1879.			
Oct. 7,	Nellie Maud Philbrick,*	Ann Maria Searles,	Billerica.
7,	Hattie Etta Jones,*	Mary Emma Hartley,	Melrose.
7,	Nellie A. Burk,*	Florence Greenwood Taber,	Malden.
7,	Fannie A. Fulcher,*	Maria Frances Fiske,	Weston.
14,	Mary Ellen Ford,*	Grace Eveline Caul,	Watertown.
14,	Daisy Mason,*	Lottie May Thomas,	Waltham.
28,	Charles Philbrick,*	Charles Bernard Tufts,	Billerica.
Nov. 11,	Mary Jane Baxter,*	Anna Maria Welch,	Lowell.
18,	Charles Hews Greenwood,*	Charles Nason Bramhall,	Cambridge.
25,	Maud Ike French,*	Maud French Marshall,	Lowell.
Dec. 2,	Madora Hawes,*	Dora Harndon Emerson,	Wakefield.
9,	Mabel Frances Durocher,*	Lulu Blanch Marsh,	Lowell.
23,	Charles W. Witherell,*	Charles Elliott Currier,	Lowell.
23,	Maud Clifton Pinkham,*	Jennie Etta Clifton,	Lowell.

WORCESTER COUNTY.

Date of Decree.	Original Name.	Name Decreed.	Residence.
Jan. 7,	Alice E. Waltzo,*	Alice Evelyn Barrows,	Brookfield.
21,	James T. Haywood,*	James T. Black,	Sturbridge.
21,	Mary Alice Haywood,*	Mary Alice Black,	Sturbridge.
21,	Elinor Alice Skinner,*	Alice Elinor Walker,	Clinton.
Feb. 4,	Delima Rabert,*	Delia Fovand,	Dudley.
4,	Joseph Rabert,*	Joseph Loiselle,	Webster.
4,	Sarah Elizabeth Johnson,*	Cora Louise Spencer,	Uxbridge.
18,	Margaret Grover,*	Jennie Amy Taft,	Upton.
25,	Bertha S. Smith,*	Bertha S. Lewis,	Fitchburg.
Mar. 18,	Harvey Clinton York,*	George Hayden Smith,	Fitchburg.
April 1,	Moses Wilber Partridge,*	Wilber Partridge Vinton,	Dudley.
15,	Mabel Caniff,*	Mabel Fessenden,	Templeton.
15,	Etta Cosseboon,*	Etta Adelia Chamberlin,	Southbridge.
15,	Clifton Eugene Parkman,*	Clifton Eugene Albee,	Dana.
15,	Pearl Parker,*	Pearl Parker Buxton,	Milford.
15,	Anna Richards,*	Anna R. Brewer,	Clinton.
May 6,	Brida Sawyer,*	Lelia Bertha Wood,	Northborough.
June 3,	Julia Nellie Kimball,*	Gertrude Tyler Gould,	Westborough.
24,	Frank F. Gates,*	Robert Franklin Fairbanks,	Fitchburg.
July 1,	Lillian Palfrey,*	Mary Josephine Johnson,	Milford.
15,	Charles Albee Chickering,*	Charles Edgar Albee,	Dudley.
Sept. 2,	Hattie Maria Morse,*	Hattie Morse Taylor,	Sutton.
Oct. 7,	Ada Louisa Smith,*	Ada Louisa Battersby,	Petersham.
Nov. 18,	Frank Eugene Preston,*	Frank Preston Bascom,	Clinton.
Dec. 10,	Frank Gilbert Hooper,*	Leon William Doane,	Warren.
23,	—— Simonds,*	Ethel Susan Brocklebank	Fitchburg.

HAMPSHIRE COUNTY.

Date of Decree.	Original Name.	Name Decreed.	Residence.
Feb. 4,	Edmund Clark,*	Edmund Miles,	Amherst.
8,	Henry Eugene Hudson,*	Henry Eugene Rawson,	Northampton.
Mar. 4,	Inez Ema Damon,*	Inez Belle Tileston,	Williamsburg.
April 1,	Jennie Maria Robinson,*	Jennie Adeline Patrill,	Greenwich.
May 6,	Archie M. Phelps,*	Archie Phelps Graves,	Hatfield.
Sept. 2,	——*	William Edward Mather,	Hadley.
2,	Alice Kershaw,	Alice Holmes,	Ware.
Oct. 7,	Kate Bakeman,	Kate Conley,	Northampton.
7,	Freddie Durand,*	Freddie Randall,	Huntington.
Nov. 5,	Mary Henrietta Blanchard,*	Etta Louise Bliss,	Amherst.

* Changed by reason of adoption.

HAMPDEN COUNTY.

Date of Decree.	Original Name.	Name Decreed.	Residence.
1879.			
Feb. 18,	Cora May Hooper,* . . .	Cora May Cady, . . .	Springfield.
18,	Henry Augustine Storey,* .	Henry Augustine Soper, .	Westfield.
Mar. 4,	Lucy Glyton Stacy,* . .	Lucy Glyton Brown, . .	Monson.
19,	Ethlyn Day Fowler,* . .	Sadie Holcomb, . . .	Enfield, Ct.
19,	Mary Frances Whittlesey,*	Mary Whittlesey Hill, .	West Springfield.
April 1,	Maggie Jarvais,* . . .	Margaret Dusseault, . .	Holyoke.
29,	Calvin Henry Fuller,* . .	George Harrison Herrick, .	Montgomery.
June 3,	Arthur Main Hughes,* . .	Arthur Hughes Whitney, .	Chicopee.
3,	Mary Almira Elizabeth Lamson, *alias* Mary Elizabeth Woodward,*	Ethel Clare Pember, . .	Vernon, Ct.
Nov. 5,	Daisy Mabel Young,* . .	Mabel Young Titus, . .	Springfield.
Dec. 2,	Adelbert Storey,* . . .	Adelbert Shipley, . . .	Westfield.
2,	Howard Stanton,* . . .	Howard Mitchell, . . .	Westfield.
2,	George Wheelock,* . . .	George Washington Albert Fox, ...	West Springfield.
2,	Florence May Jones,* . .	Emma Elizabeth Witham, .	West Springfield.
2,	Mabel Evelyn Alden,* . .	Mabel Evelyn Kendall, .	Ludlow.
16,	Grace Darling Warner,* . .	Grace Darling Maxwell, .	Westfield.

FRANKLIN COUNTY.

Date of Decree.	Original Name.	Name Decreed.	Residence.
Jan. 7,	Willie Guile,*	Willie Hume, ...	Montague.
7,	Fred. Guile,* . . • .	Fred. Hume, ...	Montague.
Feb. 17,	Martha Sophia Porter,* . .	Martha Sophia Hall, . .	Northfield.
Mar. 4,	Infant child of Caroline P. Douglass,*	Helen Frances Church, . .	Shutesbury.
11,	Florence J. Prouty,* . .	Florence J. Pratt, . . .	Orange.
June 17,	Fred. L. Rawson,* . . .	Fred. L. Phinney, . . .	New Salem.
Sept. 2,	Hattie Mabel McRay,* . .	Hattie Mabel Hall, . . .	Deerfield.
9,	Ellsworth Foster Rich,* . .	Ellsworth Foster Gardner, .	Orange.
Oct. 7,	Bessie Casey,*	Bessie Morgan, . . .	Montague.
Dec. 2,	Laura Ninette Wild,* . .	Laura Ninette Gardner, .	Ashfield.

BERKSHIRE COUNTY.

Date of Decree.	Original Name.	Name Decreed.	Residence.
April 1,	Timothy W. Welch,* . .	Timothy W. Pindergrast, .	Dalton.
May 6,	Imogene Hosford,* . .	Rebia L. Bowen, . . .	Adams.
July 15,	Etta May Nichols,* . .	Etta May Lindsay, . .	Pittsfield.
Sept. 2,	George Shear,* . . .	George Francis Murphy, .	Adams.
2,	Sara C. Shook,* . . .	Sara Shook Hutchinson, .	Richmond.
3,	Mary E. Mills,* . .	Mary E. Harper, . . .	Great Barrington.
Nov. 5,	Isabella Gould,* . . .	Isabella Wilson, . . .	W. Stockbridge.
Dec. 2,	Albert Jones,*	Albert J. Richards, . .	Richmond.

NORFOLK COUNTY.

Date of Decree.	Original Name.	Name Decreed.	Residence.
Jan. 15,	Edith Johnson,* . . .	Edith Ann Hinkley, . .	Weymouth.
22,	Mary Ellen O'Brien,* . .	Mary Ellen Sullivan, . .	Hyde Park.
Feb. 12,	Emma Louisa Zeecher,* . .	Bertha May Pye, . . .	Sharon.
Mar. 19,	Joseph Henry Evoy,* . .	Joseph Newcomb, . . .	Norwood.
19,	Frederick Stone,* . . .	Arthur Trafford Brazee, .	Quincy.

* Changed by reason of adoption.

NORFOLK COUNTY — *Concluded.*

Date of Decree.	Original Name.	Name Decreed.	Residence.
1879.			
April 2,	Ellen McLaughlin,* . . .	Nellie Wilmot Parker, . .	Stoughton.
July 22,	Susan Lunt Arnold,*. . .	Susie Lunt Glover, . . .	Quincy.
Sept. 3,	Annie Bell Newman,* . .	Annie Bell Partridge, . .	Franklin.
24,	Joseph Henry O'Brien,* .	Joseph Henry Sullivan, .	Hyde Park.
Oct. 8,	Anna Cora White,* . . .	Cora Louisa Gallagher, .	Milton.
8,	Lucy Maria De Forest,* .	Lucy Maria Talbot, . .	Quincy.
15,	Hattie Maria Fernald,* .	Hattie Maria Medan, . .	Weymouth.
Nov. 19,	Mary Brown Noyes,* . .	Harriet Allen Bedlington, .	Canton.
Dec. 17,	Emma Sumner Green,* . .	Emma Sumner Cook, . .	Foxborough.

BRISTOL COUNTY.

Jan. 10,	Alice Mabel Murphy,* . .	Alice Mabel Gibbs, . . .	Easton.
Feb. 7,	Annie Horton,*	Annie Horton Rogers, . .	Dighton.
14,	John Francis Healey,* . .	John Francis Donahoe, . .	Fall River.
21,	Ellen Scott,*	Ellen Maria Sherman, . .	Dartmouth.
Mar. 14,	Norman Lionel Brenton,* .	Norman Eli Robbins, . .	Attleborough.
14,	Alice Maud Brenton,* . .	Ella Ruggles Crossman, .	Norton.
May 16,	Carl Henry Roe,* . . .	Charles Henry Stearns, . .	Foxborough.
June 6,	———, ...	Mary Dugan, ...	Fall River.
27,	Amy Tree Gidley,* . . .	Amy Tray Royce, . . .	Dartmouth.
July 11,	Melsar Merton Peirce,* .	Melsar Merton Dean, . .	Taunton.
11,	George Durfee, ...	Thomas Durfee Robinson, .	Fall River.
Sept. 5,	John Fenwick Baker, . .	John Baker,*	Rehoboth.
Oct. 3,	Louisa Andrews,* . . .	Lotta Louisa Hardon, . .	Westport.
3,	Mary Jane Brown,* . . .	Edith May Colyar, . . .	New Bedford.
Nov. 7,	Eva Etta Bismore,* . . .	Eva Etta Burlingame, . .	New Bedford.

PLYMOUTH COUNTY.

Jan. 13,	Willie Davis,*	William B. Johnson, . .	Plymouth.
Mar. 10,	Henry Munroe,*. . . .	William A. Ruhle, . . .	Plymouth.
10,	—— Walker,* . . .	Bertha Mabel Dobson, . .	South Abington.
June 9,	William Sever Harrison, .	Alexander Madena Harrison, .	Plymouth.
Sept. 8,	Bertha Gray,*	Bertha Gray Hayes, . .	Middleborough.
Nov. 24,	—— Turner,*	Grace May Beal, . . .	Pembroke.

BARNSTABLE COUNTY.

Jan. 14,	Arthur Bingham Collins, .	Benajah Bingham Collins, .	Mashpee.
Feb. 11,	Fanny Smith Kelley,* . .	Fanny Kelley Haffards, . .	Yarmouth.
11,	Clara May Jones,* . . .	Clara May Hinckley, . .	Eastham.
Mar. 11,	Emma Winslow Foster, .	Ida Winslow Foster, . .	Brewster.
May 19,	Simeon W. Fisher,* . . .	Henry H. Baker, . . .	Falmouth.
Oct. 29,	Francis Ollar,*	Francis H. Emery, . . .	Provincetown.
Nov. 18,	John A. Nickerson,* . .	John A. Jones, . . .	Falmouth.

* Changed by reason of adoption.

SUFFOLK COUNTY.

Date of Decree.	Original Name.	Name Decreed.	Residence.
1880.			
Jan. 5,	Mabel Harvey Stone,* . .	Mabel Wortley Owen, . .	Auburn, Me.
5,	Mary Ella Geddes, . . .	Mary Ella Edmands, . .	Boston.
5,	Virginia Vanderbilt Geddes, .	Virginia Vanderbilt Edmands,	Boston.
12,	George W. Bishton,* . . .	Ralph Bishton Eastman, .	Boston.
12,	Edith Haynes,*	Mabel Edith Clough, . .	Boston.
19,	Lauretta Berry,* . . .	Lauretta Boston, . . .	Boston.
Feb. 16,	Mary Olive Philpot,* . .	Mary Olive Joy, . . .	Boston.
16,	Frank Lawrence Wyman,* .	Wilford Clark, . . .	Chelsea.
16,	Charles William Gallagher O'Connell,*	Charles William Swift, . .	Boston.
Mar. 8,	James M. Cary, ...	John Le Roach, . . .	Boston.
8,	Georgie Giles,*	Georgie Winnifred Ryan, .	Boston.
15,	Walter Wellington Doland, .	Walter Wellington Jackson, .	Boston.
15,	—— Sinclair,*	Harry Hiram Piper, . .	Boston.
22,	Frank Mack,*	Solon Edward Gilmore, .	Boston.
22,	Bertha Frances Davenport,* .	Bertha Lillian Taylor, . .	Boston.
April 5,	Joseph Lyman Andrews, . .	Joseph Andrews, . . .	Boston.
12,	Walter Cox,*	Walter Cox Green, . . .	Chelsea.
19,	Katie McCann,*	Gracie Jones Simpson, . .	Boston.
May 3,	Michael Dobrinsky, . .	Isadore Michael Dubrin, .	Boston.
3,	Alfred Poole Howard,* . .	Matthias Francis Shields, .	Boston.
10,	Adelaide Payson Schirmer,*	Adelaide Payson Vogel, .	Boston.
10,	Edwin Atherstone Damant,*	Edwin A. Stowe, . . .	Boston.
17,	Catherine Walsh,* . . .	Esther Payson Damon, . .	Boston.
31,	Catharine Wright,* . . .	Grace A. Restarrick, . .	Boston.
June 7,	Catharine Murray,* . . .	Ellen O'Neil, ...	Boston.
14,	Mary James,*	Mary Eloise Bates, . .	Boston.
14,	Lilian Logan,*	Lilian Jackson Barrus, . .	St. John, N. B.
21,	Mary Rose,*	Mary Gomes, ...	Flores, Azores.
28,	Charles O'Hara, ...	Charles Trench, . . .	Boston.
July 19,	William Armstrong,* . .	William Wallace Flagg, .	Arlington.
Sept. 6,	Herbert Warren, . . .	Herbert Langford Warren, .	Boston.
13,	John Temple,* . . .	John Benjamin Francis Rawson, ...	Boston.
13,	Frank Wilson,*	Harold Franklin Smith, . .	Boston.
13,	Emma Keene,*	Gertrude Rust, . . .	Boston.
13,	Fanny Cronin,*	Maud Louise Crowell, . .	Boston.
13,	Lora Newton Martin,* . .	Lora Maud Barbour, . .	Boston.
Oct. 4,	Alice Gertrude Homer,* . .	Alice Gertrude Keller, . .	Boston.
4,	Rubina Josephine Webber,*	Rubina Josephine Webber Martin, ...	Pueblo, Col.
11,	Ida Dobbins,*	Ida Mary McKenney, . .	Boston.
18,	Florence Naomi Safford,* .	Florence Naomi Sprague, .	Boston.
18,	Frederick Morton Currier,*	Frederick Morton Weale, .	Boston.
25,	Henry Goodsell, ...	Henry Hyland, . . .	Boston.
25,	James E. Murphy,* . . .	James E. Ballard, . . .	Boston.
Nov. 1,	John Reynolds, ...	John Phillips Reynolds, .	Boston.
8,	Daniel Graham *alias* Willie Elmer Clark,*	William Arnold Goodspeed, .	Boston.
8,	Grace Eleanor Densmore Smith,*	Grace Eleanor Smith, . .	Dover.
15,	Ida Parker Clifford,* . . .	Lillian Maud Paine, . .	Boston.
22,	Mabel Wood McLearn,* . .	Mabel Wood Johanna Helena Lehrich, ...	Boston.
22,	Mary Gallagher,* . . .	Charlotte Fitzgerald, . .	Boston.
29,	Alice Canavan,*	Alice Sharper, ...	Boston.
29,	Teresa Foster,*	Josephine Maria von Jelagin, .	Boston.
Dec. 20,	George Perry,*	George Benjamin Jerris, .	Plymouth.
20,	James McCann,*	James Cummings, . . .	Boston.
20,	—— Stickney,*	Helen Rex Keller, . . .	Boston.
20,	Edward Prouty,*	Edward Henry Cohen, . .	Lynn
27,	Elizabeth W. Southwood,*	Ada Noble, ...	Boston.

* Changed by reason of adoption.

ESSEX COUNTY.

Date of Decree.	Original Name.	Name Decreed.	Residence.
1880.			
Jan. 5,	Martin Edward Flaherty, . .	Martin Edward Ferris, . .	Gloucester.
5,	Frederick Sherwood Webb, .	Frederick Webb, . . .	Salem.
5,	Eva Belle West,* . . .	Eva Belle Perham, . . .	———.
19,	La Roy Sunderland Champion,*	La Roy Sunderland Bowler, .	Beverly.
Feb. 2,	Mary Courtney,* . . .	Annie Courtney Trask, . .	Boston.
2,	Arthur Mason Newell,* . .	Arthur Newell Cook, . .	Dover.
2,	Ethel Isabella Turgerson,* .	Allester Ethel Clarke, . .	Boston.
16,	Caroline Dunakin,* . . .	Jennie Williston, . . .	———.
Mar. 1,	Joseph Burke,*	Marshall Edwin Simmons, .	Belmont.
15,	Jennie Christie Smith,* . .	Jennie Maria Churchill, . .	Salem.
22,	Mary Ellen Smith,* . . .	Minnie Morton, . . .	Andover.
22,	Willis Lovell,*	George Willis Patten, . .	———.
April 5,	Ida Florence Dudiea,* . .	Ida Florence Cook, . . .	Salem.
5,	Robert Moore,*	Robert Moore Hulme, . .	Schenectady, N.Y.
5,	Lewis E. Woodbridge,* . .	Lewis E. Heckler, . . .	Greenfield, N. H.
19,	Alvah Woodbury Bailey, . .	Alvah Bailey Woodbury, . .	Beverly.
19,	Winifred Hamilton Lindley,* .	Winifred Hamilton Willcomb, .	Newburyport.
26,	William Patrick Foley,* . .	William Mehlman, . . .	Gloucester.
May 24,	Elizabeth Bell Ethridge,* . .	Bell E. Forbush, . . .	Boston.
June 14,	Alice Crowther,*	Alice Phinney, . . .	Lawrence.
28,	Rufina M. Thurlow, . . .	Rufina M. Kimball, . .	Lawrence.
July 6,	Joseph E. Merchant,* . . .	Joseph E. Palmer, . . .	Gloucester.
12,	Evelina Comeau,*	Evelina Conant, . . .	———.
Sept. 20,	Elvira Nelson,*	Ella Maud Webster, . .	Boston.
20,	Julia Elizabeth Young,* . .	Elizabeth Julia Griffin, . .	Middleton.
Oct. 18,	Mary Forsy.*	Mary Marcoux, . . .	Haverhill.
18,	Lavinia Anderson.* . . .	Luenia Anderson Keene, . .	Boston.
18,	Nellie Porter Battles, . .	Ellen Porter Battles, . .	Lawrence.
25,	Thomas Copley Amory, . .	Copley Amory, . . .	Nahant.
Nov. 15,	Annie Mansfield Boynton,* .	Annie Mansfield Skinner, .	Lynn.
Dec. 6,	Annie Maria Hart.* . . .	Annie Maria Lundell, . .	Gloucester.
6,	Arthur Raymond Winter,* .	Charles Hastings Breed, .	Framingham.
20,	Anna Bell Plouf,* . . .	Anna Holland Mungin, . .	Lawrence.
20,	Mary Lina Plouf,* . . .	Mary Lena Mungin, . .	Lawrence.

MIDDLESEX COUNTY.

Date of Decree.	Original Name.	Name Decreed.	Residence.
Jan. 6,	Edward Payson Marshall,* .	Edward Payson Favor, . .	Somerville.
6,	Charles Richardson Marshall,* .	Charles Richardson White, .	Cambridge.
13,	Stella Mary ———,* . . .	Stella Mary Finley, . .	Somerville.
13,	Thomas Joseph Jones,* . .	Thomas Joseph Ryan, . .	Marlborough.
27,	Edward Francis Shepard,* .	Frederick Morton Fiske, .	Weston.
27,	Etta Coleman,*	Alice Small, ...	Newton.
27,	Eva E. Bates,*	Eva Bates Corey, . . .	Waltham.
Feb. 24,	Theodore Ware,*	Horace Louis Cilley, . .	Cambridge.
Mar. 16,	John Brewer Hildreth, . .	John Lewis Hildreth, . .	Cambridge.
May 4,	Rita M. Eaton,*. . . .	Rita Maria Maloy, ...	Somerville.
18,	———,*	Mary Jane Moorhouse, . .	Lowell.
18,	Bessie Maria Knowles,* . .	Bessie Maria Lawrence, . .	Pepperell.
18,	Henry Franklin Dwinnell,* .	Franklin Russell Spear, . .	Melrose.
25,	Charles Roscoe Bassford, . .	Charles Roscoe Craig, . .	Marlborough.
June 8,	——— Heyward,*	William Albert Doucett, . .	Stoneham.
8,	Ellen L. Hammond,* . . .	Ada Florence Wright, . .	Cambridge.
8,	Joseph E. Burgeron,* . .	Joseph Elmo Leblane, . .	Lowell.
July 6,	Cora Alice Butler,* . . .	Cora Alice Groeschner, . .	Watertown.
13,	Alice Sullivan,*	Marjorie King, . . .	Newton.
27,	Charles Augustus Brinnick,* .	Charles Augustus Chamberlain, ...	Newton.

* Changed by reason of adoption.

MIDDLESEX COUNTY — *Concluded.*

Date of Decree.	Original Name.	Name Decreed.	Residence.
1880.			
Sept. 7,	Henrietta Counterway,* . .	Nettie Ella Littlefield, . .	Somerville.
21,	Hugh Short,*	Albert Tice.	Lowell.
21,	Henry Warren Taylor,* . .	James William Flynn, . .	Cambridge.
28,	Beulah Henrietta Parsons,* .	Bertha Louise Cameron, .	Cambridge.
Oct. 12,	Gracie May Thompson,* .	Gracie May Little, . .	Lowell.
12,	George Lindsey Pray,* .	Clinton Beach Haley, . .	Cambridge.
Nov. 2,	Charles Ryan,* . . .	Charles Sumner Silsby, .	Lunenburg.
9,	Mary Jane Coakley,* . .	Mary Jane Murphy, . .	Newton.
9,	William Vincent Smith, .	William Smith Carter, .	Arlington.
9,	Alice Parkman Smith, .	Alice Parkman Carter, .	Arlington.
23,	Ida Hyde,*	Dora Elizzie Leland, . .	Newton.
Dec. 7,	Henry Hay,*	Henry Kennedy, . . .	Somerville.
7,	Sarah Elizabeth Ellis, .	Sarah Lilian Ellis, . .	Marlborough.
14,	Albert Henry Putnam, .	Henry Albert Putnam, .	Marlborough.
28,	Edward Ruthvern Macdon-ough,*	Edward Ruthvern Barnes, .	Cambridge.
28,	Charles Barnes Macdonough,* .	Charles Barnes, . . .	Cambridge.

WORCESTER COUNTY.

Date of Decree.	Original Name.	Name Decreed.	Residence.
Feb. 3,	Richard Barry, ...	Charles Joseph Foster, . .	Worcester.
3,	Moses Milkman, . . .	Alfred Spencer Lowell, . .	Worcester.
17,	Annie Louisa Gay,* . . .	Belle Hallett Keene, . .	Milford.
17,	Thomas Salmon, . . .	Thomas Henry Aldrich, .	Uxbridge.
24,	Charles Edward Flint,* . .	Charles Edward Merritt, .	Fitchburg.
Mar. 2,	Charles Jones,*	Charles Corbin. . . .	Webster.
16,	George Frederick Renney,* .	George Frederick Burnell, .	Boylston.
16,	Jennie Waldmyer Foster,* .	Jennie Foster Chapin, . .	Northborough.
16,	Rose Mary Elizabeth McDon-ald,*	Effie Grace Green, . . .	Spencer.
16,	Leonia Isabell Gould,* . .	Leonia Isabell Hutchinson, .	Fitchburg.
16,	Josephine Brooks,* . . .	Clara Barton Taylor, . .	Worcester.
April 6,	Florence Edgar Benjamin, .	Frank Edgar Benjamin, .	Fitchburg.
20,	George Franklin Willard, .	George Franklin Gray, . .	Warren.
May 4,	Anna Maria C. Katherina Fahr-ing,*	Anna Maria Katherina Pfer-dekamp, ...	Clinton.
4,	Gerhard Henry Fahring,* . .	Gerhard Henry Pferdekamp,.	Clinton.
4,	Sophie M. Fahring,* . . .	Sophie M. Pferdekamp, . .	Clinton.
18,	Sarah Frances Smith,* . .	Florence Mabel Gates, . .	Worcester.
June 1,	Blanche Warren,* . . .	Blanche Warren Learned, .	Worcester.
July 6,	Ellen E. Blunt,* . . .	Nellie E. White, . . .	Northbridge.
Sept. 14,	Lillian Force,*	Lillian Sherman, . . .	Milford.
Oct. 13,	Isaletta Belle Thompson,* .	Etta Belle Smith, . . .	Petersham.
19,	Josephine Eglentine Caya,* .	Josephine Eglentine Maynard,	Southbridge.
Dec. 21,	Hattie Belle Rathburn,* .	Hattie Belle Guilford, . .	Hardwick.

HAMPSHIRE COUNTY.

Date of Decree.	Original Name.	Name Decreed.	Residence.
Jan. 6,	Annie Goss,*	Annie Goss Dolby, . . .	Worthington.
Feb. 3,	Frank L. Thayer,* . .	Frank L. Bennett, . . .	Amherst.
Mar. 2,	Bernice Ann Loring,* . .	Bernice Ann Clark, . .	Huntington.
April 6,	Henry Rawson,* . . .	Willard Francis Bryant, .	Chesterfield.
6,	Nettie Ellen Jackson,* . .	Nettie Jackson Clark, . .	South Hadley.

* Changed by reason of adoption.

HAMPSHIRE COUNTY — *Concluded.*

Date of Decree.	Original Name.	Name Decreed.	Residence.
1880.			
June 1,	Thomas McGrath, . . .	Thomas Francis McGrath, .	Hadley.
Aug. 3,	Susan M. Tilden,* . . .	Susan M. Engram, . . .	Chesterfield.
Oct. 12,	Emma Linda Jackson,* . .	Emma Linda Curtis, . .	Belchertown.
Nov. 3,	Fred Eugene Rawson,* . .	Fred Eugene Bartlett, . .	Chesterfield.
Dec. 7,	Cora E. Howe,*	Cora E. Cook, ...	Amherst.

HAMPDEN COUNTY.

Date of Decree.	Original Name.	Name Decreed.	Residence.
Feb. 16,	Florence Mabel Ritter,* . .	Olga Charlotte McFethries, .	Longmeadow.
Mar. 2,	Edward Anderson,* . . .	Edward Beiser, . . .	Springfield.
2,	Edward Franklin Bourke,* .	Edward Albert Parker, . .	Wilbraham.
2,	William Henry Bourke,* . .	William Edwin West, . .	Wilbraham.
April 6,	Zaidee Priscilla Thompson,*	Zaidee Thompson Knight, .	West Springfield.
6,	Emily M. Williams, . . .	Emily M. Ferry, . . .	Chicopee.
17,	Charles Walcott Merriam,‡ .	Charles Walcott Merriam, .	Springfield.
May 11,	Maria Waters,*	Minnie Maria Parmenter, .	Palmer.
19,	Lester Emery Converse,* .	Lester Emery Bradway, .	Wales.
July 6,	Ella Francis Barnes,‡ . .	Ella Francis Barnes, . .	Westfield.
6,	Ida May Palmer,* . . .	Ida May Presset, . . .	Springfield.
Aug. 3,	Esper Phelps,*	Esper Crosby, ...	West Springfield.
Sept. 7,	Daisy Langguth,* . . .	May Warren Farmer, . .	Springfield.
7,	Raymond T. Erwin,* . .	Raymond Irving Lewis, . .	Springfield.
21,	Fanny Bent Gowdy,* . .	Fanny Bent Bishop, . .	Springfield.
Dec. 7,	Mabel Young Titus,* . .	Mabel Young, ...	Springfield.
8,	Hattie May Dean,‡ . . .	Hattie May Dean, . . .	Springfield.

FRANKLIN COUNTY.

Date of Decree.	Original Name.	Name Decreed.	Residence.
Mar. 2,	Theresa Grollmann,* . . .	Theresa Grollmann Sommers,	Shelburne.
April 22,	Kate Leyden,*	Katie Leyden Hartley, . .	Montague.
July 6,	Arlon Orcutt Moffatt,* . .	Arlon Orcutt Holden, . .	Hawley.
Aug. 3,	Lottie Swartz,*	Lottie Russell Shirley, . .	Conway.
3,	Henry G. Bowman,* . . .	Henry G. Vincent, . . .	Heath.
Oct. 5,	Frank L. Nelson Hastings, .	Frank L. Nelson, . . .	Warwick.
Dec. 10,	Rosa Brennan,*	Rose Emma Cobb, . . .	Greenfield.

BERKSHIRE COUNTY.

Date of Decree.	Original Name.	Name Decreed.	Residence.
Feb. 3,	Anna M. North,* . . .	Anna M. Dean, . . .	Adams.
3,	Arthur Jannette,* . . .	Arthur Varno, . . .	Adams.
3,	Delia Jannette,*	Delia Murray, . . .	Adams.
Mar. 3,	Daisy E. Stone,* . . .	Daisy E. Haskins, . . .	North Adams.
May 4,	Mary Elizabeth Osborne, .	Mary Elizabeth Powers, .	Pittsfield.
4,	Charles Crew,*	Charles Thomas Kirk, . .	Pittsfield.
5,	Grace Shufelt,*	Grace Pixley, ...	N. Marlborough.
June 1,	Sarah Jones,*	Lillian B. Culverhouse, .	North Adams.
July 22,	Lida F. Moulton,* . . .	Lida F. Goodnow, . . .	North Adams.
Nov. 3,	Myrtie Hall,*	Elsie L. Boyd, . . .	North Adams.
Dec. 7,	Ivodell Tower,*	Ivodell Waters, . . .	Adams.
7,	Mary L. Mundry,* . . .	Mary L. Monteaux, . .	Pittsfield.
7,	Irena Washburn,* . . .	Rosa Adams, ...	Lee.

---

* Changed by reason of adoption.   ‡ Adopted, without change of name.

NORFOLK COUNTY.

Date of Decree.	Original Name.	Name Decreed.	Residence.
1880.			
Jan. 14,	Georgianna Glover Arnold,*	Georgianna Glover Derry,	Braintree.
21,	Harriet Allen,*	Bessie Howard Farnham,	Randolph.
Feb. 11,	Alice Levan,*	Edith Dana Tucker,	Milton.
18,	Gilbert Nathaniel Weaver,*	Harry Weston Badger,	Quincy.
Mar. 3,	William Robinson,*	William Francis Collins,	Medway.
3,	Charles Lamb,*	Charles Alonzo Thayer,	Dedham.
June 23,	Isabel Estelle Capen,*	Isabel Capen White,	Canton.
23,	Henry McCall,*.	Harry Allen Norton,	Dover.
23,	Mabel Peterson,*	Anna Mabel Newcomb,	Quincy.
Sept. 15,	Jennie Frederica Carlson,*	Hattie Ardell Poole,	Hyde Park.
15,	Jesse Cooper,*	Jessie Cooper Mears,	Quincy.
15,	Sarah Ellen Cooper,*.	Nellie S. Hanna,	Quincy.
22,	Hattie Elizabeth Shepard,*	Hattie Elizabeth Bennett,	Hyde Park.
Oct. 20,	Hattie Osgood,* .	Hattie B. Derby,	Needham.
Nov. 3,	John Wesley Kilpatrick,	John Wesley Williams,	Hyde Park.
Dec. 15,	Winnifred Camille Sampson,*	Camille Jane Osgood,	Sharon.

PLYMOUTH COUNTY.

Date of Decree.	Original Name.	Name Decreed.	Residence.
Feb. 9,	Elizabeth Marr,*	Lizzie Adams Brown,	Abington.
May 24,	George H. Stevens,*	Albert Leslie Simmons,	Plymouth.
July 12,	Sarah E. Pratt,*	Sarah E. Bryant,	Middleborough.
Sept. 13,	Bernard James,*	Fred Loring Corthell,	Hingham.
Oct. 18,	George Greeley,*	George Henry Tighe,	Brockton.
Dec. 27,	Annie Maria Parsons,*	Anna Maria Thrasher,	Plymouth.
27,	Jennie G. Walling,*	Jennie G. Hatch,	Hanover.

BRISTOL COUNTY.

Date of Decree.	Original Name.	Name Decreed.	Residence.
Jan. 2,	Alcy R. E. Young,	Alcy R. E. Swift,	Fall River.
16,	Phebe Ann Hewlett,	Annie Macomber,	Taunton.
Feb. 6,	Nellie Fits,	Winnifred Louise Harding,	Boston.
6,	Mary Ann Grady,	Mary Ann Carrot,	Fall River.
6,	Joseph Dimech,	Frederick Scholes,	Fall River.
6,	Ida M. Hanherson,	Ida M. Clemens,	Taunton.
Mar. 19,	Clara Fone,	Clara Amanda Blachler,	Boston.
19,	Sarah E. Ramsey,	Sarah E. Macomber,	Fall River.
April 2,	Ruby Marlow,	Ruby Ellen Altham,	Fall River.
May 7,	Maria Bittencourte,	Maria Sylvia,	New Bedford.
21,	Olive J. Hadwen,	Olive J. Braley,	New Bedford.
June 18,	Cora P. Wilcox,	Cora Estelle Tinkham,	Fairhaven.
July 2,	Abraham Luce,	William Aldens Johns,	New Bedford.
Aug. 6,	Maria Francisa de Rosa,	Maria Francisca Machado,	Gloucester.
6,	Martha N. Smith,	Clara May Smith,	New Bedford.
Sept. 3,	Alice Isabella Beeden,	Alice Clark,	Dartmouth.
24,	Wilbert Watts,	Wilbert Baldwin,	Boston.
Oct. 1,	Thomas Suter Palmer,	Thomas Palmer Harrison,	Fall River.

BARNSTABLE COUNTY.

Date of Decree.	Original Name.	Name Decreed.	Residence.
Jan. 13,	Angie Holway,*.	Angie Bell,	Provincetown.
June 15,	Arthur Emerson Thompson,*	Arthur Emerson Swift,	Falmouth.
Aug. 10,	Charles A. Bray,*	Charles A. Williams,	Wellfleet.

* Changed by reason of adoption.

SUFFOLK COUNTY.

Date of Decree.	Original Name.	Name Decreed.	Residence.
1881.			
Jan. 10,	Joseph Silver,*	Joseph Buswell, . . .	Boston.
10,	Sarah Anna Street,* . . .	Sarah Anna Gaines, . .	Chelsea.
17,	Anna Newton Cole,* . . .	Anna Newton Harding, . .	Ashland.
24,	Joseph Eleazar Raymond Piper,	Joseph Eleazar Raymond, .	Boston.
24,	Hattie Gertrude Henry,* . .	Hattie Gertrude Lord, . .	Boston.
Feb. 7,	Arthur Cephas Hoar, . .	Arthur Cephas Whitney, .	Boston.
14,	Grace Crowningshield Barring-ton,*	Florence Crowningshield Grout, ...	Boston.
21,	Mary Ann Dooley,* . . .	Ann Schmehl, ...	Boston.
21,	Milly Messer,*	Nettie May Clark, . . .	Boston.
21,	Elizabeth Antoinette Gould,* .	Elizabeth Gould Billings, .	Boston.
Mar. 7,	Marcia Jane Louisa Freeman, .	Marcia Jane Louisa Fogg, .	Boston.
14,	Daniel McCarthy,* . . .	Daniel Moore, ...	Boston.
21,	Herbert Leslie Woods,* . .	Herbert Leslie Woods Morse,	Brooks, Me.
21,	Mary Cynthia Dunlop, . .	Mary Cynthia Josephs, . .	Boston.
21,	Mary Elizabeth Dunlop, . .	Mary Elizabeth Josephs, .	Boston.
21,	William Henry Sullivan, . .	George William Fenlee, .	Boston.
21,	Frances Sullivan, . . .	Frances Fenlee, . . .	Boston.
21,	Edward Foster Morse,* . .	James Edward Simmons, .	Chelsea.
21,	Lulu Pearl Foster,* . . .	Lulu Pearl Whiting, . .	Boston.
28,	Loro Newton Cameron,* . .	Mildred Blanche Sampson, .	Boston.
28,	Arthur Murray,* . . .	Arthur Murray Grout, . .	Boston.
28,	Nellie Proctor,*	Jessie Helena Morrison, .	Lynn.
April 18,	Eunice Gross,*	Edith Alvena Richards, .	Boston.
18,	Elizabeth Hayes,* . . .	Hattie May Bean, . . .	Boston.
May 2,	Mary M. O'Connor,* . . .	Mary M. Whelan, . . .	Boston.
2,	Bessie Felton,*	Bessie Mildred Gammon, .	Boston.
9,	William Cameron,* . . .	Willie Castle Woodbury, .	Boston.
16,	Mary Bateman,*	Mary McCurdy, . . .	Boston.
16,	William McIntyre,* . . .	William Barker Peirce, .	Boston.
23,	Siegesmund Theodore Boetticher,	Siegesmund Theodore Becker,	Boston.
June 6,	Mary Gray,*	Mary Ella Guild, . . .	Boston.
13,	Hattie Bence,*	Hattie Elvira Harding, . .	New Haven, Ct.
13,	Frank Lester Sweetser,* . .	Frank Lester Logan, . .	Portsmouth, N. H.
13,	Nellie Palfrey Sweetser,* . .	Nellie Palfrey Logan, . .	Portsmouth, N. H.
20,	Ella Maria Mann, . . .	Ella Maria Adams, . .	Boston.
20,	Frances Floribel Mann, . .	Frances Floribel Adams, .	Boston.
20,	Horace Herbert Mann, . .	Horace Herbert Adams, .	Boston.
27,	Hannah Stone,*	Hannah Brown, . . .	Boston.
27,	Nellie Murphy,*	Mabel Alice Pittee, . .	Boston.
27,	James Rutherford Seavey,* .	Henry Beckwith Smith, .	Boston.
27,	Althea Theresa Herring, . .	Althea Theresa Butters, .	Boston.
July 11,	Midget Day,*	Annie Eugenia Crawford, .	Holyoke.
25,	William F. Luby,* . . .	William F. Stevens, . .	Boston.
Sept. 5,	Frans Albin Simmerstrom, .	Frans Albin Norman, . .	Boston.
5,	Evelyn Cecil Stanley,* . .	Bessie Evelyn Johnson, .	Boston.
5,	Annie Lizzie Morse,* . . .	Annie Lottie Anderson, .	Chelsea.
5,	Edward Haines,*	Edward Anson Kingsley, .	Boston.
5,	Lucy Austin,*	Grace Brown Dodge, . .	York, Me.
12,	Alice Gertrude Dadmun, . .	Alice Gertrude Hosmer, .	Boston.
Oct. 3,	Lottie Josephine Sessler,* . .	Lottie Melissa Johnson, .	Boston.
10,	Walter Marshall Cutler, . .	Marshall Cutler, . . .	Boston.
24,	Charles Willis Lee,* . . .	Charles Willis Lee Thornton,	St. Albans, Vt.
31,	Charles Henry Bartlett Peter-son,*	Ralph Charles Sulloway, .	Plymouth.
31,	Russell Swain Munroe, . .	Russell Munroe, . . .	Boston.
31,	Michael Granville Shean, . .	Oscar Granville Bolton, .	Boston.
Nov. 7,	Mary Ellen Doliver,* . . .	Ellen Prince, ...	Boston.
14,	Emma Gordon,*	Grace Lillian Ray, . . .	Boston.
14,	Mary Ellen Mansfield Haggerty,*	Daisy Gertrude McFarland, .	Boston.
14,	Mary Agnes Jackson,* . .	Daisy Mainjoy, . . .	Stow.

* Changed by reason of adoption.

SUFFOLK COUNTY — *Concluded.*

Date of Decree.	Original Name.	Name Decreed.	Residence.
1881.			
Nov. 14,	Dora Elizabeth McDermott,*	Mildred Eudora Smith, .	Boston.
14,	George Morris,*	George Edward Emerson,	Boston.
14,	William Caspar Sessler,* .	William John Sullivan, .	Boston.
21,	Louis Gurki, ...	Louis Crown, ...	Boston.
28,	Mabel Wilson Bishop,*	Carolina Rebecka Morise,	Boston.
28,	Mabel Davison,* . . .	Maud Ethel Quimby, .	Boston.
28,	Lillie Mabel Hall,* . .	Ellen Jane Booth, . .	Boston.
28,	Mary Josephs,*	Violet Isabel Taylor, .	Boston.
28,	Ada Pitman,*	Ida Boyce, ...	Franklin.
28,	William Shuler, . . .	George Huntington Martis,	Boston.
28,	Thomas Frederick Donahue,	Frederick Thomas, . .	Boston.
Dec. 5,	Alice Greenwood Reed,* .	Effie May Green, . .	Boston.
12,	Robert Latta Doyle, . .	Robert Henry Latta, .	Boston.
12,	Jennie Maud Henderson,* .	Jennie Maud Turner, .	Boston.
12,	Willie Concannon,* . .	William Swain, . . .	Boston.
19,	Ernest Leon,*	Percy Farnum, . . .	———.

ESSEX COUNTY.

Jan. 3,	Mary Readdey,* . . .	Lillian Swett Greeley, .	———.
10,	Joseph Judd,* . . .	Joseph Henry Stott, .	Lawrence.
10,	Margaret Judd,* . . .	Margaret M. Birch, .	Lawrence.
17,	Lillian M. Bruce,* . .	Lillian M. Thwing, . .	California.
17,	William Edward Janes,* .	William Edward Robbins,	Lynn.
17,	Edith May Janes,* . .	Helen Edith Nourse, .	Lynn.
Feb. 7,	Harry Jackson, . . .	Harry King Jackson, .	Salem.
7,	Thomas H. Pynn, . .	Thomas H. Penn, . .	Newburyport.
21,	Hattie Belle Langill,* .	Lizzie Belle Otto, . .	
Mar. 14,	Wendell Phillips Kenney, .	Stephen Wendell Abbott,	Lawrence.
14,	Martha A. Smith,* . .	Martha A. Thornley, .	Hyde, Eng.
21,	George Arthur Williston,* .	George Williston Field, .	Salem.
April 18,	Catharine A. O'Connell,* .	Catharine A. Donahue, .	Lawrence.
May 16,	William Blake,* . . .	Herbert Coryoden Dennett,	Boston.
June 20,	Ellen J. Greeley, . .	Ellen J. Tilton, . .	Newburyport.
July 8,	Harriet Eliza Reid, . .	Harriet Eliza Sargent, .	Gloucester.
18,	Bertha Adaline Zeigert,* .	Bertha Steen Flint, . .	Boston.
25,	—— Laughlin,* . . .	Ellen Kelley, . . .	Haverhill.
Sept. 12,	Carrie C. Crosby,* . .	Carrie C. Rooks, . .	Eddington, Me.
12,	Emily Robinson,* . .	Emily Heys, . . .	Lawrence.
19,	Mattie Warren,* . . .	Mabel Florence Churchill,	Marblehead.
Oct. 3,	William Sherman Harris,*	William Sherman Taylor,	Newbern, N. C.
3,	Emma Jane Whittemore, .	Emma Whittemore Crowell,	Beverly.
24,	Eva O. Spates,* . . .	Eva O. Pike, . . .	Rockport.

MIDDLESEX COUNTY.

Jan. 11,	Claude W. Ellis,* . .	Claude Wilfred Fisher, .	Malden.
Feb. 8,	Agnes Maud Marshall,* .	Agnes Maud Robinson, .	Lowell.
Mar. 1,	Jessie Shorey,* . . .	Bessie Luella Adams, .	Lowell.
22,	Eva Maud Williams,* .	Eva Maud Bolles, . .	Pepperell.
22,	Charles C. Sleeper,* . .	Charles Sleeper Young, .	Lowell.
22,	Mabel Pierce Harding,* .	Mabel Lovell Daniels, .	Holliston.
22,	Hulbert Carr Walsh,* .	Hulbert Carr Griffin, .	Lowell.
April 5,	Willard Branigan, . .	Willard Elmes, . . .	Waltham.
5,	Gertrude A. Rockwood,* .	Mary Gertrude Hemenway, .	Woburn.

* Changed by reason of adoption.

MIDDLESEX COUNTY — *Concluded.*

Date of Decree.	Original Name.	Name Decreed.	Residence.
1881.			
April 5,	Mary Elizabeth Bowden,* . .	Marilla Thompson, . .	Framingham.
26,	Walter Stover,* . . .	Thomas Henry Holland, .	Townsend.
May 10,	Edith Ella Wells,* . . .	Bessie Atkinson Little, . .	Framingham.
24,	Maggie Emery,* . . .	Carrie Emery, . . .	Belmont.
24,	Alice Gardner Sandford,* .	Alice Gardner Davis, . .	Everett.
June 14,	George Cunnabell, . . .	George Cunnabell Howard, .	Cambridge.
14,	Lilly Wilbur,* . . .	Lilla Ella Gould, . . .	Lowell.
14,	John McManus,* . . .	John Sinnott, ...	Bedford.
14,	Edward Francis Richards,* .	Edward Francis Richards Saunders, ...	Natick.
July 5,	Eva Clark,*	Eva Leavens Davis, . .	Everett.
5,	Sarah Isabel Wilton,* .	Sarah Isabel Page, . . .	Cambridge.
26,	Joseph Donovan,* . . .	Joseph Burke, . . .	Marlborough.
26,	Eva Bates Corey, . . .	Eva May Corey, . . .	Watertown.
26,	Hugh Alfred Flinn, . .	Hugh Alfred Lee, . . .	Waltham.
26,	William Herd Greenlees, .	William Herd Greenleaf, .	Waltham.
26,	Jane Herbert Greenlees, . . .	Jane Herbert Greenleaf, .	Waltham.
Sept. 6,	Mary Bird Cowdry, . .	Mary Bird Lawrence, . .	Wakefield.
6,	Frank Gunderway,* . .	Frank Morandus, . . .	Somerville.
6,	Joseph Savageau,* . .	Joseph Smith, ...	Lowell.
20,	Charles H. Swett,* . .	Ambrose Charles Thissell, .	Dracut.
27,	William Wallace Whitten,*	William Whitten Hildreth, .	Natick.
Oct. 4,	Ralph Saunders Kingsley.* .	Harry William Rockwell, .	Somerville.
11,	Abby Dorothy Tetlow, .	Abbie Dorothy Kimball, .	Malden.
25,	George N. Lucian, . .	George Nicholas Banfield, .	Lowell.
25,	Ethel Corinne Wellington, .	Ethel Corinne Boynton, . .	Cambridge.
Nov. 1,	Grace Wood, . . .	Grace Abbot Wood, . .	Lowell.
1,	George Clerendon Cotting, .	Philip Clerendon Cotting, .	Marlborough.
15,	Frederick Woodward,* .	Glenwood Frederick Braun, .	Everett.
15,	Mary Ames,* . . .	Lizzie Brandon Scofield, .	Somerville.
22,	Margaret Frances Williams Cowland,*	Emma Frances Smith, . .	Cambridge.
Dec. 6,	James Clark,* . . .	James Arthur Perkins, . .	Framingham.
27,	Edith Treadworth Gilson,*	Mary Abigail Glasgow, . .	Cambridge.
27,	Eveline Augusta Barnes,* .	Eveline Augusta Flagg, . .	Wilmington.

WORCESTER COUNTY.

Jan. 4,	—— Burns,* . . .	Edgar E. Fisk, . . .	Gardner.
4,	Lula Grafton,* . . .	Lula Rebecca Lovewell, . .	Hubbardston.
4,	Hattie Bell Rathburn,*† .	Hattie Bell Guilford, . .	Hardwick.
4,	Sarah Pyne, . . .	Sarah McFarland, . .	Worcester.
4,	Alfred Henry Damon, .	Albert Boutelle Damon, .	Fitchburg.
18,	Eva Leonora Wheeler,* .	Eva Lenora Day, . . .	Berlin.
Feb. 15,	Charles Henry Damon,* .	Charles James Powell, . .	Fitchburg.
15,	Alice Jessie Goodrich,* .	Jessie Alice Cady, . .	Grafton.
Mar. 1,	———, ...	Ethel Wheeler Lewis, . .	Fitchburg.
1,	Fannie Taylor Higgins,* .	Fannie Taylor Litchfield, .	Berlin.
15,	Octave Coron,* . . .	Octave Landerville, . .	Warren.
15,	Frank S. Coron,* . .	Frank S. Tremblay, . .	Warren.
15,	Mary Coron,* . . .	Mary Maranda, . . .	Warren.
April 5,	Carl King,* . . .	Carl King Bancroft, . .	Phillipston.
5,	Philomaine Coron,* . .	Philomaine Mathew, . .	Brookfield.
26,	Alice Estella Boughton,* .	Estella Jones Cuthbert, . .	Fitchburg.
May 3,	Nettie Garfield Oliver,* .	Mabel Maria Frost, . .	Worcester.
3,	Anna F. Mars,* . . .	Mabel Maria Reed, . .	Worcester.
24,	Allen G. Wood,* . .	Allen Gordon Buttrick, . .	Lancaster.
24,	Ralph Arnold,* . . .	Walter Chamberlain Whittier, .	Fitchburg.

* Changed by reason of adoption.　　　　　† See Dec. 21, 1880.

WORCESTER COUNTY — *Concluded.*

Date of Decree.	Original Name.	Name Decreed.	Residence.
1881.			
July 5,	Grace Evaline Pierce,* . .	Gracie Stevens, . . .	Oxford.
19,	Bertha Shaw,*	Edith Eleanor Gunn, . .	Northbridge.
19,	—— Clark,*	Ethel Susie Jordan, . .	Worcester.
19,	Florence May Holman,* .	Florence May Norwood, .	Worcester.
Sept. 6,	Adah Harriet Dorman, .	Adah Harriet Fisher, . .	Worcester.
20,	Ann Gruby,*	Ann Keveny, ...	Southbridge.
27,	Ida Sawtell,*	Ida M. Hall, ...	Fitchburg.
Oct. 4,	Sarah Wilson,* . . .	Jennie Mabel Rugg, . .	Gardner.
Nov. 1,	Abbie J. Fitton,* . .	Abbie J. Austin, . . .	Worcester.
15,	Flora Dell Reynolds,* .	Flora Dell Twitchell, . .	Fitchburg.
22,	—— Foster,*	Edith Florence Porter, .	Athol.
Dec. 6,	Josephine Read,* . . .	Josephine Maud Henderson, ...	Northbridge.
6,	James May,*	James May Austin, . .	Worcester.
20,	Mamie Jane Perry, . . .	Florence May Wheeler, . .	Athol.

HAMPSHIRE COUNTY.

Date of Decree.	Original Name.	Name Decreed.	Residence.
Jan. 4,	Elizabeth Collard,* . . .	Elizabeth Grace Kellogg, .	Goshen.
11,	Grace Maud Chamberlain,* .	Evelina Geneveive Bishop, .	Northampton.
Feb. 1,	——,*	Celia Miranda Hinckley, .	South Hadley.
Mar. 1,	H. Bessie Deacon,* . . .	Grace Maud Lindsay, . .	Easthampton.
April 5,	James Arthur Scott,* . .	James Arthur Wainwright, .	Easthampton.
May 3,	Willie H. Wormsley,* . .	Charles Frederick Wilson, .	Amherst.
3,	George Eugene Mumford,* .	George Eugene Mumford Mayor, ...	Goshen.
10,	——,*	Chester William Dunlap, .	Enfield.
Nov. 1,	Grace M. Clark,* . . .	Grace M. Shaw, . . .	Cummington.

HAMPDEN COUNTY.

Date of Decree.	Original Name.	Name Decreed.	Residence.
Jan. 4,	Harriett Louisa Warner,* . .	Mabel Ione Morgan, . .	Chicopee.
Feb. 1,	Lina Delle Moody,* . . .	Lina Delle Strong, . . .	Springfield.
8,	Lillian Eunice Miller,* . .	Lillian Eunice Wright, . .	Palmer.
May 3,	Florence Irene Strandburg,* .	Florence Irene Hibbard, . .	Springfield.
10,	Leonard Stickney Shaw,* . .	Leonard Stickney Chapin, .	Springfield.
17,	William Oliver Scott,* . .	Frederick Otis Reed, . .	Westfield.
July 5,	Alice Leonard,*	Alice Gertrude Westman, .	Black Hawk, Col.
5,	Eliza Jane Grady,* . . .	Eliza Jane Whooly, . . .	Holyoke.
5,	Wilbur Randolph Ladd, jun., .	Wilbur Allin Ladd, . .	Holyoke.
Aug. 2,	Anna Theresia Wiemer,* . .	Anna Theresia Funke, . .	Springfield.
Sept. 6,	——,*	Florence Amelia Rising, . .	Springfield.
Oct. 20,	Joseph Loiselle,* . . .	Joseph Robert, ...	Holyoke.
Nov. 7,	Georgianna Fuller,* . . .	Lena Grace Palmer, . .	Palmer.

FRANKLIN COUNTY.

Date of Decree.	Original Name.	Name Decreed.	Residence.
June 21,	Roxanna E. Davis,* . . .	Cora M. Simonds, . . .	Northfield.
July 5,	Lizzie McGee.*	Lizzie E. Miner, . . .	Greenfield.
Sept. 6,	Della F. Davis,*. . . .	Della F. Ellis,. . . .	Montague.

* Changed by reason of adoption.

BERKSHIRE COUNTY.

Date of Decree.	Original Name.	Name Decreed.	Residence.
1881.			
May 3,	Clara C. Winchester,* . .	Clara C. Church, . . .	North Adams.
July 19,	James D. Howe,* . .	James D. Harder, . . .	Pittsfield.
Sept. 6,	Mary Ann Wilson,* . . .	Mary Wilson McColgan, .	Pittsfield.
6,	Emma A. Redding,* . . .	Emma A. Crispell, . . .	W. Stockbridge.

NORFOLK COUNTY.

Feb. 16,	Georgia Augusta Stevens,* .	Edna Gertrude Wilson, . .	Wrentham.
Mar. 19,	Susie Elizabeth Newbury,* .	Susan Elizabeth Coombs, .	Wrentham.
April 20,	Emma Louisa Zeecher, *alias* Bertha Pye,*	Elsie Maud Billings, . .	Brookline.
June 8,	May Reynolds,*	Henrietta Edith Wood, . .	Wellesley.
15,	Clara Elizabeth Cargill,* .	Elizabeth Cargill Weatherbee,	Cohasset.
July 6,	Minnie Madella Carter,* .	Minnie Madella Cram, .	Weymouth.
Sept. 7,	Jessie Brown Calligan,* .	Jessie Callagan Weston,.	Needham.
7,	Albert Everett Sawyer, .	Albert Everett, . . .	Norwood.
Nov. 16,	Fanny Leonard,* . . .	Bertha Louisa Blake, . .	Franklin.

PLYMOUTH COUNTY.

May 9,	Mary Jane Ferguson,* . .	Mary Jane Luddy, . . .	South Abington.
9,	Alice Belle Joslyn,* . .	Alice Belle Lyon, . . .	Bridgewater.
Oct. 10,	Emmanuel Francis Freemefred-do, ...	Emmanuel Francis McHenry,	Plymouth.

BRISTOL COUNTY.

Jan. 7,	Benjamin Ashworth,* . .	Benjamin Forster, . . .	Safford, Eng.
7,	John Franklin Mather, .	Frank Pomery Mather, .	Fall River.
7,	Mary E. Jones,* . .	Mary E. Brown, . . .	New Bedford.
21,	Charles A. Morse,* . .	Charles A. Harvey,. . .	Taunton.
Feb. 4,	Harriet Bryon Alden,* . .	Harriet Byron Viall, . .	Fairhaven.
Mar. 4,	Elisabeth Briggs, . .	Elisabeth Stewart, . .	Attleborough.
4,	Mary Elisabeth Goff,* .	Mary Elisabeth Cox, . .	Taunton.
18,	Arthur Hayes Roberts,* .	Harrie Arthur Scribner, .	Boston.
April 1,	Ada Swain Prouty,* . .	Ida Stella Sanford, . .	New Bedford.
1,	Rosa Rich,* . . .	Cassie Leona Gold, . .	Boston
15,	George L. Root,* . .	George L. Staples, . .	Providence, R.I.
May 6,	Gertrude E. Foster,* . .	Gertrude E. Scott, . .	New Bedford.
6,	Herbert H. Jackson,* .	Herbert H. Mitchell, . .	New Bedford.
June 3,	Eugene B. Lowe,* . .	Eugene B. Lee, . . .	Attleborough.
17,	Meribah Jane Lawton,* .	Name unchanged, . . .	Fall River.
Aug. 5,	Mary Anna Sylvester Backus,*.	Mary Anna Sylvester Demers,	New Bedford.
5,	——, ...	Grace Blanchard Peirce, .	New Bedford.
Sept. 2,	Elmer A. Macomber,* .	Elmer Albert Eddy, . .	Taunton.
Nov. 4,	Nellie Folger Prouty,* .	Nellie Eudora Johnson, .	New Bedford.
4,	Louisa Harrington,* . .	Louisa Maria Taylor, . .	Fall River.

BARNSTABLE COUNTY.

June 21,	Albert Snow, ...	Albert Clarence Snow, . .	Yarmouth.
Aug. 9,	Georgianna M. Voudy,* . .	Mabel Betsie Sears, . .	Dennis.
9,	Mary Alice Morse,* . .	Mary Alice Fish, . . .	Barnstable.
9,	Cora Ada Blake,* . .	Ada Cora Fisher, . . .	Barnstable.

* Changed by reason of adoption.

SUFFOLK COUNTY.

Date of Decree.	Original Name.	Name Decreed.	Residence.
1882.			
Jan. 2,	Albert Frederick Poor, . .	Albert Frederick Winslow, .	Boston.
2,	Christina McFarland,* . .	Christina Sellon, . . .	Boston.
2,	Mary Jerome,*	Mary Farrell, ...	Martha's Viney'd.
9,	Laura Esther Barron, . .	Laura Esther Hall, . . .	Boston.
16,	George Hastings, . . .	George Henry Hastings, .	Boston.
16,	Edward Everett Powers,* .	Everett Edward Walker, .	Abington.
Feb. 6,	Alice P. Barton,* . . .	Bertha P. Hayden, . . .	Somerville.
6,	Hattie Evelyn Sessler,* .	Hattie Josephine Davies, .	Boston.
13,	Mary Elizabeth Murphy, .	Mary Elizabeth Douglass, .	Boston.
13,	Annie P. Rose,* . . .	Annie Rose Pratt, . . .	Malden.
13,	Eva Minnie Elliott,* . .	Eva Minnie Gardner, . .	Boston.
20,	William Clarke,* . . .	William Clarke Cross, . .	Chelsea.
27,	John F. Bogan,* . . .	John F. Dwight, . . .	Boston.
27,	Caroline Fuller,* . . .	Cora Edna Henshie, . .	Boston.
27,	Percy Young,*	Spurgeon Percy Gifford, .	Boston.
27,	Mary Ann Heatherstone Harvey,*	Mabel Burleigh, . . .	Boston.
Mar. 13,	——,*	Walter D. Griggs, . . .	——.
20,	Joseph McNeal,* . . .	Joseph Paul Dutram, . .	P. Edward Isl'd.
27,	Mary Ellen Powers,* . .	Mary Ellen Lawton, . .	Boston.
April 3,	Isabella Chisholm,* . .	Florence Lorette Hart, .	Boston.
3,	Helena Wallace.* . . .	Lula Dikerman, . . .	Boston.
17,	Bessie Arleen Townsend,* .	Minnie Alice Richardson, .	Bridgewater.
17,	Penelope Moore, . . .	Nellie Moore Taylor, .	Boston.
24,	John Colby,*	John Turner, ...	Boston.
24,	Curtis Adams Le Moyne,* .	William Francis Cox, . .	Boston.
24,	Gertrude Cox Le Moyne,* .	Emma Gertrude Cox, . .	Boston.
24,	Alice Maud Smith,* . .	Grace Matilda Welch, . .	Boston.
May 15,	Anna Wallace,* . . .	Annie Leah Kelley, . .	Boston.
15,	Patrick-henry McSulvin, .	Henry Sulvin, ...	Boston.
15,	Carroll Grant,* . . .	Carroll Raymond Newbert, .	Boston.
22,	——,*	Fred. H. Griffith, . .	Boston.
22,	Thomas Jones,* . . .	Bert Arthur Gordon, . .	Boston.
22,	Mary Kelly, ...	Mary Carpenter, . . .	Boston.
22,	Augusta Greenfield,* . .	Augusta Weiss, . . .	Boston.
29,	Gertrude Smith,* . . .	Gertrude Magrath, . . .	Boston.
June 19,	Leonie Cox,*	Leonie Nanine Crowell, .	Boston.
19,	Barney McAlpine,* . . .	Thomas O'Brien McCabe, .	Boston.
July 3,	Minnie Louise Holway,* .	Minnie Louise Cross, .	State of Maine.
10,	Child of Catherine Haley,*	Elizabeth Cheney Sanger, .	Boston.
10,	Bertha May Thompson,* .	Florence Edna Mears, .	Boston.
10,	Mary Ann Johnson,* . .	Mabel Elizabeth Sanford, .	Boston.
10,	Grace Elizabeth Panton,* .	Gracie Evelyn Gale, . .	Boston.
10,	Bridget Daly,* . . .	Catherine Mahon, . . .	Boston.
17,	Charlotte Gordon Hoyt,* .	Emeline Pike Walton, . .	Boston.
17,	Carrie Louise Parker Welch,* .	Carrie Louise Parker Tobias, .	Boston.
24,	William Matthews,* . .	William Clifton Redder, .	Boston.
31,	Theodore Banchor Ellis,* .	Ray Eugene Robie, . .	Boston.
Sept. 4,	Minnie Rich,*	Minnie Isaacs, . . .	Boston.
4,	Ella P. Emerson, . . .	Ella P. Bowden, . . .	Boston.
4,	Annie E. Bain,* . . .	Annie E. Coffey, . . .	Boston.
11,	Alice Henry,*	Alice Keivenaar, . . .	Chelsea.
Oct. 2,	Palmer McDonnell,* . .	James Skinner, . . .	Boston.
2,	Mabel Williams,* . . .	Lena Saloma Banister, .	Boston.
2,	Florence E. Dennett,* . .	Florence D. Sibley, . .	Brooklyn, N. Y.
9,	Arthur Harold Elliot,* . .	Arthur Harold Miller, . .	Boston.
9,	Mary O'Farrell,* . . .	Mary Esprit, ...	Boston.
16,	John Thomas,*	John McArthur Butterfield, .	Chelsea.
16,	George Emil Hoffert, . .	George Emil Homer, . .	Boston.
16,	Julia Hickey,*	Harriet Julia Green, . .	Boston.

* Changed by reason of adoption.

SUFFOLK COUNTY — *Concluded.*

Date of Decree.	Original Name.	Name Decreed.	Residence.
1882.			
Oct. 23,	Charles Henry Moore,* . .	Albert Francis Lyons, . .	Boston.
23,	Bertha ——,*	Grace Chickering Brown, .	Syracuse, N. Y.
30,	Alma Ethel Wilson,*. . .	Clara Farwell Hemingway, .	Boston.
30,	Mary Isabelle Corbett,* . .	Eva Emery Coolbroth, . .	Boston.
Nov. 6,	Ephraim Dodge Potter, .	William Potter, . . .	Boston.
6,	Joseph Boyle McGuckian,* .	George Mayott, . . .	Boston.
13,	William E. Maccue,*. . .	William E. Birkmaier, . .	Manchester, N. H.
20,	Thomas Edward Shiel,* . .	Thomas Edward McCarthy, .	Boston.
27,	Philip Carr,*	Frank Faulhefer, . . .	Boston.
27,	Mary Clyde Pain,* . . .	Florence Campbell Davis, .	Boston.
27,	John Ritter,*	John Sargent, ...	Boston.
Dec. 4,	Alice Cosman Gray,*. . .	Alice Aritta Potter, . .	Boston.
18,	Ethel R. Patter,* . . .	Ethel L. Wilson. . . .	Boston.
18,	Louise Richè McKim, . .	Rogè Coolidge McKim, . .	Boston.

ESSEX COUNTY.

Jan. 9,	Mary Louisa Rano,* . . .	Annie Louisa Currier, . .	Worcester.
Feb. 6,	Gracie Maud Bailey,* . .	Gracie Maud Whitehouse, .	Haverhill.
Mar. 6,	Bessie May Brown,* . . .	Bessie Wilson Trask, . .	Lynn.
6,	Bertie Lewis Tirrell,*. . .	Harry Lewis Howard, . .	Salem.
13,	Theodore Bird Porter,* . .	Charles Porter Noyes, . .	Camden, Me.
April 3,	Minnie Quimber Connor,*. .	Helena Perkins Mackie,. .	Brookline.
3,	Lillie Sparrow,*. . . .	Helen Florence Libbey, . .	Boston.
17,	Irene Bowley,*	Irene Bowley Usher, . .	Lynn.
17,	Joseph Warren Fields,* . .	Joseph Warren Johnson, .	Peabody.
May 1,	Rufus Gifford, ...	Rufus Babcock Gifford, .	Salem.
June 12,	Millie Belle Prescott,* . .	Millie Belle Noyes,. . .	Methuen.
26,	Georgie May Ryan,* . . .	Georgie May Ring,. . .	Boston.
July 3,	Catherine Smith,* . . .	Clara Marie Hamilton, . .	Gloucester.
3,	Annah Laskey, ...	Annie Dodge, ...	Peabody.
24,	Clemmie M. Buzzell,* . .	Clemmie M. Todd, . . .	Newburyport.
24,	Susie E. Buzzell,* . . .	Susie E. Todd, ...	Newburyport.
Oct. 9,	Estella Blanche Meady,* . .	Estella Maud Johnson, . .	Salem.
9,	Mary Sullivan,*	Mary Sullivan Fay, . .	Boston.
9,	Lulu A. Dore,*	Lulu Dore Abbott, . . .	Methuen.
23,	Everett Wellington Norris,* .	Everett Wellington McDonald,	Gloucester.
Nov. 13,	Maude Davis,*	Ella Florence Evans, . .	Lawrence.
13,	Grace Ethel Webster,* . .	Grace Ethel Butler, . .	Lawrence.
27,	—— Armstead,*. . . .	John Clifford Parker Woods,.	Newburyport.
27,	Blanche O. Ingersoll,* . .	Lillian Earle, ...	Gloucester.
Dec. 4,	Everett Herrick,* . . .	Everett Joshua Higgins, .	Gloucester.
4,	Martha Claribel Wormstead, .	Martha Claribel Stevens, .	Lynn.
18,	Sadie Mary Carlson Nelson,* .	Sarah Adaline Hinckley, .	Southbridge.

MIDDLESEX COUNTY.

Jan. 10,	Edith Young, ...	Edith Loring Young, . .	Cambridge.
10,	Jennie Emerton,* . . .	Jennie Emerton Wheeler, .	Lowell.
24,	Rosaline Coston,* . . .	Rosaline Covill, . . .	Medford.
24,	Ellen Maria McBride,* . .	Nellie Lillie Cooper, . .	Woburn.
24,	Vivia Amanda Maloney,* . .	Vivia Amanda Hathaway, .	Arlington.
24,	James Bartholemew Hartley,* .	James Bartholemew Hardy, .	Somerville.
Feb. 7,	George Edward Little,* . .	George Edward Gennery, .	Lowell.
14,	Owen Bent,*	Harry Wayne Richards, .	Lexington.

* Changed by reason of adoption.

MIDDLESEX COUNTY — *Concluded.*

Date of Decree.	Original Name.	Name Decreed.	Residence.
1882.			
Feb. 14,	Daisy Reilley,* . . .	Emily Chace Taylor, . .	Melrose.
14,	Albert Hawkins,* . . .	William John McClellan, .	Medford.
28,	Margaret Munroe Davis,* .	Flora May Chamberlin, . .	Watertown.
28,	John Golden,* . . .	Charles Fletcher Shaw, . .	Watertown.
28,	Sarah King,* . . .	Mary Julia Wheeler. . .	Stoneham.
28,	Mary Rich,* . . .	Maud Louisa Kendall, . .	Watertown.
28,	William J. Boston,* . .	William John Orcutt, . .	Cambridge.
28,	John Houston, . . .	John Houston Forsaith, . .	Lowell.
Mar. 14,	William Crooks,* . . .	William Hines, . . .	Stoneham.
28,	Lewis Webster,* . .	Herbert Louis Osborn, . .	Medford.
28,	Bessie Abbie Hall,* . .	Bessie Abbie Adams, . .	Wayland.
28,	Charles Moody Hall,* . .	Charles Moody Adams, . .	Wayland.
28,	Josephine Smith,* . .	Josephine Eliza Robinson, .	Sudbury.
28,	Abbie Clifford,* . . .	Abbie Pingree, . . .	Hopkinton.
April 4,	Herman Larch, . . .	Henry Herman Sommerman,	Cambridge.
4,	Theodore Johnson,* . .	Theodore Alaric Peck, . .	Cambridge.
11,	Sarah Etta Martin,* . .	Sarah Etta Huntoon, . .	Lowell.
25,	Florine Avesta Hogan, .	Florine Avesta Elliott, . .	Cambridge.
May 2,	Herbert Garfield McBaine,*	Herbert Garfield Blake, . .	Somerville.
23,	Orrin Sampson,* . . .	Wilmot Estes Mayhew, . .	Medford.
June 13,	Henry B. McBaine,* . .	Henry Bevins Bourne, . .	Franklin.
27,	Joseph Henry Linnell,* .	Joseph Henry Parker, . .	Woburn.
27,	Katie Chapman,* . .	Edna Blanch Cairns, . .	Cambridge.
July 11,	Lizzie Angeline Hotchkiss,*	Lizzie Allen Rockwood, . .	Holliston.
18,	Lula Bell Scott,* . .	Lula Bell Scott Mann, . .	Cambridge.
25,	Irene Rockwell,* . .	Irene Rockwell Severence, .	Medford.
25,	Theodore Baldwin,* . .	Theodore Baldwin Whitaker,	Waltham.
25,	Delia Christiansson,* . .	Delia Cornelia Anderson, .	Waltham.
25,	Frederic Ellis,* . . .	Howard Winthrop Burge, .	Waltham.
Sept. 5,	Isabella Rebecca Wilde Spinney, ...	Isabella Wilde Spinney Matthew, ...	Woburn.
5,	Hannah Thomas Crane, .	Hannah Thomas Brainard, .	Somerville.
5,	Sophia Annis Curtis, . .	Frankie Spaulding Curtis, .	Hudson.
12,	Edla Charlotte Anderson,*	Edla Charlotte Coes, . .	Cambridge.
12,	Harry W Burns,* . .	Henry Llewellyn Bixbee, .	Malden.
12,	Edward Francis Fitzgerald,*	Frank Barnard, . . .	Somerville.
12,	Mary Dudley Keane,* .	Mary Greenfield, . . .	Everett.
26,	Harry Van Duzee, . .	Harold Van Duzee, . .	Newton.
Oct. 3,	Daisey Kendrick,* . .	Amy Plimpton Fiske, . .	Newton.
10,	Hattie May Hunter,* . .	Hattie May Rich, . .	Malden.
24,	Henry Barry Conroy,* .	Franklin Theodore Meanor, .	Marlborough.
24,	Orlando Poskitt,* . .	Orlando Austin Poskitt, . .	Malden.
Nov. 7,	Etta Louise Jordan,* . .	Sybil Louise Richards, . .	Natick.
7,	Minnie Matilda Beck,* .	Minnie Emeline Hague, . .	Malden.
7,	Clarence Harrington,* .	Edward Isherwood, . .	Lowell.
14,	John W. McKenney,* . .	William Stevens, . . .	Groton.
14,	Carl Augustus Carter,* .	Carl Augustus Eaton, . .	Cambridge.
28,	Mark Chilson,* . . .	Forrest Otto Copithorn, . .	Natick.
28,	Maud Regan,* . . .	Abbie Maud Jenness, . .	Bedford.
28,	Florence Greenwood Taber,*	Nellie Alice Burke, . .	New York.
Dec. 5,	Etta S. Muzzey, . . .	Etta S. Pease, . . .	Lowell.
26,	Mabel Young,* . . .	Mabel Verne Parker, . .	Acton.
26,	Violet Gordon,* . . .	Maud Viola Dwyer, . .	Cambridge.

WORCESTER COUNTY.

Jan. 3,	Edward Sanford Fuller, . .	Edward Sanford Crawford, .	Oakham.
17,	Sarah Janette Carpenter, .	Sarah Janette Hall, . .	Upton.
17,	Alice F. Harrington, . .	Fannie Harrington Bullard, .	Westborough.

* Changed by reason of adoption.

WORCESTER COUNTY — *Concluded.*

Date of Decree.	Original Name.	Name Decreed.	Residence.
1882.			
Feb. 7,	Warren W. Blakley, . . .	Warren W. Paine, . . .	Milford.
7,	William Frank Smith, . .	William Frank Bliss, . .	Brattleboro', Vt.
7,	Caroline A. L. D. Barribeault, .	Eva Barribeault, . . .	Spencer.
7,	Ralph Ernest Bowker, . .	Ralph Ernest Jackson, . .	Winchendon.
Mar. 7,	Margaret Mitchell, . . .	Edith Elizabeth Gunn, . .	Northbridge.
April 4,	Mary Lizzie Day, . . .	Mary Lizzie Day Thompson,	Fitchburg.
4,	Edith Baker, ...	Georgiana Jeanne Spaulding,	Milford.
11,	Minnie F. Parkman, . . .	Minnie F. Bicknell, . .	Mendon.
18,	Henry Richardson, . . .	Henry Moody Mann, . .	Worcester.
18,	Mabel Louisa White, . . .	Mabel Louisa Fay, . . .	Worcester.
25,	Laura Maria Crehore, . .	Laura Minerva Sidney, .	Fitchburg.
May 10,	Leroy Alfred Goodrich, . .	Alfred Leroy Mitchell, . .	Grafton.
16,	Edith Louisa Hill, . . .	Edith Elizabeth Smith, . .	West Boylston.
16,	Ada May Clark, ...	Jennie May Burt, . . .	Northbridge.
June 6,	Addie C. Howe, ...	Addie C. Warfield, . . .	Milford.
20,	———, ...	Hattie Mabel Hudson, . .	Worcester.
July 5,	George Henry Symonds, . .	Henry Symonds Greeley, .	Leominster.
18,	Flora B. Anthony, . . .	Flora B. Aldrich, . . .	Upton.
18,	Eleanor Wight, ...	Eleanor Morgan, . . .	Worcester.
18,	Edith Howard Davis, . .	Edith Howard Robinson, .	Worcester.
Sept. 5,	Frank P. Burnham, . . .	Frank Andrews Rixford, .	Northbridge.
5,	Frank Dimond Spiller, . .	Frank Ralph Spiller, . .	Northborough.
19,	Clara Bell Barton, . . .	Clara Bell Leonard, . .	Hubbardston.
19,	Henry Francis Barton, . .	Henry Francis Leonard, .	Hubbardston.
19,	Bertha Mabel Pratt, . . .	Bertha Mabel Brewer, . .	Spencer.
Oct. 3,	Elizabeth E. Fogarty, . .	Elizabeth Norton, . . .	Webster.
Nov. 7,	Annie Louisa West, . . .	Annie Louisa Hastings, .	Westborough.
21,	Maude H. Payne,* . . .	Maude H. McConnell, . .	Worcester.
21,	Michael Angelo Breen, . .	Michael Angelo Shampagn, .	Dudley.
21,	Frederick Kennedy Grover, .	Frederick Merick Smith, .	Southbridge.
28,	Edward B Turner, . . .	Charles Frederick Batchelder, .	Worcester.
Dec. 19,	Susan B. Reed, ...	Susan E. Rolfe, . . .	Worcester.
26,	James Alfred Bishop, . .	Alfred Green Knight, . .	Southborough.
26,	Edmund Bishop, ...	Edmund Green Knight, .	Southborough.
26,	Anna Melinda Bishop, . .	Annie Mary Knight, . .	Southborough.

HAMPSHIRE COUNTY.

Jan. 3,	Agnes L. Moore,* . . .	Agnes L. Hunt, . . .	Williamsburg.
3,	Albert S. Wright, . . .	Albert S. Fairfield, . . .	Williamsburg.
3,	Clara E. Wright, . . .	Clara E. Fairfield, . . .	Williamsburg.
Feb. 7,	Emma L. Davis, ...	Emma L. Dickinson, . .	Amherst.
7,	Lilly Sullivan,*	Bertha M. Kelso, . . .	Huntington.
April 8,	Margaret Fornier,* . . .	Margaret Clapp, . . .	Northampton.
May 2,	Lillian M. Rich,* . . .	Lillian M. Smith, . . .	Amherst.
2,	Mary J. Babcock,* . . .	Mary J. Brown, . . .	Northampton.
Aug. 1,	Paul R. Bridgman,* . . .	Paul B. Lyman, . . .	Belchertown.
Sept. 5,	Michael J. Russell,* . . .	Myron J. White, . . .	Hadley.
Oct. 3,	Florence G. Rich,* . . .	Florence E. Young, . . .	Amherst.
Nov. 8,	Mabel Atkins,*	Mabel Winter, . . .	Ware.

HAMPDEN COUNTY.

Feb. 21,	Grace Buchanan,* . . .	Grace Bartlett, . . .	Chicopee.
21,	Lottie Burke,*	Charlotte Lawler, . . .	Springfield.
Mar. 7,	Elizabeth Sweeney,* . . .	Bessie May Gile, . . .	Springfield.

* Changed by reason of adoption.

HAMPDEN COUNTY — *Concluded.*

Date of Decree.	Original Name.	Name Decreed.	Residence.
1882.			
Mar. 7,	Mary Alice Sweeney,*	Mary Alice Dunbar,	Westfield.
7,	Flora Atwood,*	Florence Adeline Miller,	Springfield.
April 4,	Charlotte Emeline Buxton,*	Charlotte Emeline Hough,	Westfield.
May 2,	Margaret Griffin,*	Minnie Bryant,	Holyoke.
9,	Jennie M. Capin,*	Jennie M. Belden,	Monson.
23,	Henry Temple,*	Lewis Henry Fortin,	Springfield.
June 24,	——,*	Faith L. Atwood,	Springfield.
Sept. 5,	Emeline Chatfield,*	Emma Winchester,	Westfield.
Oct. 3,	Lucy Janet Bryant,*	Lucy Bryant Foster,	Springfield.
Nov. 9,	Jesse Alzina Flanery,*	Jesse Alzina Howard,	Chicopee.
28,	Josephine May Bond,*	Josephine May Messier,	Wilbraham.

FRANKLIN COUNTY.

Date of Decree.	Original Name.	Name Decreed.	Residence.
Mar. 14,	Lyman H. Crandall,*	Lyman H. Doolittle,	Gill.
23,	Cora Bell Ward,*	Cora Bell Marshall,	Montague.
23,	Carrie Dell Ward,*	Carrie Dell Marshall,	Montague.
May 23,	Almon Bronson Flanigan,	Almon Bronson,	Charlemont.
Oct. 3,	—— Rice,*	Bernice Rice,	Rowe.

BERKSHIRE COUNTY.

Date of Decree.	Original Name.	Name Decreed.	Residence.
Mar. 7,	Nettie C. Bates,	Nettie E. Bartlett,	Pittsfield.
7,	Maria Bevelton,	Jessie Bevelton Bartlett,	Pittsfield.
April 13,	Lena Wein,	Marion Helena Russell,	Pittsfield.
13,	Margaret McIntire, *alias* Bertha Magdalena,	Bertha Magdalena Russell,	Pittsfield.
13,	Henrietta Stephenson,	Henrietta Solert,	Pittsfield.
13,	Emon Martin,	Emon Cardinal,	Adams.
13,	Mary Powers,	Mary Snyder,	Pittsfield.
13,	Leland Jay Swan,	Leland Jay Hall,	North Adams.
June 6,	Margaret Hicock,	Margaret Collins,	Pittsfield.
Sept. 5,	Blanche Astings,	Blanche Astings Snow,	W. Stockbridge.
Dec. 5,	Elizabeth Rice,	Minnie M. Dyke,	North Adams.

NORFOLK COUNTY.

Date of Decree.	Original Name.	Name Decreed.	Residence.
Feb. 15,	William Ward Bakie,*	George William Cottle,	Norwood.
Mar. 22,	Adeline Packard Gibson,*	Grace Adeline Thayer,	Quincy.
22,	Harry Richards Marble,*	Carl Neilson Tucker,	Milton.
April 12,	Dennis Craige,*	Russell Weston Badger,	Quincy.
12,	Walter Rice,*	Raymond Palmer Delano,	Hyde Park.
12,	Harriet Powers Smith,*	Hattie Pearl Gleason,	Dedham.
19,	Edward Gardner Bowden,*	Edward Gardner Bowditch,	Braintree.
19,	William Campbell,*	William Campbell Ellis,	Walpole.
June 7,	Maud Cameron Campbell,*	Florence Everett Belcher,	Bellingham.
July 26,	Lilian Foster Bernstien, *alias* Lilian Foster Hazlett,*	Lilian Foster Turner,	Milton.
Dec. 20,	Mary Jane Bouvey,*	Mary Bouvey Smith,	Sharon.
20,	Bessie Eldridge,*	Gertrude Lfa. Sawyer,	Medfield.

* Changed by reason of adoption.

PLYMOUTH COUNTY.

Date of Decree.	Original Name.	Name Decreed.	Residence.
1882.			
Jan. 23,	Lewis F. Haskins, Jr.,*	Ernest F. Bumpus,	Wareham.
Feb. 13,	Albert W. Holmquest,*	Albert Watfried Petter,	Wareham.
13,	George E. Dempsey,*	George E. D. Eschemback,	Brockton.
April 10,	William Ives,*	William Ives Jeffries,	Middleborough.
24,	Frank Eugene Heath,*	Joseph E. Wrightington,	Middleborough.
Nov. 13,	George Henry John Ritter,	George Henry John Arnold,	Middleborough.

BRISTOL COUNTY.

Date of Decree.	Original Name.	Name Decreed.	Residence.
Feb. 1,	Minnie Rose,	Anna Thompson,	Dartmouth.
April 7,	Mary Elizabeth Harps,	Mary Elisabeth Munroe,	New Bedford.
May 5,	Elmer E. Dunn,	Elmer E. Simmons,	Fairhaven.
19,	——,	Mary Frances Ginnodo,	Attleborough.
19,	Mary Dickinson,	Mary Turner,	Fall River.
19,	Mary O'Donnell,	Mary Murphy,	Fall River.
June 2,	Agnes Carney,*	Name unchanged,	Fall River.
July 7,	Charles Edwin Manchester,	Charles Edwin Grinnell,	Attleborough.
Aug. 4,	Mary Elisabeth Carroll,	Anne Hallam,	Fall River.
4,	Helen S. D. Kent,	Mary Whitman Deane,	New Bedford.
4,	Mary J. Kelley,	Mary J. Murphy,	Fall River.
4,	Stephen Franklin Aiken,	Stephen Franklin Allen Jay,	New Bedford.
4,	Elisabeth Lowe,	Catherine Lowe,	New Bedford.
Oct. 6,	Lena Francis,	Mabel Josephine Holloway,	Taunton.
6,	Maude B. Ramsey,	Maude B. French,	Fall River.
6,	Mary Ann King, *alias* Brennan,	Delight Brown Macomber,	Fall River.
Nov. 3,	William Henry Ryder,	William Henry Frates,	New Bedford.
3,	Freddie Weston Freeman,	Charles Martin Childs,	New Bedford.
3,	Norman Burt Gilman,	Francis Lyman Gilman,	New Bedford.
3,	Michael Gardalla,	Amadeo Clorite,	New Bedford.
3,	Agnes May Haskins,	Agnes May Braley,	Taunton.
Dec. 1,	James William Everett,	William Everett Spooner,	Fairhaven.

BARNSTABLE COUNTY.

Date of Decree.	Original Name.	Name Decreed.	Residence.
May 17,	Nettie N. Totman,	Nettie Mabel Young,	Provincetown.

NANTUCKET COUNTY.

Date of Decree.	Original Name.	Name Decreed.	Residence.
Nov. 16,	William Pierce,	William Irving Sandsbury,	Nantucket.

* Changed by reason of adoption.

SUFFOLK COUNTY.

Date of Decree.	Original Name.	Name Decreed.	Residence.
1883.			
Jan. 1,	Sadie Hynes,*	Sadie Hynes Niles, .	Boston.
8,	Rose O'Hara,* .	Gracey Farrell, .	Boston.
15,	Hannah Bradbury Talcott.	Hannah Bradbury Goodwin, .	Boston.
22,	Florence Adelaide Currier,*	Edith Marcella Wells, .	Boston.
Feb. 5,	Elizabeth Stewart McLeod,*	Edith Maranda Hyatt, .	Boston.
5,	Emma Christina Leonard,*	Winifred Hopkins Moore,	Boston.
12,	William Lubben,*	Willis Mark Willoby, .	Boston.
12,	Etta Carlisle,* .	Eleanor Christina Affew,	Boston.
26,	Helen Josephine Gay,*	Mabel Josephine Eastman,	Boston.
26,	Mary Nagle.*	Florence Lyle Bent, .	Boston.
26,	Faith Rhind,* .	Ethel Euphemia Lawson,	Boston.
26,	George Philip Williams,* .	Philip Harvey Vose, .	Boston.
Mar. 5,	Edith Pearl Rich,*	Lula May Bacon, .	Boston.
12,	Oscar Peel, .	Frank Crosbie, .	Boston.
12,	Mary McGee,* .	Mary Macgee Williams, .	Boston.
12,	Bertha Louisa Cross,*	Alberta Carrie Morgan, .	Lyndon, Vt.
20,	Emily Gay,* †	Mabel Reynolds Herriman,	Boston.
26,	Mabel Miller,* .	Libby Mabel Nicholson, .	Boston.
26,	Salma Lyon, .	Louis Aldrich, .	Boston.
April· 2,	Estella Willett,*	Estella Baker, .	Burlington, Vt.
16,	Martha Barker Hall, .	Martha Wolcott Hall, .	Boston.
16,	Florence Loretta Hart,*	Florence Clark Atwood, .	Providence, R. I.
30,	Florence Edna Cowling Starr,* .	Florence Edna Cowling,	Boston.
30,	Cora May Stewart,* .	Phebe Ozeete Sawin, .	Boston.
May 7,	Mary Elizabeth Rhind,* .	Lydia Love Houck, .	Boston.
7,	Joseph Sullivan,* .	Frederick Eugene Tyler,	Boston.
7,	Lilla White Moore, .	Lilla Moore Fairbanks, .	Boston.
28,	Florence Harris,*. .	Madora Bell Hatch,	Boston.
June 4,	——,* .	James Joseph McLaughlin,	Boston.
4,	Herman L. Oakes,* .	Herman L. Robinson, .	Boston.
11,	Maud Driskell.*. .	Dora Hunter Saunders, .	Cambridge.
11,	Jacquittia McCandless,* .	Jacquittia Shafer, .	Boston.
11,	George Tyler Thornton,* .	George Jackson McNamara, .	Boston.
11,	Ethel Prescott,* .	Edna Ethel Nowell, .	Haverhill.
18,	Herbert Mulligan,* .	Herbert Jacobs, .	Boston.
25,	Alice Maud Pitman Hogan,*	Edith May Griffin, .	Boston.
July 2,	Mary Ellen Witherington,*	Mary Ellen Brannan, .	Boston.
9,	Ida Gertie Chessman,* .	Ida Gertie Joselyn, .	Boston.
30,	Daisy Norwood,* .	Myrtle Florence Freeman,	Boston.
Aug. 20,	Elizabeth Writer,*	Elizabeth Hodgkins, .	Boston.
20,	Mary Louisa Baker,*	Lillie May Robinson, .	Amherst, N. H.
Sept. 3,	—— O'Connor,* .	Herbert Cecil Daly, .	Boston.
10,	Lewis Goldberg, .	Lewis Harris Kaplan, .	Boston.
17,	William Herbert,*	William Fredrik Johnson,	——.
Oct. 1,	Ida May Griffin.*	Ida May Macdonald, .	Shelburne. N. S.
1,	Thomas John Gray, .	Turrell Fales Gray, .	Boston.
1,	Rachel Tobey, *alias* Rachel Tobey Amos Robbins,* .	Lottie Van Horten Banks, .	Mashpee.
1,	Philip Mason,* .	William Madden, .	——.
1,	Annie Louisa Hastings,* .	Annie Louisa West, .	Westborough.
8,	Eunice Hayward,* .	Laura May Bell, .	——.
8,	Anderson Alexander Reeve Kamoffsky,* .	Anderson Alexander Reeve, .	Boston.
8,	Mabel Johnson,* .	Flossie May Freeman, .	Pictou, N. S.
15,	Robert Cutler Hinckley, .	Robert Hinckley. .	Boston.
22,	—— Wilson,* .	Fannie Eleanor Guenther Winther, .	Boston.
22,	Lafayette Banks, .	Lafayette Foster, .	Boston.
Nov. 5,	Josephine McDonough,* .	Annie Josephine McDonough,	Boston.
5,	Richard Ratcliffe Bond,* .	George Henry Chase, .	Cambridge.

* Changed by reason of adoption.　　　† Changed by decree of Supreme Court, on appeal.

SUFFOLK COUNTY — *Concluded.*

Date of Decree.	Original Name.	Name Decreed.	Residence.
1883.			
Nov. 5,	Frederick Foley, . . .	Frederick Atherton, . .	Boston.
5,	Benjamin Franklin Foley, .	Benjamin Franklin Atherton,	Boston.
12,	Alfred Maurice Spalding, .	Fred Maurice Spalding, .	Boston.
12,	Gracie Harcourt, or Maggie Harcourt, or Maggie Harcove,* .	Grace Elva Kellogg, .	Boston.
12,	Mary Hughes Lane,* . .	Alice Mary Lewis, . .	Boston.
12,	Maude Gertrude Lottie Spear,* .	Maude Gertrude Tutton, .	Boston.
19,	Henry August Linnemann, .	Henry Smith Linnemann, .	Boston.
19,	William Lowell,* . .	William Augustus Stukey, .	Beverly.
19,	Hattie DeLong,* . .	Hattie Stevens Clark, .	Boston.
19,	Grace Briscoe,* . . .	Grace Maud Dickinson, .	Hull.
26,	Grace Edna Hittinghine, .	Grace Edna Martin, .	Boston.
26,	Mary Josephine Smith,* .	Mary Josephine Heath, .	Boston.
26,	Philip Burckhart, . .	William Harris, . .	Boston.
Dec. 10,	George Henry Quinland, .	George Harvey Gray, .	Boston.
10,	Frank Taylor,* . . .	Frank Wentworth, . .	Newton.
17,	John Stewart,* . . .	Walter Alexander Shannon, .	Lowell.
17,	Roswell Dash Mayhew,* .	Francis Addison Brown, .	Boston.
17,	Elizabeth Sanchez,* . .	Ella Celetta Lee, . .	Boston.
17,	Ella L. Walker,* . . .	Ella L. Heal, . . .	Chelsea.
17,	Mabel Duffie,* . . .	Mabel Agnes Stephens, .	Boston.
24,	Lydia Love Houck,* . .	Edith Houck Boyd, .	Quincy, Ill.
31.	George Roland Noyes,* .	George Roland Spinney, .	W. Newbury.

ESSEX COUNTY.

Jan. 1,	Gertie Macabe,* . . .	Eliza Ann Dickson, .	Amesbury.
1,	Maud L. Pompelio, . .	Maud L. Willey, . .	Georgetown.
15,	Nellie Lois McGrath,* .	Nellie Lois Langley, .	Lynn.
15,	Alba M. Burns, . . .	Alba Marcus Markey, .	North Andover.
Feb. 5,	Mary Elizabeth Mackey,* .	Mary Elizabeth White, .	Gloucester.
5,	Harry J. Manson,* . .	Harry Manson Moore, .	Haverhill.
19,	Susan Frances Coburn,* .	Susan Frances Johnson Coburn, ...	Lowell.
19,	Arthur Sherman,* . .	Arthur Franklin Macey, .	Boston.
Mar. 5,	Francis Martin,* . .	Francis Martin Walker, .	Lawrence.
12,	Mary A. Guard,* . .	Mary Ann Westacott, .	Methuen.
19,	Martha W. Parsons,* .	Martha W. Hewett, .	Rockport.
19,	Sarah Kate Chamberlin, .	Kate Howe Chamberlin, .	Nahant.
26,	Frank Erwin Hawkes,* .	Frank Erwin Bayley, .	Newburyport.
26,	Bertie Alvin Morse,* . .	Horace Bertrand Baldwin, .	Lynn.
April 16,	LeRoy Vincent,* . .	LeRoy Vincent Ray, .	Boston.
May 14,	Grace Edith Dunderdale,* .	Grace Edith Emmott, .	Lawrence.
14,	Annie Morton Tyler,* .	Annie Tyler Mooers, .	Lawrence.
June 4,	Daniel Campbell,* . .	Frank Woodbury Kenney, .	Athol.
4,	Samuel Smith Willey,* .	Elmer Ellsworth Bickford, .	Barrington, N. H.
18,	Annie Minahan,* . .	Mary Elizabeth Minahan, .	Lawrence.
25,	Hattie May Bradley,* .	Harriet May Dockum, .	West Newbury.
25,	Elizabeth A. Ingersoll,* .	Elizabeth Anna Elwell, .	Gloucester.
July 23,	—— Sampson,* . . .	Blanche Flora Whitney, .	West Brookfield.
23,	Lillian Josephine Sargent,*	Lillian Josephine Berry, .	Beverly.
Aug. 6,	Charles A. Nourse,* . .	Charles A. Chase, . .	Salem.
Sept. 3,	Nellie Susan Dow,* . .	Adeline Jane Graham, .	Salisbury.
17,	Anastasia Collins,* . .	Anastasia Landers, . .	Andover.
17,	John Joseph Collins,* . .	John Joseph Roche, . .	Andover.
24,	Louise Ellen Dow,* . .	Grace Hinckley Folger, .	Salisbury.
24,	Willie Munroe,* . . .	Herbert Wilson Smart, .	Tewksbury.
24,	Gladys Elizabeth Pearson,*	Constance Abbot, . .	Beverly.

* Changed by reason of adoption.

ESSEX COUNTY — *Concluded.*

Date of Decree.	Original Name.	Name Decreed.	Residence.
1883.			
Oct. 15,	—— Thomas,*	Alberta May Mansfield, . .	St. John, N. B.
Nov. 5,	Edna Alzada Matthias,* . .	Edna Alzada Smith, . .	Somerville.
5,	Hattie G. Snell, *alias* Allen,* .	Harriet Andrew Allen, . .	Beverly.
12,	Mabel Florence Foote,* . .	Mabel Florence Pressey, .	Haverhill.
12,	Charles H. Reed, *alias* Charles Henry Farrell,* . . .	Raymond Irving Marks, .	Lawrence.
19,	Alice May Douglass,* . .	Esther Maud Bunker, . .	C. Elizabeth, Me.
19,	Alice Adelaide Pease,* . .	Mabel Adelaide Lord, . .	Salem.
19,	Lilla May Peavey,* . . .	Mary Lilla Sweeney, . .	Belfast, Me.

MIDDLESEX COUNTY.

Date of Decree.	Original Name.	Name Decreed.	Residence.
Jan. 9,	Helen Francis Barney,* . .	Maud Carrie Greenleaf, . .	Watertown.
9,	Mary Wilbur Faunce,* . .	Mary Wilbur Moore, . .	Wilton, N. H.
16,	John Henry Sands,* . . .	Harold Fred Sinclair, . .	Lowell.
23,	Joseph Antona Barnedine,* .	Joseph Charles Powell, . .	Cambridge.
23,	Harold Wilson Taylor,* . .	Harold Wilson Dale, . .	Stoneham.
23,	Amos Lawrence Bond, . .	Lawrence Bond, . . .	Newton.
Feb. 13,	Adda Viola Spalding, . .	Adda Viola Knowles, . .	Somerville.
13,	Agnes Melita Spalding, . .	Agnes Melita Knowles, . .	Somerville.
27,	Alice Farquhar,* . . .	Christie Ann Kate Campbell,	Spring Hill, Wilton, Pr. Quebec.
Mar. 6,	William Frederick Schickendantz, ...	William Frederick Schick, .	Medford.
6,	Harry Davis Hearn,* . .	Gardner Holway Osgood, .	Medford.
13,	Freddie Doyle,* . . .	Frederick Bryant, . . .	Newton.
13,	Frank Eugene Risk,* . .	Frank Sanderson, . . .	Framingham.
13,	Nicholas Davis,* . . .	Charles Aubrey Kemp, . .	Stoneham.
20,	Cora Adelaide Fletcher.* . .	Cora Adelaide Turner, . .	Townsend.
27,	Franklin Calhoun Yantis,* .	Franklin Calhoun Pillsbury, .	Winchester.
27,	Joel Horace Yantis,* . .	Joel Horace Pillsbury, . .	Winchester.
27,	John Dix Yantis,* . . .	John Dix Pillsbury, . .	Winchester.
27,	William Herbert Abbott,* . .	William Herbert Abbott Whitney, ...	Malden.
27,	Addie May Happennie,* . .	Ida May Holbrook, . . .	Malden.
27,	John Manton,*	Rouello Prescott Ranger, .	Lowell.
April 3,	Lizzie Gertrude Clifford,* . .	Lizzie Gertrude Dayton, .	Somerville.
24,	Name unknown,* . . .	Albert Francis Sawyer, . .	Cambridge.
May 8,	Owen Slater,*	Owen Slater McCourt, . .	Newton.
15,	Eveline Scott May,* . . .	Florence Mabel Coburn, .	Lowell.
June 5,	Lawrence Joseph Coughlin, .	Lawrence Coolidge, . .	Framingham.
5,	Andrew McGlenn Walsh,* .	Francis Wilbur Carey, . .	Marlborough.
12,	William Francis Cook,* . .	William Francis Sullivan, .	Somerville.
26,	Sophia Little Tirrill,*. . .	Carrie Little Howarth, . .	Saxon Stat'n, Butler County, Pa.
26,	Joseph O'Connell,* . . .	Joseph Cadogan, . . .	Lawrence.
July 3,	Louisa May Brettain,* . .	Berenice Evangeline Guilford,	Waltham.
3,	Ethel Corina Newman,* . .	Ethel Corina Nichols, . .	Cambridge.
3,	Walter Whitney Newman,* .	Walter Whitney Nichols, .	Cambridge.
10,	Annie Lycholm,* . . .	Annie Lycholm Gowing, .	Wilmington.
10,	Annie Irving,*	Lillian Emma Pratt, . .	Waltham.
24,	Arthur Otis Tyler,* . . .	David Sherman, . . .	Westford.
24,	John Edward Blake,* . .	Charles Edward Felch, . .	Natick.
24,	Florence May,*	Edith May Marshall, . .	Natick.
Sept. 4,	Horace Mann Smith,* . .	Horace Mann Stetson, . .	Medford.
4,	Gertrude Lowe,*. . . .	Mabel Gertrude Mann, . .	Medford.
4,	Ada Eudora Avery, . . .	Ada Eudora Scott, . . .	Somerville.

* Changed by reason of adoption.

MIDDLESEX COUNTY — *Concluded.*

Date of Decree.	Original Name.	Name Decreed.	Residence.
1883.			
Sept. 11,	Carrie Louise Avery,*	Carrie Louise Scott,	Somerville.
25,	Mary Frances Taylor,*	Ruth Alice Gray,	Medford.
Oct. 23,	Minnie Ames,*	Minnie Irene Cross,	Medford.
23,	Julia Emma Dreiling,*	Julia Emma Axtman,	Cambridge.
Nov. 6,	Harriet Olevia Kilcup,*	Harriet Olevia Wood,	Wayland.
13,	Patrick James Wilkinson,	James Francis Wilkinson,	Cambridge.
13,	William Edgar Doucet,*	James Edgar Doucet Marygold,	Stoneham.
13,	Franklin Charles Brennan,*	Franklin Charles Henthorne,	Newton.
20,	Odessa Mettie Hendrick,*	Odessa Mettie Cummings,	Stoneham.
27,	Bertha Waugh,*	Goldy Annie Scribner,	Lowell.
Dec. 11,	Edith McBean,*	Edith Turner,	Malden.
11,	Maud Abbie Gray,*	Maud Abbie Kempton,	Richmond, N. H.

WORCESTER COUNTY.

Jan. 2,	Ralf Everett Newell,	Edgar Eugene Lamb,	Royalston.
2,	Marvin E Luby,	Marvin E. Tucker,	North Brookfield.
16,	William Taylor,	William Taylor Mitchinson,	Worcester.
16,	Mary Amelia King,	Mary Amelia Bourque,	Webster.
Feb. 20,	Louisa Green,	Louisa Toupin,	Sutton.
27,	Catharine Jackson,	Catharine Kelley,	Clinton.
Mar. 20,	Elizabeth ———,	Elizabeth Gibson,	Worcester.
20,	John Cahill,	John Cronin,	Worcester.
April 3,	Bertha C. Lawless,	Bertha Alice Pike,	Athol.
May 1,	———————,	Helen Louise Shepard,	Southbridge.
15,	William A. Flagg,	William A. Blaisdell,	Worcester.
June 5,	Elizabeth Maria Watson,	Annie Guard,	Fitchburg.
5,	George Sidney Altenburg,	George Sidney Altenburg Patterson,	Worcester.
19,	Ella Idella Ware,	Anna Idella Henshaw,	Worcester.
19,	——— Foster,*	Eva Vesta Allen,	Holden.
July 3,	David Hayward,	Edward Blanchard,	Worcester.
3,	Josephine Emmaux, *alias* Lamore,	Josephine Ward,	Webster.
17,	Jennie Gertrude Peckham,	Mabel Gertrude Gerry,	Fitchburg.
Aug. 10,	Hattie Mabel Pease,	Hattie Mabel Bolio,	Sturbridge.
Sept. 4,	——— ———,	Alvin Joseph Bouchard,	Worcester.
4,	Esther McQuestion,	Esther Isabel Knight,	North Brookfield.
4,	Richard Ellsworth McNally,	Richard Ellsworth Hazard,	Mendon.
25,	Annie O'Neil,	Hester Annie Carr,	Westminster.
25,	John Hickey,	John O'Connor,	Fitchburg.
Oct. 2,	Flora Dell Twitchell,	Flora Dell Reynolds,	Fitchburg.
2,	Jennie R. McNamara,	Mary Olive Howe,	Princeton.
16,	Lilla Hall,	Edith Lilla Newton,	Woodstock, Ct.
Nov. 6,	Henry Edwards Jackson,	Henry Edwards Bathrick,	Shrewsbury.
6,	Nellie Ducey,	Mabel Louise Hyde,	Southborough.
20,	William B. Babcock,	William Bush Holmes,	Worcester.
20,	Sadie Clark,	Sadie Luella Glazier,	Barre.
20,	Fannie Tremayne Forbes,	Fannie Forbes Hamel,	Clinton.

HAMPSHIRE COUNTY.

Jan. 2,	Gertrude F. Atkins,*	Gertrude F. Hawks,	Goshen.
Mar. 6,	Anna Dugan,*	Anna Sullivan,	Ware.
6,	Patrick J. Dugan,*	Patrick F. Sullivan,	Ware.

* Changed by reason of adoption.

HAMPSHIRE COUNTY — *Concluded.*

Date of Decree.	Original Name.	Name Decreed.	Residence.
1883.			
April 3,	Rosa Chatfield,*	Rosa Kitty Thayer,	Williamsburg.
May 1,	Grace Rogers,*	Grace Macomber,	Chesterfield
June 5,	Walter Scott Morseman,*	William Walter Skiff,	Northampton.
July 3,	Lillian Williams,*	Carrie Emma Gardner,	Plainfield.
Sept. 4,	Mary A. Estabrook,*	Mary A. Kellogg,	Amherst.
Nov. 7,	Joseph Roswell Estabrook,*	Joseph Lyman Wait,	Williamsburg.

HAMPDEN COUNTY.

Date of Decree.	Original Name.	Name Decreed.	Residence.
Jan. 2,	Delia Lillian Dickinson,*	Della Lillian Woods,	Chicopee.
2,	Pearl May Eggleston,*	Pearl Irene Browning,	West Springfield.
2,	Ann Eliza Horton,*	Ann Eliza Clark,	Springfield.
2,	Louisa Caroline Stephen,*	Minnie Wagner,	Springfield.
2,	Helen Mabel Elliott,*	Helen Mabel Bemis,	Springfield.
30,	Patrick Kelley,	William George Sherman,	Springfield.
Feb. 6,	———,*	Howard Richmond Young,	Springfield.
Mar. 6,	Emma F. Buxton,*	Emma Florence Smith,	Chicopee.
9,	Fred Braymon Clarke,*	Fred Clarke Green,	Springfield.
9,	Florence Bennett Fisher,*	Florence Bennett Cook,	Springfield.
April 3,	Arthur A. Feneuf, jun.,*	Arthur James Cranston,	Springfield.
3,	Lilly May Ward,*	Lilly May Beaudry,	Springfield.
May 5,	Eliza McCrohan,*	Unchanged,	Holyoke.
8,	Florence Butler,*	Florence Ella Sherman,	Palmer.
15,	Maud O'Donnell,*	Unchanged,	Holyoke.
June 23,	Mary Elizabeth Feneuf,	Mary Elizabeth Cranston,	Springfield.
25,	Charles Mayr,	Charles Mayo,	Springfield.
Aug. 1,	Emma Mary La Breck,*	Emma Mary Bourrassa,	Springfield.
1,	Emma Nickson,*	Emma Nickson Dunham,	Holyoke.
Sept. 4,	Maud Mason,*	Maud Rebecca Stewart,	Russell.
Nov. 3,	Terrence O'Donnell,*	Terrence William Gling,	Russell.
Dec. 18,	Carrie J. Allen,*	Carrie Jane Maxfield,	Westfield.

FRANKLIN COUNTY.

Date of Decree.	Original Name.	Name Decreed.	Residence.
Jan. 2,	Orbert Prew,*	Orbert Huguenin,	Montague.
Feb. 6,	Leroy Mitchell,*	Leroy Foster Frary,	Deerfield.
June 5,	Rosa A. Phinney,*	Rosa A. Bacon,	Orange.
5,	Jennie C. Wight,*	Jennie Culver,	Shelburne.
Sept. 4,	Rose McCabb,*	Lena M. Guilford,	Ashfield.

BERKSHIRE COUNTY.

Date of Decree.	Original Name.	Name Decreed.	Residence.
Jan. 3,	Catherine Haley,*	Catherine Manian,	Lee.
3,	Mary Ann Haley,*	Mary Ann Manian,	Lee.
Feb. 6,	Mabel Curtin,*	Mabel Grace Burns,	Lee.
May 1,	Bessie Anna Wheeler,*	Bessie Anna Merry,	Pittsfield.
1,	Mabel R. Hawkins,*	Mabel R. Pepoon,	Stockbridge.
July 19,	Eva Ashley,*	Eva Day,	Adams.
19,	Lizzie Baker,*	Lizzie Bertrand,	Adams.
Sept. 4,	Helen Mabel Kenney,*	Helen K. Parsons,	Lenox.
5,	Mabel Luella Hemenway,*	Mabel Luella Curtis,	Stockbridge.
Oct. 4,	Minnie O. Connell,*	Minnie Alice Darby,	North Adams.
Dec. 4,	Walter Wheeler,*	Arthur B. Young,	Pittsfield.

* Changed by reason of adoption.

NORFOLK COUNTY.

Date of Decree.	Original Name.	Name Decreed.	Residence.
1883.			
Feb. 7,	Laura Frances Derby,*	Laura Frances Turner,	Weymouth.
14,	Ada Dyer,*.	Ada Ives Quincy,	Brookline.
April 4,	Ethel Ninette Dalton,*	Ethel Ninette Moon,	Medfield.
18,	Roxa Isabella McGinnis,*.	Isabella Roxa Gray,	Walpole.
May 2,	Mary Olive Dalton,* .	Mary Elizabeth Haynes,	Medfield.
16,	Knoollie Walker,*	Alice Winifred Foster,	Hyde Park.
June 6,	Emma Hellen Gertrude Dalton,*	Emma Hellen Gertrude Hatch,	Dedham.
6,	Louise Lehmann,*	Marion Louise Foster,	Hyde Park.
6,	Agnes McCredie Wilson,*.	Agnes Graham Troup,	Brookline.
July 18,	Bertie Smith Colohan,*	Alfred Henry Inkley,	Weymouth.
Sept. 5,	Helen Knox Wilson,*	Helen Wilson Potter,	Brookline.
19,	Obal Keiver Thayer,*	Obal Keiver Hunter,	Medway.
26,	John Brosnan,* .	John Clifford Brosnan,	Holbrook.
Nov. 7,	Robert Wesley Pond,*	Robert Wesley Hodges, .	Foxborough.
7,	Mary Littlefield,.	Mary Long, .	Randolph.
21,	Frederick Ayer,*	Frederick Ayer Drake,	Stoughton.
21,	Mary Ann Read,	Mary Read Keith,	Stoughton.

PLYMOUTH COUNTY.

Jan. 8,	Nelly Elizabeth Gillman,*.	Nelly Elizabeth Wade,	Rockland.
8,	Bertha L. Battles.*	Bertha L. Huckins,	Brockton.
8,	George Henry John Ritter,	George Henry John Arnold,	Middleborough.
Feb. 12,	Emmanuel Francis Fiumefred-do, .	Emmanuel Francis McHenry,	Plymouth.
May 28,	Harris Lindsay,*	Henry Lindsay Sanford,	Bridgewater.
June 11,	Alfred William Mackie,	Fred William Mackie,	Brockton.
July 9,	Harriet Waters,*·	Annie Weld Edson,	East Bridgewater.
9,	Nellie Rose Reagan,*	Nellie Rose Porter, .	Brockton.
9,	Minnie Christian Atwood,*	Minnie Lee Atwood,	Brockton.
9,	Helen F. Blake, .	Helen F. Stetson,	Bridgewater.
Sept. 24,	William Arthur Bullard,	Arthur Harold Burnett, .	Brockton.
Oct. 8,	Leon Hilton Fish,*	Leon Hilton Nash,	Pembroke.

BRISTOL COUNTY.

Jan. 5,	Nellie B. Owens,	Nellie B. Chaffee,	Providence, R. I.
19,	Sadie Lawton Haigh,.	Sadie Lawrence Fisher,	Taunton.
Feb. 16,	Joseph Leslie Allen,	Leslie Allen Bedell,	Taunton.
Mar. 2,	Florence Naomi Spragg,	Florence Naomi White,	Easton.
May 4,	Freeman Everett Ward,	Freeman Frederick Baldwin,.	Easton.
June 1,	Julia Ann Padelford, .	Julia Ann Peirce,	Rehoboth.
July 6,	Margaret Elizabeth McCafferty,	Margaret Elizabeth Cote,	Fall River.
6,	Catherine W. Burns,	Catherine W. McGuire,	Fall River.
Sept. 7,	Samuel Counsel,	Samuel Counsel Sidebotham,.	Fall River.
7,	Nancy Davis.	Ida May Rounds,	Rehoboth.
Oct. 5,	Fred S. Reeves, .	Fred S. Rhodes,	Fall River.
10,	William Jackson,	William James Daily,	Mansfield.
Nov. 2,	Maud B. Child. .	Maud Child Coffin,	New Bedford.
2,	Henry Roseberry,	Frank Henry Wales,	Mansfield.
2,	Lillian Roseberry,	Fannie Lillian Wales,	Mansfield.
16,	Jeremiah Doyle,	Jeremiah Harrington,	Fall River.
Dec. 7,	Fannie D. Tripp,	Fanny Elizabeth Frasier,	New Bedford.

* Changed by reason of adoption.

DUKES COUNTY.

Date of Decree.	Original Name.	Name Decreed.	Residence.
1883.			
April 16,	Sophia M. Swain, . . .	Emma Walker Mayhew, .	Tisbury.
Sept. 3,	Presberry Luce, ...	Presberry Sherwood Luce, .	Tisbury.
Oct. 15,	Beatrice Fuller, ...	Daisy May Wesley, . .	Cottage City.
15,	Lizzie C. Harrison, . . .	Lizzie H. Rice, . . .	Cottage City.

NANTUCKET COUNTY.

–	Nellie V. Haskell, . . .	Nellie Vernon Folger, . .	Nantucket.

SUFFOLK COUNTY.

Date	Original Name.	Name Decreed.	Residence.
1884.			
Jan. 7,	Melvin Colville,* . . .	Palmer Colville Tiffany, . .	Boston.
7,	Frederick Earle Downing,* .	Frederick Cross Pittee, . .	Boston.
7,	Grace May Totman,* .	Grace Stanton Harrington, .	Brewster, Mass.
14,	Edgar Eccler,*	Alexis Edgar Trempe, . .	Boston
14,	Mary Bell McLoud,* . .	Isabella McLean, . .	Capleton, Canada.
21,	Edith Eveline Blakie,* . .	Mary Alice Cochran, . .	Boston.
21,	Mercy Grace Lubbin,* .	Flossy Maud Willoby, . .	Boston.
28,	Edward O. Griffin,* . . .	Edward O. Byrd, .	Cambridge, Mass.
Feb. 18,	Pansey Drayton,* . .	Pansey Birch, ...	Boston.
18,	—— Monroe,*. . . .	Lawrence Vinal Hill, . .	Boston.
4,	Emily Manderville Herrick Daly, ...	Emily Manderville Herrick, .	Boston.
11,	Henry Hudson,* . . .	Richard Corey Ames, .	Boston.
11,	Willie McDonald,* . .	Francis Wallace Jordan, .	Boston.
25,	Margaret E. H. Friery,* .	Colenne Frances Williams, .	Boston.
25,	Mary Milner,* . . .	Carrie Louise Bagley, .	Boston.
25,	Jacob Fitz-Herbert Sawyer,	Jacob Herbert Sawyer, .	Boston.
Mar. 3,	Mary Elizabeth Walker,* .	Marion Sarah Barber, .	Boston.
10,	Charlotte (or Lottie) Gray,*	Gertrude May Lippincott, .	Boston.
17,	Augusta Greilach,* . .	Augusta Muller, . .	Boston.
17,	George Henry,* . . .	Charles Edwin Sprague,.	Boston.
17,	Alice Maggie McDonald,* .	Alice Maggie Woodman, .	Wolfville, N. S.
24,	Sarah Jane Smith,* . .	Sarah Jane Jackson, .	Boston.
24,	Alice Towle.* . . .	Alice Elizabeth Fraser, .	Boston.
24,	Alice Welch,* . . .	Alice Walsh, . . .	Foxboro', Mass.
April 7,	Mabel F. Brainard,* .	Mabel F. Davis, . .	Boston.
7,	James Robert Johnson, .	James Robert Corey, .	Boston.
14,	Oscar Moore Eland,*. .	Oscar Alexander Ceppi, .	Boston.
14,	Ida May Fraser,* . .	Ida May Tower, . .	Revere.
14,	Dennis Haggerty, . . .	Dennis Haggerty Nettles, .	Boston.
14,	Annie Katharine Niethamer,*	Annie Katharine Nagale, .	Boston.
21,	Edward Harney.* . .	Arthur Edward Wight, .	Boston
28,	Mary Elizabeth Bullard.* .	Mary Elizabeth Underwood, .	Harrisville, N. H.
28,	Annie Elizabeth Duffie, *alias* Annie Duffie,* . . .	Annie Elizabeth Sampson, .	Boston.
28,	Walter Smith,*	Charles Harry Donovan, .	Palmer, Mass.
May 19,	Alice Bicknell,* . . .	Alice May Gore, . .	Boston.
26,	George Edgar Avery, . .	George Everett, . .	Boston.
26,	Mary Welch,*	Mabel Gertrude Clare, .	Oakham, Mass.
June 2,	Frank Stables Ramsay,* .	Frank Stables Locke, .	Boston.
9,	Frederic Lowell,* . .	John Gadsby, . .	Boston.
9,	Joseph Magoun,* . . .	Joseph Dillon,. . . .	Malden, Mass.
16,	Child of unknown parents,*	Faith Goddard, . .	Boston.
16,	Clara B. LeGallee, . .	Clara Bradbury, . .	Boston.

* Changed by reason of adoption.

SUFFOLK COUNTY — *Concluded.*

Date of Decree.	Original Name.	Name Decreed.	Residence.
1884.			
June 16,	Sarah Jane LeGallee, . . .	Sarah Jane Bradbury, . .	Boston.
23,	Ralph Haven,*	Ralph Haven Kearnes, . .	Boston
23,	Clarence Arthur Littlefield,* .	Clarence Arthur Bugbee, .	Boston.
23,	Henry John Tailliez,* . .	Henry John Nicolas, . .	New York City.
July 7,	Edgar Cephas Burnham,* . .	Edward Knapp Butler, . .	Boston.
7,	Annie Wilkinson Dillingham,* .	Annie Wilkinson Howe,. .	Boston.
7,	William Edward Lanergan, .	William Lanergan Edwards, .	Boston.
7,	Lena Toole, or Evelena Bell Bradley,*	Eleanor Marie Denslow, . .	Boston.
14,	Estrella Madrid Huston,* . .	Stella Madrid Stinchfield, .	Boston.
14,	Mary Josephine Keeler,* . .	Mary Josephine Gilmore, .	Boston.
14,	Edith Augusta Salter, . .	Edith Agnes Salter, . .	Boston.
14,	Elisabeth Sullivan,* . . .	Elizabeth Frances Owens, .	Boston.
28,	Mabel L. Mingo,* . . .	Mabel Ellen Morrison, . .	Chelsea.
28,	John Henry O'Neill, . . .	John Henry Neill, . . .	Boston.
28,	Sarah Crawford Peppard,* .	Ethel Harriet Williams,. .	Boston.
Aug. 18,	Oliver Garfield Branch,* .	Warren Gile, ...	Boston.
18,	Joseph Philip Raible, . .	Joseph Philip Ripley, . .	Boston.
18,	Ellen Frances Raible, . .	Ellen Frances Ripley, . .	Boston.
18,	Lorenzo Raible, ...	Lorenzo Ripley, . . .	Boston.
18,	Margaret Martha Raible, .	Margaret Martha Ripley, .	Boston.
Sept. 1,	Molly Garfield Brown,* .	Warrena Sawyer Phelps, .	Boston.
1,	Mary Lucas,*	Gracie May Edds, . . .	———.
1,	Sarah Eveline Tufts,* . .	Grace Adaline Ward, . .	Boston.
1,	Annie Frances Tufts,* . .	Annie Louise Fillebrown, .	Newburyport.
8,	John Russell Hurd Codman, .	Stephen Russell Hurd Codman, ...	Boston.
8,	Daniel James Murphy, . .	Daniel James, ...	Boston.
8,	William Augustus Pond,* . .	William Augustus Pond Alexander, ...	Boston.
22,	William Freeman,* . . .	William Wallace Remick, .	Boston.
22,	Frederick Hendram Gosling,* .	Charles Edward Peabody, .	Boston.
22,	Cornelia Golden Kenney,* .	Cornelia Golden Pope, . .	Boston.
29,	James Moore,* . . .	George Ernest Gillpatrick, .	Boston.
Oct. 6,	Jennie Hayden,* . . .	Helen Gertrude Bates, . .	Boston.
6,	Mary Ella Symonds,* . .	Estelle Wood Jackson, . .	Boston.
20,	Myron Fellows Bodge,* . .	Myron Fellows Ryder, . .	Boston.
20,	Mary Dempsey, ...	Mary Eaton, ...	Boston.
20,	Albert Leslie Kidder,* . .	Albert Leslie Kidder Heath, .	Manchester, N. H.
20,	Gracie Marshall,* . . .	Gracie Bell Morrissey, . .	Boston.
27,	Catherine Clark,* . . .	Katie Mary Manchester,. .	Boston.
27,	Lorena Villiers,* . . .	Lorena Quinn, . . .	Boston.
27,	Daisey Derby Welch,* . .	Daisey Derby Pulsifer, . .	Boston.
Nov. 3,	Frank Darlington Jordan Lone,*	Frank Darlington Bailey, .	Boston.
10,	Henry Thaxter,* . . .	John Howard Thaxter, . .	Boston.
17,	Grace Donovan,* . . .	Gertie May Colburn, . .	Boston.
17,	Ada Florence Hammett,* . .	Ada Florence Williams,. .	Boston.
17,	Mary Lenning,*	Elizabeth Knepel, . . .	Boston.
17,	Helen Morse,*	Flora Eugenia Warner, . .	Boston.
Dec. 1,	Flora Etta Adams,* . . .	Florenze Isabel Roath, . .	Boston.
1,	Lucy W. Clapp, ...	Alice Howland, . . .	Boston.
8,	Fanny Fisher,*	Mabel Parritt, ...	Boston.
8,	Clement Fowler,* . . .	Fred Argene Pike, . . .	Boston.
8,	Walter Albert Harvey, . .	Walter Elbert Chickering, .	Boston.
8,	John Oak,*.	Persewell John Munton,. .	Boston.
8,	Irene Sarah Rice,* . . .	Irene Sarah Homan, . .	Boston.
8,	Gertrude Stephenson,* . .	Gladdys May Woods, . .	Boston.
15,	Henry Napoli French, . .	Towneley Thorndike French, .	Boston.
29,	Lula Belle Griffin,* . . .	Josephine Louisa Isabel Greene, ...	Boston.
29,	Mary F. Vincente,* . . .	Mary F. Martines, . . .	Boston.

---

* Changed by reason of adoption.

ESSEX COUNTY.

Date of Decree.	Original Name.	Name Decreed.	Residence.
1884.			
Jan. 7,	Jeffrie Bouvie,*	William Henry Landford,	Boston.
7,	Maud G. Woodman,*	Grace Maud Sawyer,	Brooklyn, N. Y.
14,	Hattie M. Young,*	Harriet Mabel Vittum,	Gilmanton, N. H.
28,	Grace E. Thomson,	Ethel Parton,	Newburyport.
Feb. 4,	Bertha A. Harding,*	Bertha Alena Churchill,	Haverhill.
4,	William T. Dayton,	William Hardy Dayton,	Salem.
18,	Eldredge R. Morrison,*	Hermann Arthur Roeding,	Boston.
Mar. 3,	John Peckham,*	Ernest Harold True,	Adamsville, R. I.
10,	Andrew M. Lopez,	Andrew Madison Ropes,	Salem.
17,	Mildred B. Carpenter,*	Sybil Avis Clarkson King,	Lynn.
April 7,	Ruth Tarbuck,*	Ida Belle Mansfield,	Lowell.
21,	Jennie Russell,*	Jennie Rollins,	Fredericton, N. B.
28,	Rexford H. Archer,*	Rexford Henry Holt,	Haverhill.
May 5,	Blanche Beattie,	Blanche Elliot,	Peabody.
5,	Susan C. Beattie,	Susan Catharine Elliot,	Peabody.
5,	Mary Healey,*	Florence Todd,	West Newbury.
5,	Augustus L. Rhodes,*	Eugene Rhoades Fox,	Lynn.
19,	William R. Brunbridge,*	Willard Hatch Fisk,	Boston.
July 7,	Amy P. Nourse,*	Amy Porter Oliver,	Lynn.
7,	Alden G. Nourse,*	Alden Guy Oliver,	Lynn.
14,	Edith M. Chandler,*	Edith Modjeska Boardman,	Haverhill.
14,	Clara M. Dalton,*	Clara Mabel Marshall,	Deerfield, N. H.
14,	Emily Heys,*	Florence Emily Wilton,	Lawrence.
21,	Carrie J. Hutchins,*	Carrie Juliette Piper,	S. Hampt'n, N. H.
Aug. 4,	Annie J. Ryan,	Annie J. Raleigh,	Salem.
Sept. 1,	George Brigham,*	George Lislie Friend,	———.
1,	Lula J. Mudge,*	Lula Kirkland Beale,	Lynn.
8,	—— Schmidt,*	Martha Knetsch,	Lawrence.
15,	Mary E. Hanson,	Mary Ellen Very,	Danvers.
Oct. 20,	Thomas B. Martin,*	Thomas Boardman Drowne,	Newburyport.
20,	Arthur Muir,*	Edward Arthur Underhill,	Ipswich.
27,	Lucy V. Orrill,*.	Lucy Viola Warren,	Lynn.
Nov. 10,	—— Andrews,*	Fannie Emma White,	North Andover.
Dec. 15,	Marion P. Fuller,*	Marion Fuller Peabody,.	Boston.
15,	Lenora Smith,*	Lenora Porter,.	Taunton.

MIDDLESEX COUNTY.

Jan. 1,	Bernard Boland,	Charles William Ward,	Concord.
1,	William Albert Bolton, Jr.,*	William Albert Robinson,	Boston.
8,	Ellen McDonnell,*	Ella Brownell,	Newton.
8,	Edwin Esteale,*.	William Whoell,	Stoneham.
15,	Cora Mabel Cullen,*	Cora Mabel Pinkerton,	Lowell.
22,	Lucy Jane Towns,*	Lucy Jane Bickford,	Boston.
Feb. 12,	Henry John Giesin,	Henry John Gleason,	Wayland.
12,	Leora M. Chadwick,.	Leora M. Kingdon,.	Cambridge.
Mar. 4,	Lillian May Catherine Rice,*	Lillian May Catherine Ham,	Cambridge.
11,	Katie Winslow Tilden,*	Lily May Putnam,	Brockton.
11,	Joseph Alma Flannery,*	Robert Worcester,	Boston.
11,	Lucy Annie Mangar,.	Lucy Annie Hammond,	Newton.
25,	Edith Bancroft Wilkinson,*	Edith Bancroft Hayes,	Medford.
May 6,	Emma Jane Wannofsky,	Emma Jane Browne,	Hopkinton.
6,	Mary Adams Bassett,	Mary Adams Currier,	Somerville.
6,	Jennie Mabel Nilson,*	Jennie Mabel Lindqvist,	Cambridge.
6,	George Oliver Jenkins,*	George Francis Baker,	Waltham.
13,	George M. McAllister,*	George Michael Hart,	Boston.
13,	Rensselaer Worth Thyng,.	Ranford Worthing,	Lincoln.
13,	Celia Augusta Thyng,	Celia Augusta Worthing,	Lincoln.

* Changed by reason of adoption.

MIDDLESEX COUNTY — *Concluded.*

Date of Decree.	Original Name.	Name Decreed.	Residence.
1884.			
May 13,	Edwin Ellsworth Thyng, . .	Edwin Ellsworth Worthing, .	Lincoln.
13,	Eula Velma Thyng, . . .	Eula Velma Worthing, . .	Lincoln.
13,	Luissa May Thyng, . .	Luissa May Worthing, . .	Lincoln.
13,	Frederick Howard Thyng,	Frederick Howard Worthing,	Lincoln.
13,	Daisy Maud Thyng, . .	Daisy Maud Worthing, . .	Lincoln.
13,	Eva Augusta Thyng, . .	Eva Augusta Worthing, .	Lincoln.
20,	Hannah Robinson Hobson,	Etta Robinson Foster, . .	Lowell.
27,	Mary Davis,*	Mary Louise Bayard, . .	Lowell.
27,	Walter Wild,* . . .	William Walter Royal, . .	Boston.
June 3,	Josephine Nesmith,* . .	Mabel Jane Buxton, . .	Lowell.
10,	Frank Albert Norman,* .	Frank Clarence Leslie Spalding,	Lowell.
July 1,	Frederick Day Adams,* .	Eugene Adams Dakin, . .	Franklin.
8,	Michael Hinifin, . .	Michael Hannaford, . .	Somerville.
8,	Margaret Hinifin, . .	Margaret Hannaford, . .	Somerville.
8,	Mary L. Hinifin, . .	Mary L. Hannaford, . .	Somerville.
8,	Annie Hinifin, . . .	Annie Hannaford, . .	Somerville.
8,	Louisa M. Hinifin, . .	Louisa M. Hannaford, . .	Somerville.
8,	Frank H. Hinifin, . .	Frank H. Hannaford, . .	Somerville.
8,	Edward E. Hinifin, . .	Edward E. Hannaford, . .	Somerville.
8,	Robert E. Hinifin, . .	Robert E. Hannaford, . .	Somerville.
15,	Jasper Paine Blake,* . .	Jasper Leon Fisk, . .	Sanbornton, N. H.
22,	George Herbert Hebb,* .	George Herbert Gibbs, . .	Boston.
Sept. 2,	John Palmer,* . . .	Norman Brice Goodale, .	Wakefield.
2,	James Brown,* . . .	James Fleming Humphrey, .	Winchester.
2,	Ida Gertrude Parsons,* .	Ida Gertrude Hersey, . .	Bangor, Me.
2,	Etta Maud McCallum,* .	Maud Charlott Carrie Smith, .	Boston.
2,	Madeleine M. Newkirk,* .	Grace Madeleine Adams, .	New York City.
9,	Harriet James,* . . .	Margaret Georgina Doherty, .	Arlington.
9,	Josephine Ferguson,* .	Lillian Josephine Fiske, .	Sidney, C. B.
23,	Catherine Kennedy,* . .	Catherine Gildea, . .	Natick.
Oct. 7,	Martha Ella Abbott, . .	Ella Abbott Ewings, . .	Boxborough.
14,	Alice Martha Richardson,*	Alice Martha Jefts,. . .	Athol.
28,	Jane Berry,* . . .	Jane Bowler, . . .	Hopkinton.
28,	Eunice Ducey,* . . .	Maud Fremont Parmenter, .	Sherborn.
28,	Evelyn Oscanyan Emerson,	Evelyn Russell Emerson, .	Woburn.
Nov. 11,	Frederick Silas Gregory Reed, .	Frederick Reed, . . .	Cambridge.
11,	Archie Noyes,* . . .	Henry Sandow, . . .	Natick.
25,	Jerusha B. Fogg, . .	Jerusha B. Stanley, . .	Maynard.
Dec. 2,	Lena Furey,* . . .	Laura Lena Bailey, . .	Boston.
9,	Cora Dehlman,* . . .	Cora Althea Nichols, . .	North Reading.

WORCESTER COUNTY.

Jan. 1,	—— ——,* . .	Harry Augustus Warner, .	Hardwick.
Feb. 5,	Gilbert Henry O'Donnell,*	Henry Gilbert Brewin, . .	Athol.
5,	Katie Landergan,* . .	Elsie Fiske, . . .	Athol.
5,	Albert Lincoln Barrell, .	Albert Lincoln Pratt, .	Fitchburg.
19,	Carrie Eugenie Randall,* .	Carrie Eugenie Church, .	Worcester.
Mar. 4,	Agnes Williams,* . .	Emma A. Flagg, . .	Northborough.
18,	Amos F. Coburn,* . .	Amos Francis Frye, . .	Worcester.
18,	William P. Coburn,* . .	William Philip Frye, . .	Worcester.
18,	Catharine Callahan,*. .	Katie Black, . . .	Leicester.
April 1,	George Franklin Pearce,* .	George Franklin Bedore, .	Spencer.
1,	Lilla Etta Pearce,* . .	Lilla Etta Bedore, . .	Spencer.
15,	Clarence Cozzens Bates,* .	Clarence Bugbee, . .	Webster.
15,	Irving Carlos Mann,* .	Irving Carlos Hill, . .	Milford.
May 6,	Charlotte May Avery,* .	Charlotte May Dawson, .	Worcester.
6,	Edith Hope Avery,* . .	Edith Hope Dawson, . .	Worcester.

* Changed by reason of adoption.

WORCESTER COUNTY — *Concluded.*

Date of Decree.	Original Name.	Name Decreed.	Residence.
1884.			
June 3,	Jennie May Burt,*	Jennie Mary Clark,	Worcester.
3,	Walter Burton Ball,*.	Walter Burton Stockman,	Worcester.
17,	Clara Sophia Wright,*	Clara Mabel Ford,	Spencer.
17,	——— ——— ———,*	Edith May Green,	Spencer.
July 1,	Alice Newton Sprague,*	Bessie Janette Hervey,	Athol.
1,	Clarence U. Mills,*	Clarence U. Dyer,	Athol.
15,	George Noble Duke,*	George Noble Chute,	Leominster.
15,	William Henry Hewes,*	Alfred Lovell Southwick,	Douglas.
Sept. 2,	Cora Belle Moore,*	Cora Belle Hayden,	Oxford.
2,	Maude Sibley,*	Maude Sibley Chickering,	Westborough.
2,	Henry Holly,*	Frederick Henry Foster,	Worcester.
2,	William Arthur Farquhar,	William Arthur Hill,	Leominster.
2,	Florence Estella Farquhar,	Florence Estella Hill,	Leominster.
16,	William Henry Newton,*	Edmund William Duplease,	Sturbridge.
Oct. 28,	Bertha Flaglor,*	Marian Raymond Whitcomb,	Fitchburg.
Dec. 2,	Harriet Augusta Stearns,*	Harriet Darling Hoar,	Winchendon.
2,	William Carey Gosnold,*	William Carey Hoar,	Winchendon.
1882.			
Nov. 21,	Maude H. Payne,*	Maude H. McConnell,	Worcester.
1883:			
June 19,	——— Foster,*	Eva Vesta Allen,	Holden.

HAMPSHIRE COUNTY.

1884.			
Mar. 4,	Marion Matilda Moss,*	Marion Matilda Gilbert,	Hadley.
April 1,	Ellen Crane,*	Ellen Crane Egan,	Northampton.
June 3,	Emma Nancy Brown,*	Emma Nancy Clark,	Huntington.

HAMPDEN COUNTY.

Jan. 1,	Robert C. Taylor,*	Robert Charles Parsons,	Springfield.
12,	——— ——— ———,*	Pearl Deborah Hortense Hanson,	Holyoke.
Feb. 12,	Mabel Martin,*	Mabel Louise Uschmann,	Holyoke.
12,	Gracie Emmagene Lester,*	Gracie Lester Atkins,	Palmer.
April 1,	Josephine C. Cavanaugh,*	Gracie Elizabeth Smith,	Palmer.
June 3,	Willie Deffner,*	Stephen Austin Buxton,	Springfield.
3,	Elizabeth Day,*	Grace Monroe Pease,	Chicopee.
3,	Mabel Ione Morgan,*	Harriet Lovisa Warner,	Rome, N. Y.
Aug. 6,	Anna Sophia Fennyery,*	Anna Sophia Rebecka Frietag,	Springfield.
Sept. 3,	Helen Gertrude Candee,*	Helen Gertrude Bicknell,	Springfield.
3,	Lizzie S. Streeter,*	Lizzie Streeter Parsons,	Lenox.
3,	Minnie L. Streeter,*	Minnie Palmer Adams,	Orange.
17,	Edward Morse,*	Edward Erving Waterman,	Springfield.
Oct. 1,	Lucy Eliza Abbott,*	Lucy Eliza Abbott Reed,	Springfield.

FRANKLIN COUNTY.

May 27,	Emily J. Purrington,*	Emily J. Bassett,	Charlemont.
June 17,	Maud Dunkley,*	Maud E. Williams,	Orange.
Sept. 2,	Henry G. Vincent,*	Henry G. Bowman,	Montague.
Oct. 28,	Helen McGuire,*	Helen M. Peck,	Shelburne.

* Changed by reason of adoption.

NORFOLK COUNTY.

Date of Decree.	Original Name.	Name Decreed.	Residence.
1884.			
Feb. 6,	Sadie Madan,*	Ethel Cook,	Holbrook.
6,	Anna Madan,*	Anna Webster,	Holbrook.
6,	Nellie Frances Madan,*	Nellie Frances Smith,	Holbrook.
13,	Edith Helen Shaw,*	Edith Helen Bullock,	Brockton.
20,	Franklin McEachern,* sometimes called Franklin Hamilton Watson,	Franklin Loring Weston,	Natick.
Mar. 12,	John William Eccles,*	William Henry Baker,	Chelsea.
26,	Caroline Murray,*	Louise Everett Thompson,	Boston.
April 2,	Benjamin Greely Cole,	Benjamin Greeley Favor,	Dedham.
May 28,	Mary Tufts Howe,	Mary Elizabeth Tufts,	Medfield.
28,	Cora Rawson Curtis,*	Cora Rawson Ryder,	Braintree.
Sept. 10,	Frank Howard Foote,*	Frank Howard Hamlin,	Boston.
17,	Mary Linnean,*	Lucy Watson Gay,	Sharon.
Nov. 12,	Louis Gabriel Fuchs,*	Louis Edward Whicher,	Quincy.

PLYMOUTH COUNTY.

Date of Decree.	Original Name.	Name Decreed.	Residence.
Jan. 14,	Gertrude Atkins,*	Gertrude Bernice Stone,	Brockton.
Feb. 25,	Julius W. Jachimonicz,	Julius W. Paul,	Brockton.
April 28,	Mary Emma Simmons,*	Emma Mabel Ramsdell,	Brockton.
June 9,	Clara H. Snow,	Clara H. Thompson,	Rockland.
Sept. 22,	Mytell Mary Henderson,*	Mytell May Stedman,	East Bridgewater.
Oct. 13,	Sadie C. Atwood,*	Lillie Gridley,	Duxbury.
13,	Jessie Josephine Chamberlain,*	Josephine Chamberlain Walker,	Brockton.
13,	Charles Henry Goodwin,*	Charles Henry Grow,	East Bridgewater.
13,	Luzon A. Weeks,*	Luzon Anselm Damon,	Rochester.
27,	Clarence Merton,*	Clarence Merton Allen,	Brockton.
27,	Susan B. Robertson,	Susan B. Holmes,	Kingston.
Dec. 22,	Nettie Russell,*	Nettie Russell Haven,	Brockton.

BRISTOL COUNTY.

Date of Decree.	Original Name.	Name Decreed.	Residence.
Feb. 1,	Hattie Ryder,*	Georgianna Pell,	New Bedford.
15,	Bessie E. Short,*	Bessie E. Rhodes,	Attleborough.
Mar. 7,	May Jane Davis,	Name unchanged,	Somerset.
7,	Mary A. Whalley,*	Mary Whalley Whittaker,	Fall River.
7,	Olive Estella Brown,*	Olive Estella Hack,	Mansfield.
21,	Joseph Hudson Carlow,*	Joseph Hudson Howes,	Taunton.
April 4,	Mary E. Cumiskey,*	Mary E. McKenzie,	Westport.
4,	Carrie Trenholm Steves,*	Carrie Trenholm Short,	New Bedford.
18,	Lottie Mabel Smith,*	Charlotte Theresa Schneider,	Tiverton, R. I.
18,	Emma Westfall,*	Beatrice Hixon,	Attleborough.
May 16,	James Burns.	James Smith,	Fall River.
June 6,	Mabel Anthony Taylor,*	Mabel Anthony Fiske,	Providence, R. I.
6,	Abel Brooks,*	Abel Tong,	Fall River.
July 1,	James Smith,	James Callen,	Taunton.
12,	Nellie Josephine Spencer,*	Nellie Josephine Perdom,	Boston.
12,	Fred Lawrence Harvey,	Name unchanged,	Raynham.
Aug. 1,	Nameless child,*	Walter Gray,	Westport.
1,	Floretta Mabel Brown,*	Ethel May Campbell,	Fall River.
Sept. 5,	David Davis,*	David Greene,	Fall River.
Oct. 3,	Mabel E. McGann,*	Paulina Mathilda Hansen,	Woonsocket.
17,	Emma M. Burns,*	Emma M. Haskins,	Taunton.
Dec. 5,	Winnonah A. Manchester,*	Maud Elizabeth Prew,	Fall River.
5,	Howard Pratt,*	Howard Pratt Adams,	Boston.

* Changed by reason of adoption.

BARNSTABLE COUNTY.

Date of Decree.	Original Name.	Name Decreed.	Residence.
1884.			
May 21,	Helena White,*	Georgia Warren Gould, . .	Chatham.
Aug. 12,	Inez I. Chute,*	Inez M. Crocker, . . .	Provincetown.
Sept. 9,	Willie Dempster,* . . .	Albert W. Hinckley, . .	Falmouth.

DUKES COUNTY.

June 2,	George C. Wheeler,* . . .	George Cromwell Greene, .	Cottage City.
Oct. 15,	Beatrice Fuller,* . . .	Daisy Mary Wesley, . .	Cottage City.
Nov. 1,	Ruth E. Defose, ...	Ruth E. Chadwick, . .	Cottage City.

NANTUCKET COUNTY.

Apr. 10,	John R. Sylvia, ...	John M. Sylvia, . . .	Nantucket.

SUFFOLK COUNTY.

1885.			
Jan. 5,	Gilbert Lewis Pelkey, . .	Elmer Chickering, . . .	Boston.
12,	Ellen Brownell,* . . .	Clara Davis Merrill, . .	Newton.
26,	Abram A. Grodjinski, . .	Abram Albert Davis, . .	Boston.
26,	Harry Wayland Kingman Ryan,*	Harry Fred Gordon, . .	Boston.
Feb. 2,	Robert Harris Comey,* . .	Robie Harris Wentworth, .	Boston.
2,	Everett K. Hatch,* . . .	Everett Hatch Higgins, .	Boston.
9,	Mary Ellen Anderson,* . .	Edith May Force, . . .	Worcester.
9,	Grace Richards Warren, or Reynolds,*	Grace Rena Perley, . .	Boston.
16,	Annie N. Chase,* . . .	Nellie Amanda Manchester, .	Boston.
16,	Daniel McVickers,* . . .	Frederic Willis Webb, . .	Boston.
Mar. 2,	Eddie Crockett,* . . .	Harry Pearl Sheldon, . .	Boston.
2,	Harold Rogasi,*	Harold Woolf, . . .	New York.
16,	George Henry Moulton,* . .	George Henry McIntosh, .	Fitchburg.
16,	Charles Alvin Smith, . .	Charles Alvin Duren, .	Boston.
23,	Mabel Chapman,* . . .	Alta Mabel Sinclair Rich, .	Westborough.
23,	Adelaide F. Gifford,* . .	Mabel Louise Hervey, . .	Boston.
23,	Charles L. Goggin,* . . .	William Florence Wehriy, .	Boston.
23,	George F. Sellers,* . . .	George Granson Foster, . .	Boston.
May 4,	Ida Gorham, ...	Ida Chase Lee, . . .	Boston.
4,	Maude Gorham, . . .	Maude Chase Lee, . . .	Boston.
11,	Emma Frances McDonald,* .	Emma Frances Stevens, .	Boston.
18,	Elizabeth Estella Field, .	Elizabeth Estella Little, .	Boston.
18,	Sadie Hynes Niles,* . . .	Sadie Abbott, ...	Boston.
25,	William Green,* . . .	William Henry Loomis, .	Boston.
June 1,	Ruth Way,*	Ruth Cronin, ...	Boston.
8,	———— ,*	Harry Aronson, . . .	Boston.
8,	Mabel Smith Brown,* . .	Mabel Eveline Naughton, .	Boston.
8,	Mary Bryant,* . . .	Rita Grace Baker, . . .	Boston.
15,	Oscar Edmands Bryant, .	Edward Bryant, . . .	Boston.
22,	Mary Bowes,*	Mary Susan Kirker, . .	Boston.
29,	Jacob Myer Ranish, . .	Julius Leoin, ...	Boston.
July 13,	Martha Anna Proctor, .	Martha Annah Caldwell, .	Chelsea.
20,	Fannie E. Hawkins,* . .	Fannie Elizabeth Hawkins Lovesy, ...	Boston.

* Changed by reason of adoption.

SUFFOLK COUNTY — *Concluded.*

Date of Decree.	Original Name.	Name Decreed.	Residence.
1885.			
July 20,	Jere Ireland Moore, . . .	Sidney Burrill Moore, . .	Boston.
27,	Jane E Finnegan,* . . .	Jennie May Chase, . . .	Boston.
27,	George Henry,* . . .	William Calvin Arkerson, .	Boston.
Sept. 7,	Emma Bartlett,* . .	Alice Emma Bartlett, . .	Boston.
21,	John Drum,* . . .	John Lewis Robinson, . .	Cambridge.
28,	Bessie Haynes,* . . .	Bessie Haynes Wyman, .	Boston.
28,	Flora Mattie Worden,* .	Flora Mattie Danforth, .	Boston.
Oct. 5,	George F. Tessier, . .	George Francis Stacy, .	Boston.
19,	Wm. Gallagher,* . .	Adelbert Wilbur Fogg, .	Boston.
19,	Grace Phipps,* . . .	Grace Darling Mooney, .	Boston.
26,	George Leslie Friend,* .	George Orlando Nelson, .	Beverly.
26,	Margaret O'Keefe,* . .	Margaret Tierney, . .	Boston.
Nov. 9,	Alice Miller Farley,* .	Carrie Emma Jessie Kelsea, .	Boston.
9,	Leonard Pierce Smith,*	Leonard John Bartel, .	Boston.
16,	Lawrin A. Blaisdell,* .	Lawrin Alford Gaylord, .	Boston.
Dec. 7,	William Burnett Hayes,* .	William Burnett Barrows, .	Matthewson, Ks.
14,	Ellenor Miller Gowin,* .	Mary Ellen Conway, .	Cambridge.
14,	Catherine Mooney,* .	Lora Bell Haskell, . .	Boston.
14,	Ada Sims,*	Mabel Bassett, . .	Boston.
28,	Julia Riley,* . . .	Gertrude Adelaide Newton, .	Boston.

ESSEX COUNTY.

Jan. 26,	Hannah Healey,* .	Hannah Clohecy, . .	Haverhill.
Feb. 2,	Minnie R. Whitmore,* .	Mary Elizabeth Russell,	Lynn.
16,	Martha C. Williams,* .	Annie Louisa Lord, .	Ipswich.
Mar. 16,	Nellie Childs,* . .	Amelia Snow Coombs, .	———
April 6,	John B. Howes,* . .	John Burchell Howes Cahoon,	Chatham.
27,	Harry G. Clifford,* .	Harry Granville Paige, .	Plymouth, N. H.
June 1,	Charles E. Follett,* .	Charles Edwin Demeritt,	Dover, N. H.
8,	Flora M. Middleton,* .	Alice Chester Middleton,	Gloucester.
15,	——— Ames,* . .	Elizabeth Millard Montgomery, . .	Rowley.
July 13,	Mabel C. Batchelder,* .	Alice Mabel Tenney, .	Haverhill.
20,	Adelle Clarke,* .	Adelia Matthews, . .	Boston.
20,	Mabel Putnam,* .	Mabel Caswell, . .	Methuen.
Sept. 21,	Leroy E. Holbrook,* .	Leroy Holbrook Moody, .	Haverhill
Oct. 5,	Ada Russell,* . .	Ethel Putnam Sargent, .	Newton, N. H.
5,	Milton Russell,* . .	Edward Winthrop Sargent,	Newton, N. H.
12,	Nellie Pierce,* . .	Ellen Augusta Stone, .	Boston.
Nov. 9,	Eda E. Hanson,* .	Eda Evangeline Hanson Nutter, .	Wolfboro', N. H.
9,	——— Smith,* . .	Maria Elizabeth Dugdale, .	North Andover.
9,	John Wholley,* . .	John Fitzgerald, . .	Lawrence.
Dec. 7,	Carrie Wells, *alias* Florence C. Wells,* . .	Florence Carter Adams, .	Dedham.
21,	Mary E. Coburn,* .	Edith Coburn Noyes, .	Lynn.
21,	Delena J. Hiltz,* .	Delena Jane Landry, .	Gloucester.

MIDDLESEX COUNTY.

Jan. 6,	Millie Louise Bodge,* .	Millie Louise Hinckley, .	Boston.
6,	Bertha Agnes Olsson,* .	Ethel Phinney, . .	Cambridge.
13,	Helen Robinson,* .	Gladys Fogg, . .	Newton.
13,	Laura Maynes,* . .	Laura McGurk, . .	Boston.

* Changed by reason of adoption.

MIDDLESEX COUNTY — *Concluded.*

Date of Decree.	Original Name.	Name Decreed.	Residence.
1885.			
Jan. 13,	Mary Bertha McDonald,*	Mary Bertha Burke,	Marlborough.
20,	Mary Gertrude Fink,*	Mary Gertrude Brogan,	Cambridge.
Feb. 3,	David Hunter,	David Charles Fleming,	Malden.
3,	Alvah Webster Lord,*	Alvah Webster Rhoades,	Ipswich.
3,	Sarah Ellis,*	Charlotte May Carter,	Abington.
10,	Mary Jane Finnegan,*	Mary Jane Watts,	Cambridge.
10,	Willie Henry LaClair,	Willie Henry Richardson,	Stoneham.
24,	Edwin Norris,*	Edwin Norris Mason,	Pittsfield, N. H.
24,	Eva Holdsworth,*	Eva Louisa Morgan,	Brookline.
Mar. 10,	Ella Caroline Wheeler,*	Ella Caroline Abbott,	Pepperell.
17,	Minnie Odile Spearing,*	Minnie Odile Blanche Leblanc,	Lowell.
24,	Martha Augusta Godendorf,*	Martha Augusta Bettac,	Boston.
24,	Mary Lyons,*	Gertrude Ella Armes,	Boston.
28,	William A. Gordon,*	Edgar Allen Hall,	Boston.
April 7,	Sarah Ella Sherman,	Ellen Sarah Sherman,	Newton.
7,	Julia Florence Crowley,*	Florence Maria Hastings,	Boston.
14,	John Francis Maginniss,	John Innis French,	Woburn.
May 12,	Clara Olsson,*	Lina Genevra Brown,	Cambridge.
19,	Irene A. Mahoney,*	Irene Ann Looby,	Marlborough.
26,	Arnold Harris,*	Ulpian LeRoy Merson,	———.
26,	Helen Maria Krissmaul,*	Helen Maria Nudd,	Boston.
June 2,	Eben Sutton Fish,	Edward Coleman Fisher,	Natick.
2,	Myrtle Hinckey,*	Laura Dwyre Elliott,	Boston.
9,	Neal McFabyn,*	Arthur Neal Harriman,	———.
23,	Hattie Maria Hyde,*	Ida Hattie Stone,	Newton.
23,	Alice A. McKay,*	Alice Cusson,	Boston.
23,	Charlotte Gertrude O'Neal,*	Charlott Gertrude Mitchell,	Boston.
23,	Bessie Lydia Bailey,*	Bessie Lillian Handy,	Holliston.
July 7,	Willard Dalrymple Delano,	Willard Dalrymple,	Medford.
7,	Mary Alice Cushman,*	Mary Alice Lyman,	Dalton, N. H.
14,	James Irving Farquhar,*	James Irving Brigham,	Ely, Canada.
21,	Addie Battie Coggeshall,*	Addie Coggeshall Ward,	New Orleans, La.
28,	Gustavus Flynn,*	Harry Osgood Hinckley,	———.
28,	Frederick Colpits,*	Frederick Colpits Jones,	Cambridge.
Sept. 1,	Griffin Hume,*	Arthur Wilson Smith,	———.
8,	Mertie Smith,*	James Herbert Ames,	———.
22,	Gertrude DeForrest Smith,*	Gertrude Smith Watson,	Woburn.
Oct. 6,	George Emmett Fay,*	George Emmett Dowdell,	St. Law'nce, N. Y.
6,	Sadie Anderson,*	Sadie Anderson Chaplin,	Northborough.
27,	Barnie McGinness,*	Barnie Bond,	Waltham.
27,	Christina Drum,*	Agnes McCready,	Cambridge.
27,	Lewis William Edmands,*	Lewis William Gassett,	Westborough.
27,	Frank Richards,	Reuben Francis Richards,	Cambridge.
Nov. 4,	George Samuel Whitlock,	George Samuel Huntley,	Malden.
24,	Ida Bradshaw,*	Bertha Helen Bennink,	Boston.
Dec. 1,	Catherine Kelley,*	Ellen Susan Richardson	Boston.
1,	Irene Maud Ford,*	Irene Agnes Henry,	Boston.
8,	Mary Elsie Byam,*	Mary Elsie Reed,	Lowell.

WORCESTER COUNTY.

Jan. 20,	Sybil Minerva Clark,*	Sybil Minerva Smith,	Hubbardston.
20,	Mary Fahey,*	Mary Agnes Lane,	Westborough.
20,	Andrew Fahey,*	Edward Fahey Goggin,	Worcester.
Feb. 17,	Jennie Louise Anderson,*	Jennie Louise Amsden,	Gardner.
24,	Eva Belle Stiles,*	Eva Belle Seaver,	Westminster.

* Changed by reason of adoption.

WORCESTER COUNTY — *Concluded.*

Date of Decree.	Original Name.	Name Decreed.	Residence.
1885.			
Mar. 3,	Florence Mabel Ward,* . .	Delle Florence Grout, . .	Athol.
17,	Josephine Merriam,* . . .	Theodosia Alice Sprague, .	Hubbardston.
17,	Mabel Miles Baker,* . . .	Mabel Miles Mann, . .	Leicester.
24,	———,*	Florence Leone Eldridge, .	Fitchburg.
April 7,	Bertha Louisa Hunter,* . .	Bertha Hunter Ainsworth, .	Boylston.
14,	Eliza J Buckley,* . . .	Sarah Louisa Heredeen,. .	Brookfield.
21,	Emma V. Hale,* . . .	Emma Viola Whitney, . .	Leominster.
28,	Morris Kopinsky, . . .	Morris Cooper, . . .	Worcester.
May 5,	Flossie Marshall,* . . .	Flossie May Bullock, . .	Worcester.
5,	George Gill,*	George Stillman Haven, .	Worcester.
5,	Elizabeth Smith,* . . .	Elizabeth Gilligan,. . .	Leicester.
5,	Stephen Wallaston Norcross, .	Stephen Winchester Norcross,	Northborough.
5,	Alice Annie Cooke,* . . .	Alice Annie Bowdoin, . .	Worcester.
12,	Johanna Moore,* . . .	Phœbe Stone Humphrey, .	Phillipston.
19,	Jennie Mary Clark,* . . .	Jennie Mary Wilson, . .	Sutton.
19,	Katy Goodnow,* . . .	Katy Scott, ...	Worcester.
26,	Helen D. Page,*	Helen Dorsis Hills, . .	Westminster.
June 2,	Catherine T. McDonald,* . .	Catherine Therese Donnelly, .	Athol.
16,	Margret Catherine Rooney,* .	Margret Catherine Egan, .	Brooklyn, N. Y.
23,	Percy Edwards,* . . .	Percy Edwards Morrow, .	Worcester.
23,	Edward Drum,*. . . .	Edward Allen Leach, . .	No. Brookfield.
July 7,	John Nelson Boodrow,* . .	John Henry Abare, . .	Winchendon.
7,	Clara M. Wilkins,* . . .	Clara Frances Dakin, . .	Worcester.
21,	Margaret Ann Drum,* . .	Margaret Leach, . . .	No. Brookfield.
21,	Helen Elizabeth Newton,* .	Helen Elizabeth Green Knight, ...	Southborough.
Sept. 1,	Francis ———,*	Francis Charles Mackin, .	Milford.
22,	Caroline Stone,*. . . .	Bessie Louise Morse, . .	Athol.
22,	Christina Butler,* . . .	Fannie Christine Butler, .	Athol.
Oct. 6,	George Jansom,* . . .	George Lincoln Montague, .	Northborough.
13,	Anna Lauriette Moore,* . .	Anna Lauriette Carpenter, .	Royalston.
Nov. 24,	George Edward Conboy,* . .	George Edward Cornwell, .	Lunenburg.
17,	Marie Alphonsine Godette,*	Marie Alphonsine Hirbour, .	No. Brookfield.
Dec. 1,	Mary Newton Estey,* . .	Flora Louise Migneault, .	Worcester.
15,	Gertrude Evangeline Mc-Arthy,*	Gertrude Evangeline Giddings, ...	Worcester.

HAMPSHIRE COUNTY.

Jan. 6,	Celia Pluff,*	Celia Tatro, ...	Easthampton.
Mar. 10,	Winona Clark,*	Winona Estella Clapp, . .	Northampton.
May 12,	Castola Sophia Cushman,* .	Castola Sophia Dorman, .	Belchertown.
12,	Chauncey Bliss Coomes,* . .	Fred Coomes, ...	Belchertown.
12,	Lizzie Amelia Coomes,* . .	Lizzie May King, . . .	Belchertown.
July 7,	Carrie J. Piper,* . . .	Carrie J Hutchins,. . .	Southampton.
7,	Clarence Hames,* . . .	William Henry Montague, .	Belchertown.

HAMPDEN COUNTY.

Mar. 4,	George Thomas Cook,* . .	George Bissell Clark, . .	Springfield.
May 7,	Annie Funke,*	Annie Barth, ...	New Haven, Ct.
7,	Frank Gorman,* . . .	Francis Earle Moody, . .	Springfield.
July 1,	Etta Louisa Carr,* . . .	Etta Louisa Harrigan, . .	Springfield.
Sept. 2,	Leila Estelle Cook,* . . .	Leila Estelle Moore Cook, .	Springfield.
9,	——— Corttiss,* . . .	Arthur Lewis Chaffee, . .	Monson.
Oct. 7,	Frank Gardner,* . . .	Harry Blaisdale Thomas, .	Hartford, Ct.
Nov. 4,	Julia Shea,*	Julia Connor, ...	Holyoke.

* Changed by reason of adoption.

FRANKLIN COUNTY.

Date of Decree.	Original Name.	Name Decreed.	Residence.
1885.			
Mar. 3,	Mary Catharine Bean,*	Mary Catharine Stevens,	Northfield.
3,	William Bean,*	William Bean Stevens,	Northfield.
3,	Thomas Patrick Bean,*	Harrison Thomas Stevens,	Northfield.
May 12,	Waldo Ellis,*	Waldo Ellis Prentice,	Warwick.
June 17,	Willie E. Stone,*	William J Little,	Montague.
Aug. 4,	Norah Finn,*	Esther Howe,	Montague.
Oct. 27,	Ralph Haven Kearns,	Geo. Alfred Pierce Brown,	New Salem.

BERKSHIRE COUNTY.

Date of Decree.	Original Name.	Name Decreed.	Residence.
Feb. 3,	Joseph Cunningham,	Joseph Cunningham Hyndman,	Pittsfield.
Oct. 8,	Delia L. Arceman,*	Delia L. Berthiaume,	Adams.
8,	Robert Cairns,*	Robert Gow,	Adams.
Nov. 4,	Ralph Severance,*	Ralph Severance Gavitt,	Montague.
4,	Robert Wood Prior,*	Robert Munch,	Dalton.
4,	Lillian Mabel Huntley,*	Lillian Spaulding,	North Adams.
Dec. 1,	Mary Adelaine Arsino,*	Mary Adelaine Arsino Roussy,	Charlemont.
1,	Henry Arsino,*	Henry Arsino Roussy,	Charlemont.

NORFOLK COUNTY.

Date of Decree.	Original Name.	Name Decreed.	Residence.
Jan. 14,	Daisy Butler,*	Hellena May Benkindorf,	Boston.
Mar. 18,	Jennie Richards Price,*	Jennie Richards McAllister,	Meriden, Conn.
18,	Helen Howie,*	Lizzie Belle Taylor,	Quincy.
25,	Constance Emily Arrington,*	Alice Doty Sanborn,	Salem.
April 22,	Michael Richard Keeley,	Michael Richard Howard,	Quincy.
June 24,	Mora Colt,*	Florence Martin,	Boston.
July 15,	Mary Salmon,*	Marion Reardon,	Brookline.
Sept. 28,	Mary E. Field,*	Mary Ellen Cook,	Weymouth.
Oct. 7,	Rupert Funny,*.	Rupert Frederick Crowell,	Boston.
14,	Alice C. Nolan,*	Alice C. Vogel,	Quincy.
21,	—— Tisdale,*	Charles Edwin Giles,	Walpole.
Nov. 18,	Henry Brown.*	Edward Borelli,	Stoneham.
25,	Mary Agnes McCabe,*	Mary Agnes Finnegan,	Canton.

PLYMOUTH COUNTY.

Date of Decree.	Original Name.	Name Decreed.	Residence.
Feb. 24,	John Calvin Trainer,	Arthur Freeman Gibbs,	Brockton.
April 27,	Bessie Mary Howe,	Bessie Mary Bennett,	Abington.
May 11,	Julia Ann Gibbs,	Julia Ann Thayer,	Kingston.
Aug. 24,	Mabel Gertrude Chessman,	Mabel Gertrude Stenchfield,	Brockton.
Nov. 9,	Sarah Sylvester Howland,	Sarah Sylvester Stetson,	Duxbury.
23,	Willie Clark,	Edgar Amos Paun,	Middleborough.

BRISTOL COUNTY.

Date of Decree.	Original Name.	Name Decreed.	Residence.
Jan. 16,	Jessie Caliste Bryant,*	Jessie Marjorie Bryant,	Mansfield.
16,	Oscar Jones,*	Oscar Raymond Sweet,	Boston.
Feb. 6,	Elizabeth Etta Hunting,*	Katherine Kendrick Luscomb,	Boston.

* Changed by reason of adoption.

BRISTOL COUNTY — *Concluded.*

Date of Decree.	Original Name.	Name Decreed.	Residence.
1885.			
Mar. 6,	Charles H. Sisson,*	Charles Valentine Eddy,	New Bedford.
20,	Lillian M. Haskins,*	Lilly Holden,	Nantucket.
April 3,	Cornelius Cronin,*	Francis Cornelius Hourahan,	Taunton.
17,	Daniel Alden Farnum,*	Daniel Alden Chute,	Boston.
May 15,	Celina Bienvenu,*	Celina M. Paradice,	Fall River.
July 3,	Ellen Dufficy,*	Ellen Coughlin,	New Bedford.
3,	Mary E. Chace,*	Mary E. Walker,	Swanzey.
3,	Charles H. Carmichael,*	Charles H. Walker,	Attleborough.
Aug. 7,	Mabel A. Stearns,*	Mabel A. Risley,	New Bedford.
Sept. 4,	Maurice T. Bennett,	Maurice T. Fleetwood,	New Bedford.
18,	Gladys Witham,*	Annie Fenno Parker,	Fall River.
Oct. 2,	Nana Foster,*	Nana Whitney Tobey,	Boston.
Dec. 18,	Frank Reeves,*	Frank Howarth,	Fall River.
18,	Alice Oliva Kenney,*	Alice Oliva Robbins,	Brewster.
18,	Otis W. Sisson,*	Otis W. Crapo,	New Bedford.

BARNSTABLE COUNTY.

Jan. 13,	Cordelia Crowell,	Cordelia Crowell Nye,	Wellfleet.
April 21,	Hattie White,	Nellie M. Nickerson,	Provincetown.
21,	Mary Louise Peckham,	Elsie May Hill,	Falmouth.
21,	Manual Rosa,	Warren M. Young,	Provincetown.
June 16,	Ida F. Evans,	Ella Francis Swift,	Falmouth.
Aug. 11,	Charles A. Macomber,	Charles A. Kelley,	Harwich.
Oct. 26,	Alton Sidney Geggatt,	Alton Sidney Collins,	Bourne.
26,	Walter Linwood Eldridge,	Ernest Clifton Jones,	Falmouth.
28,	Antoine Rogers,	Antone Brown,	Provincetown.
Dec. 8,	John Greely,	John Barges,	Provincetown.

DUKES COUNTY.

April 20,	Warren A. Defose,*	Warren Andrew Chadwick,	Cottage City.
Dec. 7,	Grace L. Newcomb,*	Grace L. Chase,	Tisbury.

SUFFOLK COUNTY.

1886.			
Jan. 4,	Annie Crawford,*	Annie Scott,	Boston.
4,	Arthur Lyons,*	Arthur Tripp Horn,	Boston.
11,	Sybil Dent,*	Sybil Velzora Paine,	Boston.
11,	Adell Dudley,*	Adell Watkins,	Boston.
18,	Ella Mahoney,*	Henrietta Ella Brown,	Lynn.
18,	Daniel McDonald,*	Henry Cassady,	Boston.
Feb. 1,	Willie Stewart Hennigar,*	Freddie Stewart Colburn,	Boston.
1,	Mattie Isabel McLearn,*	Mattie Florence Wyatt,	Boston.
15,	Charles Porter Janes,	Charles Porter Jaynes,	Boston.
23,	Ellen Colwell,*	Fannie Elizabeth Wheaton Saunders,	Boston.
Mar. 1,	Harry Francis,*	Murry Elmore McFarland,	Boston.
15,	Andrew Welch,	Andrew Bertram Sargent,	Boston.
22,	George Murillo Bartol Turner,	George Bartol Turner,	Boston.
29,	Mary Jane Pratt,*	Gracie Burnham Williams,	Boston.

* Changed by reason of adoption.

SUFFOLK COUNTY — *Concluded.*

Date of Decree.	Original Name.	Name Decreed.	Residence.
1886.			
April 5,	Evelyn Garland Annable,*	Evelyn Annable Richardson,	Salem.
5,	Samuel Cartwright Gould,	Samuel Gould,	Boston.
19,	Mary Ellen Price,*	Mary Ellen Dawson,	Boston.
May 3,	Mary Agnes Donovan,*	Edith May Pierce,	Boston.
3,	Frederica Maynard,	Alice Frederica Maynard,	Boston.
10,	George Martin,*	George Haney,	Boston.
10,	Vivien Beatrice Page,*	Vivien Beatrice Bailey,	Manchester, N. H.
10,	Mary C. Turner,*	Mary Eliza Brown,	Boston.
17,	Susan Maria Sawyer,	Susan Maria Felton,	Boston.
17,	Addie May Tarbox,*	Addie May Goodrich,	Boston.
24,	Estelle Wood Jackson,*	Luella Edwinie Estelle Tabor,	Boston.
June 1,	David Lockhart McNutt,	David Lockhart Hanley,	Boston.
1,	Max Nachman,	Max Newman,	Boston.
7,	Clara Putnam Bowker,*	Mildred Hingdon Fogg,	Boston.
14,	Louis Albert Myerson,	Louis Ross Myerson,	Boston.
14,	Mary Alice Sharp,*	Ethel Maud Cory,	Boston.
28,	Pauline Colgan Lovell,*	Aline Morey,	Boston.
July 6,	William Joseph Sullivan,	William Joseph Saunders,	Boston.
12,	Jacob Pfaff Clark,	Jacob Pfaff Gardner,	Boston.
19,	Emma Dwinal Russell,*	Emma Adele Russell Emerson,	Boston.
Sept. 6,	—— Doyle,*	Queeny Morgan,	Revere.
13,	Ethelinda Fogg,*	Ethelinda Forbes,	Boston.
20,	Edward Franklin Jabsley,*	Edward Franklin Christopher,	Boston.
Oct. 4,	Rudolph Lipschutz,	Rudolph Libby,	Boston.
11,	Robert Dickson Smith, Jr.,	Robert Dickson Weston Smith,	Boston.
18,	David Blair,*	Robert Legume Hudson.	Boston.
18,	George Bradley,*	George Frederick Hutchins,	Boston.
18,	Arthur Fletcher Williams,	Fletcher Lambert Williams,	Boston.
25,	Elizabeth Newton Dennis,*	Mabel Viola Vornbeck,	Boston.
25,	Edith Johnson,*	Florence Mabel Marsh,	Boston.
25,	Nellie McGrath,*	Lilian Grace Gerrold,	Boston.
25,	Annie McKenna,*	Ellen Josephine Gilmore,	Boston.
25,	Sarah Roundy,	Sarah Roundy Williams,	Boston.
Nov. 8,	Frederick Jackson,*	Frederick Jackson Bell,	Boston.
8,	Francis B. Kossman,*	Francis Kossman McGrath,	Boston.
8,	Lilly M. Kossman.*	Lilly Kossman Burnham,	Boston.
15,	Charles A. Johnson,*	Henry Louis Grosslaub,	Unknown.
15,	Maria Lynn,*	Helen Gertrude Soule,	Unknown.
15,	Burton Wiswell,	Andrew Burton Wiswell,	Boston.
29,	William Johnson,*	William James Hunt,	Boston.
Dec. 13,	Mary Burgess,*	Mabel Gifford Fenner,	Boston.
20,	Elizabeth Paine Patch,	Elizabeth Paine Claggett,	Boston.
20,	Frederick Waters,*	Frederick Waters Rowe,	Boston.

ESSEX COUNTY.

Jan. 18,	Sarah A. Lambert,*	Annie Augusta Dodge,	Salem.
18,	Maud McNey.*	Maud Eliza Fiske,	Boston.
Feb. 1,	Lillian D. Ingalls,*	Helen Weston Palmer,	Lynn.
15,	Henry Wells,*	Henry Arthur Cogswell,	Saratoga, N. Y.
Mar. 1,	Mary Allen,*	Eva May Smith,	Gloucester.
15,	Mary Miller,*	Ida Florence Miller Cook,	Boston.
15,	Mary L. Gillen.*	Mary Louisa Berry,	Haverhill.
15,	Florence L. McKenney,*	Florence Lena Murphy,	Lynn.
22,	Agnes C. Maxwell,*	Agnes Catherine Andrews,	Haverhill.
April 5,	Annie M. Gillen,*	Annie May Coppen,	Haverhill.
26,	Nancy E. Rowell,*	Ethel Lewis,	Lynn.

* Changed by reason of adoption.

ESSEX COUNTY — *Concluded.*

Date of Decree.	Original Name.	Name Decreed.	Residence.
1886.			
May 3,	Genevieve C. Kent,* . . .	Genevieve Caroline Smith, .	Salem.
17,	Elliot O. Foster,* . . .	Elliot Orman Hopkins, . .	Danvers.
24,	George W. Bousley,*. . .	George Winthrop Story, .	Salem.
24,	Emma M. Porter,* . . .	Emma Maud Todd, . .	Amesbury.
June 7,	Maud Cole,*	Eunice Ryder Clukey, . .	Boston.
7,	Harriet M. Dockum,* . .	Lillian Boardman, . . .	Newburyport.
7,	Alice M. Hood,* . . .	Alice May Hamilton, . .	Ipswich.
14,	Mary A. Roche,* . . .	Harriet Estella Fellows, .	Haverhill.
14,	Earnest A. Uberschurtz, .	Earnest Albert Wiedman, .	Lawrence.
July 6,	Ruport D. Ford, . . .	George Carlton Ford, . .	Amesbury.
6,	David N. Scanlon, . . .	David Nathaniel Powell, .	Beverly.
Aug. 2,	Susan E. Bickford,* . .	Eva Gertrude Higgins, . .	Beverly.
Sept. 6,	Mary J. Montgomery,* .	Mary Jane Burke, . . .	Newburyport.
6,	John H. Montgomery,* .	Fred Webster Montgomery, .	Newburyport.
Oct. 4,	Wilbur A. Reed, . . .	Wilbur A. Coolidge, . .	Lynn.
25,	Frances Colby,* . . .	Frances Colby Rowe, . .	Manchester.
Nov. 8,	Mary A. Marcoux,* . .	Mary Angeline Marcoux Sweatt, ...	Haverhill.
Dec. 6,	Ethel M. Fisk,* . . .	Ethel May Fisk Jones, . .	Salem.
6,	Albert Gilmore,* . . .	George Greenwood, . .	Providence, R. I.
20,	Fannie V. Campbell,* .	Fannie Campbell Cook, . .	Lynn.
20,	Alice M. Dunbar,* . . .	Alice May Drew, . . .	North Andover.
20,	Hattie F. Webster,* . .	Florence Laura Abbott, . .	Lawrence.

MIDDLESEX COUNTY.

Jan. 5,	Sarah Bell Walker,* . . .	Sarah Bell Drury, . . .	Wakefield.
5,	Samuel Thomas Kirkpatrick, .	Samuel Thomas Kirk, . .	Somerville.
5,	Ida Helen Kirkpatrick, .	Ida Helen Kirk, . .	Somerville.
5,	Royden Clark Kirkpatrick, .	Roydon Clark Kirk, . .	Somerville.
5,	Hazel Ida Kirkpatrick, .	Hazel Ida Kirk, . .	Somerville.
5,	Edith Winifred Kirkpatrick, .	Edith Winifred Kirk, . .	————.
12,	Lottie Martha O'Neil,* .	Mary Elizabeth Houghton, .	Boston.
19,	Thomas Hobart Hyde,* .	Wallace Hyde Lingley, . .	Boston.
26,	Jane Agnes Murphy,* .	Jane Agnes Murphy Heaphy, .	Hopkinton.
26,	Freeman Hinckley Sampson, .	William Freeman Sampson, .	Cambridge.
Feb. 9,	Mary Hogan,* . . .	Lillian Viola Bailey, . .	Boston.
9,	Rubie May Fletcher,* .	Rubie May Oliver, . .	Brunswick, Me.
23,	Mary Alice Bulkley, . .	Alice Marean Bulkley, . .	Concord.
Mar. 2,	Thomas Strong, . . .	Thomas Benjamin Jones, .	Boston.
9,	Mary Elizabeth Henry,* .	Mary Elizabeth Hart, . .	Melrose.
16,	Annie Smith,*	Gertrude Ethel Small, . .	Boston.
16,	James Edward Tubbs, .	James Edward Wilson, . .	Marlborough.
23,	James Keenan, . . .	James Henry Parks, . .	Cambridge.
23,	Kate Gleason,* . . .	Mary Catherine Parks, . .	Somerville.
April 6,	Percy Warner,* . . .	Frederick Wayland, . .	Lowell.
6,	Maud Mahew,* . . .	Winifred Maud Twiss, . .	Reed's F'ry, N. H.
13,	William Irwin,* . . .	Arthur Middleton, . . .	Liverpool, Eng.
13,	Ida May Downing, . .	Ida May Govan, . . .	Medford.
27,	Susie Olena Goodwin,* .	Susie Olena Brown, . .	Cambridge.
27,	Minnie B. Sullivan,* . .	Minnie Braley McMeeken, .	Boston.
May 4,	Emily Gray,*	Emily Hunt, ...	Concord.
4,	Annie Mary Wigg, . .	Annie Mary Glover, . .	Dracut.
11,	Robert Everett Carlyle Robinson, ...	Carlyle Robinson Hayes, .	Boston.
25,	William Benson Chandler, .	William Benson Allen, . .	Everett.
25,	Mary Kate Peck,* . . .	Katie May Morse, . . .	Petticodiac, N. B.

* Changed by reason of adoption.

MIDDLESEX COUNTY — *Concluded.*

Date of Decree.	Original Name.	Name Decreed.	Residence.
1886.			
June 1,	Eleazer Hamilton,*	George Hamilton Harris,	Cambridge.
1,	Charles Brown,*.	Charles Brown Beattie, .	Winchester.
8,	Mary Welch,*	Theresa Dolan,	Chelsea.
22,	Nina Glive,*	Mabel Crawford Barket,	Somerville.
22,	Charlotte E. Skidmore,*	Charlotte Emily Emerson,	Boston.
22,	Zilpha Gertrude Johnson,*	Zilpha Gertrude Harris,	Lynn.
July 6,	Benjamin Petterson, .	Benjamin Petterson Watson, .	Tewksbury.
13,	Eva L. Crimmins,*	Martha Middlemas, .	Somerville.
13,	Fannie House,*	Grace Mary Smith, .	Boston.
20,	Bertha Hennessey, *sometimes called* Bertha Mackay,*	Bertha Ann Wild, .	Portsm'th, N. H.
27,	Florence Gaynor,*	Ella Florence Andrews, .	Medford.
27,	Catherine Gould,*	Catherine Danahy, .	Cambridge.
27,	Caroline Connors,*	Carrie Johnston Milliken, .	Marlborough.
27,	Ann Agnes Gosling,*.	Ann Agnes Gill,	Cambridge.
27,	Alice R. McFarland,*	Alice Ralston Benson,	Cambridge.
Sept. 7,	William Smith,*	Timothy Cahill,	Framingham.
7,	Agnes Fay,*	Agnes Guilfoile,	Wayland.
7,	Lillie May Checkley,*	Lillie May Sweat, .	New York, N. Y.
14,	Tabitha Meigs,*.	Grace Isabel Peters,	Medford.
14,	William Francis Abbott,*	William Francis Haynes,	Maynard.
14,	Patrick Francis McGaughey,*	Francis McGaughey,	Boston.
21,	James Francis Meehen,*	James Francis Lawson, .	Boston.
21,	Mary Ellen Meehen,*	Mary Ellen Lawson,	Boston.
28,	Manoel Rodriques Serpa, .	Manoel Rodgers,	Somerville.
28,	Maria Gloria Serpa, .	Maria Gloria Rodgers,	Somerville.
28,	Alfred Serpa,	Alfred Oscar Rodgers,	Somerville.
28,	Maria Serpa,	Maria Eugenia Rodgers,	Somerville.
Oct. 5,	Jane Maloney,*	Jennie Doran, .	Boston.
12,	Georgianna Jane Wood,*	Georgianna Joy,	Pepperell.
12,	Harriet Lucy Ward,*.	Harriet Lucy Southwick,	Salem.
Nov. 3,	Frederick Livingston Jennison,*	Frederick Livingston Cutter, .	Waltham.
16,	Annie Grace Snowman,*	Annie Grace Hill,	Penobscot, Me.
23,	Florence Maud Walker,*	Florence Maud Howard,	Worcester.
Dec. 7,	Martha Maria Gordon,*	Martha Maria Richards, .	Natick.
14,	Margaret Winterton,*	Belle Madge Butterfield,	Boston.
14,	Mary Shaw,*	Mary Eva Dudley,	Wayland.
14,	William Davis,*.	William Davis Bickers, .	Boston.
14,	Albertha Duke,*	Bertha May Murray,	Lynn.
14,	Agnes Duke,*	Elizabeth Jane McMeeken,	Lynn.
28,	Charles Webster,*	Charles Herbert Milligan,	Cambridge.
28,	Ella Frances Freeman,*	Ella Frances Priest,	Somerville.

WORCESTER COUNTY.

Jan. 5,	Louise S. Dorr,*.	Louise S. Mason, .	Douglas.
5,	Simeon Gaudette,*	Edward Foote,	No. Brookfield.
19,	Maud Clarisa Mills,*.	Maud Agnes Rolland, .	Athol.
Feb. 16,	Joseph ———,*	Joseph Daniel Adams. .	Brookfield.
April 6,	Nellie May Higgs,*	Helen Martha Bancroft, .	Worcester.
20,	Lulu Mabel Stone,*	Lula Mabel Morse, .	Worcester.
20,	Priestley Young,	Joseph Priestley Young,	Worcester.
20,	Otho Harold Jackson,*	Otho Harold Hartson, .	Athol.
May 4,	Etta Cummings,*	Grace Folsom Butler,	Worcester.
4,	Alice McDougal,*	Amy Grace Stedman, .	Boston.
June 1,	Florence May Jackson,*	Mabel Harwood Bemis, .	Boston.
15,	Catherine Estelle Trainor,*	Catherine Estelle Kelley,	Worcester.

* Changed by reason of adoption.

WORCESTER COUNTY — *Concluded.*

Date of Decree.	Original Name.	Name Decreed.	Residence.
1886.			
July 6,	William Gilman,*	William Donovan, . . .	Blackstone.
6,	Charles Francis Smith,* . .	Frank S. Weaver, . . .	Templeton.
6,	Georgianna Hoey,* . . .	Georgianna Baker, . . .	Worcester.
20,	———,* . . .	Bertha Kate Morse, . .	Boston.
20,	Eva Newell Johnson,* . .	Eva Newall Hurd, . . .	Worcester.
Sept. 7,	Emma Elizabeth Johnson,*	Emma Elizabeth Hadley, .	Gardner.
7,	Ethel May French,* . .	Ethel May Gould, . . .	Sutton.
7,	Annie Foley,* . . .	Mary Laura Scott, . . .	Worcester.
14,	John Hayward,* . . .	John Holmes, ...	Milford.
14,	———,* . . .	Agnes Morin, ...	Medway.
Oct. 12,	Oscar Lee,*.	Frederic Eugene Whitney, .	Phillipston.
19,	Agnes Margaret Gaffney,* .	Agnes Margaret Cunningham,	Underhill, Vt.
26,	Clara Belle Hall,* . . .	Isabelle Lyndes, . . .	Worcester.
26,	Ina Maud Moore,* . . .	Ina Maud Sawin, . . .	Worcester.
Nov. 3,	Ethel Inez Mailman,* . .	Ethel Inez Barnes, . . .	Sterling.
16,	Carrie Maria Gove,* . . .	Carrie Maria Howard, . .	Hardwick.
Dec. 7,	Arthur Briggs Woodward,* .	Arthur Briggs Wilson, . .	Worcester.
7,	Harry C. Townsend,* . .	Harry Carleton Fay, . .	Northborough.
21,	Lillian T. Doherty,* . .	Lillian T. Sullivan, . .	Leominster.
21,	Lizzie Maria Kendall,* . .	Lizzie Maria Bates, . . .	Phillipston.
28,	Winifred Vaughn,* . . .	Winifred Vaughn Carter, .	Leominster.

HAMPSHIRE COUNTY.

Jan. 5,	Marion N. Braisted,* . .	Marion N. Sawyer, . .	Easthampton.
Feb. 2,	Edith G. Bronson,* . .	Edith G. Shaw, . . .	Plainfield.
April 6,	Charles Noonan,* . . .	Forest Erskine Damon, .	Northampton.
6,	Margaret F. Carroll,* . .	Margaret F. Foley, . .	Northampton.
Sept. 7,	Lena E. Matthews,* . .	Lena Estella Hall, . . .	Northampton.
7,	Annie Foss,* . . .	Fanny M. Bryant, . . .	Chesterfield.
Oct. 12,	Lillian Ione Hall,* . .	Lillian Ione Weston, . .	South Hadley.
Nov. 3,	Josephine Floyd,* . . .	Gladys Valine Stone, . .	Northampton.
9,	Mabel Frances Tobin,* . .	Frances Louise Laidley, .	Northampton.

HAMPDEN COUNTY.

Jan. 6,	Edith M. Laurence,* . . .	Edith Myrtle Frissell, . .	West Springfield.
6,	Arthur Harper,* . . .	Albert Norman Daniels, .	Springfield.
Feb. 3,	Miriam Burke, *alias* Miriam B. Brown,*	Rachel Emily Rising, . .	Springfield.
July 7,	Richard Luther Frost,* . .	Richard Luther Davis, . .	Wilbraham.
7,	Harry Edward Christiansen,* .	Harry Edward Laurin, . .	Longmeadow.
Sept. 8,	Mary Tobin,*	Mary Agnes Offcut, . .	Holyoke.
8,	Alfred Miller,* . . .	Alfred Miller Howard, . .	Southford, Ct.
Oct. 20,	Lucy Cordelia Brock,* . .	Lucy Frostina Mooney, . .	Holyoke.
Nov. 3,	William Bailey,* . . .	William Jackson, . . .	Springfield.
24,	Susan Hayes,* . . .	Susan Elizabeth Hoag, . .	Springfield.

FRANKLIN COUNTY.

Jan. 5,	Conrad Frank,*	Conrad Alber, ...	Montague.
5,	John Frank,*	John Alber, ...	Montague.
Mar. 9,	Ernest Ingram,* . . .	Ernest Harvey, . . .	Warwick.
9,	Job Hampton,*	Warren Hampton Nims, .	Orange.

* Changed by reason of adoption.

FRANKLIN COUNTY — *Concluded.*

Date of Decree.	Original Name.	Name Decreed.	Residence.
1886.			
April 6,	John Christian,* . . .	Jay Carroll Brown, . .	Orange.
June 1,	(Infant) Crowningshield,* .	Clarence Earl Chickering, .	Greenfield.
July 6,	Francis Beacon,* . . .	Frank Wilbur Webster, . .	Warwick.
Aug. 3,	Allie Bronson,*	Almon Bronson Hale, . .	Buckland.
Nov. 2,	Earl Wayne,*	Earl Wayne Smith, . .	Orange.
Dec. 14,	Justin Lacy,*	Carl Vincent Whipple, . .	Warwick.

BERKSHIRE COUNTY.

Jan. 5,	Julie J. Arsnault,* . . .	Julie A. Charboneau, . .	Adams.
5,	Carrie Shaw Tate,* . . .	Carrie B. Breakey, . . .	Pittsfield.
5,	Bertha Watson Young * .	Bertha M. Watson, . .	Pittsfield.
Mar. 2,	Desire Adolph Sultaire,* .	Desire Adolph Stowell, .	Peru.
April 6,	Andrew Cairns,* . . .	Andrew Cairns Pow, .	Adams.
6,	Margarita Lang,* . . .	Henrietta Louisa Solert, .	Pittsfield.
June 1,	Chester Allen Potter,* .	Arthur Allen Pierce, . .	Pittsfield.
July 20,	Frederick P. Smith,* . .	Frederick Smith Potter, .	Lanesborough.
22,	Lucinda Harwood,* . .	Lucinda Harwood Coon, .	North Adams.
22,	Gracie Williams,* . . .	Gracie Sherman, . . .	Williamstown.
Sept. 7,	Delia Templin,*	Mary Ringwood, . .	North Adams.
7,	Lena Templin,*	Lena Ringwood, . . .	North Adams.
7,	Lillie Louisa Rutz,* . .	Lillie Louisa Austin, . .	Pittsfield.
7,	John Verran, ...	John DeVarennes, . . .	Lee.
7,	Byron Lincoln Verran, . .	Byron Lincoln DeVarennes, .	Lee.

NORFOLK COUNTY.

Jan. 6,	Mary Slattery, ...	Mary Morey, ...	Walpole.
Feb. 3,	Fannie Marcella Brewington, .	Fannie Marcella Thompson, .	Brookline.
Mar. 10,	Mary Alice Lester,* . . .	Mary Lester Delory, . .	Hingham.
24,	Mary Monahan,* . . .	Mary Cronin, ...	Boston.
May 12,	Thomas Holyoke,* . . .	George Albert Royce, . .	Dedham.
19,	John Tucker,*	Frank Elwood Smith, . .	Canton.
July 7,	Unknown,*	Rosalie Marion Horr, . .	Halifax, N. S.
14,	Margaret Alice Slattery,* . .	Margaret Alice McDonough, .	Montague.
Sept. 1,	Marcia Elizabeth Blackington, .	Marcia Ernestina Arnold, .	Wrentham.
8,	Effie Frances Erskine, .	Effie Florence Croak, . .	Randolph.
Oct. 6,	Annie Wardwell,* . . .	Annie Louisa Williams, .	Quincy.
Nov. 17,	Henry Kendall,* . . .	Charles Henry Crowe, . .	Sharon.
24,	Lawrence Hitchings,* . .	William Lawrence Burnham, .	Boston.
24,	Ella Moore,*	Ella Livermore Parker, . .	Boston.
24,	Rachel Watts,*	Bertha Ray Allen, . . .	Boston.
24,	John McDonald,* . . .	John Bisbee, ...	Boston.
Dec. 8,	Maud Ethel Ballou,* . . .	Maud Ethel Schell, . .	Hyde Park.
15,	Jessie Smith,*	Ada Cecilia Bailey, . .	Dover.
15,	Israel Howe,*	Harrie Israel Bailey, . .	Dover.

PLYMOUTH COUNTY.

Jan. 25,	Mamie ——,*	Mabel F. Willis, . . .	Brockton.
July 12,	Mabel Frances Reed,* . .	Mabel Frances Sullivan, .	Abington.
12,	Carrie Bell Wiley,* . . .	Amy Elizabeth Ham, . .	Bridgewater.
12,	Charles H. Ransom,* . .	Frederick Charles Burt, . .	Middleborough.

* Changed by reason of adoption.

PLYMOUTH COUNTY — *Concluded.*

Date of Decree.	Original Name.	Name Decreed.	Residence.
1886.			
Aug. 23,	Ralph D. Sproul,* . . .	Ralph D. Poole, . . .	Brockton.
23,	Charles Francis Snook,* . .	Charles Francis Kehoe, . .	Abington.
Sept. 13,	Fred Dearney,*	Fred Herbert Blake, . .	Hingham.
27,	Cuthbert Gort,*	Alberto Clifton Willis, .	Brockton.
Oct. 25,	John T. Aldoes,* . . .	John Ralph Aldoes, . .	Brockton.
Nov. 8,	Merton S. Lewis,* . . .	Merton C. Hunt, . . .	Brockton.
22,	Eldora L. Wing,* . . .	Eldora Leonard Blackwell, .	Middleborough.
22,	Eugene Kendall,* . . .	George Francis Leighton, .	W. Bridgewater.

BRISTOL COUNTY.

Date of Decree.	Original Name.	Name Decreed.	Residence.
Jan. 1,	Maria Louiza Machad.* . .	Maria Augusta Perry, . .	Fall River.
Feb. 5,	Annie E. Smith,* . . .	Annie Elizabeth Sanford, .	New Bedford.
April 2,	Frank Bassett,*	Ephrem James Desrosier, .	Fall River.
2,	Fred N. Brackett, . . .	Fred. N. Robbins, . .	Attleborough.
May 7,	William Coupe Pemberton,* .	William Coupe, . . .	Attleborough.
21,	Carrie Bell Evans,* . .	Carrie Belle Evans Chambers,	Taunton.
21,	Louis Normand.* . . .	Louis Langell, . . .	Fall River.
June 4,	William Edward Grant,* . .	William Edward Longson, .	Fall River.
July 2,	Edward North,* . . .	Edward Buckley, . .	Fall River.
Sept. 3,	Adelaide F. Aikin,* . .	Addie Alice Haskins, . .	Dartmouth.

BARNSTABLE COUNTY.

Date of Decree.	Original Name.	Name Decreed.	Residence.
Mar. 9,	Thomas Kennedy Hopkins, .	Thomas Kennedy Paine, .	Wellfleet.
April 20,	Alice Irene Baker, . .	Alice Irene Crocker, . .	Barnstable.
May 19,	Lettie Newton McMillan, .	Lettie Newton Oxnard, .	Provincetown.
Aug. 10,	Ferdinand Bacon, . .	Ferdinand Bacon Jones, .	Barnstable.
10,	George Rogers, . . .	George Arthur Kelley, .	Harwich.
Oct. 25,	Sarah L. Nickerson, . . .	Sarah L. Doane. . .	Harwich.
Nov. 16,	Susan Williston Dodge, .	Susan Webster Dodge, .	Yarmouth.

NANTUCKET COUNTY.

Date of Decree.	Original Name.	Name Decreed.	Residence.
Nov. 11,	Henry Gibbs,* . . .	Harry Gibbs, . . .	Nantucket.

SUFFOLK COUNTY.

Date of Decree.	Original Name.	Name Decreed.	Residence.
1887.			
Jan. 3,	Charles Reisner,* . .	Harry Carlton Isaac, .	Boston.
3,	Maud Turner,* . . .	Alice Maria Drake, . .	Boston.
3,	George A. Dexter,* . .	George Dexter Hammond, .	Boston.
3,	George Peter Dupris,* .	George Peter White, .	Boston.
17,	Fannie May Newell,* .	Fannie May Noble, .	Boston.
17,	Carrie McDavitt,* . .	Carrie Nadine Foster, .	Boston.
17,	Roger Crandall.* . .	Howard Lancaster Hayford, .	Boston.
24,	Harry Pearl Townes,* .	Chilson Francis Doane, Jr., .	Boston.
24,	Catherine Bates,* . .	Catherine Bates Carlton, .	Boston.

* Changed by reason of adoption.

SUFFOLK COUNTY — *Continued.*

Date of Decree.	Original Name.	Name Decreed.	Residence.
1887.			
Feb. 7,	Guy Bunker Price,* . . .	Guy Bunker, ...	Boston.
14,	Neil Kearney,*	Joseph William Lang, . .	Boston.
14,	Vanessa Madden,* . . .	Gertrude Vanessa Coffin, .	Boston.
14,	Pascal Lynch,*	William Roy Green, . .	Boston.
14,	Stella Lancey,*	Stella Elizabeth Bowen, .	Boston.
21,	Catherine Gerry, *alias* Donahoe, *alias* Dodge.*	Katherina Elizabeth Dodge, .	Boston.
Mar. 7,	Frederick William Stroinski, .	Frederick William Stroinski Pepper, ...	Boston.
7,	Edna Braman,*	Edna May Crosby, . . .	Boston.
14,	Richard Ford Scott,* . . .	George Twombly Hughes, .	Boston.
14,	Joseph McLeod,* . . .	Albert Carlton Perry, . .	Boston.
14,	Elizabeth Genevieve Johnson,*	Elizabeth Genevieve Wadleigh, ...	Boston.
14,	Fred Woodill,*	Frederick Currier, . . .	Boston.
14,	Annie Murphy,*. . . .	Bessa May Jones, . . .	Boston.
14,	Mary Reed,*	Mary Ann Clark, . . .	Bellingham.
21,	William Bourne Peabody,. .	William Oliver Bourne Peabody, ...	Boston.
21,	Elizabeth Ann Hickey, .	Elizabeth Ann Hinckley, .	Boston.
21,	Lottie Louisa Doyle,* .	Lottie Alberta Trecartin, .	Boston.
April 4,	John Edward Hanson,* .	John Edward Eldridge, .	Boston.
4,	Frederick William Oakes, .	Frederick William Holbrook,	Boston.
4,	Olive Maria Hanson, . .	Olive Maria Eldridge, .	Boston.
4,	Lucy Holbrook Oakes, .	Lucy Holbrook, . . .	Boston.
18,	Louisa Stein,* . . .	Lauria Louisa Kimball, .	Boston.
18,	Grace Flaglor,* . . .	Mabel Edith Anderson, .	Boston.
18,	Elsie Jeanette McLean,* .	Ethel May Swift, . .	Boston.
25,	Alfred Edwards,* . . .	Alfred Crawford Trenear, .	Boston.
May 2,	Lucretia Almira Taylor Hanson,*	Eleanor Gladys Sawyer, .	Boston.
2,	Julia A. Wells Swift,* .	Demareise Swift, . .	Boston.
2,	Henrietta Stevens,* . .	Mabel Hibbard, . . .	Boston.
2,	Mary Sullivan,*. . .	Augusta Garifelia Morrison,	Boston.
9,	Susan McManus,* . .	Lulu Marion Godfrey, .	Boston.
16,	Nellie Frances King,* .	Nellie Frances Gloyd, .	Chelsea.
23,	Annie Eliza Murphy, .	Annie Eliza Douglass, .	Boston.
23,	Margaret Chase,* . .	Caroline Eunice Goodwin, .	Boston.
23,	John A.— Underwood,* .	John Underwood Fowler, .	Boston.
June 6,	Ross Millmore,*. . .	Arthur Ross Nute, . .	Boston.
6,	Edith Milton,* . . .	Edith Rachel Ellis, . .	Boston.
13,	Samuel Weiss, . . .	Samuel White, . . .	Boston.
13,	Nellie Devlin, . . .	Nellie Peabody, . . .	Chelsea.
20,	John Aloysius Sullivan, .	John Aloysius Gilmore, .	Boston.
20,	Harriet Kimball,* . .	Harriet Kimball de la Vergne,	Boston.
27,	Kate Sullivan,* . . .	Edith Louise Bonner, .	Tewksbury.
27,	Mary Elizabeth Gorman, .	Mary Elizabeth Fleming, .	Boston.
July 5,	Freddie Stewart Colburn,* .	Thomas Irving Young, .	Boston.
5,	Carrie Ella Ladora Fickett,* .	Clara Ella Ladora Litchfield,	Boston.
18,	Maria Gratiala Cloutier,* .	Maria Gratiala Morin. . .	Quebec, P. Q.
Aug. 15,	Jesse Jennison,*. . .	George Burnside Maynard, .	Boston.
15,	Annie Louise Barcklett,* .	Isabel Clara Roel, . .	Boston.
15,	Annie Frances McFarland,* .	Annie Frances Bird, . .	Boston.
15,	Grace Nourse,* . . .	Grace McCarthy, . . .	Boston.
Sept. 6,	Charles Temple Ward, .	Prescott Temple Ward, . .	Boston.
12,	Alfred Bryant,* . . .	Frederick Chamberlain Richards, ...	Boston.
Oct. 3,	George Herman Coleman,* .	George Herman Bath, . .	Boston.
3,	Jennie Elizabeth Watkins,* .	Jennie Elizabeth Morrill, .	Boston.
3,	Elizabeth Wahlers,* . .	Elizabeth Goodsell, . .	Utica, N. Y.
10,	Martha Trask,* . . .	Martha Ryan,. . . .	Boston.

* Changed by reason of adoption.

SUFFOLK COUNTY — *Concluded.*

Date of Decree.	Original Name.	Name Decreed.	Residence.
1887.			
Oct. 17,	George Carlton James Cheney,*	George Carlton Cheney James,	Boston.
17,	—— Cook,*	Henry Arthur Buttrick, . .	Chelsea.
24,	John Thomas Keliher, .	John Thomas Kaler, . .	Boston.
24,	Alice Louise Wetherbee.* .	Alice Louise Meserve, . .	Boston.
31,	William Henry Loomis,* .	Walter Willie Morse, . .	Boston.
31,	Marian Bruce,*	Mabel Viola Cook, . .	Boston.
31,	Daisy Aldridge Farling,* .	Lillian Beatrice Messer, .	Boston.
Nov. 7,	Mabel Lind,*	Lottie Olena Taylor, . .	Taunton.
7,	Prudence May Harris,* .	Ettie Cushing Matteson, ˙ .	Boston.
7,	Mary Ann Agnes Martin, .	Marion Agnes Martin, .	Boston.
14,	Mary Coffee,*	Mary Frances Morgan, . .	Wyoming.
14,	Harry Clifford Brown,* .	Harry Clifford Luff, . .	Webster.
14,	Luella Hunt,*	Agnes Swain, ...	Weymouth.
28,	Nathaniel Thayer, . .	Nathaniel Francis Thayer, .	Boston.
Dec. 12,	Solomon Russell Braley, .	Russell Stanton Braley, . .	Boston.
12,	Mamie Canby,* . . .	Dora Gabel Jewell, . . .	Boston.
19,	Lottie True Austin,* . .	Lottie Alice Hall, . . .	Boston.
19,	John Frances Munroe,* .	William Francis Merrill, .	Boston.

ESSEX COUNTY.

Jan. 3,	Emma T. McCarty,* . .	Maud Gardner Favor, . .	Lynn.
10,	Annie B. Carpenter,* . .	Annie Belle Duncan, . .	Haverhill.
10,	Zita Welch,*	Eva Isabelle Curtis, . .	Boston.
Feb. 7,	Helen Grey Questrom, .	Helen Gray Hartshorn, . .	Lynn.
Mar. 7,	Mabel R. Sawyer,* . .	Mabel Runnels Porter, . .	Newburyport.
14,	Lucille Pervier,* . . .	Lucille Pervier English, .	Salem.
April 4,	George H. Matthews,* .	George Henry Robinson, .	Boston.
11,	Grace B. Johnson,* . .	Grace Belle Lurvey, . .	Haverhill.
18,	Harriet B. Poole,* . .	Harriet Belle Wheeler, . .	Gloucester.
26,	Alexander R. Porter, . .	Alexander S. Porter, . .	Beverly.
May 2,	Lizzie S. Hypson,* . .	Maud Dolphine Gault, . .	Manchester.
9,	Warren R. Buckbee.*. .	Howard Edward Winslow, .	Egremont.
16,	Blanche E. Tucker,* . .	Blanche Ethel Roberts, . .	Merrimac.
June 6,	Margaret E. O'Brien, . .	Margaret Ellen Bessom, . .	Swampscott.
July 11,	Joseph N. Mailhot,* . .	Joseph Napoleon Vallée, . .	Haverhill.
18,	Harriet E. Fellows,* . .	Harriet Estella Roche, . .	Haverhill.
Sept. 6,	Honora Gorman,* . .	Caroline Gorman Odlin, . .	Salem.
6,	Helen McCoffin Jones,* .	Helen Eliza Poole, . . .	Gloucester.
6,	Walter Smith,* . . .	Lawrence Vinton Bartlett, .	Lynn.
26,	Catherine A. Farrell,* .	Agnes Stanwood Orcutt, .	Lynn.
26,	Clara Murray,* . . .	Clara Upham, ...	Boston.
Oct. 3,	Eunice Marshall,* . .	Sarah Louise Preston, . .	Salem.
10,	Ida Perkins,*	Annie Fletcher Davis, . .	Haverhill.
17,	Frederick Cook.* . .	Frederick Cook Batchelder, .	Newbury.
Nov. 7,	Grace I. Russell,* . .	Grace Irene Hadley, . .	Lynn.
7,	Ray Wells,*	Carrie Lydia Murdock, . .	Haverhill.
28,	William H. Lewis,* . .	William Endicott Lewis, .	Lynn.
Dec. 19,	William Flynn,* . . .	William Albert Goodwin, .	Boston.

MIDDLESEX COUNTY.

Jan. 4,	Abby Barker,* . . .	Abby Lane, ...	Medford.
4,	Isabelle Allida Howard,* .	Isabelle Howard Bent, . .	Hillsboro', N. H.
11,	Edwin Earl Stackpole,* .	Edwin Earl Smith, . . .	Everett.
11,	Cora Maud Mayo,* . .	Cora Maud Howard, .	Melrose.

* Changed by reason of adoption.

MIDDLESEX COUNTY — *Concluded.*

Date of Decree.	Original Name.	Name Decreed.	Residence.
1887.			
Jan. 11,	Michael J. Kelley,*	Michael Joseph Rourke, .	Boston.
11,	Maria L. Tweedia,*	Maria Louisa Atkinson, .	Nantucket.
Feb. 23,	Annie Small,*	Maud Peterson,	Boston.
23,	Elida J. Kosman,*	Mabel Anna Heyl, .	Boston.
Mar. 1,	Eva Bryan,*	Besse Lee Spaulding,	Tewksbury.
1,	George Bryan,* .	William Martin Spaulding,	Tewksbury.
8,	Grace Bell Taylor,*	Grace Bell Brown, .	Malden
15,	Edith May Carpenter,*	Edith May Gay, .	Concord, N. H.
22,	Abbie Maud Nason,* .	Abbie Maud Dennis,	Woburn.
April 5,	Elizabeth Jane McMeeken,*	Aphia Prentiss Eastman,	Melrose.
5,	Frederick Joseph Fowler, .	Frederick Joseph Edes, .	Newton.
26,	Wallace Bloomfield Flint, .	Wallace Bloomfield Burdett, .	North Reading.
May 3,	Louis Albert Smith,* .	Louis Albert Souther,	Somerville.
3,	Eva May Smith,*	Eva May Souther, .	Somerville.
3,	Maud Watermyer,*	Mary Roberts,	Cambridge.
10,	William Newell Osgood,	William Parkman Osgood,	Cambridge.
17,	Lizzie Ellen Morris,* .	Lizzie Ellen Sherwood, .	Maynard.
24,	Austin Mann,*	Elmer Allen Bursley,	Marlborough.
24,	Mira Gillam,*	Mira Eliza Gillam, .	Lowell.
24,	Annie Tass,*	Girttrude Malinda Ward,	Cambridge.
June 7,	Henry Austin Lull,* .	Frank Edwin Pidgeon, .	Cambridge.
7,	Mollie Mutzenhauer,*	Mollie Garfield Hood, .	Dracut.
7,	Harrie Darling Abbott,	Harrie Smith Abbott, .	Malden.
7,	Charles Ralph Abbott,	Ralph Kinsman Abbott, .	Malden.
14,	Mary P. Carr.* .	Mary Carr Plummer,	Everett.
14,	Caroline Augusta Richmond Tuttle, .	Carrie Augusta Houghton,	Littleton.
July 5,	Otto Henrickson,*	Otto Henrickson Geers, .	Maynard.
5,	May Louise Carver,* .	Mabel Louise Woodward,	Melrose.
5,	Julia Thorndike,*	Julia Thorndike Dennis,	Rockland, Me.
12,	Florence May Snow,*	Florence May Faulkner,	Cambridge.
12,	Lottie Sherwood.*	Susan May Roberts,	Littleton.
26,	Jennie Hall Harback,*	Jennie Hall Nichols,	Sutton.
Sept. 6,	James Smith,*	William Frederick Jagerstan,	Boston.
6,	Rena Simonds,* .	Mabel Alice Garvey,	Medford.
Oct. 4,	George Butler,* .	George Butler Smith,	Boston.
4,	—— Thompson,*	William Francis Smith, .	Portland.
11,	Ida Springfield,*	Grace Florence Polley, .	Waltham.
25,	Georgianna Laffard,* .	Daisy Whitcomb Robbins,	Littleton.
25,	Julia Brown,*	Benita Anna Miller, .	Somerville.
25,	Mercy K. Pickering, .	Mercy Knight Sanborn, .	Somerville.
25,	Nancy E. Lee, .	Nancy Elizabeth Brigham,	Maynard.
Nov. 9,	Abbie Emma Thompson, .	Gertrude Emily Thompson, .	Billerica.
9,	Florence Adelia Pickard, .	Florence Adelia Williams,	Waltham.
15,	Hannibel Wellington Carty,	Hannibal Wellington Dennis,	Arlington.
15,	Rubie Gillis,*	Ethel Armenia Wells, .	Boston.
22,	Alonzo T. Nickerson,*	Walter Harris,	Cambridge.
Dec. 6,	Rose E. Shedd,*	Henriette Morris Pinkham,	Cambridge.
6,	Katie Hayden,* .	Katie Perry, ʻ .	Chelmsford.
6,	Ella Louisa Lord,	Eleanor Louisa Lord,	Malden.
6,	John Francis Swett, .	John Francis Robbins, .	Melrose.
13,	Pearl Wingate,* .	Ettynge Pearl Walbridge,	Medford.

WORCESTER COUNTY.

Feb. 15,	Frederick Herbert Worcester,* .	Frederick Herbert Rice, .	Worcester.
23,	Ellie Frances Munroe,* .	Ellie Frances Stone,	Leominster.
Mar. 1,	Ida Fenno,*	Ida Pelican, .	Worcester.
1,	Fred Fenno,*	Fred Pelican, .	Worcester.

* Changed by reason of adoption.

WORCESTER COUNTY — *Concluded.*

Date of Decree.	Original Name.	Name Decreed.	Residence.
1887.			
April 5,	—— ——,*	Philip Sheridan Perkins,	Worcester.
5,	Leonora Howard,*	Jennie Leonora Mason,	Southbridge.
19,	Rosana Lamoureux,*	Rosana Pinsonnault,	Spencer.
19,	Anna E. Casaubon,	Anna E. C. Purdy,	Worcester.
26,	James Harney,*.	James Harney Brennan,	Webster.
May 3,	Elvira Augusta Dean,*	Elvira Augusta Rich,	Brookfield.
3,	Alice Maude Bartlett,*	Alice Estelle Palmer,	Lancaster.
3,	Jane K. Norcross,	Jane K. Sawyer,	Gardner.
3,	Kittie Mabel Desilets,*	Kittie Mabel Chapin,	Worcester.
17,	Margaret Elizabeth Brown,	Margaret Elizabeth Graham,	Northbridge.
July 19,	Josephine Bernard,* .	Josephine Lamoureux, .	Worcester.
Sept. 6,	Philip Sidney Harvey,*	Philip Sidney Harvey Winslow,	Agawam.
6,	Mary Arabella Eddy,	Mary Arabella Austin, .	Worcester.
13,	Kate Thayer,*	Lillia Josephine Davis, .	Milford.
20,	Bertha Goldthwaite Adams,	Esther Louise Goldthwaite Adams,	Worcester.
Oct. 4,	Emma Ellen Laighton,* .	Edith Louise Ford, .	Boston.
4,	Charles Washington Oaks,	Charles Washington Holbrook,	Berlin.
Nov. 1,	Roman Kilby,* .	Frank Wendall Chase, .	Boston.
15,	Bertha Prynne,*	Alice May Taylor, .	Templeton.
15,	Arthur H. Sanborn,* .	Ernest Thompson Stone,	Westborough.
15,	Mabel Malinda Clark,*	Mabel Malinda Stone, .	Cambridgeport.
Dec. 20,	Delor Martin,* .	Albert McNair, .	Southbridge.

HAMPSHIRE COUNTY.

Jan. 4,	Nellie McQuade,*	Nellie Voigt, .	Easthampton.
11,	Fred Douglass Jackson,* .	George Frederick Jennings,	Amherst.
Mar. 1,	Wilbur Hamilton,* .	Wilfred Harold Bosworth,	Southampton.
Sept. 6,	Lillian E. Shepard,* .	Lillian E. Dunklee,	South Hadley.

HAMPDEN COUNTY.

Jan. 5,	Florence Chessman,* .	Florence Hughes, .	Cambridge.
11,	Emma Cooper,* .	Emma Cooper Holcomb,	Boston.
Feb. 2,	Frank Elmer Holt,* .	Frank Elmer Anderson,	Providence, R. I.
7,	Watson Gibbons,*	Ellis Watson Cowdry, .	Granville.
May 4,	Fannie Burbank Rice,* .	Fannie Burbank Bliss, .	Granville.
July 6,	Infant unnamed,* .	Winifred Emmons Smith,	Springfield.
6,	Harriet Flanagan,*	Harriet McDonald, .	Ludlow.
6,	Dora Lucinda Rhodes,*	Dora Lucinda Green, .	Wales.
27,	Helen May Thompson,*	Helen May Thayer, .	Springfield.
27,	Francis Holyoke,*	Francis Alvin Chapin, .	Holyoke.
Sept. 7,	Florence Opal Mulvey,*	Edith Opal Childs, .	Worcester.
7,	Angenett Petersen,*	Sarah Annie Lewis, .	Denmark.
7,	Leon Alva Tibbetts,* .	Leon Alva Aldrich, .	Springfield.
7,	Moses Kovensky, .	Moses Rivers, .	Springfield.
Oct. 5,	Walter Alonzo West,*	Walter Alonzo West Miner,	Hampden.
19,	William Hoffman,* .	William Thiele, .	Easthampton.
Nov. 2,	James Edward Baker,*	Edward James McIntire,	Springfield.
Dec. 14,	Louise Fowler,* .	Louise Fowler Hitchcock,	Westfield.

* Changed by reason of adoption.

FRANKLIN COUNTY.

Date of Decree.	Original Name.	Name Decreed.	Residence.
1887.			
Mar. 8,	James Van Dusen, . . .	Frederic James Harris, . .	Greenfield.
April 5,	Lizzie Louisa Baker, . . .	Lizzie Louisa Pennington, .	Heath.
5,	Pierre Joseph Adelard St. Germaine, ...	Pierre Joseph Adelard Asa Baribeault, ...	Montague.
June 21,	Wallace Tibbetts, . . .	Harold Arthur Sullivan, .	Orange.
Aug. 2,	John Day, ...	Chester Herbert Guilford, .	Ashfield.
Oct. 10,	Charles Roscoe Bancroft, . .	Charles Roscoe Canedy, . .	Rowe.
Dec. 13,	Adolph Ranlet, ...	Harold Eugene Humphrey, .	Orange.

BERKSHIRE COUNTY.

Date of Decree.	Original Name.	Name Decreed.	Residence.
Jan. 6,	Isabella Maude Winton,* . .	Maude Winton Cady, . .	North Adams.
Feb. 1,	Hiram M. Wing, . . .	Hiram W. Martin, . . .	North Adams.
1,	William A. Van Lone,* . .	William A. West, . . .	Stockbridge.
Mar. 1,	Walter Nicholas,* . . .	Walter Nicholas Evans, . .	Pittsfield.
1,	Stella G. Tanner,* . . .	Stella Grace Stevens, . .	North Adams.
July 21,	Napoleon Eli Alexander Bernor,*	Napoleon Beauregard, . .	Adams.
Oct. 4,	Edward Hickey,* . . .	Edward Madell, . . .	Pittsfield.
4,	Maud Sarah Yeates,* . .	Maud Sarah Bowen, . .	North Adams.

NORFOLK COUNTY.

Date of Decree.	Original Name.	Name Decreed.	Residence.
Jan. 19,	Lizzie Mabel Thayer,* . .	Lizzie Mabel Ellis, . . .	Boston.
Feb. 16,	Ignatius Jay,* . . .	Ignatius Jay Allen, . .	Boston.
16,	Laura Tupper,*	Ethel Fuller, ...	Dedham.
Mar. 9,	Eugene Newell Hawks,* . .	Eugene Newell Gardner, .	Clinton.
April 6,	Urma Carlton,*	Urmer Carlton Alden, . .	Richmond, Va.
20,	Celia Tower Ringham,* . .	Celia Tower Porter, . .	Boston.
20,	John Lowe,*	Fred Everett Bisbee, . .	Unknown.
Sept. 21,	William Everett Wortman, .	William Everett Morton, .	Walpole.
Oct. 5,	Wallace Burns Taynton,* . .	Wallace Taynton Morley, .	Elmira, N. Y.
Nov. 16,	Agnes Hawkins,* . . .	Eunice Etta Haggett, . .	Boston.

PLYMOUTH COUNTY.

Date of Decree.	Original Name.	Name Decreed.	Residence.
Mar. 14,	Corteze Elgin Hurd,* . .	Corteze Elgin Lombard, .	Brockton.
May 23,	Howard Loud Helfenstein,* .	Paul Owen Wade, . . .	Hull.
June 13,	Ella Maud Thomas,* . . .	Ella Maud Johnson, . .	Whitman.
13,	Ellen Maria Callahan,* . .	Ellen Maria Giles, . . .	Whitman.
July 11,	Idella Cushing Pratt,* . .	Idella Cushing Arnold, . .	Hanson.
Sept. 26,	Ethel May Leach,* . . .	Ethel May Ellis, . . .	Bridgewater.
26,	Florence Trafton Leach,* . .	Florence Trafton Woodman, .	Bridgewater.
Oct. 10,	Margaret Hurley,* . . .	Theodora Clare White, . .	Middleborough.
Nov. 14,	James W. Niles,* . . .	Warren Alford Allen, . .	Brockton.
14,	George Caton, Jr.,* . . .	George Edward Orcutt, . .	Hanson.
28,	Louisa West,*	Lula Irene Fletcher, . .	Brockton.
Dec. 12,	Mary McLauthlin,* . . .	Edith Mae Robinson, . .	Brockton.
27,	Lilian J. Reed,*	Lilian Turk, ...	Pembroke.

* Changed by reason of adoption.

BRISTOL COUNTY.

Date of Decree.	Original Name.	Name Decreed.	Residence.
1887.			
Jan. 7,	Peter Doane,*	Alexander Kerr, . . .	Fall River.
7,	—— Kelley,*	Benjamin O. Nickerson, .	Fall River.
Feb. 4,	Margaret C. Barlow,* . .	Margaret C. Donnelley, .	Fall River.
4,	Robert Pollard,* . . .	Robert Buckley, . . .	Fall River.
18,	Lillian Kelley,*	Lillian Darcy, . . .	Fall River.
Mar. 4,	Henry E. Booth, Jr., . .	George H. Brier, . . .	New Bedford.
April 1,	Agnes Adelaide Hampson,* .	Agnes Adelaide Fay, . .	Fall River.
1,	Nellie M. Towle,* . . .	Nellie M. Fuller, . .	New Bedford.
1,	Johanna Jarvis,* . . .	Johanna McCormick, . .	Fall River.
June 3,	Amy L. Wilson,* . . .	Amy L. Morse, . . .	Taunton.
July 1,	Blanche White,* . . .	Millicent White, . .	Gardner.
Aug. 5,	Minnie A. Gould,* . . .	Minnie Alice Lincoln, . .	Taunton.
5,	Mary Alice McCarthy,* . .	Mary Alice Devine, . .	New Bedford.
5,	Florence W. Webber,* . .	Florence W. Perkins, . .	Taunton.
Sept. 2,	Anna H. Luce,*	Anna H. Thornton, . .	Taunton.
2,	Ida Bell Chisnell,* . . .	Ida Belle Wilde, . .	Fall River.
Oct. 7,	Ida L. Williams,* . . .	Ida Luella Bradshaw, .	Taunton.
7,	Mabel Vincent,* . . .	Mabel Vincent Robillard, .	Fall River.
Nov. 18,	Rita P. Nooning,* . . .	Rita P. Tripp, . . .	Fall River.
Dec. 2,	Lina Norton.*	Clara Elizabeth Sweet, .	Norton.

BARNSTABLE COUNTY.

May 18,	Julia Victory,*	Lucy Ann Smith, . .	Provincetown.
Sept. 13,	Helen May Harlow,* . . .	Helen May Harlow Jones, .	Barnstable.
Oct. 26,	Albert Godfrey Allingham,* .	Edward Payson Shiverick, .	Falmouth.

NANTUCKET COUNTY.

Mar. 10,	Lizzie C. Coffin, ...	Lizzie Coffin Fitzgerald, .	Nantucket.

SUFFOLK COUNTY.

1888.			
Jan. 2,	Annie Maria Cecelia Brady, .	Annie Maria Cecelia Williams,	Boston.
9,	Cora Rebecca Green,* . .	Cora Rebecca Goodwin, .	Boston.
9,	Josephine Moffett,* . .	Mildred Van Schoick, .	Boston.
9,	Grace C. Currier,* . .	Grace Adell Homer, .	Boston.
16,	Percy Cliffton Greenlaw, .	Percy Cliffton Eaton, .	Boston.
16,	Frank P. Weston,* . .	Frank Preissler, . .	Philadelphia, Pa.
Feb. 6,	Joseph Lowney,* . . .	Joseph Edward Corbett, .	Boston.
13,	Florence Waters,* . .	Grace Lillian Gilmore, .	Boston.
13,	Seddie Deloria.* . . .	Burt Orlando Gilman, .	Boston.
13,	Vincenzo Patrizio.* . .	Vincenzio Argenzio, .	Boston.
13,	Sarah E. Rowland,* . .	Esther Olive Spencer, .	Boston.
27,	Josiah Edson,* . . .	Charles Winckley Cole, .	Brookline.
27,	Eva James Chisholm,* .	Eva Elinor Quint, . .	Boston.
27,	John Joseph Kelley,*. .	Louis Barr Hicks, . .	Boston.
Mar. 5,	Lizzie Stevenson,* . .	Bertha Larcom Tay, .	Tewksbury.
5,	Martin McNulty,* . .	Charles Washington Birch, .	Natick.
5,	Lulu Florence Smith, .	Lulu Florence Cunio, .	Boston.
5,	Douglas B. Rieder,* . .	Douglas Bennett Turner, .	Springfield.

* Changed by reason of adoption.

SUFFOLK COUNTY — *Concluded.*

Date of Decree.	Original Name.	Name Decreed.	Residence.
1888.			
Mar. 12,	Philip Martin.*	Albert Francis Woodward, .	Boston.
12,	Lizzie Sherman,* . .	Lizzie Hickman, . . .	Boston.
12,	Lulu Parthow White,* .	Lulu Frances Rounds, .	Woburn.
19,	Annie Frazier,* . . .	Annie Frances Charlton, .	Nova Scotia.
19,	Henry Frazier,*. . . .	Henry William Norton, . .	———.
26,	William Galloway, . .	William Lincoln Galloway, .	Boston.
26,	Alice Finley,* . . .	Dorothy Lydia Eaton, .	Boston.
April 2,	Ethel Louise Baker,* .	Ethel Mildred Wheeler, .	Boston.
2,	Eleanor Brown,* . . .	Eleanor Joslin, . . .	Boston.
9,	Alfred Bean, ...	Alfred Cobb Bean, . .	Boston.
9,	Harry Chapman,* . .	Ralph Southwick Nealy, .	Boston.
9,	Mary Ann Hathaway, .	Mary Ann Prindle, . .	———.
9,	David Quinn,* . . .	Josiah Quinn, ...	Boston.
16,	Mary Ann Martin.* . .	Annie Bohan, ...	Boston.
16,	Fred Almon Brackett,* .	Fred Almon Pushee, .	Boston.
16,	Minnie Derward,* . .	Minnie Lottie Franklin, .	Boston.
30,	Leonidas Maurice Griffin,* .	Leonidas Maurice Palmer, .	Boston.
30,	Fannie Levi,* . . .	Fannie Barry, . . .	Boston.
May 7,	George Hugo Burgholzer, .	George Burgholzer Hugo, .	———.
7,	Mildred Virginia Hughes,* .	Mildred Virginia Caldwell, .	Chelsea.
14,	Gertrude M. Geppel,* .	Gertrude May Forsyth, . .	Chelsea.
14,	Frederick Brandforth,* .	Frederick Brandforth Connolly, ...	Boston.
21,	Loise Read Patten,* . .	Loise Read Babson, . .	Boston.
21,	Catherine Mary Murray,*. .	Catherine Mary Hale, . .	Boston.
28,	George Morton,* . . .	George Carlos French, .	Boston.
June 4,	Benjamin B. Murray,* .	William Benjamin Boyden, .	Boston.
4,	Eva Elliott Leline,* . .	Bessie Torrey, . . .	Boston.
11,	William John Butler,* .	Willie J. Blake, . . .	Boston.
18,	Ida Campbell,* . . .	Mary Ann Bishop, . .	Boston.
25,	Charles Henry Moses, .	Charles Henry Moseley, .	Boston.
25,	Alice Christina Brown,* .	Alice Christina Stenman, .	Boston.
25,	Ralph Francis Handy,* .	Ralph Francis Rogers, .	New Bedford.
July 2,	Mary Ann Burns,* . .	Mary Ann Lynch, . .	Boston.
2,	William Lawrence Tucker, .	Lawrence Tucker, . .	Boston.
9,	John William Busby,* .	Ernest Chester Baker, .	Boston.
30,	Burpee Earnest Piper, .	Earnest Burpee Raymond, .	Boston.
30,	Gustave Joseph Blank, .	Edgar Theodore Thurlow, .	Boston.
30,	William Morris Austin Peters, .	Morris Austin Peters, .	Boston.
Aug. 20,	Ella May Townsend,* . .	May Ella Vilas, .	Boston.
Sept. 4,	Henry Felton,* . . .	Henry Felton Ames, .	Boston.
4,	Florence Agnes Murray,* . .	Florence Wendom Van Deusen,	Boston.
4,	Mabel Young,* . . .	Mabel Louise Towle, .	Boston.
10,	Lillian Marr Canney,* .	Lillian Marr Safford, .	Boston.
10,	Charles Henry Eltz,* .	Charles Eltz Heath, .	Boston.
10,	Eliza Somerby Prince, .	Lillian Prince, . .	Boston.
17,	Susie Ann Smith.* . .	Margaret Pfaff, . .	Boston.
24,	Sarah Helen White,* . .	Annie Laura Spinney, .	Chelsea.
Oct. 8,	John O'Beirne, . . .	John Burnes, . .	Boston.
15,	David Harry Kayes,* .	David Harry Price, .	Boston.
15,	Kate Prentice, . . .	Kate Annette Heyer, .	Boston.
22,	Florence Clement,* . .	Florence Howard Morse, .	Boston.
Nov. 5,	Ebenezer J. Foster,* . .	Ebenezer J. Foster Eddy, .	Boston.
5,	James Mack,* . . .	James Arthur Dixon, .	Boston.
5,	William Tufts Rankine,* .	William Tufts, . .	Boston.
12,	Fred Humphrey Plumb, .	Fred Humphrey, . .	Boston.
12,	Lizzie C. Baker, . . .	Beth Baker, . .	Boston.
19,	Alfred Evans Worthley,* .	Fred Evans Worthley, .	Boston.
26,	John Coffin Jones, . .	John Sumner, . . .	Boston.
26,	Austin Sumner Jones, .	Austin Sumner, . .	Boston.
26,	Marguerita Jones, . . .	Marguerita Sumner, . .	Boston.

* Changed by reason of adoption

SUFFOLK COUNTY — *Concluded.*

Date of Decree.	Original Name.	Name Decreed.	Residence.
1888.			
Nov. 26,	Ella Maria Jones, . . .	Ella Maria Sumner, . .	Boston.
26,	John James Hooper, . . .	George Hooper Merrill, . .	Boston.
Dec. 3,	Ida Helen Slack, . . .	Ida Helen Stebbins, . .	Chelsea.
3,	Roland S. Slack, . . .	Roland Stewart Stebbins, .	Chelsea.
10,	Harry Osgood,* . . .	Harry Hatch, ...	Boston.
10,	Elsie Leown Duncan,* .	Elsie Leown Coffin, . .	Boston.
17,	Herbert Eustice Cochrane,* .	George Norman Riblet, .	Newton.
17,	John Francis McCaughey,* .	William Chester Sheldon, .	Boston.
17,	Mabel Engley,* . . .	Grace Edna Hanscom, .	Hopkinton.
24,	Januario Soares de Figueiredo,	James Fred Sears, . .	Boston.
31,	Ada Souther Tarbell Jennings,*	Ada Souther Tarbell, .	Boston.
31,	Bessie P. Sullivan, . . .	Bessie P. Scates, . .	Boston.
31,	Emelie Katharina Gutberlet,* .	Emelie Katharina Israel, .	——.
31,	Eugenia Redman Highriter,* .	Eugenia Redman Highriter Jacobs,.	Boston.

ESSEX COUNTY.

Jan. 2,	Ralph Putnam Cook,* . .	Ralph Cook Putnam, . .	Danvers.
2,	Clementina Glover,* . .	Maybell Victoria Bowman, .	——.
2,	Florence Martin, formerly Mora Colt,*	Betsey Jane Pike, . . .	Needham.
16,	Mabel Estella Hood,* . .	Mabel Estella Rogers, . .	Ipswich.
Feb. 6,	Norman Edward Dunn, .	Norman Edward Crosby, .	Beverly.
20,	Lottie Bushie,*	Dora Pearl Barter, . .	New York, N. Y.
Mar. 5,	Oscar W. Clark,† . . .	Oscar Watson Frost, . .	Wenham.
5,	William H. Fitzgerald, . .	William Henry Buckley, .	Bradford.
19,	Mary E. McGovern,* . .	Mary Ellen Montgomery, .	Newton.
26,	Cassie McDougall,* . .	Eva Maud Gregware, . .	Salem.
April 2,	Angela M. Cook,* . . .	Angela May Gardner, . .	Danvers.
23,	Catherine Brennan,* . .	Sarah Frances Hincks, . .	Lynn.
May 21,	John F. Ryan, ...	John Franklin Watts, . .	Lynn.
June 4,	Mona Bell,*	Mona Bell Welch, . . .	——.
4,	Margaret E. King,* . . .	Bertha Evangeline Shaw, .	Boston.
25,	Isabelle M. Sagar,* . . .	Isabelle Maud Furber, .	Lynn.
July 2,	Jones Collins, ...	John Perley, ...	Lynn.
Aug. 6,	James Kelly, otherwise known as James Goodman,* . .	James Coughlin, . . .	Haverhill.
6,	Rose Orsikowsky,* . . .	Shirlie McKenney, . . .	Boston.
Oct. 1,	Grace E. Locke,* . . .	Grace Etta Douglass, .	Burnhamville, Minn.
8,	Alfred O. Rodien, . . .	Alfred Levi Wright, .	Haverhill.
8,	—— McSwain,* . . .	Charles Edward Sargent, .	Haverhill.
Nov. 5,	Ernest W. Smith,* . . .	Ernest Walter Rowe, . .	Gloucester.
19,	Charles A. Anderson, . .	Charles Augustus Cederberg,	Gloucester.
Dec. 17,	Mark L. Koviensky, . .	Mark Lewis, ...	Haverhill.

MIDDLESEX COUNTY.

Jan. 3,	Ormsby Albert Macready, .	Ormsby Albert Court, . .	Lowell.
3,	Lilla Blanche Macready, .	Lilla Blanche Court, . .	Lowell.
3,	John Sewall Pratt, . .	John Sewall Pratt Alcott, .	Concord.
3,	Alice McDonald,* . .	Marie Grey Hilton, . .	Boston.
10,	John William Cummings,. .	John Addison Cummings, .	Somerville.

* Changed by reason of adoption.
† May 2, 1871, Oscar W. Clark's name changed from Oscar Watson.

MIDDLESEX COUNTY — *Concluded.*

Date of Decree.	Original Name.	Name Decreed.	Residence.
1888.			
Jan. 17,	Helen Maria Hopkins,	Helen Maria Brown,	Lowell.
17,	Frances Charlotte Armstrong,	Frances Charlotte Allen,	Lowell.
Feb. 7,	William Albert Smith,	William Albert Cutter,	Wakefield.
7,	Algernon Finn,*	Frederic Ray Jewett,	Groton.
7,	Emily Jane Leckley,*	Mary Maria Ayers,	Cambridge.
14,	Ida Rachkowski,	Ida Harris,	Lowell.
14,	Joseph Rachkowsky,	Joseph Harris,	Lowell.
14,	Mary Amelia Horibin,*	Mary Amelia Sanderson,	Lowell.
Mar. 6,	Victoria Ludlow,*	Alice Crawford Marshall,	Malden.
6,	Ralph Enderly,*	Ralph William Eldridge,	Weston.
6,	George Emery,*	Walter Edward Doughty,	Boston.
13,	Irene Virginia McKean,*	Irene Virginia Merritt,	Boston.
13,	Vida Luella Wood,*	Vida Lawrence Patch,	Pepperell.
20,	Walter Ray,*	Fordyce Raymond Moores,	Marlborough.
27,	Joseph Horm,	Joseph Weissbach,	Somerville.
27,	Harry Stanley Whiting,*	Harry Augustus Newton,	Boston.
April 3,	Edwin Burke,*	James Edwin Bartlett,	Attleborough.
3,	Jennie Crowe,*	Mary Greeley,	Lexington.
10,	Lottie McAuley,*	Lottie Winsor Tufts,	Boston.
10,	Arthur Watts Taylor,*	Arthur Hartwell Douglass,	Boston.
May 1,	Henry Corbin,*	William James Drewett,	Ayer.
1,	William Albert Howard,*	William Albert Howard West,	Boston.
15,	Ina Kennedy,*	Lizzie Maude Coates,	Lowell.
22,	Maude Hutchins,*	Maude Hazelton Russell,	Boston.
June 5,	Nancy Maria Poor,	Nina Maria Poor,	Somerville.
5,	Frances Isabella Miller,	Isabella Proctor Miller,	Newton.
12,	Harriot Rust Millett,*	Harriot Burnett Newhall,	Newton.
26,	Harold Caverly Daly,	Harold Caverly,	Lowell.
July 3,	Inez Gray,*	Annie Green,	Malden.
10,	Elizabeth Langdon,*	Elizabeth Smith,	Lowell.
17,	Willard Edward Slater,*	Willard Edward Frazier,	Lowell.
17,	Harriet E. Habel,*	Hattie Elizabeth King,	Boston.
24,	Amy Palmer Morton,*	Amy Palmer Bacon,	Boston.
24,	Mary Buchanan,*	Margaret Edna Higley,	Westborough.
Sept. 4,	Irene Marie Damon,*	Irene Damon Mansir,	Somerville.
11,	Lizzie Ellen Sherwood,*	Lizzie Ellen Morris,	Maynard.
11,	Catherine Frances Magdelene Conboy,*	Catherine Frances Magdelene Rourke,	Boston.
Oct. 9,	Clara Lillian Goodhue,*	Clara Lillian Carey,	Boston.
9,	Edith Hamilton,*	Grace Arliene Hedge,	Wakefield
Nov. 7,	Alice M. Fancher,*	Alice M. Pushee,	Somerville.
7,	Grace Louise Boggs,*	Grace Louise Hodgkins,	Springfield.
7,	Samuel Wallace,*	Percy Wallace Higgins,	Weston.
7,	Lizzie Mitchell,*	Ethel May Wyman,	Newport, Me.
20,	Irene E. Butt,*	Marion Hopkins Farrar,	Boston.
20,	Willie Nugent,*	Frederick Charles Rohrer,	Boston.
27,	George Bell Kenrick,*	George Bell Kenrick Alexander,	Belmont.
27,	Clarence Kennedy,*	Clifford Henry Jacobs,	Stoneham.
Dec. 4,	Alice G. McGivney,*	Alice Gertrude McKinney,	Randolph.
26,	Joseph E. Erwin,*	Erving Garfield Hartwell,	Littleton.
26,	Flora Belle Pullen,*	Flora Belle Cooley,	Centreville, R. I.
26,	Gertrude Meriam Hartshorne,*	Gertrude Josephine Steward,	Boston.
26,	Freeman Smith,*	Freeman Davis Jennison,	Lincoln.

* Changed by reason of adoption.

WORCESTER COUNTY.

Date of Decree.	Original Name.	Name Decreed.	Residence.
1888.			
Jan. 17,	Hattie Maria Hendrick,* . .	Hattie Maria Wright, . .	Worcester.
Feb. 21,	May Elizabeth Burrage,* . .	Miriam Frances Elizabeth Smith, ...	Petersham.
Mar. 6,	May E. Russell,* . . .	Mabel Lillian Woodis, . .	Boston.
6,	Margaret Ahearn,* . . .	Margaret McGrath, . . .	Worcester.
27,	Anna Maud Smith,* . . .	Anna Maud McMullen, . .	Fitchburg.
27,	George Wallace Houghton,* .	Wallace Houghton Terrell, .	Fitchburg.
April 10,	Charles Phelps,* . . .	George Ballard Lawton, .	Lancaster.
17,	Albert Brewer,*	Albert St. Jean, . . .	Spencer.
May 15,	Samuel E. Simanovich, . .	Samuel E. Simons, . . .	Worcester.
June 19,	Tena Warren,*	Marion Warren Barton, .	Phillipston.
19,	Martha J. Butler,* . . .	Mabel Lydia Johnson, . .	Lancaster.
19,	Lyman G. Hall,* . . .	Arthur Franklin Barnes, .	Worcester.
19,	Christine Scott,* . . .	Helen Scott Ballou, . , .	Milford.
19,	Mary Elizabeth Odlum,* . .	Mary Elizabeth Converse, .	Grafton.
26,	Elmer Elsworth Cosman,* .	Elmer Elsworth Danforth, .	Fitchburg.
July 3,	Hugh James McCann,* . .	Hugh James McCoy, . .	Dudley.
Aug. 21,	Sarah Jane Mann,* . . .	Sadie Jane Coombes, . .	Thomps'nv'le, Ct.
Oct. 2,	Bessie Newcomb,* . . .	Eva May Peck, . . .	Spencer.
2,	Florence Isabel Barton,* .	Florence Isabel Cudworth, .	Worcester.
30,	Charles Henry Hillock,* . .	Charles Henry Burger, . .	Winchendon.
Nov. 23,	Joseph Raymond,* . . .	Joseph Edwin Rice, . .	Winchendon.
23,	Ethel Cruikshank,* . . .	Ethel Belle Stone, . . .	Westborough.
27,	Mary E. Smith, ...	Mary Eliza Gates, . . .	Clinton.
Dec. 4,	Addie Elfreda Barton,* . .	Addie Elfreda Burlingame, .	Rutland.
7,	Violet Harrington,* . . .	Alice Levinia Smith, . .	Boston.
7,	I. C. Bates Smith,* . . .	Isaac Chapman Bates Dana, .	Worcester.
7,	Elsie Manda Petersen,* . .	Elsie Manda Newton, . .	No. Brookfield.

HAMPSHIRE COUNTY.

Mar. 6,	Dora Goodchild,* . . .	Dora Dufresne, . . .	Northampton.
6,	Marguerite Frances Pervere,* .	Margie Cora Starks, . .	Plainfield.
May 1,	Laura Nareau,*	Laura Gaucher, . . .	Northampton.
15,	Lilla Abbie Upton,* . . .	Hattie Eliza Haskins, . .	Hadley.
June 19,	Samuel Hays,*	Samuel Hays Dickinson, .	Amherst.
Aug. 14,	Addie May Wilson Adams,* .	Addie May Wilson, . .	Belchertown.
Oct. 2,	Lizzie Bell Chapin,* . . .	Lizzie Belle Perrett, . .	Huntington.
Dec. 4,	Catherine O'Niel,* . . .	Eva Fischer, ...	Williamsburg.

HAMPDEN COUNTY.

Jan. 4,	Sarah Maud Costigan, . .	Sarah Maud Dunham, . .	Springfield.
14,	Eva May Lind,* . . .	Eva Lewis Ferry, . . .	Springfield.
Feb. 8,	Mary T. Brown,* . . .	Mary Hughes, . . .	Springfield.
8,	Lewis Springer Field,* . .	Lewis Henry Hall, . . .	Longmeadow.
Mar. 7,	Freida Clara Hetwig Baerneck,*	Winnifred Elizabeth Poskey,	Springfield.
June 6,	Maria Elizabeth Dart, . .	Maria Elizabeth Palmer, .	Westfield.
Aug. 1,	Frederic Brown,* . . .	John Jalbert, . . .	Chicopee.
1,	Dorothy Ganderton,* . . .	Dorothy Ganderton Hodgkins,	Springfield.
Sept. 5,	Blanche Leota Clough,* . .	Blanche Leota Newcomb, .	Springfield.
5,	Minnie S. Miller, . . .	Minnie S. Bramble, . .	West Springfield.
Dec. 19,	Johanna Wright,* . . .	Johanna Murphy, . . .	Chicopee.

* Changed by reason of adoption.

FRANKLIN COUNTY.

Date of Decree.	Original Name.	Name Decreed.	Residence.
1888.			
Jan. 3,	Earl Newell Thornily,* . .	George Earl Thornily, .	. Shelburne.
Feb. 14,	Frederick Rogers,* . .	Frederick Charles Allen,	. Buckland.
May 1,	George Newton,* . .	Francis Rupert Vorce, .	. Orange.
July 3,	Lewis Henry Burrage,* .	Lewis Henry Prichard, .	. Greenfield.
Sept. 25,	Martha Fulton,* . . .	Amy Florence Fenno, .	. Orange.
25,	Harold Kirby,* . . .	Harold Kirby Shaw, .	. Orange.
Oct. 23,	Mary Isabella Chandler,* .	Mary Goldie Coates, .	. Deerfield.

BERKSHIRE COUNTY.

Date of Decree.	Original Name.	Name Decreed.	Residence.
Feb. 7,	Estella Frazier,* . .	Carrie May Richmond, .	. Williamstown.
Mar. 7,	Lillian Rebecca Brierley,* .	Frances Mary Evans, .	. North Adams.
7,	Florence Jane Brierley,* .	Jennie Maude Kenyon, .	. North Adams.
June 5,	Jacob Weidman,* . .	Charles Jacob Hahneman,	. Pittsfield.
Sept. 4,	Lyn Morse,* . . .	Lyn Morse Braman, .	. North Adams.
4,	Priscilla Stone,* . .	Lena May Braman. .	. North Adams.
Oct. 2,	Curtis Aldrich Moore,* .	Curtis Aldrich Sanford,	. Sheffield.
4,	Elsie A. Haskins,* .	Agnes E. Crosier, . .	. Williamstown.
Nov. 7,	Mary Bulger,* . . .	Kate Linehan, . .	. North Adams.
7,	Nettie Curry,* . . .	Janette Curry Hastings,	. W. Stockbridge.
Dec. 4,	Etta Jane Wilson,* . .	Etta Jane Parsons, .	. Sandisfield.

NORFOLK COUNTY.

Date of Decree.	Original Name.	Name Decreed.	Residence.
1887.			
Dec. 7,	Emma Reuby Lowell,* .	Emma Reuby Reed, .	. Weymouth.
1888.			
Jan. 25,	William Miller, . . .	William James Horner, .	. Walpole.
Mar. 7,	Eliza Anna McKenney,* .	Bertha Agnes McKenney,	. Canton.
21,	Charles Frederic Jenks, .	Charles Fitz Jenks, .	. Canton.
April 11,	Mabel Florena McKenzie,*	Dorothy Florence Nash,	. Abington.
11,	Clarence Wade,* . .	Clarence Wade Cushing,	. Weymouth.
May 16,	Carl Sherman,* . . .	Nathaniel Benjamin Sanborn,	. Boston.
June 6,	Frederic Tirrell Thayer,* .	Frederic Tirrell Jones, .	. Quincy.
Sept. 5,	Nellie DeLorey,* . .	Nellie Annie Robin, .	. Quincy.

PLYMOUTH COUNTY.

Date of Decree.	Original Name.	Name Decreed.	Residence.
Feb. 13,	—— Sherman,* . .	Cora May Bent, . . .	Plymouth.
27,	Rosamond Studley Pool, .	Rosamond Studley Gardner, .	Rockland.
Mar. 12,	William Doherty,* . .	William Hartin, . . .	Plympton.
12,	Joseph Greenwood,* . .	Joseph Greenwood Binney, .	Hingham.
April 9,	John Keen,* . . .	John Melvin Thorne, .	Brockton.
9,	Mary Adeline Phillips, .	Mary Adeline Filoon, .	Brockton.
23,	Leana Durfee,* . . .	Blanche Kelley, . .	Middleborough.
May 28,	Harold Williams Reed,* .	Harold Williams Soule, .	Hingham.
28,	Charles McKuin,* . .	Charles K. Hoxie, . .	Mattapoisett.
Aug. 24,	Abraham Eastwood,* .	Charles Arthur Lowe, .	Brockton.
Sept. 10,	Bertie Foutaineau,* . .	Barbara Anna Foutaineau Raymond, ...	Hanson.
10,	Lizzie C Gray, . .	Isabella Caroline Gray, .	Hingham.
Oct. 8,	Sarah Mabel Howes, .	Sarah Mabel Howard, .	Brockton.
22,	Elsie Fox,* . . .	Elsie Fox Sampson, .	Lakeville.
Nov. 26,	Henry Davenport, . .	Henry Augustus Davenport, .	Pembroke.
Dec. 10,	Celiste G. Peckham,* . .	Celiste G. Bruce, . . .	Plymouth.

* Changed by reason of adoption.

BRISTOL COUNTY.

Date of Decree.	Original Name.	Name Decreed.	Residence.
1888.			
Feb. 3,	Elsie Jones,* . . .	Idella Elsie Holmes, . .	Fall River.
17,	Agnes Delaney,* . . .	Agnes Peckham, . . .	Fall River.
Mar. 2,	Miles Kirkwood,* . . .	Lester LeForest Savery, .	Taunton.
April 6,	Lewis Alexander Borden,* .	Lewis Alexander Vincelleto,	Fall River.
May 18,	Patrick Maney,* . . .	Patrick Judd, ...	Fall River.
18,	Lottie Douglas Lawton,* .	Lottie Douglas Hutchinson, .	Fall River.
July 6,	Henry Willard,* . . .	Henry Sumner Gilson, . .	Attleborough.
Aug. 3,	Frank Wyman,* . . .	Frank Staley, ...	New Bedford.
Oct. 19,	Albert Leavitt Brown,* .	Manton Edward Chambers, .	Taunton.
Dec. 7,	Lena Norton Parlow,* .	Lena Parlow Brayton, . .	Fall River.

BARNSTABLE COUNTY.

Date of Decree.	Original Name.	Name Decreed.	Residence.
1878.			
April 16,	Willie Kelley, ...	David William Nye, . .	Sandwich.
1888.			
Jan. 10,	Sabina J. Kossman,* .	Rena Sabina Taylor, . .	Barnstable.
10,	Eunice Lind,* . . .	Maud Lillian Doane, . .	Chatham.
April 17,	Maud Estabrook,* . .	Maud Louise Taylor, . .	Yarmouth.
May 16,	Maud Wetmore,* . .	Maud Evelyn Craig, . .	Falmouth.
June 19,	Frank Clayton, . . .	Frank C. Burrows, . .	Wellfleet.
Sept. 11,	Louisa Curley,* . . .	Louisa Nickerson, . . .	Chatham.
Nov. 20,	Roy Wilworth Bassett,* .	Roy Wilworth Nickerson, .	Brewster.
20,	Ephraim Lincoln Studley,	Ephraim F. Lincoln, . .	Falmouth.

NANTUCKET COUNTY:

Date of Decree.	Original Name.	Name Decreed.	Residence.
Nov. 15,	George E. Hitt, ...	George E. Fisher, . . .	Nantucket.

SUFFOLK COUNTY.

Date of Decree.	Original Name.	Name Decreed.	Residence.
1889.			
Jan. 7,	James I. Stevens,* . .	Thomas Francis Carr, . .	Newburyport.
14,	Agnes Meay,*	Hattie Evelyn Celley, . .	Boston.
14,	Parker Horne,*	Leonidas Palmer, Jr., . .	Boston.
28,	William Haniford or Hanifen, .	William Hannaford, . .	Boston.
28,	Catherine T. Haniford or Hanifen, ...	Catherine Theresa Hannaford,	Boston.
Feb. 4,	Mabel Swansholm,* . .	Marion Mabel Emery, .	Boston.
11,	Adolphe Belot,* . . .	Edmond Amede Drefus, .	Boston.
18,	Frederick Raymond Kennedy, .	Frederick Russell Bates, .	Boston.
18,	Beulah Locke,* . . .	Beulah Locke Wood, .	Williamstown.
18,	Aloysius James Fenwick, .	Aloysius James De Silva, .	Boston.
25,	Bernadina Gamble,* . .	Mary Bernadina Donovan, .	Boston.
25,	William Lynch,* . . .	Henry Cecil Scott, . .	Boston.
Mar. 4,	William Sargent,* . . .	Charles Franklin Morse, .	Boston.
11,	Mary Mansey,* . . .	Mary Josephine Ricker, .	Boston.
11,	Romaine Nesly,* . . .	Romaine Kaulbeck, . .	Boston.
18,	Agnes Welche,* . . .	Agnes Welche Murphy, .	———.
18,	William H. Rafferty, . .	William Henry Haskell, .	Boston.
25,	Walter Smith Fox,* . .	Walter Walker Byrne, .	Boston.
25,	Willie Adams,* . . .	Clarence Dodge Brickett, .	———.
25,	Hattie I. Winslow,* . .	Jenny Louisa Parker, . .	Boston.

* Changed by reason of adoption.

SUFFOLK COUNTY — Concluded.

Date of Decree.	Original Name.	Name Decreed.	Residence.
1889.			
Mar. 25,	Margaret E. Ducott,*	Margaret May Thompson,	Boston.
25,	Louisa Caldwell,*	Margaret Bruce,	Boston.
April 8,	Margaret Agnes Lee,*	Myrtle Helen Wallace,	Boston.
8,	Luther R. Phipps,*	Charles Robert Brooks Haskell,	Boston.
8,	William Walter Boudreau,*	Charles Walter Graber,	Boston.
15,	Edward Joseph Meehan,*	Edward Oliver Oakes,	——.
15,	Mary E. Heazle,*	Almeda Lane Ripley Colby,	Boston.
15,	Alice Galeucia,*	Alice Christiansen,	Boston.
23,	Lionel Fox,*	Lionel Fox Parker,	Boston.
23,	Clarence George,	Clarence Emerson George,	Boston.
29,	—— Southwick,*	Alton Aldrich Howard,	Somerville.
May 13,	Harry J. Bumstead,*	Harry James Hollings, 2d,	Boston.
20,	Minerva E. Newton,	Minerva Evilyn Bacon,	Boston.
20,	Frank Frederick Carstens,*	Frank Frederick Ernst,	Boston.
June 3,	Kitty Jane Lane,	Katherine Jane Lane,	Boston.
3,	William B. Drake,	William B. Goodey,	Boston.
July 1,	Mary Spooner Gaut,	Mary Spooner White,	Boston.
1,	Anna Evelina Gaut,	Anna Evelina White,	Boston.
29,	Laura Morgan,*	Roberta Gertrude Campbell,	——.
29,	Annie M. McIntosh,*	Annie May Smith,	Boston.
Aug. 19,	Edgar Jones,*	Meddie Brown,	Boston.
Sept. 3,	Joseph Wesley Hawkes,	Joseph Howard,	Boston.
3,	Harriet Fidelia Archibald,*	Harriet Fidelia Brown,	Ipswich.
30,	Hiram Alson,*	Stewart Dudley,	——.
30,	Josephine Horton,*	Josephine Dudley,	——.
30,	Charles F. Clark,*	Charles F. Guptill,	Boston.
30,	Louise Radford,*	Louise Grace Emery,	Boston.
30,	May Prospect,*	Mary Elgie Amidon,	——.
30,	Miles B. Sinnott,*	Miles Sanborn Ginn,	Boston.
30,	Harry Chase,*	Harry Chase Knight,	——.
30,	James McGann,*	William J. Schaffer,	——.
30,	Mary Kelley,*	Bessie Lelia Town,	Chelsea.
30,	George Wellington,*	John Alfred Kaveney,	——.
Oct. 7,	Sarah Grace Hypson,*	Grace Upton,	Boston.
14,	John H. Cunningham,	John Henry Lial,	Boston.
21,	Charles E. Hewitt,*	Charles Ellsworth Thayer,	Boston.
Nov. 11,	Julia Myrtle Newcomb,	Myrtle Julia Newcomb,	Boston.
11,	Eva Nixon,*	Eva Bailey,	Boston.
18,	Lorenzo A. Maynard, Jr.,	Lawrens Maynard,	Boston.
25,	Florence E. Jackson,*	Florence E. Hammond,	Boston.
Dec. 2,	Peter Thomas,	Peter James Thomas,	Chelsea.
9,	Mary Williams,*	Mary Countee,	Boston.
16,	Mary Collins,*	Dorothea Mildred Jenne,	Boston.
16,	Beatrice Pearce,*	Beatrice Wright,	Somerville.
16,	Gertrude L. Comstock,*	Gertrude Lenora Hall,	——.
16,	John Angus Livingston,*	John Angus McDonald,	Boston.
23,	Theodore Harold,	Theodore Harold Clapp,	Chelsea.
23,	Mary S. R. Harold,	Mary Stewart Robinson Clapp,	Chelsea.
23,	Stewart Harold,	Stewart Harold Clapp,	Chelsea.
30,	Mae Guiditta Allen,	Mae Guiditta Daley,	Boston.

ESSEX COUNTY.

Date	Original Name.	Name Decreed.	Residence.
Jan. 7,	Andrew D. Blanchard,	Denman Blanchard,	North Andover.
7,	Mary I Brotherton,*	Mary Isabel Fountain,	Gloucester.
21,	Neda Frances,*	Ramona Frances Hadley,	Somerville
28,	Annie Cox,*	Sylvia May Putnam Hollis,	Boston.

* Changed by reason of adoption.

ESSEX COUNTY — *Concluded*.

Date of Decree.	Original Name.	Name Decreed.	Residence.
1889.			
Feb. 4,	William Burton Bamford, .	William Burton Collins, .	Newbury.
4,	Susan Bamford, . . .	Susan Collins, . .	Newbury.
18,	Lanie M. Porter,* . .	Lanie May Barker, . .	Easton.
18,	Mamie Reed,* . .	Mary Roach, . . .	Boston.
Mar. 4,	Flora G. Lewis,* .	Flora Gertrude March, .	Lynn.
4,	Harry A. Thompson,* .	Harry Augustus Townes, .	Salem.
11,	John Highland,* .	John Crawford Bunker, .	Boston.
11,	Daisy Howe, . .	Margaret Howe, . .	Danvers.
18,	Henry J. Henley,* .	Henry Jasper Harriman, .	Peabody.
April 1,	Lucy Dawson,* . .	Lucy Conners, . .	Salem.
1,	Sarah A. Foster,* .	Sarah Alice Colesworthy, .	Essex.
1,	Mattie R. Pevere,* .	Alice Madeline Small, .	Boston.
1,	Viola P. Kitson,* .	Edwina Addie Allard, .	Lawrence.
8,	Ralph C. Stockbridge,* .	Ralph Cobb Eaton, .	Haverhill.
15,	Guy E. W. Newton,* .	Guy Edgar Weston Leighton,	Montpelier, Vt.
May 6,	Charles H. Heath,* .	Philip Sidney Williams, .	Boston.
13,	Jennie M Clark,* .	Jennie May Parsons, .	Gloucester.
20,	Sarah Anderson,* .	Ethel Crawford Fiske, .	Boston.
27,	James M. Smith, .	James Wheatland Smith, .	Salem.
June 3,	Joseph Greenberg, .	Joseph Green, . .	Lawrence.
3,	Ralph C. Stewart,* .	Ralph Cyr Heath, .	Lynn.
3,	Augustine Brisbois St. Pierre,* .	Augustine Brisbois, .	Salem.
10,	Ruth Crowell,* . .	Blanche Bell Purbeck, .	Boston.
17,	Ella Agnes Casey,* .	Ella Dixon, . .	Lawrence.
17,	Gilbert Foster,* . .	Gilbert Foster Fogg, .	Salem.
17,	Florence M Carter,* . .	Florence Miner Swain, .	Laconia, N. H.
July 1,	William Bailey Miller,* .	William Miller Hilliard, .	Lawrence.
Aug. 5,	Emma E. N. Coomes,* .	Emma Elizabeth Nason, .	Gloucester.
5,	Francis D. Foster,* .	Frank Dudley Foster, .	North Andover.
Sept. 9,	Grace B. Cunningham,* .	Grace Blanche Ordway, .	Boston.
Oct. 7,	Teresa Crimmings,* .	Teresa Rau, . .	Lawrence.
7,	Eliza Larvery,* .	Eliza Martineau, .	Lawrence.
7,	William W. Leary,* .	Willis Howes Allen, .	———.
7,	Charles A. Martin,* .	Charles Albert Russell, .	Gloucester.
7,	Sarah Ryan,* .	Sarah May Gillis, .	———.
7,	Emily B. Jackson, .	Emily B. Goodwin, .	Salem.
21,	Mette Johnson,* . .	Mette Christina Nelson, .	Newburyport.
Nov. 4,	Maggie M. Flaherty,* .	Helen Josephine Blood, .	Boston.
18,	Maud L. Swett,* .	Lillian Cassidy, .	Stoneham.
Dec. 2,	Ina Ray Hall,* . .	Ina Ray Taylor, .	Lynn.
2,	Joseph Lawrence,* .	Joseph Lawrence Clifford, .	Boston.

MIDDLESEX COUNTY.

Jan. 1,	Edith Maud Dammery,* .	Edith Maud Newcomb, .	Cambridge.
8,	Laura Noble,* .	Laura Alton Howe, .	Marlborough.
8,	Arthur Grover,* . .	Arthur Jenkins Upham, .	Melrose.
15,	Ada Hawksley,* .	Ada Amelia Hodgson, .	Lowell.
22,	Lottie Alberta Trecartin,* .	Lottie Louisa Doyle, .	Marlborough.
Feb. 5,	Lulu Marion Whitney,* .	Lulu Marion Dix, .	Boston.
5,	Chester Arthur Geldert,* .	Chester Arthur Penney, .	Cambridge.
5,	Thomas William Adams, .	Charles Thomas Reagh, .	Melrose.
12,	Charles Herbert Milligan,*	Charles Herbert Webster, .	Cambridge.
26,	Martha Dailey,* .	Annie Murdock Heuston, .	Cambridge.
26,	Joseph Roza,* . .	Joseph Silva, .	Cambridge.
26,	Walter Mahan,* .	Walter Hermann, .	Cambridge.
Mar. 5,	Abbie Louisa Wheeler, .	Abbie Louisa Walker, .	Marlborough.

* Changed by reason of adoption.

MIDDLESEX COUNTY — *Concluded.*

Date of Decree.	Original Name.	Name Decreed.	Residence.
1889.			
April 2,	Edna Marguerite Robinson,*	Edna Marguerite Mackinnon,	Boston.
9,	Estella Cressey,*	Estella Cressey Gragg.	Cumberland, Me.
May 7,	William Frederic Hurd, Jr.,	Frederic William Hurd,	Concord.
7,	Moses Hoyt Sargent Morss,	Sargent Morss,	Somerville.
7,	Mary Williams,*	Mertie Belle Etter,	Hopkinton.
14,	Leroy Taylor Prosser,*	Charles Anthony Hillers,	Malden.
14,	Patrick Lynch,*	James Atwood McVane,	Cambridge.
14,	James Conley Burke,*	Edward Andrew Marshall,	Newton.
14,	Arthur Herman,*	Arthur Percy Lawrence,	Ashby.
28,	George E. Waterhouse,	George Edwin Marsh,	Somerville.
28,	Anna S. Waterhouse,	Anna Stella Marsh,	Somerville.
June 11,	Mary E. Sullivan,*	Dulah Catherine Miller,	Townsend.
11,	John Francis Burns,*	John Francis Kirley,	Cambridge.
25,	Mary Holman Allen,	Mary Holman Avery,	Somerville.
25,	Lizzie M. Buzzell,*	Elizabeth Mary Buzelle,	Holliston.
25,	William Bradford Buzzell,	William Bradford Buzelle,	Holliston.
25,	Fannie Belle Buzzell,	Frances Mary Buzelle,	Holliston.
July 2,	Helen May Lawrence,*	Rebecca Jordan Chany,	Belmont.
9,	Richard Burke,*	Richard Irving Maynard,	Hudson.
9,	Emma Louisa Warren,*	Emma Louisa Ireland,	Somerville.
23,	Ethel G. Blaisdell,*	Ethel Monroe.	Carlisle.
23,	Ada Louise Parker,*	Ada Louise Mathason,	Lowell.
Sept. 3,	Ralph Winfield Garland,*	Ralph Garland Starbird,	Boston.
3,	Sarah Ann Nutting,*	Sarah Ann Morrison,	Lowell.
3,	Harriet Elizabeth Clark,	Katherine Hall Clark,	Reading.
10,	Carrie Black,*	Carrie Elizabeth Frost,	Ware, N. H.
10,	Bertha Bennett,*	Bertha Bennett Bacon,	Boston.
10,	Dora Archibald,*	Dora Isabel Marston,	Ipswich.
24,	Maud Sinclair,*	Maud Sinclair Tower,	Boston.
24,	Julia West,*	Julia West Hurley,	Malden.
Oct. 1,	Waldo Harper,*	Fred Waldo Wheaton,	Waltham.
8,	Mary R. Stewart,*	Mary Agnes Mahoney,	Cambridge.
8,	Arthur Brown,*	Arthur Sanborn Collieson,	Somerville.
8,	Edith Morton,*	Edith Ellen Denno,	Cambridge.
8,	Martha Thompson Adams,*	Martha Mead,	Manchester, N. H.
22,	Martha L. Demeritt,*	Helen Edgecomb Abbott,	Conway, N. H.
22,	Albert Joseph Donnelle,	Albert Joseph Kingsbury,	Lowell.
22,	Katie Belle Donnelle,	Katie Belle Kingsbury,	Lowell.
22,	Willoughby Kingsbury Donnelie,	Willoughby Joseph Kingsbury,	Lowell.
22,	Margaret Jane Donovan,*	Jessie Margaret Jones,	Cambridge.
Nov. 6,	Maud Bannister,*	Lila Maud True,	Woburn.
12,	Thomas Edward James,*	Thomas Edward Bywater,	Groton.
26,	Jesse Fisher Mattetall,*	Jessie Mattetall Stevens,	Malden.
26,	Willie Wilmot alias Willie Hanlon,*	William Cameron,	Dracut.
Dec. 3,	Hattie Harris,*	Hattie Wilson,	Chelmsford.
17,	Mary Ellen Whitford,*	Ellen Dillon,	Wakefield.

WORCESTER COUNTY.

Jan. 1,	Nellie Whitman Curtis,	Elnora Whitman Curtis,	Worcester.
1,	Rebecca Leavins Rogers,	Rebecca Leavins Field,	Worcester.
18,	Minnie Nourse,*	Florence May McDonald,	Athol.
22,	Sarah Harriet Joddrell,*	Sarah Harriet Bardsley,	Fitchburg.
Feb. 19,	Camilla Louise Brewer,	Camilla Louise Whitney,	Worcester.
26,	Ettie Lees Dole,	Dorothy Lees Dole,	Winchendon.
26,	Eben Pierce,	Eben F. Pierce,	Leominster.
Mar. 15,	Nellie Gannon,*	Nellie Hannigan,	Milford.

* Changed by reason of adoption.

WORCESTER COUNTY — *Concluded.*

Date of Decree.	Original Name.	Name Decreed.	Residence.
1889.			
April 2,	Joseph King,*	George Thomas,	Uxbridge.
5,	Grace C. Lynch,*	Grace Helen Angier,	Southborough.
May 14,	Gabriel Jacobs,*	Ralph Bertrand Kendall,	Winchendon.
21,	Clinton Davis,	George Clinton Davis,	Worcester.
21,	Ella L. Carter,	Ella L. Richardson,	Dana.
28,	Jennie Irene Moore,*	Jennie Lewella Young,	Worcester.
28,	Sarah C Babbitt,*	Sadie Estelle Tenney,	Gardner.
June 18,	Mamie Finn,*	Gracie A. Fairbanks,	Milford.
18,	Jennie Alice Sage,*	Genevieve Alice Reynolds,	Southbridge.
July 5,	May Jordan,*	Jessie May Brodgen,	Leominster.
Aug. 13,	Louis Hebert,*	Napoleon Louis Morin,	Worcester.
20,	Gertrude Adeline Barrows,*	Gertrude Adeline Shaw,	Athol.
Sept. 3,	Arthur Nye McClintock,*.	John Edwin Barlow,	Hardwick.
3,	Essie M. Decker,*	Essie May Thurber,	Worcester.
3,	Grace Isabelle Cooper,*	Grace Isabelle Harris,	Worcester.
10,	Harriet Louise Landers Jefferds,	Minnie Harriette Jefferds,	Milford.
17,	Jennie Perham,*	Jennie Alice Howard,	Milford.
17,	Thomas Edward Coley,*	Thomas Edward Jenkins,	Worcester.
Oct. 15,	Eliza Aleda Richards,*	Ruth Estelle Washburn,	Winchendon.
15,	William Augustus Russell Pearson,	William Augustus Russell,	Worcester.
18,	William Edward Ellingham,*	Robert Wallace Scott,	Worcester.
22,	Ethel Venova Gates,*	Ethel Venova McMullen,	Fitchburg.
Nov. 6,	Fanny Elizabeth Johnson,*	Edna Colleen Oliver,	Athol
19,	Alice Paine,*	Nina Gertrude Putney,	Worcester.
19,	Cora Adella Davis,	Hattie May Waterman,	Athol.
26,	Walter E. Avery,	Walter E. Green,	Leominster.

HAMPSHIRE COUNTY.

Jan. 1,	George Andrew Clink,*	George Andrew King,	Easthampton.
Feb. 5,	Clifford McManus,*	William Robinson Pillsbury,	Northampton.
12,	Lora Ellery,*	Lilly Paternande,	Ware.
Mar. 5,	Lillie L. Riley,*	Lillie L. Adams,	South Hadley.
April 2,	Valma Louise Roberts,*	Lizzie Louise Pynchon,	South Hadley.
June 4,	Frances Clementina Nahmer,	Clementina Dawes Nahmer,	Cummington.
Aug. 6,	—— Fox,*	Lincoln Allen Stewart,	Worthington.
Nov. 6,	William Henry Baker,*	William Henry Hamilton,	South Hadley.

HAMPDEN COUNTY.

Feb. 25,	Philip Newton,*	Chas. Stafford Myron Blake,	Westfield.
April 3,	Bessie Maud,*	Bessie Maud Fuller,	Ludlow.
3,	Minnie Sherman,*	Minnie May Butler,	Springfield.
May 9,	Frieda Clara Hetwig Baerneck,*	Winnifred Elizabeth Poskey,	Springfield.
June 29,	Edna Price,*	Edna Nellie Drown,	Springfield.
July 3,	Annie Rickey,*	Annie O'Callahan,	Chicopee.
Sept. 4,	Albert Arthur Crocker,*	Albert Arthur Green,	Springfield.
Oct. 2,	Frederick Miller,*	Frederick Miller Simons,	Wilbraham.
16,	Marion Belle Parks,*	Marion Belle Bray,	Springfield.
Nov. 2,	Edith Olive Morgan.*	Edith Olive Rising,	Springfield.
2,	Richard Beach Morgan,*	Richard Beach Rising,	Springfield.
2,	Alice Louisa Arms,*	Alice Louisa Tice,	Holyoke.
27,	Laura E. Miller,*	Grace Elizabeth Bullard,	Springfield.
27,	Marianne Althea Hawes,*	Eldora Annie Winter,	Springfield.
Dec. 4,	Clara Elizabeth Wheeler,*	Clara Elizabeth Doherty,	Monson.
4,	Florence Belle Wheeler,*	Florence Belle Remington,	Palmer.
7,	Clara Bristol,*	Mildred Estelle Jencks,	West Springfield.

* Changed by reason of adoption.

FRANKLIN COUNTY.

Date of Decree.	Original Name.	Name Decreed.	Residence.
1889.			
Jan. 1,	Mary E. O'Brien,* . . .	Mary E. Keyes, . . .	Springfield.
May 7,	Walter H. Woods,* . . .	Walter W. Beaman, . .	Leverett.

BERKSHIRE COUNTY.

Jan. 1,	Margaret Recor,* . . .	Margaret Lynch, . . .	Pittsfield.
1,	Joseph Recor,*	Joseph Lynch, . . .	Pittsfield.
1,	Hilie May Miller Carter, .	Frances Mary Carter, . .	Otis.
Mar. 5,	Katherine B. Davids,* .	Katherine Burr Burlingame, .	Adams.
5,	Anna Hester,*	Anna Shepard, . . .	Sandisfield.
5,	Eva La Rue,*	Eva Gaudette, . . .	North Adams.
6,	Frank Joel Jones,* . .	Frank John Lowman, . .	North Adams.
May 7,	Edmund Williams,* . .	Joseph Eben Cox, . .	North Adams.
7,	Millie Aline Crandell,* .	Aline Millie Howes, . .	North Adams.
7,	Stella May Kent,* . .	Stella May Walker, . .	North Adams.
June 4,	Mary Ludwig,*	Mary Wehner, . . .	Adams.
19,	Hattie L. Strang, . .	Hattie L. Langdon, . .	Great Barrington.
July 16,	Walter E. Duxbury,* . .	Walter Everett Scott, . .	Williamstown.
16,	Gertrude M. Pratt,* . .	Parmelia DeMary, . .	Pittsfield.
16,	Frank L. Pratt,* . . .	Charles DeMary, . .	Pittsfield.
Oct. 3,	Lillie May Hurd,* . .	Lillian May Jewett, . .	North Adams.
3,	Nellie Collins,*	Mary Maud Griffin, . .	North Adams.
Dec. 3,	William Frederic Rackemann, .	Wilfred Rackemann, . .	Lenox.
3,	Mary Prairie,* . . .	Mary Yarter, . . .	North Adams.

NORFOLK COUNTY.

1888.			
Mar. 21,	Charles Frederic Jenks, .	Charles Fitch Jenks, . .	Canton.
1889.			
Jan. 2,	Everett Carson,* . . .	Everett Frederick Reynolds, .	Boston.
6,	Bella Weld,* . . .	Bella Celia Porter, . .	Stoughton.
Mar. 6,	Austin St. Clair Matthews,*	Lawrence Earle Braddon, .	Hyde Park.
13,	Georgiana Perry,* . . .	Gertrude Georgianna Drake, .	Stoughton.
20,	Nellie Elizabeth McCarty,*	Nellie Elizabeth Murphy, .	Cambridge.
20,	Lillian May Day,* . .	Lillian May Daniells, . .	Dedham.
May 8,	Frederick Augustus Ely, .	Frederick David Ely, . .	Dedham.
15,	Helen Holmes,* . . .	Marjory Matthewson, . .	Wrentham.
15,	Charles McNeil,* . .	Charles Thomas Porter, .	Quincy.
June 5,	Abbie Theodate Raymond, .	Abbie Theodate Fuller, .	Quincy.
5,	Josephene Hunter,* . .	Josephene Haffermill, .	Norwood.
12,	Ann Griffiths,* . . .	Ann Griffiths Williams, .	Quincy.
19,	Joseph Wallace,* . .	Joseph Ambrose Maginnis, .	Medway.
Sept. 4,	Raymond Webster Guild,*	Raymond Webster Proctor, .	Franklin.
Oct. 16,	Mary Conway,* . . .	Marion Estelle Churchill, .	Stoughton.
16,	Anita Warren,*	Gladys Atwood Drake, .	Stoughton.
23,	George Alton Besse,* .	Alton George Michaels, .	Milton.
Nov. 20,	Frank Seaver Kelton, .	Frank Seaver Harding, .	Millis.
27,	Jennie Higgins,* . .	Jennie Catherine Walters, .	Quincy.

PLYMOUTH COUNTY.

Jan. 14,	Bertha Florence King Atwood, .	Bertha Atwood Wells, . .	Plymouth.
April 8,	Roderick Hall, ...	Roderick Douglass Hall, .	Bridgewater.
May 13,	Mary Graham, ...	Mabel Frances Ewell, . .	Marshfield.
27,	Frank Weatherhead, . .	Myron Henry Penniman, .	Middleborough.

* Changed by reason of adoption.

PLYMOUTH COUNTY — *Concluded.*

Date of Decree.	Original Name.	Name Decreed.	Residence.
1889.			
July 8,	Henry Herbert Gonsalus, . . .	Henry Herbert Vaughan, .	Carver.
Sept. 9,	(No name given), . . .	Florence Maude Marble, .	Brockton.
23,	Edward B. McInness, . .	Sylvanus E. Ross, . . .	Rochester.
Nov. 11,	(No name given), . . .	Mary Annie Magoun, . .	Marshfield.
Dec. 23,	Clarissa Arnold, . . .	Alice Mildred Fuller, . .	Brockton.

BRISTOL COUNTY.

Jan. 4,	Etta May Parlow,* . . .	Etta May Braley, . . .	Taunton.
Feb. 1,	Norbert Vincent,* . . .	Norbert Robillard, . .	Fall River.
1,	Samuel Koneche, . .	Samuel Koneche Grover, .	North Attleboro'.
April 5,	Marie D. Gannon,* . .	Marie D. Payson, . .	Norton.
May 3,	Grace Evelyn Perry,* . .	Grace Evelyn Weiman, . .	North Attleboro'.
3,	Emma Littlefield,* . .	Lucy Emma Williams, .	Taunton.
3,	John Craig,*	John Craig Gardner, .	Swansea.
3,	Henry Augustus Chute.* .	Henry Augustus Taber, .	North Attleboro'.
3,	William Henry McCormack,* .	John William Brown, .	Fall River.
3,	Mary Jenette Folger,* .	Mary Jenette Rogers, .	Taunton.
17,	Henry Marklevitch, . .	Henry Leavitt, . .	Fall River.
July 5,	Mary Hogan, . . .	Mary Sutcliffe, . .	Fall River.
Oct. 4,	Emma Pollard,* . .	Gertrude May Royal, .	Fall River.
Nov. 1,	Annie J. Sullivan,* . .	Marie Annette Parsons, .	New Bedford.
1,	Elsie Gertrude Dahl,* .	Elsie Gertrude Whitworth, .	New Bedford.
15,	Lillie Edith Astle,* . .	Edith Orton, . . .	Fall River.

BARNSTABLE COUNTY.

June 18,	Ethel May Pierce, . . .	Ethel May Baker, . . .	Yarmouth.

NANTUCKET COUNTY.

April 11,	Harrison Gardner, . . .	Harrison G. Gardner, . .	Nantucket.

SUFFOLK COUNTY.

1890.			
Jan. 13,	William DeWitt,* . . .	William Kittridge, . . .	———.
13,	——— Dillon,* . . .	Nellie Luna Sargent, . .	Boston.
13,	Emma J. Mitchell,* . .	Emma J. Cleaveland, .	Boston.
20,	Isaac Stiefel, . . .	Isaac Henry Caliga, .	Boston.
27,	Lizzie M. Bailey,* . .	Musetta Chin, . . .	Ashby.
Feb. 3,	Florence Gould,* . .	Rita Jones, ...	Boston.
3,	Gertrude Emerson,* . .	Mabel Estella Sargent, .	Boston.
10,	Mary Costello,* . . .	Mary Costello Wolcott, .	Boston.
17,	Crelia Iannuzzi,* . .	Angiolina Rosa DeFillippo, .	Boston.
17,	Mary Frances O'Connor,* .	Minnie Frances Joyce, .	Boston.
Mar. 3,	William Daniels Welch, .	William Welch Davis, .	Boston.
3,	Robert Richardson Everett,	Robert Maxwell Everett, .	Boston.

* Changed by reason of adoption.

SUFFOLK COUNTY — *Concluded.*

Date of Decree.	Original Name.	Name Decreed.	Residence.
1890.			
Mar. 10,	Sarah Edwards Sell,*	Sarah Edwards Porter,	Boston.
10,	Elizabeth Palmer,*	Elizabeth Kane,	Boston.
10,	Carl Alfred Carlson,*	Axel Albert Lindquist,	Worcester.
17,	Amy Hannan,*	Amy Harrison Wood,	Boston.
17,	Agnes Orenberg,*	Mary Alice McCall,	———.
April 7,	Leander Joseph Bellefleur,	Joseph Leander Belfler,	Boston.
7,	Harrie Cushing Hill,	Cushing Hill,	Boston.
7,	Hattie Melissa Merrifield,*	Hattie Melissa Roberts,	Conway, N. H.
7,	Arthur Leslie Barnes,*	Leslie Arnold,	Revere.
14,	Cecelia Leroy,*	Ellen Quinn,	Boston.
28,	Walter Vincent McCarthy,*	Walter Vincent Barry,	Boston.
May 5,	Minnie A. Osborn,*	Minnie Alice Pratt,	Chelsea.
12,	Charles Lees,*	John Bowers,	Boston.
19,	Besse Lyon,*	Besse Lyon Sinnett,	Chelsea.
19,	John Joseph Sweeney,*	Archer Irving Gilpatrick,	Boston.
19,	Eleanor Curtis,*	Eleanor Holt,	———.
26,	Minnie F. Rapson,*	Minnie F. Titus,	Boston.
June 9,	Mary Frances Hamilton,	Mary Frances Adams,	Boston.
9,	Frankie Brosnan,*	Abram Nussbaum,	Boston.
July 7,	Mona Patterson,*	Mona Hill McGregory,	Revere.
21,	Carrie B. Smith,	Carrie B: Nelson,	Boston.
28,	John F. Carroll,*	Francis Drips Bower,	New York City.
Aug. 18,	Walter Allen,	Walter Allen Walker,	Boston.
18,	Edith Agnes Pembroke,*	Edith Agnes Benton,	Malden.
18,	Frank Coulter,*	Frank Adams,	Boston.
Sept. 8,	May Lizzie Clayton,*	May Elizabeth Marshall,	Boston.
22,	Mary Cavanagh,*	Mary Richards,	Boston.
22,	Joseph Tansy,*	William Daly,	Revere.
29,	William Bell,*	Jesse William Harvey,	Boston.
29,	Maud McCaskell,*	Lucy Robbins Parker,	Boston.
Oct. 6,	Joseph W. Teufel,*	Joseph W. Dizel,	Boston.
6,	Margaret Alice Kelley,	Margaret Alice Cummings,	Boston.
6,	Mattie Bowe,*	Frances Helena Weston,	Boston.
6,	Lizzie Williams,*	Elizabeth W. Corley,	Boston.
6,	James S. Doody,*	Walter Lewis Juckett,	Boston.
6,	Mary Ethel Hogan,*	Margaret E. Waterhouse,	Boston.
6,	Agnes Kirns,*	Mary Ethel Saunders,	Boston.
13,	Edward Smith,*	Charles Adna Ross,	Boston.
13,	Frank A. Armstrong,*	Frank Armstrong Harriman,	England.
13,	Patrick L. Dolan,*	Lawrence McGovern,	Boston.
13,	Lillias Walker,*	Lillias Gibson,	Boston.
13,	Nellie Gurney,*	Nellie Gurney McLachlan,	Chelsea.
27,	Eddie West,*	Edward Tucker,	Boston.
Nov. 3,	Eleanor Frances Black,*	Eleanor Frances Carter,	Boston.
3,	Olive Johnson,*	Olive Versailles,	Boston.
3,	Clarence Dodge Brickett,*	Clarence Allison Thayer,	East Saugus.
10,	Charlotte May Powers,*	Charlotte May Johnson,	Boston.
10,	Ferdinand J. Pinsonneault,	Ferdinand J. Parsons,	Boston.
17,	Joseph Lewis Pomeroy,	Joseph Lewis,	Boston.
17,	George Clinton Ducott,*	George Clinton Rice,	Boston.
17,	Alice Adaleve Heazle,*	Alice Louise Colby,	Boston.
24,	Margaret Donovan,*	Margaret Fleming,	Boston.
Dec. 1,	Mary Frances Raymond,*	Mary Florence Frost,	Boston.
8,	Anna Doughty,*	Anna Sutton,	Lynn.
8,	Lucy Ann Smith,*	Gladys Julia Rogers,	Maynard.
15,	Mary Fox,*	Mary Elizabeth Joyce,	Boston.
15,	Mary E. Carline,*	Marie Lavinia Frances Ward,	Boston.
15,	William Charles Krauss,*	William Charles Stegmaier,	Boston.
22,	Fannie May Merrill,*	Fannie May Young,	Boston.
22,	Alice Carrigan,*	Alice McBarron,	Boston.

* Changed by reason of adoption.

ESSEX COUNTY.

Date of Decree.	Original Name.	Name Decreed.	Residence.
1890.			
Jan. 6,	Eugene Dunn,*	Eugene Augustus Howard, .	———.
6,	Mamie Loach,*	Pearl Howard Tucker, . .	Gloucester.
20,	Cora A. Boyden,* . .	Cora Boyden Thompson, .	Lynn.
20,	Herbert W. Jones,* . . .	Herbert Warren Tarbox, .	Lynn.
20,	Albert N. Jones,* . . .	Albert Nelson Tarbox, . .	Lynn.
Feb. 3,	Augusta Merchant,* . .	Louisa Marshall Towne, .	Gloucester.
3,	Samuel R. Furbush,* . .	Arthur Russell Furbush, .	Lynn.
17,	Florence A. Lynch, . .	Florence Amanda York, .	Lynn.
17,	David S. Streamberg, . .	John Fremont Streamberg, .	Beverly.
17,	Edith W. Mayberry, . .	Edith Warren Pierce, . .	Lynn.
17,	Edwin Leeds,* . . .	Harold Edwin True, . .	———.
17,	Elsie F. Turney,* . . .	Elsie Frances Ford, . .	Falmouth.
17,	Ida M. Duffy,*	Ida May Nickerson, . .	Lynn.
Mar. 3,	Helen D. Place,* . .	Helen Danforth Haskell, .	Essex.
3,	Ethel Corneille,* . . .	Ethel Corneille Burrill, . .	Boston.
April 14,	Benjamin O. Hatch,*. . .	Benjamin Osgood Congdon, .	Amesbury.
21,	Nora S. Strout,*. . .	Nora Susie Page, . . .	Haverhill.
May 5,	Lewis L. Sullivan,* . .	Lewis LeRoy Lumber Bell, .	Amesbury.
19,	Elizabeth M. Clifford,* .	Elizabeth Mary Flynn, . .	Lawrence.
June 23,	Frederick S. Frye, . .	Frederick Sheridan Morse, .	Haverhill.
July 7,	Effie Dodge,*	Effie Dodge Chase, . .	Beverly.
7,	Joseph R. Harris alias Joseph R. Lemay,* . . .	Joseph Richard Lambert, .	Methuen.
21,	Maria Barden,* . . .	Helen Gertrude Leavitt, . .	———.
Aug. 4,	Nora Clifford,*	Margery Marietta Lamprey, .	———.
Sept. 8,	Mary A. Day,*	Mary Stone, ...	Boston.
15,	Sarah E. McLellan,* . .	Grace Hammond Tobey, .	Boston.
15,	Thomas E. Faulkner,* . .	Thomas Ebenezer Berry, .	Danvers.
15,	Ora Belle Faulkner,* . .	Ora Belle Berry, . .	Danvers.
Oct. 6,	Bernard Burns,* . .	Bernard Steele, . .	Pawtucket, R. I.
6,	Mary McLeod,* . . .	Addie May Gilman, . .	Boston.
20,	Emma S. Blaisdell,* . .	Emma Sumner Brown, .	Newburyport.
20,	Frank L. Taylor,* . . .	Frank Leslie Potts, . .	Newcastle, Me.
Dec. 15,	Mary Moorehouse,* . .	Mary Moore Smith, . .	Boston.
15,	Marion Morgan,* . . .	Marion Morgan Ross, . .	Boston.

MIDDLESEX COUNTY.

Jan. 7,	Lillie Estelle Watherston,* .	Bertha Louise Needham, .	Newton.
7,	William Dennis,* . . .	William Mahoney, . .	Malden.
7,	Arthur Gustavus Thomas,* .	Arthur Gustavus Bolam, .	Stow.
14,	Edith May Holland,* . .	Edith May Goodell, . .	Somerville.
14,	Amy L. Mann,*. . . .	Amy Loella Peckens, . .	Westford.
14,	Agatha Prince,* . . .	Alice Briggs, ...	Malden.
21,	Hugo Thornton Parsons,* .	Hugo Thornton Paige, . .	Lowell.
28,	Patrick Joseph Sheehan,* .	Joseph Morris, . . .	Lowell.
28,	Josephine S. Coolidge,* .	Josephine Sophia Temple, .	Framingham.
Feb. 4,	Ella Willard Brooks,* . .	Bessie Harvey Mitchell, .	Northampton.
4,	Thomas Stonewall Jackson,* .	Frank Harmon Lee, . .	Concord.
4,	Harriet Ann Brown,* . .	Harriet Angelia Morey, .	No. Stoughton, Ct.
4,	Josephine Elizabeth Clemons,*.	Josephine Irene Walker, .	Boston.
11,	Letitia Foster,*	Katherine Harrington, .	Boston.
25,	Genevieve L. Leland,* . .	Grace Louise Trow, .	Brooklyn, N. Y.
25,	Charles Rogers,* . . .	Charles Joseph Reed, .	Boston.
Mar. 18,	Sarah Ann Morrison,* . .	Sarah Ann Curtis, . .	Lowell.
18,	Mary Eva Gourley,*. . .	Mary Eva Gourley Roe, .	Cambridge.
25,	Sadie May,*	Sadie May Gale, . .	Waltham.

* Changed by reason of adoption.

MIDDLESEX COUNTY — *Concluded.*

Date of Decree.	Original Name.	Name Decreed.	Residence.
1890.			
April 8,	Nellie Johnson,*	Nellie Jeannetta Jones,	Cambridge.
15,	Irene C. Nason,*	Irene Clifton White,	Lowell.
15,	Irene Emerson,*	Irene Young,	Cambridge.
15,	Roland Emerson,*	Roland Young,	Cambridge.
15,	Nellie Glendora Pinkham,	Nellie Glendora Laughton,	Lowell.
22,	Lillie Agnes Wilcox,	Lillian Agnes Wilcox,	Medford.
22,	Robert Palmer,*	Robert Merton Ellis,	Medford.
22,	Katie Lawrence,*	Katie Alghieri,	Cambridge.
May 6,	William Martin Bulfinch,*	William Martin Johnson,	Everett.
6,	John Otis Duigwell,*.	William Otis Barker,	Lowell.
13,	Leopold Early,*.	Joseph Leopold Smith,	Cambridge.
13,	Henry Edwards,*	Harry Gorham Spaulding,	Dunstable.
13,	Mary Ann Egan,	Mary Ann Morse,	Malden.
13,	James Martin Standish,	James Myles Standish,	Newton.
20,	Jessie Redding,*	Jessie Redding Walker,	Lowell.
27,	William Fallon,*	William Arthur Hamlin,	Melrose.
June 10,	Odessa Marietta Cummings,*	Odessa Marietta Hendrick,	Stoneham.
24,	Mary Ellen Atkins,*.	Mary Ellen O'Brien,	Cambridge.
July 1,	Robert Bacon.*	Robert Lee Spredby,	Bedford.
1,	William Driscoll,*	William Emery,	Somerville.
8,	Alice Stone,*	Alice Stone Barton,	Waltham.
15,	Mary Dugen,*	Mary Ouillette,	Lowell.
15,	Lorana S. Angier,	Lorana S Potter,	Melrose.
22,	Francois Favreau,*	Francois Leblanc,	Lowell.
Sept. 2,	Ella May Willey,*	Ella May Parker,	Waltham.
2,	Dexter Pratt Guilford,*	Dexter Guilford Pratt,	Medford.
2,	Lawrence Welch,*	Percy Lawrence French,	Malden.
2,	Ella Meader Starbuck,*	Ella Starbuck Rogers,	Newton.
9,	Curtis McQuillan,*	Curtis Vernon Ordway,	Cambridge.
Oct. 7,	William Edmund Mills,*	William Edmund Brown,	Lowell.
14,	Marion Woodward,*	Gertrude Marion Jones,	Waltham.
14,	Annie Patterson,*	Annie Elizabeth Groves,	Newton.
14,	Eva Mander,*	Ethel Crowell Dowse,	Andover.
28,	Mabel Ann Taylor,*	Mabel Ann Brusch,	Cambridge.
28,	Charles Murphy,	Charles Murphy Viles,	Cambridge.
Nov. 5,	Lena Emily Mentor,*	Mary Edna Carleton,	Melrose.
11,	Mildred Perry,*.	Mildred Burdett,	Hudson.
11,	Lolo Ruth Crawford,*	Jean Mayland Hill,	Medford.
18,	Harold Dean Blaikie,*	Rufus Stickney Scripture,	Somerville.
25,	Frank Peter McGuire,	Frank Arthur Green,	Hudson.
Dec. 2,	Ichabod Pierce Warren,	Percy Warren,	Weston.
9,	Mabel Florence Harlow,*	Mabel Florence Geisendorff,	Newton.
23,	Martha Tufts,*.	Lillian Elinor Sturtevant,	Somerville.
23,	John W. Haney,*	Wilbur Harold Moody,	Tewksbury.
23,	Alice May Hunter,*	Alice Edwina Robinson,	Lowell.
23,	Lizzie Fletcher,*	Lizzie Gertrude Nelson,	Somerville.
23,	Emma Louise Weber,*	Louise Weber Haskins,	Somerville.
23,	Silas Card,*	William Card Brock,	Cambridge.

WORCESTER COUNTY.

Jan. 14,	Edith May Furrow,*.	Edith May McKinstry,	Brookfield.
21,	—— Fosdake,*	Charles Ernest Rollig,	Worcester.
31,	Lena Chesterfield,*	Maude Chesterfield Crowell,	Worcester.
Feb. 4,	Arthur Clifford,*	Clifton Lincoln Batcheller,	Millbury.
21,	Walter Allen,*	Walter Allen Peabody,	Worcester.
21,	Gertrude Marion Blanchard,*	Mary Harwood,	Warren.

* Changed by reason of adoption.

WORCESTER COUNTY — *Concluded.*

Date of Decree.	Original Name.	Name Decreed.	Residence.
1890.			
Mar. 4,	Joseph Neylon,*	George Guyor,	Worcester.
4,	Paul Valentine Brown,*	Frederick Hoffman,	Dudley.
28,	Charles B. Swinerton,*	Charles B. Desmerais,	Millbury.
28,	Jacob Swinerton,*	Adelard Stradford.	Millbury.
May 14,	Martha C. Burbank,*	Martha Christine Wheeler,	Worcester.
16,	Mabel A. Clark,*	Mabel A. Beers,	Worcester
23,	Letitia Fay,*	Nellie Stuart Fay,	Westborough.
23,	George W. Evans,*	George Evans Robinson,	Webster.
23,	Mary Emma Gobeille,*	Mary Emma Casavant,	Webster.
27,	Carl Carlton Todd,*	Carl Carlton Chipman,	Fitchburg.
27,	Gertrude M. Parker,*	Gertrude Maria Parker Currier,	Fitchburg
June 3,	Ida J. Willis,*	Nina Belle Rice,	Leominster.
3,	John Lawrence Clark,	John Calvin Lawrence Clark,	Lancaster.
6,	Mary Henward,*	Mary Ellen Broughton,	Sturbridge.
July 1,	Nellie Bates,*	Bernice Barton,	Worcester.
1,	Harry A. Hamilton,*	Harry Crawford,	Clinton.
1,	Albina C. Chapman,	Albina C. Jacobs,	Westborough.
11,	Alma Augusta Jackson,*	Alma Harris Colley,	Worcester.
15,	William Dyer Sullivan,	William J. Dyer,	Leominster.
Aug. 12,	Eva Louisa Bowker,*	Eva Louisa Upham,	Barre.
12,	Everett Alroy Harrington,*	Everett Alfred Estes,	Westborough.
12,	Frances Grishey,*	Frances Sharkey,	Westborough.
22,	Mabel Charlotte Gay,*	Marie Mabel Moreau,	Gardner.
22,	Mary Sayre Cook,*	Mary Cook Kendall,	Worcester.
29,	Carrie Louise Weeks,*	Lillian Gertrude Carpenter,	Worcester.
Sept. 2,	Nellie R. Shaw,*	Nellie R. Wright.	Leominster.
9,	Alvan James Moody,*	Alvan James Winter,	Millbury.
16,	Elizabeth Keary,*	Corine Wedge,	Spencer.
19,	Annie L. Williams,*	Grace Tiffany,	Auburn.
Oct. 7,	Ruth Garland Perkins,*	Ruth Garland Seagrave,	Northbridge.
7,	James Russell Lowell Burnett,	James Burnett Lowell,	Southborough.
21,	Mattie L. McCrillis,	Mattie L. DeMerritt,	Worcester.
21,	Mary Suzetta Holt,	Mary Abbott Holt,	Worcester.
31,	Eileen A'Comt Annette Heazle,*	Caroline Eileen Strong,	Fitchburg.
Nov. 7,	Rosa Bell Lewis,*	Rosa Belle Jacques,	Athol.
7,	Hattie I. Parry,*	Helen Holden Craft,	Worcester.
7,	Louisa Ann Dietz,*	Louisa Ann Buttrick,	Worcester.
18,	Maud L. Norton,*	Florence Maud Chase,	Worcester
Dec. 2,	Edith Rogers.*	Olive Edith Putney,	Worcester.
16,	Grace Havey,*	Grace May Caswell,	Worcester.
19,	William Eugene Rue,*	William Eugene Wilson,	Worcester.
19,	Nellie Swan Richardson,	Helen Swan Richardson,	Worcester.

HAMPSHIRE COUNTY.

Feb. 4,	Clair Cook,*	Arthur W. Rowley,	Southampton.
Mar. 11,	Mary Ann Mason,*	Mary Ann Mather,	Belchertown.
April 1,	Blanche Simpson,*	Blanche Simpson Gleason,	South Hadley.
1,	Lillian May Sweatland,*	Lillian May Holden,	Belchertown.
May 6,	Carrie J. Farley,*	Carrie Stowell McGrath,	Ware.
6,	Mable Viola Rodelli,*	Mable Viola Hupfer,	Easthampton.
June 3,	Mary Creighton,*	June Elizabeth Stone,	Northampton.
Sept. 9,	Etta Amanda Burt,*	Harriet May Owen,	Ware.
9,	Charles Flagg,*	James I. Clark,	Greenwich.
Oct. 7,	John George Ogden,*	Alfred Lesure White,	Amherst.
Nov. 5,	Noel Bvron Lincoln,*	Noel Byron Hitchcock,	Belchertown.
Dec. 2,	Alice May Nilson,*	Caroline Pauline Blacklock,	Easthampton.

* Changed by reason of adoption.

HAMPDEN COUNTY.

Date of Decree.	Original Name.	Name Decreed.	Residence.
1890.			
Jan. 15,	Ernest Malcolm Smith,* . .	Samuel Ernest Berrett, . .	Springfield.
15,	Lura May Smith,* . . .	Lura May Berrett, . . .	Springfield.
18,	Geneva Willis,* . . .	Geneva Dimmick, . . .	Wales.
Mar. 5,	Effie Sherman Bathrick,* . .	Effie Sherman Dwight, . .	Springfield
April 2,	Flora Albena Masses,* . .	Flora Albena Wells. . .	Holyoke.
May 7,	Elizabeth Jane Croshier * . .	Elizabeth Jane Reed. . .	Springfield.
7,	Charles Thurman McNeill,* .	Clesson William Thayer, .	Springfield.
14,	Mary Collins,*	Mary Agnes Moran, . .	Palmer.
June 4,	Julia Maria Slingsby, . .	Julia Maria Clark, . . .	Holyoke.
4,	Frederick Baker,* . . .	Edward Gilligan Barry, .	Springfield.
4,	Beulah Isabel Hood,* . . .	Mary Driscoll, . . .	Chicopee.
18,	Joseph Mason,*	Joseph Alexander Arsino, .	Holyoke.
July 2,	Cora Bell Tobin,* . . .	Cora Ballou Freeland, . .	Westfield.
26,	Jane Manzie,*	Jane McCutcheon, . .	Ludlow.
26,	Bessie Manzie,*	Bessie Ann McCutcheon, .	Ludlow.
Aug. 1,	Willie Parks Cone,* . . .	Willie Parks Nichols, . .	Westfield
Sept. 3,	Lydia Florence Millett,* . .	Lydia Florence Russell,. .	Wilbraham.
Oct. 1,	Bartholomew Bradley,* . .	Bartholomew Sexton, . .	Chicopee.
11,	Warren Lester Emmons,* . .	Lester Emmons Butler, .	Wilbraham.
15,	Friederike Ahrens,* . . .	Friederike Hayden Shallies, .	Springfield.
Nov. 5,	Mary Lena Gober,* . . .	Sarah Pickering, . . .	Chicago, Ill.

FRANKLIN COUNTY.

April 2,	Leslie A. Dunton,* . . .	Leslie A. Lewis, . . .	Montague.
May 6,	Albert Alden,*	Clarence Alva Edison Brown,	New Salem.
Aug. 5,	Morris Oliver Waterman,* .	Morris Oliver Waterman, .	Shutesbury.
Sept. 23,	Grace May Senter,* . . .	Grace May Meacham, . .	Colrain.
Dec. 2,	Robert Davis,*	Robert Davis Butler, . .	Buckland.
2,	Henry Burton Barrett,* . .	Henry Burton Barrett, . .	Northfield.

BERKSHIRE COUNTY.

Jan. 7,	Lucy Rogers,*	Viola Angeline Springsteen, .	Stockbridge.
9,	Edith F. Hand,* . . .	Edith F. Ashman, . . .	North Adams.
April 1,	Walter Overbaugh,* . . .	Walter Gleason, . . .	Pittsfield.
May 6,	Minnie Ashton,* . . .	Minnie Elizabeth Aldrich, .	North Adams.
July 15,	Maggie Wilson,* . . .	Maggie McColgan, . . .	Pittsfield.
17,	Bessie May Willis,* . . .	Bessie May Nash, . . .	Pittsfield.
Sept. 2,	Henry Brown Aldrich,* . .	Henry Brown Houlihan, .	North Adams.
Oct. 7,	Eliza Thomas Willis, . .	Lila Thomas Willis, . .	Pittsfield.
8,	Charles H. Houghtaling,* . .	Charles H. O'Connell, . .	Lenox.
9,	Ike Rubinovick, . . .	Ike Goodrich, . . .	North Adams.
Dec. 2,	Mary Maria Tower,* . . .	Mary Maria Bishop, . .	North Adams.
2,	Mary B. Alley,* . . .	Mary E. Bostley, . . .	North Adams.
3,	Charles Hannibal,* . . .	Charles Harris, . . .	Great Barrington.

NORFOLK COUNTY.

Jan. 8,	Arthur Wiswall Gates, . .	Arthur Wiswall Gates-Fairbanks, ...	Dedham.
Feb. 5,	Alice Erlena Halliday,* . .	Alice Erlena Cowen, . .	Hyde Park.
May 21,	Charlotte Lyndia Feakins, .	Charlotte Lyndia Hawley, .	Hyde Park.

* Changed by reason of adoption.

NORFOLK COUNTY — *Concluded.*

Date of Decree.	Original Name.	Name Decreed.	Residence.
1890.			
May 21,	Frederick Hawley Feakins, .	Frederick Hawley, . . .	Hyde Park.
21,	Esther Catherine Feakins, .	Esther Catherine Hawley, .	Hyde Park.
21,	Harriette Savage Paullin,* .	Harriette Savage Paullin Fenton, ...	Quincy.
July 16,	Fred Newell Simmons, . .	Fred Newell Cohenno, . .	Stoughton.
Oct. 1,	Georgiana Ferguson Small,* .	Georgiana Ferguson Peterson,	Hyde Park.
15,	Mary Augusta Thayer, . .	Mary Alden Thayer, . .	Stoughton.
15,	Mabel Weston Phinney,* . .	Mabel Weston Hunt, . .	Milton.
Dec. 3,	Walter Lindsay Strong,* . .	Walter Lindsay Van Kleeck,.	New York.

PLYMOUTH COUNTY.

Jan. 13,	Rowena F. Barry, . . .	Rowena Fobes, . . .	Chelsea.
27,	——— Sherman, . .	Isabella May Briggs, . .	Carver.
Feb. 10,	Bly Gardner, ...	Walter Bly Gray, . . .	Brockton.
April 14,	Blanche Alton Hinckley, .	Fannie Stuart Hinckley, .	Hanover.
14,	Mabel Haven, ...	Mabel Haven McElroy, .	Hanson.
June 9,	Emily Stanley, ...	Emily Violet Hatch, .	Duxbury.
July 14,	Grace Caroline McCue, .	Grace Caroline Goodwin, .	Weymouth.
Aug. 25,	Eleanor Beatrice Packard, .	Beatrice Florence Bourne, .	Boston.
25,	Myra Winslow, ...	Abbie May Roads, . . .	Boston.
25,	Nellie Greeley, ...	Nellie Gertrude Dwelley, .	Truro.
Sept. 8,	Ida Belle Waterman,. . .	Ida Belle Pierce, . .	Abington.
8,	Lawrence Brooks Fuller, .	Henry Burness, Junior, .	Brockton.
22,	Mildred Allen Randall, .	Mildred Louise Jameson, .	Duxbury.

BRISTOL COUNTY.

Feb. 7,	Gracie Rowe,*	Edith Rhodes, . . .	Taunton.
7,	John Thomas Ramsbottom, .	John Thomas Reed, . .	Swanzey.
7,	Elizabeth Willis Ramsbottom, .	Elizabeth Willis Reed, . .	Swanzey.
7,	James Arthur Ramsbottom, .	James Arthur Reed, . .	Swanzey.
7,	Alfred Willis Ramsbottom, .	Alfred Willis Reed, . .	Swanzey.
7,	Annie Ramsbottom, . . .	Annie Reed, ...	Swanzey.
7,	Dora Gardner Ramsbottom, .	Dora Gardner Reed, . .	Swanzey.
7,	Nora Brown Ramsbottom, .	Nora Brown Reed, . .	Swanzey.
7,	Laurranna Villiers,* . .	Laura Tucker, . . .	New Bedford.
21,	Alzada Cobb,*	Alzada Isabel Grinnell, . .	Fall River.
21,	James Darlington,* . .	James Johnson, . . .	Fall River.
Mar. 7,	Rose Skinner,*	Grace Bassett, . . .	Berkley.
April 4,	Eva C. Bassett,* . .	Emma May Dean, . . .	Taunton.
4,	Lawrence Leach, . . .	Lawrence Leach Holden, .	Fall River.
Aug. 1,	Sarah A. Allen,* . .	Sarah Ann Delaney, . .	New Bedford.
1,	Mary Ann Hurst,* . .	Ellen Maud Dedrich, . .	New Bedford.
Sept. 5,	Abbie J. Wilcox,* . . .	Abbie J. Sherman, . .	New Bedford.
Oct. 3,	Agnes Frances Magowan,* .	Agnes Church Fox, . .	New Bedford.
Nov. 7,	Elizabeth Parkinson,* .	Elizabeth Smith, . . .	New Bedford.
Dec. 5,	Charlotte Wilson Booker,* .	Charlotte W. Wetherell, .	Attleborough.
5,	Maud Minnie Gould,* . .	Maud Minnie Freelove, .	Fall River.

* Changed by reason of adoption.

BARNSTABLE COUNTY.

Date of Decree.	Original Name.	Name Decreed.	Residence.
1890.			
April 15,	Annie,*	Annie W. Baker, . . .	Yarmouth.
May 21,	Frank Clayton,* . . .	Frank Clayton Burrows, .	Wellfleet.
June 17,	Mamie Crowell Carlin,* . .	Mary Adleta Bacon, . .	Barnstable.
Sept. 9,	Sarah Louisa Totman,* . .	Sarah Totman Freeman, .	Brewster.
Oct. 27,	Alice Elizabeth Achilles,* . .	Alma Maude Dunn, . .	Bourne.
Dec. 9,	Anna Webb Irwin, . . .	Anna Webb, ...	Barnstable.

SUFFOLK COUNTY.

Date of Decree.	Original Name.	Name Decreed.	Residence.
1891.			
Jan. 5,	Katherine L. Conine,* . .	Katherine L. Gage, . .	Athens, N. Y.
5,	Onesyi Ettinger,* . . .	Onesyi Ettinger Thurston, .	Boston.
5,	Sethantes Howland,* . .	Sethantes Howland Thurston,	Boston.
5,	Elizabeth Ray Jenks, . .	Elizabeth Ray Pritchard, .	Boston.
5,	John J. Mackeghney, . .	John J. Mack, . . .	Boston.
5,	Willie Willard Trenholm,* .	Willis Trenholm Parker, .	Boston.
26,	Quincy Alexander Shaw, .	Quincy Adams Shaw, . .	Boston.
26,	Elizabeth Tarlton, . .	Elizabeth Edwards, . .	Boston.
Feb. 2,	Lena May Pearson,* . .	Gunhilda Alfrida Miller, .	Lynn.
9,	Mary Belle McCloud, . .	Mary Belle Keith, . .	Boston.
Mar. 2,	William Harold Hickok,* . .	William Harold Tenney, .	Boston.
2,	Francis W. Higgins, . .	Francis W. Higgins Glenerne,	Boston.
2,	Bessie Marsh,* . . .	Bessie Lotty Whitney, .	Boston.
16,	Margaret Desmond, . .	Margaret Hart, . . .	Boston.
16,	Patrick Foley,* . . .	Patrick Tremaine, . .	Boston.
23,	Lizzie Graham,* . . .	Bessie Lincoln, . . .	Warren, Pa.
30,	Florence Violet Roy,* . .	Vanda Violet Maynard, .	Boston.
April 6,	Arthur Herbert Delaney, .	Arthur Herbert Dean, .	Boston.
13,	Laura May Blake,* . .	Laura May Riedy, . .	Boston.
13,	John H. Williams,* . .	John H. Blodgett, . .	Boston.
20,	Juliette Monroe,* . .	Lorna Harding Young, .	Boston.
27,	Frank Redmund Gollop, .	Frank Redmund, . . .	Boston.
27,	Jacob Knisnick, . . .	Jacob Cohen, . . .	Boston.
27,	Marion Estelle North,* . .	Marion Estelle Crowley, .	Boston.
May 4,	Margueritte McKenna,* . .	Margueritte Hanson, . .	Boston.
4,	Magdalena Wachter, . .	Magdalena Walker, . .	Boston.
4,	William Louis Wachter,* .	William Louis Walker, . .	Boston.
18,	Darwin Nugent.* . . .	Harry Fiske Blossom, .	Boston.
25,	Margaret Ann Hagerty,* . .	Margaret Ann O'Brien, .	Boston.
25,	Ellis Oechsner,* . . .	Ellis Exner Lee, . .	Boston.
June 8,	Marion Lincoln Washburn,* .	Marion Lincoln Frye, .	Boston.
15,	Wilhelmina A. Bates,* . .	Martha Augusta Tharby, .	Boston.
22,	Samuel S. Sunderland,* .	Samuel Sunderland Sherman,	Boston.
22,	Edward Kelley,* . . .	Edward Charles Hoyt, .	Dennis.
29,	Alamanza Bradley Roberts, .	Allie Bradley Roberts, .	Boston.
July 6,	Georgiana Elizabeth Speck,*	Georgiana Elizabeth Foy, .	Boston.
13,	Nellie Chaffie,* . . .	Lucy Annie Stowell, .	Eastport, Me.
13,	Joseph F. Kelley,* . .	George Francis Heald, .	Dennis.
13,	Jerome Walton,* . . .	Jerome Walton Allan, .	Boston.
20,	John Bowman,* . . .	John Blue, ...	Boston.
27,	Emma Louise Amazeen,* . .	Emma Louise Colby, .	Winthrop.
27,	Thomas Gallagher,* . .	George Harcourt, . .	Boston.
27,	Mabel Irene Taplin, . .	Mabel Irene Wheeler, .	Chelsea.
27,	Xenophon Pearce, . .	George Pearce, . .	Boston.
27,	Mabel Russell,* . . .	Gladis Dudley, . .	Boston.
Aug. 17,	Jennie Emeline Garland,* . .	Jennie Emeline Dean, .	Boston.
17,	Sibyl Adams Kohler,* . .	Sibyl Adams Hodges, .	Boston.
17,	Charles Davis Kohler,* . .	Charles Davis Hodges, .	Boston.

* Changed by reason of adoption.

SUFFOLK COUNTY — *Concluded.*

Date of Decree.	Original Name.	Name Decreed.	Residence.
1891.			
Aug. 17,	Maud E. Stedman,*	Maud E. Robinson,	Boston.
17,	Godfrey H. Stedman,*	Godfrey H. Robinson,	Boston.
Sept. 8,	Grace Blackwell,*	Ariane Goudreau,	Lynn.
8,	Elsie May Burrell.*	Elsie May Stirk,	Winthrop.
8,	Mary Anderson McCoull,	Mary McCoull Anderson,	Boston.
14,	Charles Wm. Jennison,*	Charles Wm. Whitechurch,	Boston.
14,	John Mulligan,*	John Mulhern,	Boston.
14,	Jennie Mulligan,*	Jennie Mulhern,	Boston.
14,	Sarah E Mulligan,*	Sarah E. Mulhern.	Boston.
21,	Foster Knowlton,*	Foster Clarence Poland,	Boston.
28,	Clarence Henry Doerringer,	Clarence Henry Berner,	Boston
28,	John Elliott,*	John Philip Sylvester,	Cambridge.
28,	Katie Anne Murphy,*	Katie Anne De Freitas,	Boston.
Oct. 5,	Charles Harold Coyle,	Harold Robbins Day,	Boston.
5,	Mary Emma Coyle,	Mary Emma Day,	Boston.
5,	Albert Hall,*	Howard Carter,	Boston.
5,	Wm. Jackson Onley,*	Wm. Jackson Smith,	Boston.
12,	Alice May Brennan,*	Alice Ramsey,	Boston.
19,	Frank Henry Mahoney,	Frank Henry Thomas,	Boston.
Nov. 2,	Justin Frank Carter,*	Ervin Libby Stearns,	Boston.
9,	Peter Anton Mangor Barfoed,	Peter Anton Foed,	Boston.
16,	Lena Welch,*	Mabel Adeline Welch,	Boston.
23,	Frederick P. Greenberg,	Frederick P. Green,	Boston.
23,	Theresa Josephine King,*	Theresa Stevens,	Boston.
30,	Joseph Lyman Parks,	Joseph Lyman Stone,	Boston.
Dec. 7,	Bertha Viola Sinclair,*	Ethel Collins,	Boston.
7,	Lewis Witkowsky,	Lewis Witte,	Boston.
7,	Martin Witkowsky,	Martin Witte,	Boston.
7,	Dorothea Witkowsky,	Dorothea Witte,	Boston.
7,	Saul A. Witkowsky,	Saul A. Witte,	Boston.
14,	Mabel Mitchell Wall,*	Mabel Mitchell Smith,	Boston.
14,	Henry Stanley Hearty or Haraty,*	Edwin Alfred Gatchell,	Cambridge.

ESSEX COUNTY.

Jan. 5,	Louis Nicholas,*	Charles August Pinkes,	Boston.
5,	Mabel E. Davis,*	Marie Curtis Boss,	Boston.
5,	Willie Foss,	William Albert Foss,	Haverhill.
19,	Eunice H. Phillips,*	Hazel Huntingdon Seger,	Swampscott.
Feb. 2,	Barbara M. Smith,*	Barbara May Hooper,	Beverly.
16,	Bernice M. Woodbury,*	Bernice May Allen,	Manchester.
Mar. 2,	Cora Viola Cone,*	Cora Viola Barton,	Westfield.
16,	Alice Hannefin,*	Alice May Worthen,	———.
16,	Minnie Scott,*	Minnie Helen Grover,	———.
April 6,	Mabel Giddings,	Madelaine Endicott Giddings,	Beverly.
20,	Frances Cunningham,*	Frances Wholey,	Lawrence.
20,	Agnes Cunningham,*	Agnes Wholey,	Lawrence.
20,	Lillian Perkins,*	Lillian Clements,	Newburyport.
May 4,	Glena B. Higgins,*	Glena Beal,	Haverhill.
4,	Solomon F. L. Burke,	Frank Lowell Burke,	Rowley.
4,	George G. Hicken,	Guy Reynolds Hicken,	Rowley.
18,	John H. Farley,*	John Henry Breen,	———.
18,	Maggie M. Robinson,*	Pauline Adella Rumsey,	Boston.
June 8,	Daisy L. Benson,*	Daisy Laura Kimball,	———.
July 6,	Emily F. Odell,	Nannie Lovett Odell,	Beverly.
13,	Mary A. Healey,*	Mary Ann Jennings,	Boston.
13,	Mary Lucey,*	Mary Rondeau,	Lawrence.

* Changed by reason of adoption.

ESSEX COUNTY — *Concluded.*

Date of Decree.	Original Name.	Name Decreed.	Residence.
1891.			
July 20,	Nannie Kaiser,*	Nancy Kaiser Teal, . .	Stowe, Vt.
27,	Elizabeth V. Carter,* . .	Elizabeth Victoria Carter, .	Lynn.
Aug. 3,	Edith R. Simmons,* . . .	Helen Edith Huckins, . .	Southbridge.
3,	John Barber,*	Russell Younger, . . .	Gloucester.
Sept. 8,	Jeremiah O'Connell, . . .	Joseph O'Connell, . . .	Peabody.
Nov. 2,	Roland D. Skinner,* . . .	Roland Dunbar Cummings, .	Mansfield.

MIDDLESEX COUNTY.

Date of Decree.	Original Name.	Name Decreed.	Residence.
Jan. 13,	Paul Gleason,*	Herbert Marcum Waldo Brigham, ...	Framingham.
13,	Jessie Agnes Gerry,* . .	Gertrude Carr, . . .	Somerville.
13,	Charles A. McMaster, . .	Charles Archibald Mack Masters, ...	Watertown.
27,	Harry Spencer,*	Harry Spencer Parker, . .	Medford.
Feb. 3,	Christina Drum,* . . .	Blanche Christina Horne, .	Cambridge.
3,	Cora Emma Crockett,* . .	Cora Emma Lane, . . .	Rockport, Me.
3,	Flora Ella Crockett,* . .	Flora Ella Lane, . . .	Rockport, Me.
3,	Samuella Helen Ida Pratt,*	Helen Amelia Cole, . .	Acton.
Mar. 3,	Myrtle Campbell,* . . .	Myrtle Ward, ...	Cambridge.
3,	Gertrude May Bliss,* . .	Marian Frances Whyte Hooper, ...	Medford.
3,	Julia Eagan,* . . .	Bessie Lu Priest, . . .	Lynn.
10,	Everett Bates Allen, . .	George Bates Allen, . .	Lowell.
17,	John Albert Hill McAvoy,*	John Albert McAvoy Tyler, .	Cambridge.
24,	Edwin Farnsworth,* . .	Edwin Charles Crosby, . .	Waltham.
April 7,	Wendell P. Bonney, . .	Wendell Phillips Lee, . .	Reading.
7,	Josie Bonney, ...	Josie Lee, ...	Reading.
7,	Pearl Gore,*	Pearl Foss, ...	Cambridge.
14,	Abbie Maria Newhall, .	Abbie Maria Holyoke, . .	Hudson.
28,	Annie Smith,* . . .	Annie Ruth Abbott, . .	Lowell.
28,	Everett Wellington,* . .	David Wade, ...	Malden.
May 12,	Amelia Louisa Pfaltz, . .	Annie Amelia Louisa Pfaltz, .	Framingham.
12,	Lizzie Adelade Sherman,* .	Lizzie Adelade Stetson, . .	Hopkinton.
19,	Mabel J. Buxton,* . .	Mabel Jane Hall, . . .	Lowell.
26,	Flora Edwards,* . . .	Flora Ogden, ...	Cambridge.
26,	Hattie May Allen,* . .	Hattie May Cleland, . .	Odell, Nebraska
26,	Elsie Leslie Williams,* .	Addie Leslie Foster, . .	Cambridge.
June 9,	John Beatty,*	John Danehy, ...	Cambridge.
9,	Sarah Jane McGovern,* .	Sarah Jane Reynolds, . .	Marlborough.
9,	Edna Irene Davis,* . .	Edna Irene Kendall, . .	Stoneham.
23,	John McGrath,* . . .	John Charles Wrisley, . .	Malden.
July 7,	Arthur Cary Burns, . .	Walter Francis Chapman, .	Boston.
7,	Alice Cary Burns,* . .	Maud Ethel Chapman, . .	Boston.
14,	Ruth Evelyn Sherman,* .	Ruth Evelyn Sherman Munson, ...	Medford.
21,	Elizabeth Eleanor Blood,*	Elizabeth Eleanor Griffiths, .	Pepperell.
28,	William Hastings McGaw,*	William Alexander Hastings,	Everett
28,	Mabel Linnell McGaw, .	Mabel Linnell Hastings, .	Everett.
28,	Warren Hastings McGaw,	Warren Robert Hastings, .	Everett.
28,	Bertrode Inez McGaw, .	Bertrode Inez Hastings, .	Everett.
Sept. 1,	Elizabeth Nathan Phelps, .	Elizabeth Adelma Nathan, .	Wakefield.
1,	Ruth Lee Skinner,* . .	Ruth Lee Hill, . . .	Hudson.
8,	George McCabe,* . . .	Harry Nicholas Affelhoy, .	Malden.
15,	Fannie Minerva Woodcock,*	Fannie Minerva Coffin, . .	New York, N. Y
22,	Mary Edith Chipman, . .	Esther Fenton Chipman, .	Medford.
Oct. 6,	Himan Joseph Cooperleib,.	Himan Joseph Cooper, . .	Somerville.
6,	Lizzie Mary Cooperleib, .	Lizzie Mary Cooper, . .	Somerville.

* Changed by reason of adoption.

MIDDLESEX COUNTY — *Concluded.*

Date of Decree.	Original Name.	Name Decreed.	Residence.
1891.			
Oct. 27,	Frederick Reid Coolidge,*	Frederick Coolidge Farnum,	Boston.
27,	Imogene T. Wiley,	Imogene Thompson,	Stoneham.
27,	Phebe Howard Williams,	Phebe Helen Williams,	Stoneham.
27,	Asa Balcom Stanley,	Asa Stanley Balcom,	Maynard.
Nov. 4,	William Carver Damon,	William Cotton Damon,	Concord.
4,	Margaret T. Smith,*	Margaret Thomas French,	Yonkers, N. Y.
10,	Daniel Webster Brown,*	Daniel Webster Hamilton,	Boston.
10,	Ernest J. Fortier,*	Ernest Standish,	Franklin.
10,	Bernice Hart,*	Bernice Hart Hubbard,	Cambridge.
17,	Edward Kenney,*	Edward McAvoy,	Lowell.
24,	Albert Singleton,*	Albert Osgood Ward,	Cambridge.
24,	Mattie Allen,*	Eva Mawhiney,	Boston.
24,	Louis Rudolph Niederhausern,*	Louis Rudolph Gindrat,	Waltham.
24,	Augusta Ann Smith,*	Evangeline Augusta Fletcher,	Waltham.
Dec. 1,	Bertha L. Townsend,*	Bertha Linwood Hanscom,	Wellfleet.
8,	Eden McMillen,*	Ruth Mildred Dennen,	Newton.
8,	Charles Flemming Mulhern,*	Charles Llewellyn Flanders,	Boston.
22,	Henry J. Bauer,*	Henry Joseph La Fay,	Boston.
22,	Alice G. Bauer,*	Alice Mary La Fay,	Boston.
22,	Mabel Covert,*	Mabel Goulding,	Lynn.

WORCESTER COUNTY.

Date of Decree.	Original Name.	Name Decreed.	Residence.
Jan. 9,	Ethel Winifred Pierce,*	Ethel Winifred Slater,	Uxbridge.
9,	Carrie G. Gillette,*	Carrie Belle Currier,	Ashburnham.
20,	Nellie G. Sands,*	Nellie G. Streeter,	Southbridge.
27,	Lillian T. Sullivan,*	Lillian T. Doherty,	Leominster.
Feb. 20,	Margaret A. Farren,*	Annie May Fletcher,	Harvard.
Mar. 3,	Dede Marie Nullett,*	Dede Marie Willard,	Lancaster.
24,	Archie Bradford Stanley,	Byron Archie Stanley,	Fitchburg.
24,	Emma Shambo,*	Emma Bussiere,	Fitchburg.
27,	Louis Jasmin.*	Joseph Alfred Tourigny,	Worcester.
April 7,	John Doyle, Jr.,	John J. Doyle,	No. Brookfield.
10,	Ethel Smith.*	Maud Ethel Frink,	Spencer.
17,	Laura Evelyn Fisher,*	Laura Evelyn Yeager,	No. Brookfield.
17,	Mary Sheehan,*.	Mary Sherman,	Gardner.
17,	Fred Leroy Dixon,*	Fred LeRoy Putnam,	Rutland.
28,	James Comrie,*	James Methven Comrie,	Enfield, Conn.
May 13,	Waldo Isenor,*	Ephraim Waldo Tucker,	Worcester.
June 12,	Florence May Winans,*	Florence May James,	Fitchburg.
23,	Lizzie Brennan,*	Eva Grace Nutting,	Ashburnham.
July 17,	Herbert Whiting,*	Archie Berthold Codding,	Conway.
17,	Mary Ethel Franklin,*	Mary Ethel Coolidge,	Worcester.
21,	Amy Edson,*	Leone Margery Morse,	Athol.
Aug. 11,	William Dresser Clegg,*	William Dresser Knight,	Putnam, Conn.
Sept. 1,	Harland L. Goodnow,*	Harland L. Neal,	Winchendon.
1,	Frank R. Hood,	Frank R. Warren,	Worcester.
1,	Edgar Smith,*	Edgar Nichols,	Worcester.
Oct. 6,	Charles A. Hypson,*	Alfred Wilson,	Hopedale.
6,	Harry James Parker,*	Harry James Power,	Southborough.
6,	Leon Carter,*	Leon Edwards,	Worcester.
20,	Lena Etchells,*	Dora Eliza Allen,	Worcester.
Nov. 17,	Helen Clark,*	Helen Hemenway,	Gardner.
17,	Willie Elwin Ball,	William Elwin Ball,	Westborough.
17,	Emeline T. Knight,	Emeline P. Tenney,	Worcester.
17,	Harry C Dunn,*	Harry William Nelson,	Fitchburg.
24,	Lester W. Towne,*	Lester W. Sanders,	Athol.
Dec. 1,	Frederick Coomes Hale,	Frederick Coomes Garfield,	Northborough.
22,	Ethel Curley,*	Mabel Ethel Nutting,	Ashburnham.

* Changed by reason of adoption.

HAMPSHIRE COUNTY.

Date of Decree.	Original Name.	Name Decreed.	Residence.
1891.			
Jan. 6,	Tuma Sarafian,*	Esther Sarafian,	Diarbekia, Arm'ia.
Feb. 3,	Agnes Brown,*	Pearl Lorence Patrell,	Northampton.
3,	Eugene L. Knowlton,*	Eugene L. Knowlton,	Wilbraham.
Mar. 3,	Elmer Channing,*	Robert Elmer Edwards,	Worthington.
3,	William Mahor,*	William Henry Tencellent,	Westfield.
3,	Flora F. Shepardson,*	Fannie F. Hofman,	Lenox.
3,	—— Daniels,*	Charles Francis King,	Unknown.
April 7,	—— Harrington,*	Charles Henry Walker,	Willimantic, Conn.
May 5,	Robert Clifford,*	Robert Williams,	Vermont
5,	Bessie Viola Damon,*	Bessie Viola Hathaway,	Chesterfield.
July 25,	Thomas Sullivan,	Thomas O'Sullivan,	Ware.
Aug. 4,	Fred Warren Beals,*	Freddie Eugene Canterbury,	Amherst.
Sept. 1,	Ella J. Sweet,	Ellen J. Vail,	Northampton.
1,	Ernest Sweet,	Ernest Vail,	Northampton.
1,	Carroll E. Sweet,	Carroll E. Vail,	Northampton.
Nov. 4,	Philip Moen Washburn,	Philip Washburn,	Northampton
10,	Mather Humphrey Neill,*	Mather Humphrey Neill,	Highland Park, Ill.
Dec. 8,	Hannah Sullivan,*	Josephine Brown,	Ware.

HAMPDEN COUNTY.

Jan. 7,	Charles Lindsey Chick,*	Lindsey Chick Brigham,	Monson.
7,	Mary Ellen Hogan,*	Mary Ellen Riley,	Palmer.
7,	John William Hogan,*	John William Riley,	Palmer.
7,	Lizzie Hogan,*	Lizzie Riley,	Palmer.
7,	Edward Richard Hogan,*	Edward Richard Riley,	Palmer.
7,	Jennie May Hogan,*	Jennie May Riley,	Palmer
Feb. 26,	Margaret Helen Moynahan,*	Margaret Helen Dougherty,	West Springfield.
Mar. 23,	Alice Josephine Graham,*	Alice Josephine Mason,	Springfield.
May 6,	Elizabeth Brown,*	Marion Chase Severance,	Holyoke.
13,	Bessie May Bambush,*	Lillian May Dodd.	Springfield.
July 31,	Myrtle Pease,*	Myrtle Mildred Blight,	Springfield.
Oct. 7,	Emma Louise Norcross,*	Marjorie Christine Lane,	Springfield.
21,	No name.*	Ruth Cleaves Merrill,	Springfield.
Dec. 2,	Blanche Morrison,*	Marion Blancne Clark,	Holyoke.

FRANKLIN COUNTY.

Sept. 22,	Blanche A. Davis,*	Blanche A. D. Elmer,	Buckland.
Oct. 27,	Florence Mildred Brown,*	Florence Mildred Bishop,	Buckland.
Dec. 1,	Frederick E. Ellis,*	Frederick E. Blanchard,	Greenfield.

BERKSHIRE COUNTY.

Feb. 5,	Lucy L. Bourk,*	Viola Marguerite Mandeville,	Pittsfield.
5,	Elise Masse,*	Elise Terrien,	Clarksburg.
Mar. 3,	Rosa Mary Hebert,*	Rosa May Mottor,	Dalton.
3,	Noel Hebert,*	Noel Mottor,	Dalton.
3,	Cheri Joseph Hebert,*	Cheri Joseph Sarrissin,	Hinsdale.
3,	Archibald Stannard,*	Archibald Armstead,	New Marlborough.
May 5,	Howard L Wilcox,*	Howard L. Pratt,	North Adams.
5,	Harold L Wilcox,*	Harold C. Pratt,	North Adams.
6,	Clara Lillian Wilcox,*	Clara Lillian Cormier,	North Adams.

* Changed by reason of adoption.

BERKSHIRE COUNTY — *Concluded.*

Date of Decree.	Original Name.	Name Decreed.	Residence.
1891.			
June 2,	James F. Lewis, ...	Frederick J. Hatch, . .	Great Barrington.
2,	Marguerite Daisy Roso,* .	Marguerite Daisy Clement, .	Richmond.
2,	Louisa Cadrin,*	Louisa Clairmont, . . .	North Adams.
July 21,	Barbara Lacy,* . . .	Nellie Lacy, . . .	Pittsfield.
21,	Mabel Elizabeth Witherell,*	Mabel Elizabeth Roberts, .	Pittsfield.
Oct. 6,	John Allen Atwood,* .	John Atwood Allen, . .	Pittsfield.
8,	James W. Magee,* . .	Frederick E. Terry, . .	North Adams.
Dec. 1,	Elizabeth E. Norton,* .	Elizabeth E. Coughlin, . .	Cheshire.

NORFOLK COUNTY.

Jan. 7,	Michael Francis Clarke, .	Francis Clarke, . . .	Randolph.
7,	Effie Maud Tuttle,* .	Effie Maud Stanton, . .	Needham.
Feb. 4,	Ernest Hermann Seifert,* .	Ernest Halbauer, . . .	Dedham.
18,	John Arthur Healy,* . .	John Arthur Lyman, . .	Cambridge.
April 1,	Thomas Lester,* . .	Frederick Cushman Runnels,	Boston.
8,	Willie Wesson,* . .	William Meehan, . . .	Lowell.
15,	Mary Ella Robinson,* .	Mary Ella Gay, . . .	Hampton, N. B.
June 10,	Frederick Lawrence,* .	Frederick Lawrence Vinal, .	Methuen.
July 1,	Gertrude Anna Stirckler,*.	Gertrude Anna Packard, .	Worcester.
Sept. 2,	Georgie Pearl Tower,* .	Alice May Bickley, . .	Boston.
23,	John Chapman,* . .	Charles Richard Stewart, .	Boston.
23,	Rose Murphy,* . . .	Gertrude Hazel Frye, .	Boston.
Oct. 28,	Ethel Smith,* . . .	Mildred Ethel Haggerty, .	Groton.
Nov. 11,	Ruth Beatrice Sinclair Pieterse,*	Beatrice Tucker, . .	Boston.
11,	Herbert Harrison Pieterse,*	Herbert Loring Doble, . .	Boston.
18,	Kathrine Belle Crawford,*	Kathrine Belle Bacon, .	Scotland.

PLYMOUTH COUNTY.

Jan. 12,	Julia S. Stanley,* . .	Julia May Woods, . . .	Pembroke.
12,	Victoria Stanley,* . .	Mabel Victoria Hunt, . .	Duxbury.
Mar. 9,	Alice Caroline Damon,* .	Alice Caroline McKenney, .	Abington.
9,	George Henry Downey, .	George Henry Downing, .	Hingham.
April 13,	Edwin Forest Page, . .	Edwin Forest Cobb, .	Brockton.
May 25,	Rose McCloskey,* . .	Rose Ellen Conroy, . .	Whitman.
June 22,	Infant,*	Pearl Aleda Packard, .	Brockton.
22,	Esther Maude Wright,* .	Esther Maude Stetson, . .	Bridgewater.
Sept. 28,	Hugh McCloskey,* . .	Hugh Churchill McAdams, .	West Bridgewater.
Oct. 26,	Blanche Maud Crowell,* .	Louise Flavella Field, .	Brockton.

BRISTOL COUNTY.

Jan. 2,	Jeremiah Harrington,* .	James Harrington Doyle, .	Fall River.
2,	Eva Carlton Vincent,* .	Eva Carlton Leach, . .	New Bedford.
Mar. 6,	Isadore Abby Bradley,* .	Isadore Abby Colyar, . .	New Bedford.
6,	Benjamin Keith,* . .	Clayton Simpson Robinson, .	Seekonk.
April 3,	Anna Margerite Otes,* .	Anna Margerite Bourgeois, .	Norton.
May 1,	Elizabeth Defley,* . .	Elizabeth Lavelle, . .	Fall River.
15,	Joseph Sylvia,* . . .	Joseph Sylvia Mello, . .	Fall River.
June 5,	Mary Martha Jones,* .	Martha Jones Adams, . .	New Bedford.
5,	Alice Mayo,* . . .	Mabel Rhodes, . . .	Taunton.

* Changed by reason of adoption.

BRISTOL COUNTY — *Concluded.*

Date of Decree.	Original Name.	Name Decreed.	Residence.
1891.			
July 3,	Nellie Golding,*	Nellie Shea, ...	Fall River.
3,	Arthur William Leonard,*	Arthur William Larson,	Norton.
Aug. 7,	Ida May Gorman,* . . .	Ida May Harvey, . . .	Taunton.
Nov. 6,	Manuel Silveira,* . . .	Manuel A Brazil, . . .	New Bedford.
20,	Ethel Woodward,* . . .	Ethel Tretheway, . . .	Fall River.
Dec. 4,	Emma Parkinson,* . . .	Emma Taylor, . . .	New Bedford.

BARNSTABLE COUNTY.

April 21,	Bessie May Eldridge,* . .	Bessie May Chase, . . .	Yarmouth.

DUKES COUNTY.

Oct. 19,	Frank L. Stuart, . . .	Frank Leonard Norton, . .	Edgartown.

SUFFOLK COUNTY.

Date of Decree.	Original Name.	Name Decreed.	Residence.
1892.			
Jan. 11,	Arthur Henry,*	Arthur Ford, ...	Boston.
18,	John S. Dalton,* . . .	John Suinburne Dalton Mills,	Boston.
25,	Daisy Rogers, ...	Marguerite Rogers, . .	Boston.
25,	Bertha Ford,*	Bertha Sands, ...	Boston.
Feb. 1,	Joseph E. Longbois, . .	Joseph E. Long, . . .	Boston.
8,	Gertrude Pauline Knight,* .	Gertrude Pauline Potter, .	Amesbury.
8,	Annie Elizabeth Cashman,*	Christine Larain Mansfield, .	Newburyport.
15,	Mildred Hatch,*	Mildred Hastings, . . .	Boston.
15,	Herbert Washington Chase,*	Herbert Washington Zarro, .	Boston.
23,	Della Sidney Cullen,* . .	Dorothy Lucas, ...	Malden.
29,	Mary Josephine Pitts,* . .	Mary Josephine McCarthy, .	Boston.
29,	George McDuff,* . . .	George Nelson Dawes, . .	Boston.
Mar. 7,	Harry Proctor or Harry Harding,*	Jesse Allen Holton, . .	Boston.
14,	Isabella Sebley,* . . .	Isabella Williams, . . .	Winchester.
14,	Charles E Staples,* . . .	Charles E. Kimball, . .	Boston.
14,	Mary M. Lynch,* . . .	Mary M. Cluney, . . .	Lubec, Me.
14,	Marion Frances Graves, .	Marion Frances Reed, . .	Boston.
21,	Geo. Widgery Brown, . .	Geo. Widgery Andrews, .	Boston.
21,	Joseph Sullivan,* . . .	William Henry Parry, . .	Boston.
21,	Hattie Comeford,* . . .	Harriet Fellner, . . .	Boston.
21,	Mertys Ada Schrebler,* .	Mary Ethel Langtry, . .	Methuen.
28,	Isabella Weiss, ...	Isabella White, . . .	Boston.
28,	Max Weiss, ...	Max White, ...	Boston.
28,	Charles Louis Sheidegger, . .	Charles Delmont, . . .	Boston.
28,	Frederick Siedel,* . . .	Frederick Reisser, . . .	Boston.
April 4,	John Darney,*	William Saunders, . . .	Boston.
18,	Ruth McDonald,* . . .	Mary Ruth Clark, . . .	Boston.
25,	Lilly M. Godfrey,* . . .	Lilly M. Lester, . . .	Boston.
25,	Hattie Irene Sherman,* . .	Hattie Irene Pond, . . .	Boston.
25,	Josephine Thayer,* . . .	Maude Good, ...	——.
May 9,	Lawrence Sincock, . . .	Lawrence Simcox, . . .	Boston.
9,	John Rowe Wright, . . .	John Wright Rowe, . . .	Boston.
16,	Willie H. Grieves,* . . .	Willie Grieves Carter, . .	Boston.
23,	Ralph Kingston,* . . .	Ralph Kingston Riggs, . .	Boston.

* Changed by reason of adoption.

SUFFOLK COUNTY — *Concluded.*

Date of Decree.	Original Name.	Name Decreed.	Residence.
1892.			
May 23,	Nellie Roughsedge, . . .	Elinor Amelia Smith, . .	Waltham.
23,	Walter Grafton,* . . .	Wm. Stewart Colburn, . .	Chelsea.
24,	John Killam McEacham,* .	John Killam Daley, . .	Chelsea.
31,	Joseph Ness, ...	Joseph Van Ness, . .	Boston.
31,	Lillie Katie Dixon, . .	Lillie Dixon Fay, . . .	Boston.
31,	Collinwood Taylor,* . .	Archibald Emerson, . .	Boston.
June 9,	Winifred Izozelia Bruce,* .	Winifred Bruce Jacobs, . .	Boston.
13,	Thomas William Daley, .	Thomas William Dale, . .	Boston.
13,	Olivia Kirstine Johnson,* .	Olivia Kirstine Cutter, .	Boston.
18,	Aurelius Richards,* . .	Frank Leslie Richards, . .	Boston.
25,	Marion Elizabeth Corish,*	Marion Elizabeth Gilman, .	Boston.
25.	Mary Keohane,* . . .	Mary Gilogly, ...	Boston.
25,	Ellen Keohane,* . . .	Ellen Gilogly, ...	Boston.
July 7,	Herbert Hasty,* . . .	Herbert Whiting Russell, .	Boston.
14,	Leopold Paul Weiss, . .	Leopold Paule White, . .	Boston.
21,	Ruth Notman, ...	Ruth Sloane, ...	Boston.
21,	Bertha Houghton Notman,	Bertha Houghton Sloane, .	Boston.
21,	George Sloane Notman, .	George Sloane, . . .	Boston.
28,	Harry M. Pakulski, . .	Harry M. Parker, . . .	Boston.
28,	Johan C. W. Stolzenwaldt,	John Charles Carlson, . .	Boston.
Aug. 18,	Samuel Webber,* . . .	Samuel Augustus Goddard, .	Boston.
18,	Edward Murray,* . . .	Francis Edward Sindona, .	Boston.
Sept. 1,	May Ella Aldrich, . .	Ella Aldrich, ...	Boston.
1,	Joseph Barrett,* . . .	Joseph Flagg, ...	Boston.
1,	John William Ellis, . .	John William Marshall, .	Boston.
8,	Ella May Leahy,* . .	Mary Elizabeth Foley, .	Boston.
8,	Barnard Lecherzach, . .	Barnard L. Bernard, . .	Boston.
8,	Alexander Steiner, . .	Alexander Steiner Stanley, .	Boston.
15,	Maud Gretchen Hanna, .	Maud Gretchen Sutherland, .	Boston.
22,	Eva May Folsom, . .	Eva May Butler, . .	Boston.
22,	Delia E. Brown,* . .	Elizabeth Brown Allen, . .	Boston.
29,	Alice Bertha Hinds,* . .	Alice Bertha Langille, . .	Boston.
Oct. 13,	Mary Emily Moore,* . .	Mary Emily Conway, . .	Boston.
20,	Charles McAllister, . .	Charles Arthur Marston, .	Boston.
Nov. 3,	Lillie Chantrey,* . . .	Lillian Mildred Dixon, . .	Lawrence.
10,	Sophia Mary Dousett,* .	Sophia Mary Bundy, . .	Boston.
10,	Frank O'Bryant,* . .	Nathaniel LeRoy, . .	Boston.
17,	Rowena Carver,* . .	Clara May Anderson, . .	———.
17,	Francis P. Riordan,* . .	Francis P. O'Connor, . .	Boston.
23,	Clara Blanche Patten,*	Clara Blanche Castle, . .	Boston.
25,	Ernest Arthur Paige,* .	John Lowell Brigham, . .	Chelsea.
25,	Ruth Donovan,* . .	Ruth Marion Parker, . .	———.
25,	Edward Wall,* . . .	Edward May Pease, . .	———.
Dec. 1,	Carrie A. Dowlin, . .	Carrie A. Patterson, . .	Boston.
22,	Mary Elizabeth Bemis,* .	Mary Elizabeth Ormsby, . .	Boston.
29,	Mary J. Long,* . . .	Mary Kiernan, . . .	Boston.
29,	Charles Rasmussen, . .	Charles Robertson, . . .	Boston.
29,	Annie Roth,*	Annie Moore, ...	Boston.
29,	Grace Viola West,* . .	Grace Viola Rich, . . .	Boston.

ESSEX COUNTY.

Jan. 4,	Effie M. Hersey,* . . .	Ethel Marie Trask, . .	Lynn.
18,	Mary F. Murphy,* . . .	Mary Frances Weld, . .	Boston.
Feb. 15,	Joseph Birmingham,* . .	Joseph Ahern, . . .	Peabody.
Mar. 7,	Augustine W. Rich (second), .	Augustine Hall Rich, . .	Swampscott.
14,	Milton L. Goodere,* . .	Roy Henry DeLand, . .	Lynn.
14,	Helen M. Hall,* . . .	Helen Meredith Hall Ellison,	Haverhill.

* Changed by reason of adoption.

ESSEX COUNTY — *Concluded.*

Date of Decree.	Original Name.	Name Decreed.	Residence.
1892.			
Mar. 14,	—— Roberts,*	Ruth Charlotte Josephine Mortenson, ...	Gloucester.
April 4,	Philomine Lapointe,* . .	Philomine Coté, . . .	Lynn.
11,	Frank E. Higgins,* . .	Frank Ellis Jellison, . .	Lynn.
18,	—— Siefert,* . . .	Marion Leroy Janvrin, . .	Boston.
June 6,	Nettie Palm,* . . .	Hildah Myers, . . .	Tewksbury.
20,	Emma C. Loftus,* . .	Emma Christina Blomquest, .	Lawrence.
July 18,	—— Page.* . . .	Rebecca Mercy Eldridge, .	Lynn.
Aug. 1,	Leola M. Verrill,* . .	Leola Morton Kimball, . .	——.
1,	Eva M. Nutter,* . .	Eva May Bowen, . . .	Haverhill.
Sept. 6,	Raymond H. Pool,* . .	Raymond William Sargent, .	Rockport.
Oct. 3,	Thomas Huggup,* . .	James Arthur Byers, .	Beverly.
3,	Paul Webber,* . . .	Stanley Webber Annable, .	Boston.
10,	Ralph C. Eaton,* . .	Ralph C. Stockbridge, .	Haverhill.
17,	Raymond McGlynn,* .	Raymond George Robinson, .	Lawrence.
17,	Agnes Mabel Bogart,* .	Agnes Mabel Pyne, . .	Lynn.
24,	Annie O'Leary,* . .	Annie Maud Mercer, . .	——.
Nov. 7,	Alexander Hissoire, . .	Alexander Hissoire Brown, .	Haverhill.
14,	Alice L. Armstrong, . .	Alice Lillian Jenkins, . .	Lynn.
21,	Alonzo H. Grant,* . .	Roy Alonzo Hainer Torrey, .	Haverhill.
Dec. 19,	Charles E. Whittier,* .	Charles Edward Shackleton, .	Lawrence.
19,	William Ropes, . . .	William Colby Ropes, . .	Lynn.

MIDDLESEX COUNTY.

Date of Decree.	Original Name.	Name Decreed.	Residence.
Jan. 5,	Archie R Sweatland,* . .	Archie Harmon, . . .	Belchertown.
12,	Harrison Otis Barnes,* .	Harrison Otis Pickering, .	Everett.
19,	Clara Frances Murphy,* .	Clara Frances O'Keefe, .	Somerville.
26,	Gertrude Foster,* . .	Elsie Theresa Collins, .	Cambridge.
Feb. 2,	William Herbert Folsom, .	William Gray Folsom, .	Newton.
9,	Kate Ayers Claflin, . .	Kate Ayers Green, . .	Arlington.
9,	James Snow,* . . .	Harwood Dillon Granger, .	Medford.
9,	Ellen Collins.* . . .	Ellen Shea, . . .	Marlborough.
16,	Laura Maud Kingsley,* .	Effie May Hurlbut, . . .	Wakefield.
23,	Gertrude Sylvester,* . .	Gertrude Sylvester Harrington, ...	Boston.
Mar. 1,	Horatio Fogg Tibbetts, .	Horatio Fogg Twombly, .	Framingham.
1,	Annie Dean,* . . .	Jessie May Snow, . .	Wakefield.
8,	Nellie Matthews,* . .	Helen Amelia Dimon, . .	Lowell.
22,	Daisy Watrous,* . .	Mary Anna Clark Dexter, .	Melrose.
22,	Robert Moran,* . . .	Robert Chester Smith, .	Milton.
22,	Emma Amelia Park,* . .	Emma Amelia Sylvester, .	Newton.
22,	William Austin Dakin,* .	William Austin Perkins, .	Hopewell, N. B.
April 5,	Florence Minetta Capron,* .	Florence Minetta Butters, .	Wrentham.
19,	Laurice Taylor Russell,* .	Laurice Taylor Moreland, .	Arlington.
19,	Mary Simpson Whitman,* .	Leslie Field Farrington, .	Lowell.
May 17,	Frederick Owen Coombs,* .	Frederick Owen Stuart, .	Malden.
24,	Sarah Elvira Williamson,* .	Sarah Elvira Blake, . .	Lowell.
June 7,	Edward Emil Horm, . .	Edward Emil Weisbach, .	Cambridge.
14,	Dora Sumner,* . . .	Dorothy Bouvé, . .	Cambridge.
14,	Emma Maria Knight,* . .	Emma Marie Taylor, .	Everett.
21,	Elmer Augustus Wright,* .	Elmer Augustus Gilson, .	Lawrence.
21,	Frank Eagan,* . . .	Frank Irving Melvin, .	Cambridge.
28,	William Albert Smith, .	William Albert Somers, .	Somerville.
28,	Agness Gertrude Bruce,* .	Agness Gertrude Phelps, .	Hudson.
July 5,	Ida Bell Gromer,* . .	Ida Bell Percy, . .	Cambridge.
26,	Flora Barton,* . . .	Florence Rose Nichols, .	Monson.
Sept. 6,	Beatrice Akisson,* . .	Beatrice Emma Bishop, .	Boston.

* Changed by reason of adoption.

MIDDLESEX COUNTY — *Concluded.*

Date of Decree.	Original Name.	Name Decreed.	Residence.
1892.			
Sept. 6,	Charles S. Barrows,*	Charles S. Carr,	Everett.
6,	Walter A. Felker,	Albert Johnson Stackpole,	Lowell.
6,	Charles F. M. Fisher,	Charles Fordice Meade Fish,	Chelmsford.
6,	Katie Fogarty,*	Katie Murphy,	Waltham.
6,	Ethelwyn Sophia Matthews,	Ethelwyn Sophia Bailey,	Malden.
6,	Charles Raphael McIntyre,*	Clarence Eugene Foster,	Boston.
6,	Lucinda B Pocknett *	Lulu Frances Martin,	Cambridge.
6,	Ethel Gertrude Townsend,*	Ethel Gertrude Ormsby,	Malden.
6,	Frank Lester Wyman,*	Frank W. Bulette,	Ludlow, Vt.
Oct. 4,	Augusta Severin,*	Myrtle Gladys White,	Boston.
11,	Ebba Robinson,*	Mildred March,	Easton.
11,	George W. Garland,*	George Washington Phinney,	Boston.
11,	Dora Murray,*	Dora Louise Collier,	Chelsea.
18,	Mildred Louise Gee,*	Mildred Louise Finney,	U. Wicklow, N. B.
25,	Annie L. Garbit,	Annie Louise Ralph,	Cambridge.
25,	Clara F. Garbit,	Clara Frances Ralph,	Cambridge.
25,	Frederick E. Garbit,	Harold Edward Ralph,	Cambridge.
25,	Roy Horton,*	Clayton Roy Fuller,	Lynn.
Nov. 9,	Mabel Bruce,*	Mabel Ethel Newell,	Boston.
15,	Rhoda Eunice Judd,*	Mildred Eleanor Blodgett,	Stanstead, P. Q.
22,	Mabel Swett,*	Mabel Barss,	Boston.
22,	Otis Henry Bamford,*	Harold Everard Carleton,	Haverhill.
22,	Harry J. Smith,*	Harry Johnson Colby,	Cambridge.
Dec. 6,	George Dionne,	George Gibson,	Newton.
6,	Phillip Dionne,	Phillip Gibson,	Newton.
6,	Bertha Leona York,*	Ruth Miles Bailey,	Harrison, Me.
13,	Ralph Eaton,*	Ralph Eaton Brown,	Waltham.
13,	John Trull Swords,	John Swords Trull,	Belmont.
20,	Irene Coffey,*	Mildred Alice Linnell,	Somerville.
20,	Harry Dwight Corey,	Harold Dwight Corey,	Newton.
27,	Susie Victoria Lehr,*.	Florence Louise Campbell,	Boston.

WORCESTER COUNTY.

Date	Original Name.	Name Decreed.	Residence.
Jan. 15,	Jane Comrie,*	Gladys Wetherbee Beane,	Worcester.
26,	Mary Jane McNeill (alias Bessie Prindle),*	Mildred Joy Ladd,	Ashburnham.
Feb. 2,	Edgar R. Davie,	Edgar R. Webber,	Worcester.
2,	Frederick Albee,*	Bertie Edwin Bemis,	Barre.
2,	Florence Campbell,*	Florence Gertrude Nash,	West Brookfield.
2,	Herbert Ready,*	Herbert Cowden,	Worcester.
2,	Walter Clifford Barstow (alias Robert Alexander),*	Clarence Henry Ladd,	Sturbridge.
5,	——,*	Luther William Hayward,	New Haven, Ct.
23,	Lydia E. Lebeau.*	Lydia E. Wilmot,	Uxbridge.
Mar. 4,	Francis Wilmot Woodman,*	Angelo Capuro,	Worcester.
15,	Hattie Louise Amsden,*	Lizzie Ella Grimes,	Petersham.
15,	Marion Hawes Chute,*	Marion Hoyt Chute,	Northborough.
15,	Florence M. Pease *	Florence May Pease Fuller,	Charlton.
25,	Agnes Etta Magowan,*	Madeline Russell,	Worcester.
April 1,	Annie Whitehead,*	Blanche Isetta Graves,	Milford.
5,	William Francis Sharkey,*	William Francis Crane,	Leicester.
5,	Mary Manning,*	Adele Bullard,	Westborough.
5,	Nellie Josephine Fanning,	Helen Josephine Fanning,	Worcester.
12,	Walter Pomeroy,*	Charles Milton Scollay,	Worcester.
12,	Lucia Corning,*	Lucia Barnard,	Worcester.
19,	Sarah R. Howe,	Sarah R. Fuller,	Athol.
19,	Emily Isabel Oakley,	Harriet Emily Lane,	Worcester.

* Changed by reason of adoption.

WORCESTER COUNTY — *Concluded.*

Date of Decree.	Original Name.	Name Decreed.	Residence.
1892.			
May 3,	Agnes Lemieux,* . . .	Alice Maud Tibbetts, . .	Worcester.
17,	Adelia Marion Hill, . . .	Adelia Marion Fay, . .	Worcester.
24,	—— ——,*	Louis Sargent Rockwood, .	Ashburnham.
24,	Mary Ellen Leary,* . . .	Elizabeth Hennessey, . .	Fitchburg.
June 7,	George Lucier,*	George Lajore, . . .	Worcester.
24,	Etta Jane Skinner,* . . .	Etta Jane Sprague, . .	Harvard.
July 8,	George W. Eastman,* . .	George W. Freeman, . .	Gardner.
Aug. 9,	George Nelson Cutler,* . .	George Nelson Rose, . .	Fitchburg.
Sept. 6,	May Etta Kelley,* . . .	Bertha Rosa Dugar, . .	Oxford.
Oct. 7,	Ralph Benway,* . . .	Charles Otis Warner, . .	Worcester.
18,	Emma Jane Young (otherwise known as Grace Boynton), .	Grace Boynton Gould, . .	Worcester.
21,	Arthur Judisch.* . . .	Arthur Bonat, . . .	Webster.
25,	Carrie L. Getchell,* . . .	Carrie L. Page, . . .	Leominster.
25,	Gertrude Evans.* . . .	Gertrude Eva Barnes, . .	Sterling.
Nov. 1,	William Christian Niedermeyer,*	Christian William Jacobson, .	Fitchburg.
4,	Fred Nason Whittier,* . .	Fred Beaman Woodbury, .	Sutton.
22,	Edith Ammon,*	Edith Agnes Dell Whitaker, .	Lancaster.
22,	Eva E. Lord,*	Eva E Pierce, . . .	Leominster.
23,	Mildred Alice Thresher,* .	Mildred Alice Hastings,. .	Spencer.
Dec. 6,	—— ——,*	Mildmay Ozro Crawford, .	Oakham.
30,	Faith Hunter,*	May Houghton Gates, . .	Worcester.

HAMPSHIRE COUNTY.

Mar. 1,	Susan P. Wesley,* . . .	Susan Wesley Steele, . .	Hyde Park.
1,	Milicent Wesley,* . . .	Milicent E. Hawley, . .	Hyde Park.
April 5,	Bertha K. Bates,* . . .	Bertha Hattie Morrison, .	Southampton.
5,	Lois Ethel Cushman,* . .	Lois Ethel Angell, . . .	Huntington.
June 5,	Frank Tufts, ...	Frank Kinne, . . .	Chesterfield.
July 5,	Catherine Hiner,* . . .	Catherine O'Donnell, . .	Easthampton.
Aug. 9,	Elmer Arthur Brigham,* .	Harrison Franklin Wilbur, .	Amherst.
Sept. 6,	Nellie Grace Culver,* . .	Nellie Grace Streeter, . .	Worthington.
13,	Euclid Geoffrion,* . . .	Euclid Charbonneau, . .	St. Anne, Canada.
13,	Louis Geoffrion.* . . .	Louis Charbonneau, . .	St. Anne, Canada.
Dec. 6,	Laura Pearl Gilman,* . .	Pearl Gilman Scott, . .	Boston.
6,	William Hall,*	Eugene Norman Durkee, .	Boston.
13,	Lena Kuntzel,*	Lena Kuntzel Gates, . .	Agawam.
13,	Margaret Thompson,* . .	Bertha Louise Rice, . .	Worcester.

HAMPDEN COUNTY.

Jan. 6,	Clarence Chamberlin,* . .	Clarence Woodbury Cilley, .	Woonsocket, R. I.
20,	Caroline Koch,*	Emily May Randall, . .	Westfield.
Feb. 3,	Clarence Cook,*	Elwood Clarence Keith, .	Concord, N. H.
3,	Charles Shipman,* . . .	Charles Alfred Hadd, . .	Springfield.
Mar. 16,	Delia Barcumb,* . . .	Delia Deforge, . . .	Wilbraham.
16,	Loise Barcumb,* . . .	Loise Le Due, . . .	Wilbraham.
April 6,	Rosa Gravel,*	Rosa Belleville, . . .	Springfield.
6,	Ruth Mabel Woodcock,* .	Ruth Mabel Griffin, . .	Springfield.
June 1,	Ann Eliza Phillips, . . .	Ann Eliza Watson, . .	Chicopee.
15,	Isaac Covensky,. . . .	Isaac Coven, ...	Springfield.
15,	Frances Eggleston,* . . .	Gladys Emeline Chapin, .	Westfield.
July 22,	Charles Raymond Savage,*	Charles Raymond Mitchell, .	Springfield.
Sept. 14,	Harry Andrew Carroll,* .	Harry Andrew Russell. .	Springfield.
Oct. 5,	Mabel Zeigler Benjamin,*.	Mabel Zeigler Olmstead, .	Springfield.
19,	Catherine Curtin,* . . .	Catherine Cavanaugh, .	Holyoke.
Dec. 7,	Frederick Connor,* . . .	Frederick Stevenson, . .	Holyoke.

* Changed by reason of adoption.

FRANKLIN COUNTY.

Date of Decree.	Original Name.	Name Decreed.	Residence.
1892.			
Jan. 5,	David Manning Purrington,* .	David Manning Purrington Bassett, . . .	Charlemont.
Mar. 1,	Robert Foley,* . . .	George Francis Cohen, .	Greenfield.
April 5,	Weston Kent,* . . .	Edwin Crandall Harris, .	Deerfield.
5,	Eddie (Stevens ?),* . .	Charles Edward Stuart, .	Orange.
May 3,	Grace Hutchins,* . .	Grace Emily Wheeler, .	Orange.
17,	Lillian Rand,* . . .	Lillian May Sanderson, .	Whately.
Sept. 17,	John Montgomery,* . .	Albert Henry Knight, .	Whately.

BERKSHIRE COUNTY.

Date of Decree.	Original Name.	Name Decreed.	Residence.
Jan. 5,	Mary McNulty,* . . .	Mary Hourahan, . .	North Adams.
5,	William McNulty,* . .	William Cassidy, . .	North Adams.
Feb. 2,	Ida Decker,* . . .	Ruth Laura Phillips, .	Cheshire.
Mar. 1,	Guy Asahel Campbell,* .	Guy Asahel Campbell Lawrence, ...	Lenox.
1,	Marguareta Perce,* . .	Hazel Lorrenna Shultis, .	North Adams.
1,	Fred Burnside Place,* .	Fred Burnside White, .	North Adams.
2,	Ora I. Clark,* . . .	Ora I. Lees, . . .	Florida.
Nov. 9,	Harry Decker,* . .	Harry Dearing, . .	Great Barrington.
9,	Alice Woods Jacobs,* .	Mabel May Stearns, .	Dalton.
9,	Annie Pratt,* . . .	Mertie A. Allen, . .	North Adams.

NORFOLK COUNTY.

Date of Decree.	Original Name.	Name Decreed.	Residence.
Jan. 6,	Maud Barrows Upson,* .	Maud Barrows Dutton, .	Plantsville, Conn.
6,	Mabel Lillian Upson,* .	Mabel Lilian Dutton, .	Plantsville, Conn.
6,	George Abbot Weld, .	Abbot Morse, . . .	Stoughton.
6,	Catherine Alice Weld, .	Catherine Alice Morse, .	Stoughton.
6,	Herbert Abbot Weld, .	Herbert Abbot Morse, .	Stoughton.
6,	Eugene Weld, . . .	Eugene Morse, . .	Stoughton.
20,	Harold Reynolds,* . .	Harold Reynolds Tucker, .	Stoughton.
Feb. 3,	Edith Munson,* . . .	Pansy Edna Allen, . .	Boston.
3,	Florence Beatrix Phillips,*	Florence Beatrice Sabray Diman, . . .	Boston.
10,	Elsa Dahl,* . . .	Elsa Frolund, . . .	Sweden.
June 8,	Maybell Lee Batson,* .	Maybell Lee Wood, .	New Brunswick.
22,	Emma Forbes, . . .	Emma Morton, . .	Sharon.
July 20,	Louis Albert Hall,* . .	Louis Albert Langsdale, .	Newton.
27,	Mary Frances Murphy,* .	Frances Althea Smith, .	Denver.
Sept. 7,	Lilias Jordan Rattray,* .	Lilias Jordan Rattray McIntosh, ...	Ontario.
21,	Samuel McGlynn,* . .	Samuel James Bunker, .	Weymouth.
28,	—— Milchell,* . . .	George Weston Abbott, .	Chelsea.
Nov. 16,	Ashton Fay McQuarry,* .	Ashton Fay McLeod, .	Boston.
Dec. 7,	George Washington Eliot, .	George Worcester Eliot, .	Brookline.

PLYMOUTH COUNTY.

Date of Decree.	Original Name.	Name Decreed.	Residence.
Feb. 8,	Mildred Ellis Cole,* . .	Mildred Cole Cushman, .	Kingston.
Mar. 22,	Martha J. Kimball, . .	Martha J. Perkins, . .	Brockton.
28,	Franklin Cahoon,* . .	John Franklin Ryder, .	Wareham.
April 25,	Richard Stevenson,* . .	Richard Tolman, . .	Hingham.
May 9,	Ullie Cushing,* . . .	Annie May Morey, . .	Brockton.
June 27,	Bertha Augusta Beyerlieb,*	Elvira Augusta Johnson, .	Brockton.
27,	Warren Bickford,* . .	Warren Henry Tobey, .	Brockton.
Sept. 12,	Esther Herff, . . .	Eva May Bumpus, . .	Brockton.

* Changed by reason of adoption.

BRISTOL COUNTY.

Date of Decree.	Original Name.	Name Decreed.	Residence.
1892.			
Mar. 4,	Francis Dowd,*	Francis Dowd Mannion, . .	New Bedford.
April 1,	Louisa Harriet,*	Louisa Alice Wetherell, . .	Dighton.
1,	Louise E. Adshead, . . .	Louise E. Goddard, . .	Fall River.
May 6,	Fred Manchet, ...	Fred Mansfield, . . .	Raynham.
July 1,	Clarinda Bouthiette,*. . .	Clarinda Plante, . . .	New Bedford.
Sept. 16,	Madeline Dwart,* . . .	Madeline Sampson, . .	New Bedford.
Nov. 4,	Geo. H. Stephens,* . . .	Charles Bradly Gustin, . .	Attleborough.
Dec. 2,	Mary A. Connelly,* . . .	Hester Crawford Wade, . .	Easton.
2,	Horace Lincoln Cushing,* .	Horace Cushing Mills, . .	New Bedford.
2,	Malvinia F. Holman,* . .	Malvinia Holman Goff, . .	Fall River.

BARNSTABLE COUNTY.

Date of Decree.	Original Name.	Name Decreed.	Residence.
Jan. 12,	Frederick Reed,* . . .	Paul Alexander Clark, . .	Wellfleet.
April 19,	Edwin Ray,*	Edwin Ray Snow, . . .	Yarmouth.
19,	Phebe S. Eldridge, . . .	Phebe Shurtleff, . . .	Yarmouth.
June 21,	Alton B. Wixon,* . . .	Alton B. Long, . . .	Dennis.
Dec. 13,	Ossie W. Chase,* . . .	Franklin Thomas Dean, .	Dennis.

DUKES COUNTY.

Date of Decree.	Original Name.	Name Decreed.	Residence.
Feb. 10,	Chester Campbell,* . . .	Walter Loyd Mayhew, . .	Chilmark.
April 5,	Dorothy Clark,* . . .	Eliza May Stratton, . .	Cottage City.

* Changed by reason of adoption.

INDEX OF ORIGINAL NAMES.

* Adopted — name unchanged.

* Adopted. Name unchanged.

* See note page 165.

* Adopted. Name unchanged.

* Wife and three children.   † Wife and two children.

358   INDEX OF ORIGINAL NAMES.

* Adopted. Name unchanged.

* Wife and son.

* Adopted — name unchanged.

* See note page 165.

* Adopted. Name unchanged.   † And minor daughter.

* Five children take surname Rogers.   † See note, page 143.

* Name unchanged.

* And two minor sons.

* Wife and two children.

INDEX OF ADOPTED NAMES.

* See December 21, 1880.

* Wife and three children.   † Wife and two children.

* Adopted. Name unchanged.

* And minor son.

* Adopted.

* Adopted. Name unchanged.

* See note on page 145.

* And five children.

* Wife and two children.

* Wife and son.

www.ingramcontent.com/pod-product-compliance
Lightning Source LLC
Chambersburg PA
CBHW072038020426

42334CB00017B/1320